W9-BUY-643

Educational Programming for the Severely and Profoundly Handicapped

Ed Sontag, *Editor*

Judy Smith *Associate*
Nick Certo *Editors*

A Special Publication
of the
DIVISION ON MENTAL RETARDATION
The Council for Exceptional Children

CONSULTING EDITORS

Technical Assistance by: The National Learning Resource Center of Pennsylvania, RRC-Region 11 (Constance Burton, James B. Duffey, Evelyn Richardson); and the Montgomery County, Pennsylvania, Intermediate Unit #23 (Peter Boardman, William Wartman).

Additional copies of *Educational Programming for the Severely and Profoundly Handicapped* are available at $14.95 per copy. This price includes postage and handling. Order from the CEC Division on Mental Retardation, 1834 Meetinghouse Road, Boothwyn, Pennsylvania, 19061.
Cover photos by Robert Coleman, Nebraska Psychiatric Institute, Omaha, Nebraska.

Library of Congress Catalog Number 76-45231
Printed in the United States of America

The Division on Mental Retardation

The Council for Exceptional Children

The Division on Mental Retardation, with over 10,000 members, is the largest Division within the Council for Exceptional Children. The purposes of the Division are to advance: the education and welfare of the mentally retarded, research in the education of the mentally retarded, competency of educators in this field, public understanding of mental retardation, and legislation needed to help accomplish these goals. The Division encourages and promotes professional growth, research, and the dissemination and utilization of research findings.

The Division's journal, *Education and Training of the Mentally Retarded*, is sent to all members of the Division. All Division members must first be members of the Council for Exceptional Children. Division membership is on an annual basis. Dues are $5 for regular members and $2 for full-time students. Subscription to *Education and Training of the Mentally Retarded* is available without membership: domestic, $12.50 per year; PUAS and other countries, $14.50 per year. For information concerning CEC and CEC-MR membership or subscription to the Division's journal, contact the Division on Mental Retardation, The Council for Exceptional Children, 1920 Association Drive, Reston, Virginia 22091.

Foreword

JOHN W. KIDD

Executive Director, Division on Mental Retardation, Council for Exceptional Children

The Division on Mental Retardation of the Council for Exceptional Children came into existence as a petitioning division in April, 1963. It became a full-fledged division among CEC's family of units at the end of its required two-year probationary period in April, 1965. Its newsletter became its quarterly professional journal, *Education and Training of the Mentally Retarded*, in October, 1966, under the editorship of Floyd E. McDowell.

Now, ten years after the appearance of CEC-MR's first journal, the publication has grown to 100 pages per issue. Now that CEC-MR has grown to more than 10,000 members, and now that it has employed its first Executive Director, the division has reached a new pinnacle of eminence in the publication of this, its first special bonus volume.

The Division on Mental Retardation of the Council for Exceptional Children at its best is exemplified by the unselfish efforts of the major architect of this production, Ed Sontag. He has obtained remarkable contributions from persons of note and knowledge, and he has most ably orchestrated these discrete parts into a fluid synthesis second to no other contribution to the field of education for the severely and profoundly handicapped.

The Division on Mental Retardation, its state affiliates, its members and officials express sincere gratitude to Floyd McDowell, whose vision brought this volume into focus; to Ed Sontag, whose devotion to our less fortunate fellow beings is unstinting; to Judy Smith and Nick Certo, who, as Associate Editors, carried this work into production; to Lester Mann, who provided vast technical assistance; to the consulting editors, who played a major role in the quality of this publication; and to the contributors, without whose expertise and cooperation this book could not have evolved. To all of these, we offer our appreciation with deep humility and utmost sincerity. May they be the happier for their efforts, and may those for whose benefit the messages herein are intended find life ever more meaningful as a major consequence of what has here been fashioned.

Dedication

We dedicate this book to the severely and profoundly handicapped: to those who have been served in the developing programs described herein and who have thereby become part of a significant educational and social change; to those whom we shall, hopefully, better serve in the future; and to the proposition that we never lose sight of the reason we entered this profession—to serve these individuals.

E.W.S.
J.S.
N.C.

CONTENTS

I The Population, the Profession, and Public Education: A New Era

If it is possible to speak of the genius of a culture, the focus or concentration of its energies, or the ends toward which it historically inclines, the genius of the American culture might be the idea and ideal of the individual. For us, the worth of the individual is the foundation of value; the well being of the individual is the chief object of social purpose and action.

William V. Schipper, William C. Wilson, and Judith M. Wolf

The Severely and Profoundly Handicapped as Catalysts for Change

FLOYD E. McDOWELL

Editor, *Education and Training of the Mentally Retarded*

ED SONTAG

Bureau of Education for the Handicapped

The educational strategies and concepts conveyed by the authors of this book collectively convey a larger message—that the severely and profoundly handicapped are serving as catalysts for major changes in public education. First, this group has brought us to the long overdue realization that effective education for all students is and must be a science, not an art. Simply pick up your daily newspaper and consider the declining college board scores of *non-handicapped* students, the *non-handicapped* students who graduate from high school unable to read, the *non-handicapped* students who advance from grade to grade without mastering basic living skills. These failures alone, well documented and publicly acknowledged, are sufficient to emphasize the importance of objective assessment for educational planning, of task analysis and individualized programming, of continuous evaluation of performance, and of data collection that can verify student progress. The fact that such scientific procedures are being proven effective in the education of the severely and profoundly handicapped does not detract from, but in fact underscores, the recognition that they should be the bases for other educational practices.

Second, some current divergent thinking regarding the definition of the severely and profoundly handicapped proposes a restructuring of our ideas on the whole of service delivery in special education. There is, and rightly should be, questioning of the prevailing system of defining this low-incidence population on the basis of intelligence quotients and specific characteristics that may or may not be present in a given individual. (For example, the severely handicapped may be "defined" as having IQ's between 20 and 35, and as being characterized by self-stimulation, self-mutilation, aggression toward others, severe sensory or physical defects, poor communication skills, and so on, while the profoundly handicapped may be described as having IQ's of less than 20, and as having only a few reflexes, extreme feeding problems, inability to sit in an erect position, numerous associated physical disorders, and the like.) Because such definitions lack relevance for educational programming, and because they are conducive to false negatives and false positives when placement occurs, our intellectual and practical struggle with them is now leading to the questioning of static definitions in all areas of special education. A few conceptual alternatives are, consequently, beginning to emerge.

Sontag, Smith, and Sailor (1977) suggest that the severely and profoundly handicapped be identified not in terms of individual characteristics, but in terms of effective educational programming and teacher competencies. Specifically, they consider a reorganization of the whole of special education which would create three global instructional areas: general special education (remedial academic instruction), severely handicapped education (basic skill development), and early education (divided into areas of skill development and pre-academic remediation), with emphasis on the flexibility that allows students to move from severely handicapped education, to general special education, to the least restrictive environment, according to their progress and individual needs. Teachers with competencies in basic self-help, motor, perceptual, social and communication skill development would teach in severely handicapped education, while teachers with competencies in pre-academic and academic instructional areas would handle general special education. This type of definition would not only facilitate the progressive inclusion of the low-incidence population into the school and community, but would also cut across disability areas and create a programmatic and need-centered model of service delivery for all handicapped children.

Similarly, Haring, Nietupski, and Hamre-Nietupski (Note 1) question the assumption that a finite number of static characteristics distinguish the severely handicapped as a group, and cast doubt on the validity of the traditional definitions. The dynamic definition they suggest in relation to the severely and profoundly handicapped is: "the level of resources necessary to produce acceptable educational progress, on accepted curricula, toward independent functioning, which greatly exceeds the level of resources provided in regular education" (p. 4). Again, what is defined and what must be defined is the educational framework.

Our work with the severely and profoundly handicapped is, in other words, making it abundantly clear that defining, labeling, and categorizing have little point unless they lead directly and specifically to appropriate placement and programming. In this and other areas of special education, we may have spent too much time defining students and too little time determining effective services.

This book is an initial attempt to present some educational models, intervention strategies, and concepts for the education of the severely and profoundly handicapped. It is not put forth as a comprehensive and complete view, because this area of special education is in its formative stage, with much research and development remaining to be done. In this sense, the contents collectively convey another larger message—that of the relative strengths and weaknesses of the current status of educational programming for the severely and profoundly handicapped. For example:

- We have presented far more information pertaining to the severely handicapped than to the profoundly handicapped, who are the most seriously involved of all exceptional children. The larger part of our professional work has been devoted to the severely handicapped, however, and we must take steps to rectify this imbalance.
- The implications of Public Law 94-142, as presented here, reflect our dilemma in meeting the demand for services while we are as yet unready to provide sufficient numbers of well trained personnel to work with the severely and profoundly handicapped.
- The entries on community reintegration are forceful arguments for deinstitutionalization and local support services, yet how much of a social revolution will be necessary before meaningful changes are implemented?
- In this book and in the field, more attention is being devoted to important early intervention strategies than to the also important programs for the opposite age group—adolescents and adults. Yet, in the long run, public acceptance of the severely and profoundly handicapped will hinge on their relative independence. We have a long way to go in bridging that gap.
- In terms of specific teaching strategies, the contents of this book show at a glance that more progress has been made in language and communication development than, for instance, in curriculum development or the training of sensorimotor skills.
- The viewpoints of a parent advocate and of a clinician underscore the role of parents as the real movers in the education of the severely and profoundly handicapped, while at the same time revealing the continuing frustrations and despairs of these parents in their search for answers and services.
- The section on the educational team emphasizes the importance of an interdisciplinary approach, and the effectiveness of medical personnel and a variety of therapists can be no better documented than in the excellence of the work they have contributed to this book. Moreover, the information on personnel preparation underscores the continuing commitment of the Bureau of Education for the Handicapped to the expansion and upgrading of the education of the severely and profoundly handicapped.

In practical terms, the public education of the severely and profoundly handicapped is not yet five years old. In that short time, remarkable strides have been made by a small and devoted group of professionals. Much more must come and will come, from those whose work is represented here and from many others who are now beginning their careers in this field.

Reference Note

1. Haring, N. G., Nietupski, J., and Hamre-Nietupski, S. Guidelines for effective intervention with the severely handicapped: Toward independent functioning. Unpublished manuscript. Seattle: University of Washington, 1976.

Reference

Sontag, E., Smith, J., and Sailor, W. The severely and profoundly handicapped: Who are they? Where are we? *Journal of Special Education*, March, 1977, *11*, 1.

FLOYD E. McDOWELL is Program Director, Keystone Learning Center, Boothwyn, Pennsylvania, and Principal of Meadowood School, Stanton School District, Wilmington, Delaware. He is Editor of *Education and Training of the Mentally Retarded*, and has served as President, Division on Mental Retardation, The Council for Exceptional Children; President, the National Association of Recreational Therapists; Vice-President, General Division, The American Association on Mental Deficiency; and as Charter Member of the National Commission on Accreditation of Residential Facilities for the Mentally Retarded. He completed his Doctorate in Educational Administration and Special Education at George Peabody College for Teachers.

ED SONTAG is Chief, Program Development Branch, Division of Innovation and Development, U.S. Office of Education, DHEW, Washington, D.C. He has been a classroom teacher, university instructor, state department administrator, and national level coordinator. Contributions to the field include his reality-based simulation materials for the training of special education administrators, and his extensive writing and advocacy in behalf of effective programming for the severely and profoundly handicapped in the public schools.

Public Education of the Handicapped

WILLIAM V. SCHIPPER
WILLIAM C. WILSON

National Association of State Directors of Special Education

JUDITH M. WOLF

University of Minnesota

If it is possible to speak of the genius of a culture, the focus or concentration of its energies, or the ends toward which it historically inclines, the genius of American culture might be the idea and ideal of the individual. For us, the worth of the individual is the foundation of value; the well being of the individual is the chief object of social purpose and action. This ideal, however, has not always been achieved.

Historically, the United States has denied educational and employment opportunities to its handicapped population in appreciable measure. Of the more than eight million handicapped children in this country today, fewer than half receive the appropriate educational services that would give them full equality of opportunity. It is estimated that one million of the handicapped children in the United States are entirely excluded from public school systems and do not experience the educational process in any fashion. Further, there may be additional handicapped children in this country whose handicaps are undetected and who are participating in regular education programs. Fortunately, this situation can now be rectified. New technology which compensates for handicapping conditions has been developed. Right-to-education court decisions have been delivered, and governors, state legislatures, and chief state school officers have made education for the handicapped a priority issue. To emphasize equal educational opportunity for the handicapped, the United States Congress has recently passed landmark legislation (Public Law 94-142), which, if adequately funded, will help the states assure that all handicapped children, including the most severely/profoundly handicapped, have available to them a full, appropriate public education which emphasizes special education and related services designed to meet their unique needs (Wilson, 1975).

This legislation will mean that children who have traditionally been completely excluded from public education, or who were automatically placed in state residential institutions, will now be placed in public school programs. Such a serious effort to educate all of a nation's handicapped individuals is without precedent in other countries and cultures.

This article provides a brief conceptual overview of past, present, and possible future developments affecting the overall status of education for the handicapped. Specifically, the article will provide an overview and chronology of the developments leading up to this historical legislation; a presentation of the essential characteristics of the law as they pertain to public education of the handicapped; a discussion of how we came this far in educating the handicapped (including a brief synopsis of significant right-to-education court cases); and ideas on where we might be going in the future of public education for the handicapped.

Developments Leading to the Passage of Public Law 94-142

Public Law 91-230, the Amendments to the Elementary and Secondary Education Act (ESEA) created, as of July 1, 1971, the Education of the Handicapped Act (EHA). Part B of the Act authorized grants to the states and trust territories to assist them in initiating, expanding, and improving programs for the education of handicapped children. In 1974, the role of the federal government in the education of handicapped children was significantly increased with the passage of the Mathias Amendment to S. 1539, included in the Amendments to ESEA of 1974. At full funding, the amendment authorized more than $660 million to be made available to states under Part B, for fiscal year 1975 only. The intent of the amendment was to provide financial assistance to states in order to meet mandates established by the Act to identify, locate, and evaluate all handicapped children; to establish full educational opportunities for all handicapped children; and to establish a full-service timetable. In that S. 1539 was signed into Public Law 93-380, the new provisions of Part B (Aid to States) laid the basis for comprehensive planning, additional financial assistance to states, and protection of the rights of handicapped children by due process procedures and assurances of confidentiality.

The Education for All Handicapped Children Act was introduced in the 93rd Congress on January 1, 1974, as S. 6 was reintroduced in the 94th Congress on January 15, 1975, with the intent of amending Part B, in order to ensure the expansion of the provisions for handicapped children enacted in the 93rd Congress. In June, 1975, S. 6 was passed by the Senate and the companion measure, H.R. 7217, was passed by the House in July. The Conference Report on the Education for All Handicapped Children Act was passed on November 18, 1975, in the House of Representatives by a vote of 404 to 7. The report also passed the Senate by an overwhelming majority of 87 to 7. Such support reflected the turnabout in social attitudes toward the handicapped and seemed to be an appropriate and natural extension of the civil rights movement.

On November 28, 1975, President Ford reluctantly signed the act into Public Law 94-142. His reluctance was expressed in the following portion of his message:

> . . . this bill promises more than the Federal Government can deliver and its good intentions could be thwarted by the many unwise provisions it contains. Everyone can agree with the objective stated in the title of this bill—educating all handicapped children in our nation. The key question is whether the bill will really accomplish that objective. (White House Press Release, December 2, 1975)

Although the President supported full educational opportunities, it was his feeling that the bill not only carried unrealistic authorization levels, but also contained costly administrative requirements which would lead to unnecessary Federal control over traditional state and local government functions. Whether one agrees with President Ford's objections or not, the burden of responsibility is now clearly on society and its institutions to take into account, plan for, and include the handicapped in all possible social milieus in order to guarantee the brighter future which P.L. 94-142 promises for the nation's handicapped children and youth.

Essential Characteristics of Public Law 94-142

The major purposes of P.L. 94-142 are to assure that all handicapped children are provided with special education and related services designed to meet their unique needs, to protect the rights of handicapped children and the rights of their parents, and to assist the state in providing and evaluating services to handicapped children. If properly implemented, P.L. 94-142 should begin to address these issues by providing supplemental monies, guidelines, and assistance from the federal government to state and local education agencies so that they can provide equal educational opportunity to all children with handicapping conditions.

Beginning in the 1977–78 school year, states will receive entitlements based on the number of handicapped children receiving service (ages 3 through 21), plus a possible additional allocation for serving the preschool handicapped child. Although state education agencies (SEA's) may not count more handicapped children than 12% of the 5 through 17 age group in the state, a significant increase in the federal contribution to education of the handicapped will be realized. Although federal appropriations for state assistance programs have quadrupled since 1973, even higher federal entitlements may be allocated in the future. Public Law 94-142 contains an escalating authorization for funding which, beginning in school year 1977–78, would allow for more than $300 million for the program and would gradually increase the federal contributions to over $3 billion by 1982.

The new law provides that local education agencies (LEA's) will receive direct flow-through funding. In fiscal year 1978 (beginning October 1, 1977), 50% of the state entitlement will flow through the state agency to local school districts. In 1979 and after, 75% of the funds will flow through to LEA's. The congressional intent of this mechanism was to place the dollars with the direct service provider, the local school district.

Before any federal dollars leave Washington, D.C., the SEA must have a state plan for services to handicapped children which has been approved by the United States Office of Education (USOE). In addition, the state must furnish the following written assurances and procedures to the federal government before it can receive funds:

- Full educational opportunity available to all handicapped children;
- A date by which the state intends to accomplish full service to all handicapped children, which must be by September 1, 1980, for all children aged 3–21, unless inconsistent with state law or court order;
- A description of the kind and number of facilities, personnel, and services necessary throughout the state in order to meet the goal;

- A program to identify, locate, and evaluate all handicapped children;
- Protection of confidential information and personally identifiable data;
- Due process procedures for children and parents;
- An assurance that the results will be used in a nondiscriminatory manner;
- Appointment of a surrogate parent for the child should it be deemed necessary;
- A comprehensive program for personnel development;
- Requirements that any private school which is receiving funds for serving referred children must meet SEA standards and have SEA certified personnel in leading positions.
- Assurance that the handicapped child will be educated with normal children to the maximum extent possible;
- Written communication with parents in their own native language prior to placement of a child in any program.
- An active SEA program to promote education of the handicapped, as well as an information dissemination program related to the latest developments in education of the handicapped;
- An individualized educational program for each handicapped child, to be developed jointly by an LEA representative, the teacher, the parents, and the child (when appropriate) which provides, in writing, the child's current level of educational performance, a date for initiation of service, the type of service the child is to receive, long-range goals and short-term objectives, as well as an evaluation schedule to be reviewed at least once annually to determine whether the child is benefiting from a particular program;
- An assurance that the dollars will be spent to provide programs first for the previously unserved child and second for adequate services to children with the most severe handicapping conditions which were inadequately served in the past.

A public advisory panel must be maintained to inform the state of unmet educational needs of the handicapped, and each state plan must become a public document, submitted for public review. Under the new law, the SEA is responsible for the general supervision of all public education programs for the handicapped within a state; it must maintain LEA's for compliance with the law and must decide whether these agencies can provide a program of sufficient size and scope to qualify for "pass-through" funds. (Pass-through funds are allocated to state agencies and passed through to local agencies upon receipt of a compliance application.)

Although the SEA will have overall and ultimate responsibility for the education of handicapped children, the local education agency will be responsible for providing a program which will be in compliance with the federal law and in line with state priorities. Before an LEA can receive pass-through funds from the state, an application which meets all the requirements of the law must be submitted to, and approved by, the SEA. The applications must contain not only procedures for meeting the eligibility requirements which the state must submit to the federal government, but must also assure that the federal dollars will be spent to pay only those costs that are in excess of the costs for educating normal children in a given locality. The LEA must also use federal funds to supplement its budget and must assure that the local contribution for education of the handicapped will remain as high in the year that the locality receives funds as it had been in the previous fiscal year. Additionally, a comparability requirement will ensure that programs for handicapped children in an LEA will be equal, whether or not federal funds are being utilized. The LEA must maintain records of identification, evaluation, and placement of handicapped children, and these records must be accessible to the state education authorities.

Implications of Public Law 94-142

Obviously, the public responsibility for education of the handicapped will be realized upon implementation of Public Law 94-142. Its implications for states and localities are many. However, the greatest administrative implication will be that of inservice training. Not only will regular and special education teachers need specific types of training in the development of individualized educational programs, but inservice training will be needed for state and local educational personnel, if states are to maintain local programs adequately, conduct child-find programs, track statistical data, provide for training of due process officials, increase written communication with parents, and provide uniform financial accounting.

Administrative implications also exist for those private and institutional facilities currently providing an educational program for handicapped children. In the future, such programs must meet state education agency standards and must be conducted by qualified personnel.

Although the administrative implications of

the new legislation are complex, the benefits to children should be significant. Many states either have in existence, or have pending in committee, state laws that are as comprehensive as P.L. 94-142. However, some states still provide special education and related services on a piecemeal basis. The Education for All Handicapped Children Act guarantees that every handicapped child in the United States will now receive a free, specially designed public education to meet his unique needs. Furthermore, the rights of handicapped children and their parents will be protected through the specific due process provisions of the law. The law also affords an opportunity for the renewal of our educational priorities for all handicapped children in the United States.

How Did We Come this Far?

There are two important forces affecting present trends in special education. One such force is the judicial system. There is no question that court cases in the areas of classification, education, employment, and treatment have had profound effects on public education services for the handicapped. Judgments in several precedent-setting cases dealing with issues of classification of handicapped persons forced states to discontinue the use of tests that are biased toward special populations; to provide for a due process hearing to contest any special class placement; to allow an independent review by an outside examiner; to provide a thorough medical and psychological examination for each child considered for placement; and to submit a detailed timetable for compliance with each of these requirements.

Right-to-education cases have been fought in Arizona, California, Colorado, Connecticut, the District of Columbia, Florida, Illinois, Indiana, Kentucky, Maryland, Michigan, New York, North Carolina, North Dakota, Ohio, Pennsylvania, Washington, West Virginia, and Wisconsin. In each of these cases, parents or parent advocate groups brought suit in behalf of children who, for one reason or another, were excluded from public school. Courts have ruled in favor of the excluded children, and have further stated that such children are clearly entitled to alternative free public educational programs. In the famous Mills *vs.* Board of Education of the District of Columbia case (Note 1), Judge Joseph C. Waddy not only ruled that the plaintiffs be placed in school, but ruled that no child eligible for publicly supported education in the District's schools shall be excluded from a regular public education by rule, policy, or practice of the school board or its agents, unless the child is provided with adequate alternative educational services suited to his needs. In that event, a prior hearing and a periodic review of the child's status, progress, and the adequacy of the educational alternative must take place. Further, Judge Waddy ruled that insufficient resources may not be used as a basis for exclusion. The Mills decision expanded the PARC (Pennsylvania Association for Retarded Children) case, which gave the right to an individually appropriate public education not only to mentally retarded children, but to all children who suffer from mental, behavioral, emotional, or physical handicaps or deficiencies (Note 2). Also, the Mills case ended not with a consent agreement, as in many other decisions, but with a pure constitutional holding, and so was of even greater value as a precedent. A monitoring system was also included in the Mills case, by which a special master was appointed to oversee the implementation of the court's ruling.

One employment case concerning the handicapped in Florida (Roebuck et al. *vs.* Florida Department of Health and Rehabilitative Service et al., 1974) is related, although indirectly, to the nondiscriminatory testing provisions of previous court decisions and present law (Note 3). This case concerned persons who had been classified as "handicapped" when the classification was not related to the job task to be performed. Although the court has not reached a final verdict in this case, the implications for public schools seem clear. Public education systems may be called upon to prove that tests used to determine educational handicap actually measure skills and knowledge related solely to performance in school.

Court cases dealing primarily with right-to-treatment issues have been introduced in Alabama, California, the District of Columbia, Florida, Georgia, Hawaii, Illinois, Maryland, Massachusetts, Michigan, Minnesota, Mississippi, Missouri, Montana, Nebraska, New York, Ohio, Pennsylvania, Tennessee, and Washington. These cases concern the right of mentally retarded and mentally ill patients confined in institutions to treatment for their diagnosed problems. In a landmark case in Alabama, Wyatt *vs.* Hardin (formerly Wyatt *vs.* Stickney), the ruling established a detailed procedure for treatment implementation, which included many provisions to ensure a humane psychological environment, minimum staffing standards, provision for individualized evaluation of residents, habilitation plans and programs, and a requirement that every retarded person be placed in the least restrictive setting necessary for habilitation (Note 4). A similar class-action suit brought on behalf of residents at six state hospitals for the mentally retarded in Minnesota (Welsch *vs.* Likins) served to generalize the provisions of the Alabama case (Note 5). The court agreed with the plaintiffs' contentions that mentally retarded persons confined to state institutions have the right to a humane and safe living environment, which include the right to protection from danger, access to exercise, and provision for basic hygienic needs. Moreover, institutional violations were noted in the excessive use of seclusion, physical restraint, and tranquilizers. In addition, the court required the defendants to devise a written plan to provide community placement for all residents capable of such placement. (This requirement has implications for the educational planning now required of SEA and LEA officials in behalf of every handicapped child to be served in the schools.) Other right-to-treatment suits emphasized the right to normalization and to treatment in less restrictive environments than institutions. Handicapped Acts, both in 1974 and 1975, have been affected by these decisions.

The second growing force which is operating to modify public education for the handicapped is social awareness—a desire to serve the severely and multiply handicapped child. It is no longer appropriate for this country to continue to deny education to those children in our midst who are most in need of our services. With the present concern for the severely profoundly handicapped child, and given the present inability of most states to serve this group due to the lack of trained personnel and the scarcity of available programs, monies available through P.L. 94-142 will most certainly be directed in good measure to this population. This will significantly alter the pattern of services as it presently exists in our schools.

A conference sponsored by the National Association of State Directors of Special Education (NASDSE), entitled "Strategies for Planning for the Severely, Multiply Handicapped," produced several crucial imperatives for this population which incorporate the essential characteristics of the court mandates and of humanistic ideals:

- Zero reject concept—all children will be served;
- Development of pilot programs to serve the total handicapped population;
- Recognition that state institutions are being vacated as more and more handicapped are returning to the community;
- Need for early intervention;
- Design of an individual educational plan and provision of a team to manage each child;
- Provision of special training for persons to work with this population.

The need for comprehensive services for all handicapped individuals has been recognized both at the judicial level and at the state educational administrative level. This recognition has been summarized by Engelman (1974):

> Conventionality, or just progress is not enough. We have resources to not only demonstrate progress or evolution in our states, but we have the resources to demonstrate dramatic new kinds of comprehensive care, the kind of total care—not bandaids, but the kind of total care that honors and brings dignity to a life as it is, whatever station. (p. 10)

Where Are We Going?

Historically, we have denied educational and employment opportunities to many of our handicapped population. However, several national forces are working to create changes in this situation. New technology is being developed; right-to-education court decisions have been delivered; P. L. 94-142 has guaranteed a free and appropriate education for every handicapped child as a priority issue; and the values of our society suggest a more humanistic attitude toward all individuals who have special needs. Clearly, our educational institutions will be affected by all of these forces. What might our future look like? In an attempt to answer this question, NASDSE conducted a futuristic study of special education, using the Delphi methodology (Helmer, 1965). The basis for the study came from more than 800 predictions about the future. The pool of experts was composed of 121 special education administrators from all over the country, who represented subgroups of chief state school officers, state directors of special education, SEA staff, national and regional special education administrators. Data were collected in two rounds, according to the Delphi methodology. Participants recorded the probable year when an event might occur and the value they attached to the occurrence of that event. The data indicated some basic trends which can be grouped into four categorical areas for ease of discussion: legal/statutory; administrative; instructional; and teacher education (Schipper & Kenowitz, 1975).

Legal and statutory trends suggest that, by 1995, all exceptional children, including the severely and multiply handicapped, will be receiving educational services; due process procedures will be guaranteed; and educational opportunities will be uniform and will transcend state and district boundaries. Also, sophisticated evaluation of private as well as public school programs by SEA's was predicted.

Forecasts of administrative trends included a growing movement toward regional resource sharing, such as information systems and consortia. Participants predicted greater steps toward deinstitutionalization, while indicating a corresponding increase in public school programs for the handicapped. The year-round school concept was foreseen as a way to provide greater services for the handicapped. Also, special education administrators seemed to recognize the impact and value of increasing parental input into school matters.

Predicted instructional trends included more extensive use of instructional technology, such as mobile vans, instructional media services, and individualized prescriptive instruction. Also, preschool programs for early identification and remediation, and a continued national swing toward mainstreaming were predicted to take place by 1985.

Substantial changes were also forecast in teacher education by 1985. It was suggested that general educators will need a minimum of six credits in child exceptionalities for certification, as well as required courses in behavior modification. Other predictions indicated that performance-based criteria would replace traditional campus-based instruction, and that teacher training would shift from universities to local school systems and teacher associations. The notion of SEA's and LEA's providing inservice training for teachers and administrators was seen as a "somewhat valued" rather than as a "highly valued" event. The authors of the NASDSE report suggested that one use of these data might be as an aid to strategic decision makers who ask, "What do we have to do today to be ready for an uncertain tomorrow?" In some ways, the state of the art has changed drastically since the completion of the NASDSE futures report. Public Law 94-142 has become a reality and, with its enactment, certain policies and procedures are no longer recommended, but mandated. But the survey shows that, prior to the enactment of the law, special education administrators were aware of the weaknesses of the present system, and of areas which, if expanded, would begin to address the general goal of comprehensive educational services for all handicapped individuals.

The NASDE survey looked at the future from a long-range perspective. Our new legislation suggests more immediate implications, most notably that school systems and our states will have to reach out to populations that have generally been ignored, in order to identify, locate, and evaluate all handicapped children, as mandated. In order to fulfill this requirement, we may choose to form new supportive relationships and revolutionary coordinative patterns and structures. We are further mandated to develop systems of multicultural testing, in response to the need to screen and assess all children for special education services. Further, an essential facet of the identification, assessment, placement, and instruction procedures has been virtually ignored by most of our states. This concerns the development of sophisticated and comprehensive screening, monitoring, and data processing systems. Such development would require a screening procedure to evaluate all the children in a school district, including preschool children, and a data-processing system to furnish output on each child concerning a treatment plan, a placement decision, and a provision for annual review.

Changes will be made in the typical referral system for identifying and placing a child with educational problems. Traditionally, the classroom teacher refers a child to the building principal or the school psychologist. Someone then examines the child and recommends a placement and possibly an educational program. This approach is referred to as a "linear" or "straight line" placement system. A more futuristic approach to student placement is a team approach. Whether the team is organized at the building, district, or cooperative level, it represents a non-linear approach to referral, diagnosis, and placement. This is a revolutionary concept in that it alters the traditional roles of psychologist, teacher, and school administrator. The concept of a placement team implies the following:

- Inclusion of regular and special educators on a team;
- Inclusion of school administrator(s) and special service personnel on a team;
- Inclusion of parents or care givers at all decision levels of team activity;
- Strict adherence to all due process regulations;
- Knowledge and skills relating to diagnostic techniques on the part of team members (e.g., nondiscriminatory testing);
- Knowledge of costs and resource requirements for serving handicapped children;
- Knowledge of all program options and clear understanding of the concept of least restrictive alternative;
- Ability to recommend and implement a

written individual educational program for each special education student;
- Decision to review the educational program and placement of each exceptional child at least annually.

Educators have recognized that some children learn better under certain conditions than under others. Given this concept, school personnel have tried to offer alternatives for students who learn in different ways. The system has been fairly successful in describing the prescriptive needs of a given learner. It has been fairly successful in describing the characteristics a learner must demonstrate in order to have an effective learning experience in a given environment. However, the match between learner characteristics and qualities of a specific learning environment have not yet been fully understood (Dunn & Dunn, 1974). An individual educational plan, designed to achieve this match, can be described in two global components: child characteristics and service requirements.

One set of child variables might include emotional characteristics, such as attitudes toward school, motivation of learner, persistence to task, ability to accept criticism, tolerance of frustration, and risk-taking tendencies. Another set of variables should include the physical needs of the learner: some learners achieve best through auditory stimulation, some through visual means, and for other learners a multimodality approach works best. Attention span and need for mobility are characteristics that reflect interaction between learner and learning environment. Children react differently to other students, to adults, and to the process of learning. Needs for interaction and communication differ greatly among children; some perform best in a small group situation, while others prefer to learn with a large group of children, or alone. Children also differ in their responsiveness to directions from persons in authority, and will show idiosyncratic limit-testing or limit-setting patterns. Reactions to conflict situations will also differ, depending on interpersonal skills and self-concept. A final set of variables includes all traditional achievement characteristics that are available and used in diagnosing the child's initial educational problem.

Once these variables have been phrased objectively, it becomes possible to employ a multifaceted assessment system to describe each learner on each characteristic. The next step is to describe the environmental options available to each learner by a similar set of characteristics.

Each educational option offers a distinct set of environmental, emotional, social, physical, and academic possibilities. For the child who demonstrates a significant disparity between ability and achievement, the best individual educational program might be that which offers small classes, tutoring, behavior modification, frequent staffing conferences, and ongoing evaluation and monitoring. If these characteristics describe a particular kind of resource room operating in a specific elementary school building, then this would be recommended as the appropriate placement (adhering to all due process and least restrictive alternative guidelines) for that child. If the individual is a severely handicapped secondary school-aged student, the incorporation of such programmatic features in a self-contained class within a local high school may be the most appropriate placement, since high schools may be the only environment where the social and emotional needs of such learners can be met in an age-appropriate manner.

Each service option would be described in accordance with the variable clusters listed above, and these components would be matched to learner characteristics. Ideally, together with frequent observation and monitoring, placements would be based on data, rather than on arbitrary decision processes or on convenience.

We are entering a stage which requires enormous creative energy to make appropriate changes in public education for the handicapped. Legislative modifications and societal forces push us toward new and revolutionary systems. To assist us in producing such change, P.L. 94-142 should provide monies and guidelines; growing instructional and mechanical technologies should aid in expanding viable service options; and multidisciplinary team evaluation linked to computerized data collection and monitoring should yield a closer approximation of the goal of comprehensive educational service, based on individual student needs. But only through the complete utilization of our resources, human as well as material, will we be able to reach our full-service goal—a free appropriate public education for all handicapped children.

Reference Notes

1. *Mills vs. Board of Education of the District of Columbia*, 348 F. Supp. 866 (D.D.C., 1972).
2. *Pennsylvania Association for Retarded Children vs. Commonwealth of Pennsylvania*, 334 F. Supp. 1257 (1971).
3. *Roebuck, et al. vs. Florida Department of Health and Rehabilitative Services, et al.* 502 F. 2nd 1105 (5th Cir., 1974).
4. *Wyatt vs. Hardin (formerly Wyatt vs. Stickney)*, 325 F. Supp. 781 (M.D. Ala., 1971, 344 F. Supp. 1341 M.D. Ala., 1971) 344 F. Supp. 373, 387 (M.D. Ala., 1972, aff'd. in part, modified in part sub. nom. *Wyatt vs. Aderholt*, 503 F. 2nd. 1305, 5th Cir., 1974).
5. *Welsch vs. Likins*, 373 F. Supp. 485 (U.S. D. Ct. Minn., 1974).

References

Dunn, R., and Dunn, K. Learning styles as a criterion for placement in alternative programs. *Phi Delta Kappan*, December, 1974, 275–278.

Engelman, V. *Planning for the severely handicapped.* Washington, D.C.: National Association of State Directors for Special Education, July, 1974.

Helmer, O. J. *Analysis of the future: The Delphi method.* New York: Rand Corporation, March, 1967.

Schipper, W., and Kenowitz, L. *Special education futures: A forecast of events affecting the education of exceptional children, 1975–2000*. Washington, D.C: National Association of State Directors of Special Education, February, 1975.

White House Press Release, December 2, 1975.

Wilson, W. C. *An analysis of Public Law 94-142*. Washington, D.C: National Association of State Directors of Special Education, 1975.

WILLIAM V. SCHIPPER has been with the National Association of State Directors of Special Education for the past three years and has served as training director of the BEH funded project. As an Associate Director of NASDSE, Dr. Schipper has been primarily responsible for a number of training activities and publications which address the needs of special education administrators, including development of a kit on individualized education programs for use by placement committees in local education agencies.

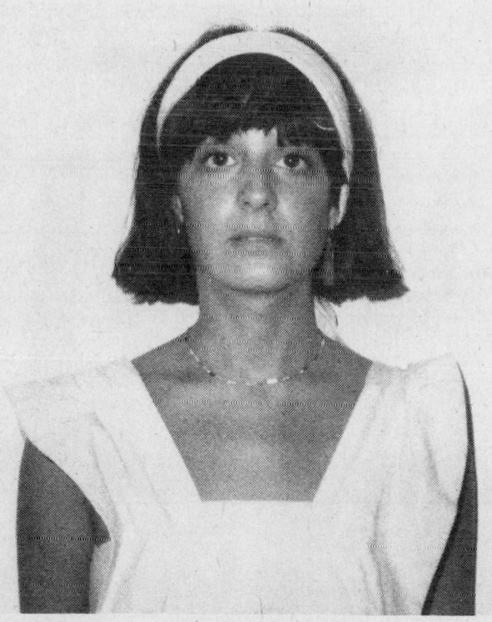

JUDITH M. WOLF is an Assistant Professor in Educational Administration at the University of Minnesota. She has been Project Coordinator in the Special Education Administrators Training Project, funded by the Bureau of Education for the Handicapped.

WILLIAM C. WILSON is an Associate Director at the National Association of State Directors of Special Education in Washington, D.C. He has coordinated legislative activities for NASDSE and has directed NASDSE's information dissemination efforts on Public Law 94-142, the Education for All Handicapped Children Act of 1975.

ESTIMATED NUMBER OF HANDICAPPED CHILDREN SERVED AND UNSERVED BY TYPE OF HANDICAP

U.S. OFFICE OF EDUCATION, BUREAU OF EDUCATION FOR THE HANDICAPPED, AID TO STATES BRANCH 1976

	1975–76 Served[a] (Projected)	1975–76 Unserved	Total Handicapped Children Served & Unserved	% Served	% Unserved
Total age 0–19	4,310,000	3,577,000	7,887,000	55%	45%
Total age 6–19	3,860,000	2,840,000	6,700,000	58%	42%
Total age 0–5	450,000	737,000	1,187,000	38%	62%
Speech impaired	2,020,000	273,000	2,293,000	88%	12%
Mentally retarded	1,350,000	157,000	1,507,000	90%	10%
Learning disabilities	260,000	1,706,000	1,966,000	13%	87%
Emotionally disturbed	255,000	1,055,000	1,310,000	19%	81%
Crippled & other health impaired	255,000	73,000	328,000	78%	22%
Deaf	45,000	4,000	49,000	92%	8%
Hard of hearing	66,000	262,000	328,000	20%	80%
Visually handicapped	43,000	23,000	66,000	65%	35%
Deaf-blind & other multi-handicapped	16,000	24,000	40,000	40%	60%

[a] Estimated total numbers of handicapped children served—obtained from SEA's Fall and Winter 1975–76. Information by type of handicap was not available and is projected from data provided by SEA's for School Year 1972–73.

[b] Total number of handicapped children ages 0–19 provided on basis of estimates obtained from various sources, including National agencies and organizations, plus State and local directors of special education. According to these sources the incidence levels by types of handicap are as follows: speech impaired 3.5%, mentally retarded 2.3%, learning disabled 3.0%, emotionally disturbed 2.0%, crippled & other health impaired .5%, deaf .075%, hard of hearing .5%, visually handicapped .1%, deaf-blind & other multi-handicapped .06%. The total number of handicapped children in the above categories represents 12.035% of all school age children from 6–19 and 6.018% of all children age 0–5. The population figures to which the incidence rates were applied, were obtained from the Bureau of Census and reflect the population as of July 1, 1974.

USOE/BEH/ASB
March 1976

II Community Reintegration of the Severely and Profoundly Handicapped

. . . It can be suggested that there is a direct relationship between one's level of functioning and the detrimental effects that may accrue to him as a result of institutionalization. That is, institutionalization may be least likely to harm an individual who possesses superior intellectual and behavioral abilities, and most likely to damage an individual who has intellectual and behavioral handicaps. If this is the case, and I believe that it is, then we have just made another huge error in our human services system. Instead of devoting most of our attention to deinstitutionalizing the mildly and moderately handicapped, we should be seeking to deinstitutionalize the severely and profoundly handicapped. In fact, if our institutions are going to continue to exist, residence in them should be limited to those who have *no* behavioral or intellectual deficiencies.

Lawrence A. Larsen

Community Services Necessary to Program Effectively for the Severely/Profoundly Handicapped

LAWRENCE A. LARSEN

Johns Hopkins University

Few would argue that our institutions for the handicapped have provided so much as humane care, let alone effective training and treatment programs, for their charges. The original purpose of the first institution, to make each resident ". . . more of a man and less of a brute by patience and kindness directed by energy and skill" (Howe, quoted by Baumeister, 1970), has been subverted over the years, as the number and size of residential centers for the handicapped have increased. With the exception of a minority of individuals for whom the institution represents an improvement in living conditions, the available evidence unequivocally shows that normal home care is more conducive to healthy growth and development than is institutional care (Klaber, 1970). In fact, the overcrowded and sensorily deprived environments in most institutions probably account for much of the bizarre and disturbed behavior exhibited by many institutionalized persons (Kreger, 1971). And Wolfensberger (1971a) has characterized the average public residential facility as ". . . a de-individualizing residence in which retarded persons are congregated in numbers distinctly larger than might be found in a large family; in which they are highly regimented; in which the physical or social environment aims at a low common denominator; and in which all or most of the transactions of daily life are carried out under one roof, on one campus, or in largely segregated fashion" (p. 15).

The American public seems slow to become aware of its social problems, quick to react vigorously and with outrage when it is made aware of those problems, and unfortunately prone to forgetting quickly, after an initial flurry of effort and action, that the problems still exist. This seems to have been the case with our public residential facilities for the mentally retarded. Although many Americans were aware of the deplorable and inhumane conditions that existed in our institutions for many years, it was not until the late 1960's and early 1970's that these conditions were made public on a national basis. Two of the most significant contributions here were news media accounts of Senator Robert F. Kennedy's reactions to what he witnessed during several visits to different facilities, and Blatt and Kaplan's photographic essay of life in the back wards of five institutions in four different states (Blatt & Kaplan, 1966). A parents' group in Alabama initiated a lawsuit, *Wyatt V. Stickney*, that led to a landmark decision in which a federal court mandated massive changes and sweeping reforms in a state-suported residential facility. In the professional domain, Wolfensberger (1969; 1971a; 1971b), among others, called for phasing out large residential facilities in favor of community services and programs, and Nirje (1969), Wolfensberger (1972a), and Roos (1970) recommended normalization as a guiding principle in the provision of services for the handicapped. As early as 1963, President Kennedy called for reducing the residential population of our mental hospitals and retardation centers by "hundreds of thousands" over a period of years (Kennedy, 1963), a challenge that ultimately led to a policy of deinstitutionalization, a term first used in a speech by former President Nixon in 1971, as a major goal of our efforts on behalf of the handicapped in the 1970's. A number of federal and state laws were enacted, culminating with the 1975 passage of P.L. 94-142, which sought to improve the quality of life for all handicapped individuals, and to make available community-based alternatives for their care and treatment.

This paper was supported in part by Grant No. G007603409 to Johns Hopkins University from the Department of HEW, USOE, Bureau of Education for the Handicapped, Division of Personnel Preparation, Washington, D.C.

Given this background of public, professional, political, and judicial action, major changes should have been made, and most problems should have been resolved. Unfortunately, although some progress is evident, this is not the case. If major changes have been made within institutions, or in the development of community alternatives, it is impossible to discern them. With the exception of a relatively small number of exemplary programs in a few locations, and with the exception of a general upgrading of most of our institutions, life for the severely and profoundly handicapped goes on pretty much as it has for many years.

The public notoriety gained by institutions for the mentally handicapped has had at least one lasting effect, however. Compared with our history of services to the handicapped, we can sense a new durable commitment to better serving the severely and profoundly handicapped, a commitment that we must and can provide them with better services, more effective programs, and improved living conditions. There is no longer any question of *whether* the lot of the severely and profoundly handicapped will be improved. The only arguments that remain are where, when, how, and at what cost.

Institutional versus Community Services

There are two points of view about where the severely and profoundly handicapped should be served. Some believe that institutions are the only, if not the best, alternative for this group, while others argue that services should be provided to all individuals, irrespective of their level of functioning, in community settings.

It is clear that there is a trend toward serving only the severely and profoundly handicapped in residential settings. In 1968, the severely and profoundly handicapped accounted for 60% of the residents in public residential facilities (Baumeister, 1970). This increased to 63% of the residents in 131 institutions surveyed by the National Association of Superintendents of Public Residential Facilities for the Mentally Retarded (NASPRFMR) in 1972 (Rosen & Callan, Note 1), and to 71% of the residents in 177 public facilities in a 1974 NASPRFMR survey (Scheerenberger, 1976). Although institutional discharges may reflect administrative or legal decisions more than institutional program effectiveness, it is hoped that this trend toward discharging borderline, mildly, and moderately retarded institutional residents reflects an increased ability on the part of our institutions to prepare their less handicapped residents for community living.

It should also be pointed out that many institutions have revised their requirements for admission to exclude all but the severely and profoundly handicapped; that there are more community programs available today for the less severely handicapped than in previous years; that the less severely handicapped are much easier to place and integrate into community settings; and that the parents of less handicapped individuals object less frequently and less strenuously to their discharge than is the case with the severely and profoundly handicapped. If the current trend continues, it will not be long before our public residential facilities are given over completely to the severely and profoundly handicapped.

While there seems to be a general consensus that the moderately, moldly, and borderline handicapped should be served in community settings, many continue to believe—and argue—that institutionalization is the only alternative for the severely and profoundly handicapped. A 1969 conference, sponsored by the National Association for Retarded Children, concluded ". . . that institutions are with us, they are going to continue to be with us and we had better accept the fact that this is one facet in a total program for the retarded" (National Association for Retarded Children, 1969). This point of view was also expressed in a recent position statement on residential programming prepared by NASPRFMR (1974):

> . . . the development of community programming should not be accomplished by sacrificing quality of services for retarded persons requiring residential care. It is not a question of residential or nonresidential programming. Both are essential, and both, in reality, constitute community services. (p. 3)

Many arguments have been proposed to justify our continued support of institutions for the severely and profoundly handicapped. First, it is sometimes argued that the burden of caring for these individuals is so great that we cannot expect parents to be up to the task. The parents of severely and profoundly handicapped individuals have come to expect institutional services, and they are unwilling to maintain their children in, or reintegrate them back into, their natural homes. After all, it is argued, the state has usurped parental responsibilities for many years, and it is impossible and unfair to terminate such services now. An opposing point of view holds that most parents can—and want to—meet their parental responsibilities in rearing their handicapped children if they are only given the minimal assistance that this requires. Parent education programs, early intervention services, respite care and baby-sitting services, family subsidies, and the like are proposed as alternatives that most parents would find more acceptable than placing their child in an institution.

Second, we are sometimes told that the handicapped are happiest and best adjusted when they associate only with their "own kind," rather than competing with their more able peers, where they usually experience failure. Institutionalization, according to this view, is the best choice for the severely and profoundly handicapped, because they differ the most from their normal peers. The advocates of community services, on the other hand, argue that the severely and profoundly handicapped benefit more from association with normal individuals of their own age group, and with their parents and other adults, than they do from associating only with others who are similarly handicapped. Institutionalization denies the individual many opportunities to acquire normal behavior patterns through the mechanisms of modeling and imitation. Segregating large numbers of severely and profoundly handicapped individuals in large institutions can only facilitate and prolong retarded behavior.

A third point of view is that the severely and profoundly handicapped are so different from the general population that the public will never accept them into the mainstream of community life. This argument is similar to the previous one, and it is probably based on an honest concern for the welfare of the individuals concerned. But those holding this opinion are more concerned with the detrimental effects of social ostracism than they are with the beneficial effects of segregated living in institutional settings. The proponents of community services believe that community acceptance of the severely and profoundly handicapped is possible, although it will never be a reality until they are integrated into community life. People probably will find it difficult to completely assimilate the severely and profoundly handicapped into society. The process will take time and it will be painful for some. However, the severely and profoundly handicapped will never be accepted into communities as long as they are permanently shuttled to isolated residential centers at an early age.

Fourth, some argue that institutions are not intrinsically bad (after all, even Harvard is a residential institution). It is held that institutions can, if given adequate financial support, become developmentally healthy places for the severely and profoundly handicapped. This argument implies that institutionalization has been deleterious to the handicapped because insufficient resources have prevented the provision of adequate programs and care. Those opposed to institutions, on the other hand, believe that increasing our financial support of institutions will not substantially improve their ability to serve their residents. Institutions, it is argued, have several essential features, among them their separation of the individual from emotional ties with family and friends, their isolation from the mainstream of community life, and the inconsistency found in any group care situation that cannot be rectified with any amount of financial support.

A fifth argument is that the range of medical, psychological, educational, social, and other services required by the severely and profoundly handicapped is so extensive that it is impractical to provide them in the community. The only economically feasible alternative is to centralize such interdisciplinary services in a residential setting. Community services proponents suggest, as an alternative, that generic community services are sufficient for all but extreme cases and, even then, specialized services can be provided at reasonable cost. This suggests that the problem is not so much one of *insufficient* services as it is one of excluding the severely and profoundly handicapped from services that are already available.

Sixth, some argue that it is generally less expensive to serve large groups in centralized institutions than it is to serve small groups in dispersed community programs. The costs of providing comprehensive programs and services to small groups of severely and profoundly handicapped individuals in a large number of communities are held to be prohibitive. In view of the skyrocketing costs of institutional care, community services advocates claim that community services may be cheaper. The annual per capita costs of residential care in a facility that meets the requirements for accreditation set forth by the Accreditation Council for Facilities for the Mentally Retarded (1971), for example, are estimated at somewhere between $20,000 and $25,000, excluding the initial capital improvement expenditures that will also be required. It is hard to imagine community services, even those that include residential care, costing this much.

Seventh, some have argued that community services can be, and often are, just as restrictive, just as de-individualizing, and just as segregated as institutional services. Although the individual may be no better off, he often is no worse off in an institution than he is in the community. This point is made in the NASPRFMR position statement on residential programming (NASPRFMR, 1974), and made even more forcefully in a recent publication commissioned by the American Federation of State, County, and Municipal Employees (Santiesteven, 1975). Most community services advocates would agree that community services may be just as bad as institutional services, and that geographic location alone is no guarantee that a particular residence will provide freedom from unnecessary restrictions, that it will be responsive to individual need, or that it will lead to integration into the mainstream of society. Yet, it is generally held that the opportunities for freedom, individualization, and integration are greater in community settings. All other things being equal, community residences and community programs are more likely to meet the tests of least restrictive environment, individualized treatment and programming, and normalization.

Summation

Although one may wish that it were otherwise, the arguments for and against community services for the severely and profoundly handicapped are likely to be waged for many years to come. It would be far better if a consensus could be reached in favor of one or the other. We should choose between either continuing our efforts toward renewing and reforming our institutions, or redoubling our efforts toward serving all handicapped individuals in community programs. We already have a tremendous financial and philosophical investment in institutions, and it will be very difficult to abandon this investment in favor of community alternatives. However, we simply cannot afford high quality services for some in institutional settings and high quality services for others in community settings. Although financial considerations alone should not determine our efforts on behalf of the handicapped, they must be carefully considered. The resources available to us are already scarce, and we cannot afford to be irresponsible in their allocation. We must either devote our full efforts and energies, and the bulk of our money, to creating effective and humane services in institutions, or we should dismantle our institutions as quickly as possible and allocate those resources to community programs.

The wisdom of rededicating our institutions to serve only the severely and profoundly handicapped must be questioned. We have a tradition in human services that those who have the greatest needs and the most severe handicaps receive the least in the way of services, and the conversion of our institutions to serve only the severely and profoundly handicapped seems to be another example of "the least getting the least" in human services. If community programs are better suited to meet the needs of the mildly and moderately handicapped, why are they not also better equipped to meet the needs of the severely and profoundly handicapped? Are the severely and profoundly handicapped so different that they are immune from the potentially detrimental effects of institutionalization?

Although there is little evidence bearing on this point, it can be suggested that there is a direct relationship between one's level of functioning and the detrimental effects that may accrue to him as a result of institutionalization. That is, institutionalization may be least likely to harm an individual who possesses superior intellectual and behavioral abilities, and most likely to damage an individual who has intellectual or behavioral handicaps. If this is the case, and I believe that it is, then we have just made another huge error in our human services system. Instead of devoting most of our attention to deinstitutionalizing the mildly and moderately handicapped, we should be seeking to deinstitutionalize the severely and profoundly handicapped. In fact, if our institutions are going to continue to exist, residence in them should be limited to those who have *no* behavioral or intellectual deficiencies.

Arguments and opinions aside, the choice between institutional and community services is difficult, and each person must arrive at his or her own decision. The point of view expressed here is that community alternatives appear to have greater potential for providing better services and programs, at smaller or equal costs, than do institutions. If our goal for the severely and profoundly handicapped is the development of normal behavior patterns in normal settings, then community programs must be preferred to institutionalization.

According to Scheerenberger (1974), deinstitutionalization consists of three interrelated processes. These processes can be phrased in the form of priorities for the severely and profoundly handicapped. Our first priority should be to prevent the institutionalization of all severely and profoundly handicapped individuals through the provision of community programs and services. Our second priority should be to return as many of those who are currently institutionalized to community life as we can, through the creation of community services that are designed for this purpose. And our third priority should be to provide humane care and improved services for all those who must be retained in their current institutional residences. In keeping with these priorities, the remainder of this article is primarily concerned with community programs and services for severely and profoundly handicapped individuals who are below age 21 and who have, so far at least, escaped institutionalization.

Essential Community Services

General Considerations

The central tenet of this paper is that *all* individuals, irrespective of their level of functioning or the nature of their handicaps, can be served in community settings. Before this goal can be accomplished, however, some drastic revisions in our approach to providing human services will be required.

Our human services industry is not in good condition. All too often, one has the uneasy feeling that, when effective services are provided, it is more accidental than purposeful. The number and variety of agencies, task forces, consortia, bureaus, divisions, sections, authorities, offices, committees, councils, and departments that comprise our human services apparatus at the local, state, and federal levels has made it unresponsive to individual needs and nearly incomprehensible to those who work within it, let alone to the average citizen.

The indirect process of service development and change, in which administrative bureaucracies, judicial systems, and legislative bodies stand as buffers, if not barriers, between the identification of human needs and the delivery of services, makes meaningful change slow at best and, at times, impossible. Interagency and interdisciplinary conflicts consume too much of our collective energies, at the expense of our consumers. Government mandated and government operated services are subject to the vagaries of political, administrative, and judicial processes, with the result that programs come and go in discontinuous fashion. Funding programs are often categorical, serving only certain age groups or certain target populations, with the result that many individuals in need are excluded from services.

We cannot afford to repeat the past and present errors of our human services when it comes to community services for the severely and profoundly handicapped. This is a new endeavor, and we must carefully plan a network of services and a delivery system that does not become overly bureaucraticized and which retains its original commitment to meeting the needs of individual consumers.

Specific Community Services

It seems to be generally agreed that the special and multiple needs of the severely and profoundly handicapped are so extensive and so diverse that they cannot be met by a single service or program. Few would disagree that full services for this population will require a coordinated, multi-component system in which each service component complements the others.

Some service components, however, are more important than others. Three major components are critical to retaining and serving the severely and profoundly handicapped in community settings: (a) early intervention programs; (b) educational services in public schools, beginning no later than age three and lasting at least until age 21; and (c) community residential services for those individuals who cannot live in their natural homes. The demand for residential placements would be greatly reduced if all severely and profoundly handicapped children had the benefit of early intervention programs to prevent the development of behavioral disabilities, and if parents were assured that their children would have access to a free public school education.

Early Identification and Intervention. Intervention is predicated on identification, and the earlier the identification and intervention, the better (Nielsen, Collins, Meisel, Lowry, Engh, & Johnson, 1975). This being the case, our identification efforts should begin with neonatal screening to identify handicapped and at risk infants. The most commonly used screening methods, the Apgar Scale (Apgar, 1953) and pediatric neurological examinations (Parmalee & Michaelis, 1971; Prechtl & Beintema, 1964) can detect gross abnormalities. They cannot, however, detect somewhat milder forms of dysfunction (Tronick & Brazelton,1975). Two scales of more recent origin, the Brazelton Neonatal Behavioral Assessment (Tronick & Brazelton, 1975) and the Graham/Rosenblith Neonatal Test (Rosenblith, 1961; 1975) more accurately differentiate between abnormal, at risk, and normal infants.

Besides neonatal screening tests, there are a number of instruments available for screening purposes during infancy and childhood. These include the Developmental Screening Inventory originally developed by Gessell and Amatruda (Knobloch & Pasamanick, 1974), the Denver Developmental Screening Test (Frankenburg & Dodds, 1966), and the Lexington Developmental Scale (United Cerebral Palsy of the Bluegrass, 1973). A comprehensive developmental evaluation, which should be repeated at regular intervals, is indicated whenever an infant is identified as handicapped. There are many scales available for this purpose, the best of which appear to be the Bayley Scales of Infant Development (Bayley, 1969) and the Gessell and Amatruda developmental assessment procedures (Knobloch & Pasamanick, 1974). The identification of handicapping conditions without appropriate intervention is meaningless, however. As soon as an individual is identified as handicapped, he should be placed in an effective early intervention program.

The weight of evidence suggests that the first few years of life are extremely important in determining the course and rate of subsequent development. The manner in which parents structure the infant's environment, and the quantity and quality of their interactions with their children, have substantial effects on later development (Streissguth & Bee, 1972). Depriving infants of social, sensory or maternal stimulation for prolonged periods of time has been shown to have adverse effects on development (Dennis, 1960; Goldfarb, 1955; Spitz, 1946), and Down's syndrome children reared at home fare much better than those reared in institutions (Centerwall & Centerwall, 1960; Stedman & Eichorn, 1964). There is also evidence that at least short-term developmental gains can be obtained through even minimal environmental enrichment and stimulation at an early age (Casler, 1965; Dennis & Sayegh, 1965; White & Castle, 1964), and an early classic study associated long-term gains with a regimen of stimulation, enrichment, and mothering over a prolonged period (Skeels, 1966; Skeels & Dye, 1939). (The terms "maternal" and "mother," as used in this article, do not necessarily refer to a biological parent of the female sex. While the role of the "mother" is critical to development, this role can be fulfilled by a father, sibling, relative, foster parent, or other adult serving in this capacity.)

Beginning with the initiation of the Head Start program in 1965, and continuing through the present day, most of our early intervention efforts have been aimed at the socio-economically disadvantaged or cultural-familial retarded, sometimes with limited success (see Bronfenbrenner, 1974, and White, 1970, for reviews of the efficacy of Head Start) and occasionally with reported dramatic gains (Heber & Garber, 1975). While it is hoped that longitudinal data will eventually show that early intervention programs can prevent or minimize many of the behavioral deficits of severe and profound handicapping conditions, a word of caution is in order. We cannot afford to repeat the history of the Head Start movement, promising more than we can deliver and expecting more than we can achieve, with the result that we have a "period of optimism" followed by a "period of disillusionment" (Caldwell, 1974). However, we can prevent the development of those disabilities that stem from inadequate stimulation and care during the first few years of life.

Stone (1975) and Brassell (1975) have presented cogent arguments for extending our early intervention efforts to the biologically impaired. According to Stone, we should focus our efforts on parent-child relationships because (a) parents are critical as resources and mediators in the transactions between the infant and his world; (b) adverse effects are usually noted in cases in which the quality and quantity of infant-mother interactions are deficient; (c) biologically impaired infants have an even greater need for the mother to assist them in the development of information processing and response systems than do normal infants; and (d) there is sufficient data to indicate that parents who have been taught special training techniques have positive effects on the development of their children. Early intervention efforts should be directed toward developing mutually reinforcing mother-child systems before they are aimed at training the child in specific skill areas. Such systems can facilitate and enrich the transactions that occur between the child and his environment, making it more likely that healthy development will occur as a function of specific training efforts. This approach is supported by evidence that negative experiences can alter the course and impede the rate of development, when mothers either cannot or will not provide their children with adequate learning environments (Heber & Garber, 1975). Handicapped infants are more likely to have these negative experiences in the course of their interactions with their mothers (Fraiberg, 1975; Greenberg, 1971). Several programs for developmentally delayed, high-risk, or atypical infants (Cornwell, Lane, & Swanton, 1975; Dunst & Brassell, 1975; Nielsen, et al., 1975), Down's syndrome children (Hayden & Dmitriev, 1975; Rynders & Horrobin, 1975), blind infants (Fraiberg, 1975), and for mixed groups of developmentally delayed and normal infants and toddlers (Bricker & Bricker, 1971, 1972;

Vonderweidt, 1975) are demonstrating the efficacy of early intervention programs in which parents play an active and important role.

Several features appear to be critical to the success of early intervention programs for the severely and profoundly handicapped. First, it is mandatory that parents be actively involved in all aspects of the intervention process, and that they serve as primary change agents. Not only should parents and professionals enter into partnership, but parents should be the senior partners. Early intervention programs, and indeed all services for the severely and profoundly handicapped, must be responsive to consumer, rather than to professional, needs. This can be accomplished by recognizing that the primary focus of our early intervention efforts should be on the development of mutually reinforcing parent-child relationships, by involving the parents in all diagnostic and developmental evaluations, by responding to parental suggestions and wishes in planning intervention programs; and by seeking to develop parental self-sufficiency in caring for and teaching their own children. It is only through active parent involvement that we can discontinue the dangerous practice of having professionals assume parental responsibilities and that we can assure that early intervention efforts have durable, long-term effects.

Second, because the parent is the primary change agent, most early intervention efforts should be conducted in the home, rather than in clinic, settings. The process of teaching parents specific intervention techniques should be conducted in the natural surroundings of the home where the services will be delivered and the programs conducted, rather than in the artificial surroundings of an office building or a clinic.

Third, parents should participate in groups whenever possible and individually only as often as necessary. There are benefits, both economic (in terms of staff salaries and travel costs) and social (in terms of the dynamics of group membership) that can be obtained through facilitating the development and maintenance of small groups of parents who have the common bond of a severely or profoundly handicapped child.

Fourth, effective programs require interdisciplinary services that should be mediated through a single professional who works with each family. Termed the cross-modality (Crosby, 1976) or transdisciplinary (Nielsen, et al., 1975) model, this approach requires that the professionals involved be secure enough in their own abilities to permit them to release their roles and impart their skills to other professionals. The members of the interdisciplinary team conduct evaluations and make recommendations for programs and services; their recommendations are then carried out by a single professional who works directly with the family. This individual, in turn, should seek to pass these skills along to the parents as quickly as possible, in keeping with the primary goal of parental self-sufficiency. It goes without saying that there are some services that cannot be delivered except by professionally trained individuals. Every effort should be made, however, to keep direct services delivered by professionals at a minimum, through the use of transdisciplinary teamwork.

Fifth, early intervention programs should be guided by a longitudinal, sequenced curriculum that specifies both long-range goals and short-term behavioral objectives that are related to the long-range goals. The specific activities or experiences being afforded at any point should have a definite relationship both to the long-range objectives of the intervention program and to the child's developmental level.

Sixth, as Rynders and Horrobin (1975) have emphasized, the specific activities in an intervention regimen should have sufficient structure to assure that they will have a positive impact on development, but at the same time be flexible enough to allow the mother to assert her own maternal style. These authors also suggest a number of principles, based on their work with the mothers of Down's syndrome children, that serve as an excellent guide for the provision of home-based intervention services.

Public School Services. In addition to early intervention programs, the severely and profoundly handicapped must have access to public school services if they are to be served in community settings. Termed the "zero exclusion" model (Crowner, 1975; Sontag, 1976), and stipulated by P.L. 94-142 (see Ballard, Nazzaro, & Weintraub, 1976 for a detailed discussion of this legislation), it guarantees a free, public school education to all severely and profoundly handicapped individuals, irrespective of their level of functioning or the nature of their handicap.

The term "public school," as it is used here, refers to neighborhood schools. It does not refer to special schools that serve only handicapped students, nor does it refer to educational services provided at public expense in institutional settings or through contractual arrangements between state or local education agencies and third parties, such as a local Association for Retarded Citizens or United Cerebral Palsy organization. The severely and profoundly handicapped must be able to attend the same public schools that they would attend if they were not handicapped.

Adopting the zero exclusion model presents a number of problems to school administrators, teachers, and parents. The high incidence of physical handicaps among this population has sometimes been used to justify their continued exclusion from neighborhood schools. Most of our school buildings are old, and nearly all of them have architectural barriers that make wheelchair locomotion difficult. Yet someone must be responsible for students in wheelchairs, and to say that this is not the responsibility of public school personnel is only to say that someone else should do the work. Serving a relatively small number of physically handicapped children in a public school is not an insurmountable task. Most school buildings can accommodate wheelchairs through minor modifications that can be made at a reasonable cost. The difficulties of serving a few students in wheelchairs in a public school are minor when they are compared to the problems of serving a large group of nonambulatory individuals in a large residential facility or a special school.

Full-day, five-day-a-week nursery schools are not generally recommended for normally developing children below the age of 18 to 24 months, and severely and profoundly handicapped children should probably not be placed in full-day programs until they are at least three years of age (Knobloch & Pasamanick, 1974). Entry into school should also be preceded by a preschool program that begins at 12 to 24 months of age, in which the children attend school for two or four hours each day, three to four days each week. Nielsen, et al. (1975) suggest that preschools of this type can provide a natural bridge between home-based intervention and entry into full-day school programs, and that they have several other advantages including opportunities for socialization and the acquisition of new behavior through imitation, more intensive intervention than can be provided by parents over extended periods of time, and relief for mothers from the demands of caring for their handicapped children on a full-time basis.

The issue of integrating the severely and profoundly handicapped with their normal agemates is often raised when it is suggested that they be enrolled in public schools. As a general rule, the severely and profoundly handicapped should be placed in segregated classes only when necessary, and they should be integrated with their normal counterparts whenever possible. Although some segregation is usually required for instructional purposes, at the least these children can be integrated during recreation periods, mealtimes, and non-instructional activities.

It is sometimes felt that the severely and profoundly handicapped will suffer by being compared with more competent students if they are served in integrated classrooms. Although no controlled studies have been reported, there is no evidence that their self-concepts are substantially lowered as a consequence of integration. The potential for the severely and profoundly handicapped to acquire more normal behavior, and greater public acceptance, through an association with more competent students, outweighs any disadvantages.

It is understandable that some parents object when their normally developing children are integrated with the severely and profoundly handicapped, because they fear that their children may acquire inappropriate or aberrant behavior through "downward imitation." Such imitative behavior was observed in one integrated day care program, but the imitated responses quickly extinguished in the minority of children who exhibited them, presumably because they were not functional and because such behavior was not reinforced by parents or staff members (Vonderweidt, 1975). The evidence suggests that integrated preschool and day care programs result in measurable developmental gains for both handicapped and nonhandicapped children (Bricker & Bricker, 1971, 1972, 1973; Vonderweidt, 1975).

The heterogeneity of student ability that stems from integrating severely and profoundly handicapped students with their normal peers also poses instructional problems for teachers. Providing each student with an individualized instructional program that is matched to the student's developmental level becomes much more difficult if the students are extremely heterogeneous. This difficulty can be overcome, however, if each teacher is given adequate paraprofessional assistance and technical consultation; if teacher-pupil ratios are maintained at realistic levels; and if the teacher instructs students in small, developmentally homogeneous groups, rather than individually, whenever possible.

Community Residential Services. The demand for costly residential services would be substantially reduced if all severely and profoundly handicapped students were served in early intervention and public school programs. However, some severely and profoundly handicapped individuals cannot be kept at home (as is also the case with some normal individuals), and residential services must be provided for them.

In large measure, the impetus for community residences stems from the normalization principle (Nirje, 1969; Wolfensberger, 1972a). According to this principle, residential services for the handicapped should be patterned as closely as possible after the norms and patterns of the mainstream of society. Although the handicapped require extraordinary, i.e., abnormal, treatment at times (Throne, 1975), and although the road to normalization is not without some pitfalls (Vitello, 1974), the principle of normalization can still be an important guide for our efforts. If our ultimate goal for the handicapped is normal behavior patterns occurring in normal environments, the former will not be easily obtained in the absence of the latter.

The term "community residential service," refers to any community-based domicile that provides short or long term care on a 24-hour-per-day basis for individuals or for small groups of handicapped persons. Skarnulis (1976) has used the term "alternative living unit" to refer to the variety of community residences that have been successful in serving a wide range of handicapped individuals, including group homes, developmental homes, staffed apartments, cluster apartments, intensive training homes, apartments, duplexes, condominiums, single family homes, foster homes, and so on. With respect to the severely and profoundly handicapped, there are four basic types of community residences that should be made available: respite care services, adoptive home placements, foster care, and group homes.

Respite care refers to provisions for families to obtain brief periods of relief from the continuous care of a handicapped child. In some cases, respite care alone can mean the difference between a child's being retained at home and his being institutionalized. Respite care is an especially important service during periods of family stress or crisis. It can also be a means of providing short-term intensive training that is designed to teach specific skills to individual students. Several institutions are currently offering respite care services (Aanes & Whitlock, 1975), although it would be better to offer these services in community facilities or homes where they would be more accessible to the families requiring them.

If a severely or profoundly handicapped child cannot be retained in his natural home, adoptive placement is the preferred alternative. Until recently, most handicapped children were considered unadoptable. Fortunately, this has changed in recent years, as the number of children available for adoption has decreased and as public attitudes towards the handicapped have improved. In many cases, foster placements eventually result in adoption, after the foster parents have accepted the handicapped child into their family. The Child Welfare League of America operates the Adoption Resource Exchange, a clearinghouse for placing children who are available for adoption, including handicapped children, in appropriate homes. Since 1968, some 1,400 "hard to adopt" children have been placed in adoptive homes through this one program (Soeffing, 1975). Adoptive placements for the severely and profoundly handicapped are difficult to obtain. They would be easier to locate, however, if the potential parents could be assured of effective educational programs in public schools, and if subsidy payments were available to reimburse them for excess costs (for example medical expenses) which they incurred because of the child's handicap.

We have also seen a dramatic increase in the availability of foster homes for handicapped children in the past few years. Project MEMPHIS (Quick, Little, & Campbell, 1973) and the Macomb-Oakland family care training program (Rosen, Note 2) are two examples of foster home programs that also provide for home-based education and training. In Project MEMPHIS, children ranging in age from birth through five are placed, at the earliest possible time, with foster parents who are paid for their services. The children and their foster mothers are seen twice each week, and individualized lesson plans that are implemented in the foster homes are developed on the basis of extensive assessment data. One of the primary objectives of project MEMPHIS is to intervene early, so that the foster child will be more likely to be adopted by his foster family. In the Macomb-Oakland program, foster parents are selected and trained to provide care and training services for handicapped individuals. In addition to receiving payment for residential care and services, the "family care managers" are paid additional, but modest, stipends for providing two hours of daily active instruction for their foster children.

Community group homes should be available for all severely and profoundly handicapped children who cannot be kept in their natural homes and for whom adoptive or foster care placements are not possible. In keeping with the general trend toward community services for the handicapped, there has been an increasing emphasis on group homes in recent years. O'Connor and Sitkei (1975) surveyed 611 facilities that provided services to small groups of ". . . mentally retarded and/or otherwise developmentally disabled persons who are presently or potentially capable of functioning in the community with some degree of independence" (p. 35). They found that 75% of the facilities surveyed had been in existence for less than five years and that 46% of them had been operating for less than two years. The majority of the residents (89%) served were mentally retarded, and about one-half had been transferred to their community homes from institutions. Although O'Connor and Sitkei do not present data on this point, it can be assumed that few of the residences served severely or profoundly handicapped clients. At least two group homes have successfully served these individuals, however. Martin and Lowther (1973) have reported that substantial behavioral gains were made by a group of formerly institutionalized severely and profoundly retarded girls after they were transferred to a group home, and Favell, Larsen, Sellers, Boyd, St. Clair, Fleeman, and Jackson (1976) have presented data indicating that five severely retarded boys, who were transferred from an institution to a group home, made substantially greater gains on both standardized and criterion-referenced measures than did a matched contrast group that was retained in the institutional setting.

A recent bibliography of printed and audio-visual materials (Council for Exceptional Children, 1975) lists many resources that are available to agencies and organizations involved in community residential services development. Two additional publications, by Patterson & Byrne (1973) and by Behavior Analysis Research Associates (undated), are especially helpful in providing step-by-step instructions for planning and operating community group homes. All of the problems that are encountered in developing community residences for any handicapped group (for example zoning restrictions, transportation, fire and safety codes, community acceptance, employment and training of houseparents, and funding) are compounded in residences for the severely and profoundly handicapped. Yet the success of group homes for less severely handicapped individuals indicates that these obstacles can be overcome.

Other Community Services

There are three additional service components that should be available to support the retention of the severely and profoundly handicapped in community settings. These components—family counseling, in-home services, and protective services—should provide whatever support and assistance are required for parents to retain their handicapped children in their natural homes.

Family Counseling. Using a broad definition of the term "counseling," Townsend and Flanagan (1976) have described an in-home pre-admissions program consisting of: (a) instruction in child-training procedures; (b) discussions of available community resources; and (c) counseling about attitudes towards mental retardation, the needs of the child, child-rearing, and homemaking. This program tended to improve the chances that severely and profoundly retarded children would be kept at home. According to these authors, counseling with the mother alone tends to increase marital conflict—a problem that may be minimized by working with both parents or with the entire family. The instruction that they provided in child-training procedures effectively reduced the frequency of objectionable child behavior, and this also tended to induce a decision to keep the child at home. In a 10-week group counseling program, Lewis (1972) obtained significant improvements in both parental attitudes toward their handicapped children and in parental knowledge about mental retardation. The results of these two studies suggest that counseling and related services can improve parental attitudes and reduce the likelihood of institutional placement.

In-Home Services. Skarnulis (1976) has proposed a number of in-home family support services which can make it much easier for a parent to care for a severely or profoundly handicapped child. In the area of material options, he suggests providing: (a) appliances or equipment that eliminate architectural barriers for physically handicapped children; (b) time-saving appliances, such as dishwashers, laundry equipment, and transportation, that would make it possible for parents to devote more of their energies to caring for their children; and (c) medical and behavior modification equipment, such as oxygen tents when they are needed, alarm systems to alert the parents when their child is in need of something or wandering, and special toilet-training apparatus. Skarnulis also lists a number of staff services that could be made available, including: (a) parent support employees to assume some household and child care duties; (b) home handyman services, to make household repairs and construct specialized equipment for child care and training purposes; and (c) skilled babysitting services.

Protective services. Protective services, of which advocacy is the most common form, are required whenever an individual is unable to manage his own affairs, and whenever the services available to him are qualitatively or quantitatively deficient. In many respects, protective services are responses to deficiencies in our human services system—more often than not, they are needed to protect the individual consumer from the very agencies and institutions that were created to serve his needs. There are three major forms of protective services, including operational advocacy, personal or case advocacy, and legal advocacy, all of which seek to make human services responsive to human needs.

Operational advocacy can be defined as the presence of a system for delivering human services that focuses on: (a) ease of access to services at the local level; (b) delivery of full preventive and remedial services to all who need them; and (c) the provision of consumer-oriented, rather than institutionally-oriented, services (Lourie, 1975). Operational advocacy seems to be what the Joint Commission on Mental Health of Children (1969) had in mind when it recommended a nationwide, four-level advocacy system to cover the entire human services apparatus. The closest we have come to developing a functional operational advocacy system is in the Eastern Nebraska Community Office of Retardation (ENCOR) program, which provides comprehensive community-based services to all mentally handicapped individuals in a five-county region of Nebraska (Barker, 1971).

Personal or case advocacy is the most common approach to protective services. A number of models, including citizen advocacy (Wolfensberger, 1972b), child advocacy, and the European educateur (Linton, 1971), exemplify its essential features. These models have in common that they: (a) serve individual consumers who are unable to represent their own interests, (b) make provisions for meeting the expressive needs of the individuals that they serve, (c) assure that the individual contacts and is served by appropriate services, (d) protect the individual's human and civil rights, and (e) provide the individual with continuity across time and services.

Legal advocacy covers any activity that seeks to obtain needed services, when such activities involve making or interpreting laws through legislative action, court decision, or administrative rule-making. It has become the single most important form of protective services, as witnessed by a recent report on the status of current court cases (President's Committee on Mental Retardation, 1975) which reviews 104 pending lawsuits that concern architectural barriers, classification, commitment, custody, education, employment, guardianship, protection from harm, sterilization, treatment, voting, and zoning.

Conclusion

If there is a final solution to the problem of serving the severely and profoundly handicapped, it is to be found only in maintaining the vast majority of these individuals in their natural homes. The astronomical costs of inadequate care and treatment in large residential centers makes it clear that institutions are not an acceptable alternative, on either programmatic or financial grounds.

We should seek to abandon our institutions at the earliest possible time, not by dumping those who currently reside within them into "mini-institutions" that are even worse, but by preventing the admission of any more handicapped individuals to them. We have failed to adequately care for and serve the severely and profoundly handicapped who are already in our institutions, and we cannot give them back the years that we have taken from them or the opportunities that we have caused them to lose. It is within our power, however, to assure that we do not repeat these same errors with younger—and future—generations of severely and profoundly handicapped children.

This is not to say that we can forget the obligation that we have to those who are currently residing in our institutions. It is within our financial and technical resources to provide them with at least humane care and treatment. This can be accomplished at the same time that we create the community programs and services that are necessary to prevent the institutionalization of any more handicapped individuals.

The task of serving all severely and profoundly handicapped individuals in community settings is not insurmountable. In fact, community services for this group will be neither more expensive nor more difficult to provide than it would be to maintain our current fragmented and ineffectual service system for this group. We should begin by basing our services and programs on a firm commitment to our consumers, and by creating a network of services that is aimed at meeting the special needs of severely and profoundly handicapped individuals rather than meeting our own needs or the needs of our institutions or agencies. If we are to be successful, this is where we will have to start.

The specific community services that are required for the severely and profoundly handicapped do not have to be constructed from nothing. There are a number of exemplary programs throughout the country that have demonstrated the efficacy of early identification and intervention, public school programming, and community residential services that can guide us in this task. These model programs can be adapted to and emulated by other states and regions to create comprehensive and effective services in community settings. To date, not a single state nor region has developed a service network that uses the knowledge and technology that is already available. With your help, perhaps *your* state will be the first to accomplish this important task.

Reference Notes

1. Rosen, D., & Callan, L. B. *Trends: Residential services for the mentally retarded*. Unpublished manuscript. Sterling Heights, Michigan: Macomb-Oakland Center, 1973.
2. Rosen, D. *Family care training program*. Unpublished manuscript. Sterling Heights, Michigan: Macomb-Oakland Center, undated.

References

Aanes, D., & Whitlock, A. A parental relief program for the MR. *Mental Retardation*, 1975, *13*(3), 36–38.

Accreditation Council for Facilities for the Mentally Retarded. *Standards for residential facilities for the mentally retarded*. Chicago: Joint Commission on Accreditation of Hospitals, 1971.

Apgar, V. A proposal for a new method of evaluation of the newborn infant. *Current Researches in Anesthesia and Analgesia*, July–August 1953, 260–267.

Ballard, J., Nazzaro, J. N., & Weintraub, F. J. *P.L. 94-142, The Education for All Handicapped Children Act of 1975*. Reston, Va: Council for Exceptional Children, 1976.

Barker, E. Current and significant: ENCOR—A community's alternative to institutionalization. *Education and Training of the Mentally Retarded*, 1971, *6*(4), 185–190.

Baumeister, A. A. The American residential institution: Its history and character. In A. A. Baumeister & E. Butterfield (Eds.). *Residential facilities for the mentally retarded*. Chicago: Aldine Publishing Company, 1970.

Bayley, N. *Bayley scales of infant development*. New York: The Psychological Corporation, 1969.

Behavior Analysis Research Associates. *An operating manual for group living homes*. Tallahassee, Fl: Florida Division of Retardation, undated.

Blatt, B., & Kaplan, F. *Christmas in Purgatory: A photographic essay on mental retardation*. Boston: Allyn & Bacon, 1966.

Brassell, W. R. The case for very early intervention. *North Carolina Journal of Mental Health*, 1975, 7(3), 10–21.

Bricker, D., & Bricker, W. Toddler research and intervention project report—Year I. *IMRID Behavioral Science Monograph*, No. 20. Nashville, Tn: George Peabody College, 1971.

Bricker, D., & Bricker, W. Toddler research and intervention project report—Year II. *IMRID Behavioral Science Monograph*, No. 21. Nashville, Tn: George Peabody College, 1972.

Bricker, D., & Bricker, W. Infant, toddler, and preschool research and intervention project. *IMRID Behavioral Science Monograph*, No. 23. Nashville, Tn: George Peabody College, 1973.

Bronfenbrenner, U. Is early intervention effective? In B. Friedlander, G. Sterritt, & G. Kirk (Eds.). *Exceptional infant, Volume 3: Assessment and intervention*. New York: Brunner/Mazel, 1975.

Caldwell, B. M. A decade of early intervention programs: What we have learned. *American Journal of Orthopsychiatry*, 1974, *44*(4), 491–496.

Casler, L. The effects of extra tactile stimulation on a group of institutionalized infants. *Genetic Psychology Monographs*, 1965, *71*, 137–175.

Centerwall, S., & Centerwall, W. A study of children with mongolism reared in the home compared to those reared away from the home. *Pediatrics*, 1960, *25*, 678–685.

Cornwell, S. O., Lane, A. B., & Swanton, C. H. A home-centered, regional program for developmentally impaired infants and toddlers: The first years. *North Carolina Journal of Mental Health*, 1975, 7(3), 56–65.

Council for Exceptional Children. *Reintegrating mentally retarded people into the community*. Reston, Va: Author, 1975.

Crosby, K. G. Essentials of active programming. *Mental Retardation*, 1976, *14*(2), 3–9.

Crowner, T. T. A public school program for severely and profoundly handicapped students: Zero exclusion. In L. Brown, T. Crowner, W. Williams, & R. York (Eds.). *Madison's alternative for zero exclusion: A book of readings*. Madison, Wis: Madison Public Schools, 1975.

Dennis, W. Causes of retardation among institutional children: Iran. *Journal of Genetic Psychology*, 1960, *96*, 47–59.

Dennis, W., & Sayegh, Y. The effects of supplementary experience upon the development of infants in institutions. *Child Development*, 1965, *36*, 81–90.

Dunst, C., & Brassell, W. R. The utility of Piaget's concept of decalage for the construction of cognitively-based infant curricula. *North Carolina Journal of Mental Health*, 1975, 7(3), 22–31.

Favell, J. E., Larsen, L. A., Sellers, V., Boyd, L., St. Clair, J., Fleeman, G., & Jackson, L. *Belvedere House: A group home program for severely retarded boys*. Paper presented at the annual meeting of the American Association on Mental Deficiency, Chicago, June 1976.

Fraiberg, S. Intervention in infancy: A program for blind infants. In B. Z. Friedlander, G. M. Sterritt, & G. E. Kirk (Eds.). *Exceptional infant, Volume 3: Assessment and intervention*. New York: Brunner/Mazel, 1975.

Frankenburg, W. K., & Dodds, J. B. *Denver developmental screening test*. Denver: University of Colorado Medical Center, 1966.

Goldfarb, W. Emotional and intellectual consequences of psychological deprivation in infancy: A reevaluation. In P. H. Hoch & J. Zubin (Eds.). *Childhood psychopathology*. New York: Grune & Stratton, 1975.

Greenberg, H. A. A comparison of infant-mother interactional behavior in infants with atypical behavior and normal infants. In J. Hellmuth (Ed.). *The exceptional infant, Volume 2: Studies in abnormalities*. New York: Brunner/Mazel, 1971.

Hayden, A. H., & Dmitriev, V. The multidisciplinary preschool program for Down's syndrome children at the

University of Washington Model Preschool Center. In B. Z. Friedlander, G. M. Sterritt, & G. E. Kirk (Eds.). *Exceptional infant, Volume 3: Assessment and intervention*. New York: Brunner/Mazel, 1975.

Heber, R., & Garber, H. The Milwaukee project: A study of the use of family intervention to prevent cultural-familial mental retardation. In B. Friedlander, G. Sterritt, & G. Kirk (Eds.). *Exceptional infant, Volume 3: Assessment and intervention*. New York: Brunner/Mazel, 1975.

Howe, S. G. *Report made to the legislature of Massachusetts upon idiocy*. Boston: Collidge & Wiley, 1848.

Joint Commission on Mental Health of Children. *Crisis in child mental health: Challenge for the 1970's*. New York: Harper & Row, 1969.

Kennedy, J. *Message from the president of the United States*. Washington, D.C.: House of Representatives (88th Congress), Document No. 58, 1963.

Klaber, M. M. Institutional programming and research: A vital partnership. In A. A. Baumeister & E. Butterfield (Eds.). *Residential facilities for the mentally retarded*. Chicago: Aldine Publishing Company, 1970.

Knobloch, H., & Pasamanick, B. (Eds.). *Gessell and Amatruda's developmental diagnosis*. Hagerstown, Md: Harper & Row, 1974.

Kreger, K. C. Compensatory environment programming for the severely retarded behaviorally disturbed. *Mental Retardation*, 1971, *9*(4), 29–33.

Lewis, J. Effects of a group procedure with parents of MR children. *Mental Retardation*, 1972 *10*(6), 14–15.

Linton, T. E. The European Educateur model: An alternative and effective approach to the mental health of children. *Journal of Special Education*, 1971, *3*(4), 319–327.

Lourie, N. V. Operational advocacy: Objectives and obstacles. In I. N. Berlin (Ed.). *Advocacy and child mental health*. New York: Brunner/Mazel, 1975.

Martin, G. L., & Lowther, G. H. *Kin Kare: A community residence program for severe and profound retardates in a large institution*. Paper presented at the International Symposium on Behavior Modification, Minneapolis, October 1972.

National Association for Retarded Children. *Final report of the National Conference on Residential Care* (Houston, Texas, July 1969). New York: National Association for Retarded Children, 1969.

National Association of Superintendents of Public Residential Facilities for the Mentally Retarded. *Residential programming*. Washington, D.C.: President's Committee on Mental Retardation, 1974.

Nielsen, G., Collins, S., Meisel, J., Lowry, M., Engh, H., & Johnson, D. An intervention program for atypical infants. In B. Friedlander, G. Sterritt, & G. Kirk (Eds.). *Exceptional infant, Volume 3: Assessment and intervention*. New York: Brunner/Mazel, 1975.

Nirje, B. The normalization principle and its human management implications. In R. Kugel & W. Wolfensberger (Eds.). *Changing patterns of residential services for the mentally retarded*. Washington, D.C.: President's Committee on Mental Retardation, 1969.

O'Connor, G., & Sitkei, E. G. Study of a new frontier in community services: Residential facilities for the developmentally disabled. *Mental Retardation*, 1975, *13*(4), 35–39.

Patterson, G., & Byrne, R. (Eds). *The right to choose: Achieving residential alternatives in the community*. Arlington, Tx: National Association for Retarded Citizens, 1973.

Parmalee, A. H., & Michaelis, R. Neurological examination of the newborn. In J. Hellmuth (Ed.). *Exceptional infant, Volume 2: Studies in abnormalities*. New York: Brunner/Mazel, 1971.

Prechtl, H., & Beintema, O. *The neurological examination of the full term newborn infant*. London: Wm. Heinemann, 1964.

President's Committee on Mental Retardation. *Mental retardation and the law: A report on status of current court cases* (DHEW Publication No. 76-21012). Washington, D.C: Author, 1975.

Quick, A. D., Little, T. L., & Campbell, A. A. Early childhood education for exceptional foster children and training of foster parents. *Exceptional Children*, 1973, *40*(3), 206–208.

Roos, P. Normalization, de-humanization, and conditioning: Conflict or harmony? *Mental Retardation*, 1970, *8*(4), 12–14.

Rosenblith, J. F. The modified Graham behavior test for neonates: Test-retest reliability, normative data and hypotheses for future work. *Biology of the Neonate*, 1961, *3*, 174–192.

Rosenblith, J. Prognostic value of neonatal behavioral tests. In B. Friedlander, G. Sterritt, & G. Kirk (Eds.). *Exceptional infant, Volume 3: Assessment and intervention*. New York: Brunner/Mazel, 1975.

Rynders, J. E., & Horrobin, J. M. Project EDGE: The University of Minnesota's communication stimulation program for Down's syndrome infants. In B. Friedlander, G. Sterritt, & G. Kirk (Eds.). *Exceptional infant, Volume 3: Assessment and intervention*. New York: Brunner/Mazel, 1975.

Santiestevan, H. *Out of their beds and into the streets*. Washington, D.C: American Federation of State, County, and Municipal Employees, 1975.

Scheerenberger, R. C. A model for deinstitutionalization. *Mental Retardation*, 1974, *12*(6), 3–7.

Scheerenberger, R. C. A study of public residential facilities. *Mental Retardation*, 1976, *14*(1), 32–35.

Skarnulis, E. Less restrictive alternatives in residential services. *AAESPH Review*, 1976, *1*(3), 40–84.

Skeels, H. M. Adult status of children from contrasting early life experiences. *Monographs of the Society for Research in Child Development*, 1966, *31*, Serial No. 105.

Skeels, H. M. & Dye, H. B. A study of the effects of differential stimulation on mentally retarded children. *Proceedings and addresses of the American Association on Mental Deficiency*, 1939, *44*, 114–136.

Soeffing, M. Families for handicapped children: Foster and adoptive placement programs. *Exceptional Children*, 1975, *41*(8), 537–543.

Sontag, E. Zero exclusion: Rhetoric no longer. *AAESPH Review*, 1966, *1*(3), 105–114.

Spitz, R. A. Hospitalism: A follow-up report. *Psychoanalytic Study of the Child*, 1946, *2*, 113–117.

Stedman, D., & Eichorn, D. A. A comparison of the growth and development of institutionalized and home-reared mongoloids during infancy and early childhood. *American Journal of Mental Deficiency*, 1964, *69*, 391–401.

Stone, N. A plea for early intervention. *Mental Retardation*, 1975, *13*(5), 16–18.

Streissguth, A. P., & Bee, H. L. Mother-child interactions and cognitive development in children. In W. W. Hartup (Ed.). *The young child: Reviews of research* (Volume 2). Washington, D.C: National Association for the Education of Young Children, 1972.

Throne, J. M. Normalization through the normalization principle. *Mental Retardation*, 1975, *13*(5), 23–25.

Townsend, P. W., & Flanagan, J. J. Experimental preadmission program to encourage home care for severely and profoundly retarded children. *American Journal of Mental Deficiency*, 1976, *80*(5), 562–569.

Tronick, E., & Brazelton, T. B. Clinical uses of the Brazelton Neonatal Behavioral Assessment. In B. Friedlander, G. Sterritt, & G. Kirk (Eds.). *Exceptional infant, Volume 3: Assessment and intervention*. New York: Brunner/Mazel, 1975.

United Cerebral Palsy of the Bluegrass. *The Lexington developmental scale*. Lexington, Kentucky: Author, 1973.

Vitello, S. J. Cautions on the road to normalization. *Mental Retardation*, 1974, *12*(5), 39–40.
Vonderweidt, J. A developmentally integrated day care center: A new concept in early intervention. *North Carolina Journal of Mental Health*, 1974, 7(3), 32–40.
White, B. L., & Castle, P. W. Visual exploratory behavior following postnatal handling of human infants. *Perceptual Motor Skills*, 1964, *18*, 497–502.
White, S. H. The national impact study of head start. In J. Hellmuth (Ed.). *Disadvantaged child, Volume 3: Compensatory education, a national debate.* New York: Brunner/Mazel, 1970.
Wolfensberger, W. Twenty predictions about the future of residential services in mental retardation. *Mental Retardation*, 1969, *6*(7), 51–54.
Wolfensberger, W. Will there always be an institution? I: The impact of epidemiological trends. *Mental Retardation*, 1971, *9*(5), 14–20(a).
Wolfensberger, W. Will there always be an institution? II: The impact of new service models. *Mental Retardation*, 1971, *9*(6), 31–37(b).
Wolfensberger, W. *The principle of normalization in human services*. Toronto: National Institute on Mental Retardation, 1972 (a).
Wolfensberger, W. *Citizen advocacy*. (DHEW Publication No. OS 72-42). Washington, D.C: President's Committee on Mental Retardation, 1972 (b).

LAWRENCE A. LARSEN is the Project Director of the Severely and Profoundly Handicapped Training Program at Johns Hopkins University in Baltimore. Previously, he was a Research Associate at the Parsons Research Center, and later Director of Psychology and Special Education at Western Carolina Center. His major professional interests are the implementation of community services for the handicapped, the development of competency-based training programs, and the application of behavioral principles in classroom settings.

Generic Services for the Severely Handicapped and Their Families: What's Available?

LEONARD A. KENOWITZ
JILL GALLAHER
EUGENE EDGAR

University of Washington

The recent trend toward deinstitutionalization of the handicapped has engendered the belief that, with proper training, any disability can to some degree be ameliorated, regardless of its severity. However, the purpose of training to achieve community integration is twofold: first, training the handicapped individual to be as normal as possible (for example, to feed himself and to learn how to use existing community resources) and, second, training those in the service programs, such as health and recreation, that the handicapped individual uses in daily living to accomodate his needs.

Although many university and public school programs are training the severely handicapped in such "normal" activities as eating in restaurants and using public transportation, there are few community programs which adapt programs or train personnel to promote community integration of the handicapped. When this is the situation, it is paradoxical to train the handicapped to use public transportation if they are denied access to or face obstacles in using such services.

Most professionals have recognized the fact that the severely/profoundly handicapped will require a wide range of special professional services that, though expensive, are necessary if these individuals are to survive and be normalized in society. What has not been as readily acknowledged is the need for providing the handicapped and their families with nonspecialized, typical services that are readily available to families with nonhandicapped children—generic services.

We have heard so much from families of the handicapped in our community about the difficulty and expense of obtaining services that we surveyed generic services in the greater Seattle area and thereby obtained at least an informal view of the problems confronting these families. Although this survey is not necessarily representative of other areas, it may offer some useful stimulus to programs and professionals across the country. If findings in other areas are similar, this will be an indication of how much work we have to do in order to make life more livable for the severely/profoundly handicapped and their families. One recently proposed solution to this service problem is presented in the final section of this article. The focus of this paper is, therefore, to present an analysis of some data which suggest that generic services are not readily available to the severely/profoundly handicapped and their families.

Definition of Generic Services

Generic services are here defined as the typical services which families with nonhandicapped children either receive outright (the use of public transportation, the freedom to have a meal in a restaurant, the freedom to take part in religious activities of their choice), or to purchase for a standard price (a dental examination, treatment of a skin rash, dancing lessons, life insurance). These are the services that typical families take for granted and consider a necessary part of everyday life. Most of these services are provided to the individual on a profit basis, i.e., the provider must make a profit in order to continue to give the service. Although some services are underwritten by federal funds (public transportation) or state monies (state parks), the majority must show some type of profit in order to continue operating. As a result, these services are organized to serve the greatest number of people at the lowest possible cost. When an

All data mentioned in this article were gathered by students in the Special Education-Early Childhood master's program at the University of Washington. The authors acknowledge these students' assistance and their zeal in the accumulation of this information, specifically Jeff Brewster in data collection for Tables 1 and 2, and Elizabeth Tracy Barsh in data collection for Table 3. The authors also acknowledge the editorial assistance of Gael McGinness and Sharon Talbert in the preparation of this paper.

individual differs significantly enough from the majority to require special treatment, either the purchaser or the provider of the service must assume the added cost. In most cases, this cost is passed on to the purchaser, or the service is denied outright. In either case, families of severely/profoundly handicapped children are often denied services, either because of prohibitive cost or because the service simply is not available to them.

Examples of Generic Services

Medical Care

Most families are able to purchase competent medical care for their children locally. At times, specialized care may require transporting children some distance in order to obtain the most appropriate treatment. Still, for common childhood illnesses, medical care is a fairly typical available service. The families of handicapped children, on the other hand, are often frustrated in their attempts to procure medical treatment. In far too many instances, when parents take a severely handicapped child to a primary care physician for treatment of a cold, they are told that the physician does not treat mental retardation, and that they should seek treatment elsewhere. To compound the problem, many primary care physicians are not aware of the services for the handicapped in the community.

In a recent survey of eighteen pediatricians in a local residential area, eight expressed willingness to treat handicapped children, five preferred not to treat such patients, and five were hesitant to provide such service. The physicians in this survey were called by a student who told them she had a friend with a moderately handicapped five-year-old who needed treatment for a severe cold. Seven of the physicians referred the caller to the local Child Development and Mental Retardation Center at the University of Washington.

The findings of this survey were generally positive in that eight of the physicians were willing to treat the child. However, the number of referrals to the Child Development and Mental Retardation Center is quite disturbing. There is little wonder that parents become angry and frustrated when they are referred to an inappropriate agency and then often accused of shopping for a "better" diagnosis of their children.

Dental Care

The survey also revealed a surprising number of dentists who chose to refer the handicapped either to another dentist or to the University of Washington Dental School, which has a special program for handicapped children. The rationale for these referrals was that the expense involved in treating the handicapped prevents most dentists from treating this population.

Dental care for the severely/profoundly handicapped is quite expensive. One dentist who uses a general anesthetic charges $60 just to open the child's mouth; all additional treatment is extra. Another, who often recommends the hospitalization of severely/profoundly handicapped children for dental treatment, charges $120 just to begin treatment. Certainly these costs are exhorbitant. Referring children to the local university, although ensuring appropriate and reasonably priced care, does not solve the transportation problem. In communities that do not have access to a dental school for specialized treatment, dental care for the severely handicapped may be neglected altogether.

Insurance

Medical and life insurance are typical services most parents purchase for their children. Not so for the handicapped. Medical insurance is virtually impossible to purchase if the child was not insured from birth because the potential cost to an insurance company is unlimited in the case of a severely handicapped child. The question is: should parents of the severely handicapped carry the burden of excessive medical expense because insurance companies do not wish to take such a risk?

Life insurance policies for the severely/profoundly handicapped, when available, also require unrealistic premiums. Again, the families of the handicapped find themselves deprived of services that are available to others. In our survey, only one insurance company had a ready-made plan for the retarded at no extra cost. The other insurance companies had no established policy and were noncommittal about insuring the handicapped. Most companies decide each case individually, using a physician's prognosis as the major determinant. The best advice for prospective parents is to enroll in a group insurance program before the birth of a child, to be sure of receiving coverage. (There are plans in the State of Washington, to introduce legislation at the state level requiring insurance companies to provide medical insurance to the retarded.)

Religion

The purpose of the church survey was to determine whether there were opportunities for handicapped children and/or their families to participate actively as church members through specific programs or child day care services. On the positive side, there were nine programs, three of them on Saturday mornings. Programs were offered for young children, for those of elementary age, and for adolescents. One church offered a summer camp program. One denomination provided respite care services for handicapped children from birth to age 12 and was in the process of developing a parent outreach group.

A second survey generated the following comments from church personnel, with each major denomination represented:

"Never has come up, so we don't know how to answer."

"Possibly; parents should call first if the child needs constant supervision. Possibly child care at 9:30 mass."

"Child care at 10:00. Mothers volunteer, so it depends on the particular mother working. Call first to make special arrangements. Minor handicaps, probably; severe, probably not."

"Can't answer the question; the problem has never come up before. They do have handicapped adults attending church. Would need special consideration."

"High school girls handle Sunday child care, so we probably could not handle a special child."

Although some promising programs are being developed, there is indecision on the part of a number of churches. Some have not considered developing programs or providing child care during the worship service so that parents could continue to be active members of the church. Again, the case-by-case phenomenon is present, and severity of the handicap is a prime factor in obtaining services. A number of parents have reported that they stopped attending church after their handicapped child was born. Their reasons included child care problems and lack of support from church members.

Restaurants

The survey of urban and suburban restaurants, of varying levels of expense and different ethnic themes, questioned whether or not a person afflicted with cerebral palsy and confined to a wheelchair would be served. The interviewer stressed the term "cerebral palsied," and the basic approach was: "I would like to make reservations for a party of five. We would like to come to your restaurant for dinner. However, one of the people in the party has cerebral palsy and is confined to a wheelchair. Will that make a difference?".

Of the 31 restaurants surveyed, the unanimous response was that there would be no problem, and the individual could be served. Some answered as follows:

"No problem at all."

"No, why should it?"

"We have a pathway for wheelchairs. Cerebral palsy is okay."

"Oh sure! We have a two-door back entrance. We have regular customers who have cerebral palsy."

"When making reservations, note wheelchair. Park in the unloading zone by the Space Needle. There is a pathway to get the chair up to the elevators."

It is interesting that the restaurant that gave the response, "No, why should it?", was the impetus for this survey, in that a woman with cerebral palsy had been requested to leave that same restaurant while dining, her contention being that it was due to speech and eating difficulties caused by her disability.

Transportation

Intra-city and inter-city transportation services are very limited for handicapped individuals, particularly for those with physical disabilities. The limited assistance provided is mainly in the form of fare reduction rather than in provisions for physical accessibility.

The survey of the urban public transportation system revealed that only one special service was provided: free bus service for legally blind individuals. The requirements for obtaining the pass included an annual application, an annual income of $4,800 or less per couple or $3,600 or less for a single individual, and a document signed by an opthalmologist declaring the degree of visual acuity.

In a recent legal suit, initiated by a quadriplegic, charging discrimination against the physically handicapped, the transit system in question concluded.:

> (Metro) does not exclude wheelchair-bound handicapped persons in general nor the plaintiff in particular from use of its transit services by actively refusing to provide services or increasing fares. The case is concerned with just the physical problem inherent in a step-entry vehicle in view of the plaintiff's wheelchair bound condition. Metro does not distinguish between handicapped and nonhandicapped. (King County File #795806)

The alternatives to public transportation are private vehicles. In an effort to assist handicapped individuals who drive to ride in private cars, a decal system for preferential parking has been instituted. How effective is this system? In November 1975, the Governor's Subcommittee on Transportation in Washington stated that "the Department of Motor Vehicles has a service that they are not publicizing. Parking stalls are reserved but the requirements are not enforced. The Committee suggested that police departments be contacted about reserved parking and parking tickets." Recently, however, at a restaurant parking lot, a city police vehicle was parked in the space clearly designated for handicapped drivers while the officers were dining inside.

Public transportation for the handicapped is little better at the national level. Regarding physically handicapped individuals travelling on AMTRAK, the stated policy is: "If a person is limited to a wheelchair, the only solution is to travel in the sleeping car, which entails being put onto a stretcher and lifted through a window, as the stairwells are too narrow and very winding and thus cannot accommodate a wheelchair." When told that one person would be accompanying the handicapped individual, the AMTRAK Special Services representative replied that this was out of the question, because at least two or three persons would be necessary, and no AMTRAK personnel are allowed to physically assist anyone at any time unless specifically hired by the travelling individual to do so. It was emphasized time and time again that travelling by train under these conditions was very, very difficult.

The Greyhound Bus Corporation has made strides in this area through instituting its "Helping Hand" service, and Greyhound should be commended for this effort. It is ironic that the provision of such a basic, essential service as transporation is news, but an article entitled "Compassionate Greyhound" appeared in the January 11, 1976, issue of *Parade*, a nationally circulated Sunday newspaper feature:

> Companions of handicapped individuals who need help in boarding, exiting, or travelling on any Greyhound bus can now travel free. Both people travel on a single ticket, and non-motorized wheelchairs, walkers, crutches and other ambulatory devices are carried without charge in the baggage compartment of all buses. Greyhound inaugurated its "Helping Hand" service several weeks ago. (p. 14)

Social

Recreation and leisure time activities are an important adjunct to educational and vocational services, and most people depend on their communities for these services. However, many of the handicapped are not receiving any form of professional recreation or leisure service, and many of the services that are provided are underfinanced or offered only infrequently.

In a survey of 31 parents with Down's syndrome children aged 6 to 12 living at home, there was an alarming response to the question, "What types of recreational services have you wanted for your child, but have not been able to receive or find?". The recreation services mentioned by these parents were dance, tumbling, swimming, day camp, Sunday School, music lessons, Camp Fire Girls, and Boy Scouts, all of which are supposedly available in this particular community. If these services are provided, why are they not being delivered? It is important to realize that there is a disparity between provision for and delivery of services, an issue that needs to be investigated.

Although the area of recreation is by far the strongest in offering generic services for the handicapped, the only specific program for the severely/profoundly handicapped is the newly expanded Special Olympics program of 1976. Recreation program staffs of park department, and private organizations have said, "We have had virtually no referrals for severely/profoundly handicapped individuals but would provide service through our other programs, unless their numbers warranted specific programs."

The social activities of handicapped adolescents are also limited. A case in point is that of two cerebral palsied adolescent boys enrolled in a class taught by a team of teachers. The teachers rated one of the boys as a socially active student outside the school environment, and the other boy as socially isolated. Each boy was interviewed for 45 minutes to develop a chart showing how he spent his time out of school. Although the data are displayed in a one-week format, they are an assimilation of out-of-school activity over a period of one month (Tables 1 and 2).

As the daily schedules indicate, the handicapped students had very little contact with individuals outside of the school program. Most leisure time was spent in isolation or with their parents. Both boys were totally dependent on their parents for transportation away from home. Other than a few telephone conversations, their social lives seemed to center around the public school program and organized activities for the handicapped. There was no indication that there were any meaningful contacts with females of their own age, or that they had a group of friends, or even one friend.

Another study was instituted in an urban-suburban area in order to discover how retarded adolescents actually spent their leisure time, as opposed to how they might spend it.

TABLE 1

Raw Data Sheet–Student A (Socially Active)

	Monday	Tuesday	Wednesday	Thursday	Friday	Saturday	Sunday
Morning 7–8 a.m.	*7:00 a.m.* 1. Get up 2. Dress 3. Eat (mother feeds) 4. Bathroom *8:10 a.m.* Take bus to school—Mom helps walk	Same	Same	Same	Same	1. Get up when wishes independently 2. Feed self breakfast	Same as Saturday
School 9–3						Afternoon	Afternoon
After School 3–6 p.m.	1. TV—self 2. Talk to Mom 3. Walk around w/friend or self 5. "Mess around"	Same May go window shopping —self	Same	Same	Same	1. "Mess around" w/handicapped friends 2. Play chess 3. Young peoples church group (monthly—normal peers)	Same
Dinner 6–7 p.m.	Feed self	Same	Same	Same	Same	Same	Same
After Dinner 7–10 p.m.	1. TV—self 2. Radio—self 3. Talk w/parents 4. Telephone calls to handicapped school friends 5. Magazines—self	Same	Same May have a friend for dinner	Same	1. Park Dept Soc Prog w/handicapped peers (monthly) 2. TV—self & parents	1. TV—self 2. Sports event—normal and handicapped peers 3. Party—normal & handicapped peers	1. TV w/ family
Bed	To bed & bathroom by self	Same	Same	Same	To bed independently	Same	Same as Monday

Initially, ten adolescents were contacted: five who were trainable mentally retarded (TMR) and five normal high school students. Data were collected via an individual weekly schedule of activities, indicated by day and time for seven consecutive days. Eight adolescents participated: four TMR and four normal (Table 3).

The special education group was transported to most social activities by parents; presumably the high school group had greater mobility. All the parents of the special education boys reported that they found it difficult to provide transporation, and no parent in this group felt confident in allowing his or her son to travel on his own.

Whereas sports comprise the major activity for the high school group (averaging at least 10 hours per week in play or practice), listening to records and watching television seems to take up the bulk of the special education group's free time (averaging approximately 25.6 hours television time per week for the group). Although it is possible for a high school student to watch as much television as any special education adolescent, three of the four high school boys watched considerably less than their special education peers. In fact, three of the special education adolescents even watched television in the morning after breakfast before the school bus arrived. Watching television simply to fill up time seems to indicate a lack of opportunity, or the inability to develop creative

TABLE 2

Raw Data Sheet–Student B (Socially Isolated)

	Monday	Tuesday	Wednesday	Thursday	Friday	Saturday	Sunday
Morning 7–8 a.m.	*7:15 a.m.* 1. Get up 2. Dress—self 3. Bathroom—self 4. No breakfast *8:00 a.m.* Mother helps out to bus	Same	Same	Same	Same		
School 9–3						Get up late (about 10 a.m.)	Same
After School 3–6 p.m.	1. Go for walk—self 2. Write letters to normal peers (camp counselors) and relatives 3. TV—self and sister 4. Radio—self 5. Help father in yard	Same	3–5 p.m. Monthly Park Dept Gym Prog Same	Same as Monday	3–4 p.m. Sports Club with handicapped peers: Father picks up Twice month: Park Dept social event (handicapped peers)	Father feeds breakfast *Afternoon* 1–3: Seattle Handicapped Club	*Afternoon* 1. TV w/ family 2. Visit relatives
Dinner 6–7 p.m.	Fed by father	Same	Same	Same	Same	Same	Same
After Dinner 7–10 p.m.	1. TV w/family 2. Radio—self 3. Telephone calls mostly to non-handicapped peers	Same Monthly: dinner with last year's teacher	Same	Same Every fortnight: dinner out with family	1. TV 2. Monthly: football (normal peers) 3. Telephone	1. Monthly: social event (handicapped & normal) 2. TV—self, sister, family	Same as Monday; especially TV w/ family
Bed 10 p.m.	To bed & bathroom	Same	Same	Same	Same (later)	Same (later)	Same as Monday

uses of free time. For example, only one special education student had a hobby (building model airplanes), whereas each boy in the high school group engaged in challenging activities (skiing, band practice, extra sports practice) of his own choosing sometime during the week. This points up the qualitative difference between being taken to a swimming lesson as part of a school program and creatively choosing a particular activity or program, based on personal likes and interests.

Home Aid Resources Program

A proposed answer to the many dilemmas of home life for the handicapped individual and his family is the newly instituted Home Aid Program. This program is designed to serve developmentally disabled individuals and their families by providing: home care (short-term respite care and temporary in-home care and supervision of the handicapped individual on an emergency basis); parent-to-parent outreach (experienced volunteer support to parents of a newly identified, developmentally disabled child in such areas as friendship, advocacy, counseling, education, and consultation); resource therapy (professional services in the home of the client in such areas as physical, occupational and recreational therapy, nutri-

TABLE 3

Organized Social/Recreational Activities (times per week)

	High School				*Special Education*			
Ss	1	2	3	4	a	b	c	d
#	6	7	8	5	2	3	2	4

High School	Special Education
Sports (basketball, wrestling)	Young Generation Club
School dances	Boy Scouts
Dancing lessons	Bowling at school
Karate lessons	Swimming lessons

Unorganized Social/Recreational Activities

	High School				*Special Education*			
Activity Ss	1	2	3	4	a	b	c	d
Friends	0	3	0	2	0	2	0	0
Going out	2	0	2	3	0	0	0	4
Eating out	2	0	0	0	0	0	2	1
Stores (shopping)	0	0	0	0	0	0	1	3

Television and Records (hours per week)

	High School				*Special Education*			
Ss	1	2	3	4	a	b	c	d
TV	5	4	21.5	2	11.5	27.5	29.0	35.0
Radio	0	1	0	0	6.5	3.0	1.0	5.5

tion and health maintenance, dental hygiene, behavioral management, and communication therapies); program/skill development (community based program for client skill development in such areas as socialization, recreation, education, vocational skill training, religious nurture activities, and other specialized activities to meet the individual client's training needs); and further assistance (such as transportation) to enable the handicapped individual and his family to participate in local skill development programs. These services are intended to: strengthen the family as the primary resource; lower the individual's cost to the state, as compared with the cost to the state when individuals are institutionalized; benefit the handicapped individual and increase his independence; and develop a community living situation.

Recently, one of the teachers at the Experimental Education Unit of the University of Washington tried to secure such services for a mother of a severely handicapped infant. The teacher, with the assistance of a medical advocate for families of the handicapped, tried everything possible to prevent the parent from becoming frustrated with the social system bureaucracy. Even with the help of these "system wise" individuals, an aide was secured for 12 days of work only after 59 phone calls to 18 individuals, three trips to the state capital, and six meetings over a 41-day period! Even with this massive expenditure of energy, the aide had still not received payment two weeks after the work had been completed.

Service delivery systems such as this often consume more time and energy than they seem to be worth. The great majority of parents would not have the energy or endurance to persevere long enough to secure the services they were seeking.

Cosmetic

The counseling staff of a state residential school for the mentally retarded reports that a number of their members regularly take the men and women into the community for haircuts and stylish clothes. Their stated purpose was to get away from the institutional look, especially the outdated hairstyles provided by the institution's barbers and beauticians.

When asked how a barber or beautician was selected, the reply was: "You have to feel the person out; it's an experience-type thing." Before taking an individual for a haircut, the counselor personally finds out what sort of reception to expect. The selection of professionals in providing the service is carefully made ("Why subject them to stares and rude, ignorant remarks?"). For the most part, personal barbers and beauticians of the staff are selected according to expertise and personal qualities. Obviously, the selection of these generic services for the handicapped require extra time, energy, and thought.

Long-Term Care

A critical service for handicapped individuals and their families is that of planning for long-term care—specifically, estate planning.

Many parents of handicapped children, especially those who have chosen not to institutionalize a moderately to severely involved youngster, are concerned about how they can provide for that child in his later years. Yet few undertake the legal procedures essential to securing the future. Some fear the complicated procedures involved; others are intimidated by the legal profession; the majority are simply uninformed, or misinformed, about their rights and opinions in estate planning.

A parent must consult a competent attorney, making sure that the advisor is familiar with all the facets of the law which pertain to the handicapped, and prepare a will. In so doing, the parent must, in fact, disinherit the child from any bequest because an individual who has funds of his own will automatically be disqualified from state aid. That person will no longer be eligible for Supplemental Security Income, group home care, Medicare/Medicaid coupons, state assistance benefits, or services offered by the Department of Vocational Rehabilitation. Furthermore, many of these services cannot be bought at any price (e.g., those of the Department of Vocational Rehabilitation). In other cases, the cost is prohibitive. If a parent does not leave a will or does not isolate the money properly, and the handicapped person is the only beneficiary, the estate will be transferred directly to the child and, if the child is already institutionalized, indirectly to the state. If he is not institutionalized, that inheritor is expected to begin supporting himself, without benefit of financial counseling or any other state services.

Child Care

Day care centers are widely used by working parents for child care, but they are not readily available to parents of handicapped children, particularly the severely involved. In a survey of 34 urban and suburban day care centers, the responses to the question, "Would you accept a handicapped child into your program?", were as follows: twelve yes; eleven no; ten case-by-case; one would not answer directly. At a glance, these data may lead the reader to believe that day care is available to the handicapped. However, after a closer look at the responses, the interpretation changes.

Yes: "At present we don't have any vacancies."
"Will accept slow learners. Feel we are not able to deal with severely delayed."
"Do take slow learners and would consider children with motor disabilities."
"Would welcome handicapped child. Serve children with adjustment and home problems. Presently serving a child with a limp."

No: "No. Will refer to Child Development and Mental Retardation Center at the University of Washington."
"No, not licensed to accept Mongoloid children." (Obviously, there is no such license!)

An alternative to day care services is babysitting. Is babysitting available? What is the quality of service? On the surface, private babysitting businesses gave the most positive responses:

"Would sit for the handicapped and have in the past. The price is usually the same, but, for a severely handicapped nursing case, they may charge more. Sitters have no special training."

"Would consider on a case-by-case basis."

Prices are $1.60 an hour, minimum four hours, plus $1 for transportation. However, the responses included the following:

"Case-by-case, may cost a little more."

"Mildly handicapped only."

"Five dollars per day."

"Has had one boy with open spine. Will take handicapped, $6 per day. May charge more if the child requires extra supervision."

"Consider case-by-case."

"Child would have to be able to walk."

Child care is not readily available to handicapped children, particularly the severely handicapped, either in the form of day care centers or babysitting. When the service is available, the quality is questionable, because of the lack of training of the staff.

Who Is Responsible?

This paper has attempted to demonstrate that few services are equally available to the handicapped and the nonhandicapped, and that even more inequity exists for the severely handicapped. This report has also shown that some services are offered, but for some reason are not much used by families of the handicapped. An obvious gap exists, and it is not simply a communication gap between families of the severely handicapped and the available services. A larger task, that of developing a process for the sensitization of community generic services so that they will serve the severely handicapped and their families, must be undertaken.

The most viable arrangement seems to be the development of community action networks. These networks would exist in every community and might be centered or coordinated at a local Association for Retarded Citizens Center, university hospital, fraternal organization, parent group counseling center, or public school. The primary responsibility of this network would be to bring together families of the severely handicapped and all agencies responsible for delivering some type of service.

The authors are currently engaged in conceptualizing and field testing a process for setting up communications to develop a community action network. While the margin between availability of services and the use of existing services by the handicapped is a formidible one, there is an order to the process of reducing this margin. First, every community must recognize its responsibilities and avail itself of the necessary services, while, simultaneously, the handicapped must be trained in using these services. The next step is to match or bring the two together for optimal integration of the handicapped into the community. The third is to identify service deficiencies and begin to develop service programs. Only when all services are readily available to the severely/profoundly handicapped and their families will community reintegration move from a dream to a reality.

References

King County file #79505.

Parade. January 11, 1974, 14.

LEONARD A. KENOWITZ, is the Inservice Training Coordinator for the Severely Handicapped Personnel Preparation Program at the Experimental Education Center of the University of Washington. Dr. Kenowitz previously held positions as teacher, counselor, researcher and teaching fellow. He has also served as a post-doctoral fellow with the National Association of State Directors of Special Education, Inc. His articles have appeared in *Education and Training of the Mentally Retarded* and *The Journal of Special Education.*

JILL GALLAHER is an educator in the Communications Preschool of the Experimental Education Unit at the University of Washington in Seattle. She also is a candidate for a master's degree in the area of early childhood education at the university.

EUGENE EDGAR, is an Assistant Professor at the University of Washington, Seattle. He is affiliated with the school's Experimental Education Unit, Child Development and Mental Retardation Center. A Peace Corps graduate, he also worked for Cumberland House Elementary School, a Project Re-Ed Center in Nashville, Tennessee. He has published in *Exceptional Children, Education and Training of the Mentally Retarded*, and *The Psychological Record.*

From Institution to Community: A Conversion Model

BURTON BLATT
ROBERT BOGDAN
DOUGLAS BIKLEN
STEVEN TAYLOR

Syracuse University

For too long, teachers have viewed their roles in society in terms of what takes place in the schoolhouse. Although we do not believe that such a model works very well for any child or, for that matter, any teacher, it works especially poorly and leads to serious problems when the children are the so-called handicapped and the teachers have been charged with the development of responsible programs to serve these children. All education is part of a larger social context, and seldom is it more important to recognize this than in dealing with children who are at high risk for placements in institutional environments. This paper addresses itself to that larger social context and its relevance for teachers and other professionals associated with the schools.

This article begins with a brief discussion and definition of our Conversion Model, with the expectation that the reader will be receptive to the conclusion that deinstitutionalization is only one facet of any bona fide system of community options for individuals with special needs. We next describe the elements of a community model, followed by a discussion of the processes involved in conversion. The paper continues with a plan of action and, based on our analysis of relevant literature and our own investigations, an assessment of the magnitude of the problem. We conclude with a summary which sets forth the relevance of these issues for teachers and others connected with the schools. Finally, because we believe that a serious barrier to achieving a workable conversion model stems from imprecision in definitions of the population and in estimates of incidence and prevalence, the appendix delineates information on the magnitude of this problem.

Conversion Defined

If we do not reconceptualize deinstitutionalization, it will fail, either by inertia or by backlash. Deinstitutionalization is a federal policy mandated as a priority by Title XX Social Security legislation, and by the Developmental Disabilities Act of 1975. Both as a policy and a philosophy, it has received general acceptance by state human service agencies, and by the public. Nevertheless, the practice of deinstitutionalization is occurring at a snail's pace (Conroy, 1976). The reasons are myriad, but the common denominator is our definition of deinstitutionalization.

Too often, deinstitutionalization has simply meant releasing people from state facilities by moving traditionally institutionalized people into community institutions. These have usually been nursing homes of two or three hundred people, or group homes, foster homes, and boarding homes that sometimes provide little more than bed and board. However, the goal of deinstitutionalization should not be simply to move people from one building to another, from one location to another, from a total-care institution to a partial-care one, or from a custodial-care facility to a non-care facility. The goal should be to transform a dehumanizing, segregated institutional model of services into a humanizing, integrated community model.

The task of achieving this goal has proven more difficult than first thought, mainly because it involves so much more than simply releasing people from institutions. There are several reasons for the difficulty. First, we have lacked a clearly articulated plan for community-based human services. Such a plan should address itself to these questions. Which children should enter public schools? Who will require special instruction? Who will need only resource assistance? Who will need more intense and individualized programming? What kinds of residential options will be necessary? Second, the states have vested interests in maintaining institutions whose construction has been financed by state and municipal bonds and loans. Institutional residents' Social Security, Medicaid, and insurance payments will be needed to repay lenders in the future. This mandates a continued full house in state-supported institutions. Third, deinstitutionalization will require changes in attitude throughout our culture. If the community is to offer experiences different from those offered by institutions, it must rid itself of prejudice and stereotyping and of the segregating, discriminatory policies that result from those attitudes. Fourth, the conduct of service providers must conform to principles of normalization (Wolfensberger, 1972), and of human dignity.

The roadblocks to deinstitutionalization will not be overcome by either moral or legal commitments to release institutional residents. What is demanded is a systematic approach to transforming institutions—a *Conversion Plan. By conversion, we mean an orderly transition from an institutional to a community-based system of services with concomitant plans to transform existing physical facilities, staff resources, institutional ideologies, community attitudes, and agency policies to alternative, more humanizing uses and postures.*

When industries shift their direction and begin new production, they almost always attempt to convert existing facilities and staff to the new or alternative effort. It is time for institutions and communities to proceed in similar fashion in moving toward deinstitutionalization. Without conversion, deinstitutionalization will fail to yield its expected positive results and may possibly produce a powerful backlash.

Conversion to What?

We must conceptualize the problem of institutions and community programs as the *conversion* of a system, rather than as the deinstitutionalization of individuals. But what kind of system do we want? Are we advocating a transition from large institutions to smaller ones? Do we speak only for the mildly or moderately retarded? Are we asking for a new generation of enlightened professionals to decide how the retarded are to live? No. We have a vision of a world with dramatically different assumptions about the rights of people, and their potential for growth, individuality, and dignity. And we have a vision of a sysytem of services that reflects the following principles:

1. Services must be provided as a right of citizens, rather than as a privilege (Biklen, 1974). Traditionally, services for those with disabilities have been considered a matter of charity and good will. As such, they have been denied on the basis of insufficient funds and other considerations. In the system we foresee, services will be offered to all who need them. This implies that all disabled individuals can benefit from community residential, educational, and vocational services and that they are capable of unlimited growth and development (Blatt & Garfunkel, 1969). It also means that no person will be deprived of services without due process procedures, whereby the burden of proof as to the appropriateness of any service shall be upon the service agency. All persons, regardless of nature or degree of disability, shall be entitled to a full range of appropriate programs and services.

2. Services must be provided on a *non-categorical* basis. That is, a person's needs, and not his category or label, will determine the services he receives. No agency will categorize people as "mentally retarded," "emotionally disturbed," "learning disabled," or as any other disability type.

3. Services must constitute a *continuum* to ensure that each individual's needs are met in the most appropriate manner. Programs shall be designed to fit individual needs, rather than vice versa. Rather than group homes, there will be a range of community residences—short and long term group facilities—offering foster care, respite care, and a chance for independent and semi-independent living. Rather than special schools, there will be a range of educational programs. Individuals will be able to move from one program to another as their needs require.

4. Services must be provided under the *least restrictive, most normalized* circumstances possible (Wolfensberger, 1972). Every individual must have the maximum opportunity to be integrated into the community and to be among typical peers. This implies a preference for independent, rather than supervised, living; for integrated, rather than segregated, schooling; for regular, rather than sheltered, employment.

5. The agencies providing services must be *accountable* to consumers. There must be active and significant consumer involvement in the planning, implementation, monitoring, and operation of services at agency, local, regional, state, and federal levels.

There are some who will dismiss our vision as idealistic or impractical. And they may be correct. From our viewpoint, however, there has been far too much realism and far too little idealism in the past. We have written plans without goals, provided services without a purpose, and constructed a world without a vision. If nothing else, a vision offers hope and direction.

Barriers to Community Conversion

We have presented one way of conceptualizing the problem of institutions and deinstitutionalization, and some of the components of the system into which we are attempting to convert. It is also important to consider the barriers that interfere with our efforts at conversion, for it is possible that one reason for their persistence is our seeming reluctance to identify them.

Handicapism

Handicapism has many parallels with racism. It is a set of assumptions and practices that promotes the differential and unjust treatment of people because of apparent or assumed physical, mental, or behavioral differences. Handicapism pervades our society and, overall, presents the most important barrier to the development of community programs. Prejudice, stereotyping, and discrimination are its major components. (See Yinker, 1965, and Allport, 1954, for a discussion of the use of these terms in the study of ethnic relations.)

Prejudice toward the handicapped is indicated by assumptions that they are innately incapable and naturally inferior. It is revealed in the belief that the handicapped have personalities and characteristics so extraordinary that they have little in common with non-handicapped persons, and should therefore be kept "with their own kind" (Goffman, 1963; Wright, 1960).

Prejudice is a general disposition, while stereotyping refers to the content of the prejudice that is directed toward specific groups. Thus, the mentally retarded are believed to be forever childlike, to enjoy boring, routine activities, and to be oversexed (Wolfensberger, 1975). The blind are supposed to be melancholy (Scott, 1969). Stereotypes are frequently used to justify particular modes of treatment. Thus, the retarded are often treated like children, given boring work, and isolated from others.

Despite their inaccuracies, stereotypes are maintained by many processes. They are transmitted and constantly reinforced by the culture and by peers. Since the handicapped are isolated and have few opportunities for close or sustained relations with normal people, they have little chance of disproving the stereotypes about themselves. Since handicapped people are treated in ways that correspond to their stereotypes and are rewarded for stereotypic behavior, they learn to act out the role of the handicapped and fall victim to self-fulfilling prophesies (Merton, 1957).

Prejudice and stereotyping point to the cognitive and ideological substance of handicapism and lead to discrimination. At one time, slaves and women were considered to be not unfairly treated. Laboring in the field for the economic benefit of others, or serving their husbands was viewed as their natural condition. Similarly, handicapped people are thought to have relative equality in our society, especially since the advent of categorical social service programs. Nevertheless, their differential treatment is evidence of deep discrimination.

Recognizing handicapism in a general way is important, but we must be more specific if we are to bring down this barrier. We must recognize that prejudiced assumptions are transmitted by the mass media—television, films, books, and newspapers. For example, in horror movies we see a clear association of physical and mental handicaps with acts of violence and hatred. In children's stories, there are the inevitable hunchbacks, trolls, and other deformed monsters who frighten pretty, normal children.

Cartoons, too, are important carriers of handicapist images. "Stupid idiot," "moron," "dumb," and "crazy" dot the landscape of such comic strips as *Beetle Bailey* and *Archie*. These comics not only confirm prejudicial and stereotypic attitudes, but also prove that disability labels have become general terms of derogation.

In hundreds of ways, the mass media transmit and reinforce negative concepts of the handicapped that create barriers to their placement and acceptance in the community. (For a full discussion of the concept of handicapism, see Biklen and Bogdan, 1976. Authors who have described various categories of the handicapped as minority groups include Dexter, 1964; Wright, 1960; Yuker, 1965; and Gellman, 1959.)

Economics

Special education is big business. The Rand Corporation recently reported that government agencies expend $2.8 billion annually to serve mentally retarded youth (Kakalik, 1973). Mental health is also big business. Governor Carey of New York has recommended a $924 million Department of Mental Hygiene budget for the 1977 fiscal year, "part of the Governor's $10.7 billion austerity budget . . ." (*Mental Hygiene News*, January 30, 1976, p. 1). Contrast this with the $640.2 million appropriated for fiscal year 1973 in New York State.

Institutionalization is big business in New York, and in a fundamental sense, New York, our case example, reflects the national situation. The 1975 appropriation for the Willowbrook Developmental Center was approximately $62 million, more than a $20,000 expenditure per resident. In 1965, the per capita expenditure at Willowbrook, and at virtually every other state institution for the mentally retarded, was less than $4,000 a year.

Even deinstitutionalization is big business, for those engaged in trust-busting and monolith-wrecking and for others who create and manage community alternatives to institutions. There is no way to avoid the fact that special education-mental health-mental retardation is big business. We can, in fact, talk of a handicap industry (Blatt, 1976).

And it is sacred business too! How many people noticed recently that a presidential candidate's ill-fated $90 billion federal budget cut proposal avoided assault on allocations for the handicapped? Our pariahs have become holy untouchables, for the most part segregated and lacking normal opportunities, but surrounded by government and philanthropic agents who are committed to protect to the end their right to be different, and to back that right with big dollars. In this modern era, we seem to insist on creating problems, and then on spending heavily to support them.

The handicapped are big business, although the business resembles more closely the game of Monopoly than the work of people who buy, or sell, or grow. Like Monopoly, the handicap business appears unreal, the money expended seems like paper, the promises not really meant or taken seriously. Handicap monopolies are easily created and almost as easily destroyed; this moment's idea is the next moment's joke; today's victory is tomorrow's embarrassment.

When Rockefeller, Carnegie, Mellon, and others invented the philanthropy business, their efforts led to significant changes in the extent and manner in which the federal government aids those in need. Big business has taught us how to organize our philanthropies to serve the people and, further, how to organize the people—the state—to serve both business and philanthropy.

This is America. There is enough for everyone, for the rich and the poor, the healthy and the sick, the sound and the unsound, the philanthropist and the businessman. Some data:

Item. In 1965, New York State embarked upon a five-year $500 to $600 million mental hygiene construction program as part of a master plan for the mentally disabled (Legislative Commission on Expenditure Review, 1973). Forty major projects were approved, at a construction cost of $320.3 million. Furthermore, the program included an additional $188 million for modernization of existing facilities, plus $100 million to help construct community mental health facilities. By 1972, 23 of the original 40 major projects had been completed or were under construction; these exceeded cost estimates by 50% ($94 million), a discrepancy that inflation in construction costs cannot fully explain. When the revised total plan is implemented, 28 projects will have been completed at a cost of $343.5 million, $23 million over the original estimates. If there are no further delays, inflationary increases, union demands, or bright new ideas, the 7,500 beds that will be the basic product of New York's master plan will cost the state's taxpayers approximately $45,000 each for construction, and an additional one and one-half to two times that amount ($65,000 to $90,000) to meet fund obligations, to the banks, foundations, and other bondholders who underwrote the cost.

Item. A recently completed study by the New York State Department of Mental Hygiene disclosed that residents in group homes for the mentally retarded required expenditures of $6,700 yearly, while institutionalized residents required $34,000.

Item. A recent report issued by the New York State Assembly (Swift & Melby, 1976) revealed that family care for the mentally ill and retarded requires approximately $7 a day, while residential services cost from $50 to almost $90 a day. While family care and other community placement admittedly may require additional educational and treatment services, such services are frequently available through resources provided by insurance, city, county, or state programs.

There are fixed costs, some of gigantic proportions, which are not accounted for above: pension costs, government and other grants, various kinds of interest rates, and hidden costs that even the most penetrating search has yet to uncover. The question that crops up again and again is: Why New York State (and other states) continue to construct and support segregated facilities? Perhaps because there are currently 64,000 union employees in the New York State Department of Mental Hygiene, an increase of 10,000 in little more than three years. Perhaps because there are also contractors, builders, architects, real estate entrepreneurs, and many other people anxious to provide the best construction to any state for any purpose. Perhaps because there are merchants and manufacturers who would rather sell carloads of merchandise to institutions than run corner five-and-dime stores.

In 1963, at the behest of Governor Rockefeller, the New York Legislature created the Health and Mental Hygiene Facilities and Improvement Fund (HMHFIC), an organization that has had several name changes since, but has remained steadfast in its mission to execute the construction program of the Department of Mental Hygiene (Legislative Commission on Expenditure Review, 1973). Its original responsibilities included completing work on a $350,000,000 mental hygiene bond issue. However, since its January 1964 takeover date, HMHFIC (or you may use its new name, the Facilities Development Corporation), has spent over one billion dollars on mental hygiene construction. Financing is arranged through the State Housing Finance Agency, which issues bonds to institutional and individual investors, who purchase them because they are tax-free and offer the lender a virtually fail-safe guarantee of earning from 3½ to 7% interest on his money. You must remember that these bonds are tax-free (an important benefit to those in high tax brackets) and are rated as very safe by Standard and Poor and by Moody, even in the face of New York City's and New York State's various fiscal crises. One reason for the safety of these bonds and their high ratings is that income to mental hygiene facilities (income directly from patients or their families, or from federal or third-party sources, such as income from Title 19 of the Social Security Act) *is pledged first to the mental hygiene facilities improvement fund.* The bondholders must be paid first, as in any good business.

How do we convert segregated facilities for the handicapped and the elderly to useful purposes? How can these thousands of people return to normal community life, without the state's bankrupting itself in attempts to meet bond obligations and other commitments to the business community? First, we must recognize the depth and extent of commercial involvement in supposedly non-profit, philanthropic, and service agencies. Second, we must seek to interest other clientele in the segregated facilities and programs we have set up for the handicapped and the aged. A modest beginning might be to explore with business and state officials the possibilities for converting segregated facilities to new uses. To carry out the conversion, institutional operating budgets would be transferred to the community as each segregated facility is evacuated by so-called mental patients, state school residents, and the aged. This may require public support, special tax measures, and other inducements. The farmers have these advantages and so do others. Why not the handicapped?

The Schools

In its first five years (1971–1976), the Center on Human Policy (a Syracuse University facility devoted to the promotion of community-based environments for people with special needs) received over 4,000 requests for assistance from parents of children with disabilities and from teachers and other professionals in education. The vast majority of these requests concerned school placement and the right to education. The requests and complaints fell into several groupings. Some involved children who were excluded from school for behavioral reasons or because of severe disabilities. Others came from parents and guardians who sought to improve the quality of school instruction, or desired more specialized instruction. There were complaints about absence of auxiliary services, such as transportation and speech therapy. There was a recurring pattern of non-service; institution and social service agency professionals often found local school districts reluctant or unwilling to accept "state" children.

This last category is particularly significant. We found that, while parents were often willing to advocate tirelessly and for months on end to secure adequate services for their children, professionals were often as concerned with interagency harmony as with the fate of an individual child. Consequently, agency professionals often gave up trying to place institutional children in local schools, for fear of jeopardizing interagency harmony. These findings have been reiterated in several local and national reports (Task Force, 1971; Children's Defense Fund, 1974), as well as in our own research (Biklen, 1973; Blatt & Blank, 1971).

Numerous parent and professional cases brought the *Center on Human Policy* staff into frequent contact with school officials. Here we learned the language of exclusion, and its familiar ring from school district to school district, from professional to professional. We began to catalogue the many phrases that signalled exclusion. In some instances, they were typical bureaucratic doubletalk; in other cases, they reflected not so much the bureaucratic ethos as the social context in which prejudice toward the disabled is commonplace. *Taken as a whole, these phrases and the attitudes they reveal constitute a formidable barrier to successful deinstitutionalization.*

In the bureaucratic tradition, we frequently heard:

"We do not have the funds to create a program for your child."

"We agree with your philosophy, but we must be practical."

"The child is not in our jurisdiction. It is beyond our sphere of influence."

"Sorry, we do not make the rules."

"The unions will never buy it. They will not take on any extra work."

"We cannot change all at once. It will take time. We do not want to rush into things and possibly make it worse for everyone."

"We need evidence before we can act."

"We will need more time. You must learn to be patient."

There were other built-in biases against disability, expressed in exclusionary language:

"This child is an exceptional child among exceptional children. She just doesn't fit any category of student in our schools."

"Your child is too severely disabled."

"The schools cannot solve every need. We are not a babysitting service."

"If we included your child, we would have to cancel an art teacher for the typical children."

"We have always sent such children to the institutions or to private schools."

"We need at least ten of them with the same disability before we can set up a specialized program."

"We do not have a program for children at that level."

"We would like to help, but we need teachers first."

The effect of such phrases is immense (Task Force, 1971). Schools provide the core of every child's developmental experience, apart from home life. School exclusion, perhaps more than any other agency policy, threatens the whole deinstitutionalization process. Without schooling, community placement becomes a kind of custodial placement. So we must again turn to conversion, this time with an eye to overcoming prejudices, stereotyping, and bureaucratic red tape.

In part, that has already occurred in the form of court rulings, such as the PARC vs. Commonwealth of Pennsylvania litigation and the Mills vs. Board of Education case; national legislation, such as PL 93-380 and PL 94-142 (Abeson, 1974; Abeson, et al., 1975; Gilhool, 1973); and consumer advocacy (Biklen, 1974, 1976; DesJardins, 1971; Ruskin, 1975). Court decisions like these and laws established on their basis insist on the right of children with disabilities to public education in the least restrictive (most integrated) setting possible. Children and their parents have also won due process rights by which they may question and challenge placement and exclusion decisions. Thus, there is an emerging new language replacing the language of exclusion. We are beginning to hear more about "rights": "every child can benefit from an education," "least restrictive services," "zero reject," "mainstreaming," and "individualized planning." These new words and phrases can be regarded as part of the conversion process.

Professionalism

Ironically, those who have been given the responsibility to provide services to the handicapped often erect additional barriers to changing our categorical service-segregated system to an integrated non-categorical one. Many professionals working with the handicapped think in terms of categories and segregated services. This is the way they have been taught to diagnose and prescribe. Thus, they may not have the philosophy or the skills needed to meet the requirements of conversion. Retraining can provide only a partial remedy; professionals do not change easily. Furthermore, not only is retraining a technical problem, but professional resistance to it can lead to a major undermining of conversion efforts.

Next, there is the brick-and-mortar, formal organization of the professions—physical and organizational elements that stand as defenses against the onslaught of change. For example, our buildings have been constructed to foster segregation and isolation. State schools dot the landscape of our countrysides, and day schools for the handicapped form part of the skyline of our cities. These represent great financial, as well as career and life, investments. Similarly, professional societies and professional schools have been organized in ways that may be detrimental to conversion, i.e., according to diagnostic categories. There is, for example, the American Association on Mental Deficiency. Special education departments have specific programs in emotional disturbance, mental retardation, learning disabilities, speech and hearing disorders, and so on.

Another barrier to conversion is the profession's insistence that special children need specially trained professional people to take care of them. While, to some extent, this is true, it is not wholly or always the case. A major challenge for the professional lies in demystifying himself and freely sharing some of his understanding with others, so that they too can join in helping the handicapped.

Bureaucratic Structures

As we have seen, deinstitutionalization means nothing more than the exodus of individuals from an institution. Usually, it has resulted in "dumping" and re-institutionalization (Conroy, 1976). But who is responsible for the failure of deinstitutionalization? Is it the institution that sends people into the community? Or the community that fails to provide local services? Or perhaps the private agencies that refuse to serve the formerly institutionalized? The institution points to the local community, the local community to the institution, the private agencies to both, and all to the legislature that balks at additional appropriations, in an endless display of buck-passing and rationalization (Biklen, 1974).

This brings us back to our original question. Who is responsible for the failure of deinstitutionalization? Perhaps everyone in general, yet no one specifically. The deinstitutionalization process has been based on faulty assumptions and models. In this section, we identify three major deinstitutionalization models and show how they have been doomed to failure (see also President's Committee on Mental Retardation, 1976). Most states have adopted one of these models with only slight variations. Some have combined two or more, to further complicate matters. Still others have adopted no model at all.

Institutional expansion. In many states, the same agencies that operate institutions have been expected to develop community-based programs. However, whether for ideological, economic, or pragmatic reasons, these agencies remain committed to the institutional model. As a matter of ideology, many state and institutional officials believe in segregation. As a matter of economics, they strive to meet minimal standards of institutional care in order to obtain federal monies. As a matter of pragmatism, they wish to avoid scandal and exposés. "We can only have community programs," these officials state, "after we have good institutions." Thus, they may continue to pour resources into the institution endlessly even though this may drain away funds necessary for community services. Or they may alleviate institutional overcrowding and understaffing through the haphazard release of people into the community, as though small warehouses were better than large ones. In the context of an institutional system, then, resources for the community-based services, like minorities in the job market, are the last to be employed and the first to be cut.

Dual systems of services. Some states have turned to local governments or regions to develop community programs, while themselves maintaining a state institutional system (Goldman, 1975). Typically, these states offer to reimburse localities if they allot a certain proportion of their expenditures for community services. For example, a state may underwrite one-half to three-fourths of the net operating expenses of programs in the community. As currently established, such schemes are certain to fail. In times of fiscal austerity, which is almost always, localities will hesitate to pay even a part of the costs of services as long as the state will pay the full cost of institutionalization. Thus, even the mildly retarded will be labelled as "the state's problem," being "too retarded to live in the community," or "in need of specialized services only the institution can offer." Under a dual system of services, the local government's incentive to institutionalize people all too often offsets its incentive to serve those people in the community.

Laissez-faire. Finally, some states have adopted a laissez-faire system, based on the assumption that private agencies will develop a range of services if sufficient funds are allocated for that purpose. Yet a continuum of services cannot evolve through the voluntary actions of service providers. In the absence of proper planning and coordination, small agencies will flounder, because they lack the expertise to obtain funds and to establish programs; large agencies will operate mini-institutions, with little accountability; and services will be congregated in low-income areas of the community. Under a laissez-faire system, service providers also tend to engage in "creaming" (Miller, et al., 1970; Bogdan, 1976) and "bounty hunting" (Bogdan, 1976). That is, they serve those who are the easiest to serve and those who may not require services at all, rather than those with the most severe disabilities. In short, laissez-faire guarantees neither quality services, nor services for all who need them.

Unlike these deinstitutionalization models, the conversion model implies an orderly and planned transition from an institutional to a community-based system of services. As such, it requires administrative structures with fixed lines of responsibility to prevent bureaucratic buck-passing. In a later section of this paper, we describe the administrative precondition to conversion.

The Institutions

We have seen how handicapism and school exclusion policies act as obstacles to conversion. Because of their disabilities, the institutionalized are discriminated against by society and excluded from typical school programs. They face further discrimination as well, for institutions foster the very behaviors which society and the schools find least acceptable.

In response to progressive ideologies, the custodial institutions of the past have gradually become "training schools" and "developmental centers." However, today's institutions, like yesterday's custodial asylums, foster dependence and incompetence among their residents (Blatt, 1970; Butterfield, 1967). At institutions, both new and old, residents' meals are selected, prepared, and served at specific times; the inmates' clothes are laundered; their routines and activities are planned by others (Biklen, 1973; Bogdan, et al., 1974). They are told what to do and when to do it. As a staff member at one institution we have studied put it:

> "The staff has a lot of power here and they do use it. The staff tells them when to get up in the morning, when to go to bed at night, when to eat, when to brush their teeth . . . The residents are virtually completely dependent on the staff for everything."

In some instances, the brutal realities of institutional life have even more dramatic implications. For the sake of convenience, staff members feed residents, rather than teach them to feed themselves, or change the children's diapers, rather than toilet-train them (Bogdan, et al., 1974). Thus, residents are denied opportunities to develop the skills needed for adjustment to the community.

Institutions also tend to accentuate the behaviors they claim to treat (Blatt, 1970). As a response to boredom or lack of stimulation, many residents develop habits such as head-banging, rocking, and self-abuse. In the absence of proper exercise, their limbs may atrophy and wither away (deGrandpré, 1973). Because they have never known privacy, residential inmates urinate, defecate, or masturbate in public. Since they have had to fight for social-psychological rewards at the institution, residents and former residents attempt to ingratiate themselves with strangers by such inappropriate remarks as "I love you," or "You're my friend." Ironically, institutional staff members often cite such behaviors as the reason why "the community will never accept this kind of person." So they breathe life into handicapism and provide school officials with rationales for exclusion and segregation.

Institutionalization itself is therefore a major barrier to the integration of the formerly institutionalized into society. In deinstitutionalizing the residents of state schools and centers, we must take the institution out of the people, as well as the people out of the institution.

Relevance for Teachers

The transition from institution to community is a complex process. Deinstitutionalization has failed because its proponents have ignored this reality. Such factors as societal discrimination; funding mechanisms and construction costs; school exclusion; professionalism; bureaucratic structures; and institutional dependence have acted as barriers to the movement of individuals from the institution.

We have discussed a different way of thinking about deinstitutionalization: in the context of the larger society, and in terms of specific elements of the conversion system. We must now articulate the relevance of conversion to teachers and to schools.

1. Teachers cannot control the course of deinstitutionalization. The process of bringing children from institutions back into the community involves many groups, and interests other than those connected with the schools. For example, in a handicapist society, a teacher cannot pretend to overcome prejudice toward children with disabilities by using a new curriculum that emphasizes positive attitudes toward the disabled.

2. However, if the teacher wishes to do more than add a new curriculum or subtract an old one, his actions can surely influence society's treatment of disabled children. How?

3. The answer is found in the term itself: conversion means societal efforts to eradicate handicapist attitudes and practices. Obviously, teachers, as members of a larger society, can play a role in such efforts. Conversion means rechannelling funds to support community placements for the handicapped. This process will ultimately provide resources for the schools. Conversion means retraining institutional staffs and community personnel. Teachers can play major roles in such programs. Conversion means creating noncategorical systems of educational treatment. Such policies will eventually affect the design, the appearance, and the functioning of all school classrooms and curricula. Conversion means changing attitudes of school administrators toward acceptance of zero reject policies. Conversion means planning community services, of which education is a major component. Conversion means the appointment of professional and consumer advocates for community programming. Last, conversion means developing classroom strategies that focus on promoting integration of disabled

children into regular school programs. This implies efforts to increase awareness, understanding, and acceptance of disabled students by non-disabled students and, obviously, acceptance by teachers, principals, and other school officials.

Teachers and their colleagues can promote new understanding and positive values about individuals with special needs. They can learn, and teach others to learn, to recognize handicapist assumptions and to work to eliminate them. If conversion is to succeed, the schools must change. For the schools to change, and for children to change, teachers must change.

Appendix

When President Ford signed into law the Education for all Handicapped Children Act of 1975, he intensified our need to know, fairly precisely, the incidence and the prevalence of children with special needs. Without such knowledge, there could be no funding, and even more important, it would be impossible to plan effectively for the resources we do have. Without such knowledge, conversion could fail.

A substantial portion of the new federal money (authorized at $387 million for fiscal year 1977–1978 and escalating to an authorization of $3.1 billion by 1982) will flow through local school districts and through state-operated programs. Among its many provisions, the act requires, for funding eligibility, the identification of specific children.

While labels have always been important in contributing to the definition of a person and, thus, to how that person is regarded and indeed regards himself, in recent years some labels have been anchored to various funding schemes. This is seen as a serious problem by those who believe that many so-called handicaps are neither diseases nor conditions which presuppose certain characteristics and predictable occurrences. Nonetheless, we have one committee reporting that there are six million mentally retarded individuals in the United States (an application of the 3% estimate), while other committees report or claim a 1% estimate, or a 2% estimate, or more, or less. Of course, some discrepancies and confusion attend all attempts to define, discuss, or enumerate anything in any significant manner metaphorical; incidence and prevalence data are not grounded in objectively based disease entities. One example is the definition of homosexuality, changed by vote of the Board of Trustees of the American Psychiatric Association in December of 1973, whereby it was decided that homosexuality should not be designated a "psychiatric disorder" and, instead, should be labelled a "sexual orientation disturbance" (Blatt, 1976). A second example is the 1973 revision of the American Association on Mental Deficiency's definition of mental retardation.

Prior to 1959, there was more or less general agreement that the incidence of mental retardation is approximately 3%. That is, mental retardation was assumed to be normally distributed in the population and it was further agreed that the psychometric "cutoff" would be 75 I.Q. or 1½ standard deviations away from the mean. In 1959, the Association's Terminology and Classification Committee, chaired by Rick Heber, redefined mental retardation and, included in the revised definition, there was the statement that subaverage intellectual performance refers to a psychometric score which is greater than one standard deviation below the population mean on tests of general intelligence (Heber, 1959). With that change in definition, 16% of a typical population would be, psychometrically at least, eligible to be designated as "mentally retarded."

In 1973, a subsequent committee of the Association, now chaired by Herbert Grossman, again revised the definition to include as mentally retarded only those who are "significantly" subaverage in intellectual functioning, where "significantly" means performance which is two or more standard deviations from the mean or average of the tests (Grossman, 1973). With the figurative, and possibly literal, stroke of Herbert Grossman's pen, a committee sitting around a conference table reduced enormously the potential incidence of mental retardation, never having to see or dose or deal with a client, only having to say that, hereinafter, mental retardation is such and such, rather than this or that. We cannot redefine measles, or cancer, or pregnancy with such external procedures. It is obvious; mental retardation and emotional disturbance, and even such seemingly objective conditions as blindness and deafness, are less objective disease entities than they are administrative terms; and they are metaphors more than anything else (Blatt, 1976).

The Grossman Committee is back at work and very shortly will be issuing a revised definition, again increasing the psychometric cutoff. Unfortunately, added to the metaphorical nature of labels associated with special education, is the unpleasant fact that careful epidemiologic research cannot be conducted without a great deal of effort and resources and, consequently, there are relatively few such reports in our literature. Therefore, in spite of the influence preparative labels have on the treatment of the handicapped, and in spite of the ever-increasing chaining of resources to identified clients, incidence and prevalence estimates vary so remarkably and change so frequently to fit certain pragmatic needs that they are relatively unhelpful, if not altogether untrustworthy.

However, there have been several attempts to estimate the occurrence of various handicaps in our schools and in other program areas. We believe some general statements can be made, based on our own research (Finn & Blatt, in Blatt, 1973) and the work of others. Table I summarizes estimates drawn from several of these studies (Blatt, 1976).

TABLE 1

Prevalence Estimates of Various Types of Handicapped Children

Handicap	Prevalance Estimates by Percent 1[a]	2[b]	3[c]	4[d]	5[e]
Educable Mentally Retarded	.5	2.0	2.3	1.30	1.30
Trainable Mentally Retarded				.24	.24
Hearing Impaired	1.1	1.5	.575	.10	.575
Visually Handicapped	.6	.2	.1	.05	.1
Speech Impaired	3.4	2.0	3.5	3.60	3.5
Physically Handicapped	1.0	1.5	.5	.21	.5
Brain Injury & Learning Disabled	1.7	N.E.	1.0	1.12	1.0
Emotionally Handicapped	1.0	2.0	2.0	2.0	2.0
Multiply Handicapped	N.E.	N.E.	N.E.	.07	.07
TOTALS	9.3	9.2	9.975	8.69	9.285

[a] Estimates based on a Syracuse University-Systems Research Incorporated Head Start questionnaire; T.M.R. and E.M.R. combined; no estimate (N.E.) on "Multiply Handicapped."

[b] Estimates by Mackie, R. P., & Dunn, L. M., *College University Programs for the Preparation of Teachers of Exceptional Children.*

[c] Estimates prepared for *Estimates of Current Manpower Needs in Education for the Handicapped, 1968–69.*

[d] Estimates used by Rossmiller, R. A., Hale, J. A., & Frohreich, L. E., *Educational Programs for Exceptional Children: Resource Configurations and Costs.*

[e] Conservative estimates used by *The Fleischman Report on the Quality, Cost, and Financing of Elementary and Secondary Education in New York State.*

It should be noted that, with the exception of our own preschool estimates, reports here are for age groups 5 through 19. Second, none of these estimates accounts for what is now termed minimum learning disability. Third, multiple handicaps are not included as a category in three estimates and, with the exception of mental retardation, severity of handicap is not considered. What Table 1 does illustrate is the significant range of such estimates. The relatively recent Rand study provides additional documentation in support of this contention (Kakalik, 1973).

Because there is an important difference between, for example, psychometric mental retardation (at the present time, approximately 2% of the total population) and known mental retardation (approximately 1% of the total population), and because other disability areas show similar discrepancies, we believe it is both reasonable and in the best interests of clients to use incidence and prevalence estimates that are based on available studies of known cases in the various categories. As we recently concluded, and as Table 2 shows: from our own demographic studies of mental retardation, our evaluation of the epidemiologic literature in the field, and from a careful analysis of the data obtained from both our Head Start questionnaire survey and our observational studies of selected Head Start programs, we estimate that 1% of the total population (incidence) needs special services because of their mental retardation, another 1% requires it because of behavioral disturbances, and another 1% because of moderate and severe sensory and/or physical disorders. We would not include the so-called speech-impaired in such designations; nor would we include the so-called learning disabled. We believe it is not in the best interests of either the children or the programs to label children with mild disabilities, who could otherwise be adequately dealt with in ordinary classes, as "handicapped," "retarded," "speech impaired," etc. We believe it is in the interest of both the children who have been heretofore so labelled, and those others who are now denied a normal interaction with them, to reserve the categories of handicap only for those who have such severe and moderate needs where they will not be able to be served adequately in ordinary classes under ordinary conditions. For that group with such special needs, we estimate that there is no more than a 3% incidence across populations and age categories and, possibly, a 4%, and no more than 5%, prevalence during the pre-school and school years. Therefore, mild speech impairments, as mild retardation or disturbance, could not be considered a handicap requiring special attention in the traditional sense. Those children with mild disabilities should be served within the context of regular school settings. Those with severe or moderate speech impairments will be found to have general language disabilities and, more probably than not, learning, behavioral, sensory, or physical disorders (Blatt, 1976 pp. 144–146).

While the experts in the field of special education have argued that 3%, or as much 5%, of the population is "psychometrically mentally

TABLE 2

Estimated Needs for Special Community and Residential Services for Children and Adults in a Model Region of 50,000 Population

Category	Percent of Total Population in Categories	Estimated Number in Categories
Major categories		
1. Percent of total population needing special services due to mental retardation	1% of total population: .75% EMR; .20% TMR; .05% SMR	5,000
2. Percent of total population needing special services due to behavior disturbances	1% of total population: .50% severely ED or SM; .50% moderately or mildly ED or SM	5,000
3. Percent of total population needing special services due to moderate and severe sensory and/or physical disorders	1% of total population: .03% blind; .08% deaf; .14% severely sensory and/or PH; remainder partially disabled	5,000
Sub-categories		
1. Mental retardation		
a. Individuals in need of special programs in public school at any one time	1% of total school population (125,000)	1,250
b. Individuals in need of only minimum services other than special programs during school years	50% of entire mentally retarded population	2,500
c. Individuals in need of residential placement, at any one time, with alternative programs available	.1% of total population	500
d. Individuals requiring other services:		
Nursery and preschool programs	5% of known mentally retarded population	250
Day care programs	5% of known mentally retarded population	250
Sheltered workshop activities, vocational training, adult day activities	10% of known mentally retarded population	500
2. Behavioral disturbances		
a. Individuals in need of special programs in public school at any one time	1% of total school population (125,000)	1,250
b. Individuals in need of only minimum services other than special programs during school years	50% of entire emotionally disturbed population	2,500
c. Individuals in need of residential placement, at any one time, with alternative programs available	.1% of total population	500
d. Individuals requiring other services:		
Nursery and preschool programs	5% of known emotionally disturbed population	250
Day care programs population	5% of known emotionally disturbed population	250
Sheltered workshop activities, vocational training, adult day activities	10% of known emotionally disturbed population	500
3. Sensory and/or physical disorders		
a. Individuals in need of special programs in public school at any one time	1% of total school population (125,000)	1,250
b. Individuals in need of only minimum services other than special programs during school years	50% of entire sensory and physically handicapped	2,550
c. Individuals in need of residential placement, at any one time, with alternative programs available	.1% of total population	500
d. Individuals requiring other services:		
Nursery and preschool programs	5% of known sensory and physically handicapped population	250
Day care programs	5% of known sensory and physically handicapped population	250
Sheltered workshop activities, vocational training, adult day activities	10% of known sensory and physically handicapped population.	500

retarded," our own studies indicate that a 1% estimate is more valuable for program planning and development. Similarly, estimates as high as 20% to 50% in the relatively new category called "learning disabilities" are provocative, but do not appear to be helpful for those planning or implementing programs. The studies that have been completed suggest that there are substantial differences between what we might call "administrative disability" and "objective disability." We believe it is reasonable to base our estimates on whatever studies of known cases are available (administrative disability). That advice might lead to a general conclusion that not more than 3% of a representative population will be moderately, severely, or multiply handicapped.

References

Abeson, A. Movement and momentum: Government and the education of handicapped children—II. *Exceptional Children*, 1974, *41*, 109–115.

Abeson, A., Bolick, N., & Hass, J. *A primer on due process*. Reston, Va.: The Council for Exceptional Children, 1975.

Allport, G. W. *The nature of prejudice*. Boston: Beacon Press, 1954.

Biklen, D. Advocacy comes of age. *Exceptional Children*, 1976, *42*, 308–313.

Biklen, D. Exclusion. *The Peabody Journal of Education*, 1973, *50* (3), 226–234.

Biklen, D. Human Report: I. In B. Blatt (Ed.). *Souls in extremis: An anthology on victims and victimizers*. Boston: Allyn & Bacon, 1973.

Biklen, D. *Let our children go*. Syracuse, N.Y.: Human Policy Press, 1974.

Biklen, D., & Bogdan, R. *Handicapism*. Syracuse, N.Y: Human Policy Press, 1976 (slide show with script).

Blatt, B. *Exodus from pandemonium. Human abuse and a reformation of public policy*. Boston: Allyn & Bacon, 1970.

Blatt, B. Instruments of change—the executive. In R. B. Kugel (Ed.). *Changing patterns in residential services for the mentally retarded* (2nd ed.). Washington, D.C: President's Committee on Mental Retardation, 1976.

Blatt, B., & Blank, H. D. *Children with special needs in New York State: A report for the New York State Commission on the Quality, Cost and Financing of Elementary and Secondary Education*. Syracuse, N.Y: Syracuse University, Center on Human Policy, 1971.

Blatt, B., & Garfunkel, F. *The educability of intelligence*. Washington, D.C: Council for Exceptional Children, 1969.

Bogdan, R. National policy and situated meaning: Head Start and the handicapped. *American Journal of Orthopsychiatry*, 1976, *46* (2).

Bogdan, R., Taylor, S., deGrandpré, B., & Haynes, S. Let them eat programs. *Journal of Health and Social Behavior*, 1974, *15*.

Butterfield, E. C. The role of environmental factors in the treatment of institutionalized mental retardates. In A. A. Baumeister (Ed.). *Mental Retardation: Appraisal, education, and rehabilitation*. Chicago: Aldine, 1967.

Conroy, J. *A review of trends in deinstitutionalization of the mentally retarded*. Unpublished manuscript, Temple University, Developmental Disabilities Center, 1976.

Construction of mental hygiene facilities. New York Legislative Commission on Expenditure Review, October 3, 1973.

Children's Defense Fund. *Children out of school in America*. Cambridge: Washington Research Project, 1974.

deGrandpré, B. *The culture of a state school ward*. Unpublished doctoral dissertation, Syracuse University, 1973.

DesJardins, C. *How to organize an effective parent group and move bureaucracies*. Chicago: Co-ordinating Council for Handicapped Children, 1971.

Dexter, L. *The tyranny of schooling*. New York: Basic Books, 1964.

Ensher, G. E. (Ed.). *Final report on assessment of the handicapped effort in experimental and selected other programs serving the handicapped*. Syracuse, N.Y: Report to the Office of Child Development, Department of Health, Education, and Welfare, October 1974, 199–230.

Estimates of current manpower needs in education for the handicapped 1968–69. Washington, D.C: United States Office of Education, 1968.

Finn, F., & Blatt, B. The demography of a mental retardation region. In B. Blatt (Ed.). *Souls in extremis: An anthology on victims and victimizers*. Boston: Allyn & Bacon, 1973.

Fleischman, M. *The Fleischman report on the quality, cost, and financing of elementary and secondary education in New York State* (Vol. II). New York: Viking Press, 1972.

Gellman, W. Roots of prejudice against the handicapped. *Journal of Rehabilitation*, 1959, *25*, 1–6.

Gilhool, T. An inalienable right. *Exceptional Children*, 1973, *39*, 597–609.

Goffman, E. *Stigma*. Englewood Cliffs, N.J: Prentice-Hall, 1963.

Goldman, E. R. A state model for community services. *Mental Retardation*, 1975, *13* (5), 33–36.

Grossman, H. J. (Ed.). *Manual on terminology and classification in mental retardation*. Washington, D.C: American Association on Mental Deficiency, 1973.

Heber, R. (Ed.). A manual on terminology and classification in mental retardation Monograph supplement to the *American Journal of Mental Deficiency*, 1959, *64*.

Kakalik, J. S. *Services for handicapped youth: A program overview*. Santa Monica: The Rand Corporation, 1973–74.

Mackie, R. P., & Dunn, L. M. *College university programs for the preparation of teachers of exceptional children*. USOE Bulletin No. 13. Washington, D.C: U.S. Government Printing Office, 1954.

Merton, R. *Social theory and social structure*. New York: Free Press, 1957.

Miller, S. M., Roby, P., & de Vos van Steewijk, A. Creaming the poor. *Trans-Action*, 1970, 7 (8), 38–45.

New York State Department of Mental Hygiene. Governor Carey recommends $924 million DMH budget. *Mental Hygiene News*, January 30, 1976, p. 1.

Persons released from state developmental centers. New York Legislative Commission on Expenditure Review, December 18, 1975.

President's Committee on Mental Retardation. *Mental Retardation: Trends in state services*. Washington, D.C: U.S. Government Printing Office, 1976.

Rossmiller, R. A., Hale, J. A., & Frohreich, L. E. *Educational programs for exceptional children: Resource configurations and costs*. Madison: University of Wisconsin, Department of Educational Administration, 1970.

Ruskin, M. *Parent power*. New York: Walker, 1975.

Scheff, T. J. *Being mentally ill: A sociological theory*. Chicago: Aldine, 1966.

Scott, R. *The making of blind men*. New York: Russell Sage Foundation, 1969.

Swift, S., & Melby, R. *A report to Speaker Stanley Steingut*. Albany: The Assembly Joint Committee to Study the Department of Mental Hygiene, March, 1976.

Task Force on Children Out of School. *The way we go to school*. Boston: Beacon Press, 1971.

Wolfensberger, W. *The origin and nature of our institutional models*. Syracuse, N.Y: Human Policy Press, 1975.
Wolfensberger, W. *The principle of normalization in human services*. Toronto: National Institute of Mental Retardation, 1972.
Wright, B. *Physical disability: A psychological approach*. New York: Harper, 1960.
Yinker, M. *A minority group in American society*. New York: McGraw-Hill, 1965.
Yuker, H. Attitudes as determinants of behavior. *Journal of Rehabilitation*, 1965, *31*, 15–16.

Robert Bogdan, Steven Taylor, Burton Blatt, Douglas Biklen

ROBERT BOGDAN is Associate Professor of Special Education and Sociology at Syracuse University. He has published books on research methods and mental illness. His articles have appeared in such diverse journals as: *The American Psychologist, Phi Delta Kappan, Social Work, Orthopsychiatry, Journal of Health and Social Behavior, Educational Technology,* and *The American Behavior Scientist.*

STEVEN TAYLOR is a staff member of the Center on Human Policy, Syracuse University, and is currently working on his Ph.D. in Sociology. He has done extensive research on institutions and the effects of institutionalization. He has authored and co-authored a number of publications, including *Introduction to Qualitative Research Methods* (with Robert Bogdan).

DOUGLAS BIKLEN is Director of the Center on Human Policy and Associate Professor of Special Education and Rehabilitation at Syracuse University. He is author of the book *Let Our Children Go: An Organizing Manual for Parents and Advocates* and has written numerous other articles on advocacy, the legal rights of children with disabilities, institutional life, and the politics of behavior modification.

BURTON BLATT is Centennial Professor and Dean, School of Education, Syracuse University. He is author of approximately 150 books, monographs, and papers, among these *The Preparation of Teachers: An Unstudied Problem in Education* (with Seymour Sarason and Kenneth Davidson), *The Intellectually Disfranchised, The Educability of Intelligence* (with Frank Garfunkel), *Christmas in Purgatory* (with Fred Kaplan), *Exodus from Pandemonium, Souls in Extremis*, and *Revolt of the Idiots.*

Establishing a Public School Program for the Severely Handicapped: A Case Study

JEAN B. McGREW

Superintendent of Schools, East Grand Rapids, Michigan

Social barriers of many types are breaking down across the country. Courts have been particularly active in mandating services to segments of the population that heretofore had been ignored. Legislators, probably taking a cue from the judicial decisions, have plowed boldly into new "rights" territory that only a few years ago was considered a political mine field. There is little doubt that the historians will look back on the '70's as a decade in which the country used its judicial and legislative machinery to realign societal values. However, historians have pointed out before that court and legislative decisions only set the pre-conditions for implementation, and that implementation does not necessarily occur with "all the deliberate speed" that the statutes and court decisions might call for. For example, the United States Supreme Court determined that racially segregated schools were inherently unequal over two decades ago. Still there are many school systems considered in non-compliance of the desegregation order. The reasons for such non-compliance are often complicated and do not lend themselves to easy conclusions. In a vein somewhat similar to the desegregation cases, numerous federal and state courts have determined in the last several years that the state, through its local school districts, must provide services to *all* students, including those with handicapping conditions. Federal legislation (and in many cases state legislation) has both supplemented and reinforced the judicial decisions.

While *all* handicapped students may expect to benefit from these new mandates, it is the student defined as severely/profoundly handicapped who may expect to benefit the most, as he has most often been excluded from public school programs. Such exclusion was often based on the school district's posture that it had neither the resources, programs, nor competency to provide adequate education. Whether or not we will have non-compliance two decades hence remains to be seen. It is certainly hoped that sound public school programs can be offered to all severely/profoundly handicapped students at a compliance rate much more rapid than that of school desegregation. Still, the process will undoubtedly proceed much more slowly than some would wish or expect. The purpose of this paper is to provide a case history of one school system's implementation of school based programs for the severely/profoundly handicapped student. Hopefully, the case history will be helpful to those currently addressing the problem and may perhaps serve as a catalyst in speeding events along.

Before describing the Madison (Wisconsin) experience, a few preliminary definitions may add some clarity. Most professionals in the field recognize that definitions or labels can in themselves be a source of controversy, but in order to present an historical development it is necessary to use historical labels in context. The three labels used in this paper include "trainable," "severe," and "profound" and reflect the degree of a handicap's severity, i.e., "trainable" representing the least severe handicap in the continuum discussed in this paper, and "profound" representing the most severe.

Programs for the trainable, severely, and profoundly handicapped in the Madison Public Schools evolved through a series of four steps. Each step developed the prior condition for the next step. This is not to suggest that each step is a *necessary* prerequisite, but only that each step was part of an *historical* continuum. The first step began approximately seven years ago in the late 60's with the determination by school authorities that an elementary school (Sunnyside) was no longer needed to serve the general school population. Special educators were quick to lay claim to the building, and requested that it become a self-contained school for trainable students from 5 through 18 years old. The experience with the trainable student was sufficiently successful that some more severely handicapped students were quickly added. It was soon apparent that this second

---

Prior to July, 1976, Dr. McGrew was Assistant Superintendent of the Madison, Wisconsin, Public Schools.

step, the cautious addition of severely handicapped students, was well founded.

It is doubtful that such service would have been provided nearly a decade before legally mandated had it not been for several critical factors. The first and perhaps most critical factor was the availability of an idle building. This is obviously not a very altruistic reason for the establishment of such a program, but was nonetheless an important first obstacle to be cleared. Availability of space under the current legal mandates is probably less a contention than it was ten years ago, but, without the advantage of any legal mandates in the mid 1960's, it was an absolute necessity to have some physical location where the program could be initiated. The common argument of having to build new facilities for such a program was considerably diluted by the availability of space. Even with the availability of a building for such a program, some decision makers felt that the taxpaying public would be better served if the building were sold than if it were used for a new program. Arguments against the selling of the building prevailed, through the following lines of persuasion: (a) the altruistic argument that trainable and severely/profoundly handicapped students had been neglected and should be served; (b) the educational argument that enough technology had been developed to indicate that such students could learn at a faster rate than previously believed; (c) the practical argument that the student population was still increasing (at that time) and that the school might have to be reopened at some later date; (d) the fiscal argument that the land value of the site was bound to appreciate in the next several years.

Second, there were strong advocates both inside and outside the school system who maintained continuing support and pressure on decision makers to make some kind of affirmative move. These advocates included parent organizations and community groups, as well as a strong director of special education. The role of the special education director as a knowledgeable advocate cannot be underestimated. Many directors in special education have had little training or experience with the severely/profoundly handicapped. The lack of such training and experience limits the advocacy role, and in some cases may even do it harm. For example, when it appears to decision makers that the chief administrative officer in special education shows uncertainty as to how such a program might work, an equal uncertainty can develop on the part of the decision making group. Such was not the case with the Madison program. The director had both training and experience with severely/profoundly handicapped students and thus could speak from an experiential knowledge base. The availability of a major university with individuals wishing to assist in the development of a program for this population added constant reassurance and assistance. Not only did the university provide the psychological backstop for launching into such a program, but provided some assurance that trained teachers would be available to carry on and expand the program if it proved successful.

Some other factors that helped to launch the program were the fact that a sizable population of students for this program existed within the metropolitan boundaries of the Madison school system. Many of these students were receiving education and treatment in private day-care facilities. With the population readily available, the problems of extensive busing and foster family arrangements were only minimal. Finally, the state law had provided for significant financial assistance to support special education programs in the state. This meant that the out-of-pocket cost to the district was not extraordinary. Still, with all these positive conditions, there was a counter argument (not without some credibility) that, should such a program be successful, it would encourage the state to promote tuition students into the program from outlying districts. This argument was mollified by emphasizing that such tuitions would be at full costs, and that the addition of students would probably create a better critical mass, i.e., enough students to justify the expense of valuable support personnel. Not only would those from the outlying district benefit from such support services, but so would students residing in the district, and all at a lower per-capita cost.

A number of important outcomes were gained from this initial, self-contained program at Sunnyside. It showed conclusively that trainable and severely handicapped students could learn a variety of skills, both academic and social, beyond what was originally believed to be the case. This expanding range of skill development was documented and such documentation served as a base for even further expansions in development. In addition, it placed these students well within the domain of public education by demonstrating educational gains. It further showed that such a program did not necessarily need new and specialized facilities. Other than an occasional wooden ramp for wheelchairs, the typical schoolhouse is quite adequate to the task. Funds, then, could be spent on direct rather than indirect service needs. One might recognize today the concern that some groups might have about relegating such programs to cast-off buildings. This is more often a concern about equitable treatment for handicapped students vis-a-vis regular students than it is a question about the adequate use of the building itself. This may be a separate argument, but the point was fairly well established that a traditional building is quite useful. It was further learned that students ranging from trainable to severely handicapped could be managed in a school and group situation. Early concerns about the need for excessive individualization, and whether severe or profound students would aggress toward other students or staff were diminished as experience and teaching techniques were expanded. In general, this early experience demonstrated to special educators and to many regular educators that trainable and severely handicapped students could benefit from all-day school programs, and that the range of what they could learn was considerably beyond what was initially suspected.

The successfulness of this early program, coupled with the increased knowledge of effective teaching techniques and skill sequences, led to a more open attitude on the part of the school system to expand the Sunnyside program. But simply a more open administrative posture was not enough to bring about this transition. Once again, available space set the stage for further development. When a secondary elementary school was declared surplus, the entire program was moved to Badger School. The move to Badger School was the third step in the development of educational services for severely/profoundly handicapped students.

As a facility, Badger School provided a gym, multipurpose work rooms, and more classroom space. This extra space made it possible for the program to begin to include more students. Since the Sunnyside program had focused the majority of its efforts on trainable students, the remaining unserved population fell into the severe and profound range. Gradually Badger School began admitting more severely handicapped students. There was one essential step left before profoundly handicapped students were served. This step involved the incorporation of self-contained trainable and severely handicapped *classes* within regular elementary and middle school buildings.

The development of the two early programs in self-contained *schools* brought on a moderate amount of opposition. Most of the opposition centered around costs, the mechanics of administering the program, and the question of whether or not this was an appropriate function for a school district to perform, since it was not legally mandated. The fourth step in the service expansion, the determination to move some of the programs into the regular elementary and middle schools, was altogether different. The most apparent problem, though seldom articulated among parents, teachers, and administrators, was the concern of aggressive behavior of the severely handicapped toward the regular student population. The argument that this kind of behavior had been diminished in the self-contained school setting to a minimal degree was helpful but not convincing at the outset. Here again, it must be recognized that the knowledge and experience of the typical person with the severely handicapped was quite limited, and it was not unnatural that there would be some apprehension. A second concern was a feeling that the special classes would take up an extraordinary amount of space and building resources allocated to that particular school. Space at that time of expanding enrollment was at a considerable premium.

Finally, there was only a vague concept of what mainstreaming meant, and some of the regular teachers had visions of severely handicapped students mainstreamed into their regular programs. The state of the art was not well defined at that point among special educators either, and some of the pronouncements by some of the more zealous advocates undoubtedly compounded this fear of mainstreaming among the regular teaching staff. Through the patience and dedication of several principals, however, self-contained classrooms were opened in the elementary schools and became quickly accepted by the staff when they understood that their worst fears were not to be realized. (It should be noted here that the key element to introducing any such classes into a regular school setting is the principal. Without overt and positive support on the part of the principal, the chances of success are greatly diminished.) While many of the service delivery resources in the schools were integrated to include service to trainable and severely handicapped students, as well as the regular students, it would be inaccurate to say that the student populations themselves experienced any substantial integration. Over time, parallel integration did take place in gym, lunchroom, playground, and art classes. Such close proximity of programs, however, expanded universal acceptance within the buildings, and such acceptance allowed an expansion of integration for handicapped students into various facets of school life.

When this baseline of experience had been established, efforts to integrate profoundly handicapped students and to develop a more sophisticated service delivery system were appropriately pursued. With assistance from the University of Wisconsin, proposals to develop model programs for the 5 through 21 year old, and for the infant and preschool severely/profoundly handicapped student were submitted for federal funding. Both were funded. Project MAZE (Madison Alternative for Zero Exclusion) focuses on the development of curricular materials, a delivery system for such materials, and the training of teachers.

The infant and toddler project focuses on early intervention of students with identified handicaps, and also serves as a training center for teachers of very young handicapped students. It is expected that the technology, curriculum materials, and insights into teacher training developed out of these two federally funded projects will provide some needed assistance to those school districts just in the initial stages of developing their own program.

There are several lessons that have been learned over the decade of development in the Madison program. Experience indicates that the average individual, whether professional educator, taxpayer, teacher, or student, has an initial uneasiness and uncertainty concerning the severely/profoundly handicapped student. Sometimes parents and advocates for such students perceive this to be a lack of sensitivity or a lack of concern about a disabled population. Neither is usually the case. More often such people lack exposure to severely/profoundly handicapped youngsters and are concerned that their own behavior or lack of information could result in something damaging to children they do not understand. In the minds of many of these people, the severely/profoundly handicapped individual is perceived as quite fragile. The developments of the past decade have also demonstrated that students ranging from trainable to profoundly handicapped can learn a great deal more than was originally expected. Such learning, however, does not take place randomly or incidentally, but must be highly structured and sequenced, and considerable trial and error must take place before the right formula is found. In addition, retarded students, like their normal counterparts, will learn best if there is a constant expectation on the part of the teacher that they can and will learn. What applies to Pygmalion and regular students also applies to retarded students. Programs designed to coddle retarded students with a baby-sitting service may keep some students and parents happy, but will result in little learning on the part of the student. To provide structured and sequenced learning to this student population, it is clear that teachers need rigorous training and practicum experience in the area. A class or two in the education of the severely retarded and a few observations of programs in operation will not be adequate to the task. It has also become apparent that the rigors required in such teaching can burn out teachers in a relatively short period of time, as programs of this kind expand across the country and supply lags behind demand. Strategies must be devised to rotate teachers out of these programs periodically to prevent extensive dropout after only a few years' experience. Finally, it is apparent that close cooperation must be developed between school systems with such programs and universities in the business of training teachers in this area.

By comparison, the technology in this area is relatively young. To become more comprehensive will require direct research in the classroom and a smooth flow of research findings to the practitioner. A strong joint effort between the researcher in the university and the practitioner in the school seems to give the best possibility for practical developments with this student population. Such joint university/public school cooperation is greatly facilitated where the location of two institutions is close, as in the case of Madison. But even for those not in proximity, it should be noted that many universities are developing more of an outreach program than ever before and appear to be more receptive to cooperative efforts in the field. In addition to university assistance, other agencies can be tapped to provide technical assistance. The whereabouts of such agencies can usually be secured through contacts with the State Department of Education or through the Bureau of Education for the Handicapped, on a national level. Finally, advocacy groups are usually well grounded in the sources of technical assistance and can be a valuable source of such information. The point remains that school systems, especially those lacking much experience with the severely/profoundly handicapped, are well advised to seek the assistance of some external agencies with experience and expertise. Such assistance will diminish "rediscovering the wheel," and usually will make for a smoother and more rapidly developed program.

The problems of incorporating a comprehensive program for the severely and profoundly handicapped in a typical school district program can be overcome, but it is essential that those charged with that responsibility exercise patience (without acquiescence), take logical steps one at a time, provide adequate information to all concerned, and feel confident that their teaching staff is adequately trained. Given these caveats, there is no reason that, twenty years from now, the public should be debating the role of the public school system in the education of the severely and profoundly handicapped.

JEAN B. McGREW became Superintendent of Schools for East Grand Rapids, Michigan, on July 7, 1976, after completing six years as Assistant Superintendent of the Madison, Wisconsin, Public Schools. He had the primary responsibility for introducing and implementing the Management by Objective (MBO) program in the Madison Public Schools five years ago. He is the author of numerous articles, co-author of a book on MBO, has conducted workshops on MBO for school systems throughout the country, and has taught graduate courses on Management by Objectives in Education at the University of Wisconsin.

III Services: Family Involvement

Parents need guidance, they need comfort, and they need to be periodically freed from their heavy and lonely burden of providing for a child whose care requires more than the usual amount of parenting and nurturing. The needs of the children are great; the needs of the family are often even greater. The needs of the children are frequently met; the needs of the family are too seldom recognized or satisfied.

Ronnie Gordon

Special Needs of Multi-Handicapped Children Under Six and Their Families: One Opinion

RONNIE GORDON

Institute of Rehabilitation Medicine, New York University Medical Center

"It is no exaggeration to say that in the background of every individual handicapped child there is always a handicapped family" (Sheridan, 1965, p. 100). Among most professionals concerned with children with deviant development, there is increased awareness and recognition that not only are the children unusually vulnerable but the families with young children "at risk" are too often themselves "at risk." Experience and study suggest both the need for and the value of early and ongoing support for the family, as well as the need for early identification, screening, extended assessment, and intensive developmental therapy for the very young multi-handicapped child. Although these needs can be approached and treated individually, when they are dealt with simultaneously, the results appear to be more than a summation of the effects of two components—treatment for the child and service for the family. Our clinical impression is that the addition of one component to the other results in a total effect that is greater than the sum of the parts.

If the young multi-handicapped child is left undiagnosed and untreated, he will in time demonstrate increasingly more deviant patterns of development and the major effects of delays and chronic handicapping conditions in early childhood will be evident in ". . . later motor-linguistic, adaptive, and social behavior. Thus, one firmly established principle is to aim to establish the most normal sequence of development possible" (Ingram, 1973, p. 421).

The Families' Needs

The impact of a handicapped child on the resources of a family (psychological, social, physical, and financial), on the relationship between husband and wife, on the stability and normalcy and mental health of other siblings, and on the quality and quantity of the family's interactions with friends and relatives cannot be minimized or ignored. Every family with a handicapped child or one with chronic disease has an ongoing, onerous, and unenviable task (Morris, 1974).

Several comments from our recorded interviews with parents illustrate this:

"Neighbors with children kept away from us. . . ."

A need to move away was based on the explanation, "Neighbors are too nosy" (about the child's condition).

"I don't visit nobody; nobody visits me. I just stay inside with the family . . . (but) there are times when you need somebody. . . . We don't go no place since he was born."

The extended families are not as supportive as would be hoped. "The grandparents think there's really nothing wrong. Why is she a patient at the Institute?"

"My father can't face the problem. He thinks that one day he (my son) will wake up."

Another parent: "You see, his (my husband's) mother doesn't think there's something wrong with her."

Another family: "My mother (grandparent) talked about a couple of dreams she had. She sees T getting up and suddenly walking."

These statements reflect the commonality of problems in families from London and in families served at the Institute of Rehabilitation Medicine (IRM) in New York who share the life experience of having children with developmental disorders (Fox, 1975; Gordon, Jacobson, Gitler, Schwartz, Ezrachi, & Brenner, 1975b).

Parents need guidance, they need comfort, and they need to be periodically freed from their heavy and lonely burden of providing for a child whose care requires more than the usual amount of parenting and nurturing. The needs of the children are great; the needs of the family are often even greater. The needs of the children are frequently met; the needs of the family are too seldom recognized or satisfied.

The views expressed in this article are those of the author and do not necessarily represent those of the institution with which she is affiliated.

A fundamental need of the families of handicapped children is for support and a nonjudgmental audience for their expression of feelings related to parenting a child who is different—different from the normal child they had expected and whom their world could easily accept. Frustration, anger, and anguish related to the scarcity or inadequacy of services or insensitivity in the attitudes of personnel responsible for helping parents of this special child are dramatically stated in the title of a document prepared in England by a pediatrician after conducting a series of interviews with parents. His queries were directed to parents' assessment of the quality of services given to their children and to the attitudes of professionals toward them personally. Fox quoted a parent who said about physicians: "They get this training, but they don't really know how you feel" (Fox, 1975, p. 8).

A study of the interaction of parents with our program was completed at this Institute (Gordon et al., 1975b). This study was based on data generated from 500 hours of audio tapes of semi-structured but open-ended weekly sessions with parents of children in one of the inpatient service programs at IRM. Interview sessions focused primarily on short and long term educational goals for the child, interpretation of the developmental program offered in the setting, and ways in which parents can realistically interpret and incorporate elements of the stimulation program at home. However, because of the intensity, frequency, and relationship of the discussants (the project director and the parent), these changes also resulted in serendipitous findings—the parental sense of immediate stresses, anxieties, and specific crisis situations. In addition, many parent statements were remarkably and dramatically similar to those of the London parent who talked to Dr. Fox.

Parents' needs are many. Concretely, they need service from the first moment their child is identified as exceptional—service delivered *to them* rather than service that they have to seek, service organized *for them* rather than service that they have to mobilize for themselves. In specific situations, when a family has a history of problems related to previous births of children with developmental difficulties, many believe that the family should be scheduled immediately for guidance and for medical and genetic counseling prior to the birth, prior to the gestation, or even prior to the conception of another child. Parents of handicapped children need other parents of handicapped children with whom to speak, if only to know, as one parent put it: ". . . that other mothers can live (through this) and can survive with these awful burdens, and sometimes can even smile and laugh."

Parents need professionals who are sound academically, stable emotionally, and ready to face the situation with them, empathize with them, and translate for them a realistic picture of the handicapped child's current status, as well as projections that can be made, while admitting that there are some projections that cannot yet be made about the child's future development and potential. Evasion or use of professional jargon (one parent termed it "polysyllabic intimidation") is too often reported by parents who are dissatisfied and upset with the quality of professional care rendered.

Families who have already arrived at a point of questioning the existence of developmental dissonance or of a special problem in their youngster's development describe a history of physicians' ignoring their initial concerns and observations of "something different" in their child's growth and maturation, different either from other children in their family or from other children they have observed. Parents describe a pattern of frustration while shopping around for medical clarification in response to their refusal to accept passively the too frequently reported reaction of physicians: "Don't worry, just give him time; he'll outgrow it." Another frequently reported comment is: "Doctors tend to withhold information."

Such comments are documented too often to be ignored or treated as mere emotional outbursts unrelated to the reality of the situation. If these recurring reports are dignified as accurate descriptors of the unmet needs of families with handicapped children, then we must address ourselves to the subject of what indeed is interfering with the delivery of effective support and guidance to these parents, which in turn, we believe, influences their interactions with their children.

Over 14 years of clinical experience in the design, organization, and implementation of developmental-therapeutic programs for multihandicapped children aged 18 months to 6 years, and parallel supportive and interpretative programs for their parents, including the more formal study of the data generated from the audio-taped parental interviews previously described, suggests several issues and raises many questions related to the quality and patterns of delivery of services for both the parents and their handicapped children. Although there is increased agreement with and investment in the position that parents have a critical role to play in their children's therapeutic program, little is known or documented about how profoundly parents are affected by the manner in which they are initially told of their child's abnormal medical and developmental condition. Perhaps the greatest initial assistance that can be offered to parents is respect for their feelings of shock, fear, and anxiety. During this critical period, the primary person involved with the family is usually the physician, who often assumes a therapeutic role. To do this well, as we have all learned, requires considerable allocation of time, as well as the ability to listen and to comfort. Parents need to express feelings, rather than merely listen to reassurances that everything will turn out all right (Morris, 1972). Reality is more difficult and painful to describe and to prescribe for than is optimism, tempered with verbal placebos.

Of tremendous concern to those who are privy to later reactions of parents (who are so very articulate when describing their frustrations) is the knowledge that, in reality, most physicians often do not have the time (cannot have the time in our system of health service) that is needed for the extended dialogue required to translate concrete medical and associated psycho-educational information to parents and, at the same time, to empathize with the family in this catastrophic situation. Our experience suggests that, in the initial discussion of problems related to a new diagnosis of a handicapping condition, seldom do the parents reach an understanding of the actual medical condition, its associated sequelae, its implications for the future development of the child, and the impact of the specific disability on his educational and vocational potential. Frequent and repeated exchanges and interactions are needed between the family and those professionals involved in the child's care to clarify the actual dimensions and severity of the multi-faceted problems associated with the disability. Time is also needed for the parents to establish sufficient rapport with the professionals to express their reactions to this unexpected, unwanted, and ongoing burden.

The comments of a parent prior to the discharge of a child who had been in an intensive in-patient program at IRM, illustrates better than any theoretical discussion the burden, the ambivalence, and the stress borne by parents of severely handicapped children. With the date of release from IRM becoming imminent, one parent said: "Do I want him back? Don't I want him at all?" The psychological impact of having a handicapped youngster upon all members of a family was well articulated in another quote: "We have never turned away from our responsibilities. I wanted to send him away a long time ago, but I don't know whether I could. No, I didn't want him to come home . . . but my husband has placed tremendous burdens on me. . . . He (the child) is part of us and can't be forgotten. I don't know at this point. . . . He will have to leave us at some time. We both know this."

We believe that our program at the Institute assisted this family by providing a respite from the ongoing problem of caring for this child. The parent's comment was: "This program has helped me cope with the problem by letting me get out of it for a while. I don't know what I'll be like when I have to go back. . . . " In an undated post-discharge interview approximately one year later, the same parent had made a decision: "I want him to die in an institution. I couldn't cope with him at home."

Findings in our study of 40 children and their families indicate that, in many cases, the handicapped child has an impact on the family milieu. Withdrawal behavior of the teenaged siblings of one youngster was reported, as well as unrealistic attitudes and behavior of the father. It was also reported that the sisters of a child who was in one of our in-patient programs offered all kinds of excuses as to why they could not play with him during the weekend, when the child was at home. "What is behind it is the wish that we could go back to the days when we didn't have him. I imagine that is certainly what is on everyone's mind."

Feelings of inadequacy emerge frequently in interviews with parents: "I feel a parent can't do enough when compared to what teachers do." Another parent reported: "This is all so new (the educational stimulation program). . . . I'm totally ignorant. I don't know where to begin." In her analysis of interaction between program and parents, Jacobson (in Gordon et al., 1975b) reports several conclusions that relate to the study mentioned previously:

> That the overwhelming majority of parents are not fully cognizant of the mental deficiencies of their children—putting stress on motor handicaps primarily, and that almost all the parents are unaware of the implications of play (interactions with materials) for the cognitive development of their children. Therefore, prior to their participation in the program, parents did not know how to stimulate their children and select developmental-appropriate materials. (p. 34)

These findings are not unique. Parallel findings were reported in a study carried out by Shere (1971). She wrote:

Mothers of children with severe physical handicaps were mainly concerned about the physical handicap. . . . The mothers wished primarily for their children to progress in the area of physical development, with 'walking' given as the most important activity wished." (p. 55)

An object-impoverished environment with few opportunities for needed play experience was reported by Shere and Kastenbaum (1966). As a result of their findings, we initiated a guidance program for parents, which is educational in nature. The inclusion of parents in our programs, as well as the ongoing translation for them of educational objectives and strategies, has been a basic component of our operational model at IRM since the inception of our first program. The evaluation of the impact of the program upon the parents was initiated 10 years later. Basing our efforts on clinical knowledge, we continuously try to assist parents in understanding the need to provide a richer environment for their children who, because of their physical handicapping conditions, have had too limited contact with the objects and people in their world. In her conclusion, Jacobson states (in Gordon et al., 1975b).

> It may be interesting to point out that parents turned to the educational staff for guidance when they encountered periods of special stress and seemed most incapable of coping with their handicapped children. At such times parents were most suggestive and malleable and more open to change of behavior patterns. It may be that the maximum impact of counseling has occurred at such periods, when there was a great tendency to depend on the educational-therapeutic team for help for themselves and their children. (p. 34)

The Children's Needs

Besides reducing the workload of the physician in charge of a young child's case, the use of a multi-disciplinary pediatric team can result in more precise knowledge of the patient's abilities and disabilities in all aspects of development, not only those related to his physiological functioning or dysfunctioning. Utilization of the pediatric habilitation team approach is not only most appropriate but is also critically needed, in our opinion, in serving a population of children with multihandicapping conditions, many of whom require the specialized and sophisticated expertise of staff from many disciplines, including education, psychology, social service, speech and hearing therapy, physical and occupational therapy, and pediatric nursing. These professionals are needed to augment the medical findings of the pediatrician in consultation with physiatrist, neurologist, audiologist, ophthalmologist, and orthopedist.

The value of this kind of comprehensive team diagnostic evaluation and treatment model for all children with developmental disabilities has been questioned. One study suggests that patient contact (child and family) be limited to the pediatrician and psychologist (Kleinberg & O'Connor, 1972). This simple and less costly evaluation approach is open to question when it involves dealing with young children with a mosaic of intellectual, communicative, sensory, affectual, and motor disorders. Questionable, too, according to Denhoff (1972), is the competence of the average pediatrician to have a "keen knowledge of the theoretical and technical roles played by the different professional members of the team" (p. 548). Denhoff's thesis is that a pediatrician, if he is "to serve as the central diagnostic figure for the rich diversity of these cases, must have had the same exposure to skills assessment that therapists and teachers receive" (p. 548).

This exposure is not part of the content of academic training or clinical preparation of most medical personnel. The quality of another aspect of training of pediatricians has been questioned in an article in *Developmental Medicine and Child Neurology*, by MacCarthy (1974):

> Pediatricians are few who have had a personal analysis or have put in a period of training in child psychiatry. Most of us have to get the little we know from psychiatrists' journals or from attending psychiatric meetings or from frequent associations with child psychiatrists. Child psychiatrists do not write much in journals about the organic disciplines, unfortunately. (p. 279)

MacCarthy also suggests that pediatricians borrow some of the tools of child psychiatrists. Others may indeed question the use of these tools by those without prior training, or in the absence of in-depth training before this therapeutic responsibility is assumed.

Not only is the interactional process of medical personnel with parents being questioned today (by physicians themselves as well as by professionals from other disciplines), but, in addition, the quality of interactional patterns of pediatricians with children is being opened to scrutiny.

> It is rather a sad admission that, on the whole, pediatricians have very little relationship with children in the sense of a one-to-one confiden-

> tial relationship. . . . But the longer one works in this field the more one can see that children, given the opportunity and a little time, can convey to a doctor personally quite a lot more about themselves. . . .
>
> A child undergoing surgery, or treatment of injuries, or medical investigation, has problems which have to do with the inner meaning of these things for him and the stress he may be experiencing. (MacCarthy, 1974, p. 279)

This comparatively new but healthy self-evaluation and probing related to the quality of communication between physician and child is analagous to the questioning described earlier in parents' comments about communication barriers with professionals. We have previously discussed the amount of time needed for effective interactions between physicians and parents. The following is a physician's interpretation of the amount of time needed for effective interactions between pediatrician and child—the time needed to establish rapport with a child, and to assess him:

> To be 'a privileged listener' seems to be the best definition of the idea of 'communication between child and doctor' and the best guide as to what to do or not to do from the most serious situation to the most trivial. It cannot take place on a ward-round. . . . We must use time better so as to have more available when required and we must be prepared to cut other obligations if there is some serious listening to be done. (MacCarthy, 1974, p. 284)

This statement suggests that there *is* some serious listening to be done, not only listening to the parent of the handicapped child but "listening" to the handicapped child himself. Both our long clinical experience and our studies wholeheartedly confirm this contention.

When the child is very young, however, just listening is not enough, for listening becomes secondary to observing. In the preschool-aged child (and in particular, in the preschool-aged multi-handicapped child), much of the information related to the child's current affective, social, cognitive, and physical status must be extrapolated from observational data and records. In the absence of mobility as well as of expressive speech, or in the presence of immature patterns of expression or different modes of communication, assessment of the child's developmental level must be based on data from alternative sources and interdependent aspects of developmental milestones.

The physician's medical evaluation of a young child with multi-handicapping conditions does not provide sufficient data to guide a teacher in the prescription of educational goals for this child. It has long been our contention that a medical diagnosis cannot and should not be equated with an educational diagnosis or prescription. A treatment program should not be based on stereotyped expectations for a child based upon his or her medical diagnosis, but should rather be based upon what that particular child can or cannot do. Knowledge of the medical diagnosis and the presence or absence of sensory deficits of this very special population of children is helpful if a teacher is to be effective in minimizing the influence of physiological differences as depressors of educational performance. This knowledge alone, however, is insufficient. Findings from one study completed in 1975 (Gordon et al., 1975b) clearly indicate that medical diagnosis gives little more than entry information about very young multi-handicapped children. Chronological age is not a factor that can be used for educational prescription for this population.

Mental age, based on psychometric testing, yields more information but not as much as ongoing educational assessment and reassessment, using educational materials and activities designed to explore both the child's current competency and his quality and style of response. These problem-solving work sessions have provided the most significant information for assessment-prescription when working with multi-handicapped young children. The work-samples, when documented on video tape, provide the teacher with concrete information and guidance which can be immediately transferred to and utilized in the classroom, enabling educators to design appropriate learning experiences for a particular child at a particular time. (See Appendix A for protocol of a diagnostic work sample.)

These conclusions are based on the experience of the author and, therefore, are directly related to clinical work involving a population of over 2,000 young children whose development has been interfered with by a wide range of multi-handicapping conditions, including physical and sensory deficits—conditions which impinge, in varying degrees, upon intellectual, social, and emotional development.

Shere and Kastenbaum (1966), describing Haeussermann's position, speak from their own extensive experience:

> . . . delay, difficulty or inability in manipulation additionally restricts experiential learning about the nature and properties of everyday

> things in the environment. Inability to speak, delay in learning to speak . . . will all contribute in some measure to a delay in learning or to a reduction in the amount of learning; . . . (p. 259)

Perhaps the most eloquent theoretician on the subject of learning by doing was John Dewey (1939). He stated:

> . . . even the simplest sort of activity has to be *learned*, it is not merely physical, but is mental, intellectual, in quality. The first problem set [for] the human young is learning to use the organs of sense—the eye, ear, touch, etc.—and of movement—the muscles—in connection with one another. Of course, some of the mastery achieved does not involve much mental experimentation, but is due to the ripening of physiological connections. But nevertheless there is a genuinely intellectual factor when the child learns that one kind of eye-activity means a certain kind of moving of the arm, clasping of the fingers, etc., and that this in turn entails a certain kind of exploring with the fingers, resulting in an experience of smoothness, etc. In such cases, there is not simply an acquisition of new physical capacity; there is also learning in the mental sense; something has been found out. (pp. 608–609)

We too have found these areas of development to be interdependent, not independent (Gordon et al., 1975a). Findings indicate that interference in one area will have repercussions in another area. Skills gained in one area or increased mastery in that area will have an effect upon growth in other areas. The findings of Gordon et al. (1975a) support this position:

> As hypothesized, the dimensions are interdependent, yielding a picture of interactive change across several dimensions. . . . This finding suggests that programs should be implemented to work with multiple areas of development rather than on acquisition of segregated skills. (p. 53)

The population of children served and studied in programs at IRM includes youngsters with a wide range of disabilities, including insult to the nervous system: cerebral palsy, congenital or acquired; spina bifida with myelomeningocele and associated hydrocephalus; congenital skeletal abnormalities; muscular atrophy and dystrophy; uncommon birth defects. It also includes youngsters with delays in development of unknown etiology.

This population of children is similar, we believe, to populations served and studied in other medical facilities, certainly in other rehabilitation centers. The presence of an educational department in a medical setting can precipitate questions related to professional autonomy, parity, or subservience. In a traditional medical setting, there is little doubt about the pattern or order of the hierarchy. In the best interests of the child, we would suggest that whoever is on top is not as important as whether the status of professionals or patients is of primary concern.

Within the framework of a medical model, belief in the omnipotence of physicians (and this is the thinking of an unusually large number of families served and, not infrequently, the belief of some physicians) is being questioned, and so is the efficacy of the model itself. Concerns about the fallibility of medicine are obviously not new. In a recent editorial in *Developmental Medicine and Child Neurology*, Mac Keith (1974) quoted Proust:

> 'To believe in medicine would be a great error were it not that not to believe in medicine would be a greater error still, for out of all its mistakes has emerged much wisdom'. (p. 277)

The sensitive use of the combined expertise of a multi-disciplinary team can not only add information related to the status of the multi-handicapped child and give dignity to the feelings of the parents, but can also enhance the possibility of emergent integrated wisdom while reducing the possibility of mistakes.

Medical information is surely needed. Familiarity with specific medical diagnostic entities and the patterns of dysfunction associated with the many types of cerebral dysfunction that interfere with, restrict, distort, or limit intellectual development does furnish general information to child development specialists prior to their own evaluation of each child's current cognitive status. It permits more effective planning of each young child's individualized educational program, one designed to raise the child's performance to the optimum, within the limits that are imposed by organic deficits. There are, however, clear ceilings on performance which are related to the degree of neurological insult. Ranges in capacities do exist in multi-handicapped children. Understimulation and lack of developmental therapy for these children can restrict their performance, but even intensive stimulation and extensive therapy cannot restore a damaged organism to normal capacity.

A distinction is purposely being made between performance and capacity (Bortner & Birch, 1970). Extended assessment and reassessment is always indicated, but not always provided, in working with young children with multi-handicapping conditions. To evaluate capacity reliably, one performance (one test) of a very young child is not a valid indicator of the child's potential as a learner or of his cognitive ability or style, but more usually tests the child for comfort in the testing situation, previous exposure to similar tasks, level of motivation of work, interest in the specific activity or material presented, and rapport with the examiner. Discrepancy or congruence between educational performance and capacity (capacity representing the potential of the child and performance representing the level of response in one situation) can be established only after very sensitive and extensive assessment by academically sound and experienced educational staff in a natural and relaxed learning environment. Intervention strategies should be based on this developmental-profile type of assessment. Only then can curricular goals be projected, based on concrete information about the child's current level of performance in defined areas of development. (Appendix B shows a sample anecdotal log record; Appendix C shows sample curricular goals.) Efforts should then be organized and integrated by the educator (together with the other members of the multidisciplinary staff responsible for the child's therapeutic program) to gradually extend each child's ability to respond to more complex problem-solving situations, as well as to more differentiated social, emotional, and physical demands.

Staffing Needs

Further comment is warranted on staffing needs, especially the academic and experiential qualifications of the educational staff. A teacher of multi-handicapped children has in common with them an unusual share of problems. The educator of special children must be able to recognize rapidly and readily those areas of strengths and deficits which together provide the best image of the child's developmental status. The educator should be capable of identifying the presence and loci of cognitive dysfunction. In this multi-handicapped population, there exists a wider range of differences than in the normal population. In order to recognize uncommon patterns of learning behavior, the teacher must be thoroughly versed in normal patterns of learning and behavior.

Conventional ratios of teacher to child do not allow opportunities for optimal interactions of multi-handicapped children in child-to-child or child-to-teacher relationships. Conventional physical environments do not offer optimal opportunity for action and interaction for children with restricted mobility, reduced stamina, with missing or abortive limbs, or for children whose neurological disability interferes with perceptual and spatial organizations.

The objectives of an educational program are as clearly reflected in the design of the physical learning environment and selected learning materials as they are in the design of individualized curricular goals in which active engagement of the child with his environment is of primary concern (Gordon, 1969; 1972). With normal children, we assume that a normal environment will provide these opportunities. With deviant children, that assumption cannot be made casually. Modifications and adaptations of physical space, equipment, and materials are clearly needed to enhance the possibilities for success in the multi-handicapped child's activities and in his encounters with objects and people.

Assessment/Evaluation—Child, Parent, Program

The knowledge gained from extended assessment of the very young child and the strategies developed for implementing educational therapeutic programs should be transmitted on an ongoing basis to staff from other disciplines involved in the treatment program. They should also be described to the family of the child. This exchange increases the likelihood that the methods developed in the school setting for maximizing the child's functioning will be understood and used by everyone responsible for the child's care. Cooperation, coordination, and communication among the disciplines involved in the child's program, as well as among staff and parents, are essential. Active parent participation in the young child's program has been found to be the most effective means of demonstrating and clarifying educational objectives and methods.

Findings from our analysis of interviews with parents did indicate (as mentioned earlier) that parents tend, upon their child's admission, to focus primarily on children's motor deficits and speech production—overt symptoms of problems in development (Gordon et al., 1975b). It is our thesis that equal concern should be devoted to the child's affectual state, his level of social responsiveness, his awareness of the environment, and his ability to interact purposefully with educational materials. The holistic view of the child should be presented and interpreted to the parents, families, or other caretakers of these children.

In a final interview, responding to a comment by the author, a mother made the following comments, suggesting that her concerns for her son seemed to have shifted away from a primary focus on physical development:

> I expected a lot of other things and I got a lot. I didn't get what I really expected, but I'm happy with what I got. After 3 months here, he's sitting up all by himself and he's been using his hands already and I figure—I expect a miracle—that's what I do, but he's still doing just as good. He's not doing what I expected. I know he understands whatever I tell him. Before I didn't think he really understood. But now I know that he does. . . .
>
> The toys he used to have are no good. I got him a few new toys—simple little things: You put on a peg. And I got him a little puzzle. It keeps his interest. I could sit there and he doesn't start crying right away. I give him mechanical things: he'll look at it two seconds and start crying. Now you give him something, like his hand. . . .
>
> Most of the stuff they have around the Infant Room—that's the kind of toys now that I look for. And they're really simple, little nothings, you know that really amuses him, which amazes me. I'll go out and get all these rare, rare looking toys that do amazing things and he doesn't like any of them. And pegs and blocks and things like that is what he really likes.
>
> Everybody who saw him before, they kept telling me they didn't see any mental damage. So being they told me that, I just assumed that everything was all right and I never bothered . . . I thought there was nothing mentally wrong with him. I wanted help with physical problems. I see now he needs more mentally—not that he's retarded. I hope if I talk to him and make him understand more, he can help himself more physically because then he'll know what I want him to do.

Our position, educationally, is that one cannot separate the child's emotional status from his mental and physical status. Affective and cognitive processes are not compartmentalized. We support the view that there is constant interweaving and interdependence of affective, cognitive, and physical development in handicapped young children, as well as in normal children. Emerging new patterns of responding to people and trusting new people, as well as the more complex and differentiated patterns of expressing feelings, are very clearly goals of the educational process for children with developmental disorders.

Our clinical observations and progress reports and our more formal investigations all indicate that changes in performance related to intervention are most frequently first observed in changes in a child's emotional status, in the degree and complexity of his social responsiveness, and in the quality and quantity of self-initiated independent movement toward people and objects. Our findings further suggest that these changes take place concurrently with positive changes in the child's communicative skills, reasoning processes, and overall cognitive growth. These changes nurture each other; they are dependent upon each other (Gordon et al., 1975a). All children do change, but there is no single pattern of change associated with every child. Progress or change in any multi-handicapped child is best described when that particular child's performance, style of response, and behavior are independently studied through measures that reflect and describe where that child was and what he did and where that child is and what he does now, qualitatively as well as quantitatively.

Both clinical and research experience suggest that simplistic checklists of accomplishment, or discrete gains of skills over limited periods of time, or pre and post responses to questionnaires, are inadequate to assess the impact of intervention programs on multi-handicapped children or on their families. The factors that contribute to or inhibit change are as multi-variable as the group of children subsumed by the descriptive label "multi-handicapped." Instruments for reporting change are most easily designed and most readily used when they measure the most concrete objectives at one point in time. However, gains related to a program may very well emerge at a later period in time. Neither the children, nor their families, nor the school setting, nor the teaching staff, nor the situation-specific characteristics of testing or responding can be disassociated from the day-to-day variations that are the reality of human interactions.

Given this type of thinking, our commitment is to sound and quality programs with ongoing observational recording, documentation, and analysis of the change and progress that occur in the natural setting of school programs where intervention strategies are employed with both children and families. Research using data directly generated from these settings can best reflect and mesh with the overall intent and philosophy of the developmental programs offered to the children we serve.

This approach, we believe, respects the similarities, the differences, and the limitations in both the children and their families in their ability to respond to any one pattern of treatment, however sensitively and individually it is designed and implemented.

Appendix A. Protocol of Diagnostic Work Sample

I first gave N.D. the Montessori Cylinders. He had just come from a very active session in the playground, and it was my feeling that he might need a very structured, controlled material to bring him down to very directed play. As I observed N.D. attempting to remove the cylinders in a chaotic, impulsive way, it was clear that I would have to structure the task even further. I did this simultaneously with an attempt to assess whether N.D. understood the concepts of larger, smaller, largest, smallest, bigger, and so on. By controlling the speed at which he removed the cylinders as well as replaced them, I was able to get a better understanding of his ability to recognize and differentiate sizes. At the same time, it was apparent that the more external controls the teacher provided, the more effective N.D. could be. He was able to discriminate sizes, and he understood the labels associated with gradations of size.

I next presented matching plaques of faces. This required the kind of investment of attention and visual concentration that is most difficult for this boy, particularly because many people were entering and leaving the room in his direct line of vision. He had more trouble with this exercise. Although he was able to differentiate a face in which one eye was open and the other eye was closed, in contrast to matched plaques in which the face drawing had both eyes open, the task was too complicated for him to do under the environmental conditions. (I think that in a quieter atmosphere, he would be more effective with this task.) Interestingly, N.D. was not able to close one eye himself (wink) even though I demonstrated this action.

I changed materials and went on to the puzzle of the boy and girl, once again assisting him orally in making choices as to which piece should be approached at a particular time. I felt that this structuring of the demands of the puzzle improved his performance. I had the impression that, left alone, he would have been too disorganized to do it. Yet, with help, he was able to complete the task, even the rotations of the bent arms of the girl and boy.

Earlier, I had offered the form box and structured this already defined material even further by having N.D. group the objects by their different shapes as he took them out of the box. This he did well. He labeled them and was reasonably accurate in counting the number of objects in each group (two or three). With this type of initial grouping, he was able to insert the pieces in sequence into their correct holes, having difficulty only with the C-shaped form and the triangle. His problems were more those of attention, I suspect, than of ability.

Ronnie Gordon, Examiner, and N.D.

Appendix B. Sample Anecdotal Log Record Used in Prescribing Curricular Goals

In crib lying down. Seemed very tired. Looked at me, smiled, but did not sit up when I went to the crib.

I sat him at the table for psychological evaluation. I observed for a while. He built a tower of three cubes, attempted the fourth, but because of his incoordination and lack of stabilization, it collapsed. This frustrated him, and he began throwing cubes. With the form board (circles and squares only), he managed with quick success, including the rotation of the square pieces. When the psychologist presented the second board (circle, square, triangle), he removed the pieces and threw them (see sample goal 3 in Appendix C.) I did not understand the action. It was probably not frustration since he had previously done similar tasks with ease.

After the evaluations, he was taken down to physical therapy. He returned, smiling broadly and walking very well indeed for his first experience on the rollator. The physical therapist reported that he had learned to walk with it immediately and "loved it." He cried when she tried to remove him until I placed the cookie tin on the table. He recognized it and crawled right over to his chair. Pulled to standing at the chair and struggled to pull it out. I helped.

Once he was seated, he helped himself to a cookie. When his juice was served, he pulled little pieces of cookie out of his mouth and placed them carefully (in pincer grasp) on the table. This was apparently to make room for the juice. He held his covered cup in two hands and drank. The pulp of the orange juice clogged the spout of the cup. I removed the cover, and he managed pretty well in drinking without it. There was a little spilling and drooling. When he finished, he held out his cup for more.

After his snack, I placed him on the floor. He crawled, pulled to standing, and cruised. Using this combined means of transport, he followed Jory all about the room. He watched Jory and touched him exploratively. Binnie pushed him when he grabbed at a toy he was holding. Made some vowel sounds in a conversational manner.

Did not cry when I returned him to his crib. This was new. He usually does. I waved good-bye and, for the first time, he waved back by extending his arm and opening and shutting his palm.

In bed when we came. Sat up when he saw us. Smiled. Pulled to standing and walked along crib side. He continued to smile as he watched me move about, readying the room.

I took him from the crib and sat him at the table where I had arranged the easel, paint brush, and dish of red paint. He quickly got the sequence of dipping and brushing after I demonstrated one stroke. He continued to paint with fascination. It was a pleasure to watch his enjoyment. His style was very mature for his age, and he showed above age level interest in watching the paint cover the paper. He really enjoyed that more than the tactile experience and exploration. This was illustrated in a paint-spilling incident in which he briefly put his hand in and smeared. He quickly returned, however, to the brushing, showing a preference for that. He covered nearly the whole piece of paper, both sides, the top and the bottom. (See sample goals 4 and 6 in Appendix C.)

During the cleanup, he showed more age-appropriate behavior by splashing so vigorously that it was next to impossible for me to control it. The vigor and enjoyment made me laugh. When he saw me laugh, he laughed too; I got the mirror and showed him a spot of paint on his face. He seemed to understand. Smiled some more and watched his reflection as I washed it off. (See sample goal 1 in Appendix C.)

I put him on the floor to crawl and he moved about, seeming to enjoy the sheer physical pleasure of the movement. When we brought out the snacks, he crawled to the table and pulled to standing at his chair.

During the snack, his mother arrived for her participation day. He looked up at her and smiled. She sat next to him. I blew bubbles, and he visually tracked them in all directions. He "caught" them in his two hands and smiled when they popped. His mother tried to hold the wand in front of his mouth so he could blow. He struggled with her for possession of the wand. She did not want him to hold it. This made him very angry, and he expressed his anger by grabbing her arm and scratching. She would not let him have it. I broke the deadlock by suggesting that she put him down for a little exercise.

He crawled to the cabinets and pulled out blocks, puppets, cars, everything. His mother tried, by demonstration, to get him to put some back. Each time she put some back, he took them out. At this point, I suggested a walk in the hall. (It was raining, so no playground.) They left.

They returned in time for him to join the group in sliding down the ramp. He smiled as he slid down.

D. Clyde Brenner
Master Teacher, Infant School

Appendix C. Sample Curricular Goals; Methods and Materials for Implementation

1. Focusing on faces and lip movements when spoken to. We will begin by turning his head toward us when we speak in combination of speech and gestures. We will tape small objects to various parts of our faces and encourage him to pull them off, in order to make the face a more interesting thing to look at. We will also sit in front of the mirror with him and work to get focus on our reflections as well as his own.
2. Independent exploration of space and objects. We will provide two periods a day for free movement, with cabinet doors open for each access to materials.
3. Stacking large blocks, bowls, and other objects, towards eventual cube stacking and stabilizing ability.
4. Painting, scooping, and pouring, for improved coordination and age-appropriate fun.
5. Experiencing vibration and wind movement from rhythm instruments and squeaky toys, as compensatory training and for the understanding of the action of such toys in absence of auditory feedback.
6. Extension of existing strengths. We will provide a variety of activities with forms, colors, and size differentiations to help him hold onto and grow in the concepts he has.
7. Walking with rollator or holding a teacher's hand as extension of physical therapy goals.

D. Clyde Brenner, Master Teacher
Infant School

References

Bortner, M., & Birch, H. G. Cognitive capacity and cognitive competence. *American Journal of Mental Deficiency,* 1970, *74,* 735–744.

Denhoff, E. Editor's Note: Appraising the effectiveness of a simple evaluation approach to problems of retardation and behavior in childhood. *Clinical Pediatrics,* 1972, *11,* 547–548.

Fox, A. M. *They get this training but they don't really know how you feel.* London: Institute of Child Health, 1975.

Gordon, R. The design of a pre-school "learning laboratory" in a rehabilitation center. *Rehabilitation Monograph* (#39). New York: Institute of Rehabilitation Medicine, New York University Medical Center, 1969.

Gordon, R. The design of a pre-school therapeutic playground. An outdoor "learning laboratory." *Rehabilitation Monograph* (#47). New York: Institute of Rehabilitation Medicine, New York University Medical Center, 1972.

Gordon, R., White, D., & Diller, L. Performance of neurologically impaired preschool children with educational materials. *Exceptional Children,* 1972, *38,* 428–437.

Gordon, R., Gitler, D., Schwartz, B., Ezrachi, O., and Brenner, D. C. *Evaluation of behavioral change. Part I: Study of multi-handicapped young children. Final report,* U.S. Department of Health, Education and Welfare, Office of Education, Bureau of Education for the Handicapped. Project No. HOO50SJ, Grant No. OEG-0-72-5386, August, 1975a.

Gordon, R., Jacobson, C., Gitler, D., Schwartz, B., Ezrachi, O., & Brenner, D. C. *Evaluation of behavioral change. Part II: Interaction between program and parents. Final Report,* U.S. Department of Health, Education and Welfare, Office of Education, Bureau of Education for the Handicapped. Project No. HOO50SJ, Grant No. OEG-0-72-5386, August, 1975b.

Ingram, T. S. Habilitation and rehabilitation. *Developmental Medicine and Child Neurology,* 1973, *15,* 421–422.

Kleinberg, W., & O'Connor, P. A. Appraising the effective ness of a simple educational approach to problems of retardation and behavior in childhood. *Clinical Pediatrics,* 1972, *11,* 545–548.

MacCarthy, P. Communication between children and doctors. *Developmental Medicine and Child Neurology,* 1974, *16,* 279–285.

MacKeith, R. Medicine and the people. *Developmental Medicine and Child Neurology,* 1974, *16,* 277–278.

Morris, D. Coming to terms with social implications. *General Practitioners Magazine,* January 18, 1972.

Shere, E. S. Modes of child-rearing in cerebral palsy: Effects upon the child's psychological development. *The Israel Annals of Psychiatry and Related Disciplines,* 1971, *9,* 52–59.

Shere, E. S., & Kastenbaum, R. Mother-child interaction in cerebral palsy: Environmental and psycho-social obstacles to cognitive development. *Genetic Psychology Monographs,* 1966, *73,* 255–335.

Sheridan, M. *The handicapped child and his home.* London: National Children's Home, 1965.

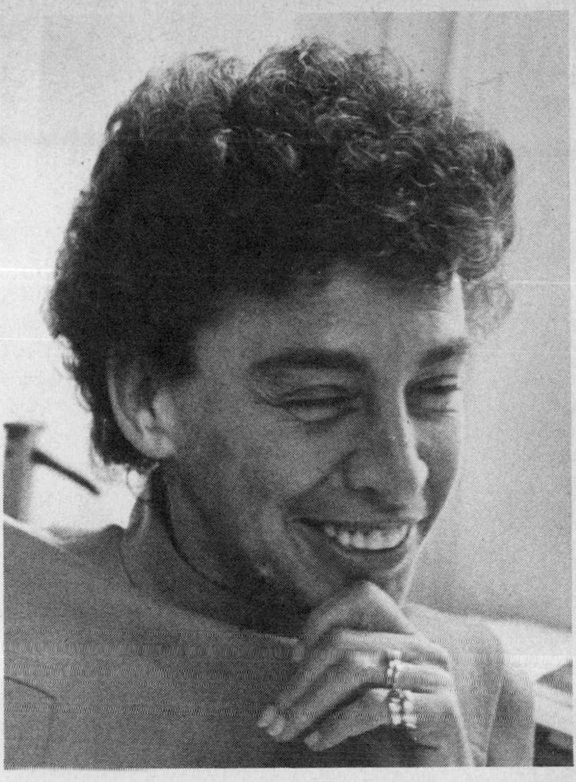

RONNIE GORDON is Associate Professor of Clinical Rehabilitation Medicine at the New York University School of Medicine, and Director of Preschool and Infant Developmental Programs at the Institute of Rehabilitation Medicine. She has had extensive experience in the developmental evaluation of young multi-handicapped children, the development of prescriptive individualized curricular goals, and the organization of engineered environments for the multiply-handicapped child. Professor Gordon is the author of many articles on these and related subjects and she has also lectured widely in the United States and abroad.

A Parent's View of What Public Education Should Accomplish

PHILIP ROOS

National Association for Retarded Citizens

Education is essential to all human beings; without it no individual can hope to survive, much less become a contributing member of society. Yet, until recently most mentally retarded children were denied access to adequate public education (National Association for Retarded Citizens, 1974c; Roos, 1971). Ironically, those in greatest need, the severely and profoundly retarded and the multiply handicapped, were least likely to be served. It is not surprising that parents of retarded children, and particularly the National Association for Retarded Citizens (NARC), formerly National Association for Retarded Children, have long agitated for adequate public education for the mentally retarded.

In recent years, NARC and its state and local units have become increasingly militant, challenging the nation to meet its constitutional mandates through national policies (NARC, 1968, 1971, 1973b, 1974b, 1975c, in press-b), litigation (New York Association for Retarded Children v. Rockefeller, 1972; Pennsylvania Association for Retarded Children v. Pennsylvania, 1972; Roos, 1972; Wyatt v. Stickney, 1972) and support of national and state legislation (Felicetti, 1975; Roos, 1972). Parent advocates have been joined in these efforts by professionals and administrators and have, with increasing frequency, found strong allies in such organizations as the Council for Exceptional Children (CEC) and the American Association on Mental Deficiency (AAMD).

Counterproductive Parent-Professional Interactions

Parents and professionals have not always worked harmoniously together. Indeed, the genesis of NARC has been attributed in part to parental frustrations stemming from professional apathy, neglect and indifference (Roos, 1970, 1975a). Years of unfortunate interactions between parents and professionals have generated negative stereotypes, many of which still linger.

Professional Mishandling

Professional mishandling of parents of retarded individuals has, unfortunately, been common. Some of the most frequent types of mishandling include the following:

Professional Ignorance. Even today, many professionals in the medical and behavioral sciences have little knowledge of mental retardation. Some fail to recognize mental retardation or, when they suspect its presence, they dispense misinformation. For instance, some parents are still advised that their child will outgrow the difficulty, while others are told of the "hopelessness of their child's condition and the necessity for immediate institutionalization.

Professional Hopelessness. Medically oriented professionals, in particular, tend to consider mental retardation as an incurable disease, and hence as hopeless. This attitude generates self-fulfilling and self-limiting prophecies which impede the development of retarded individuals. Parents usually detect such defeatist attitudes and either adopt similar expectations or resent those who hold such negative expectations toward their child.

Referral Ad Infinitum. The tendency of some parents to shop around in the vain hope of obtaining a satisfying answer to their unresolved questions is well known, but in many cases professionals have initiated the referrals for which parents are later held responsible. Often such referrals reflect lack of professional expertise in mental retardation and/or reluctance to confront parents with the traumatic conclusion that their child is retarded. Ironically, some professionals are less able to accept retardation in a child than the child's own parents, leading to the peculiar situation of parents trying to convince the professional of the retardation of their own child.

Veil of Secrecy. Some mental retardation professionals have adopted the approach once popular among medical and mental health professionals of withholding information from clients, allegedly because the information would be too threatening, too uncomfortable, or in some other way would be destructive to the client. The erection of this veil of secrecy may belie the more fundamental reason that some professionals minimize their own feelings or insecurity by maintaining a monopoly on information of potential value to their clients.

Deaf Ear Syndrome. Parents have at times become infuriated when their most earnest requests of professionals have been totally ignored. They sometimes feel that any suggestion made by a parent regarding his own child is categorically dismissed. This not uncommon professional disregard for parental suggestions or information may be the result of destructive stereotypes of parents.

Professional Omniscience. Whereas some professionals candidly admit ignorance regarding mental retardation, others exude extraordinary confidence in their own pronouncements. Although they may hint that they possess the key to all ultimate knowledge, they often hoard much of this precious commodity behind the veil of secrecy mentioned above, perhaps suggesting that the naive parents would be totally overwhelmed by exposure to the fountain of knowledge available to the professionals. Their ready recourse to esoteric jargon helps to convince the unfortunate parents of the professionals' omniscient status.

Professional Omnipotence. Related to professional omniscience is the myth of professional omnipotence—the assumption that professionals have the wisdom to make sage decisions about other people's destinies. Even when sophisticated multidisciplinary teams conduct evaluations and develop individual program plans, the child's parents (and the child himself) are still frequently excluded from the deliberations and decision-making process. Instead, parents are informed after the fact of the conclusions reached by the team.

Parents as Patients. Since many professionals have developed a stereotype of parents of retarded children as emotionally disturbed people, it is not surprising that they tend to consider parents as prime candidates for psychotherapy. Parents may thus be thwarted in obtaining desperately needed concrete information regarding their child's condition and the availability of services to meet his needs. They are likely to be confronted by professionals eager to unravel their intrapsychic conflicts and to explore their marital problems and other areas of maladjustment.

Two popular objectives in counseling parents of the retarded are getting parents to accept mental retardation and lifting the depression which seems to be a common parental reaction. Unfortunately, neither of these objectives is realistic. While parents may fully understand that their child is mentally retarded, it is unrealistic to expect them to accept this situation with blandness and equanimity; our society places too high a value on intelligence. Likewise a state of chronic sorrow has been described as the normal (in contrast to pathological) response of parents to having a retarded child (Olshansky, 1966).

Parental Reactions to Mental Retardation

The impact on parents of having a mentally retarded child typically precipitates reactions which, though not necessarily pathological, tend to frustrate professionals. These reactions may interfere with effective parent-professional interaction and may, in some cases, impair parents' capacity to deal constructively with their retarded child. Common parental reactions to having a retarded child include loss of self-esteem, shame, increased ambivalence, depression, self-sacrifice, and defensiveness (Roos, 1963). Extreme degrees of any of these reactions can obviously interfere with helpful parent-child interaction, as well as with constructive parent-professional relationships.

Whereas many professionals are relatively aware of these parental reactions and of ways of coping with them, they are usually unaware of, and unresponsive to, the serious existential conflicts which are likely to overwhelm parents. Knowledge that one's child is retarded tends to reactivate anxieties which are common to most members of our culture, but which tend to lie dormant in most relatively normal human beings. Many professionals seem to feel uncomfortable discussing these existential conflicts and effectively avoid doing so. They much prefer dealing with the traditional "parental pathology." They may have no easy answers to the existential conflicts which threaten to overwhelm parents of retarded children, and they may experience personal discomfort as their own unresolved conflicts are reactivated.

The degree of impact on parental adjustment resulting from having a retarded child is a function of many factors, including the importance the parents place on having children and whether or not the retarded offspring is an only child. Some of the most critical existential conflicts common to parents of retarded children include the following:

Disillusionment. Our society propagates myths which generate totally unrealistic expectations. As children, we learn to expect success, achievement, wealth, and status. We are taught in innumerable ways to expect wise parents, loving and lovable mates, and perfect children. Experiences gradually erode these unrealistic expectations of ourselves and others, leading to a long series of disillusionments in ourselves, in others, and in life in general.

Many of us channel our yearning for perfection into our children. We hope to realize through them our own frustrated aspirations and our thwarted dreams of achievement and happiness. Since a retarded child is usually an unsuitable vehicle for realizing parental hopes, he presents a major disillusionment, often the culmination in a long series of disappointments. If a retarded child symbolizes failure as a parent, the parent may experience serious disillusionment in self. If no other children are present, the hope of eventual fulfillment through one's children is lost forever, and the parent may seek desperately for other avenues toward self-enhancement or he may adopt a pervasive attitude of hopelessness.

Aloneness. Our need for intimacy is never completely fulfilled. We have no way of transcending our personal boundaries and fully sharing our feelings and perceptions with another. Neither our parents nor our mate can ever completely meet our desire for complete sharing with another. Many of us yearn to overcome our loneliness through our children; products of our bodies, shaped into our images, literally extensions of ourselves, they represent our last hope for reaching true intimacy. Yet a retarded child may thwart this hope because of his limited ability to communicate, or because he is unresponsive to his parents' attempts to achieve intimacy. As a result, feelings of aloneness are likely to be intensified when a parent realizes that his child is retarded. He may feel he has lost the final opportunity to achieve intimacy and that he is henceforth condemned to a life of aloneness.

Vulnerability. A child's early fantasy of omnipotence is soon shattered as he is confronted by his dependency on others and his helplessness to cope with the world. Gradually he learns that others, too, are helpless, including his parents, his teachers, and his heroes. Pain, injury, illness, and failure all attest forcefully to personal vulnerability, to the tenuousness of one's control over the world, and indeed to the fragile nature of life itself.

Mental retardation in one's child reactivates feelings of helplessness by dramatically reminding the parent that his most precious possessions and dearest dreams can be totally annihilated, and that neither he nor any other—human or divine—can do anything about it.

Inequity. Our nation is founded on the premise of justice for all, and we are conditioned from earliest childhood to believe that fairness and justice ultimately prevail. Our world view is predicated on the premise that good will triumph and that, should our judicial system falter, some greater force will ensure that heroes are rewarded and villains are punished. When faced with retardation in one's child, the natural reaction is to ask, "Why me?". The enormity of the apparent inequity is overwhelming. In his desperate search for an answer to this question, the parent is likely to entertain two alternatives: either he has sinned grievously and is getting his just rewards, or he is living in a world in which fairness and justice are fictitious constructs. The former alternative leads to guilt, remorse, and self-recrimination; the latter may threaten basic ethical, moral, and religious beliefs.

Insignificance. As young children, we imagine ourselves to be important figures occupying a central role in the scheme of things, but with maturity comes the realization that we are relatively insignificant, that we are unimportant individuals on a minute planet of a small sun in a mediocre galaxy spinning in an infinite universe. In spite of history which attests to the insignificance of billions of human beings whose trivial lives have been less than noticed, we are raised to strive—some more desperately than others—to achieve greatness or at least "meaning." When greatness escapes us, as it usually does, we are prone to compromise with our early dreams by seeking meaning in fulfilling important and satisfying social roles: husband, wife, father, mother, and so forth. Thwarting of parental roles, as is likely to occur when one's child is retarded, may confront parents with their insignificance by depriving them of one of their few opportunities to achieve meaning.

Past Orientation. Man is unique among our planet's living organisms in his capacity to travel through time; he can recapture his past, dwell in the present, or project himself into the future. Avoiding the present and future by clinging to the past is associated with various morbid states, while projecting oneself into the future tends to be associated with mature planning and optimism. Future projection is related to the anticipation of happy and satisfying events, whereas the anticipation of unhappiness and frustration tends to block future projection and to foster orientation toward the past.

Generally, parents anticipate their child's future with enthusiasm, looking forward to such events as attending school, scholastic achievement, excellence in sports, graduation, marriage, birth of grandchildren, and career achievements. They are likely to hold an optimistic future orientation. Parents of a retarded child, on the other hand, are prone to view their child's future as a source of increasing frustration and anxiety. They fear their child will face such trauma as scholastic failure, exclusion from schools, inability to work, problems in sexual adjustment, inability to live independently, and a life of loneliness and isolation. Furthermore, as the retarded offspring grows older, services usually become increasingly inadequate, adding to the parents' frustrations. Hence, for many parents of retarded children, the future holds little promise, and they tend to shift from future to past temporal orientation and from an optimistic to a pessimistic attitude toward what lies ahead.

Loss of Immortality. Man's ability to transcend the present and anticipate his own death is a major source of human existential anxiety. Many individuals achieve a type of symbolic immortality through their children; they think of themselves as living on through their children and their children's children. Grandparents' legendary preoccupation with their grandchildren attests to the symbolic significance of continuation of the family line. When a child is retarded, this potential avenue to immortality is threatened; when the retarded child is an only child, this form of immortality is denied the parents, and they are faced with the inescapable prospect of their own finiteness and ultimate loss of identity.

Constructive Parent-Professional Interactions

In recent years parents and professionals have increasingly shifted from adversary stances to cooperative interactions. By joining together and forming voluntary organizations, parents have gradually gained potency as social change agents. They have developed considerable sophistication in the mechanics of fostering social change, as well as in the technical aspects of programming for mentally retarded individuals (Roos, 1970, 1975a).

Parents as Members of Multidisciplinary Teams

Parents are becoming increasingly active participants in multidisciplinary teams, in contrast to their traditional role of being passive recipients of professional services. This significant change reflects not only the impact of voluntary organizations, such as NARC, but it is also the result of several relatively recent scientific developments, including the following:

* The relevance of mothers' teaching approaches to their children's performance has been experimentally substantiated (Brophy, 1970; Hess and Shipman, 1965; Wiegerink, 1969).
* The impact of early intervention on children's subsequent intellectual and emotional development has been impressively demonstrated (Gray, 1971; Gray and Klaus, 1970; Haywood, 1967; Heber, Garber, Harrington, Hoffman and Falender, 1972; Hunt, 1961). Long-term effects of a deprived environment during the first five years of life seem particularly potent and apparently may significantly lower a child's intelligence quotient (Bloom, 1964).
* Curricula, training materials and audiovisual aids specifically designed to assist parents in training their handicapped children are now readily available (Bijou, 1968; Gray and Klaus, 1965; Ferritor, 1970; Wahler, 1969; Wildman, 1965).

Pilot demonstration programs have already impressively documented the success of using parents as implementors of systematic training programs with their own handicapped children. These parents typically are trained to function as extensions of the professional team. They assume a major role in conducting formal training activities, which at times reach considerable sophistication. Pre-school programs (Bijou, 1968; Luterman, 1971), programs for severely and profoundly retarded young children (Smith and Murphy, 1969), and programs for brain-injured children (Salzinger, Feldman, and Portnoy, 1970) have been successfully implemented. NARC is currently engaged in a national program, funded by the Bureau of Education for the Handicapped, of developing materials, workshops, and audiovisual presentations designed to equip parents of severely and profoundly retarded children to orchestrate training efforts with professionals. The program is using the association's almost 1900 state and local units as the conduit for reaching individual parents.

It would be unrealistic to assume that all parents of retarded children will embrace the role of trainer of their handicapped children with equal enthusiasm. Parents of normal children vary greatly in the degree to which they actively participate in the education of their children, and there is no reason to suspect that parents of retarded children differ from them in this regard. Yet in many cases, assuming this new role will mitigate the feelings of frustration and helplessness which are common in parents of retarded children. It is likely to enhance their self-concept and increase their self esteem. Furthermore, as parents adopt formal training responsibilities, their new role should bring them into a closer relationship with professionals by fostering mutual understanding and respect.

Parents as Decision Makers

Parents as well as professionals have been gradually redefining their respective roles. In the past professionals have tended to either assume almost total programming responsibility for severely handicapped children, or they have attempted to avoid any involvement. Parents have adopted reciprocal roles, either totally relinquishing the child to the professional or assuming complete responsibility for his care. Hence, until relatively recently, parents of retarded children had only two practical options available to them: either they could institutionalize their child or they could retain him at home and attempt to meet all his needs through their own efforts.

The genesis of parent organizations can be attributed to frustrations resulting from lack of services (Mead and Brown, 1966; Roos, 1970, 1975a). These early groups were deeply involved in developing services for their own children, a pattern which has only gradually been altered as appropriate public services for retarded individuals become available (Roos, 1970, 1975a).

In recent years, public services for the retarded have greatly expanded, and professionals have become increasingly committed to these programs. In general, parents have welcomed these changes, and most favor further expansion of appropriate specialized services for the retarded as well as increasing access to generic services of all kinds. Yet most parents insist on retaining a key role in all decisions affecting their children.

Parental concern with decision-making is primarily focused on two distinct types of situations: they want to be involved in decisions affecting their own child, and they want to participate in decisions affecting the delivery of services to the mentally retarded in general. With regard to decisions affecting their own child, parents are primarily interested in the selection of objectives and goals. An important function of professionals in the decision-making process is to provide parents—and the mentally retarded client himself, if possible—with information on which informed decisions can be based. Preferably alternative courses of action can be objectively described so that choices can be intelligently made among several desirable alternatives. Once the decision has been reached regarding goals, professionals have the primary responsibility for selecting the specific methods and approaches for reaching these goals. Parents might also wish to participate in the selection of methods, however, when several alternative approaches are available. In such instances, professionals would describe the available alternative methods, the advantages and disadvantages of each and, if applicable, their own preferences and proficiencies.

The involvement of parents in making decisions affecting their own children is becoming widely recognized as an essential component of programming for handicapped individuals. National accreditation standards (e.g., Joint Commission on Accreditation of Hospitals, 1973), federal court mandates (e.g., Wyatt v. Stickney, 1972), and federal guidelines (e.g., regulations governing intermediate care facilities for the mentally retarded) already incorporate provisions ensuring the direct participation of clients and/or their parents or parent surrogates in making major programmatic decisions. Policy statements developed by major national organizations likewise reflect this stance. For example, at its 1975 national convention, NARC adopted a resolution on Biomedical and Pharmacological Research on Mentally Retarded Persons in Residential Facilities (NARC, 1975c) which included, among several requirements needed for approval of such research, that: "there shall be competent, voluntary and individual informed consent which is knowledgeable and autonomous and given by the individual, his parent or legal guardian without coercion or duress . . . " (p. 2). Similar requirements have been proposed by NARC regarding participation in behavior modification programs (May, Risley, Twardosz, Friedman, Bijou, and Wexler, 1975). The AAMD advocates a similar position, as evident from the following statement regarding individualized program plans: "Recipients of services and their personal or legal representatives should be given a full opportunity to participate in all phases of the development and review of their individual program plan. Where appropriate, parents should be asked to participate in carrying out the plan, as well" (AAMD, 1975, p. 30).

With regard to parents' decision-making role relative to the delivery of services, recent years have brought a noticeable shift in the attitude of parents toward professionals, administrators, and governmental bodies. The trend has been toward activism and even militancy, in contrast to the passivity and dependency of the past. Furthermore, parent organizations have become increasingly effective as social change agents.

Parents as Social Change Agents

The development of parent organizations, such as NARC, has been described in detail (Boggs, 1963; Dybwad, 1959; Katz, 1961; Mead and Brown, 1966; Roos, 1970, 1975a; Segal, 1970). Specific phases have been identified in their evolution from small groups of parents joining together for mutual support to complex organizations with paid staff (Katz, 1961). The functions of these groups have shifted over the years. The most dramatic change has been the gradual relinquishing of the operation of direct services in favor of assuming roles related to catalyzing social change (Roos, 1970, 1975a).

One of the most impressive achievements of Associations for Retarded Citizens (ARC's) has been their highly sophisticated legislative activities at the state and national levels (Felicetti, 1975; Roos, 1972). These groups have buttressed their legislative efforts by articulating their activities with state and federal operating agencies. Typically, they have established continuing liaisons with key staff of agencies delivering services to retarded persons. Often they are involved in drafting and modifying regulations promulgated by agencies to implement new legislation.

ARC's are increasingly joining forces with other organizations to form coalitions and gain potency relative to issues of common interest. These coalitions frequently include professional organizations, such as the AAMD, CEC, the American Orthopsychiatric Association, and many others. Another approach by parent organizations to fostering social change has been to place key members on state and national boards, task forces, and advisory committees. Hence the Developmental Disabilities Services and Facilities Construction Act has furnished a particularly fertile arena for ARC's direct participation in planning and evaluating services for the developmentally disabled at the state and national levels. NARC has been instrumental in establishing major entities designed to serve as national advocacy and monitoring bodies, including the National Center for Law and the Handicapped and the Accreditation Council of Facilities for the Mentally Retarded. ARC representatives serve on these organizations' boards of directors, as do administrators and professionals. As a result of such activity, parents have had increasingly direct input in shaping services for the retarded.

In spite of the obvious gains achieved by parent organizations, services to mentally retarded persons are still often fragmented and of questionable quality. For example, a recent national survey conducted by NARC (1974c) revealed that only 40% of school aged children had access to appropriate public education. Likewise institutional services for the retarded have come under increasing criticism (e.g., Blatt, 1966, 1970, Kugel and Wolfensberger, 1969; Roos, 1976). As a result, parent organizations have grown increasingly militant. Parents have gradually abandoned their traditional stance of begging and pleading for desperately needed services in favor of demanding services predicated on constitutional rights.

Parents have often been joined by professionals in litigation designed to improve services to the retarded. Litigation to date has focused principally on issues related to right to education and right to treatment (Friedman and Beck, 1975). In general, the courts have upheld the contention of ARC's and individual parents that institutionalized retarded persons are entitled to treatment meeting minimally acceptable standards (e.g., New York State Association for Retarded Children v. Carey, 1973; Welsh v. Likins, 1974; Wyatt v. Stickney, 1972) and that all children of school age—regardless of handicap—are entitled to a public education (e.g., Mills v. Board of Education of District of Columbia, 1972; Pennsylvania Association for Retarded Children v. Pennsylvania, 1972).

When confrontations on these legal issues occur between parents and professionals or administrators, they typically result from problems of timing rather than from conflicts in basic goals or philosophy. Administrators usually concede that services are deficient, but they justify delays in improving situations on the basis of budget limitations, inadequacy of physical plants, lack of staff, bureaucratic obstacles and other "realistic" impediments to change. The typical method for placating parents has been the presentation of plans which incorporate comprehensive services based on such currently popular concepts as normalization and developmental programming. However, parents are no longer willing to accept plans and rhetoric as substitutes for action. They have grown impatient waiting for an idyllic future which never comes.

Formal training programs have been developed to assist parents in assuming monitoring and advocacy functions. For example, NARC recently developed a curriculum and set of manuals (NARC, 1972) to train its units in the evaluation of residential services for the retarded. The manuals include objective rating scales and concrete strategies for articulating efforts with administrators and other professionals. NARC has also designed training programs designed to increase consumer groups' effectiveness as change agents. Modular training materials and related workshops were recently developed to increase the expertise of NARC's state units in relating to federal programs and in ensuring maximum effectiveness in using federal funds to benefit retarded persons. A similar approach has been used to assist the association's local units to foster the development of community-based residential services (NARC, 1973a).

A new approach to advocacy by consumer groups is the establishment of citizen advocacy programs (NARC, 1974; Wolfensberger and Zauha, 1973). These formal, professionally directed programs pair a mature, interested citizen of "normal" intelligence (the advocate) with a mentally retarded person (the protege). The resulting one-to-one relationship can focus primarily on meeting the retarded person's emotional needs, his needs for guidance and assistance in dealing with practical issues, or a combination of both. Advocates are systematically screened, oriented and professionally supervised. An advisory committee, usually including persons sophisticated in legal and programmatic areas, is available as a resource to the advocate. NARC has mounted a federally funded national program designed to train its units in establishing and operating citizen advocacy programs, and the enthusiastic involvement of many of its state and local units suggests that citizen advocacy will emerge as a major function of many ARC's.

These recent developments suggest that parent organizations in the United States, primarily under the aegis of NARC, have matured into potent, sophisticated advocates for the retarded and their families. No longer alone and helpless, parents have demonstrated that they can influence the course of social change in behalf of retarded and other handicapped people.

Potential Problems in Parent-Professional Interactions

Although parents of retarded children and professionals have obviously been drawing more closely together in recent years, it would be naive to conclude that their interactions are uniformly productive and free of conflict. The very complexity of the task of teaching a retarded child and the resulting frustrations are likely to generate tensions. Furthermore, potential difficulties between parents and professionals can often stem from destructive stereotypes, from professional mishandling or from unresolved parental emotional problems. In addition to these common sources of difficulty, other factors which usually remain unrecognized may contribute to problems. They can be particularly troublesome when neither parents nor professionals recognize their existence. Probably the most common of these factors are issues related to values, objectives and priorities, temporal orientation, and competitiveness between parents and professionals.

Values

Although programs for retarded persons are invariably predicated on underlying values, they are seldom made explicit by either professionals or parents. Usually, they remain implicit and may be unrecognized, even by the very professionals who are implementing services designed to achieve goals based on these values. To the degree that the values held by parents and professionals are incompatible, conflicts are likely to emerge regarding program objectives and long-range goals.

An important issue, which is seldom addressed, is the question of "whom does the program serve?". The assumption that programs for retarded persons obviously serve retarded persons is by no means always valid. Other possible beneficiaries of programs include the retarded person's family (e.g., reduce the parental frustrations resulting from having a retarded child in the home), the agency operating the program (e.g., justify increased budgets and expanded staffs), the professional in charge of the program (e.g., establish a favorable reputation), and society (e.g., decrease the number of tax burdens). Obviously the needs of these potential beneficiaries are not always identical, and programs which succeed in meeting the needs of some may thwart the needs of others. It is well recognized that even the needs of parents and their children are not always compatible, and the establishment of human rights committees, ombudsmen, and legal guardians attests to the growing concerns that parental needs not usurp the needs of their handicapped children.

Even when the issue of "whom does the program serve?" has been clearly resolved in favor of the mentally retarded client, lack of clarity may still exist regarding the implicit values on which program objectives are predicated. Examples of commonly held implicit values, which may at times be mutually incompatible, include the following:

* Optimizing the retarded person's level of development so that he functions as close to his potential as possible.
* Providing the retarded person with conditions which are as much as possible like conditions experienced by normal persons.
* Achieving the highest possible level of contentment and happiness of the retarded person.
* Establishing the greatest possible degree of economic independence of the retarded person.
* Achieving behavior of the retarded person which is as similar as possible to behavior of normal persons.
* Establishing the greatest possible degree of emotional independence of the retarded person.

Each of the values has been rather widely endorsed in recent years, although when applied to a specific individual they can obviously lead to incompatible program objectives. Consequently, if parents, professionals, and retarded clients themselves hold incompatible values, problems are likely to develop.

Objectives and Priorities

Even when parents and professionals share basic values, important differences may exist regarding specific program objectives and their prioritizing. Whereas professionals may tend to stress abstract and academic objectives, parents are more prone to place high priority on practical objectives which have direct implications for their interactions with their retarded child. When such differences exist, professionals may become frustrated and puzzled by the parents' lack of enthusiasm regarding the achievement of certain program objectives. Parents, on the other hand, may feel that no significant gains are being made, since they detect no progress toward reaching those objectives which they consider to be of high priority. In general, professionals tend to emphasize development of new skills (e.g., number concepts, identification of colors, spatial concepts), whereas parents emphasize elimination of socially undesirable and stigmatizing behaviors (e.g., screaming, talking too loudly, irritability). Hence while a professional may derive a feeling of real achievement because of successfully teaching a child to count to three, the child's parents may feel no progress is being made because the child still yells loudly in social situations, thus effectively ostracizing himself and his parents from normal social interactions.

Temporal Orientation

Educators tend to be future-oriented in their preparation of their pupils. Parents, however, are often threatened by what they fear the future holds in store for them and their retarded children. Hence, long-range goals may hold little attraction for parents and may, on the contrary, be perceived negatively. For example, middle-class parents may reject the ultimate goal of having their child work in a marginal service job, whereas this same goal may seem highly desirable to the child's teacher. Conversely, parents may place much greater emphasis on immediate objectives than do professionals, and they may appear to professionals to be unduly concerned with what appear to be unimportant objectives, relative to long range considerations. Yet to the parent who has to cope on a daily basis with the retarded child's behavior, eliminating present frustrations may seem much more urgent than building toward distant goals whose very desirability they may question.

Competition

Parents and professionals may feel, often unconsciously, competitive toward each other in their efforts to educate retarded children. It may be painful for a parent to admit to himself that a stranger is more successful with his retarded child than he has been himself. As a result, parents may inadvertently downgrade professional successes or may even (without being aware of it) undermine professional efforts. On the other hand, professionals may feel threatened that parents, while untrained and unsophisticated, may succeed where they have failed. Some professionals are prone, therefore, to withhold assistance from parents and/or to hold them responsible for their children's problems and failures.

Recommendations for Productive Parent-Professional Interactions

The following recommendations are designed to foster constructive cooperative relationships between professionals and parents. If implemented, they should minimize many of the potential problems previously described.

* Parents should be considered as fully participating members of the educational team. Other team members should relate to parents as peers and colleagues and should treat their contributions to the team process with respect, even though they might completely disagree with them.
* Professionals should try to accept parents where they are and develop the skill to listen and encourage full disclosure. They should resist the temptation to criticize parental attitudes which conflict with their own beliefs, since doing so would tend to discourage parents from fully expressing their feelings and could reinforce parental feelings of guilt or worthlessness. In order to assist parents in developing constructive attitudes toward their retarded children, it is often helpful to let them verbalize destructive feelings so that they can deal with them and work them through.
* Professionals should share all relevant information with parents as the basis for planning and decision-making. Unless there are compelling reasons to do otherwise, parents should have access to the same information, including test findings and written reports, as other team members.
* Whereas professionals should have the major responsibility for selecting methodology and technology, parents—or, when appropriate, the clients themselves—should have the principal responsibility for selecting goals and objectives. In reaching these decisions, parents should be furnished with as much relevant information as possible, including a description of all available alternatives. In cases where professional members of the team seriously question the soundness of a parental decision on the basis that it is not in the best interests of the retarded client, the matter should be referred to an independent committee charged with review of ethical and legal issues. The establishment, composition, and functions of such committees have been described in detail (AAMD, 1975; May et al, 1975; Wyatt v. Stickney, 1972), and they are now commonly assigned to programs and facilities serving retarded clients.
* Since clear communication is vital to meaningful interaction between parents and professionals, professional jargon should be minimized. Reports should be presented using everyday language rather than specialized technical terminology, and when technical concepts are inescapable (e.g., "I.Q.," "hydrocephalus," "timeout"), their meaning should be clarified in operational terms.
* Parents often need support and encouragement as they struggle to cope with the problems and frustrations of raising a retarded child. Professionals can be extremely helpful by systematically reinforcing parents' efforts and furnishing parents with positive feedback regarding their child's progress. Letting parents know that professionals recognize that parents are facing difficult situations can also prove to be highly supportive.
* Professionals should guard against entering into covert competition with parents. They need to be constantly aware of the possibility of entering into such competitive rivalries and of the temptation to use parents as scapegoats or to undermine parental efforts with their retarded child.

General Principles

Since parents of retarded children differ considerably from each other in almost any dimension, it would be inaccurate to claim that they all concur on some general principles for serving the mentally retarded. Nonetheless, NARC has succeeded in promulgating general policy statements and in advocating implementation of several basic principles through such diverse avenues as legislation, federal regulations, national standards, and court decisions. Although these principles are not necessarily subscribed to by all members of the association, nor by all parents of retarded children, they do reflect values generally held by many such parents (Roos, 1975b).

Developmental Programming

First proposed as an alternative to destructive stereotypes of mental retardation by Wolfensberger (1969), the developmental model of mental retardation was subsequently operationally defined and applied to programmatic and administrative issues (Roos, McCann, and Patterson, 1971; Roos, 1972). It has since been widely adopted as a sound basis for programming for handicapped individuals and it has been incorporated in national standards (e.g., Joint Commission on Accreditation of Hospitals, 1973) and court decisions (e.g., Wyatt v. Stickney, 1972).

The developmental approach to programming is predicated on the assumptions that (a) all human beings are in a constant state of change, (b) they change in predictable, sequential ways, in compliance with specific stages, and (c) environmental variables exert a potent influence on the rate and direction of individual development. All human beings are considered to be malleable and to have potential for growth and development, no matter how seriously handicapped they might be.

Three fundamental criteria were proposed by Roos et al (1971) as the basis for selecting program goals. Programs should increase the complexity of the client's behavior, increase the client's capacity to cope with his environment, and enhance the client's human qualities, as culturally defined.

Normalization

When first enunciated by Nirje (1969), the principle of normalization referred to ". . . making available to the mentally retarded patterns and conditions of everyday life which are as close as possible to the norms and patterns of the mainstream of society" (p. 181). This concept referred to a process rather than to a goal or objective, but subsequently Wolfensberger (1972) expanded the principle to include both process and goal by defining normalization as "utilization of means which are as culturally normative as possible, in order to establish and/or maintain personal behaviors and characteristics which are as culturally normative as possible" (p. 28).

Although it seems safe to assume that normative approaches usually foster normative behavior, this is not necessarily the case. Hence, deviations from normative techniques are warranted to the degree that they prove more successful in reaching developmental goals when applied to specific individuals (Roos et al, 1971).

Individualization

This principle has been defined as "recognizing the uniqueness of each handicapped person and the need to individualize all services to best meet his individual needs" (Roos, in press). Inherent in this concept is emphasis on the potential dangers of regimentation and labeling. Regimentation tends to reduce all individuals to the least common denominator and has been particularly destructive in institutional programs designed to handle large groups as efficiently as possible. Labeling not only oversimplifies complex individual situations, but it also tends to generate self-fulfilling and self-limiting prophecies. General recognition of the importance of individualization is now evident in the emphasis on individual program planning contained in national standards, regulations, and court decisions.

Self-actualization

Borrowing the term from Maslow (1968), Roos (1974) has defined this principle by stating that "each handicapped person should be given the opportunity to determine his own course, to shape his own destiny. This means that each individual should be given maximum opportunities for making choices among acceptable alternatives" (p. 6). Traditionally, handicapped persons have been restricted in the number of desirable alternatives available to them, and hence their freedom has been curtailed. This restriction in freedom has been partly a function of others (often parents or professionals) making decisions for handicapped individuals, but it has also been a function of environmental conditions. The complex environments in which most of us live are designed for nonhandicapped persons and frequently present serious physical and psychological obstacles to handicapped persons. Modification of the environment is therefore crucial in fostering self-actualization, and must include development of new prosthetic environments designed to allow handicapped persons greater control over their surroundings and hence greater freedom of choice (Bensberg, Colwell, Ellis, Roos, and Watson, 1969; Roos, 1974).

Conclusion

There seems to be enough agreement among parent organizations to warrant summarizing what the majority would currently consider as the most desirable approach to the education of mentally retarded persons. The following are some of the major components of this approach:

* All mentally retarded children should be provided appropriate public education.
* Education should begin as early in life as possible and continuing education services should be available throughout life to retarded adults.
* Education should focus on practical skills which will foster developmental goals.
* Normative approaches are to be preferred unless deviations from such approaches prove to be more effective in achieving developmental objectives.
* Parents and, when possible, retarded students themselves, should be fully participating members of the educational team, with primary responsibility for deciding on the priority of program objectives.

* Every pupil should have an individualized program which is periodically reviewed and appropriately modified.
* Each pupil should be given the maximum possible opportunity for making his own decisions and shaping his own future.

Major strides have been made toward achieving adequate public education for all retarded individuals, yet many critical needs are still unmet. Parents have played a key role in progress to date. As they grow in sophistication and assume an increasingly active involvement as social change agents, they will doubtless contribute even more to the future of handicapped persons.

References

American Association on Mental Deficiency. *Position papers of the American Association on Mental Deficiency.* Washington: American Association on Mental Deficiency, 1975.

Bensberg, G., Colwell, C., Ellis, R. N., Roos, P., & Watson, L. S. *Report on symposium on environmental modifications for the profoundly retarded.* Albany, New York: New York State Department of Mental Hygiene, 1969.

Bijou, S. W. *Research in remedial guidance of young retarded children with behavior problems which interfere with academic learning and adjustment.* Washington: Office of Education, Bureau of Research, ED 024-196, GPO, June, 1968.

Blatt, B., & Kaplan, F. *Christmas in purgatory: A photographic essay on mental retardation.* Boston, Mass: Allyn and Bacon, 1966.

Blatt, B. *Exodus from pandemonium.* Boston, Mass: Allyn and Bacon, 1970.

Bloom, B. S. *Stability and change in human characteristics.* New York: John Wiley and Sons, 1964.

Boggs, E. M. New hope for the retarded. *The Rotarian Magazine*, July, 1963.

Brophy, J. E. Mothers as teachers of their own preschool children: The influence of socioeconomic status and task structure on teaching capacity. *Child Development,* 1970, *41,* 79–94.

Dybwad, G. *Community organizations for the mentally retarded.* Columbus, Ohio: National Conference on Social Welfare, 1959.

Felicetti, D. A. *Mental health and mental retardation politics.* New York: Praeger Publishers, 1975.

Ferritor, D. E. Modifying interaction patterns: An experimental training program for parents of autistic children. *Dissertation Abstracts,* 1970, *30,* 3114–3115.

Friedman, P. R., & Beck, R. L. *Mental retardation and the law: A report on status of current court cases.* Washington: President's Committee on Mental Retardation, U. S. Department of Health, Education, and Welfare, 1975.

Gray, S. W. Children from three to ten: The early training project. *DARCEE Papers and Reports* (Vol. 3). Nashville, Tenn.: George Peabody College, 1971.

Gray, S. W., & Klaus, R. A. An experimental preschool program for culturally deprived children. *Child Development,* 1965, *36,* 887–898.

Gray, S. W., & Klaus, R. A. The early training project: The seventh year report. *Child Development,* 1970, *41,* 909–924.

Haywood, H. C. Experimental factors in intellectual development: The concept of dynamic intelligence. In J. Zubin & G. A. Jervis (Eds.), *Psychopathology of mental retardation.* New York: Grune and Stratton, 1967.

Heber, R., Garber, H., Harrington, S., Hoffman, C., & Falender, C. *Rehabilitation of families at risk for mental retardation.* Madison, Wisc: University of Wisconsin, 1972.

Hess, R. D., & Shipman, V. C. Early experience and the socialization of cognitive models in children. *Child Development,* 1965, *36* (4), 869–886.

Hunt, J. McV. *Intelligence and experience.* New York: Ronald Press, 1961.

Joint Commission on Accreditation of Hospitals. *Standards for residential facilities for the mentally retarded.* Chicago: Accreditation Council for Facilities for the Mentally Retarded, 1973.

Katz, A. H. *Parents of the handicapped.* Springfield, Ill.: Thomas, 1961.

Kugel, R. B., & Wolfensberger, W. (Eds.), *Changing patterns in residential services for the mentally retarded.* Washington: The President's Committee on Mental Retardation, 1969.

Luternan, D. M. A parent-oriented nursery program for preschool deaf children. *Volta Review*, 1971, *73,* 106–112.

Maslow, A. *Toward a psychology of being,* (2nd ed.) New York: Van Nostrand Rheinhold, 1968.

May, J. G., Risley, T. R., Twardosz, S., Friedman, P., Bijou, S., & Wexler, D. *Guidelines for the use of behavioral procedures in state programs for retarded persons.* Arlington, Texas: National Association for Retarded Children, 1975.

Mead, M., & Brown, M. *The wagon and the star.* Chicago: Rand McNally, 1966.

Mills v. Board of Education of District of Columbia. 348 F. Supp. 866 (D.C.D.C., 1972).

National Association for Retarded Children. *Policy statement on residential care.* Arlington, Texas: National Association for Retarded Children, 1968.

National Association for Retarded Children. *National conference on residential care*. Arlington, Texas: National Association for Retarded Children, 1969.

National Association for Retard Citizens. *Policy statements on the education of mentally retarded children.* Arlington, Texas: National Association for Retarded Citizens, 1971.

National Association for Retarded Citizens. *Residential programming for mentally retarded persons* (4 vols.). Arlington, Texas: National Association for Retarded Citizens, 1972.

National Association for Retarded Citizens. *The right to choose.* Arlington, Texas: National Association for Retarded Citizens, 1973 (a).

National Association for Retarded Citizens. *Teacher preparation and certification.* Arlington, Texas: National Association for Retarded Citizens, 1973 (b).

National Association for Retarded Citizens. *Avenues to change* (4 vols.). Arlington, Texas: National Association for Retarded Citizens, 1974 (a).

National Association for Retarded Citizens. *Competencies of persons responsible for the classification of mentally retarded individuals.* Arlington, Texas: National Association for Retarded Citizens, 1974 (b).

National Association for Retarded Citizens. Public enrollment practices are surveyed. *NARC Research News,* December 1974 (c), 1–2.

National Association for Retarded Citizens. *Educating the 24-hour retarded child.* Arlington, Texas: National Association for Retarded Citizens, 1975 (a).

National Association for Retarded Citizens. *Proceedings of national conference on housing for the handicapped.* Bethesda, Md.: Health and Education Resources, Inc., 1975 (b).

National Association for Retarded Citizens. *Resolution on biomedical and pharmacological research on mentally retarded persons in residential facilities.* Arlington, Texas: National Association for Retarded Citizens, 1975 (c).

National Association for Retarded Citizens. *Vocational and life skills.* Arlington, Texas: National Association for Retarded Citizens, 1975 (d).

New York State Association for Retarded Children v. Carey, 393 F. Supp. 715 (E.D.N.Y. 1975).

New York State Association for Retarded Children v. Rockefeller, C.A. No. 72-365 (E.D.N.Y. filed 1972).

Nirje, B. The normalization principle and its human management implications. In R. B. Kugel, & W. Wolfensberger (Eds.). *Changing patterns in residential services for the mentally retarded.* Washington, DC: The President's Committee on Mental Retardation, 1969.

Olshansky, S. Parent responses to a mentally defective child. *Mental Retardation,* 1966, *4,* 21–23.

Pennsylvania Association for Retarded Children v. Pennsylvania, 343 F. Supp. 279 (E.D. Pa. 1972).

Roos, P. Psychological counseling with parents of retarded children. *Mental Retardation,* 1963, *1,* 345–350.

Roos, P. Parent organizations. In J. Wortis (Ed.), *Mental retardation: An annual review* (Vol. 3). New York: Grune and Stratton, 1970.

Roos, P. Current issues in the education of mentally retarded persons. In National Association for Retarded Citizens (Eds.), *Conference on the education of mentally retarded persons.* Arlington, Texas: National Association for Retarded Citizens, 1971.

Roos, P. Mentally retarded citizens: Challenge for the 1970's. *Syracuse Law Review,* 1972, *23,* 1059–1074.

Roos, P. *Current trends in mental retardation.* Paper presented at the John Umstead Lecture Series. Raleigh, North Carolina, February, 1974.

Roos, P. Parents and families of the mentally retarded. In J. M. Kauffman, & J. S. Payne (Eds.), *Mental retardation: Introduction and personal perspectives.* New York: Charles E. Merrill Company, 1975 (a).

Roos, P. Remarks. In Bureau of Education for the Handicapped. *Proceedings of the conference on research needs related to education of the severely handicapped.* Princeton, NJ: Bureau of Education for the Handicapped, U.S. Office of Education, 1975 (b).

Roos, P. Trends in residential institutions for the mentally retarded. In University Council for Educational Administration (Eds.). *Trends in Education.* Columbus Ohio: University Council for Educational Administration, 1976.

Roos, P. Consumer involvement—Advocacy and the role of private agencies. In Texas Tech R & D Center (Eds.), *Interagency approaches to working with the mentally retarded.* Lubbock, Texas: Texas Tech R & D Center, in press.

Roos, P., McCann, B., & Patterson, E. G. *A developmental model of mental retardation.* Arlington, Texas: National Association for Retarded Citizens, 1971.

Salzinger, K., Feldman, R. S., & Portnoy, S. Training parents of brain-injured children in the use of operant-conditioning procedures. *Behavior Therapy,* 1970, *1,* 4–32.

Segal, R. M. *Mental retardation and social action: A study of the associations for retarded children as a force for social change.* Springfield, Ill.: Charles C Thomas, 1970.

Smith, D., & Murphy, W. K. A new world for Lori. *Mental Retardation in Illinois,* 1969, *3,* 3–5.

Wahler, R. G. Setting generality: Some specific and general effects of child behavior therapy. *Journal of Applied Behavior Analysis,* 1969, *4,* 239–246.

Welsch v. Likins. 373 F. Supp. 485 (U.S.D.Ct., Minn. 1974).

Wiegerink, R. A. A comparative study of the teaching behaviors of advantaged and disadvantaged mothers. *Dissertation Abstracts,* 1969, *30(A),* 3808–3809.

Wildman, P. R. A parent education program for parents of mentally retarded children. *Mental Retardation,* 1965, *3,* 17–19.

Wolfensberger, W. The origin and nature of our insitutional models. In R. B. Kugel, & W. Wolfensberger (Eds.), *Changing patterns of residential services for the mentally retarded.* Washington: The President's Committee on Mental Retardation, 1969.

Wolfensberger, W. *Normalization.* Toronto: National Institute on Mental Retardation, 1972.

Wolfensberger, W., & Zauha, H. *Citizen advocacy and protective services for the impaired and handicapped.* Toronto: National Institute on Mental Retardation, 1973.

Wyatt v. Stickney, 344 F. Supp. 373 (M.D. Ala. 1972).

PHILIP ROOS, is Executive Director of the National Association for Retarded Citizens. He has extensive experience as an administrator and program specialist in mental retardation, including posts as Associate Commissioner in the New York State Department of Mental Hygiene and as Director of Psychological Services, Texas Department of Mental Health and Mental Retardation. A former Associate Professor at Texas Christian University, he has held clinical appointments with the Baylor University Medical School and the University of Texas.

What are the "Badger Books"?

. . . They are eight yearly publications that describe many of the successful programs the Madison, Wisconsin, public schools have provided for the severely and profoundly handicapped. The programs described in the Badger Books have demonstrated effectiveness in leading to skill acquisition in a variety of areas, and the authors try to communicate in detail exactly *what* skill sequence was used, *why* it was developed, and *how* it was taught. The books are intended to assist teachers in adapting, extending, or replicating these programs. Each volume has different topical areas of focus.

Volume 1. Self-help and prevocational skills

Volume 2. Prevocational and academic skills

Volume 3. General academic skills, particularly language and reading

Volume 4. Math, reading, sex education, social telephone skills, and language

Volume 5. Reading, math, assessment, bus transportation, telephone skills, social skills

Volume 6. Part I — Community programs for secondary students
Part II — Tracking/scanning, communication, integrated uses of therapy services, motor skills
Part III — Primary and intermediate programs

Volumes 1 and 2 are available only through ERIC. Volumes 3 through 5, and the three parts of Volume 6, are available at $8.00 each. (This fee is used solely to offset printing costs and postage.)

Write to: Badger School
501 East Badger Road
Madison, Wisconsin 53713

The Badger Books were produced by Madison Public School personnel involved in Project MAZE (Federal Contract No. OEC-74-7993), under the direction of Dr. Timothy Crowner, and by personnel involved in a preparation program of the University of Wisconsin (Federal Grant No. OEG-0-73-6137), under the direction of Dr. Lou Brown.

IV Services: Rural and Sparsely Populated Areas

The final option for educational placement of the severely handicapped would involve least restrictive programs: preschools, day care, and Head Start programs, or home-based programs for the very young, and regular class placement for those of elementary and secondary school age. Although a monumental challenge, . . . this most normalized placement will be sought in Vermont. In this way, severely handicapped individuals can remain in their communities and live with their parents; attend community schools which do not require extensive transportation systems; and receive the benefits of interaction, instruction, and assistance from their more normal peers. In addition, these peers will have the opportunity to participate in the instruction and assistance of the severely handicapped.

Hugh S. McKenzie, Mildred G. Hill,
Susan P. Sousie, Robert York,
and Ken Baker

Cooperative Special Education Services in Remote and Sparsely Populated Areas

JUDY SMITH
ROBERT PASTERNACK

University of New Mexico

During the past decade, legislative mandates and judicial decrees have brought about an increase in special education services throughout the United States. Many rural communities have thus been asked to consolidate their school systems in order to create an adequate financial base for the provision of appropriate special services to children. Local education agencies, however, frequently have been reluctant to relinquish their locus of control. Desirous of preserving their autonomy, school districts in remote and sparsely populated areas are seeking alternative models for providing special services.

Public Law 94-142 requires the additional task of providing an individualized educational plan for each exceptional child, including the severely and profoundly handicapped. It will be difficult indeed for schools in sparsely populated areas even to come close to meeting this requirement without establishing a cooperative effort among school districts in geographic proximity to one another. Moreover, Public Law 93-380 (the Federal Education Amendment of 1974) requires that, in order to retain eligibility for federal funds for the education of the handicapped, each state must establish procedures to ensure that programs in the least restrictive alternative setting are available to handicapped children (Abeson, 1974). This means that, under Title VI-B, provisions must be made to educate handicapped children alongside children who are not handicapped. It also means that public schools receiving federal funds must begin to develop innovative programs to serve these children.

Severely handicapped children in remote and sparsely populated areas have sometimes received no professional treatment, education, or training. Those who have received such services have generally been institutionalized in order to receive them, often at a considerable distance from their families. In some cases, the severely handicapped in remote locations have been served by itinerant therapists who traveled from metropolitan bases of operation on a weekly or monthly basis. This kind of outreach work includes efforts to train parents to work therapeutically with their children, but the limited capabilities of some parents, coupled with the intermittent nature of the training, often inhibit consistency and continuity in the child's program and impede his progress. In the Southwest, the efforts of itinerant therapists are sometimes further hampered by barriers of language and custom between the therapist and the family.

In a small and remote community, there may be only one handicapped child, whose treatment and education have been handled in one of the ways described above. Ideally, such a child would receive consistent and appropriate services within his community and, legally, this ideal is now required of his public school system. A number of states have developed approaches to this problem. In Vermont, for example, consulting teachers assist and train regular classroom teachers to provide successful learning experiences for exceptional children (Fox, et al., 1975). In California, the Los Angeles Community College District operates an educational telephone network which provides coursework and lends itself to the development of inservice training of teachers in rural areas (Los Angeles Community College District, 1973). Many states, including Georgia (Hulbright, et al., 1974), offer extension courses for teachers in rural areas, and some rural sections of Tennessee (Murfreesboro City Schools, 1973), Colorado (Thornton, 1975), and Virginia (Ford, 1972) are served by mobile units which offer instructional and/or diagnostic services to exceptional children, as well as some inservice training to teachers. The Department of Special Education at the University of New Mexico offers two programs for regular and special education teachers in remote areas: Project Outreach (funded by the Division of Personnel Preparation, Bureau of Education for the Handicapped) provides inservice training on

---

The authors acknowledge the assistance of Dr. Gary Adamson and Dr. James Everett, University of New Mexico, in the preparation of this manuscript.

More information on the proposed cooperative for Lincoln County and surrounding areas of New Mexico may be obtained from the liaison officer of the project, Mr. Sid Miller, Ruidoso Public Schools, Ruidoso, New Mexico.

site, while the second program provides on-campus graduate training during the summer.

Although such approaches are underway in some areas, many remote communities, not only in New Mexico but in other states as well, are being short-changed in the delivery of special education services because they are unable to support adequate special programs to meet the needs existing in their school districts. Furthermore, in such miniscule townships, the power of parents and concerned professionals to improve available services is drastically curtailed by their small numbers. Although there are innovative professionals who want to provide appropriate services, they have difficulty in solving these problems as individuals or as small groups in isolated districts. In addition, many states lack a comprehensive model that can be used for special education programs in sparsely populated regions. Some remote areas in New Mexico have formed consortia, in attempts to provide a greater number of special education personnel, but alliances such as these have focused on itinerant programs. Although the consortium concept represents one answer to the problem of service delivery, total reliance on itinerant services is not adequate and points up the need for a more comprehensive model.

The Sparsely Populated Areas of New Mexico

Like rural areas, sparsely populated and remote areas usually have a population base of no more than 2500. The inhabitants live in very small and widely scattered clusters. In such an environment, the problem of service delivery is more complex than it is in areas that are classified simply as rural. Besides the shortage of qualified personnel, complications are caused by vast expanses of rugged terrain with few or widely separated population centers, limited accessibility by conventional modes of transportation and communication, serious limitations in available educational resources, inadequate funding, and low enrollments.

The 121,666 square mile area of New Mexico is divided into 32 counties and 88 school districts, and the state's population is very unevenly distributed. One school district, Albuquerque, contains approximately 40% of the total school and state population; eleven districts share another 30% of the population; and the remaining 30% is distributed across the 76 other districts. Moreover, New Mexico's population is multicultural.

In November 1975, four New Mexico organizations (Association for Children with Learning Disabilities, Association for Retarded Citizens, Council for Exceptional Children, and the University of New Mexico Student Council for Exceptional Children) petitioned the U.S. District Court to compel the state's public school systems to provide appropriate services for all exceptional children currently in or out of school. Even though this litigation is still pending, during its most recent session the State Legislature voted to nearly double the number of special education programs in the state.

In their concern for establishing such programs, school systems in sparsely populated areas are stymied by low enrollments, inadequate funds, geographic isolation, distance from resources, and often by the social and ethnic uniqueness of their educational groups. There is also the expressed need to continue self-determination at a local level and to offer services that do not require consolidation over broad geographic areas in order to maintain high educational standards. Education seems best if it is community based, and the only way a small district can maintain local control over educational programs that will meet the needs of its specific clients is by offering services that do not mandate consolidation. The purpose of this article is to outline procedures that may be used by small remote communities to devise a cooperative program of special education to meet the needs of their exceptional children.

The Release-Time Consultation Model

The University of New Mexico's Release-Time Model for technical assistance to remote areas places heavy emphasis on working with local school staffs, so that university consultants may become thoroughly informed about the training needs of educators in the field. This process forces people in the local school district to examine and identify the special education needs of children and teachers, while the university staff acquires an intimate understanding of the services they should provide to improve the quality of special education.

Appraising and Mapping the Organization

A group of staff members from the university visits the local education agency in the area targeted for service. This multiplicity of training personnel is necessary to ensure an objective appraisal of the school district's needs. It also offers immediate opportunities for discussion among the training staff regarding these needs and the strategies for meeting them.

The appraisal staff visits each school in the

designated area, meeting with teachers and administrators to identify existing programs and resources, and to discuss the types of training desired. These data-collection visits are coordinated by a liaison agent from the local education agency. To open lines of communication, the university signs a contractual agreement with the liaison agent to develop a partnership which specifies that both local and university personnel will develop a program appropriate to the locality. This agreement also ensures that both groups are accountable for providing the required services.

Once the needs of administrators and teachers have been identified, a modified Delphi process is employed to assign priorities to those needs. In this procedure, all personnel from the areas interested in forming a cooperative attend a workshop at which the identified needs are listed randomly and prominently displayed (on a blackboard or on large sheets of newsprint). Each participant then determines his own rank ordering of priorities. University personnel combine these prioritized needs into training and service components, which are then subjected to an input-process-output discrepancy evaluation, as well as to a time and cost analysis.

The results of this process are furnished to the local school districts in a list of identified training and service needs. Local personnel then select those components which they need immediately and are capable of financing. This procedure guarantees that localities will receive the information they desire, based on their own perceptions of their needs, rather than having someone else's concept imposed upon them.

Release Time

At the same time that training and service components are selected by school personnel, arrangements are made to provide release time for the teachers who will be receiving inservice training. The release-time arrangement provides substitute instructors for all teachers who must be released from teaching duties to receive training. In sparsely populated areas, where substitutes are scarce, the best procedure seems to be the use of graduate students in special education who are certified to teach as substitutes. While the classroom teachers are participating in a series of inservice programs, the same graduate students should substitute for the same teachers to provide consistency for both staff and students. This not only facilitates communication between teacher and substitute, but also provides an excellent educational opportunity to the graduate student. The Release-Time Model promotes involvement of and communication between teachers and administrators, gives the school system an opportunity to observe the skills of prospective teachers, and allows the university staff to give immediate feedback to graduate students about their teaching experiences. This approach also diminishes any fear or hostility which might have impeded joint attempts of universities and public schools to develop solutions to special education problems.

Planning for Integration of the Severely Handicapped

When the foregoing procedures are used in planning programs for severely handicapped individuals, it is essential that all school administrators participate in the workshops. Even more essential is the inclusion of a demonstration classroom component. The majority of public school personnel have had little or no contact with the severely handicapped. Thus, an important first step toward programming for the integration of these children into the public schools is the provision of first-hand experience for teachers and administrators. Ideally, this experience should come through a series of experiential visits to programs in which the severely handicapped are being successfully trained and educated. Experiences with ongoing programs give teachers opportunities to develop beginning competencies for working with the severely/profoundly handicapped, and they give all personnel insights into the possibility that these children can become part of the public school population. When the developing program is located in a remote part of the state, and the demonstration sites are some distance away, visitors are transported to the sites and given continuous interpretation and explanation of the procedures in which they participate during the demonstration.

A Model for the Cooperative Delivery of Services

The New Mexico communities of Ruidoso, Hondo, Capitan, and Cloudcroft (Lincoln County and surrounding areas), aware of the need to develop a more comprehensive approach to the education of their exceptional children, began in 1974 to institute workshops focusing on their existing capacities for serving exceptional children, and the means by which they might cooperate to bring actuality and potentiality into balance. They were aided in these efforts by the New Mexico State Department of Education, Title VI-D (Education of the Handicapped Act), and by consultation from the University of New Mexico's Department of Special Education.

These workshops produced specific recommendations from administrators and teachers in the four communities as to what was needed and wanted in the delivery of special education services. This gathering of ideas was followed by a joint meeting of community administrators and teachers to outline a delivery model. The model for Lincoln County and surrounding areas is essentially an operational and administrative design for a special education cooperative that meets the specific needs of remote and sparsely populated areas.

Functions of a Cooperative

The initial and formative functions of a cooperative must, of necessity, be to develop relationships that will pull together manpower, resources, and professional expertise, and to develop procedures for integrating separate existing programs. When these preliminary functions have been initiated, additional functions will include:

1. Coordination of services between and within school districts, public and private agencies and educational centers, colleges and universities, community and adjacent resources.
2. Sponsorship of inservice training, with emphasis on materials, diagnosis and prescription, parent counseling, and the political processes and issues involved.
3. Development of systematic procedures for educational diagnosis.
4. Establishment of procedures for quality control and continuous evaluation of the total cooperative program.
5. Development of a regional service center for use as a materials depository, as a center for the development and evaluation of programs, and as a focal point for funding.
6. Initiation of public relations and dissemination activities that will involve the communities, inform the state, and contribute to the enhancement of special education programs throughout the field.

Objectives

Although the objectives of a cooperative special education program will vary from one area to another, the following are essential:

1. To inform educators in the area of the cooperative that the term "exceptional children" implies the inclusion of all children at both ends of the spectrum in public education and that a cooperative exists to provide services that will benefit all children and their families.
2. To identify all out-of-school handicapped children in need of special education services in the remote and sparsely populated areas.
3. To comply with the guidelines of Public Law 94-142 in establishing an information tracking system for all exceptional children.
4. To provide a continuum of special education services and the necessary support systems to implement these services in remote and sparsely populated localities.
5. To identify and evalute all existing services for exceptional children and their families in the general area of the cooperative.
6. To coordinate and integrate all existing services for exceptional children and their families in a remote and sparsely populated area.
7. To identify those professionals in close geographic proximity who are capable of providing services to exceptional children and their families.
8. To compile a list of agencies to which children with highly specific needs can be referred.
9. To develop a depository of materials proven useful in the education of exceptional children.
10. To include in the materials depository a compilation of materials developed by the teachers in the targeted area.
11. To identify the areas in which the professionals in the cooperative's schools require training in the provision of services to exceptional children and their families.
12. To provide inservice training for those teachers and other professionals who deal with exceptional children and their families.
13. To provide training to teachers in the assessment of existing educational materials, and instruction in techniques of developing teacher-made materials.
14. To provide consistent and specific training to parents in the techniques useful in the management of their children's behavior.
15. To provide a vehicle for the dissemination of information regarding exceptional children and the services which are available to them in remote and sparsely populated areas.
16. To develop a model demonstration program for the delivery of services.
17. To develop a manual on the procedures for using the services that the cooperative will provide.
18. To develop a general public awareness in the target area about the characteristics and special needs of exceptional children and their families.
19. To provide assistance to any interested person in obtaining information or services for exceptional children.

A time line is evolved for completion of the objectives, which are planned to be accomplished gradually over a period of possibly two years. Included with the time line are criteria for the evaluation of the success of each accomplishment.

Preliminary Activities

Prior to the implementation of a cooperative special education program, it is necessary to:

1. Form an advisory committee of professionals, parents, and community leaders.
2. Employ a coordinator of services.
3. Establish an information system for disseminating plans and proposed innovations to all school personnel of the cooperative.
4. Integrate the separate existing programs.
5. Develop a manpower and resource pool from within the communities and outlying areas.

Employment of a Coordinator of Services. The advisory committee of the cooperative prepares a position description applicable to the coordinator of services and develops the salary scale for the position. Applications for this position are solicited by local, state, and national advertisements, and appropriate interview procedures are arranged. There is also decision making on the locality and facility where the coordinator will initially be housed, and consideration is given to the hiring of clerical personnel. Once a coordinator is engaged, the remainder of the preliminary activities become his responsibility.

Establishment of a Preliminary Information System Among School Districts. The coordinator establishes a system for informing all school personnel (special education, general education, administration, aides and ancillary personnel) on the purposes and functions of the cooperative and a time schedule for implementation. This dissemination activity is carried out through a newsletter, open faculty meetings, small group meetings, and the provision of a central information source. When school personnel have been informed, parents of exceptional children are given information through letters and parent meetings, and information is released to the media that serve the localities.

Integration of Programs and Pooling of Resources. Information on existing services, resources, and personnel is gathered through questionnaire surveys, telephone inquiries, and personal contact with school staffs; agencies, facilities, and professionals in private practice in the area; consultants and staff at colleges and universities in the state; and the Division of Special Education of the State Department of Education. This information-gathering effort is structured to bring the following results:

1. Elimination of unnecessary duplication in the services and functions of the cooperative.
2. Full utilization of the talents and skills of personnel already employed in the school districts.
3. Identification of needs for further training of personnel already employed in the school districts.
4. Mutual awareness of facilities and materials currently available in the school districts.
5. Assessment of needs for new personnel, materials, and facilities.
6. Information on the availability of the services of a communication disorders specialist, physical therapist, and other specialists.
7. Development of a pool of professionals and resources existing in outlying areas which may be utilized by the cooperative.
8. Development of a list of referral sources for children with highly specific special problems.

Continuum of Services

A recommended model of delivery of special education services in a cooperative is the Fail-Save Program (Van Etten & Adamson, 1973), with modifications that make it practical for use in sparsely populated areas. The Fail-Save Program provides a continuum with different levels of service for children, depending on the severity of a child's problems and the intensity of the treatment he needs. It also includes guidelines for placing a child in any level of the continuum, as well as criteria for moving him from one level to another. The model limits the time that a child can spend in any one phase and, consequently, limits the time available for the achievement of a programmed goal. The time limit forces accountability, as a child is given every possible opportunity to show that he can succeed in the mainstream of education. The Fail-Save Program also makes possible the integration of the severely handicapped into public education systems.

This model requires a resource room arrangement, which already existed in some of the Lincoln County schools before this cooperative plan was established. With appropriate inservice training and a materials depository, it should not be difficult for other cooperatives to arrange resource rooms.

Phase 1. A methods and materials consultant-teacher is an integral part of the Fail-Save Program, particularly in its first phase, when the referred child is observed and evaluated by the consultant within the child's regular classroom. The consultant then works with the classroom teacher to develop an educational prescription for the student. Beginning with one specific task, the consultant monitors the child's performance and behavior and assists the teacher in tutoring the child individually. The consultant also works with the teacher to develop plans and strategies to use with the student, and this consultation evolves into a team approach to teaching in which the consultant's role diminishes as the classroom teacher's role grows. At the end of ten weeks, the student is again evaluated to determine whether he can continue without further special help, whether he should repeat Phase 1, or whether he should be moved to the second phase.

In a developing rural cooperative, it is recommended that the coordinator of services initially assume the consultant role, while simultaneously training resource room personnel to assume the dual roles of resource room teacher/methods and materials consultant teacher. Again, the emphasis is on assisting the teacher in devising appropriate instructional strategies for the child within the regular classroom.

Phase 2. This phase calls for a combination of individualized resource room instruction and regular class instruction for the child who needs more intensive services after Phase 1. Phase 2 placement is made for a maximum of 90 school days. During this phase, the classroom teacher continues to work with the consultant to tailor instruction to the child's needs, while the resource room teacher provides individualized instruction geared to his special needs, all the while communicating these interventions to the regular classroom teacher, who proceeds with follow-up activities. Depending upon the student's rate of achievement, two program actions are possible at the end of Phase 2: if achievement increases satisfactorily, the child is returned to Phase 1; if achievement does not meet the stated objectives, the child is moved to Phase 3.

Phase 3. This phase consists of placement in a special class/resource room program for a maximum of nine months. The requirements of this phase pose a problem to many remote school districts as they currently operate, in that not every district has a self-contained classroom. Therefore, two alternatives are offered to solve the problem of providing Phase 3 placement to all children in remote, sparsely populated areas who need it:

1. Establish a self-contained classroom in one community, so that all Phase 3 students in the cooperating districts can be served in that district. In large geographic areas, a second self-contained classroom can be set up, with consideration of the most equidistant points among the cooperating school districts. The composition of students in such self-contained classrooms is heterogeneous in terms of exceptionalities, but such a population could be accommodated in a structure similar to that of the Madison School Plan (Hewett, Taylor, & Artuso, 1970).

This solution requires the transportation of students. A bus or van for this purpose could also be used for transporting parents to the regional service center for training and counseling, for transporting students to specialists, and for various other purposes.

2. Make partial use of a large resource room as a self-contained setting, by placing Phase 3 students in a designated area of the resource room for the full day, with an aide to supervise their programs, under the direction of the resource room teacher. The students who are self-contained in this manner would participate with resource room children in selected activities during specified periods of the day, and would also participate with the general school population in as many appropriate activities as possible.

This alternative would necessitate retraining of teachers to the extent that resource room teachers would also function as teachers of self-contained classrooms, precluding any additional duties as methods and materials consultant-teachers. Additional aides would be necessary, and this need might be met by additional hiring or by the use of parent and community volunteers trained for this purpose by the cooperative.

At the end of Phase 3, if the child's academic performance shows no improvement, a placement decision is made on the basis of his social development. Two outcomes are possible: he can be returned to Phase 2, or he can be referred to Phase 4.

Phase 4. This phase is the entry point for severely/profoundly handicapped children and provides for long-term placement in a special class, with a well developed and tested curriculum, such as the persistent life-problems approach (Bransford, 1969), or a social learning curriculum (Goldstein, 1969), or a sequential curriculum designed for the severely handicapped. Implementation of this phase depends on the alternative selected for the establishment of a self-contained classroom in Phase 3. Special arrangements should be made to introduce vocational education teachers to special education by means of additional training and thereby employ their skills in Phase 4. The ultimate goal of this phase is the maximum adjustment of the severely handicapped to the normal environment of home, school, and community, and the maximum development of their potential for productivity. Toward this end, the proper use of community support and community resources is invaluable.

A child's academic performance determines his progression through the continuum of services available in the Fail-Save Program. The mildly handicapped child progresses downward from Phase 1 to Phase 4, if necessary. This progression occurs because most children begin their academic careers in the regular classroom. However, the severely handicapped student will usually enter the continuum in Phase 4, the self-contained classroom, but with provision for maximum possible integration with non-handicapped students and with the regular activities of the school. Like the other components of the Fail-Save continuum, Phase 4 decisions are reviewed regularly. At the end of 36 weeks, the child is eligible to move to a different phase of the program if he is ready.

Materials Depository

The development of a regional service center makes a cooperative relatively self-sufficient in terms of availability of materials and also provides a central office and training site. The functions of a regional service center include:

1. Materials and descriptor service. Materials are purchased through a matching-money plan, whereby the school districts contribute a certain amount of money which is matched from a grant or from an extra allocation designed to stimulate the purchase of materials. Individual teachers and schools then purchase or borrow materials directly from the center.
2. Training center on the uses of materials. Individual teachers and groups of teachers from general and special education receive consultation from the coordinator of services and others on the uses of materials in prescriptive teaching.
3. Center for motivating teacher-made materials. Sessions on teacher-made materials, as well as other forms of emphasis and reinforcement for these activities, provide stimulation and can lead to conference presentations and written forms of dissemination.
4. A training site for: inservice training of teachers and aides in regular and special education; inservice training for ancillary professionals; parent training; training of high school tutors for exceptional children.
5. A location for public information programs.
6. A central office for coordination of the cooperative, and for the coordination of activities of student teachers.
7. A site for meetings of the cooperative's advisory committee.
8. A central location for a professional library.
9. A depository for records of the cooperative.
10. A central office for personnel of the cooperative.
11. An information clearinghouse, facilitated by the installation of a toll-free number which school personnel in the cooperative's school districts can call to obtain advice or assistance.

Public Relations and Dissemination Activities

The major purposes of disseminating information about the cooperative are: to create an understanding of the importance of providing appropriate educational programs for exceptional children; to evoke changes in attitudes toward the handicapped; to make people aware of the types of services that are available; to offer information to other geographic areas and to the field of special education so that effective programs may be duplicated by others.

The targets of public information are: the public at large, parents, teachers, legislators, church organizations, physicians and health-related professionals, clubs, agencies and advocacy groups, and other professionals in education. Although all of these targets may not be present in a small, remote community, nearly all will probably exist in the group of communities participating in the cooperative. Moreover, even if a small township has no daily newspaper nor radio station, the possibilities for public information remain great, in that information can reach each and every member of the community, often on a personal basis.

The activities to be developed for public relations and dissemination include:

1. Discussions with the teaching and administrative staffs of schools in the cooperative's participating districts to prepare them for the innovations that will take place as a result of the cooperative effort in special education.
2. Publication of an informal newsletter to keep school districts and their personnel informed of the activities, progress, and goals of the cooperative.
3. Presentations by the staff of the cooperative and personnel of the participating school districts to local groups and town meetings, with emphasis on the new programs as a source of community pride.
4. Circulation of handbills on the cooperative to all citizens of smaller communities, and for posting in businesses and stores.
5. Inclusion of special education information in the newsletters of local and state agencies and advocacy organizations concerned with exceptional children.

6. Contact with media serving the geographical area and the state to promote features describing the cooperative to other sparsely populated areas.

7. Development of a brochure or information packet describing the services and functions of a cooperative.

8. Presentations, demonstrations, and workshops at state and national professional conferences.

9. Responses to requests for information.

10. Development of tours of facilities within the cooperative.

11. Production of a slide presentation on the services and facilities of the cooperative.

12. Contributions, by professionals in the cooperative, of articles and information to journals and newsletters.

13. Provision of technical assistance to other communities interested in establishing special education cooperatives, through demonstration models and consultation.

Conclusion

Local education agencies in the sparsely populated areas of Lincoln County and surrounding areas in New Mexico have proposed these procedures for improving their delivery of special education services to meet a need that, because of national legislation and state litigation, is on the verge of becoming critical and whose resolution will shortly become mandatory. Attempts to transpose urban administrative patterns to less populous areas would be futile. We feel that the answer lies in cooperative programs that combine resources of two or more school districts which are unable to support special education programs on an individual basis.

References

Abeson, A. Movement and momentum: Government and the education of handicapped children-II. *Exceptional Children*, October 1974, 109–115.

Bransford, L. *A total assessment program for the mentally retarded*. Albuquerque: University of New Mexico Press, 1969.

Ford, F. G. Project helping hand: Innovative special education service center for a rural area. In *Innovation in Special Education.* U.S. Department of Health, Education, and Welfare Publication No. (OE) 72-30. Washington, DC: U.S. Government Printing Office. 1972, 31–36.

Fox, W. L., Enger, A. N., Paolucci, P. E., Perelman, P. F., McKenzie, H. S., & Garvin, J. S. An introduction to a regular classroom approach to special children. In E. N. Deno (Ed.). *Instructional Alternatives for Exceptional Children*. Reston, Virginia: Council for Exceptional Children, 1975, 22–46.

Goldstein, H. Constructions of a social learning curriculum. *Focus on Exceptional Children*, 1969, *1*(3), 1–7.

Hewett, F., Taylor, F., Artuso, A., & Quay, H. The learning center concept. In R. H. Bradfield (Ed.). *Behavior Modification of Learning Disabilities*. San Rafael, California: Academic Therapy Publications, 1974, 127–137.

Hulbright, R. L. *Teacher training in a rural Georgia community*. Statesboro, Georgia: Georgia Southern College, 1974 (ERIC Document Reproduction Service No. ED 085 057).

Los Angeles Community College District. *A plan for development of an educational telephone network (ETN) to extend access to educational programs*. Los Angeles: Los Angeles Community College, California Division of Educational Planning and Development, 1973 (ERIC Document Reproduction Service No. ED 085 057).

Murfreesboro City Schools. *Classroom on wheels*. Murfreesboro, Tennessee: Murfreesboro City Schools, 1972 (ERIC Document Reproduction Service No. ED 969 341).

Thornton, S. M. A preschool on wheels for isolated tots. *The National Observer*, November 15, 1975, 6.

Van Etten, G., & Adamson, G. The Fail-Save Program: A special education service continuum. In E. N. Deno (Ed.). *Instructional Alternatives for Exceptional Children*. Reston, Virginia: Council for Exceptional Children, 1975, 156–166.

JUDY SMITH is a staff member of the Department of Special Education, University of New Mexico, currently serving as Senior Program Director of *Teacher Education/Special Education*, a national dissemination project for professional preparation programs. In this capacity, she is associated with the Division of Personnel Preparation, Bureau of Education for the Handicapped, U.S. Office of Education, Washington, D.C. Her background includes the development and administration of educational programs for severely disturbed adolescents, as well as a number of positions and consultancies involving public information, public relations, technical writing and editing.

ROBERT PASTERNACK is a doctoral fellow and teaching assistant in the Department of Special Education, University of New Mexico, and has served as a diagnostic consultant to several school districts in Arizona and New Mexico. He also directs Villa Santa Maria, a residential facility for disturbed boys in Albuquerque. Currently, he is involved in an investigation of possible relationships between learning disabilities and juvenile delinquency.

Special Education Training to Facilitate Rural, Community-Based Programs for the Severely Handicapped

HUGH S. McKENZIE
MILDRED G. HILL
SUSAN P. SOUSIE
ROBERT YORK

University of Vermont

KEN BAKER

Vermont State Department of Education

Vermont is a rural, sparsely populated state with over 9,000 square miles of mountains and river valleys, and a population of approximately 450,000. (See Figure 1.) Because 90% of the state's 252 school districts have fewer than 500 school-aged children and youth, it is difficult for each district to make available several kinds of special education classes. In fact, in terms of geography, population, and financial status, many traditional special education delivery systems are financially and demographically unlikely.

State statutes provide for special education for exceptional children from birth to age 21. Thus, the total school population of 176,000 is composed of 40,000 preschool children, 116,000 in the 6-through-18 age range, and 20,000 aged 19 to 21. The Vermont State Department of Education estimates that 19,000 of the school-aged (6 to 21) population, and 1,800 of the preschoolers are candidates for special education. In the entire school-eligible population, there are approximately 1,600 individuals who fit the definition of severely handicapped provided by the Bureau of Education for the Handicapped (*Federal Register*, 1975). Many of these individuals are institutionalized in Brandon Training School (the state's institution for the retarded), Waterbury State Hospital for the Mentally Ill, and various other private and semi-private institutions in the state. Others are maintained in their homes by their families, some with tutors provided by the state. Since 1974, several special classes have been formed for the severely handicapped, two located in the Rutland area in the central part of the state, and two in the Burlington area in the northwestern part of the state.

To help answer the need for service delivery to exceptional children, the University of Vermont in 1968 established a personnel preparation program in special education, in a cooperative effort with the State Department of Education. The purpose of this program has been to furnish consulting teachers to regular classrooms to train the mildly to moderately handicapped in basic academic skills, and to begin to integrate the severely handicapped in the public school setting.

An initial pilot project was undertaken in 1968 to develop a training-based model (Lilly, 1971) wherein a consulting teacher would train and consult with regular classroom teachers, parents, school administrators, volunteers, and paraprofessionals to improve the quality and effectiveness of educational services to be delivered in least restrictive environments, at the early education level, in the home, day care center, or Head Start program; and at the elementary and secondary levels, in regular classrooms. Experienced classroom teachers were trained to become consulting teachers, and, simultaneously, the special education model was being piloted, evaluated, and continuously revised in five school superintendencies in the vicinity of the University of Vermont.

In 1972, the Vermont State Department of Education, with the support of the state legislature and governor, inaugurated a ten-year plan to provide special education to every school-aged individual who required it. One of the major components of this plan was the training and placement of approximately 300 consulting teachers in Vermont school districts to provide least restrictive special education at the preschool, elementary, and secondary

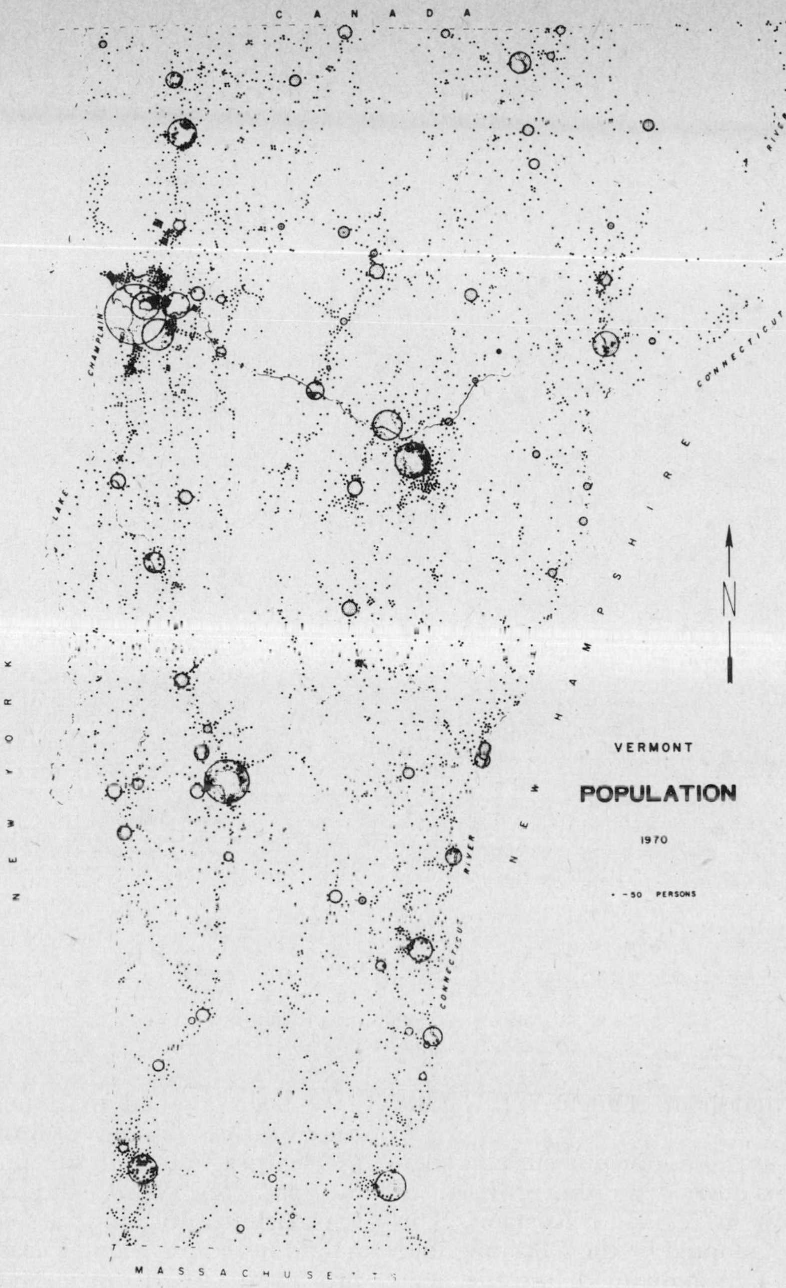

Figure 1. Vermont.

levels. Currently, graduates of the program are employed by 27 of Vermont's superintendencies. (Figure 2 shows the location of consulting teachers within the state of Vermont.)

In the 1974–75 school year, consulting teachers provided special education services to over 1,300 children while those students remained in regular classrooms. This approach defines successful services to students as reliably-measured acceleration in the rates of mastering essential basic academic skills. Moreover, certified consulting teachers employed in Vermont schools receive associate faculty appointments to the Special Education Area of the College of Education and Social Services, University of Vermont, and, in 1974-75, consulting teachers conducted graduate level courses in special education for more than 300 regular classroom teachers. The consulting teacher's goal is to train teachers to accelerate eligible students' rates of learning basic skills (Christie, McKenzie, & Burdett, 1972; Egner & Lates, 1975; Fox, Egner, Paolucci, Perelman, & McKenzie, 1973; McKenzie, 1972; McKenzie,

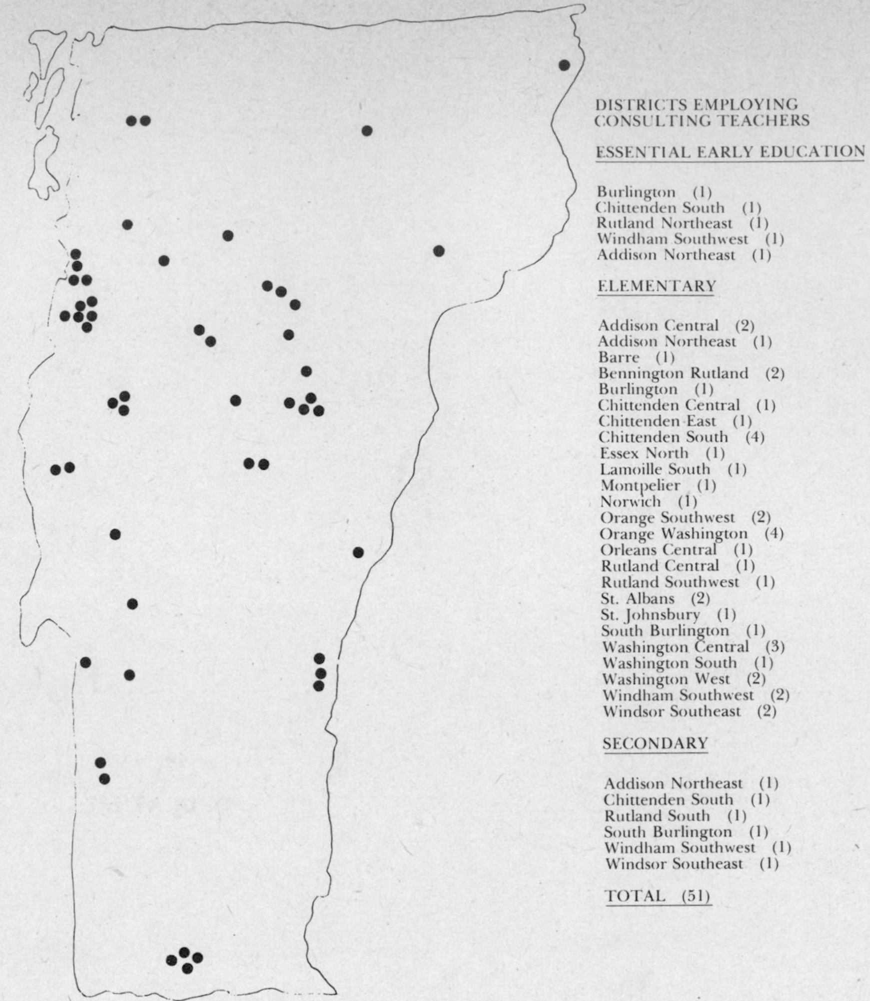

Figure 2. Locations of consulting teachers in Vermont.

Egner, Knight, Perelman, Schneider, & Garvin, 1970).

During program development, an accountability system was devised for the provision of special education in regular classrooms. This system has been adopted by the Vermont State Department of Education to define the eligibility of students for consulting teacher services; to evaluate the effectiveness of these services; and to determine when services should be terminated (Christie & McKenzie, 1974; McKenzie, 1976). Also developed was a system which combines the Discrepancy Evaluation Model (Provus, 1971) with criteria from performance-based teacher education and which led to a specification of the training program modules in a systems analysis format. Data have been collected about the effectiveness of these training modules, and the results have been evaluated through performance-based teacher education criteria. Thus, consistent standards have been applied to evaluate the effectiveness of the training program by examining the learning rates of the pupils served. Over the past few years, the consulting teacher approach to educating the mildly to moderately handicapped in regular classrooms has been proven effective (Christie, McKenzie, & Burdett, 1972; Hanley, 1975; McKenzie, 1976).

A major concern of the Special Education Area and of the Division of Special Educational and Pupil Personnel Services of the State Department has been that special education services to the severely handicapped were non-existent or inadequate in many parts of the state. Thus, in 1973 a decision was made to create the Center for Special Education as part of the University of Vermont's Special Education Area. The major initial responsibility of the Center was the planning and development of appropriate educational programs for severely handicapped children and youth. Toward this end, the staff of the Center began to work with officials at the Brandon Training School. As a result, in January, 1975, six profoundly retarded, multiply-handicapped individuals were transferred from Brandon Training School to the Burlington Convalescent Center, a nursing home close to the Special Education Area offices. Six paraprofessionals were hired and trained by the Center staff to develop educational programs for these severely handicapped individuals. Their efforts were aimed at defining an appropriate educational program for the severely handicapped, and developing, implementing, and evaluating the results of that program. Additionally, in the Spring of 1975, the staff of the Center began to offer coursework and technical assistance to teachers and other individuals involved in the education of the severely handicapped.

These experiences and related studies clearly showed that the development of appropriate, humane, and effective educational programs for the severely handicapped requires a major effort by individuals from many disciplines. Not only special education professionals, but communications specialists, medical professionals, occupational and physical therapists, and engineers are needed to develop educational programs and to train teachers. An interdisciplinary team is also necessary to design a model for service delivery to this population. The Center for Special Education is establishing such an interdisciplinary team to:

1. Develop an interdisciplinary model for educating the severely handicapped;
2. Define the competencies required of the special educator to work successfully in this model and develop training programs which will lead to the achievement of these competencies; and
3. Assist advocacy groups and state agencies in the planning for and implementation of community-based services, including education for the severely handicapped.

The following sections will present the educational model, delivery system, and training programs designed for the education of the severely handicapped population of Vermont.

The Educational Model

The educational model planned for use with individuals with severe handicaps will be adapted and developed from the model used by the consulting teachers who work with mildly to moderately handicapped students (McKenzie, 1972; Fox, Egner, Paolucci, Perelman, McKenzie, & Garvin, 1973). This model, originally termed a *behavioral model of education,* is now more appropriately named a *data-based, individualized model of education*. In the data-based, individualized model, a learner's eligibility for special education is based on the number of critical instructional goals he has achieved relative to the number specified by the school as appropriate to his grade level. This criterion-referenced way of determining eligibility has the advantage of indicating those critical areas and levels of instructional goals toward which special education should be directed. Next in the model, teaching/learning procedures are developed specifically for each learner. These procedures are implemented with frequent, careful measures so that their effectiveness in helping pupils reach instructional goals can be regularly evaluated. The teaching/learning procedures are considered effective if the pupil demonstrates increased rates of achieving appropriate instructional goals. If the student's instructional program does not meet this criterion, the procedures are changed until his learning rates improve. Regular measures also record the achievement of the sequenced instructional goals so that it is clear when one goal or set of goals has been achieved and which set of goals should become the next target.

A fundamental aspect of this educational model is the *minimum objective system,* which is based upon the following assumptions:

1. That there exists a behavioral repertoire consisting of a set of skills, knowledge, and attitudes which is the basic minimum required for a reasonably happy, healthy, and productive life.
2. That there are observable and measurable indicators of this repertoire, and that measures of these indicators demonstrate achievement and approximations to achievement of this repertoire.
3. That this repertoire, through such tools as task analysis, can be ordered into a sequence of skills, knowledge, and attitudes which begin at birth.
4. That all human beings have the potential to achieve this repertoire, given adequate teaching/learning environments, appropriate nutrition and medical services, and necessary prosthetic devices and adaptive environments.
5. That formal education furnishes a significant part of this repertoire, and, in the case of handicapped learners, that special education is responsible for all of this basic repertoire.

The basic minimum repertoire should include skills, attitudes, and knowledge in the following areas:

1. *Communication*: Reading, writing, and speaking, as well as non-verbal forms of communication, such as sign language.
2. *Self-Care*: Feeding, dressing, hygiene, diet, and exercise.
3. *Motor*: Walking, standing, jumping, climbing, sensorimotor coordination, fine motor skills, or skills which through prosthesis are functionally equivalent to the norm.
4. *Social*: Skills, attitudes, and knowledge necessary to develop and maintain interpersonal relationships involved in work, play, and learning.
5. *Counting*: The use of arithmetical operations and concepts.

Other areas of the repertoire fall into such categories as career/vocational, family and home, citizenship, recreational, independent information gathering, independent decision-making, aesthetics, ethical/religious/philosophical, continued personal growth and development, and self-actualization.

From these examples of the basic minimum repertoire, it is possible to conceptualize an ordered set of precisely written instructional objectives which begin at birth and lead to the minimum repertoire required for a happy, healthy, and productive life. These minimum objectives may be distributed across, or paired with, school years so as to indicate a measure of instructional growth. For example, a child comes to school at about age six to attend the first grade. He is presumed to have certain entry level skills which are a part of, or approximations to, the conceptualized minimum repertoire. Under this model, the public schools have 12 years in which to teach the child to fulfill the remaining minimum objectives that make up the basic repertoire. A school could determine that every child should learn at least a certain number of minimum objectives in each of the areas of the basic repertoire for each year. (This is represented graphically in Figure 3.) In Figure 3, the vertical axis shows the minimum objectives which the public school is responsible for developing, arrayed by or paired with years. That is, the minimum number of objectives that must be taught to every child during each year of instruction is displayed on the vertical axis and represents instructional growth. Years of instruction are indicated on the horizontal axis, and a 45° line can be drawn which shows the minimum rate of progress each child should make through the ordered set of instructional objectives. This is called the *minimum rate line.* For convenience, objectives have been paired with years on the vertical axis in such a way that a straight line with a slope of 1 is formed as this minimum rate line. Through the conceptualization depicted in Figure 3, we have a complete accountability system for special education. In our view, an accountability system should specify precise criteria for the following:

1. Who is eligible for special education and, if eligible, what should he be taught first?
2. How may special education services be evaluated?
3. When may a child exit from special services?

Sue, in Figure 3, is clearly not eligible for special education. In fact, her rate of learning the instructional objectives is so rapid that it appears that she will be ready early for enrichment activities, or that she will enter college at a very early age. Sam, on the other hand, is not achieving minimum objectives as rapidly. He is eligible for special education because he is achieving below the minimum rate line. With this determination of eligibility and because minimum objectives are ordered, special education services would be directed toward the next set of minimum objectives appropriate for Sam to learn. The choice of special services for Sam would be based on his rate of achieving minimum objectives after special education intervention. One criterion to evaluate Sam's special education would involve drawing a new minimum rate line for Sam from the point at which he was identified as eligible for special education to the point at which he would achieve the minimum repertoire (Figure 3). Special education services would be evaluated positively insofar as Sam achieved at the rate of this new minimum rate line and, conversely, procedures would be changed insofar as Sam did not achieve at the rate specified by this new line. If drawing a new minimum rate line from a student's current skill level to the essential life repertoire level would set a prohibitively high evaluation criterion (e.g., a minimum rate line with slope exceeding two or more than two years of instructional growth per one year of instruction), a minimum rate line of slope equal to 2 is drawn to evaluate special education. (Both of these criteria are employed by the Vermont consulting teacher approach to special education.) Termination of special education services would be warranted when the learner had reached the appropriate skill level for his age and was continuing to achieve at or above the minimum rate line

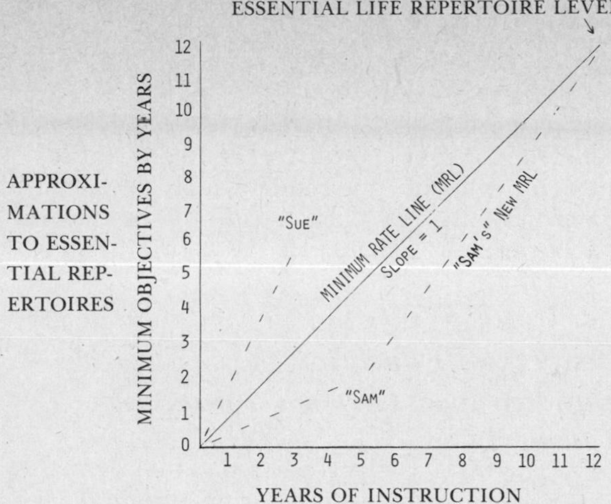

Figure 3. Conceptualization of public school minimum objective system.

with slope equal to one. Follow-up checks would be warranted in most cases.

Although the minimum objective system does provide for accountability of special education services through criteria for eligibility, evaluation of services, and exit from services, it does not determine who is eligible for the very intensive services required by the severely/profoundly handicapped. Thus, we posit a sixth assumption to follow the five assumptions stated earlier:

6. That an individual who falls below the minimum rate line for achievement of the birth-to-two-years span of minimum objectives is eligible for the very intensive education services for the severely handicapped.

In Figure 4, the area of eligibility for severely handicapped services is depicted by the cross-hatched area. Thus, any child who needed to learn the minimum objectives paired with birth through two years on the minimum rate line would qualify for the intensive services for the severely handicapped. The graph of Figure 4 is extended to 21 years of age, since Vermont's special education laws specify birth to 21 years of age as eligibility limits for special education. It should also be noted that identification of individuals eligible for education of the severely handicapped would be possible under this conceptualization before an individual is two years of age. Also included are those individuals who, because of accident or trauma after the age of two, fall below the minimum rate line.

Eligibility and instructional objectives parallel the pairing system used with the years of public school instruction. Again, evaluation of special education services could be recorded by drawing a new minimum rate line from entry point to repertoire level, or by drawing a minimum rate line of slope 2, depending on which is more appropriate. Exit from services for the severely handicapped is determined in the same way as in the consulting teacher approach. Although these may be good starting points for positive evaluation of educational services for the severely handicapped, experience will tell us if these criteria are appropriate.

Work is currently underway at the University of Vermont's Center for Special Education to develop sets of minimum objectives for the range of birth to two years. These objectives will include communication, social, self-care, and motor development and will draw information from several disciplines. These minimum objectives will be field-tested over the next several years and revised until the system is refined, workable, and acceptable to the Vermont State Department of Education as an accountability system for the education of the severely handicapped.

The Center for Special Education is also continuing to conceptualize the essential life repertoire, as well as to conceptualize research, development, and demonstration efforts which may define this repertoire and lead to its analysis in a minimum objective system. The Center staff hopes to increase these efforts in the near future.

Severely Handicapped as Learners

A basic assumption of this educational model is that each individual, no matter how severely handicapped, has the potential to achieve the minimum repertoire, given appropriate medical intervention, prosthetic devices, adaptive en-

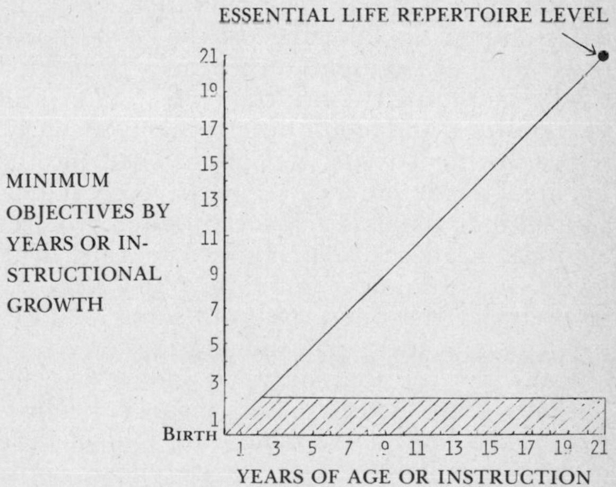

Figure 4. Conceptualization of minimum objective system for the severely handicapped.

vironments, and skilled application of principles of learning. Principles of learning involve respondent behaviors, or those behaviors that are controlled or elicited by preceding stimuli. Principles of controlling respondent behaviors seem to be more critical for effective educational programs for the severely handicapped than they are for the mildly to moderately handicapped. With such deficits as the lack of development of appropriate reflexes, or the persistence of reflexes no longer appropriate to the age, principles of respondent behavior are vital. These principles would be applied by the conditioning of new eliciting stimuli, as well as by using the fact that certain respondent behaviors inhibit or are incompatible with other respondent behaviors.

Additionally, the systematic principles associated with the control of operant behavior would be applied for the benefit of the severely handicapped. Operant behaviors are controlled by stimuli which follow the behaviors, so that the rates of the behaviors may be increased or decreased through these stimuli. Schedules of stimuli that follow behaviors can lead to specified rates of behavior, maintenance over long periods of time, and high resistance to extinction. Behaviors may be task-analyzed into simpler components and systematically built from a child's entry level up to the more complex goal behaviors. Antecedent events and stimuli to operant behaviors act as signals for certain behaviors (e.g., as in spoken words) and such signals can be developed in the severely handicapped to facilitate their achievement of the minimum functional repertoire. (See Bijou and Baer, 1961, and Holland and Skinner, 1961, for fuller treatments of respondent and operant behaviors.)

The medical profession provides other interventions which may be required with the severely handicapped as a part of the educational program. For example, surgery may be needed to alleviate muscle contraction which interferes with postural and motor development. Similarly, seizure control is of vital importance for the maximal development of some severely handicapped individuals. Such control often requires a critical balance to keep both seizures and drug levels at absolute minimums so that the severely handicapped are sufficiently alert to participate in their educational program.

Many severely handicapped individuals apparently have sensory and response deficits which are not correctable through medical intervention nor through the systematic application of principles of learning. In these cases, prosthetic devices and adaptive environments must be developed as supplements to learning and medical interventions so that these individuals may also attain the essential life repertoire in every functional sense, even though the responses the students make to achieve these repertoires may be different from those of students who do not require such devices and environments. (A case study of a severely handicapped learner is presented in the appendix.)

Delivery of Education to the Severely Handicapped Through Consulting Teachers

Although the original consulting teacher approach to special education was aimed at providing services for the mildly to moderately handicapped, this model is now being extended to the severely handicapped. In Vermont, education is currently provided to the severely handicapped primarily in institutions, secondarily in home-based programs, and last in regional programs operated by public schools. As we proceed in developing community-based programs for the severely handicapped in Vermont, with the goal of promoting deinstitutionalization, it is becoming clear that the 1,600 severely handicapped individuals are widely scattered throughout the state. In the circumstances, there are only three options for public school placement. The first involves placement in self-contained classrooms in the public schools. This will provide education to only a small number of the severely handicapped, since only three or four areas of the state have the population density necessary to predict numbers of students required for self-contained, special classrooms.

A second possibility is to place severely handicapped students in classes for the trainable mentally retarded; these classes are based in regional programs throughout the state. Although this arrangement could work, with some extension of the current system, there are two factors which mitigate against it. The first involves the extensive busing required to transport the severely handicapped to and from these programs. Since many of them have motor disabilities, a transportation system would have to be specially developed, would be costly, and would involve many hours of travel. It is also thought that to burden the less handicapped with assisting the development of the severely handicapped is neither equitable nor educationally sound. Why should students who are themselves finding it difficult to become integrated into society be required to take the lead in the integration of the severely handicapped? A more viable approach would be for more normal students to lend their greater skills to achieving this integration.

The final option for educational placement of the severely handicapped would involve least restrictive programs: pre-schools, day care, and Head Start programs, or home-based programs for the very young, and regular class placement for those of elementary and secondary school age. Although a monumental challenge, and one for which no successful models are available, this most normalized placement will be sought in Vermont. In this way, severely handicapped individuals can remain in their communities and live with their parents; attend community schools which do not require extensive transportation systems; and receive the benefits of interaction, instruction, and assistance from their more normal peers. In addition, these peers will have the opportunity to participate in the instruction and assistance of the severely handicapped. Moreover, education professionals and other citizens in the community will have an opportunity to become acquainted with the severely handicapped, to understand and appreciate their special needs and characteristics and, thus, to develop more positive, humane attitudes than are possible when severely handicapped individuals are isolated.

Consulting teachers will receive additional training to enable them, in time, to train others in the management and education of the severely handicapped, and to provide leadership in the integration of these individuals into least restrictive environments. This program, which began in the summer of 1976 for 20 consulting teachers, will include training in the skills and knowledge needed to work with interdisciplinary teams in the development of productive educational programs for the severely handicapped. Consulting teachers will also be trained in the skills required to work with non-educational agencies and departments which serve the severely handicapped (e.g., community mental health services, rehabilitative services, residential services, health services, and so on.)

To support consulting teachers in these endeavors, highly skilled interdisciplinary teams will be needed. Such a team was formed in the spring of 1976 and includes special educators, physicians, communication specialists, occupational and physical therapists, and engineers skilled in developing prosthetic devices and adaptive environments. This team is conversant with the data-based, individualized model of education for severely handicapped individuals. Consulting teachers are trained to work with the members of this team and to provide appropriate data and feedback to them.

This team provides instruction to consulting teachers, regular classroom teachers, and tutors who are involved with the severely handicapped during the 1976–1977 school year. Team members will also give follow-up technical assistance to consulting teachers as they develop, implement, and evaluate education for the severely handicapped through the school year.

Training Programs

Four types of training programs are required in Vermont to implement community-based education services for the severely handicapped.

1. *Consulting teachers*. Consulting teachers will be employed in Vermont to implement training-based, least restrictive educational services for the severely handicapped. This training program will be a post-master's program offered during summers and, on an inservice basis, during the school year.
2. *Special class teachers and tutors*. This would be a master's level program for those having direct responsibility for the education of the severely handicapped, including regular classroom teachers, day care, Head Start, and nursery school teachers, home tutors, and others.
3. *Interdisciplinary professionals*. Professionals from such fields as communication disorders, engineering, occupational and physical therapy, and pediatric neurology will need training in the data-based, individualized model of education, as well as in the attitudes and principles required to implement community-based services for the severely handicapped.
4. *Others*. This category includes group home managers, health workers, rehabilitation workers, and others who will have contact with the severely handicapped in community-based programs. Their understanding and support of the data-based, individualized model of education is important in developing total programs for the severely handicapped.

Only the training program for consulting teachers, as it is now conceived, will be outlined and briefly described here. The training program for the other three categories will include parts of the training program for consulting teachers. Also, it is planned that consulting teachers will ultimately provide most of the training to the other groups, with summer programs and special workshops being offered by the Special Education Area of the University of Vermont.

Consulting teachers will enter the post-master's training program with 60-hour master's degrees and demonstrated competencies in the following: applied behavior analysis; individualizing instruction; school district development of mainstreamed special education programs; consultation and training of regular classroom teachers, parents, administrators, and other professionals and paraprofessionals; research and dissemination skills; and a record of successful implementation of the data-based, individualized model of education for mildly to moderately handicapped learners in least restrictive environments.

It is currently projected that 12 additional training modules will be offered to consulting teachers on a post-master's basis to prepare them for the education of the severely handicapped.

1. *History of services for the severely handicapped.* This will cover early workers (such as Itard), issues of institutional expansion, problems of institutional care, formation of special classes, and modern trends.
2. *Etiology.* Major etiological factors for severe handicaps, as contrasted with normal human development, and correlated medical aspects will be included in this module.
3. *Curriculum for the severely handicapped.* Initially, this will include the motor, communication, self-care, and social areas of development for the birth-to-two-year minimum objective range being covered. Eventually, these curriculum areas will be expanded into academics, occupational skills, and so forth.
4. *Intervention methodologies.* Here, respondent and operant learning will be specifically applied to individuals with severe handicaps. The use of occupational and physical therapy techniques, medical intervention, and the engineering of prosthetic devices and adaptive environments will be covered.
5. *Assessment and evaluation.* The data-based, individualized model of education, with accompanying minimum objective systems, will be applied specifically to individuals with severe handicaps. In addition, the use and misuse of intelligence tests and adaptive behavior scales will be covered, as well as the use of normal developmental guidelines as evaluation and assessment devices.
6. *Multiple handicaps.* Here, sensory deficits and motor disorders will be covered, with analysis of the origin of the disorder and possible treatments.
7. *Adaptive/prosthetic procedures and devices.* This will involve such things as positioning, lifting and carrying, commercially available furniture, and the use and development of such devices and procedures.
8. *Working with others.* This module covers working with parents, teachers, interdisciplinary team members and others, in a coordinated effort to serve the severely handicapped.
9. *Training others.* Consulting teachers will receive instruction in working with and training parents of the severely handicapped, paraprofessionals, special and regular class teachers, interdisciplinary team members, recreation, mental health, transportation, vocational and rehabilitation workers, and group home parents. Consulting teachers will also be trained in the support of school administrators and other personnel who manage and evaluate the education of the severely handicapped child.
10. *Research.* This module deals with the methods and results of research in the area of severe handicaps, as well as the methods and results of single subject research. It includes training in the evaluation, adaptation, and application of research for the severely handicapped, as well as supervised design and implementation of research.
11. *Development of community-based services.* Here, training will emphasize the values and principles of establishing and maintaining community-based services. This will include relationships with the home and support to the home in maintaining the severely handicapped; alternatives to living at home; education, recreation, transportation, work, and family; the role of community mental health agencies; and the role of such state agencies as Mental Health, Health, Social Welfare, Social and Rehabilitative Services, and Education.
12. *Systems management.* Consulting teachers will receive training in the development, implementation, and evaluation of systems designed to provide education for the severely handicapped.

These 12 modules comprise the post-master's training of consulting teachers. These module areas are the near equivalent of 18 to 30 semester-hour credits of coursework beyond the master's level. When trained, consulting teachers will train others to provide humane and effective education for the severely handicapped in least restrictive environments.

Conclusion

Vermont's community-based education plan is indeed ambitious. There are no data to indicate that such an undertaking can be successful, even in a state where the consulting teacher model has been under development for the last eight years, under the direction of public school districts, the State Department of Education, and the University of Vermont. The future, however, will determine whether approximations to the implementation of such a model are being made, and thus give us data to predict ultimate success or failure.

Other questions remain. Will the birth-to-two-year minimum objective system eliminate all but the most profoundly handicapped individuals, or will it also include the less profoundly—though still severely—handicapped? Under what conditions will regular classroom teachers receive severely handicapped individuals in their classrooms? What effective interdisciplinary team model can be developed that allows for cost efficiency and maximum effectiveness in providing education for the severely handicapped? How can all community-based services required for the severely handicapped be coordinated in the most humane and effective way? How can parents be best supported so that they can maintain their severely handicapped children at home for the time their more normal peers live at home? How can such parents' special knowledge of their severely handicapped children be effectively utilized in educational programs? Productive answers to these questions will be enabling goals for achieving community-based, effective education for Vermont's individuals with severe handicaps.

Appendix: Developing Rudimentary Communication Through Eye Contact–A Case Study

This case study is presented to support our opinion that severely handicapped individuals should be viewed as learners, and that they can acquire basic skills if the appropriate educational program is provided.

The importance of communication in human development hardly needs to be documented here. However, for a large number of severely handicapped individuals, no systematic means of communication exists. Often, this is due to severe physical handicaps that impede the development of a consistent response pattern, such as pointing or vocalizing. This case study reports a procedure used to teach a severely, multiply handicapped boy to use his eyes for rudimentary communication.

Student

Greg was born in 1969 with congenital hydrocephalus, spastic quadraplegia, and a seizure disorder. Four weeks after birth, an otrioventricular shunt was implanted to inhibit continuing enlargement of Greg's head. At two months of age, Greg was placed in a foster home, remaining there until the age of three, when he was placed in Brandon Training School.

When Greg was transferred to the Burlington Convalescent Center in January, 1975, he exhibited profound retardation, an extension pattern of his entire body, and a left-facing asymetrical tonic neck reflex. His limbs and trunk could be described as being "stiff as a board." In addition, Greg had severe respiratory problems which required daily postural drainage. At mealtimes, he ate blended, liquidified foods. Since Greg was unable to suck from a bottle, the liquids were administered by dropping several drops into his mouth with a straw. Feeding was excruciatingly slow and intake very slight. On the positive side, Greg had a wonderful smile which was elicited by human contact and music.

Greg was functioning in the birth-to-two-years developmental range for communications, motor, self-care, and social skills. Most functioning levels were at or below six months. Thus, Greg was eligible for intensive special education services for the severely handicapped.

The Center for Special Education began planning an educational program that would utilize Greg's entry skills and cumulatively build on new skills as he acquired them. Like most programs for the severely handicapped, the planning and design required an interdisciplinary effort. We will not describe Greg's overall educational program, but will describe the sequence of the tasks taught in the communication area and will include a detailed description of one program in this curriculum area.

Anne Wallace, Milly Hill, and Robert York developed and implemented the procedures presented in this case study, and special thanks go to Barbara DeMatteo, Physical Therapist, for her help in the planning and design of this educational program.

Objectives

Greg vocalizes only a few sounds. The spasticity of his limbs prevents their effective use as tools of communication. His greatest voluntary control seemed to be the use of his head and eyes, so initial programming focused on further development of these skills. Programs were designed to teach Greg to make eye contact, track by moving his eyes and turning his head, and shift his gaze; at the same time, motor programs were carried out to help him gain some independence from his total body reflex patterns. The terminal objectives for these initial programs follow:

Attending. Given the command, "Greg, look at me," he will look at the teacher so that eye contact is made for 3 seconds on 18 of 20 trials conducted on two consecutive days.

Turning Head to Right. With Greg placed supine on a mat, his head positioned by the teacher so that his right cheek is flush against the mat, Greg will hold his head in this position independently for a 2-minute period.

Eye Tracking. Placed in a prone position on the table with a bolster under the armpits, Greg will track horizontally and vertically for a total of 3 minutes out of a 5-minute block of time, as judged acceptable by the teacher and one independent observer.

Shifting Gaze. In a quiet room, properly supported in his wheelchair so that his head is free to turn to the left and right when two toys are held 18 inches apart and alternately squeaked or "rattled," Greg will shift his gaze from one toy to another within 5 seconds of the sound on 80% of the trials on three out of four consecutive days.

When these objectives were achieved, instruction was begun on the next objective:

Indicating More. Given a position: (a) on teacher's legs; or (b) on the ball (as described under *Procedures*), Greg will make eye contact with the teacher within 5 seconds on nine out of ten trials on three out of four consecutive sessions.

Instructional Procedure

Instruction took place in two separate situations: with Greg on the teacher's legs and with Greg supported prone on a big ball. Since instructional procedures remained the same in both positions, the procedure will be explained only once, using "on the teacher's legs" as the setting.

Greg was placed prone on the teacher's legs, straddling the teacher's ankles, his arms hooked around the teacher's legs. The teacher supported Greg above the elbows and bounced him up and down while singing a rhythmical song. Occasionally, the teacher stopped bouncing and singing, waited 20 seconds or until Greg looked up and made eye contact. If Greg made eye contact with the teacher, she smiled, asked, "You want more?," and immediately started bouncing Greg and singing to him again. After another 10 seconds, the teacher again stopped and repeated the procedure. If 20 seconds elapsed without Greg's making eye contact with the teacher, she prompted him by wiggling her fingers in front of his eyes, having him follow the fingers to his eye level. When eye contact was made, the teacher smiled, said, "You want more?," and repeated the procedure.

Each day Greg was given one 10-trial session on the teacher's legs and one 10-trial session on the ball. (Figure 5 shows the data sheet that was used.)

Scoring was conducted so that if Greg made independent eye contact with the teacher on any of the trials, a circle was drawn around the corresponding number. If Greg did not make independent eye contact and required prompting (wiggling fingers) to make the correct response,

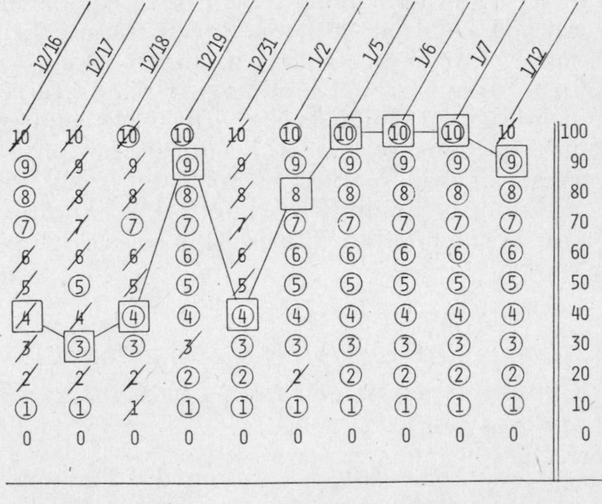

Figure 5. Example of data sheet (Saunders and Koplik, 1975). Circles represent correct responses. Slashes represent incorrect responses. Connected squares represent total number of correct responses per session.

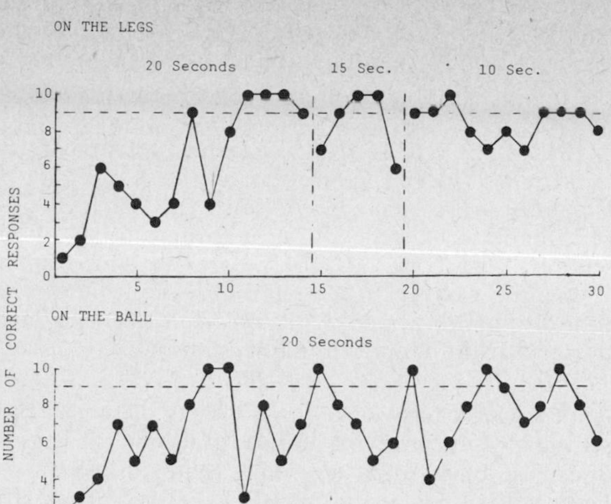

Figure 6. Number of correct reponses per daily session on the legs (upper graph) and on the ball (lower graph).

a line was drawn through the number corresponding to that trial. Criteria for successful completion of the first phase program was nine out of ten correct responses on three out of four days. Initially, eye contact had to be made within 20 seconds of the cessation of bouncing. As instruction progressed, the time criterion was lowered to first 15 and then 10 seconds.

Results

Figure 6 shows the results of this procedure in each of the settings. Greg met the objective under each time criterion on the teacher's legs. He has yet to meet the 20-second criterion on the ball. The program is still in progress.

Discussion

Eventually the exercises of "shifting gaze" will be combined with the skill of signaling, "I want more," so that Greg can show preferences by looking at toys, food, or activities, and then make eye contact with his teacher. Sequenced communication objectives will continue to be devised with specific teaching/learning procedures for each one until Greg achieves a more functional communication system. Also, programs are underway to increase his rate of vocalizations, as well as imitation of sounds, in the hope that eventually he will master vocal communication.

References

Bijou, S. W., & Baer, D. M. *Child development I: A systematic and empirical theory*. Englewood Cliffs, N.J: Prentice Hall, 1961.

Christie, L. S., & McKenzie, H. S.: *Minimum objectives: A measurement system to evaluation of special education in regular classrooms.* Reston, Virginia: CEC Information Center, 1975 (ED 102 786).

Christie, L. S., McKenzie, H. S., & Burdett, C. S. The consulting teacher approach to special education: Inservice training for regular classroom teachers. *Focus on Exceptional Children*, 1972, *4*, 1–10.

Egner, A., & Lates, B. J. The Vermont consulting teacher program: Case presentation. In C. A. Parker (Ed.). *Psychological consultation: Helping teachers meet special needs.* Minneapolis, Leadership Training Institute/Special Education, University of Minnesota, 1975.

Federal Register, 40, 35, Thursday, February 20, 1975, 7412.

Fox, W. L., Egner, A. N., Paolucci, P. E., Perelman, P. F., McKenzie, H. S., & Garvin, J. S. An introduction to a regular classroom approach to special education. In E. N. Deno (Ed.). *Instructional alternatives for exceptional children.* Reston, Virginia: The Council for Exceptional Children, 1973.

Hanley, E. Evaluation of the consulting teacher approach to special education, 1972–1975 Unpublished manuscript, Special Education Area, College of Education and Social Services, University of Vermont, 1976.

Holland, J. G., & Skinner, B. F. *The analysis of behavior.* New York: McGraw-Hill, 1961

Lilly, M. S. A training-based model for special education. *Exceptional Children*, 1971, *37*, 745–749.

McKenzie, H. S. Special education and consulting teachers. In F. Clark, D. Evans, & L. Hammerlynck (Eds.). *Implementing behavioral programs for schools and clinics.* Champaign, Ill: Research Press, 1972.

McKenzie, H. S. Higher education's role in mainstreaming: An example. In J. B. Jordan (Ed.). *Teacher, please don't close the door–the exceptional child in the mainstream.* Reston, Virginia: The Council for Exceptional Children, 1976.

McKenzie, H. S., Egner, A., Knight, M., Perelman, P., Schneider, B., & Garvin, J. Training consulting teachers to assist elementary teachers in the management and education of handicapped children. *Exceptional Children*, 1970, *37*, 137–143.

Provus, M. *Discrepancy evaluation*. Berkeley, Cal: John McCutchan Publishing Company, 1971.

Saunders, R. R., & Koplik, K. A multi-purpose data sheet for recording and graphing in the classroom. *AAES/PH Review*, 1975, *1*, 1–8.

HUGH S. MCKENZIE is Director of the recently formed Center for Special Education at the University of Vermont, where he supervises the development of educational programs for the severely handicapped. Prior to this appointment, he was the first Chairman of the Special Education Area at the University of Vermont, a program that evolved from a pilot project he directed in training consulting teachers.

MILDRED G. HILL is affiliated with the Center for Special Education at the University of Vermont, where she has trained tutors and developed procedures for the education of the severely and profoundly handicapped in a convalescent center setting. Mrs. Hill's previous experience includes work as a technical associate with the Consulting Teacher Program and as a participant in reading and math research projects.

SUSAN P. SOUSIE is a staff member of the Center for Special Education at the University of Vermont where her work includes the development of educational programs for the severely and profoundly handicapped. She had previously been a research assistant and a parent trainer for a home-based special education project for two years.

ROBERT YORK is the Associate Director of the Center for Special Education at the University of Vermont. He has been both a teacher and consultant to special education programs in public schools. Mr. York has also worked at the Central Wisconsin Colony, teaching the severely and profoundly handicapped. He received his graduate training at the University of Wisconsin.

KEN BAKER has worked in a variety of special class settings while studying for a graduate degree in Special Education at Potsdam State and Syracuse Universities. Following a BEH Fellowship at the University of Vermont, he joined the Vermont State Department of Education and Pupil Personnel Services, where he is a consultant for school district consulting teacher programs as well as programs for severely handicapped students.

V Services: Secondary and Adult Populations

Deviant behavior and skill deficits lead to exclusion from society. For example, an employer will not consider hiring an individual who is obviously incompetent and unable to perform the job. Unfortunately, many people in our society assume that severely handicapped persons are necessarily incompetent, and therefore deny them all opportunities to succeed. Conversely, denial of opportunity leads to incompetence and deviance. When individuals are consistently excluded from the environments where socially appropriate behavior and skills are learned, their development will become increasingly retarded. The conditions that still exist in many institutions for the severely handicapped represent an extreme example of this phenomenon.

David J. Pomerantz and David Marholin II

A Review of Secondary-Level Educational Service Delivery Models for Severely Handicapped Students in the Madison Public Schools

NICK CERTO
LOU BROWN
University of Wisconsin–Madison

KEN BELMORE
TIMOTHY CROWNER
Madison Public Schools

". . . twenty years of schoolin' and they put you on the day shift, look out kid, they keep it all hid. . ." B. Dylan, Subterranean Homesick Blues, 1965, BMI.

During the past ten years there has been a dramatic increase in public school educational services for severely handicapped students. Educational service delivery models are being devised, longitudinal curricular sequences are being attempted, and instructional programs focusing upon a wide range of traditional academic and non-academic skills are being developed. Most of these laudable efforts are oriented toward severely handicapped students from infancy through late elementary school age. Unfortunately, relatively little effort of a longitudinal, systematic, and comprehensive nature has been devoted toward creating specialized educational services for secondary-level severely handicapped students. At the present time, there is a dire need for viable secondary educational service delivery and curricular models for severely handicapped late adolescent and young adult students.

Chronological age is only one criterion for determining appropriate delivery models for educational services. Many essential components of service and curriculum models designed for younger severely handicapped students generally are applicable to older ones. In addition, the problems of providing educational services to secondary-age severely handicapped students may be similar to those confronted in regular secondary education. Educational service delivery problems do, however, differ between younger and older severely handicapped students and between severely handicapped and non-handicapped secondary students. Usually, these differences relate primarily to distinctions in the choice of tasks and instructional settings, rather than in differences in the skill clusters that need to be acquired. For example, regardless of age, many severely handicapped students will need to learn to track moving objects or scan stationary arrays. For younger severely handicapped students, visually tracking the movement of a ball within a play situation might be an appropriate task. For secondary-age severely handicapped students needing to acquire age-appropriate leisure skills, it might be more relevant and functional to teach visual tracking skills while following the movement of a ball when learning to operate a pinball machine. The objective of teaching visual tracking skills remains the same, but the task changes for many practical reasons. In regular secondary classrooms, non-handicapped students are taught the equivalence between various amounts of money and purchasable goods and services. Teachers infer that students will use those "in-school skills" in natural settings. Rarely would one expect to see a teacher instructing students from a regular high school on the fine points of grocery shopping at an actual community supermarket. In our opinion, with secondary-age severely handicapped students, teaching or verifying purchasing skills within natural community contexts is mandatory.

This paper provides a cursory review of several secondary education models for severely

This paper was supported in part by Madison Public School Federal Contract No. OEC-0-74-7993 and in part by Grant No. OEG-0-73-6137 to the University of Wisconsin-Madison, from the Department of Health, Education, and Welfare, USOE, Bureau of Education for the Handicapped, Division of Personnel Preparation, Washington, D.C. A revision of this paper will be published in *Education and Training of the Mentally Retarded.*

Appreciation is expressed to Ms. Nancy Dodd, University of Eastern Montana, for her contribution to the final version of this manuscript.

handicapped students that have been used in the past and are currently in operation within the Madison (Wisconsin) Public Schools. Although Madison is a small urban community of approximately 180,000 residents, the possibility exists that the essential issues and information presented will be of benefit to other school systems of different size. Other school systems addressing the issue of secondary education for severely handicapped students may, therefore, find such a review relevant.

For organizational purposes three non-mutually exclusive, secondary service delivery models will be presented along an historical continuum. The first (Phase I) focuses on the earliest model employed, a totally self-contained elementary school model. (By self-contained school, the authors are referring to a school whose sole function is to serve only one of the many possible populations of students. In this case, the population was almost totally severely handicapped.) The second (Phase II) relates to a traditional secondary level departmentalized model and the third (Phase III) is concerned with the components of a current model which can be described as an interactive public school-community model. A fourth model (Phase IV) is just beginning. It is concerned with an interactive public school-community approach that utilizes self-contained classrooms within regular middle and senior high schools. Space does not permit an explanation of the four models in their intricate entirety. Thus, three models will be described in reference to what in retrospect appears to have been their more salient potential advantages and disadvantages from student, parent, teacher, and administrative perspectives. The fourth model will be described only briefly.

It should be emphasized that the authors are not implying that the four models discussed are the only service approaches that exist for severely handicapped secondary students. Moreover, the models presented in Phases III and IV are not final models. They do represent our current efforts. As with our previous service models, their organizational structure yields educational advantages and disadvantages. Over time, concurrent with changes in educational goals, funding, parent input, student progress, and so on, the current service approaches probably will also be improved upon. What is presented, then, is an explanation of the various service models employed, the reasons for using them, and the reasons for changing them.

Phase I. The Single Teacher-Single Class Model

In the fall of 1969, the Madison Public Schools entered into a relationship with the University of Wisconsin in an attempt to develop systematic and comprehensive educational services for severely handicapped students. This relationship was manifested primarily at Sunnyside School, a self-contained, two-story school for severely handicapped students. Sunnyside school was endowed with most of the trappings of educational services for the severely handicapped of the time, including its optimistic name, and a building previously rejected for other uses by the school administration.

A traditional elementary school service delivery model was adopted in that all students were assigned to self-contained classes within this self-contained school. Within each self-contained class, a single teacher was responsible for the total educational programming of the students. The following is a presentation of selected presumed or potential advantages that were expected to accrue from utilizing the self-contained classes within a self-contained school model.

Selected Presumed Advantages of the Phase 1 Model

There were fewer students per teacher per day. Since the students to be served reliably executed few educationally relevant skills, and were considered to acquire new skills at exceedingly low rates, a need for as close an approximation of individualized instruction as possible was considered essential. If teachers dealt with only a few students each day for the entire day, it was argued that teaching time could be more easily adapted to the acquisition rates and styles of each student, i.e., with few (8–10) students per day, it was expected that teachers would have more flexibility in arranging and carrying out instruction than if they were required to relate either to larger groups of students or to larger total numbers of students, which would be the case if instruction were departmentalized as in the general secondary education model.

Working with fewer students was supposed to make it easier for the teacher to spend more time with each student. These one-to-one interactions were thought to increase the effectiveness of individualization by placing teachers in situations in which they could adapt to idiosyncratic acquisition styles. Including fewer students in each class also reflected recognition of the paucity of available information regarding what and how to teach severely handicapped students. Having fewer students would presumably provide the *teacher* with more freedom to create. Teachers were, therefore, to be given an opportunity to determine the "what" and "how" by experimenting on line in the classroom.

Fewer instructional materials per class were needed. Most, if not all, commercially available materials were determined to be of little direct instructional value. These materials assumed prerequisite skills that had not yet been acquired by the severely handicapped students. Due to this large discrepancy between required and existing prerequisite skills, it was also difficult to adapt materials to individual student needs. Thus, teachers not only had to determine what and how to teach, but also had to devise appropriate instructional materials. As a result, catalogs from hardware stores became more commonplace in classrooms than those from educational publishers. With fewer students per day, teachers had at least the opportunity to develop individualized instructional materials.

There were fewer parents per teacher. Most of the skills taught to severely handicapped secondary-age students presumably were targeted for use in the home or other community environments. Therefore, parents needed to be apprised of the skills their children were acquiring and how they might be able to facilitate the performance of those skills in non-school settings. As all teachers are aware, effective interaction with many parents on a continuing basis is a very time-consuming task. For teachers of the severely handicapped, the task is compounded by the time demands associated with instructional material and program development. With fewer parents to relate to, home visits by teachers, classroom visits by parents, and other forms of direct parent-teacher contact were easier to schedule. With more direct contact, the chance for effective two-way communication was improved, and parents were provided with an opportunity to express their concerns and objectives regarding the education of their children. In addition, the concentration of parents in one school and the visibility of that school in the community enhanced the probability of effective parental actions in the political arena.

Students had intimate knowledge of a small group of peers. Working together in small groups was expected to increase the opportunities for socialization and sustained interaction with other students, especially since many students previously had not experienced close interactive contact with peers. It was expected that the exclusive association with a peer group that could be achieved in the self-contained classroom would produce a less threatening environment which was devoid of unequal competition. The arrangement of such an environment was considered a potential facilitator of social development. In addition, it was believed that a self-contained class in a self-contained school was a less punitive atmosphere than placement in a self-contained class within a regular public school where non-handicapped peers and adults might be less accommodating and more critical of the appearance and actions of severely handicapped secondary-age students. Secondary-age severely handicapped students, having outgrown much of their childhood "cuteness," were considered prime targets for ridicule in a regular public school.

These severely handicapped students were, therefore, in somewhat of a "Catch-22" position. If they were placed according to functioning level, they would end up in an elementary school where the parents of non-handicapped students might lobby for their exclusion on the basis of irrational fears that their own children's development might be jeopardized. On the other hand, parents of severely handicapped students might present the same argument against an age-appropriate regular senior high school placement, focusing the same prejudices against the non-handicapped high school students. For at least these reasons, a self-contained school was viewed as an advantageous educational environment.

Students learned to work well with at least one adult. Another presumed advantage associated with a self-contained class was the close interaction that could be achieved with an adult authority figure. Learning to respond to reasonable demands made by authority figures is a crucial community living skill. It was argued that, if the students could learn to respond to at least one authority figure, this skill would generalize to other authority figures in other community settings.

Teachers could work in a variety of curriculum domains. In a self-contained class, one teacher is responsible for providing instruction across all curricular domains in which students need to acquire skills. Thus, each secondary teacher was required to teach at least reading, mathematics, language, self-help and community functioning skills. Therefore, it was presumed that the teacher could pace the emphasis given to separate curricular areas on the basis of the students' educational needs and could also integrate the learning experience across curricular domains.

Administration was simplified. A self-contained school, and to a lesser extent, self-contained classes, present an aura of efficient cost-effectiveness ratios and reductions in physical management problems. Resource persons (e.g., speech, occupational, physical, and psychological therapists) essential to the education of severely handicapped students can be centrally located. The amount of time available for providing direct supportive services would therefore be increased, since travelling from building to building, as in decentralized models, is eliminated. A principal presenting a request for a physical therapist to a school board might be more successful if he could maintain that the majority of the therapist's time would be spent providing direct services to students. Instructional materials and especially major equipment could be shared across a number of classrooms, resulting in less duplication than might be necessary in decentralized models.

From an administrative point of view, it also seemed that the principal could deal with staff problems and needs more effectively because the staff was housed in the same building. A principal who had direct knowledge of the problems and needs of the staff members would have an essential part of the information necessary to ensure appropriate program development and would have a better understanding of the administrative support required to facilitate programmatic changes.

The teacher-training setting was simplified. The Madison Public School system has for many years assumed the responsibility of providing practicum experiences for University of Wisconsin students preparing to be teachers. A self-contained school simplified much of the difficulty often encountered in providing adequate supervisory time for teachers in training, inasmuch as a supervisor had only one site to visit. All university students preparing to work with severely handicapped children at a self-contained school could be observed in one school day. Since the supervisor did not have to travel to different schools, more time could be scheduled for critical feedback regarding classroom performance.

Self-contained classes required that student-teachers learn to teach only one group of severely handicapped students. Additionally, as student-teachers working with severely handicapped students must learn to solve an unusual array of behavior management problems *while* they are teaching other skills, a self-contained school with self-contained classes was believed to present them with a more manageable setting in which to learn.

Homogeneous grouping was feasible. In self-contained classes within self-contained schools, students could be easily grouped for instruction on the basis of the skills they had acquired and how those skills were to be used. A small number of students in each class made it easier for teachers to make such homogenizing determinations. It was assumed that homogeneous groupings would make instruction more efficient by allowing the teacher to individualize programming without eliminating group instructional arrangements. Individualization was supposed to decrease the time necessary to acquire a skill, while group arrangements reduced the personnel costs associated with totally individualized instruction.

Inter-teacher communication was feasible. A self-contained school not only allows for homogeneous student groupings, but it also clusters teachers in a homogeneous fashion. Teachers in self-contained schools are usually trained in special education and possess a common reference base of theories, jargon, and techniques. With such a common base, it was presumed to be easier for teachers to communicate effectively with one another. In addition, placing people together who had similar professional training was expected to create a situation in which teachers would be interested in learning about the successes and failures of each other.

It was also assumed that major benefits would result from increased inter-teacher interactions. First, instruction could be improved by learning how someone else had already solved an instructional problem and time could be saved by capitalizing on someone else's efforts. If the teachers used each other as sounding boards for their ideas, instruction might be improved by feedback regarding the feasibility and completeness of the sequences planned. Second, teachers of similar professional backgrounds who faced similar problems daily might more readily develop relationships that could improve or maintain staff morale by providing built-in empathy, encouragement, and support. When one teacher walked up to another teacher and said, "Maria looked at me today for 10 seconds," the significance would be understood immediately.

Instructional programs were not segmented across time and domain. As self-contained classes required each teacher to teach skills in many curriculum domains, it was assumed that teachers would have first-hand knowledge of each student in each domain. Thus, they would be in a unique position to ensure general curriculum continuity. Teachers, for example, would have the information needed to require verbal responses during reading and math which were either the same as, or one step behind, those acquired in verbal language instruction. Skills that were acquired in math (e.g., one-to-one correspondence, time telling, etc.) could then be incorporated and/or expanded upon in the community work skills curriculum domain.

Flexible programming related to individual needs was feasible. Since students would remain in one class for the majority of the school day, teachers would not have to adhere rigidly to prearranged schedules but could adjust them to individual educational needs. If students were demonstrating a high degree of interest in a particular task, teachers could continue instruction. If major instructional goals were being accomplished, there could be variability in such factors as the time of day in which a skill was taught, the number of occasions a student was given to respond, and the exact materials being used.

Sole responsibility led to increased accountability. Accountability for student achievement, a major consideration in education, is becoming an *especially* salient issue as educational institutions are receiving more and more community scrutiny. Public school administrators have the responsibility of ensuring that students are provided with opportunities for educational growth. Teachers have the responsibility to utilize their skills to maximize the chances that student progress actually occurs. It was assumed that, since student progress in self-contained classes was the responsibility of one teacher, accountability could be assessed. It was also assumed that having sole responsibility for student growth might provide extra motivation to teachers, no matter how small or slow the progress, since with severely handicapped students the number of teaching failures often outnumbers successes.

In the fall of 1969 the Madison Public Schools considered these assumptions about the potential advantages of the self-contained school and self-contained class model. Based on this reasoning, they chose the Phase I model as an initial approach for providing educational services to severely handicapped students within the public schools.

Selected Presumed Disadvantages of the Phase I Model

In the considered judgment of many, the student gains expected to accrue from the self-contained school and class model were not realized. In practice this model had many disadvantages. The following is a presentation of some of the more salient of these disadvantages.

No involvement with nonhandicapped peers was possible. The students in the self-contained school had no exposure to nonhandicapped peers during the school day. As a result they did not have the opportunity to witness and experience normal age-appropriate skills. Teachers, continually confronted with students whose interpersonal, dress, and grooming habits were inconsistent with those of normal students, began to adapt to and tolerate such differences. Typical adolescent concerns regarding clothing, hair style, current slang, and other fads were virtually nonexistent. In short, the environment created by the self-contained school did little to reduce the severely handicapped appearance of the students.

Interactions with adults were constricted. The assumption that, if students learned to function well with one adult, they would concommitantly develop the skills necessary to function with other adults did not seem to hold in practice. In retrospect it seems entirely possible that in many cases the teacher-student interactions fostered in self-contained classes resulted in students performing only in the presence of their teacher. Self-contained classes rarely allow for the systematic performance of skills across a number of persons. Traditionally structured self-contained classes may, therefore, inadvertently teach students to perform in the presence of one adult and not in the presence of others. Research with handicapped students that has varied the number of adults involved in instruction seems to support this hypothesis (Barrett & McCormack, 1973; Certo & Vincent, Note 1; Corte, Wolf, & Locke, 1971; Garcia, 1974; Johnson & Johnson, 1972; Kale, Kaye, Whelan, & Hopkins, 1968; Martin, 1975; Stokes, Baer & Jackson, 1974).

Homogeneous grouping misrepresented the heterogeneity of the post-school world. While self-contained classes do not need to be comprised of students who share similar skills or characteristics, they often are. The logic of homogeneity (Brown, Nietupski, & Hamre-Nietupski, 1976), which forms the basis for the formation of many self-contained schools, generally filters into policy decisions regarding the composition of individual classes.

Homogenized classes provide a relatively consistent environment in which severely handicapped students can function. The community provides a diverse, changing, heterogeneous environment in which individuals are required to function. The self-contained service delivery model may prepare severely handicapped students to become dependent on consistency when, in reality, they need to learn how to adapt to inconsistency. Severely handicapped students need to learn that at times they should respond differently to similar situations; that some people allow interruptions in their conversations, but some people expect you to wait; that some stores stock one brand of milk while other stores stock another; that, in some parts of city, bus stops have signs with printed words, but in other parts international symbols are used.

If severely handicapped students learned readily to generalize from one situation, material, language cue, and person to others, homogeneous groupings would not necessarily impede community functioning. However, severely handicapped students often manifest only rudimentary generalization skills. One of the major goals of education for severely handicapped students is preparation for community living. Therefore, a heterogeneous model which systematically introduces variation in persons, situations, and so on, will probably facilitate this goal.

Experiences in community settings were limited. The quest for a consistent environment, and the unwarranted inference that well developed generalization skills existed, interacted with other factors to produce a situation in which criterion performance in a simulated school setting was accepted in lieu of empirically verified criterion performance in community settings. On the rare occasions when students were taken into town, the skills performed in the simulated school settings were either quantitatively deficient (e.g., they counted money too slowly at a check-out counter in a grocery store) or they were not performed at all. Gradually, it became clear that instruction conducted only in school was inadequate, if the final goal was acceptable community performance.

Teachers' skills became circumscribed. When working only with homogeneous groups of students, the teachers often learn only how to teach students who function within a restricted skill range. In a field where federal and state legislation, executive and judicial rulings, economic insecurity, variable funding patterns and movement of teachers from one school to another are common, a service delivery system that prepares teachers to adapt to diversity is needed. Stated another way, self-contained schools and classes breed self-contained teachers.

Teachers' skills and interests were not equal across curriculum domains. It was unrealistic to expect teachers to be sufficiently knowledgeable or interested in each content area that needed to be taught. It was also unrealistic to expect that each teacher would possess a repertoire of teaching styles diverse enough to motivate and pace all students. Self-contained schools and classrooms do not easily provide the flexibility necessary to link teacher knowledge and interests with subject areas, or student motivational needs with particular teaching styles.

Inter-teacher interactions were minimized. Simply placing teachers of similar training in the same building does not necessarily engender educationally productive communication. In retrospect, having self-contained classes seemed to reduce the need to interact, because no two teachers had responsibility for the *same* students.

Recognizing these disadvantages of self-contained classes and schools, the Madison Public Schools began to evaluate available options. An alternative model appeared to be the use of self-contained classes within a self-contained school by means of a departmentalized model. This option appeared to offer some advantages over the previous model.

Phase II. A Departmentalized Model

Many of the difficulties emanating from self-contained service delivery models can be organized into two main clusters. One cluster of problems relates to issues pertaining to the generalization of skills across adults, peers, situations, language cues, and materials. These generalization problems seem directly related to such issues as the fact that one teacher cannot be all things to all students; that inter-teacher communication is often lacking; and that the model did not adequately prepare prospective teachers to adapt to diversity of student populations. In the fall of 1971, a revised service delivery model was implemented for secondary-level severely handicapped students within the Madison Public Schools. A traditional departmentalized secondary model was chosen. This model involved giving the responsibility for specific curriculum domains to five different teachers. That is, Teacher A would teach reading to *all* severely handicapped secondary students; Teacher B would teach vocational skills to *all* severely handicapped secondary students; and Teachers C, D, and E would teach math, domestic living, and community functioning skills, respectively.

Coinciding with the change in service delivery model was a change in schools. Sunnyside School was officially retired from the public school roster. It was replaced by Badger School. Like Sunnyside, Badger was a self-contained school, but it had a small gym so that indoor recreational programming could be expanded. Initially, Badger School provided more space for approximately the same number of students, and the extra space was to be used to simulate vocational and domestic settings.

The advantages provided by the change to the new school building and the change to the departmental model were considered promising in that the changes seemed to provide a means to eliminate or attenuate at least some of the disadvantages of the self-contained classroom model. The following is a presentation of several of the presumed advantages of the self-contained school-departmentalized model.

Selected Presumed Advantages of the Phase II Model

Students learned to function with a variety of adults and in a variety of places. Perhaps the most distressing problem encountered with the totally self-contained class model was the failure of students to perform skills across persons, situations, etc. The departmentalized model was designed to ensure that students would have the opportunity to perform across persons, since each curriculum domain was taught by a different teacher. Then, too, it was assumed that the ability to perform across settings would be improved because the students were required to perform skills in at least five different instructional settings within the school.

Teachers focused expertise on specific curriculum domains. The departmentalized model provided an opportunity to capitalize upon the teaching skills and interests that had developed during Phase I. Many teachers had indicated definite interests in and had developed effective strategies for teaching skills in a particular curriculum domain. Additionally, as some of the teachers did not have the interest or skills necessary to teach across the various secondary skill areas, the departmental approach seemed to offer a reasonable alternative. That is, it could lead to an improved learning environment for students, and an improved work environment for teachers.

Teachers could develop highly specialized materials. Development of specific expertise in a curriculum domain was expected to facilitate continued improvement in the instructional materials that were being constructed or adapted by a teacher. A shift to a focus upon one curriculum domain allowed a teacher to spend the necessary time creating, refining, and empirically verifying crucially important instructional materials.

Teachers learned to apply skills across a variety of functioning levels. By teaching skills in one curricular area to all the secondary severely handicapped, teachers could not only capitalize upon their interests, but also could expend their knowledge within a curricular domain and absorb and accommodate students who exhibited varying levels of prerequisite skills. The teacher was not solely confined to devising, for example, vocational tasks for students, using only an artificial match-to-sample presentation for acquisition. The teacher also could work with students who could learn the task from a variety of different strategies. This, of course, increases the individualization skills of teachers. A secondary gain anticipated from such varied teacher-student interactions was an appreciation for reasonable longitudinal curriculum sequences. Teachers could also be expected to have a more concrete conceptualization of which auxiliary skills a particular student needed to learn before being exposed to a more complex task. It appeared that suppressed student development due to limited teacher expectations might be avoided or minimized with this model.

In summary, it was anticipated that the general advances that have been realized from departmentalized models for normally functioning students would accrue for severely handicapped students as well.

Selected Presumed Disadvantages of the Phase II Model

It was the considered judgment of almost all who were directly involved that the change from a self-contained class in a self-contained school model to a self-contained school-departmentalized model generally resulted in qualitatively improved educational services. However, in addition to the disadvantages of the self-contained school model of Phase I, there seemed to be disadvantages that were particular to the departmentalized model. The following is a presentation of some of the major disadvantages of that model.

Necessary communication between teachers was often questionable. The simple movement from room to room reduced the amount of time available for direct teaching. Reductions in the amount of total instructional time made it difficult for teachers to introduce the flexibility necessary to address individual student needs. From a broader perspective, teachers did not have or did not take the time to discuss student progress in other curricular domains. As a result there was a lack of continuity in the skills students were acquiring *across* various curricular domains and in some cases a decrease in student progress *within* a domain due to the reduction of individualization.

Distributing instruction across five teachers divided the responsibility for student change. This divided responsibility made it difficult to clearly delineate the accountability of individual teachers. A departmentalized model does not by its structure necessarily lead to such a result, but as the model discussed here was organized, time was not set aside for teachers to meet as a team to decide upon general program goals. For example, Teacher A often complained that Teacher B was not effective and that the skills Teacher B was supposed to produce were not present. Thus, the progress of Teacher A was retarded. In addition, the principal was approached by teachers demanding more teaching time for their curricular domain. Common arguments centered around the issue that some curricular domains were more important than others and, therefore, should be given more instructional time. This controversy between teachers, combined with the lack of communication, impeded student learning.

Necessary communication between parents and teachers was often questionable. In the departmentalized model, each teacher was responsible, in part, for all secondary students. Two outcomes resulted: 1) parents needed to communicate with at least five teachers; 2) with such a large number of parents to contact, teachers had to rely upon indirect methods of communication (e.g., notes). The sustained interactions so vital between home and school suffered.

Student performance across persons and settings within curriculum areas was lacking. One advantage cited in support of the departmentalized model was the opportunity it presented for students to perform skills across a number of people and in a variety of settings. Although students did, in fact, perform skills across a variety of people and settings, one variable that was not accounted for was that the *same skills* were always performed with the *same teacher* and in the *same classroom*. Skills acquired with one teacher were not being performed with other persons and in other settings. Generalization was, therefore, still a problem. If generalization was to be dealt with, a service delivery model which required performance of skills across persons and places *within* and *between* curricular domains was mandatory.

Related to the generalization problems, homogeneous groupings of students, a lack of involvement with nonhandicapped peers, and infrequent interactions within crucial community environments were still prevalent. Students were still not being taught to adapt to the diversity of the post-school world. Since it had been demonstrated that generalization could not be expected or inferred, a model which incorporated heterogeneous interactions as a daily course of events began to surface as a priority which could not be ignored.

Phase III. A Self-Contained School Combined with Community Settings

> The criterion of ultimate functioning refers to the everchanging, expanding, localized, and personalized cluster of factors that each person must possess in order to function as productively and independently as possible in socially, vocationally, and domestically integrated adult community environments. Since severely handicapped citizens will ultimately function in settings which contain less handicapped and nonhandicapped citizens, the majority of the developmental environments to which most severely handicapped citizens are now exposed will have to be changed substantially. Longitudinal segregation, whether manifested in residential institutions or self-contained schools, homes, or classes will not culminate in the realization of the criterion of ultimate functioning. (Brown, Nietupski, & Hamre-Nietupski, 1976 p. 8).

In reference to the realization of this criterion Brown, Nietupski, and Hamre-Nietupski further state:

> . . . (eventually) severely handicapped citizens will attend church, shop, wait in the offices of physicians, ride public buses, wash dishes, attend movies, use restrooms, cross streets, and cheer at football games with less handicapped and nonhandicapped citizens.(1976, p. 8)

It should be readily apparent when the general skill levels of most severely handicapped adults are considered, that significant training efforts will be required if younger severely handicapped students are to learn to perform in accordance with their capacity. As new training efforts are designed, there is no doubt that traditional public school service models will need to be changed. For example, the concept of a school must be expanded to include regular involvement in community environments. For far too long the programs that have been designed and implemented for severely handicapped students have inadvertantly ensured that such students would not learn to function as independently as possible in integrated adult public communities.

The current secondary-age educational service delivery model for severely handicapped students in the Madison Public Schools represents a significant departure from the models described in Phases I and II. This departure reflects a commitment to produce graduates with more independent community functioning skills than those who have graduated in the past. The earlier service delivery models did not include consistent instruction in community settings and were not designed so that criterion performance on tasks taught in a school building could be empirically verified in community settings. Model III is designed to provide systematic instruction that would clearly demonstrate the existence of the required skills *prior to graduation*. Students who had graduated would, therefore, possess the necessary skills to function in heterogeneous adult communities.

The educational service delivery model presently operating in the Madison Public Schools includes systematic attempts to combine teaching severely handicapped students in public school classrooms with teaching them in local community settings. In addition, if skills are taught in simulation in school, attempts are made to verify criterion performance empirically in actual community settings.

Selected Potential Advantages of the Phase III Model

Students are taught to perform skills within and between curricular domains, and across persons, places, materials, and language cues. A school-community instructional model reduces the probability that severely handicapped students will become "stimulus bound" to the circumscribed consistent characteristics of self-contained classrooms or schools. Such a model allows the teaching of a set of skills in one setting by one person using a particular set of materials and language cues, and then verification that these same skills are performed in community settings in reaction to different adults and to more natural materials and language cues. For example, in a school-community model a severely handicapped student can be taught a set of vocational skills by a classroom teacher, a vocational teacher, and ultimately by an actual work supervisor, yet all three trainers would probably use different language cues and the settings would differ. In addition, within a school-community model a student may be required to perform skills in a school at a simulated work station, and ultimately at an actual job site. In effect, a school-community model forces the student to learn appropriate reactions to continuous environmental changes.

The development of functional post-school skills is enhanced. In the past, post-school environments available to severely handicapped adults in Madison have been relatively limited in that graduates have had few residence and employment options. Graduates could reside at home, in a limited number of group homes, or in an institution. Vocational options were almost exclusively of the sheltered variety: an ARC day-care program and a non-profit sheltered workshop.

More recently, however, there has been a concerted effort on the part of parents and professionals to improve and expand the post-school environments available to severely handicapped citizens. Residential opportunities still include living in natural homes and in institutions. These options are, however, exercised by fewer and fewer persons. Graduates now also live in group homes and semi-sheltered apartments that involve only minimal supervision. Post-school vocational options also have been expanded to range from placement in highly supervised sheltered workshops to competitive work.

One of the primary reasons for developing a school-community service delivery model is to attempt to produce a closer alignment between the training a student receives in school and the skills needed to function as independently as possible in adulthood. Thus, home living skills are now taught at school, but also at home and in group homes. Vocational skills are taught at school, in simulated job settings and at actual job sites. The goal is to teach individual severely handicapped students post-school skills that reflect places and situations where the students are *currently* functioning *and* those places where the students may *ultimately* function.

The gap between school and community is reduced. When students started to receive systematic instruction in natural community settings, the dichotomy between school and community seemed to become more nebulous. Consistently teaching skills in natural settings has had a pronounced effect upon the content covered in various school programs. For example, teachers are no longer satisfied with simply teaching students to count coins. Instead, they are imbedding coin counting within a purchasing format (Certo & Swetlik, 1976). In the past, teachers were content to teach students to prepare meals at school. Meal preparation is now taught in group homes and natural homes as well. In addition, the scope of meal preparation has been expanded to include purchasing necessary items at a supermarket (Nietupski, Certo, Pumpian, & Belmore, 1976). Motor skills, math skills, purchasing skills, transportation skills, and social skills are no longer viewed as separate entities. A beginning has also been made toward viewing the broad spectrum of community leisure facilities as ideal vehicles for providing extra training for the development of academic, pre-academic, and functional academic, pre-academic, and functional academic skills.

Closing the gap between school and community creates the potential to increase the time available for developing skills needed to function effectively in the community without sacrificing academic skill development, because the academic skills that are taught will by necessity more closely coincide with those needed in community environments. There are many ways, some attempted, some planned, and some inevitable, to reduce the gap between school and community that are a natural outgrowth of a school-community service delivery model.

Exposure to non-handicapped peers and adults in the community is increased. At this writing, some students are based in a self-contained school, not even directly connected to a public bus line. Thus, it is difficult to provide consistent exposure to and interaction with non-handicapped peers and adults. Unfortunately, the fears and concerns of many parents further reduce the number and kind of interactions with non-handicapped individuals. However, many severely handicapped students are able to interact with non-handicapped peers. Almost all secondary age students have been exposed to and have interacted with normal peers and adults on public buses and in public libraries and restaurants. Admittedly, too few sustained interactions have occurred, but severely handicapped students did request food, learned to avoid pushing and shoving in line, learned to function quietly because other people were reading and learned to sit down in an empty seat on a public bus. These interactions produced many positive social gains in the absence of systematic direct training. The student's choosing more age and style appropriate clothing for scheduled travel about town, or the student's occasionally combing his hair after removing a hat upon entering a public building are but a few examples. In addition, many students successfully sustained interactions with store clerks, librarians, waitresses, and other service-providing persons. Finally, at least 15 secondary-age, severely handicapped students successfully maintained relatively complex interactions with non-handicapped peers who were fellow employees and with Citizen Advocates (persons who volunteer to spend after-school hours with handicapped citizens under supervision of the local ARC).

Parents become more directly involved in school programs. Since the school-community service delivery model was a novel approach locally and one that involved a certain amount of risk on the part of both students and teachers, most parents requested information pertaining to the nature of community activities and the degree to which their sons and daughters would be exposed to potentially hazardous, embarrassing, or punishing situations. When initial parent meetings were held, many parents thought that the new community-oriented program simply meant more field trips. However, as some students began to learn to work in competitive job settings, make purchases at real grocery stores and perform other newly acquired skills at home, parents became better informed about the goals and potential benefits of the model. As the school year progressed, the content of parental questions began to focus upon gaining information about exactly what their son/daughter had learned and was learning, and toward requesting extensions of the skills that were being taught. A shift into community instruction generated a situation in which both parents and teachers found increased communication both necessary and natural.

Students may adapt to negative affect, rejection, and ridicule. If severely handicapped students are to venture into heterogeneous adult community environments daily, it can be expected that they will eventually experience forms of negative affect, rejection, and ridicule. Unfortunately, there are members of our society who feel the need to fear, physically harm, ignore, ridicule, harass, and attempt to confuse our students. There is no doubt that severely handicapped students will find it necessary to cope with other peoples' prejudices when away from the protective scrutiny of parents, teachers, and schools. The position offered here is that it is beneficial to allow such situations to occur, but under circumstances where a teacher can intervene for reasons of protection *and* training. One strategy that seems to have merit is, for example, when teaching public bus skills, to arrange for an adult volunteer, whom the severely handicapped students have never met, to ride the buses *without* the student's knowledge. In this way, many difficulties can be dealt with as they happen, providing a means to teach students how to adapt to real problem situations.

Students are expected to perform as non-handicapped citizens. One way to deal effectively with the problems of ridicule, harassment, or indifference might be to minimize individual characteristics which secure unnecessary attention. For example, in the domain of self-help skills, students should be taught not only how to dress, but to wear age and style appropriate clothing. Although a more age-appropriate appearance will probably help, other crucial skills must be developed before general community acceptance is realized. In the past, when students rode public buses or shopped at grocery stores, inconsistencies in bus stop signs or arbitrary separations of similar food items on shelves proved frustrating. Teachers often voiced implicit expectations that society should be reorganized to accommodate to the needs of severely handicapped individuals. Such expectations may provide a pleasant cathartic experience, but will do little in the way of increasing community acceptance of severely handicapped adults. As professionals, we can no longer be satisfied with skill acquisition, if the skill is performed in an unreasonably slow, impolite, inconsistent, and adult-dependent manner. Such performance will only maintain the social barriers which already make the community inaccessible for many severely handicapped citizens. Only when performance begins to approximate that of non-handicapped individuals can we expect to see needed changes in community acceptance.

Community and professional expectancy stereotypes are attenuated. Stereotypic expectations can not only result in harassment, but can also place limitations upon the kinds of interactions severely handicapped students might have in the community. For example, when bus riding skills were initially taught, actual bus riding was delayed by two months of classroom instruction. One major reason was skepticism about the ability of the students to adapt to the demands of public bus riding. When the students finally started to ride public buses, they were taught always to get on or off the bus at a particular bus stop to minimize the chance that they would get lost. Of course, the inevitable happened one afternoon: a bus arrived without a student. The student left the bus at a different bus stop by accident, but easily found his way to the pre-arranged destination. By bringing the severely handicapped students into the community, actions that were believed beyond their skill repertoires continually surfaced.

Changes in expectations have occurred in persons after regular interaction with severely handicapped students. Three employers, each of whom reluctantly rewarded perseverative phone calls with competitive employment for one student are now ready to employ more students than are currently available. One supermarket manager who initially allowed his store to be used as a training site, simply because the school maintained an active charge account, now offers suggestions on how to teach severely handicapped students to use the facility efficiently. The shift to a school-community model has not only surfaced unexpected skills, but has also shown that the presence of severely handicapped individuals in a store, on a bus, or on a job does not necessarily equal bizarre disruptive actions.

Longitudinal program goals are made salient. The shift to a school-community model has fortunately surfaced student skills of which teachers are unaware, and has made salient several important shortcomings of exclusive classroom instruction. These shortcomings are generally expressed in two ways. First, when a community functioning skill, such as reading a restaurant menu and ordering food, is taught *solely* in the classroom, the skill rarely, if ever, transfers to natural settings. A longitudinal program objective for restaurant skills could only be met when a student visited an actual restaurant and, without a teacher present, read the menu and ordered food appropriately.

Second, there are ancillary skills related to every isolated skill that is taught in a school that are crucial to effective functioning in a natural setting. When severely handicapped students were placed in remumerative jobs, it was determined that simulated job training had not included many necessary, though supplemental, skills. Although students had been taught to tell time, they had not been taught to keep appointments. Therefore, before it could be expected that these students would arrive on time for work, additional training was necessary. Many students involved in vocational preparation had been taught to respond to diverse language cues during a number of years of language instruction. However, they had not been taught to respond to commands that were frequently issued by their actual job supervisors (e.g., "We need a picker."). In short, the content of the school-based language training had not included idiomatic and/or idiosyncratic language content common in actual vocational settings. Obviously, excursions into the community have initiated a realignment of classroom goals and curriculum content.

Students learn to perform without teachers as supervisors. In service delivery models where most instruction occurs in schools, teachers, student teachers, and aides serve as primary supervisors. When teaching personnel serve as primary supervisors on a regular basis, severely handicapped students often become dependent upon them to provide cues that indicate when and how to perform a skill. Until supervision is *eliminated* and skills are performed in natural settings in reaction to naturally occurring context cues, it cannot be assumed that a skill has acquired functional significance. Many community related skills such as cooking, shopping, riding buses, and janitorial job responsibilities serve as clear reminders to the teaching staff that self-initiated student performance of crucial skills is mandatory.

Student development is a function of teachers and non-teachers. When severely handicapped students receive a significant amount of their instruction outside the classroom, they will inevitably interact with non-teaching persons. Unfortunately, these non-teaching persons have often had little, if any, previous dealings with severely handicapped students. In effect, severely handicapped students must perform skills for community persons who often consequate actions in a manner different from that of teachers. These community persons often do not use consistent cues, and are not particularly informed of the rights and unique needs of severely handicapped citizens.

While the vocational training component of the school-community model involves extensive use of on-the-job instruction, the ultimate supervisors of a severely handicapped worker will almost always be non-teaching persons whose foremost concerns revolve around the operation of a profitable business. Fortunately, work supervisors primarily concerned with the production skills manifested by severely handicapped employees often become facilitators of student growth.

A more demanding test of teacher accountability emerges. The criterion of longitudinal program success for severely handicapped students includes the empirical verification of functional skill performance in natural settings, without teachers present. These parameters of skill verification are certainly more demanding for teachers than the more limited verification possible in schools. For example, when a vocational teacher removes himself completely from instructing a severely handicapped worker on an actual job, his ability to teach work skills is evaluated by the level of success or failure demonstrated by the student. In addition, when a teacher suggests to severely handicapped students and to their parents that the students can and should perform, in many ways, as non-handicapped persons, the responsibility to provide the skills necessary for success is placed upon the teacher.

Staff and student morale improves. It is the judgment of almost all persons involved in the school-community model that, when students become aware that they will have opportunities to perform school-learned tasks in real life situations, excitement, morale, and interest increase dramatically. In addition, the reaction of teachers to the school-community model has been enthusiastic, to say the least. When the model was initially implemented, teachers had a number of well-founded reservations and several of these reservations are presented below as potential disadvantages. However, after several basic problems were resolved, teacher reservations were replaced with cautious optimism. At this point, there is not one teacher who would return to the departmentalized model. Indeed, the teachers are actively planning more and more community involvement for the future.

Selected Potential Disadvantages of the Phase III Model.

Despite the overriding advantages of the school-community service delivery model for secondary level severely handicapped students, it would be unrealistic to project the model without delineating several of the more pronounced disadvantages. Thus, in the following section some of these disadvantages will be presented.

Before the school-community service delivery model was put into operation, teachers and parents raised a number of reasonable reservations. Some of these reservations were:

1. Since systematic community instruction is a relatively new concept locally, why should severely handicapped students be used as experimental subjects to determine the validity of such programming?
2. What sort of community programming would be most effective with lower functioning students of secondary age? Would these students have to wait until they had a number of prerequisite skills *before* they

could be involved in community programming?

3. How will scheduling be arranged and who will be ultimately responsible for the students when they are out of the building?
4. Will administrative support for the program be there when it is needed?
5. How many students can be served realistically in an effective school-community program?
6. Will there be enough community support and tolerance when the students are taken into community settings?
7. What about student transportation?

In the remainder of this section issues related to the above questions will be presented.

The minimum wage law presents problems. A crucial component of the school-community service delivery model relates to vocational training. The goal of vocational training is actual employment in the most competitive jobs possible. If severely handicapped students are to leave school with marketable vocational skills, it is crucial that training be conducted in real work settings. In order to receive permission to use actual work settings for training purposes, it was often necessary to convince employers that the training would supplement rather than interfere with actual production. However, according to at least one interpretation of recent labor laws, anyone who performs a service or produces a product which is ultimately marketed must be compensated. As a result, it was necessary to arrange and tolerate simulations of complex job skills that required relatively long training periods. In an attempt to avoid many of the pitfalls of the past, work sites within the Madison Public School System were chosen, e.g., industrial equipment at a high school cafeteria was used to teach dishwashing skills. Considering that the educational statutes of Wisconsin clearly refer to education for handicapped students in terms of individual needs, and that the vocational settings were sanctioned by school administrators and within public school facilities, state labor officials were satisfied that the vocational training was educational and did not require compensation. When employment opportunities that allowed for payment arose during the school year, students performed the work for payment at actual worksites, rather than in school facilities.

Liability insurance presents problems. Whenever a teacher, an aide, or a student teacher instructs one or more students, liability insurance is required. However, liability insurance coverage does not always include instruction outside school facilities. Students and teachers involved in community training could be covered by liability insurance *only* when the students were in the charge of certified teachers. Thus, aides, student teachers, psychologists, etc., could not instruct students at community settings *unless* a certified teacher was present. In many ways, these insurance-related problems limited the scope of community training. For example, it could not be verified that a severely handicapped student could use a public grocery store unless a certified teacher looked on from a distance.

Traditional public school models must be revised. The school-community model defies the scheduling simplicity of self-contained and departmentalized service models. There are three factors which generate enormous scheduling difficulties: travel time to and from town; the need for staggered arrivals and departures of students to avoid overcrowding at community training sites; and the difficulties presented by the insurance requirement that a certified teacher must always be present in situations where only two or three students can benefit from training at *any one time*. These three factors clearly indicate that some of the benefits of community instruction are paid for by a reduction in direct teaching time.

In addition to scheduling factors, the content of instruction in a school-community model is radically different from that of a traditional school environment. Severely handicapped students learn how to order food at restaurants, cross streets, work, shop, and ride public buses. Academic classroom instruction becomes focused upon practical community applications. Such an applied orientation sets restrictive limits upon the content of academic programs and instructional materials. For example, a situation might arise in which students are taught to use money to make purchases, but are not taught underlying concepts of equivalence, set formation, or one-to-one correspondence. Without these related concepts, money use might become limited to the exact items the students are taught to purchase. Thus, it probably would be difficult for the student to shop when a store has run out of a particular item. Certainly, severely handicapped students could be taught alternative problem-solving skills, but a completely applied curriculum is probably not the route for such an objective.

Small group instructional arrangements are more prevalent. Although small group instructional arrangements probably net a higher cost effectiveness return than one-to-one instructional arrangements from both acquisition and economic perspectives, they are more costly initially than large ratio instructional arrangements. The eventual goal of most if not all educational skills is the self-initiated performance of those skills in natural settings. Transitioning a severely handicapped student toward independence, especially when that student has a long history of adult dependence, is a time consuming and often frustrating task. For example, teachers must learn to do more observing than interacting. With direct teacher intervention reduced, the probability increases that the student will encounter failure. Initially, teachers might have to accept qualitatively lower performance, if it is self-initiated.

Teaching roles have to be expanded. As a result of the school-community model, it has been necessary to expand teacher roles, especially in the areas of teaching hours and the locations in which instruction takes place. If a teacher is arranging for the eventual independent performance of a set of leisure skills (e.g., movie attendance and viewing), at least two assumptions can be made. First, criterion verification of movie attendance and viewing will take place in real movie theatres and a significant number of teaching trials must be attempted in real facilities. Second, empirical verification of acceptable movie skills should probably take place during typical recreation time periods and not only during the school day. The working hours of teachers will change, and teachers will be working in community facilities as well as in schools. Needless to say, some of the difficulties resulting from necessary changes in the teaching day and in teaching locations are unsettling to some classroom-oriented teachers and to some extent to teachers in training who are unprepared for community instruction.

The model is more expensive in the short run. Obviously, the cost of transporting and instructing students at community sites is more expensive than conducting classes in schoolrooms. Some of the factors that contribute to the increased costs of school-community programs are listed below.

1. Reduced student teacher ratios are needed.
2. Transportation costs which include public bus, private bus rental, public taxi, and teacher reimbursement for private auto use are vital.
3. The consumable instructional materials needed for community programming (e.g., coins/bills, food items, work clothing, safety items, etc.) are increased.
4. The basic cost of liability insurance is increased.
5. Miscellaneous rental fees (e.g., rental of bowling alleys, bowling shoes, archery equipment, etc.) increase.

However, despite the short-term expenses incurred from a school-community model, it is argued that the potential for long-term gains outweighs the initial financial investment. Listed below are selected long-term gains that seem reasonable:

1. Increases in independent functional skills lead to reductions in the costs of supervision;
2. Competitive employment reduces government welfare and disability payments;
3. Increased independent home living skills reduce the need for low-ratio adult maintenance care;
4. Competitive employment skills reduce the supervision costs incurred in subsidized sheltered workshops;
5. Independent shopping and transportation skills reduce domestic supervision costs.

Individualization requires staff increases. In order to verify empirically that individual severely handicapped students can perform a series of independent adult skills in natural settings, students are required to perform many skills *alone* in a *variety* of natural settings. In addition, it appears that acquisition is smoothest when the student-teacher ratios for most community programs approximates 4:1. Obviously, the quality of any community-based program will be a direct function of the number of teachers available. On the other hand, it should be noted that the school-community model was able to provide community instruction to approximately 53 secondary-age severely handicapped students by adding only two teachers to a staff of seven. While staff increases are required by a school-community model, hopefully such increases can be kept to a minimum through efficient scheduling.

Parent concerns and fears are made salient. Parental fears surfaced as soon as the school-community model was discussed. There are many valid reasons why parents of severely handicapped students should be concerned about the independent functioning of their children in community settings. In years past, many secondary-age severely handicapped citizens were denied public school education. From a parent's perspective, past exclusionary arguments and professional descriptions have probably shaped many fears concerning the inability of their children to function independently. Many parents and educators are skeptical concerning the overall skill performance of severely handicapped students. In effect, many parents will continue to be concerned until their children can demonstrate adult skills across several domains.

Competition for jobs emerges. One of the goals of the school-community model was to demonstrate that some severely handicapped students could maintain themselves in competitive employment. In order to reach this goal potential, jobs were selected that were frequently considered to be of low status in the community, specifically dishwashing and janitorial jobs. However, it was quickly determined that preconceived notions of job status were irrelevant when severely handicapped students competed for jobs previously handled exclusively by nonhandicapped workers. For the most part, nonhandicapped workers resented the possibility that their job could be handled satisfactorily by a severely handicapped worker. Thus, it became necessary to reduce the visibility of handicapping conditions and to teach as many work skills as possible *before* severely handicapped students applied for competitive jobs.

Time required per task is difficult to arrange. One of the most important factors of all instructional programs for severely handicapped students is the need for the repeated practice of clusters of skills. Without repeated practice across extended time periods, it is difficult to acquire community-acceptable performance criteria. School-exclusive models are ideal arrangements for providing repeated practice opportunities. However, the school-community model presents problems in this regard, in that it is often difficult to arrange for sufficient practice. Practice trials are limited by the length of time that can be spent at a site and by the non-functional nature of repeated training trials. For example, in one community program students were taught to dine in a cafeteria and one specific skill involved the proper use of trash receptacles. During visits to various cafeterias, there was not time to practice using trash receptacles more than twice. In addition, teaching the students to use the trash container (e.g., 20 times during one cafeteria visit) would have been non-functional and quite unrealistic. One solution was to afford repeated practice in simulation at school and then to extend the skill to other community settings.

Program continuity problems arise. The overall logistical problems encountered daily are possibly the most difficult aspects of a school-community model. The constant need to rearrange schedules, transport students, and plan for new community sites requires inordinate amounts of time. Program continuity problems can be resolved only when efficient scheduling and inter-teacher cooperation are operating. If a small cluster of students is to receive instruction at a public grocery store during the same interval that another cluster of students is to receive vocational training in a laundry, several logistical problems arise. Obviously, it is crucial to find appropriate community training sites. These sites can only be found by teachers with adequate time designated for this purpose. Each student's daily routine must be organized in a consistent manner so that the schedule is predictable for the student, parents, and classroom teachers. Scheduling should be arranged so that, whenever feasible, each student receives community instruction across all major curricular areas.

Summary of School-Community Service Delivery Model

Before leaving this rather cursory discussion of the school-community model, it seems appropriate to summarize several of the major issues related to such a model. First, it seems reasonable that teaching independent community-functioning skills is best accomplished when the skills are taught in both school and community settings. Thus, decisions as to the skill clusters that can be taught best in school, as opposed to those that are best acquired in natural community environments, are crucial.

Second, in the past when teaching students selected skills, the instructors chose to teach *all* the school components before teaching functional components in community settings. Many times such a clearcut dichotomy between school and community is unnecessary. For example, severely handicapped students acquiring bus riding skills probably should have practiced rudimentary forms of actual bus riding concurrent with related instruction in school (Certo, Schwartz, & Brown, 1976).

Third, it is imperative that skills taught in schools be verified empirically in natural community settings with community accepted performance criteria. It cannot be inferred that a student who can make grocery purchases in a simulated school store will be able to make similar purchases in real supermarkets. There are innumerable characteristics of supermarkets, indeed, of almost any natural community setting, that can never be simulated in schools.

Fourth, in a school-community service delivery model, realistic student-teacher ratios are crucial. The protective boundaries of a classroom or of a simulated street crossing in the school gym are not present in natural community settings. The option of having four students working on Task A and four students working on Task B is untenable when one teacher takes 8 severely handicapped students to a public market place. Student-teacher ratios of three or four to one will probably be required for training in natural settings.

Fifth, there are thousands of sub-skills, attitudes, and values that contribute to the successful performance of almost any skill necessary for independent community functioning. Unfortunately few, if any, generally acceptable instruments that allow for the precise assessment of community functioning skills exist at this time. Thus, it is necessary for the teacher to arbitrarily generate non-inclusive clusters of skills that are presumably necessary for severely handicapped students to do such things as shop, ride buses, or engage in recreation independently (Belmore & Brown, 1976; Certo, Schwartz, & Brown, 1976; Nietupski, Certo, Pumpian, & Belmore, 1976; Schwartz, Note 2).

Finally, instruction in community settings requires the degree of program precision and preparation similar to that employed daily in classrooms. Community instruction for severely handicapped students should *not* imply that a student group is embarking on a field trip. Rather, such instruction should imply that the school in which functional skills are taught has been moved to more natural settings, that the walls of the school have been decreased, and that those walls are permeable.

Phase IV. Self-Contained Classes within Regular Middle and Senior High Schools and Community Settings

At the start of the 1976-77 school year, only 10 severely handicapped students of secondary age will be placed in self-contained classes in a self-contained school; 22 severely handicapped students will be placed in two different regular middle schools; and 18 severely handicapped students will be placed in two regular senior high schools. It is intended that self-contained schools will not be a component of the service delivery model for handicapped students of any age and any functioning level in the Madison Public School system by the start of the 1977-78 school year.

Since the majority of secondary-age severely handicapped students will be served in regular middle and senior high schools, it is anticipated that the school community model described in Phase III will be expanded to allow for more community involvement and more realistic social-emotional development. That is, it is intended that severely handicapped students of all functioning levels from birth through young adulthood will interact with non-handicapped students throughout their school years.

There is no doubt that placing severely handicapped students in regular middle and senior high schools has the potential of creating both real and irrational problems. However, the advantages that can be realized from extensive exposure to nonhandicapped peers, more realistic involvement in complex social and emotional environments, more assessible age-appropriate leisure activities, and more sophisticated performance expectations will result in longitudinal gains that could never be realized from confinement in self-contained schools.

Reference Notes

1. Certo, N., & Vincent, L. Teaching handicapped students to perform across persons and places. Unpublished manuscript. Madison, Wisc: University of Wisconsin, 1976.
2. Schwartz, R. *Teaching severely handicapped workers to function as dishwashers in simulated and natural settings.* Unpublished master's thesis. Madison, Wisc: University of Wisconsin, 1976.

References

Barrett, B. H., & McCormack, Jr., J. E. Varied teacher tutorials: A tactic for generating credible skills in severely retarded people. *Mental Retardation*, 1973, *11*, 14–19.

Belmore, K., & Brown, L. A job skill inventory strategy for use in public school vocational training program for severely handicapped potential workers. In L. Brown, N. Certo, K. Belmore, & T. Crowner (Eds.) *Selected papers related to secondary programming with severely handicapped students, Vol. VI, Part 1*. Madison, Wisc: Madison Public Schools, 1976.

Brown, L., Nietupski, J., & Hamre-Nietupski, S. The criterion of ultimate functioning and public school services for severely handicapped students. In M. A. Thomas (Ed.). *Hey! Don't forget about me: New directions for serving the severely handicapped*. Reston, Va: Council for Exceptional Children, 1976.

Certo, N., Schwartz, R., & Brown, L. Community transportation: Teaching severely handicapped students to ride a public bus system. In L. Brown, T. Crowner, W. Williams, & R. York (Eds.). *Madison's alternative for zero exclusion: A book of readings, Vol. V*. Madison, Wisc: Madison Public Schools, 1975. (Republished: N. G. Haring & L. Brown (Eds.). *Teaching the severely handicapped: A yearly publication of the American Association for the Education of the Severely/Profoundly Handicapped, Vol I.* New York: Grune & Stratton, 1976.

Certo, N., & Swetlik, B. Making purchases: A functional money-use program for trainable level retarded students. In L. Brown, N. Certo, K. Belmore, & T. Crowner (Eds.). *Selected papers related to secondary programming with severely handicapped students, Vol. VI, Part 1*. Madison, Wisc: Madison Public Schools, 1976.

Corte, H. E., Wolf, M. H., & Locke, B. J. A comparison of procedures for eliminating self-injurious behavior of retarded adolescents. *Journal of Applied Behavior Analysis*, 1971, *4*, 201–213.

Garcia, E. The training and generalization of a conversational speech form in nonverbal retardates. *Journal of Applied Behavior Analysis*, 1974, *7*, 137–149.

Johnson, J. M., & Johnson, G. T. Modification of consonant speech-sound articulation in young children. *Journal of Applied Behavior Analysis*, 1972, *5*, 233–246.

Kale, R. J., Kaye, J. H., Whelan, P. A., & Hopkins, B. L. The effects of reinforcement on the modification, maintenance and generalization of social responses of mental patients. *Journal of Applied Behavior Analysis*, 1968, *1*, 307–314.

Martin, J. A. Generalizing the use of descriptive adjectives through modeling. *Journal of Applied Behavior Analysis*, 1975, *8*, 203–209.

Nietupski, R., Certo, N., Pumpian, I., & Belmore, K. Supermarket shopping: Teaching severely handicapped students to generate shopping lists and make purchases functionally linked with meal preparation. In L. Brown, N. Certo, K. Belmore, & T. Crowner (Eds.). *Selected papers related to secondary programming with severely handicapped students, Vol. VI, Part 1*. Madison, Wisc: Madison Public Schools, 1976.

Stokes, T. F., Baer, D. M., & Jackson, R. L. Programming of a greeting response in four retarded children. *Journal of Applied Behavior Analysis*, 1974, *7*, 599–610.

NICK CERTO received his doctorate in special education from the University of Wisconsin under the direction of Dr. Lou Brown. His areas of professional concentration include teacher training, and programming for preschool and secondary severely handicapped students. During the 1975–76 academic year, Dr. Certo co-developed a service delivery system for secondary severely handicapped students within the Madison Public Schools. He is currently a Project officer with the Division of Innovation and Development, Bureau of Education for the Handicapped, Washington, D.C.

LOU BROWN is a Professor in the Department of Studies in Behavioral Disabilities at the University of Wisconsin, Madison. His professional career has been concentrated on developing public school service for severely handicapped students from birth through young adulthood.

TIMOTHY CROWNER is Coordinator of Specialized Educational Services for Madison Metropolitan School District. His major responsibility has been to develop programs for severely handicapped students in the public school and community. He has been active in curriculum development, inservice training, and transdisciplinary service delivery.

KEN BELMORE is currently Vocational Coordinator of Community Based Vocational Training Programs for Moderately and Severely Handicapped Students at Badger School, Madison Metropolitan School District, Madison, Wisconsin. He has assisted in the design and implementation of a vocational training model that emphasizes instruction in real work settings. He has taught handicapped students in a residential institution and in public schools.

Vocational Habilitation: A Time for Change

DAVID J. POMERANTZ
University of Illinois at Urbana-Champaign

DAVID MARHOLIN, II
Boston University

Recent developments in special education have provided an empirical basis for the elevation of expectancies and goals for severely handicapped individuals. Perhaps the most important development has been in the area of applications of learning principles and behavioral intervention programs. Although applications of learning theory are not new, training programs specific enough to be replicable and powerful enough to produce significant behavior change in severely handicapped individuals have only recently become available (for reviews cf. Barrett, in press; Birnbrauer, 1976). We now have the technology to teach the handicapped those skills which will allow them to live in community-based settings without strong dependence on large institutions.

Behavior modifiers have developed teaching procedures to deal with several primary categories of skill deficits. The earliest programs demonstrated how one might effectively teach a variety of self-help skills, including dressing (Watson, 1973), personal hygiene (Lent, 1975), care of one's environment (Girardeau & Spradlin, 1964), and toileting (Foxx & Arzin, 1973). The teaching of appropriate eating habits (Barton, Guess, Garcia, & Baer, 1970) and cooking skills (Steed, 1974) have also been demonstrated. In addition, a variety of social interaction skills have been taught, e.g., basic imitation skills (Baer, Peterson, & Sherman, 1967), speech (Guess, Sailor, & Baer, 1974), sign language (Wilbur, 1976), cooperative play (Redd, 1970; Whitman, Mercurio, & Caponigri, 1970), attending to another adult (Brown & Foshee, 1971), and appropriate hetero-sexual activities (Lent, 1975). A wide variety of academic survival skills such as telling time, counting change, and recognizing particularly important written words have also been acquired by severely handicapped individuals (Bijou, 1972; Bijou, Birnbrauer, Kidder, & Tague, 1966). Finally, in the area of vocational habilitation, behavior modification principles have been used to increase productivity, accuracy, and various work-related social behaviors (Brown, Bellamy, Perlmutter, Sackowitz, & Sontag, 1972; Brown & Pearce, 1970; Marholin & Burleigh, Note 1). Other research has demonstrated the capabililty of the severely handicapped to learn skills once considered far too difficult or complex for them (Gold, 1968, 1972, 1973, in press; Levy, Pomerantz, & Gold, in press). This research employs methods of careful task analysis in which target behaviors are broken down into components and the behavior of the trainer is systematically planned and closely monitored. Gold (1975) reports that the use of task analysis in training complex assemblies has been extremely effective with moderately and severely retarded learners. In teaching tasks involving 15 and 24 piece bicycle brake assemblies, printed electronic circuit boards, and other relatively difficult tasks, only a small percentage of the severely handicapped individuals trained by Dr. Gold and his colleages have failed to reach criteria of skill acquisition (Gold, in press). Gold provides a dramatic indication that expectancies for the severely handicapped have been far too low. Severely and profoundly retarded blind individuals successfully learned and completed a 15-piece bicycle brake task. Apparently, the technology for teaching competitive work skill is on the way.

If technology is to solve human problems, however, effective service delivery systems are needed. The focus of this paper is on vocational service systems for severely handicapped individuals. Its purpose is to determine whether current systems are reaching severely handicapped persons with available technology and whether they are delivering the technology in an effective problem-solving manner.

In order to evaluate a problem-solving system, one must look closely at the nature of the problem being addressed (Watzlawick, Weakland, & Fisch, 1974). The challenge of habilitating severely handicapped individuals is not exclusively one of remediating behavioral deviance and skill deficits. Societal factors must also be considered (Wolfensberger, 1972). Farber (1968) argued that mental retardation is largely a social phenomenon, based on the need of an industrial society for "surplus populations." Whatever the reason, severely handicapped persons have limited opportunity to participate in culturally desirable activities and to share in our society's rewards.

In our view, the problem cannot be understood when psychoeducational or societal factors are analyzed independently. An interaction of both sets of variables has determined the existing situation: deviant behavior and skill deficits lead to exclusion from society. For example, an employer will not consider hiring an individual who is obviously incompetent and unable to perform the job. Unfortunately, many people in our society assume that severely handicapped persons are necessarily incompetent, and therefore deny them all opportunities to succeed. Conversely, denial of opportunity leads to incompetence and deviance. When individuals are consistently excluded from the environments where socially appropriate behavior and skills are learned, their development will become increasingly retarded (Bijou, 1966). The conditions that still exist in many institutions for the severely handicapped represent an extreme example of this phenomenon (Blatt, Note 2; Blatt & Kaplan, 1966; O'Leary & Wilson, 1975). Commenting on a building for older women patients at Willowbrook, a New York State institution, Dr. Michael Wilkeins pointed out that:

> These patients do have clothes on today, but as you can see, the one thing that can't be hidden is that there are no training programs here. All these patients do is sit all day. They are not occupied. Their life is just hours and hours of endless nothing to do; no one to talk to, no expectations, just an endless life of misery and filth. When you see this, it makes you think it's hopeless. But you know they look this way because they haven't ever had the opportunity for training. If you or I were left to sit on a ward surrounded by other mentally retarded people, we would probably begin looking like this too. (Rivera, 1972, p. 62)

Recent analyses have criticized existing human service systems for their failure to recognize societal determinants of human problems (Rappaport, Note 3; Ryan, 1971). Programs for severely handicapped individuals are open to such criticisms unless their interventions are based upon the interactional perspective that has been described. If an interaction of behavioral deviance and societal exclusion has caused the problem, solution strategies must be aimed at both sets of factors. Thus, all programs would attempt to open up opportunities for severely handicapped individuals to participate in normative activity, and to provide the skills necessary for success in those activities. If training technology were applied according to such a service model, stated goals such as independence, autonomy, and dignity for service recipients might be realized.

An interactional view of the problem dictates that the general goal of vocational services for the severely handicapped is to prevent their exclusion from normative and remunerative work roles. Specific criteria for achievement of these goals are defined as the individual's performance of useful jobs (i.e., jobs that are needed in some sectors of the economy), and earning normative wages. At present, severely handicapped adults are untrained for existing jobs and have little access to useful work (Bellamy, Peterson, & Close, 1975; Gold, 1973). Therefore, the role of vocational habilitation programs is to identify or provide useful job opportunities and to teach the skills needed for the successful performance of these jobs. This role might be criticized as too narrow in scope by professionals who regard rehabilitation as responsibility for the welfare of the whole person (Trevethan, 1971). However, our position is that in the case of severely handicapped clients, the provision of useful and remunerative work is a necessary first step toward helping the whole person. Considering society's emphasis on vocational activity and income level in determining the status of an individual, it is logical to expect that changes in these variables would produce generalized change in attitudes toward the severely handicapped. Furthermore, earned income would lead to opportunities for more independent functioning in the community. Parents might be less likely to behave in an overprotective manner if their handicapped children were economically more self-supporting. They might be willing to allow their sons or daughters to attempt independent or semi-independent living in apartments or group homes. As opportunities of this sort become available to severely handicapped individuals, habilitation programs should increase their emphasis on whole-person programming.

The vocational service models we shall discuss are sheltered workshop and prevocational school programs. Participants in sheltered work programs will be referred to as clients because this term is commonly used in adult services. The terms used are important only because they carry implications about the relationship between service providers and service recipients. We fully recognize the need to change the quality of this relationship, but we do not believe that choosing new descriptive terms will lead to such change. Perhaps future papers can accurately refer to service recipients as consumers, indicating that service programs work directly for them, providing services that have been specifically requested.

The Sheltered Workshop

Sheltered work programs serve handicapped clients by placing them in competitive jobs and by providing long-term employment within the workshop (Conley, 1972). The objectives of vocational services might be attained through either function. With reference to long-term employment within the workshop, these objectives would be realized if clients performed jobs that were comparable to those in the competitive sector and paid competitive wages. Thus, the difference between sheltered and competitive work settings would be in the special services available in the sheltered workshop (e.g., training, prosthetics), which allow clients to perform normative work.

Placement

In general, sheltered work programs attempt to place only those clients who are evaluated as having potential for rehabilitation (Greenleigh Associates, Inc., 1975). Rarely are severely handicapped individuals included in this category. Only 10–13% of all sheltered workshop clients are placed, and only a small fraction of these clients are severely handicapped (Greenleigh Associates, Inc., 1975). The assumption that severely handicapped clients have little or no potential for competitive work should be re-examined. Placing severely handicapped persons in competitive employment is a challenging task, but the difficulty of the task should not inhibit placement efforts. On the contrary, one function of vocational services is to develop and assess strategies for overcoming such problems.

The placement programs that currently exist in shelterd workshops are generally inadequate for placing severely handicapped workers. Typically, only one of two staff people, if any, are responsible for the complete placement function (Leslie, 1967). Thus, there can be little on-the-job training or support for clients as they move into new jobs. This suggests the need to develop new and more intensive approaches, rather than to completely discard placement as an alternative for severely handicapped clients.

One new approach involves the full-time services of trainer-advocates, or staff members who are responsible for all aspects of integrating clients into the competitive labor market. They contact people in business or industry who are potential employers. Trainer-advocates "sell" clients to employers, stressing the research and demonstration projects which illustrate the untapped work potential of the client population. Risk to employers hiring severely handicapped individuals is minimized if the trainer-advocate takes full responsibility for skill and adjustment training and promises to stay with the client on the job until specific performance criteria have been reached. When commitments from employers are secured, trainer-advocates work on the job themselves until its demands have been thoroughly assessed. At that point, training methods are developed and clients are trained in the work setting. If client performance is monitored carefully and trainers gradually phase out their assistance, the transition to competitive employment can be made smoothly. The trainer-advocate model has been applied in the schools of Bucks County, Pennsylvania, for the past four years (Bucks County Public Schools, 1974). Three full time staff workers concentrated their efforts on securing jobs and training moderately and severely retarded young adults to perform jobs in the community. The program reported that, for the 1972–1973 school year, 14 full-time placements out of 23 attempts were successful. Criteria for successful placement were established by the employers; that is, the employers decided which trainers were no longer needed in the work setting. Mean training time per client was reported to be 70 hours. Client wages during the training period averaged $2.13 per hour. Evidently, direct placement and on-the-job training are viable and promising options for habilitation programs serving the severely handicapped.

In general, sheltered workshops are not now using available instructional technology in ways that lead to job placement of severely handicapped clients. Workshop programs rely on production and adjustment training within the workshop, in the hope that a general upgrading of client skills may lead to future placement. The Greenleigh (1975) data indicate how ineffective this strategy has been. Although job placement is a stated goal that is used to justify much of a program's activity, it is not accomplished very often.

To alter this state of affairs, sheltered workshops must separate their placement and production functions. When placement is the objective, it should be approached directly. That is, instead of waiting for job opportunities to open up, the program must increase its efforts to promote openings. Such efforts should begin with increased staff allocation for finding and securing jobs. Several skilled staff members must become knowledgeable about the employment market in the community and acquainted with as many potential employers as possible. If jobs are secured, specific training goals for individual clients can be set. Instead of a vague curriculum of loosely defined general work skills and personal adjustment, clients would be trained in the specific skills needed for a particular job.

Workshop Tasks

Currently, almost all severely handicapped clients in sheltered work programs remain in the workshop on a permanent basis. According to the survey by Greenleigh Associates, Inc. (1975), four basic programs are offered to these clients. The activity that accounts for the greatest amount of client time is supervised production, Unfortunately, little or no training in new skills is offered during supervised production (Gold, 1973; Greenleigh Associates, Inc., 1975). As they now function, sheltered workshops have little need to engage in skill training because of the kinds of work contracts that they make. The Greenleigh report states:

> "It is difficult to assess the relation between wages paid in sheltered workshops and those paid for comparable work elsewhere, since it was found that work performed in workshops is seldom comparable to that in the competitive sector. Jobs allocated to workshops are generally so low skilled, tedious, unrewarding, and unremunerative that they are seldom found in the competitive sector. Frequently, the operations are so inefficient that, if employers had to pay full labor costs, they would automate the process instead. (1975, p. 14)

Thus, the major activity of the sheltered workshop is usually supervised production of nonhabilitative, non-normative jobs.

Workshop tasks frequently are subdivided into multiple work stations, each of which covers one or two basic operations (Nelson, 1971). The more difficult stages of the production process are generally performed by the clients whose functioning level is highest and by the staff. For example, quality control procedures are considered to be a major problem for sheltered workshop programs, and are often carried out by production supervisors (Leslie, 1967). Hence, sheltered workshops fail to take advantage of the potentially habilitative activity inherent in their production design.

The subcontract work that sheltered workshops rely on is becoming increasingly scarce. As a result, there is a substantial amount of down time, or time spent on the production floor without work. On the average, the workshop client spends 10 hours per week in forced nonproduction. The Work Activity Center, a form of vocational program that serves a large proportion of severely handicapped clients, has approximately 20 hours of down time per client-week (Greenleigh Associates, Inc., 1975).

In summary, sheltered employment provides severely handicapped individuals with neither the opportunity nor the skills to perform useful work. The failure of workshops to achieve defined objectives is also documented by client remuneration data. The average hourly wage for all sheltered workshop clients in the United States is approximately 75 cents, while Work Activity Center clients average only 33 cents per hour (Greenleigh Associates, Inc., 1975).

In order to furnish severely handicapped adults with useful, normative, and remunerative work within the workshop, programs must regularly obtain habilitative contracts. Gold (1973) has described the five major characteristics of such contracts. First, the work should require skills that must be learned, rather than skills already in the clients' behavioral repertoires. Second, the contract must have sufficient lead time (time set aside to prepare for production). This allows for the development of effective training strategies and efficient production designs. Third, the amount of shop space required for the contract should be proportionate to the number of clients employed on it. Fourth, the task should consist of enough operations to provide significant work at a variety of job stations. Finally, the contract should be profitable for the workshop and for the clients.

Organizational Variables

As sheltered workshops are now organized, they are not equipped to obtain or carry out habilitative contracts. Basic organizational changes are needed if the workshops are to attain their goals, and one important modification will involve staff allocation. A dichotomy now exists between rehabilitation-oriented and production-oriented personnel (Nelson, 1971). Rehabilitation staff includes psychologists, evaluators, counselors, social workers, and special educators who are responsible to the institutions that fund the program (e.g., the Department of

Mental Health, the Division of Vocational Rehabilitation). Production staff includes business managers, job procurement personnel, and production supervisors who are accountable to the businesses with which the contracts are signed.

Unfortunately, rehabilitation and production staff frequently see themselves as working at cross purposes (Braun, 1976). Rehabilitation personnel often view production time as an annoyance which interferes with the more important activities aimed at changing some aspect of client behavior. Conversely, production staff are concerned with meeting contractual deadlines; time spent training clients in areas that do not involve production is frequently seen as wasted. In general, the more powerful staff positions in sheltered workshop programs are the rehabilitation staff positions. Thus, the individuals with advanced training hold these positions and are not directly involved in production. Responsibility for implementing production is generally given to floor supervisors, who are trained least and paid least. Considering the great number of demands placed on them, they cannot be expected to design and execute the training necessary for the production of habilitative contracts. Younger and more skilled floor staff members often become frustrated with their difficult assignments and leave their jobs to enter more rewarding vocations or to acquire the additional education needed for higher positions in service agencies (Berkson, Note 4). Hence, there are few people with extensive workshop experience who are also able to develop quality programs related to production.

With a dichotomized staff, it is difficult for sheltered workshop programs to improve habilitative services. Only when the normalization of the work setting itself becomes a common objective for staff can this be achieved. Training and behavior modification would then be tied into production needs, and the complex work skills needed for specific job contracts would be taught to clients.

A Sheltered Workshop as a Business

A glaring weakness of the average sheltered workshop is its lack of personnel with business expertise. At best, a few staff members have a limited understanding of business practices, and they are generally not the ones who make major policy decisions for the program (Braun, 1976). As a result, production designs used to fulfill workshop contracts are usually inefficient and somewhat disorganized (Gold, 1973; Greenleigh Associates, Inc., 1975). However, the severely handicapped worker needs normal industrial procedures and superior job designs to compensate for possible physical and behavioral problems. As suggested by Stroud (Note 5), a skilled industrial engineer should be employed by the workshop to develop sophisticated production designs that are efficient and well coordinated with training demands.

Typically, the equipment in sheltered workshops is inadequate for production design. The available tools and machines are generally antiquated and in substandard condition (Greenleigh Associates, Inc., 1975). Furthermore, workshop personnel, feeling that mechanization might further cut the already limited supply of work, are hesitant to use automated procedures. Hence, clients produce goods without the technology that is available to factory workers. Automation must be incorporated, where appropriate, with necessary adjunctive tools and machinery. The current challenge is to design man-machine interfaces that maximize the productive potential of handicapped workers (Gold & Wade, in press; Jordan, 1963).

Another production-related weakness of sheltered workshops is their failure to specialize (Braun, 1976). Workshop contracts tend to be completely unrelated to one another, so that new production strategies must be developed that would enable the workshop to secure a particular type of habilitative contract.

In the absence of production expertise, job procurement personnel have little basis on which to bid for contracts. Even if they are able to assess the job adequately, the poor production designs and lack of equipment that characterize sheltered workshops do not permit them to bid at competitive rates (Greenleigh Associates, Inc., 1975). In practice, rather than remediating its inadequate production system and providing more training to the clients, the workshop bids at competitive prices and pays its workers a small percentage of regular industrial wages (Conley, 1972).

Small manufacturing companies that rely on subcontract work might serve as models for the development of business expertise in the sheltered workshop. In general, these companies specialize in one product-related service (e.g., packaging, electronic circuit board assembly, tool and die manufacture). One of the few sheltered workshops in this country operating with a profit margin, exclusive of service-related funding, has specialized in the production of sterilized paper supplied to hospitals (Gold, Note 6).

It might be argued that increased specialization would work against habilitative goals. That is, reliance on specialized contracts would limit the kinds of skills that are taught, thereby reducing clients' chances for placement and restricting their production to a few operations. However, general programs of in-workshop training have not led to placement of severely handicapped clients either. Training for placement must be specifically designed for the individual who is to be placed and for the job that has been secured. Contract specialization does not necessarily limit production to a few fixed operations. Although most jobs would be related, it is reasonable to assume that each contract would involve a range of challenging tasks. This assumption appears valid, in that specialization should enable workshop programs to obtain work of a generally higher level than is now possible. The possible narrowing of the range of skills to be learned is a hypothetical problem, since sheltered workshops are teaching so few skills of any kind. The availability of useful and remunerative work that might result from specialization more than compensates for its possible disadvantages.

Evaluation vs. Training

Evaluation is the second common sheltered workshop activity identified by Greenleigh Associates (1975). Criticisms of the theoretical and empirical foundations of vocational evaluation have been presented elsewhere (e.g., Gold, 1975). Still, it should be emphasized that evaluation of severely handicapped individuals alone does not lead to the solution of their problems (Bijou & Grimm, 1975). Since these individuals are not placed in competitive employment or provided with complex jobs in the workshop itself, it is difficult to understand why information about their potential to perform high-level work is needed. Normative vocational assessment data, even if valid and reliable, are not particularly useful for the individual who has no opportunity to join a productive labor force. Although evaluators are among the most highly trained staff in the workshop, they spend considerable time and energy obtaining data that generally will not be used. It would be more productive to have these staff members engaged in placement and skill training activities.

A second evaluative function carried out by the sheltered workshop is the time study (Stroud, 1970). The production rates of individual clients are computed in percentages of the industrial norm and then used to determine client wages on a piece rate basis. Considering the subnormal production environment characteristic of sheltered workshops, this practice is unacceptable. It is doubtful whether a physically and intellectually normal, experienced factory worker could achieve the industrial norm under sheltered workshop conditions. It is noteworthy that labor unions accept the piece rate scale in only a few industries (e.g., garment production), and only when production is tightly controlled and carefully monitored (Korn, 1964; Rothman, 1964).

Other common workshop activities for the severely handicapped focus on personal adjustment training (modification of social behaviors) and daily living skill training. Given the tedious nature of workshop tasks and the extensive down time, clients tend to exhibit a high frequency of inappropriate behavior. Modifying this behavior without changing the work setting is a necessary but insufficient condition for maintaining appropriate social behavior (Marholin & Siegel, in press). Similarly, teaching daily living skills without building in opportunities to use them is not very functional. It would be far easier and more practical to teach these skills in a community environment (Wolf, Phillips & Fixsen, 1972). It must be concluded that the standard nonproduction programs in sheltered workshops contribute little to the habilitation of severely handicapped individuals.

School Pre-Vocational Programs

Pre-vocational programs in secondary schools have only recently begun to emerge. As Meyen and Altman (1976) have emphasized, these programs currently lack direction and are inadequate in the area of curricula design. As a general observation, school pre-vocational programs appear to be using the sheltered workshop as a model, and are in danger of incorporating its habilitation deficiencies. The problem of low expectancies exists in pre-vocational courses, as indicated by their reliance on simple, workshop-like tasks for training purposes. School programs must not limit their role to pre-sheltered workshop experience. By accepting the challenging goals of providing students with job-related skills and placing them in work settings where they can perform remunerative work, these programs can create significant change.

Secondary pre-vocational programs must employ "seeking" rather than "waiting" approaches to service delivery (Rappaport & Chinsky, 1974). That is, they must work actively in the community, rather than continue the traditional reliance on classroom teaching. If vocational training for severely handicapped students is to be implemented, the pre-vocational teacher must function as an advocate as well as an instructor. Thus, teachers should become involved in such activities as job procurement, teaching work and community living skills in appropriate settings, and working with non-handicapped individuals who are important in the students' lives, such as job supervisors and other workers. The seeking mode of education is critically important for two reasons. First, the severely handicapped need advocates who will create for them opportunities they now lack. This aspect of service delivery is of primary importance but usually is neglected. Second, training in the community circumvents many aspects of the problem of generalization (Tharp & Wetzel, 1969). Behaviors taught in one setting cannot be expected to generalize automatically to other settings which are characterized by different stimulus conditions and reinforcement contingencies (Marholin, Siegel & Phillips, 1976; Wahler, 1969). Teaching in the community helps to ensure that newly acquired skills will be used in appropriate settings. Educators using this approach must be careful to fade out of the instructional settings systematically, once target behaviors have been established. Otherwise, the learner is likely to become dependent on the particular cues of the teacher, and his performance will deteriorate when the teacher is not present (Marholin, Steinman, McInnis & Heads, 1975; Pomerantz & Redd, Note 7).

Placement of students in competitive employment represents an excellent application of the teacher-advocate role. The schools appear to be the service agencies that are best suited for placing students, as they have no production demands and a relatively low student-staff ratio (Conley, 1972).

Non-handicapped students in pre-vocational settings receive training in specific skill areas such as drafting, welding, driving, and typing. With skilled teachers applying task analysis methods, severely handicapped students could also acquire competencies that would greatly enhance their chances for placement in skilled or semi-skilled jobs. When possible, the schools could contract with local business operations for the initiation of on-the-job training programs. Teachers would apply the procedures needed to train severely handicapped persons in actual work settings. Although businesses would have no obligation to hire the students, they might do so if competence and skill were clearly demonstrated.

One major problem in teaching specific skill areas is that few special educators are familiar with these areas themselves. Therefore, it is essential that university programs preparing teachers of severely handicapped students provide information about the business world, as well as teaching expertise.

Debilitating Contingencies

The need for operational change in vocational programs has been stated by others (e.g., Gold, 1973) but, in general, proposed solutions have yet to be effectively implemented. One of the reasons that these solutions have been ineffective is that the problems are conceptualized in ways that do not suggest strategies to solve them.

Every solution depends upon the way the problem is presented. The precise terms of the problem's definition determine the general orientation and specific techniques of intervention, as well as the criteria for subsequent evaluation. Social critics often provide perceptive analyses, but their criticisms are usually at a global, descriptive level. Zifferblatt and Hendricks (1974) have pointed to an analogue in traditional diagnostic procedures in psychotherapy in which a client is often classified by a global label, such as "schizophrenia." Unfortunately, such diagnoses are often made on the basis of diagnostic tests that have limited validity and reliability (Mischel, 1968; Stuart, 1970). Hence, the diagnosis and labeling provide little useful information for solving the client's problem (Marholin & Bijou, in press). Similarly, current diagnostic terms related to social systems (e.g., disorganization, self-perpetuating) do not readily suggest solutions (Ehrlich, 1970; Slater, 1969; Toffler, 1970). A technology designed for changing social systems, as well as individual client behavior, is needed.

Applied behavior analysis offers social change agents the same principles as it offers the behavior modifier working with an individual client: an empirically-validated technology that is effective for changing individual behavior. There is no reason to believe that this technology cannot be useful in changing larger behavioral systems (Craighead, Kazdin, & Mahoney, 1976). Such an analysis would entail, among other things, assessment of institutional objectives, delineation of target behaviors implied by the objectives, and identification of reinforcement contingencies that would facilitate or obstruct the establishment of these target behaviors.

Behavioral technology can also be applied in some operational and procedural aspects of institutional change, particularly when it is combined with systems design and analysis (Berrien, 1968; Zifferblatt, 1972). A first step in applying behavior analysis to the problems of vocational programs is to outline the contingencies that exist in the service system, as a basis for possible changes in the system. In this paper we shall identify some contingencies that are central to the problems of vocational programs.

Inadequate Accountability

Under the authorization of the Fair Labor Standards Act, sheltered workshops which promote the employment of the handicapped may be certified as exempt from minimum wage requirements of the Federal Department of Labor. Certification also qualifies the workshops for federal grant-in-aid funds which are allocated through state vocational rehabilitation agencies. Finally, certification allows workshops to receive income under the Developmental Disabilities Act, usually through state departments of health, mental health, and mental retardation. Although there are multiple sources of funding for workshop programs, there are no national standards regarding qualifications to receive funds (Greenleigh Associates, Inc., 1975). As a result, workshop programs are not monitored closely, and few evaluative data are collected. Without such data, differential funding is impossible. Innovative and successful programs have little more chance of obtaining funds than do the least effective programs.

Funding for Quantity Rather than Quality

In general, vocational programs are reimbursed by state social service agencies on a per-client-day basis. Funds are allocated according to the number of clients in the program rather than by qualitative changes in the client population, placement in competitive jobs, or upward movement within a workshop system (Marholin, White & Knowles, 1975). Marholin *et al.* (1975) present a case in which a privately-owned and operated sheltered care facility for severely handicapped individuals in Illinois received state funds for vocational services, contingent upon the number of residents in its workshop program. This is a typical example of how economic contingencies operate to systematically punish the functional gains and increased independence of clients (Grossman & Rowitz, 1973). Fewer dollars come into a program if it meets its stated habilitative goal of providing clients with the opportunity and skills for placement into the most normalized work setting possible. Furthermore, there is minimal incentive for placement built into the system to counteract these negative economic consequences. On a long-term basis, programs that successfully place handicapped individuals in competitive employment are contributing to their own destruction. It is not clear exactly how this economic policy influences the personnel who design and execute programs. It is likely, however, that such economic contingencies pave the way for agency policies that de-emphasize or completely inhibit attempts to place severely handicapped persons in the community.

Consequences of Placement

Due to production demands, sheltered workshops tend to hold onto clients who function on a relatively high level, rather than place them outside the workshop. In order to maintain high production rates, workshops need the most qualified workers. Retaining the faster workers on the production line is particularly important because the contracts obtained by workshops generally do not provide much lead time. Thus, there is little time to train other clients. Such training would require considerable staff time, reduce production during training time, and remove staff from supervisory roles on the production floor. In addition, the process of placing handicapped individuals takes many valuable staff hours, and there are few tangible rewards delivered to a workshop program for placing clients in competitive employment.

Consequences of Increased Earnings for Clients

A subtle but often devastating contingency on clients in sheltered work and school programs involves their rights to financial benefits from various sources. If the severely handicapped person is going to make the transition from dependent to at least semi-independent community living, he will have to receive sufficient financial support. Presently, this support can be provided by several sources, including Social Security, medical assistance, welfare insurance, and mental health monies. When the client has demonstrated his ability to earn a sustained income and has a stable living environment and adequate community living skills, these supporting funds would be gradually withdrawn. In this way, the all-important first steps toward independence would be reinforced, and money would be released for other severely handicapped individuals making the same transition to independent community living. At present, the system is undercut by the stipulation that client income from any source, in excess of $60 monthly earnings, significantly reduces the amount of Social Security and medical assistance that a person may receive (Greenleigh Associates, Inc., 1975). In other words, should an individual progress to the point that his earnings, based on job performance, exceed $60 per month, some of the funds needed for a transition to more normal community settings would be lost. This potential loss of benefits presents an extreme threat to clients, parents, and program administrators. Thus, administrators are less likely to initiate programs aimed at client self-sufficiency, and parents are less likely to allow their children to participate in such programs.

Work activity centers are licensed to serve only inconsequential producers. Individuals can be classified as inconsequential producers only if they earn approximately 25% or less of the minimum wage. Therefore, it is illegal for these programs to provide genuinely remunerative work to clients. Since many work-activity programs are not associated with regularly licensed sheltered workshops (Greenleigh Associates, Inc., 1975), clients would have no available program if their earnings were to increase. Unfortunately, one cannot expect these programs to meet vocational goals if the changes necessary to meet those goals entail serious legal risks.

Rearranging Existing Contingencies

Several systematic variables contributing to the ineffectiveness of vocational services have been identified. The final task is to suggest approaches to instituting change. In order to improve the services offered by sheltered workshops and prevocational school programs, counterproductive contingencies should be examined. Accordingly, the following section will deal with the reorganization of existing service models and the establishment of alternative models.

Increased Accountability Procedures

There are two basic requirements for a truly accountable system. First, objectives must be defined in clear and measurable terms. If funding sources explicitly state their criteria for successful programming, service agencies could establish priorities consistent with those criteria. It is essential that funding agencies raise their expectations and direct workshop programs toward the goals that represent significant changes in vocational services. If program administrators knew that providing useful and remunerative work was the priority of the funding sources and that a long-term commitment to this priority existed, they would be able to initiate long-range program modifications. The second requirement for an accountable system is the development of procedures to monitor program effectiveness. Such procedures must allow for the collection of reliable data on the degree to which various programs are meeting predetermined criteria. Implementation of monitoring procedures should be widespread, rather than specific to particular agencies, and the evaluative criteria employed must be defined in terms of quantifiable outcome measures (e.g., number of clients in community placement, and mean weekly wages of clients).

Funding for Quality Rather than Quantity

A policy of differential funding is suggested, whereby programs meeting specific criteria would receive more money than less successful programs. Incentive funds should be provided to service agencies for increasing the number of clients placed in competitive employment, increasing average client earnings, and providing clients with competence in specific skill areas such as complex assembly tasks, welding, machine operation, and the like. With the additional monies acquired by meeting such criteria, vocational programs might further develop the particular endeavors that brought them the incentive funds (e.g., hire additional placement personnel or purchase new equipment). Initially, the cost of improving vocational programs will be high. The improvements, however, would eventually reduce the need for money that is now spent on ineffective services. Clients placed in competitive jobs should no longer need sheltered employment or disability benefits. Sheltered workshops might become self-supporting. Thus, the funds currently allocated to vocational programs would be redirected, but not necessarily increased.

Encouragement of Client Independence

Legislation should be initiated to allow severely handicapped clients to maintain Social Security insurance and medical benefits as they begin to earn normative wages. Although one goal of human services is to reduce client dependence on state support, this is not likely to occur unless adequate support is guaranteed during transitional periods. External support should be gradually reduced and terminated when predetermined criteria for self-support are met (e.g., 6 months of steady employment). A sliding scale or income supplement approach could be used in this process.

Client wage limits should be removed from work activity center licenses. In fact, these programs should be reinforced for turning inconsequential producers into productive workers.

Future Directions

Legislative action and policy changes by funding agencies are needed to rearrange contingencies in the vocational service system. Advocacy groups can play an important role by lobbying for improved vocational programs. These groups have already been successful in obtaining more services for handicapped persons. The emphasis of their political action in the field of vocational services should now shift toward qualitative change.

Many vocational programs are directed and staffed by individuals who recognize the problems inherent in the service system. There are several things that vocational service personnel can do to facilitate change. First, they can concentrate their efforts on one aspect of the program, developing a high quality of service on a small scale. For example, one skilled staff member might institute the trainer-advocate approach for placement with a few clients. If the positive results of placing severely handicapped workers are clearly demonstrated in the community, the chances of a greater change, encouraging more placement efforts, will be enhanced. Second, vocational programs should systematically document and publicize whatever progress they are able to make. Finally, program personnel should continually remind their funding sources about the counterproductive contingencies that are in effect. For example, on the forms that report how many clients were served, program administrators might include data that they consider to be better indicators of program effectiveness (e.g., increased client wages). They should also discuss programs that should be initiated but which, if undertaken, might result in a lower funding level for one program, under existing funding criteria.

Change in the vocational service system will not occur rapidly or easily. Vocational services are usually controlled by large bureaucratic agencies whose policies are well established and will not be suddenly discarded. In this regard, Sarason (1972) has suggested the development of new settings, or models, rather than the rearrangement of older malfunctioning ones. However, alternative models must be carefully designed to avoid the mistakes and shortcomings of the ones they are intended to replace. Thus, accountability for teaching skills and for opportunities provided to use skills productively should be programmed into alternative habilitation models. Several alternatives for vocational service are briefly presented.

Habilitation in the Private Sector

One way of escaping the counterproductive contingencies operating in service programs is to leave the service domain altogether. Businesses that employ integrated labor forces could be established in the competitive sector. Integrated labor is an excellent means of maximizing the work potential of severely handicapped persons. In this manner, particularly difficult operations requiring intensive, long-term training could be performed by non-handicapped workers. Thus, severely handicapped employees would be responsible only for the specific tasks for which they are very well trained.

The business might hire educational specialists to execute whatever training is needed to develop a skilled and integrated work force. This arrangement makes all parties highly accountable for performance. In order to survive in the competitive market, a business must provide all available resources to enhance the efficiency of the operation (e.g., machinery and sophisticated job designs). Although workers would be assured of earning normative wages, they would not retain their jobs unless their performance was of good quality. By the same token, individuals hired to train handicapped workers would be required to demonstrate instructional effectiveness, or their service would be terminated and the same service purchased from other sources.

Clearly, everyone involved in vocational service programs cannot go into private business. Expertise and capital are necessary if this is to be a viable alternative. Under the right conditions, however, it represents an exciting and effective way to increase the participation of severly handicapped individuals in the labor market.

The Enclave

Enclaves are groups of handicapped individuals working as units under special supervision within regular factories. The enclave model retains many of the special services, such as training, that are, in theory, provided in sheltered workshops. However, the limited expertise and resources for production that characterize sheltered workshops would not be problems in the enclave. Quality-based accountability is more important in this model than in the traditional workshop. Trainers and supervisors are responsible for maintaining an adequate production rate and production accuracy within the enclave. If they should be unable to do so, the private employer would replace the enclave work force with more productive employees. However, the service agency's participation would still be publicly funded and, therefore, subject to many of the same contingencies that control sheltered work programs. Greenleigh Associates, Inc. (1975) reports that enclaves have worked well in their few domestic applications.

Cooperative Programming

The task of providing normalized work opportunities to severely handicapped individuals might best be accomplished by the organizations that regularly deal with business and industry. An alliance between service providers and labor unions, for example, should prove beneficial. Unfortunately, organized labor is often an obstacle to the placement of handicapped workers in competitive jobs. The resistance of unions, however, may be little more than an untested assumption of vocational service personnel. Labor unions have been consistently critical of sheltered workshop practices (Korn, 1964; Rothman, 1964), and they might be willing to represent handicapped workers. The unionization of a trained work force could occur only if labor organizations were made aware of the demonstrated work potential of severely handicapped clients. Possibly, unions could organize placement programs and hire trainers from service institutions. Trainers would then be accountable to the unions, which represent the clients' interests. Labor unions' areas of expertise (working with business and negotiation) are among the weakest areas of vocational service programs. Conversely, the strength of human services for the severely handicapped, such as training ability, is not well developed in organized labor. Cooperative programs would both maximize the skills of participants and minimize their deficiencies. Programs of this kind have rarely been attempted. Yet, they represent a promising direction for vocational habilitation and should be explored.

Conclusion

The development of a training technology suited to the needs of severely handicapped individuals has made re-examination of service-delivery models necessary. One can no longer be satisfied with programs that provide "someplace to go during the day and something to do." Instead, vocational programs must put instructional technology to good use, thereby increasing the social participation of severely handicapped persons. Clearly, there is a long way to go. Significant change must occur in the service system as a whole and in individual vocational programs. At present, there is little empirical basis for suggesting any particular strategy for creating change. Solutions will begin to appear when the inadequacies of current service models are discussed more openly, when many small-scale change efforts are initiated in various communities, and when the impact of program modifications is systematically assessed through experimental or quasi-experimental procedures.

Reference Notes

1. Marholin, D., II, and Burleigh R. An analysis of stimulus control in a prevocational workshop setting. Manuscript in review, 1976.
2. Blatt, B. Personal communication. April 29, 1976.
3. Rappaport, J. *Toward a community psychology: In search of new paradigms.* Unpublished manuscript, University of Illinois at Urbana-Champaign, 1976.
4. Berkson, G. Sheltered workshop adaptation of retarded adults residing at home or in public facilities. Paper presented at the Downs Syndrome Congress, Las Vegas, Nevada, November, 1975.
5. Stroud, R. R. Industrial engineering in the sheltered workshop. Paper presented at the National Training Institute for State Facility Specialists, Dallas, Texas, September, 1969.
6. Gold, M. W. Personal communication, 1976.
7. Pomerantz, D. J., and Redd, W. H. Programming generalization through stimulus fading in 1 to 1 instruction of retarded children. University of Illinois at Urbana-Champaign, 1976.

References

Baer, D. M., Peterson, R. F., & Sherman, J. A. The development of imitation by reinforcing behavioral similarity to a model. *Journal of Experimental Analysis of Behavior,* 1967, *10*, 405–416.

Barrett, B. Behavior modification. In J. Wortis (Ed.), *Mental retardation and developmental disabilities: An annual review* (Vol. 8). New York: Brunner Mazel, in press.

Barton, E. S., Guess, D., Garcia, E., & Baer, D. M. Improvement of retardates' mealtime behaviors by time-out procedures using multiple baseline techniques. *Journal of Applied Behavior Analysis,* 1970, *3,* 77–84.

Bellamy, G. T., Peterson, L., & Close, D. Habilitation of the severely and profoundly retarded: Illustrations of competence. *Education and Training of the Mentally Retarded,* 1975, *10,* 174–186.

Berrien, F. *General and social systems.* New Brunswick, N.J.: Rutgers University Press, 1968.

Bijou, S. W. Functional analysis of retarded development. In N. Ellis (Ed.), *International review of research in mental retardation* (Vol. I). New York: Academic Press, 1966.

Bijou, S. W. The technology of teaching young handicapped children. In S. W. Bijou and E. Ribes-Inesta (Eds.), *Behavior modification: Issues and extensions.* New York: Academic Press, 1972.

Bijou, S. W., Birnbrauer, J. S., Kidder, J. D., & Tague, C. Programmed instruction as an approach to the teaching of reading, writing, and arithmetic to retarded children. *Psychological Record,* 1966, *16,* 505–522.

Bijou, S. W., & Grimm, J. A. Behavioral diagnosis and assessment in teaching young handicapped children. In

T. Thompson & W. S. Dockens III (Eds.), *Applications of behavior modification*. New York: Academic Press, 1975.

Birnbrauer, J. S. Mental retardation. In H. Leitenberg (Ed.), *Handbook of behavior modification*. Englewood Cliffs, N. J.: Prentice-Hall, 1976.

Blatt, B., & Kaplan, F. *Christmas in purgatory: A photographic essay on mental retardation*. Boston: Allyn & Bacon, 1966.

Braun, K. M. The role of the sheltered workshop in the habilitation of severely handicapped individuals: A proposal to modify the model. Unpublished manuscript, University of Illinois, 1976.

Brown, L., Bellamy, T., Perlmutter, L., Sackowitz, P., & Sontag, E. The development of quality, quantity, and durability in the work performance of retarded students in a public school prevocational workshop. *Training School Bulletin,* 1972, *68,* 29–36.

Brown, L., & Foshee, J. G. Comparative techniques for increasing attending behavior of retarded students. *Education and Training of the Mentally Retarded,* 1971, *6,* 4–11.

Brown, L., & Pearce, E. Increasing the production rates of trainable retarded students in a public school simulated workshop. *Education and Training of the Mentally Retarded*, 1970, *5,* 15–22.

Bucks County Public Schools. *Methods in vocational education: Program report to Pennsylvania Department of Education, Bureau of Vocational, Technical, and Continuing Education.* Doylestown, Pa., 1974.

Conley, R. *The economics of mental retardation.* Baltimore: Johns Hopkins Press, 1972.

Craighead, W. E., Kazdin, A. E., & Mahoney, M. J. *Behavior modification: Principles, issues, and applications.* Boston: Houghton Mifflin, 1976.

Ehrlich, P. *The population bomb.* San Francisco: Ballantine Books, 1970.

Farber, B. *Mental retardation: Its social concept and social consequences.* New York: Houghton Mifflin, 1968.

Foxx, R. M., & Azrin, M. H. *Toilet training the retarded.* Champaign, Ill.: Research Press, 1973.

Girardeau, F. L., & Spradlin, J. E. Token rewards on a cottage program. *Mental Retardation,* 1964, *2,* 345–351.

Gold, M. W. Preworkshop skills for the trainable: A sequential technique. *Education and Training of the Mentally Retarded,* 1968, *3,* 31–37.

Gold, M. W. Stimulus factors in skill training of the retarded on a complex assembly task: Acquisition, transfer, and retention. *American Journal of Mental Deficiency,* 1972, *76,* 517–526.

Gold, M. W. Research on the vocational habilitation of the retarded: The present, the future. In N. R. Ellis (Ed.), *International review of research in mental retardation* (Vol. VI). New York: Academic Press, 1973.

Gold, M. W. Vocational training. In J. Wortis (Ed.), *Mental retardation and developmental disabilities: An annual review* (Vol. 7). New York: Brunner Mazel, 1975.

Gold, M. W. Task analysis: A statement and an example using acquisition and production of a complex assembly task by the retarded blind. *Exceptional Children,* 1976, in press.

Gold, M. W., & Wade, M. G. Limitations of the retarded worker when maximizing the man-machine interface. *Human Factors,* 1976, in press.

Greenleigh Associates, Inc. *The role of the sheltered workshop in the rehabilitation of the severely handicapped.* Report to the Department of Health, Education, and Welfare, Rehabilitation Services Administration. New York, 1975.

Grossman, H., & Rowitz, L. A community approach to services for the retarded. In G. Tarjan, R. Eyman, & C. Meyers (Eds.), *Social behavioral studies in mental retardation.* Monograph of the American Association of Mental Deficiency, 1973.

Guess, D., Sailor, W., & Baer, D. M. To teach language to retarded children. In R. L. Schiefelbusch & L. L. Lloyd (Eds.), *Language perspectives: Acquisition, retardation, and intervention.* Baltimore: University Park Press, 1974.

Jordan, N. Allocation of functions between man and machines in automated systems. *Journal of Applied Psychology,* 1963, *47,* 161–165.

Korn, A. Fair labor standards and workshops. *Rehabilitation Record,* 1964, *5,* 30–31.

Lent, J. R. Teaching daily living skills. In J. M. Kauffman & J. S. Payne (Eds.), *Mental retardation: Introduction and personal perspectives.* Columbus, Ohio: Charles E. Merrill, 1975.

Leslie, G. R. *Supportive personnel in rehabilitation centers: Current practices and future needs.* Washington, D.C.: Association of Rehabilitation Centers, Inc., 1967.

Levy, S. M., Pomerantz, D. J., & Gold, M. W. Work skill development. In N. G. Haring & L. Brown (Eds.). Teaching the severely handicapped: A yearly publication of the American Association for the Education of the Severely/Profoundly Handicapped (Vol. I). New York: Grune & Stratton, 1976.

Marholin, D., II, & Bijou, S. W. A behavioral approach to the assessment of children's behavior disorders. *Child Welfare*, 1977, *56*, in press.

Marholin, D., II, & Siegel, L. J. Beyond the law of effect: Programming for the maintenance of behavioral change. In D. Marholin II (Ed.), *Child behavior therapy.* New York: Gardner Press, in press.

Marholin, D., II, Siegel, L. J., & Phillips, D. Transfer and treatment: A search for empirical procedures. In M. Hersen, R. M. Eisler, & P. M. Miller (Eds.), *Progress in behavior modification* (Vol III). New York: Academic Press, 1976.

Marholin, D., II, Steinman, W. M., McInnis, E. T., & Heads, T. B. The effect of a teacher's presence on the classroom behavior of conduct-problem children. *Journal of Abnormal Child Psychology,* 1975, *3,* 11–25.

Marholin, D., II, White, S., & Knowles, D. The right to treatment: Uses and abuses. *Social Work Today*, 1975, *6*, 418–420.

Meyen, E. L., & Altman, R. Public school programming for the severely/profoundly handicapped: Some researchable problems. *Education and Training of the Mentally Retarded,* 1976, *11,* 40–45.

Mischel, W. *Personality and assessment.* New York: John Wiley & Sons, 1968.

Nelson, N. *Workshops for the handicapped in the United States.* Springfield, Ill.: Charles C. Thomas, 1971.

O'Leary, K. D., & Wilson, G. T. *Behavior therapy: Application and outcome*. Englewood Cliffs, N.J.: Prentice-Hall, 1975.

Rappaport, J., & Chinsky, J. M. Models for delivery of service from a historical and conceptual perspective. *Professional Psychology,* 1974, *5,* 42–50.

Redd, W. H. Generalization of adult's stimulus control of children's behavior. *Journal of Experimental Child Psychology,* 1970, *9,* 286–296.

Rivera, G. *Willowbrook.* New York: Random House, 1972.

Rosenthal, R. *Pygmalion in the classroom: Teachers' expectation and pupils' intellectual development.* New York: Holt, Rinehart, & Winston, 1968.

Rothman, J. F. Organized labor and sheltered workshops. *Rehabilitation Record,* 1964, *5,* 28–29.

Ryan, W. *Blaming the victim.* New York: Random House, 1971.

Sarason, S. B. *The creation of settings and the future societies.* San Francisco: Jossey-Bass, 1972.

Slater, P. *The pursuit of loneliness.* Boston: Beacon Press, 1969.

Steed, F. R. *A special picture cookbook.* Lawrence, Kansas: H & H Enterprises, 1974.

Stroud, R. R. *Work measurement in rehabilitation workshops: Time study and predetermined motion time systems.* College Park (Md.): Regional Rehabilitation Research Institute, University of Maryland, Monograph No. 2, 1970.

Stuart, R. *Trick or treatment*. Champaign, Ill.: Research Press, 1970.

Tharp, R., & Wetzel, R. *Behavior modification in the natural environment.* New York: Academic Press, 1969.

Toffler, A. *Future shock.* New York: Random House, 1970.

Treuethan, P. J. Development and utilization of sheltered workshops and rehabilitation facilities in the United States. In N. Pacinelli (Ed.), *Research utilization in rehabilitation facilities.* Washington, D.C.: Social and Rehabilitation Service, U. S. Department of Health, Education, and Welfare, 1971.

Urban Report. *Executive summary of the comprehensive needs study of individuals with the most severe handicaps. Report to the Department of Health, Education and Welfare.* Washington, D.C., 1975.

Wahler, R. G. Setting generality: Some specific and general effects of child behavior therapy. *Journal of Applied Behavior Analysis,* 1969, *2,* 239–246.

Watson, L. S. *Child behavior modification: A manual for teachers, nurses, and parents.* New York: Pergamon Press, 1973.

Watzlawick, P., Weakland, J., & Fisch, R. *Change: Principles of problem formation and problem resolution.* New York: W. W. Norton, 1974.

Whitman, T. L., Mercurio, J. R., & Caponigri, V. Development of social responses in two severely retarded children. *Journal of Applied Behavior Analysis,* 1970, *3,* 133–138.

Wilbur, R. B. The linguistics of manual languages and manual systems. In L. Lloyd (Ed.). *Communication assessment and intervention strategies.* Baltimore: University Park Press, 1976.

Wolf, M. M., Phillips, E. L., & Fixsen, D. L. The teaching family: A new model for the treatment of deviant child behavior in the community. In S. W. Bijou & E. Ribes-Inesta (Eds.), *Behavior modification: Issues and extensions.* New York: Academic Press, 1972.

Wolfensberger, W. *The principle of normalization in human services*. Toronto: National Institute on Mental Retardation, 1972.

Zifferblatt, S. Analysis and design of counselor-training systems: An operant and operations research perspective. *Counseling Psychologist*, 1972, *4*, 12–31.

Zifferblatt, S. M., & Hendricks, C. G. Applied behavioral analysis of societal problems: Population change, a case in point. *American Psychologist,* 1974, *29,* 750–762.

DAVID POMERANTZ, a doctoral candidate in human development at the University of Illinois, is a Research Assistant in the Institute for Child Behavior and Development. He has served as a consultant to public school and sheltered workshop programs involved in vocational training of severely handicapped individuals and currently is developing and supervising a series of practical courses for students in a mental health paraprofessional training program.

DAVID MARHOLIN is Assistant Professor of Special Education at Boston University. His major interests include applications of behavior therapy techniques to juvenile corrections and mental health delivery systems, and to the effects of phenothiazines on specific social and cognitive behaviors of the retarded. He previously served as program director of Webster Hall, a community-based treatment program for delinquent females in Decatur, Illinois.

Simulating Real-Life Situations in a Classroom Setting: The Montgomery County Training Module

JEROME T. POTTER
Montgomery County Intermediate Unit

ANTHONY J. BIACCHI AND EVELYN A. RICHARDSON
National Learning Resource Center of Pennsylvania

Tom flipped the wall switch, but nothing happened. He shook his head and tried again. Still no light. He checked to see if the lamp was plugged into the receptacle. It was. He changed the light bulb and turned the lamp switch twice. Still nothing.

Must be the wall switch, he thought to himself. He went to the circuit breaker and flipped the lever, turning off the electricity. Then, returning to the switch with a tool box, he proceeded to replace the faulty device.

The scene created here might be a common occurrence for a normal teenager. But Tom is not normal. He is a 14-year-old trainable mentally retarded (TMR) child. And what he has done here—replace the defective electrical switch—demonstrates an ability that might well not have been demonstratable as recently as 10 years ago.

Historically, the plight of the mentally retarded has been one of almost total exclusion from the mainstream of society. This segregation typically began in the child's early years, in schools that all too often provided little more than custodial care. Special education classes often were mere repositories for children who were unable to adjust to regular education, and instructional efforts usually consisted of little more than watered-down curriculum or busywork (Mann, Note 1). Any attempt to prepare the retarded to become productive individuals focused on training them to live and work within a sheltered environment.

That situation is changing rapidly, however, as legislation and empirical research prompt exciting new efforts directed at teaching the mentally retarded to become truly functional citizens. Researchers (Gold, 1969, 1974; Bellamy, Peterson & Close, 1975; and Levy, 1975, among others), by demonstrating that the retarded can be taught to perform tasks previously considered beyond their intellectual level, have provided the impetus for curriculum specialists (such as Brown, Scheuerman, Cartwright & York, 1973; Brown & Sontag, 1972; Brown, Williams & Crowner, 1974) to develop new avenues for teaching the retarded. The results have proved fruitful as new methodology is being implemented successfully within the classroom setting.

Such cliches, therefore, as "*if* the mentally retarded can acquire certain vocational skills" and "*if* the mentally retarded are capable of tending to their basic home maintenance needs" should be discarded. The question today is: *how* should these skills be taught (Brown, 1973)?

In Pennsylvania, the Montgomery County Intermediate Unit stresses vocational training as a critical ingredient in its curriculum for mentally retarded students. This emphasis was adopted when an informal survey of retarded youngsters in county programs revealed that the children were lacking both vocational employment and basic home repair skills. Remediating these deficiencies in an environment that simulated a typical home setting became the goal of intermediate unit educators.

A prototype of an electrical training device (Figures 1 and 2)—called the Montgomery County Training Module (MCTM)—was constructed, and the intermediate unit began a four-month study to assess the utility of the device and the feasibility of its testing/instructional pro-

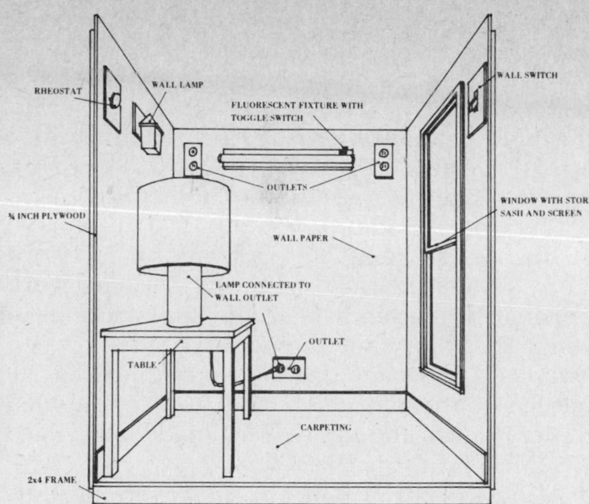

Figure 1. Front View—Montgomery County Training Module.

gram. Subjects who participated in this investigation were 30 pupils from two self-contained classes. In each class, approximately half the students, most of whom were boys, were functioning at the TMR level, and the other half, at the severely mentally retarded (SMR) level. Two teachers and two aides monitored the pilot study.

Teachers and students alike appeared eager to try out the module when it was unveiled. The children seemed relaxed and confident in this natural setting. (Brown [Note 2] stressed the importance of naturalizing instruction during a tour of Intermediate Unit Special Education facilities.) Those who were able were allowed to work the electrical switches. They had, of course, seen such items before, but they had never tried them. Most of the children, for example, had never pushed on a switch and seen a room light up. Enthusiasm was found to be a built-in feature of this new training device.

Testing began. Eight of the students were found to be capable of such preliminary tasks as turning lights on and off and plugging and unplugging an electrical cord. When the tasks became more complex, individual differences were noted. Thus, the assessment procedure used was found to be a viable means of determining entry-level skills of the students. (Entry-level skills are those abilities and knowledge in a particular content area an individual brings to the instructional situation.)

Based on the success of these early studies, instruction in vocational/home living skills has been formally incorporated into the intermediate unit's educational plan for the mentally retarded, and the MCTM has become a major means for channeling such instruction.

Modular teaching is now being carried out in a second intermediate unit-sponsored prevocational class for adolescent TMR students. Training here is focusing on painting and wallpapering skills and window and screen work, in addition to electrical tasks.

Description of the Module

The MCTM is a three-sided, floored device that is made to represent a typical room of a house. Appropriate fixtures and furnishings are included. The wall panels measure 4 × 4 ft. and the floor panel, 4 × 5 ft. The floor panel is mounted on four 2 × 4-in. × 4 ft. support beams and the side panels are attached to the base by four winged nuts. All panels are one-half inch thick. The hinged side panels can be extended to form a 4 × 12 ft. wall for group instruction, or they may be constricted to a 4 ft., three-sided unit for individualized instruction/demonstration. The module can be collapsed within minutes into a 4 × 5 ft. × 5-in. unit for easy transportation or storage.

This design was chosen because its developers wanted something that was large enough to represent a room, yet small enough that the device could be put into a station wagon and taken from school to school. Flexibility was another consideration in determining design. The module had to be constructed so that it could be opened for large group instruction, but small enough so that one child working

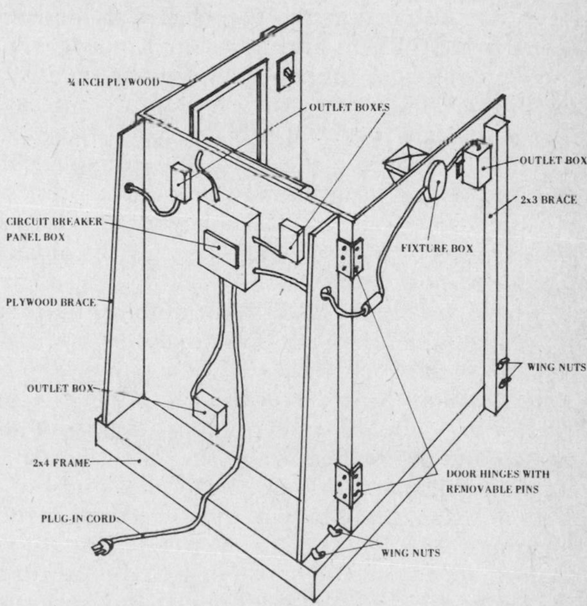

Figure 2. Rear View—Montgomery County Training Module.

within it would feel as if he were actually in a small room. The module also had to be sturdy, yet inexpensive and relatively easy to build.

The initial module was designed to provide instructional/experiential opportunities in the operation, repair, and maintenance of electrical apparatus. Included with this unit are such items as wall sockets, wiring, light bulbs, fluorescent tubes, and circuit breakers, all of which normally are found in the home.

Each unit contains a complete set of the tools needed to repair and restore components of the module to their original condition. Vocabulary lists, tools, and task-analyzed assessment/instructional procedures for accomplishing en-route objectives (Peter, 1972) accompany each module. The instructor's vocabulary list contains the jargon typical of the particular profession under study, in addition to the formal words regularly used. Both the words, "electricity" and "juice," for example, are included on the electrical module vocabulary list because "juice" is the term typically used by an electrician and the word the student would be more likely to hear used in the community or on the job.

It should be noted, too, that once the student learns to function within the module, components can be programmed by the teacher to contain certain defects, thus providing the opportunity for the student to locate and correct, or repair, these defects.

MCTM Evaluation Procedure

With construction on the electrical module nearing completion and additional modules in the design stage, the next step in the creation of the MCTM's was the development of an assessment/instructional procedure.

After considering the complexity of some of the operations programmed into the modules, it was decided to merge task analytic procedures with aspects of industrial engineering to formulate a pre-post test format.

Minge and Ball (1967) were among the first to realize the merit of task-analyzed instruction in their work with retarded patients in a state hospital. More recently, Knapczyk (1975) cited the value of task analysis as a tool to assess and program for the severely retarded, including instruction in prevocational education. Use of this methodology was underscored in the October, 1976, issue of *Exceptional Children*, when Gold stated that the most important product of his research with moderately and severely retarded individuals was task analysis.

The applicability of industrial engineering techniques, specifically Methods Time Measurement (MTM), a system that analyzes basic body movement and manual operations an individual performs during a human control activity (Antes, Honeycutt, & Koch, 1973), has been cited as a useful tool in the instruction of retarded students (Gold, 1973; Coombe, 1976). MTM may be explained as a work study system in which methods of doing work are analytically subdivided into basic motions to which predetermined time values have been assigned. The standards are determined by the nature of the movement and the condition(s) under which the motion is made (Maynard Research Council, 1962).

Also incorporated within the criterion-referenced assessment procedure are "decision verbs" (decisions the student makes during performance of the task), and method verbs (specific actions necessary to perform the activity, as described in the *Handbook for Analyzing Jobs*, 1972).

Collectively, these sources of information provide a test procedure that can indicate that the student performed a task successfully, possessed en-route abilities, or lacked the prerequisite skills necessary to perform the operation. This information is then used to individualize a unit of instruction.

Test format and student data sheets are included for each of the 12 assessment measures contained in the electrical module. In many instances, the same procedure and data sheets are appropriate for assessing more than one electrical apparatus, e.g., the same format can be used to test turning on a light, regardless of whether a wall switch, a rheostat, or a lamp switch is used. A three-step segment from Pretest #8 and its accompanying student data sheet are presented in Tables 1 and 2.

The test administration form for Pretest #8 (Table 1) consists of: the entry-level skills that should be mastered by the student; the decision verbs the student should be able to perform before entering the test situation; the method verbs and MTM motions the student will exhibit when changing a wall switch, rheostat, or wall outlet, and a list of the METWA (Materials, Equipment, Tools, Work Aides) required to test or teach the skill.

The actual test procedure, which starts at Step #1 at the lower segment of Table 1, contains two components: the step sequence required to complete the task, and the METWA needed. Included within an individual step, printed in capital letters, is the MTM motion, the decision verb, or the method verb spe-

TABLE 1.

Excerpt from Pretest #8—Changing a Wall Switch, Rheostat, or Wall Outlet.

8

TEST FORMAT FOR CHANGING A WALL SWITCH, RHEOSTAT, OR WALL OUTLET

Included in this pretest are the following:

Entry-Level Skills		Decision Verbs	Method Verbs
on - off	loose - tight	label (name)	bending
in - out	remove - replace	locate (find)	matching
			screwing
			tightening

MTM Motions	METW (Materials, Equipment, Tools, Work Aids) Needed		
apply pressure	wire - color coded	wall box	wall switch or
disengage (pull)	needle nose pliers	screws	rheostat or
engage (insert)	circuit breaker	screwdriver	wall outlet
grasp			
move			
position			
reach			
turn			

Because of the potential danger involved in working with live electrical wires, this pretest is broken down into three parts.

Part 1 takes place at a work table. It starts at Step 7 and terminates at Step 16.

Part 2 takes place in the electrical module, but the module has no electricity coming into it. This pretest starts at Step 1 and terminates after Step 21.

Part 3 follows Steps 1 through 22. However, the instructor is to terminate the pretest, if the student forgets to turn off the electricity at the circuit breaker in Step 1.

NOTE: Part 1, the pretest at the work table, starts at Step 7.

PRETEST FOR DISASSEMBLY	METWA
Step # 1. Turn off the electricity at the circuit breaker.	circuit breaker
a. LOCATE the circuit breaker.	
b. LOCATE circuit switch.	circuit breaker switch
c. Place (POSITION) hand on the switch.	
d. GRASP the switch.	
e. APPLY downward PRESSURE to the switch.	
f. RELEASE hand.	
2. LOCATE wall switch to be changed.	wall switch in wall
3. Remove (unscrew) both screws of the cover plate.	cover plate
a. LOCATE screwdriver.	screws
b. GRASP screwdriver.	screwdriver
c. LOCATE wall cover plate.	
d. LOCATE the two screws.	
e. INSERT (ENGAGE) screwdriver into screws.	
f. APPLY inward PRESSURE to the screwdriver.	
g. TURN (counterclockwise) the screwdriver.	
h. GRASP the screws and cover plate.	
i. Place (POSITION) screws and cover plate down.	
j. Maintain GRASP on screwdriver.	

cific to that step, and the METWA, which is underlined. For example, in Step #1a, the decision verb is LOCATE; the METWA to be located is *circuit breaker*. In Step #1c, the MTM motion to be performed is POSITION; the hand is to be placed, or positioned, on the circuit breaker *switch*.

The general instruction sheet for test administration (which is not included here) suggests that before pretesting a student, the teacher

TABLE 2.

Excerpt from Student Data Sheet for Pretest #8.

STUDENT DATA SHEET FOR CHANGING WALL SWITCH (✓), RHEOSTAT ( ), WALL OUTLET ( ) Pretest # 8

Coding System for Entry Level Skills & Decision Verbs:
P - Previously Taught
N - New Concept, First Contact

Part 1 ( )
Part 2 (✓)
Part 3 ( )

STEP	NAME:	Tom D.											
	DATE:	11-2-76	11-5	11-3	11-3	11-3	11-3	11-4	11-4				
ENTRY LEVEL SKILLS		Pre	Post	~~Pre~~	~~Post~~	~~Pre~~	~~Post~~	~~Pre~~	~~Post~~	Pre	Post	Pre	Post
	on-off	P	P										
	in-out	P	P										
	loose-tight	P	P										
	remove-replace	N	N										
	wall switch	P	P										
	rheostat	X	X										
	wall outlet	X	X										
DECISION VERBS													
	label (name)	P	P										
	locate (find)	P	P										
STEP	"Tom, change the wall switch."												
1.	LOCATE	✓	✓										
	LOCATE	✓	✓										
	POSITION	✓	✓										
	GRASP	✓	✓										
	APPLY PRESSURE	✓	✓										
	RELEASE	✓	✓										
2.	LOCATE	✓	✓										
3.	LOCATE	✓	✓										
	GRASP	✓	✓										
	LOCATE	✓	✓										
	LOCATE	✓	✓	✓	✓	✓	✓	✓	✓				
	ENGAGE (INSERT)	O	✓	O	✓	✓	✓	✓	✓				
	APPLY PRESSURE		✓		✓	✓	✓	✓	✓				
	TURN		✓		O	O	O	✓	✓				
	GRASP		✓					✓	✓				
	POSITION		✓					✓	✓				
	GRASP		✓					✓	✓				

should determine the child's entry-level skills. If the student is found to lack these prerequisite skills, assessing his manipulation of the electrical apparatus is not advised. Rather, instruction should begin with the entry-skills, and testing should be postponed until the prerequisite skills are demonstrated.

Some pretests contain more than one test phase because some electrical tasks are potentially injurious if performed improperly. In Pretest #8 (Table 1), for example, rather than risk subjecting a student to possible electrical shock while changing a wall switch, rheostat, or outlet, the instructor should first assess his ability to perform the operation(s) with the apparatus placed on a worktable (Part 1). In Part 2, the student, working in the module, is assessed with the wall box connected to a dead electrical line. Finally, the child is tested with the wall box connected to a live circuit (Part 3).

The student should successfully complete each step of the worktable pretest (both assembly and disassembly of the wall switch, and so on) before taking the same pretest using the electrical module with a dead circuit.

The same steps used in Part 2 testing (the dead circuit) are appropriate for Part 3 testing, assessment using the module with live electricity. The test format for Pretest #8, Part 1, differs from that of the other two phases because Part 1 testing is performed at a worktable. As a result, Part 1 assessment does not involve as many operations as Parts 2 and 3 pretests (e.g., turning off the circuit breaker and then turning it on again after replacing the wall switch is not included). Part 1 testing starts at Step 7 in the task-analyzed test sequence and terminates at Step 16. Parts 2 and 3 test procedures have 22 and 23 steps, respectively.

Table 2 contains three of the more than 20 steps taken from the student data sheet that accompanies Pretest #8, the test format presented in Table 1.

The top portion of the data sheet provides space to indicate the electrical apparatus being tested and the appropriate test phase. Below this section is space for the name of the student being assessed and the date of test administration. As can be seen in Table 2, the same data sheet can be used for both pretest and posttest administration. If the teacher blocks out the words "pre" and "post" from the form, the data sheet also can be used during remediation. Thus, the data sheet can be used a number of times with one student or simultaneously with several students.

The marking system suggested for the student data sheet is fairly simple. As noted earlier, the test administrator should determine the student's entry-level skills. If these concepts have been taught or if the tester is confident that the child can demonstrate such knowledge, the teacher marks a "P" under the student's name/test date column and across from the particular skill. When a concept required for successful manipulation of the electrical apparatus is new to the child, the teacher may mark an "N" in the appropriate space.

When the teacher finds that the student possesses the prerequisite skills, test administration begins. The examiner should simply tell the student, verbally or through gesture, to perform the entire task, rather than its individual steps, e.g., "Tom, remove the wall switch."

This procedure assesses the student's competence without outside cues. Teacher input and prompting should be reserved until instruction is initiated. As each step or substep is performed, the examiner makes the appropriate notation on the student data sheet.

The scope of the pretest embodies the electrical operations and the sequence of steps within a skill area which are required for successful manipulation of the apparatus. The pretest results, then, become the blueprint for instruction, and the pretest steps failed by the child become the instructional objectives within a teaching unit. This task-analyzed format also can be used to assess and teach the students using an end (backward) chaining instructional procedure, where the last part of the task is taught first, then the next to the last part is taught, and so on. Because remedial techniques and instructional materials may differ according to the needs of each student, no other mention of specific teaching procedures is made in this article. However, the instructor should be cognizant of safety factors, as well as of appropriate vocabulary, when formulating an individual educational prescription.

Following instruction, a posttest is administered to measure the student's degree of success in acquiring the skills presented. The pretest format may be used for this purpose. The posttest sequence need differ only if the pretest contains more than one part, or if the examiner decided to forego Parts 1 or 2 posttesting. The example presented in Tables 1 and 2 could be included in this category, since replacing a rheostat and an outlet are tested after the student has changed the wall switch. An example of how to use the data sheet follows. Tables 1 and 2 may be referred to for clarification.

Example

A student was administered Pretest #8, Part 2, to determine his ability to replace the wall switch on the electrical module. The results contained on the data sheet (Table 2) show that the student possessed the necessary entry-level skills and that he previously had been able to label (name) and locate appropriate objects upon request. The student then was told, "Tom, replace the wall switch." Actual test results revealed that he knew, first, to locate and turn off the electricity at the circuit breaker (Step 1), and that he could locate the wall switch to be replaced (Step 2). However, he was unable to complete Step 3, which required removing the screws that support the coverplate; the student was unable to engage the blade of the screwdriver into the recess of the screw.

An "0" (or whatever symbol the teacher chooses to indicate the student's inability to perform the task) was placed in the column across from "INSERT (ENGAGE) screwdriver into screw(s)," and also under 11-1-76, the date of the pretest. The remaining operations within Step 3 were left untested because of the student's earlier failure.

The baseline for instruction thus had been established; remediation would begin with instruction on how to insert a screwdriver into the notch of a screw.

To document student progress during instruction, the data sheet was again used. However, specific curricular content and methodology were not recorded on the data sheet. This information could be recorded on a separate document.

As can be seen in the third, fourth, and fifth rows of Figure 4, the teacher recorded the dates of instruction, crossed out the words "pre" and "post," and documented progress made during each instructional trial.

When the teacher was confident that the student could perform all of the tasks within a step, the child was posttested. Posttest results are reported in the second row (under the date, 11/5/76) of the data sheet.

What has been described is only a suggested procedure for using the data sheet. Teachers are encouraged to modify the recording system, based on individual teaching style and student needs.

Also, it should be noted that the assessment and instructional procedures described above are actually the eighth of 12 tasks incorporated into the electrical module evaluation and management system. Examples of more basic operations include: turning a switch on and off, plugging and unplugging an electrical cord and changing a light bulb or fluorescent light. These are the types of repair tasks a severely impaired student should be capable of handling.

Safety Considerations

Safety should be considered an integral part of electrical modular instruction. Careful supervision during training on all tasks is essential since possibilities for injury abound. The wisest course is to train the student to act safely and carefully when manipulating the electrical devices, thereby avoiding accidents. However, the instructor should be prepared to meet any emergency with calm, efficient action.

Among the safety considerations that should be emphasized in using the electrical module are:

—Have dry, clean hands when touching an electrical appliance.
—Remove an electrical plug by pulling on the plug, not the cord.
—Keep electrical outlets from being overloaded.
—Do not use frayed wiring.
—Keep hands away from illuminated light bulbs and lamps.
—When cutting, always point knife or other cutting utensil away from body.
—Never substitute METWA for the sake of convenience. If an analysis calls for a specific piece of equipment, use only that apparatus.

Conclusion

The MCTM was designed for use primarily with trainable and educable mentally retarded students, although, as has been pointed out, the device has been used successfully with the severely impaired as well. Based on preliminary success with the electrical module, its developers believe that this and other units also can be used effectively with other special education students; namely, learning disabled and the emotionally disturbed. The authors view the module as an adjunct tool to complement the home economics and workshop programs typically offered retarded students. In addition, they suggest that the device has value for use in regular elementary schools to acquaint children with the dangers of such home fixtures and to teach them the need for care in handling such devices.

The developers of the MCTM acknowledge that not all retarded students will be able to successfully complete all the tasks contained within a particular teaching unit. Many of the more severely retarded, for example, may not be capable of actually repairing defective electrical devices. But they can be taught to perform simple related tasks, to recognize when something is broken or not working properly, and to know when it is time to call for help.

The MCTM was not designed to make full-fledged plumbers or electricians of these retarded pupils. The value of the module lies in providing these students with a working knowledge of the tools and language used in particular trades. As a result, many retarded individuals can, for example, become plumber's or electrician's helpers.

And, perhaps, more significantly, many will be able to assume home maintenance duties, thus assuring them a new degree of self-sufficient living once they leave school and go out into the community. As Wehman (1975) noted, vocational training and self-sufficient home living go hand-in-hand: "A major factor in habilitating mentally retarded adults into community living is effective vocational training" (p. 342).

Reference Notes

1. Mann, L. Personal communication, June 8, 1976.
2. Brown, L. Personal communication, March, 1976.

References

Antes, W., Honeycutt, J. N. Jr., & Koch, E. N. *The basic motions of MTM*. Naples, Fla.: The Maynard Foundation, 1973.

Bellamy, G. T., Peterson, L., & Close, D. Habilitation of the severely and profoundly retarded: Illustrations of competence. *Education and Training of the Mentally Retarded*, 1975, *10*, 174–185.

Brown, L. Instructional programs for trainable level retarded students, In L. Mann & D. A. Sabatino (Eds.), *The first review of special education* (Vol. 2). Philadelphia: Journal of Special Education Press, 1973.

Brown, L., Scheuerman, N., Cartwright, S., & York, R. (Eds.). *Design and implementation of an empirically based instructional program for young severely handicapped students: Toward the rejection of the exclusion principle*. Part III. Madison, Wis: Madison Public Schools, Department of Specialized Educational Services, 1973.

Brown, L. & Sontag, E. (Eds.). *Toward the development and implementation of an empirically based public school program for the trainable mentally retarded and severely emotionally disturbed students*. Part II. Madison, Wis: Madison Public Schools, Department of Specialized Educational Services, 1972.

Brown, L., Williams, W., & Crowner, T. (Eds.). *A collection of papers and programs related to public school services for severely handicapped students*. Part IV. Madison, Wis: Madison Public Schools, Department of Specialized Educational Services, 1974.

Coombe, E. J. Human factors engineering. In D. N. Lapedes (Ed.). *McGraw-Hill yearbook of science and technology*. New York: McGraw-Hill, 1976.

Gold, M. W. *The acquisition of a complex assembly task by retarded adolescents*. Final Report, May 1969, University of Illinois at Urbana-Champaign.

Gold, M. W. Research on the vocational habilitation of the retarded: The present, the future. In N. R. Ellis (Ed.). *International review of research in mental retardation*. New York: Academic Press, 1973.

Gold, M. W. Redundant cue removal in skill training for the retarded. *Education and Training of the Mentally Retarded*, 1974, *9*, 5–8.

Gold, M. W. Task analysis of a complex assembly task by the retarded blind. *Exceptional Children*, 1976, *43*, 78–84.

Knapczyk, D. R. Task analytic assessment of severe learning problems. *Education and Training of the Mentally Retarded*, 1975, *10*, 74–77.

Levy, S. M. *The development of work skill training procedures for the assembly of printed circuit boards by the severely handicapped*. Final Report, June 1975, University of Oregon, Eugene, Oregon.

Manpower Administration, U.S. Department of Labor. *Handbook for analyzing jobs*. Washington: Government Printing Office, 1972.

Maynard Research Council Inc. *High achievement multimedia training course*. Pittsburgh: Author, 1962.

Minge, M. R., & Ball, T. S. Teaching of self-help skills to profoundly retarded patients. *American Journal of Mental Deficiency*, 1967, *71*, 864–868.

Peter, L. J. *Individual Instruction*. New York: McGraw-Hill, 1972.

Wehman, P. H. Toward a social skills curriculum for developmentally disabled clients in vocational settings. *Rehabilitation Literature*, 1975, *35*, 342–348.

ANTHONY J. BIACCHI is Evaluation Specialist for the National Learning Resource Center of Pennsylvania, King of Prussia, Pennsylvania.

JEROME T. POTTER is Supervisor of the Center for Developmental Education, Norristown, Pa., which is sponsored by Montgomery County Intermediate Unit #23, Pennsylvania.

EVELYN A. RICHARDSON is a Product Development Specialist for the National Learning Resource Center of Pennsylvania, King of Prussia, Pennsylvania.

Important Right-to-Education Decision: Pennsylvania

PENNSYLVANIA ASSOCIATION FOR RETARDED CITIZENS v. PENNSYLVANIA, 334 F. Supp. 1257 (E.D. PA. 1971) and 343 F. Supp. 279 (E.D. PA 1972)

In May 1972, a three-judge federal court ratified a consent agreement assuring all retarded children in the state the right to publicly supported schooling appropriate to their needs. The agreement specifically required that:

- The state locate all excluded children.
- Local school districts evaluate all retarded children in their jurisdiction.
- All retarded children in special classes be reevaluated every two years
- Children be placed in programs appropriate to their capacity.
- Parents be extended all rights of due process.

Important Right-to-Education Decision: District of Columbia

MILLS v. BOARD OF EDUCATION OF DISTRICT OF COLUMBIA, 348 F. Supp. 866 (D.D.C. 1972)

The landmark decision by Federal Court Judge Joseph Waddy extended the right to education to all children previously denied the benefits of an education. Specifically, Waddy ordered that every school-aged child residing in the District of Columbia shall be provided ". . . a free and suitable publicly supported education regardless of the degree of the child's mental, physical, or emotional disability or impairment . . . ."

Important Right-to-Education Decision: North Dakota

IN THE INTEREST OF G. H., A CHILD (N.D. Supreme Court, C. A. No. 8930, 1974)

The North Dakota State Supreme Court affirmed that the right to a public school education is guaranteed by the State Constitution. It also ruled that the residence of a child determines the identity of the school district responsible for providing an education. Placing a child in a special program outside the district does not change the residence of the child.

Important Right-to-Education Decision: Maryland

MARYLAND ASSOCIATION FOR RETARDED CHILDREN v. STATE OF MARYLAND, Equity No. 100-182-77676 (Circuit Court, Baltimore City, Maryland, 1974)

The Court stated that Maryland law guarantees free education to *all* handicapped children in the state. Mental retardation is not a condition that justifies home teaching instead of classroom instruction, and placement in private facilities is outlawed unless such facilities provide accredited educational programs and can admit the child to the program rather than placement on a waiting list.

Information furnished by the Council for Exceptional Children

VI Services: Infant and Preschool Populations

Early experience does have an influence, and that influence affects all areas of functioning. Research has shown that there may be critical periods for the development of certain skills, and that most of these periods may occur during the first three years of life. Failure to provide a stimulating early environment leads not only to a continuation of the developmental status quo, but to actual atrophy of sensory abilities and to developmental regression.

Alice H. Hayden and Gael D. McGinness

Bases for Early Intervention

ALICE H. HAYDEN
University of Washington
GAEL D. McGINNESS
University of North Carolina

With the recent passage of Public Law 94-142, public education for the severely/profoundly handicapped child has become a matter of recognized right. While we applaud the passage of this legislation, we cannot help but be concerned that it extends this right only to those children over the age of three, whereas all that we now know about early development suggests that it is the first three years that are of major importance:

> After 17 years of research on how human beings acquire their abilities, I have become convinced that it is to the first three years of life that we should now turn most of our attention. My own studies, as well as the work of many others, have clearly indicated that the experiences of those first years are far more important than we had previously thought. In their simple everyday activities, infants and toddlers form the foundations of *all* later development. [White, 1975, p. xi]

Until we are able to point to a well-established system of public education for the handicapped child from the moment when his handicap is identified, we cannot rest content. Even then, there will need to be refinements and continued efforts to make the system more efficient and effective. That task is one of such scope that today our first order of business must be that of public education. Charting a future course for the care of the infant and preschool child with a severe handicap must begin with informing society about basic issues, such as what intervention can and cannot do.

Why Early Intervention?

> *Responsibility implies always asking whether one is justified in intervening, and considering what value the goal has for both the individual and society.*
> –*William Yule*, Behavior Modification with the Severely Retarded, *Study Group 8 of the Institute for Mental and Multiple Handicap, ISBN 90 219 5006 6 and 0-444-14191-5.*

No one involved in early intervention escapes asking himself why one ought to engage in such an effort, if only because the question is asked of us so often by others. Self-questioning inevitably follows questioning by parents, legislators, and colleagues in behavioral sciences. We would like to begin by offering a brief list of reasons for early intervention, and then go on to develop some of these rationales at greater length, on the basis of some of the more dramatic or more recent evidence in favor of early intervention. The following list is not intended to be complete or exhaustive, but it does offer some of the most salient responses of educators to the question: "Why do you want to start with an infant who can't even talk (or walk or sit up) yet?"

When a child is shown to have a handicap or to be at high risk for developmental disabilities, we intervene as early as possible because:

1. Early experience *does* have an influence, and that influence affects all areas of functioning.
2. Research has shown that there may be critical periods for the development of certain skills, and that most of these periods may occur during the first three years of life.
3. Failure to provide a stimulating early environment leads not only to a continuation of the developmental status quo, but to actual atrophy of sensory abilities and to developmental regression.
4. All systems of an organism are interrelated in a dynamic way; failure to remediate one handicap may multiply its effects in other developmental areas, and may produce other handicaps (particularly social and emotional ones) that are secondary to the initial insult.
5. With a delay in remediating an intellectual or cognitive handicap, there is a cumulative achievement decrement even within a *single* area of functioning, apart from the danger of secondary emotional or social handicaps; that is, the condition is progressive—the child's developmental status inevitably becomes worse with respect to other children as he grows older.
6. Early intervention *has* been shown to help: it can work to reduce the effects of a handicapping condition, and can do so more surely and rapidly than later intervention.

7. The cost-benefit ratio of early intervention usually makes it more economical than later intervention.
8. Parents need support during early weeks and months, before patterns of parenting become established.
9. Parents need models of good parenting behavior with a handicapped child, and specific instructions for working with the child.

The Dependency of Nature on Nurture

Early experience does *have an influence, and that influence affects all areas of functioning.*

Primacy of Natural Influences

The day is long gone when educators believed that a newborn child is simply a blank slate upon which experience might write any sort of story. We know now that the biological organism is the basis for all behavior. One indication of this is that very considerable repertoires of reflexive behavior exist at birth. Such behavior is used by physicians to conduct rapid screening of infants in the delivery room, where an Apgar score is derived 60 seconds after birth from five separate criteria (color, heart rate, muscle tone, reflex irritability, and respiratory effort) and is used to indicate which infants need further follow-up or intensive care.

The infant is not merely a vegetative organism, as once was thought. The range of capabilities the infant is born with attests to the important part nature plays in what we later come to see as intelligent behavior. Protective reflexes and such adaptive behaviors as the ability to cry to summon help are indications of the primacy of natural influences on behavior. Indeed, using more fine-focus indicators than the Apgar rating to determine the presence or absence and relative strength of these reflexive behaviors, Brazelton (1973), Prechtl and Beintema (1964), and many others have devised neonatal assessment scales that have fair predictive validity with respect to later functioning.

You Can't Change Nature

Lay persons and even developmental psychologists have occasionally claimed that intervention with a handicapped child is probably useless. They have said that the developmental outcome (barring a major environmental insult) probably depends more on heredity or "nature" than on the environmental experiences of the organism after birth. Their theory was that a child's development could be likened to that of a flower, whose entire life course is contained in the seed from which it grows. We intend to challenge this theory and to develop the thesis that nurture in the life of a child—and particularly of a handicapped child—is of critical importance.

Before we do so, we would like to acknowledge the other side of the question, that of nature, because we believe that the only valid viewpoint is the one which holds the development of a child to be a dynamic, interactive process involving components of both nature and nurture. Because we are inclined to stress the environmental component rather strongly, it is important to give a balancing emphasis to biological or natural factors.

Maturation

There are significant indications that nature has a great deal to do with behavior development. For example, a child will occasionally progress along some behavioral lines during a vacation from a training program at the same rate as during training, despite the fact that he has had no practice. We have found this in working with infants in the Experimental Education Unit's Center for the Severely Handicapped. Occasionally, an infant who is being trained in visual discrimination or some such task will go off on holiday and come back further advanced in the skill, although he has had no practice (Gentry, 1975). One study in which identical twins were being taught to ride tricycles (one twin at an early age and the other twin at a later age) implied more or less the same thing about the influence of maturation. The twin taught to ride the tricycle at an early age learned to ride only after much training, but the twin not taught until much later quickly caught up, once his training began, to the level that the other twin had reached earlier. Neither twin ever reached a greater level of skill in tricycle riding than the other. The investigators who conducted this study concluded, therefore, that the major antecedent of some motor skills was neither training nor practice, but rather the maturation of certain muscular systems, of the ability to perform those skills at the biological level (Sears, Maccoby, & Levin, 1957).

Similar studies with twins have shown the influence of nature on performance with respect to intelligence (Bodmer & Cavalli-Sforza, 1970; Kagan, 1971); several studies have also been reported on the inheritance of schizophrenia (Kallman, 1959). Collectively, these highly controlled and frequently replicated investigations leave no doubt that genetic, or inherited, influences profoundly affect developmental outcomes. The following quotation from the Bodmer & Cavalli-

Sforza article indicates how, with respect to intelligence, the press of inheritance is heavy indeed:

> Effects of environment can be measured by comparing correlation coefficients of individuals with similar genetic backgrounds reared in different environments and those with different backgrounds reared in the same environment. Published data collected by Erlenmeyer-Kimling and Jarvik show that unrelated persons reared together have coefficients that range from about .15 to slightly over .30. Coefficients for foster-parents and children range from .16 to almost .40. Siblings reared apart have coefficients that range from more than .30 to more than .40. Siblings reared together have coefficients that range from .30 to almost .80. Monozygous twins reared apart have coefficients that range from more than .60 to above .80, and monozygous twins reared together have coefficients of more than .70 to more than .90. *It appears that environment affects intelligence but not as strongly as heredity does*. [1970, p. 127]

Interactive Nature of Experience/Heredity on Intelligence

Many investigators have therefore concluded, as we have, that it is simplistic to view intelligence as a fixed potential or a trait, latently present in early infancy and gradually unfolding with maturation. Nor can we say that experience is prepotent. Most insist that intelligence must be viewed as an interaction phenomenon:

> Since the organism brings to each adaptive act certain properties, both those of an intrinsic biological nature and those which are the result of the impact of previous experience upon the organism, it is correct to say that intelligence development is at all times dependent upon what the organism is like. Yet, since it requires environmental circumstance to mobilize the organism, and since the kind of transaction which develops depends on the objective content of that to which the organism must adapt, it is equally true to say that the development of intelligence depends at all times on the experience encountered by the growing child. [Escalona & Moriarty, 1961, p. 597.]

The Influence of the Nurturing Evironment

As mentioned earlier, some investigators have at times been so strongly impressed with nature's influence that they conclude that nurture is of little significance in behavioral development. They claim that, provided an even moderately nurturing environment is available, the child will develop to the level he was "destined" to reach, despite minor variations in experience (Evans, 1975). Nevertheless, most recent investigations have demonstrated that environment is extremely important to the growth process. Sandra Scarr-Salapatek and Richard Weinberg reported in a recent issue of *Psychology Today* (December, 1975) that early intervention in the form of adoption of a disadvantaged child can prevent a learning handicap from occurring. They were interested in finding out whether a black child adopted by a white family would or would not show the usual 15-point decrement in IQ that children of black families in the United States characteristically display. On tests of intelligence, black children ordinarily score 15 points below white children from a presumably comparable environment and economic status. Scarr-Salapatek and Weinberg suspected that the environments probably were not really comparable; they looked at families adopting black infants from disadvantaged backgrounds to see just what the results of this adoption would be later in the child's life. They found that a black child adopted by a white family would indeed match almost exactly the other white siblings in the family on tests of intelligence.

The implication, again, is that providing an appropriately nurturing environment is extremely important to the development of normal or near normal behavior. Among the longitudinal studies demonstrating this conclusively, one thinks in particular of the work of Burton White as described in his two recent books, *Experience and Environment* (1973) and *The First Three Years of Life* (1975). Both books are based upon extensive research to discover which elements in the environment may or may not influence intellectual or adaptive-behavior development, and, even in the most rudimentary reflexive and sensory areas of behavior, environment has been shown to be critically important.

Early Experience: Effects on Behavior

The importance of environmental or experiential impact was clearly shown when three or four day old infants were examined in a study conducted by Lipsitt and Kaye (1973) to see if classical conditioning of sucking behavior could occur at such an early age. A non-nutritive nipple was used to elicit a sucking response. It was paired with an auditory tone lasting 15 seconds. The experimental group subsequently exhibited significant numbers of sucking responses to the sound of the tone alone.

An attempt was made by Connolly and Stratton (1973) to condition the Bablin reflex (a wide opening of the mouth, turning the head toward the midline from the tonic-neck-reflex position, frequently followed by raising the head in the midline position) to an auditory stimulus (a burst of white noise). In this study, the subjects were infants only 50 to 90 hours old, yet they were successfully conditioned by manipulating environmental events. Such demonstrations of early receptivity to conditioning in the newborn imply that early intervention can be effective.

Influence on Vision

In 1965, Haynes, White, and Held investigated several parameters of visual ability in the young infant. They found that, although at the age of one month the infant has a certain amount of difficulty in focusing on objects, by the time the infant is four months old his visual development is the same as that of a young adult. However, if the young organism lacks appropriate early visual experiences, this ability is markedly decreased. Riesen, in 1950, demonstrated that chimpanzees reared in total darkness from birth to 16 months of age never developed normal vision: ". . . it appears that lack of practice, at least if sufficiently prolonged, can interfere with the development of behavior which is basically instinctive or reflexive in nature" (Riesen, 1973). This clearly suggests that the experiences provided in the environment can be very important. Gibson and Walk (1973), in similar investigations into the development of visual ability, showed that depth perception appears as soon as most infants can move about and that hearing, taste, touch, and kinesthetic sensibilities are also present in very early behavior.

However, not only vision but every sensory system is capable of being damaged by deprivation of early experience. Indeed, probably the largest number of studies that have been done on the effects of experience on behavior in animals involve introducing some deprivation of sensory input or social stimulation and then measuring the effects of that deprivation. Virtually all studies we have reviewed confirm that the lack of experience to stimulate sensory systems is damaging to those systems.

Influence on Social Behavior

In the area of social behavior, Harlow, whose early experiments with monkeys (Harlow, 1973; Harlow & Harlow, 1973) offered further evidence about the importance of the maternal-infant tie, has demonstrated conclusively that deprivation of an early mother-infant relationship has a devastating effect on the organism's functioning as an adult. This is true not only in the areas of social interaction, but in cognitive functioning and even in sexual behavior. Even partial social deprivation (in which monkeys could see and hear others but could not touch them) resulted in bizarre personal-social behavior, such as "sitting and staring, stereotyped repetitive patterns, self-aggression" (Harlow, 1973, p. 826). Spitz (1973) and Yarrow (1961) observed an analogous phenomenon in babies who had been separated from their mothers, particularly (in the Spitz study) during the London bombings of World War II.

Influence on Actual Physical Growth—Deprivation Dwarfism

So important is the stimulating environment to adequate social and emotional development, that Lyte Gardner, in 1972, began studying infants who had been raised in apparently deprived environments in an attempt to uncover the underlying mechanism in social deprivation. He found, in particular, that a child who is raised in an emotionally deprived environment will typically (over time) show deprivation dwarfism, or a lower rate of growth in height and weight than is normal for children in his earlier-projected growth grid. Such children actually show inhibition of pituitary hormone secretion, including the growth hormone; this constitutes a very dramatic example of the interactive dynamics of the biological and physical organism with the social environment.

In fact, as these studies show, the biological organism itself can be influenced by the emotional environment to change physio-chemically. The child is simply not the same child in his very hormone secretions if he is deprived of a normal, stimulating environment and, in particular, if he is deprived of a normal mother-child relationship.

Influence on Cognitive Functioning

Stimulus deprivation effects show up clearly in such areas as cognitive functioning and exploratory behavior, but investigators have shown that normal "handling" experience in any complex environment provides a healthy level of stress (Levine, 1973) which frequently results in beneficial brain and central nervous system changes. This has been demonstrated primarily in monkeys and other animals which have been used for deprivation experiments and later sacrificed. At autopsy, these animals showed distinct differences from those which had been stimulated (by handling or even electric shock) in the environment. Apparently, stimulative handling is so important to the development of normal behavior, that even painful stimulation is better than no stimulation:

> When in 1954 we began our investigation into the broad area defined by this question, we naturally turned first to presumably more obvious effects [on development] of early painful or traumatic experience. We subjected a group of infant rats to mild electric shocks, scheduled at the same hour each day. For control purposes we routinely placed the members of another group in the shock cage for the same length of time each day but did not give them shocks. A third group of infant rats was left in the nest and not handled at all. We expected that the shocked rats would be affected by their experience, and we looked for signs of emotional disturbance when they reached adulthood. To our surprise it was the second control group—the rats we had not handled at all—that behaved in a peculiar manner. The behavior of the shocked rats could not be distinguished from that of the control group which had experienced the same handling but no electric shock. Thus, the results of our first experiment caused us to reframe our question. Our investigations . . . have since been concerned not with the effects of stressful experience—which is after all the usual experience of infants—so much as with effects of the absence of such experience in infancy. [Levine, 1973, p. 55]

Influence on Language

The most easily appreciated environmental influence on the organism has been language. Although even a deaf infant will babble at 4 to 6 months, babbling in the deaf child drops off after a time because of lack of feedback, lack of reinforcement. Similarly, although at a less dramatic level, the language development of any child is compromised if that development is not supported by an environment that stimulates the child, offers the child examples of names for objects, asks questions, and in general responds to communication that the child initiates.

Because language development so obviously depends on the environment, intervention to promote better language experiences has had a long history of public acceptance, assisted by research findings such as the following: data consistently indicate that there is a positive correlation between maternal response to infant behavior, such as vocalizing and crying, and the cognitive development of the infant as measured by response decrement (Lewis & Goldberg, 1973). Furthermore, the correlations indicate that "the latency of the maternal response and contingency of maternal response . . . are important variables. Mother must act contingently toward the infant for him to learn to expect his actions to have an effect on the environment" (p. 963).

Unfortunately, knowledge of the importance of language development has not disseminated to all social and economic groups; Tulkin and Kagan (1973) found a difference in verbal, but not non-verbal behavior, between middle and working class mothers. "Some working class mothers did not believe that their infants possessed the ability to express 'adult-like' emotions or to communicate with other people. Hence, the mothers felt it was futile to attempt to interact [verbally] with their infants" (p. 953).

Influence on "Purely" Biological Processes

Apparently, too, in the area of biological functioning, even an ostensibly genetic phenomenon (for instance, the inherited metabolic dysfunction phenylketonuria or PKU) responds to dietary manipulation. Diet, of course, is an environmental matter; it is therefore unnecessary to conclude that intervention is fruitless where nature seems to be most influential, no matter how "purely" biological a process or development may be. It may be the case that an environmental change can redirect a "natural" course. Since this is so, the discovery that a handicap is natural in origin should not keep us from trying to find an environmental remedy. Although this may seem obvious, it is surprising how many parents and teachers tend to despair when a handicap is shown to result from a biological condition.

A recent example of intervention in an inherited biological disorder involved the use of amniocentesis to diagnose the condition. It has been known for some time that amniocentesis could alert the prospective mother and her physician to the presence of a number of seriously handicapping conditions. But the only alternative offered to the mother, in the event that the procedure showed her to be carrying a developmentally disabled child, was until recently the alternative to abort the pregnancy. As we have discussed in a previous publication (Hayden, McGinness, & Dmitriev, in press) we have found many parents reluctant to consider this alternative and anxious to maintain any pregnancy out of a very deep wish to have a child, regardless of its potential handicaps. Recently, however, it has been reported even in the popular press (Galton, 1976) that amniocentesis can be used to diagnose methylmalonic acidemia, "an inherited disorder characterized by abnormal accumulation of acids, recurrent vomiting, developmental retardation and failure to thrive," (p. 13) and then to treat it in the developing fetus. The physician involved, Dr. Mary Ampola, conjectured that administering large doses of vitamin B_{12} to the mother while the child was still in utero would help to correct the condition. The baby so treated was delivered and is now, at one and a half years, entirely normal. We have often insisted that the critical variable in early intervention is identification (Haring, Hayden, & Beck, 1976); unless we know that a problem exists, we are unlikely to do anything to help correct it.

"Nature versus Nurture" Is the Wrong Issue

All the research available to us leads to the same conclusion that we stated earlier: the development of any human ability results from a complex dynamic interaction, one to which both nature and nurture contribute in an almost incredibly complicated way. Someone has said that the answer to the age-old question, "Which is more important?", is "It is 100% nature and 100% nurture." That is only apparently a paradox; in fact, it seems to be literally the best answer to the old question at this stage of the game. Again, we believe that what is needed is more research to tease out how much of the variation in each particular behavioral system is accounted for by nature and how much by nurture. Exactly what amounts of both factors do influence the development of specific appropriate behaviors? This is the area that is most exciting at the moment.

Exploiting Critical Periods

Research has shown that there may be critical periods for the development of certain skills, and that most of these periods may occur during the first three years of life.

Early intervention is important, not only to prevent handicaps, but also to take advantage of those critical periods which occur in the life of every organism for developing certain skills and abilities.

> In addition to the process of learning about the environment, there seem to be a number of cases in which basic systems of the organism, which will allow it to interact with its surroundings, are fine-tuned by stimuli present in the surroundings during the organism's early development. Since the organism is maturing quite rapidly during the period following its birth, the time span during which certain types of environmental events have their maximal effect on development is often quite short. Such a limited time span, during which the organism is most sensitive (or at all sensitive) to some aspect of its environment, is often called a 'critical period.'
>
> A useful way to view critical periods is as a time of *lowered threshold* for certain experiences. Following the critical period of lowest threshold, the threshold may remain sufficiently low that the same, or a more intense, experience will result in normal development; alternatively, the threshold may rise to such an extent that naturally occurring stimulation cannot have its developmental effect. [Greenough, 1973, pp. 46–47]

Failure to provide a stimulating early environment leads not only to a continuation of the developmental status quo, *but to actual atrophy of sensory abilities and to developmental regression.*

Although an infant is born with basic visual equipment and can often see at birth or within four months almost as well as an adult can on many measures, particularly pattern discrimination (Fantz, 1973), deprivation of early visual experience (at least in animals) has resulted in atrophy of the physical structures of vision and, therefore, permanent blindness. With vision, nature provides the structure, but nurture (or stimulating visual experiences) is absolutely required to keep that structure functional.

Interestingly, in terms of our own views on early intervention, not only may actual atrophy of the retina and optic nerve occur because of visual deprivation, but the danger of damage to the basic structure is greatest if it occurs during the critical period for development. If the deprivation occurs later in life, it will have some serious effects, but they will not begin to approximate the very damaging effects of infantile deprivation.

Further, minor deprivation in the critical period may be compensated for later in life, but it will take much more intense and prolonged experience to bring the organism back to near-normal functioning than if the same deprivation had occurred later in life. These few findings about visual development, critical periods for learning visual skills, and developmental regression following stimulus deprivation are taken from a single article (Riesen, 1973), yet they are rich in implications for early intervention in special education. Reading the literature on early development from the standpoint of preventing developmental disability and correcting it if it should occur despite prevention efforts, one is struck by the force of the evidence which this critical period issue provides for early intervention.

Examples of such critical periods are found not only in visual development but also in feeding skills. There is a defined period when a child is most receptive to learning how to chew textured foods. At about 9 months of age, the child develops the skill of opposing his finger and thumb and can pick up small bits of food from a food dish or high chair tray. Since he tends to explore objects by putting them into his mouth, he will frequently learn the skill of chewing textured foods very naturally at about the same age. Unfortunately, if the child's mother continues to spoon-feed the child, it may be very difficult to teach him the skill of chewing textured foods later on. He may insist on clinging to the bottle or to very soft pureed baby foods and not develop chewing skills without a great deal of intervention. It is therefore very economical, and perhaps even essential, to intervene with a child who is delayed in developing one of those skills for which there is a critical period of learning.

Failure to Treat Handicap in One Sensory System May Produce Impairment in Others

All systems of an organism are interrelated in a dynamic way; failure to remediate one handicap may multiply its effects in other developmental areas, and may produce other handicaps (particularly social and emotional ones) that are secondary to the initial insult.

One of the most startling of all findings about the effects of early handicapping conditions is that a handicap in one sensory system, such as vision, will produce handicaps in another system. Thus, when the "sensory felicitation" which one system ordinarily provides for another breaks down, the effect of the original handicap is multiplied. Myklebust and Brutten (1953) reported, for example, that deafness has a deleterious effect on visual perception: ". . . when hearing is deprived in early life, visual perception is disturbed" (p. 47).

The mechanism here may be related to the need for frequent stimulation of any sensory system in order for normal development to occur. One is tempted to speculate that a child with a hearing impairment would miss some of the sound cues that ordinarily alert a child to an interesting visual event in the environment, and would therefore not experience as many visual perception learning opportunities as would a normal child. Perhaps, too, parents might begin to diminish the number of stimuli provided to the child because of his frequent lack of response to hearing his name called, to verbal play or conversation, to lullabies, or to sound toys, such as rattles and squeak toys. Particularly if there is a delay in their realization that the child's lack of response is due to a hearing difficulty, the parents may perceive the child as rejecting and dull. Thus, a vicious cycle can be set up in which the very handicap a child is born with leads to less effective caregiving from those around him. However, early intervention can reverse this unhappy course and lead to redoubled efforts on the parents' part to give their disabled child the stimulation he needs (Hayden, McGinness, & Dmitriev, in press).

Progressive Deterioration Without Early Intervention

With a delay in remediating an intellectual or cognitive handicap, there is a cumulative achievement decrement even within a single *area of functioning, apart from the danger of secondary emotional or social handicaps; that is, the condition is progressive—the child's developmental status inevitably becomes worse with respect to other children as he grows older.*

Cumulative achievement decrement is the term Jensen (1966) used to describe the performance of an intellectually handicapped child relative to his normal peers. The fact that a child whose condition makes him rank at only one standard deviation below the mean in IQ or other tests of ability will tend to rank even lower by adolescence makes the importance of early intervention quite clear. Part of the reason for this progressive deterioration in a child's relative standing, developmentally, may be that the fact of his handicap tends to alter the responses of parents and other caregivers in the environment. This is shown in studies exploring the complexity of stimuli provided to normal children as opposed to handicapped children. For example, in a study of the linguistic environment provided to children with Down's syndrome, investigators observed and recorded verbalizations of mothers to their Down's syndrome children and of mothers to their normal children in situations where the mothers were asked to play and talk naturally with the children. The records measured the verbalizations in terms of their frequency and complexity. The authors note: "At this time it can be stated that in some verbal situations, certain parameters of the linguistic input to the Down's syndrome children are different in terms of frequency of occurrence . . . the Down's syndrome children's linguistic acquisition device must operate on linguistic data that are somewhat different than the data provided to normal children" (Buium, Rynders, & Turnure, 1974, p. 57).

The second significant finding is that mothers of Down's syndrome children seem to "talk down" (speaking in simpler, shorter phrases) to their children more than the mothers of normal children do—so that their children's opportunities for acquiring complex language skills would be more limited than a normal child's. The implications of this study are fascinating and a bit horrifying: as if the syndrome itself is not bad enough, the effects it has on caregivers in the environment, who respond so much less adequately to a Down's syndrome child than to a normal child, multiply the disabilities. Such a finding suggests that parents of an exceptional child may need special training themselves, in order to learn how to respond to their children in a naturally stimulating way.

Intervention Can Be Effective

Early intervention has *been shown to help: it can work to reduce the effects of a handicapping condition, and can do so more surely and more rapidly than later intervention.*

The one basis for early intervention that overrides all others is that such intervention can be effective; it can raise the developmental prognosis for a child at risk or even a child displaying an established handicap. Urie Bronfenbrenner (1973) reviewed some of the most prominent attempts at preschool intervention and concluded that though such attempts were vulnerable to failure and were still relatively unsophisticated, some of the programs did produce significant developmental gains in the children who were enrolled.

Other research has shown that intervention can work to benefit a child with a severe handicap or a high degree of developmental risk. In 1971, Logan Wright reported on a pilot study he had undertaken with premature infants. His goal was to determine whether providing the infant with a stimulus-rich environment (as opposed to the stimulus-poor surroundings of the usual premature isolette) would improve the infant's performance on such indices as rooting reflex behavior and glucocorticoid chemistries. He compared this with the performance of a control group which received the traditional nursery treatment for premature infants. Wright concluded that "the vulnerability of prematures is increased significantly if, during infancy, they are reared in an environment providing minimal sensory-motor stimulation." Instead, the premature baby should be given the sort of stimulation offered in this study, as a minimum: vestibular stimulation from being rocked; tactile, kinesthetic and visual stimulation from handling by a nurse; auditory stimulation from music and talk on a radio; color and pattern stimulation of vision from striped sheets and other patterned stimuli. The differences exhibited by the experimental group over the control group were measurable when the infants were only three weeks old.

Katz (1971) produced some significant gains in premature infants (as measured after 36 weeks of life) by using auditory stimulation alone, but the overall stimulation employed in the Logan Wright study has been used with dramatic effects in at least three other instances. In a Philadelphia hospital in 1972, Scarr-Salapatek and Williams used early stimulation and several kinds of intervention-support with infants who were very premature at birth. These infants had been born to unwed, impoverished mothers (and were consequently at high risk for developmental disabilities). The infants were given visual stimulation in their isolettes; they were held, talked to, rocked, and cuddled during eight half-hour feeding sessions in the nursery. These things alone produced significant gains over a control group within a month. (Note again the very rapid changes when early stimulation is provided.) When the babies were discharged to go home with their mothers, a social worker visited the home to continue providing stimulation, toys, and other assistance to the infant in the home and also offered advice to the mother concerning child care and community services. At the end of one year, most of the infants in the experimental group were at normal or nearly normal levels of development with only 21% having IQ's below 90. Infants in the control group scored an average of one standard deviation below the norm; 67% had IQ's below 90. Kugel (1974), working with Down's syndrome infants at the University of Nebraska, found that a stimulus-rich simulated home environment contrasted most favorably with the usual hospital ward environment in producing a markedly higher developmental level in the treated children. The widely-reported Milwaukee Project (Heber, Garber, Harrington, Hoffman, & Falendar, 1975) selected children from disadvantaged backgrounds, with mothers of subnormal IQ, and provided them with a stimulating intervention program from birth to school age. The results showed that all of the children participating in the project had at least normal intelligence, and the group average was at least one standard deviation above the mean. This study did not involve children who presented a serious handicap at birth. However, the thesis that intervention may prevent those handicaps which are largely environmental in origin gained support from this investigation. This study provokes us to ask what part of the variation in intelligent performing by a child with a genetic disorder is due to environmental changes or, to look at the question slightly differently, what part *could* be affected by environmental manipulation, whether it usually is or not.

Advances in Earliest Intervention

In 1957, Drillien (among other investigators) began to study the effects of technological advances in improving the survival rates of those infants who might have died because of prematurity or perinatal complications in the days before Intensive Care Units for infants were established. The researchers were encouraged to find that many more babies were surviving prenatal or perinatal developmental insults, but they predicted that this survival would mean an increase in the number of handicapped children in the population. They reasoned that the conditions that would have killed these infants in more primitive times would at least impair their functioning now, when we are able to sustain life but not to guarantee a normal functioning level.

This prediction, happily, is proving to be false. Stewart and Reynolds (1974) reported on a long-term follow-up of all infant survivors cared for in the Neonatal Unit of University College Hospital, London, from 1966 to 1970. Although the survival rate for babies of low birth weight is still low (23% for infants from 501 to 1,000 gm and 69% for those from 1,001 to 1,500 gm), babies who did survive showed highly encouraging effects of the early care they received. Of the 98 surviving children, 95 were followed up with repeated physical examinations and developmental assessments. Sixty-five of the older children were also given IQ tests. The results showed that 86 (90.5%) of the children *had no detectable handicap*; 4 (4.2%) had physical handicaps only, and 5 (5.3%) had mental handicaps (of these, two also had physical handicaps). The authors conclude that ". . . intensive care can both increase the chance of survival for infants of very low birth weight and reduce the incidence of serious handicap in survivors" (Stewart & Reynolds, 1974, p. 724).

Cost Benefit of Providing Intervention

The cost-benefit ratio of early intervention usually makes it more economical than later intervention.

As in any kind of endeavor which involves a considerable outlay of staff time and resources, we question ourselves about the cost effectiveness of intervention. In the case of providing intervention to a group of children, we have to ask ourselves whether we can identify with certainty those children who need intervention, whether we can be sure that intervention will do no harm, and whether we can be thoroughly confident that intervention will benefit a child who is handicapped.

The answer to the first question is only a qualified one. We really cannot identify with complete confidence all the children who need intervention. We still routinely have some false positives and some false negatives—some children who are never identified do need intervention and some children are identified as needing intervention who do not (Gallagher & Bradley, 1972). Our present screening devices are only barely adequate, and are too often not applied. Fine-focus assessment of handicapping conditions in infancy and early childhood is still primitive, and no national effort at such assessment has yet been implemented (Haring, 1976; Hayden, McGinness, & Dmitriev, in press). The ones who need our help but who are not identified should be our primary concern. The child who is identified as needing intervention and who is provided with a program will experience all the benefits of being enrolled in a program that will give him instruction in many important behavioral skills. There is, admittedly, the danger that the child will suffer from being labeled as a handicapped child, but this danger is diminishing all the time as we move further and further away from the use of deleterious labels for handicapping conditions.

The second question, whether we can be sure that intervention does not harm a child, has therefore been answered in the context of the first. We really feel that intervention does no harm. In the Model Preschool Center for Handicapped Children at the Experimental Education Unit, we have for several years integrated normal children, children who serve as models of normal behavior for the handicapped pupils, with children who have handicaps. The effects of this integration effort have been uniformly good. The children who are normal models do not seem to acquire any inappropriate behaviors as a result of being in a classroom with children who have handicaps. In fact, they seem to acquire additional appropriate behaviors. They develop a helpfulness and a wish to be of use to their classmates that we do not always see in children of their ages who have not had the opportunity to help a child with less ability.

The children who have handicaps, on the other hand, seem to benefit from having good examples of normal behavior in children who are their age mates. They do not suffer the growing atypicality of behavior that sometimes develops when children who have handicaps are grouped exclusively together. So there seems to be, at least on the basis of this firsthand experience, some evidence that intervention will not do any harm. On the basis of results from many different studies, we can say with some confidence that intervention can help a child who is handicapped. Investigators have reported less than ideal results in programs where parents have not shown much motivation (Bronfenbrenner, 1973). But in programs where parents can be relied on to continue the work of the classroom at home, and where parents provide good, nurturing home environments for their children, a program of early intervention can help a great deal. The cost of early intervention can also be substantially reduced if parent volunteers can be enlisted for actual classroom work, and paraprofessional workers employed for a variety of tasks.

Ideally, we would make no false identifications. We would serve only those children who need help, and would not serve those who do not. We can, however, rest fairly content with the present cost effectiveness of providing intervention. The problem at the moment is that there are not enough high-quality programs for those severely handicapped children who could be identified as needing help.

In a study of the effects of providing very early medical intervention, Quilligan and Paul (1974) reported on the cost-benefits of monitoring fetal heart rate during delivery, working on the assumption that monitoring fetal heart rate during labor could reduce perinatal mortality and morbidity by 50%. They compared the cost for total monitoring of 3000 deliveries per year with the savings realized by preventing one-half of the mental retardation that would have developed in the group, had the subjects not been monitored. Their cost-analysis concludes that "total intrapartum monitoring as described would require a yearly expenditure of an estimated $100 million. By merely halving the incidence of handicapped individuals, an estimated $2 billion long-term expenditure would be prevented. Additionally, 6000 intrapartum fetal deaths might be avoided and this immeasurable resource provided to society and the nation. . . . The use of fetal monitoring seems to present attractive potentials for enhancing the quality of maternal-fetal health care and the future of its recipients" (Quilligan and Paul, 1974, 99–100).

The economic appeal is not one that special educators like to use to promote early intervention, because they usually feel impatient with public failure to acknowledge education as a legal right for every child. But, as we stated at the beginning of this article, such a right has not yet been extended to the handicapped child under the age of three. As a basis for intervention, cost-effectiveness is one point we may do well to emphasize in our dealings with the general public.

Parents' Need for Early Intervention

Parents need support during the early weeks and months, before patterns of parenting become established. Parents need models of good parenting behavior with a handicapped child, and specific instructions for working with the child.

If children need early intervention to overcome their handicaps, parents are often just as much in need of intervention to help them execute their critically important tasks in the early weeks and months of the child's life. The parents of a handicapped child typically appear at a center where they are seeking help for their child in the same state that emotionally disturbed people appear at a crisis clinic. They are typically in shock or in a state of acute distress, and they very much need direction from a trained professional. They need, in particular, to develop some specific skills and some knowledge of tasks they can perform that will help their child move toward nearly normal behavior.

In his recent (1975) book, written for parents of normal children as a guide to early childhood care and development, Burton White points out that a parent is at great risk of being unable to do the job of child-rearing well, for three reasons. First, there is ignorance: specialists until very recently did little more than descriptively catalogue the rough sequence and timing of the appearance of such major developmental milestones as walking, talking, and so forth. What should be done to facilitate the appearance of these skills was poorly explained, if at all. Second, parents are under stress because of the several burdens of child-rearing: responsibility for the 24-hour care of a child who, at eight months, begins moving about the home and posing a major hazard to his own safety and to that of treasured possessions, as well as attracting the displeasure and even overt hostility of his older siblings. Third, there is lack of assistance: in our society there are often no readily available sources of advice and help in child care. The family—and usually it is the mother who bears the major responsibility for child care—must go it alone.

Those of us who have set as a goal the involvement and training of parents whose children are handicapped, particularly parents of severely handicapped children, must often sigh at such reasons for parenting risks. Of course, they are quite accurate: child-rearing is indeed stressful, and calls for additional knowledge and assistance. But the parents of a handicapped child who hear some parents of normal children complain about the difficulties they are having must be saying to themselves, "You think *you* have it so hard." They must feel other parents are indeed lightly burdened, because the problems of caring for a severely handicapped child often require that the parent become his or her own minor expert in nursing, physical therapy, education, and psychology, to name only a few.

In the face of such heavy demands it is easy for parents of handicapped children to give up the struggle altogether. We are only too familiar with parents who are so worn down by shock, grief, and sheer physical fatigue that they have become passive "do-littles," defeated at the threshold. One antidote for this is early intervention: intervention to support parents in their grief and relative helplessness and to model a positive interventionist role for them to assume in working with their child. If a parent assumes a change-agent role from the first few months of parenthood, defeat and passivity may never develop.

Improving Tomorrow's Bases for Intervention

Early childhood education, including infant intervention, for the handicapped is likely to become widespread in the next few years. The message that we cannot afford to wait until the child's condition has progressed for three years before we begin our prevention/remediation efforts is now clear to most professionals. It is even beginning to reach the wider nonprofessional audience that must accept this proposition if infant intervention is ever to be supported by legislation and funding.

The harbingers of the current "season" of the very young child have been with us for years. Burton White (1975) has remarked that the move to establish Head Start programs in the 1960's was only one beginning of education's focus on children under six years, and that others multiplied the public attention to the early years. Moreover, the focal age for this interest has been moving rapidly downward toward infancy. The special education literature certainly supports White's point. The March 1976 issue of *Exceptional Children* examines both the past history and present directions of special education and, in a section titled "Into the Crystal Ball," looks at what the future holds. Significantly, the first future development mentioned is the following:

> Our concerns for children now extend into infancy, the pre-school years, and even the prenatal period. The studies of Merle Karnes and Rick Heber are just two of the many symbols of this vital trend based on early diagnosis, identification, programming and parent education. [p. 334]

Are we prepared for this wave of the future? Do we really have adequate bases for intervention? Not in any ideal sense. Ideally, we would know much more about the precise variables that account for the success of early intervention in some cases and its failure to produce results in others. When we read, for example, in Urie Bronfenbrenner's (1973) review of early childhood programs, that those in which some gains were shown also involved "motivated parents," we know only enough to ask more intelligent questions. We still do not know how a motivated parent's behavior differs on an everyday basis, in specific ways, from that of an unmotivated one. But neither can we afford to wait until all the research results are in to begin applying the little we do know. For one thing, there are handicapped children here and now whom we must not abandon, who need even the imperfect help we can give now. What we usually do is to offer gross, undifferentiated guidelines about "parent involvement" and "motivating good parenting skills." We know enough to be sure that good parenting is important, and we make large, clumsy efforts to promote it, even though we are not sure exactly which of the several components of good parenting are truly the keys to some parents' success.

Adequate bases? No. We must go on working for better ones, but we cannot wait for perfect bases. It may be an illusion to think that the ground under our feet will ever keep still. In a recent and brilliant article summarizing his presidential address to the Eastern Psychological Association, Jerome Kagan (1976) speaks of "Emergent Themes in Human Development." Reading the article, one is struck with a sense of Kagan's care in choosing the word "emergent" for his title: he clearly takes nothing for granted. Instead, he pays humorously tentative homage to what we have been learning in developmental psychology in the past few years:

> The recent crest of interest in developmental psychology has produced a *tiny* corpus of *moderately firm* facts that invite reexamination of the presuppositions that have guided so much past work. [p. 186]

We can serve handicapped children best by acknowledging the frailty of professional understanding at the present time. We are, and should be, our own severest critics, based on the data we gather on our programs' effectiveness and efficiency. By constructive criticism of our own efforts and especially by offering to share the information we have generated with our colleagues in the field, we can perhaps improve the bases for intervention that we stand on today.

References

The dates in parentheses following the titles of some articles in this reference list show the date the study was originally published.

Abraham, W. The early years: Prologue to tomorrow. *Exceptional Children*, 1976, *42*, 330–335.

Bodmer, W. F., & Cavalli-Sforza, L. L. Intelligence and race (1970). In W. T. Greenough (Ed.), *The nature and nurture of behavior, developmental psychobiology*. San Francisco: W. H. Freeman, 1973.

Brazelton, T. B. *Neonatal behavioral assessment scale.* Philadelphia: J. B. Lippincott, 1973.

Bronfenbrenner, U. *A report on longitudinal evaluations of preschool programs: Is early intervention effective?* (Vol. II) Washington, D.C: DHEW publication NO. (OHD) 76-30025, 1973.

Buium, N., Rynders, J., & Turnure, J. Early maternal linguistic environment of normal and Down's syndrome language-learning children. *American Journal of Mental Deficiency*, 1974, *74*, 52–58.

Connolly, K., & Stratton, P. An exploration of some parameters affecting classical conditioning in the neonate (1969). In L. J. Stone, H. T. Smith, & L. B. Murphy (Eds.). *The competent infant.* New York: Basic Books, 1973.

Drillien, M. Growth and development in a group of children of very low birthweight. *Archives of Disease in Children*, 1958, *33*, 10–18.

Escalona, S. K., & Moriarty, A. Prediction of schoolage intelligence from infant tests. *Child Development*, 1961, *32*, 597–605.

Evans, E. D. *Contemporary influences in early childhood education.* New York: Holt, Rinehart, and Winston, 1975.

Fantz, R. L. Visual perception from birth as shown by pattern selectivity (1965). In L. J. Stone, H. T. Smith, & L. B. Murphy (Eds.). *The competent infant.* New York: Basic Books, 1973.

Gallagher, J. J., & Bradley, R. H. Early identification of developmental difficulties. In I. J. Gordon (Ed.). *Early childhood education: The seventy-first yearbook of the National Society for Education.* Chicago: The University of Chicago Press, 1972.

Galton, L. Prenatal tests help cure defects and save babies. *Parade: The Sunday Newspaper Magazine*. April 11, 1976, 12–14.

Gardner, L. I. Deprivation dwarfism (1972) in W. T. Greenough (Ed.). *The nature and nurture of behavior, developmental psychobiology*. San Francisco: W. H. Freeman, 1973.

Gentry, D. Personal communication, 1975.

Gibson, E. J., & Walk, R. D. The "visual cliff" (1960). In W. T. Greenough (Ed.). *The nature and nurture of behavior, developmental psychobiology*. San Francisco: W. H. Freeman, 1973.

Greenough, W. T. Introduction to critical events in the shaping of basic systems. In W. T. Greenough (Ed.). *The nature and nurture of behavior, developmental psychobiology*. San Francisco: W. H. Freeman, 1973.

Haring, N. G. The educator looks at the severely handicapped infant. Presentation to the Council for Exceptional Children's Invisible College, January 12–14, 1976.

Haring, N. G., Hayden, A. H., & Beck, G. R. General principles and guidelines in "programming" for severely handicapped children and young adults. *Focus on Exceptional Children*, April, 1976.

Harlow, H. F. Early social deprivation and later behavior in the monkey (1964). In L. J. Stone, H. T. Smith, & L. B. Murphy (Eds.). *The competent infant*. New York: Basic Books, 1973.

Harlow, H. F., & Harlow, M. K. Social deprivation in monkeys (1962). In W. T. Greenough (Ed.). *The nature and nurture of behavior, developmental psychobiology*. San Francisco: W. H. Freeman, 1973.

Hayden, A. H., McGinness, G. D., & Dmitriev, V. Early and continuous intervention strategies for severely handicapped infants and young children. In N. G. Haring & L. Brown (Eds.). *Teaching the severely handicapped: A yearly publication of the American Association for the Education of the Severely/Profoundly Handicapped* (Vol. I). New York: Grune & Stratton, 1976.

Haynes, H., White, B. L., & Held, R. Visual accommodation in human infants (1965). In L. J. Stone, H. T. Smith, & L. B. Murphy (Ed.). *The competent infant.* New York: Basic Books, 1973.

Heber, R., Garber, H., Harrington, C., Hoffman, C., and Falender, C. *Rehabilitation of families at risk for mental retardation.* Madison, Wisconsin: University of Wisconsin, 1975.

Jensen, A. R. Cumulative deficit compensatory education. *Journal of School Psychology*, 1966, *4*, 137–147.

Kagan, J. *Change and continuity in infancy.* New York: John Wiley, 1971.

Kagan, J. Emergent themes in human development. *American Scientist*, 1976, *64*, 186–196.

Kallman, F. J. The genetics of mental illness. In S. Arieti (Ed.). *American handbook of psychiatry*. New York: Basic Books, 1959.

Katz, V. Auditory stimulation and developmental behavior of the premature infant. *Nursing Research*, 1971, *20*, 196–201.

Kugel, R. B. Early "enrichment" programs for Down's syndrome children. Presented at the Charles R. Strother Seminar, Child Development and Mental Retardation Center, University of Washington, Seattle, Washington, May, 1974.

Levine, S. Stimulation in infancy (1960). In W. T. Greenough (Ed.). *The nature and nurture of behavior, developmental psychobiology.* San Francisco: W. H. Freeman, 1973.

Lewis, M., & Goldberg, S. Perceptual-cognitive development in infancy: A generalized expectancy model as a function of the mother-infant interaction (1969). In L. J. Stone,

H. T. Smith, & L. B. Murphy (Eds.), *The competent infant.* New York: Basic Books, 1973.

Lipsitt, L. P., & Kaye, H. Conditioned sucking in the human newborn (1964). In L. J. Stone, H. T. Smith, & L. B. Murphy (Eds.). *The competent infant.* New York: Basic Books, 1973.

Myklebust, H. R., & Brutten, M. A study of the visual perception of deaf children. *Acta Oto-Laryngonogical Supplement*, 1953, *105*, 45–56.

Prechtl, H., & Beintema, D. *The neurological examination of the full-term newborn infant.* London: Spastics Society Medical Education and Information Unit, 1964.

Quilligan, E. J., & Paul, R. H. Fetal monitoring: Is it worth it? *Obstetrics and Gynecology*, 1974, *45*, 97–100.

Riesen, A. H. Arrested vision (1950). In W. T. Greenough (Ed.). *The nature and nurture of behavior, developmental psychobiology.* San Francisco: W. H. Freeman, 1973.

Scarr-Salapatek, S., & Weinberg, R. A. The war over race and I.Q.: When black children grow up in white homes. *Psychology Today*, December, 1975, *9*(7) 80–82.

Scarr-Salapatek, S., & Williams, M. L. A stimulation program for low birth weight infants. *American Journal of Public Health*, 1972, *62*, 662–667.

Sears, R. R., Maccoby, E. E., & Levin, H. *Patterns of child-rearing.* Evanston, Ill.: Row, Peterson, 1957.

Spitz, R. A. Hospitalism: An inquiry into the genesis of psychiatric conditions in early childhood (1945). In L. J. Stone, H. T. Smith, & L. B. Murphy (Eds.). *The competent infant.* New York: Basic Books, 1973.

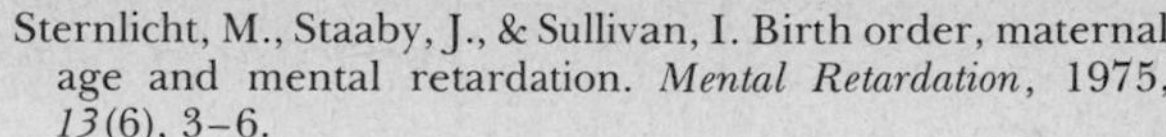
Sternlicht, M., Staaby, J., & Sullivan, I. Birth order, maternal age and mental retardation. *Mental Retardation*, 1975, *13*(6), 3–6.

Stewart, L., & Reynolds, E. O. Improved prognosis for infants of very low birthweight. *Pediatrics*, 1974, *54*, 724–735.

Tulkin, S., & Kagan, J. Mother-child interaction in the first year of life (1972). In L. J. Stone, H. T. Smith, & L. B. Murphy (Eds.). *The competent infant.* New York: Basic Books, 1973.

White, B. L. *The first three years of life.* Englewood Cliffs, N.J.: Prentice-Hall, 1975.

White, B. L., & Watts, J. C. *Experience and environment.* Englewood Cliffs, N.J.: Prentice-Hall, 1973.

Windle, W. F. Brain damage by asphyxia at birth (1969). In W. T. Greenough (Ed.). *The nature and nurture of behavior, developmental psychobiology.* San Francisco: W. H. Freeman, 1973.

Wright, L. The theoretical and research base for a program of early stimulation care and training of premature infants. In J. Hellmuth (Ed.). *The exceptional infant* (Vol. 2). New York: Brunner/Mazel, 1971.

Yarrow, L. J. Maternal deprivation: Toward an empirical and conceptual re-evaluation. *Psychological Bulletin*, 1961, *58*, 459–490.

ALICE H. HAYDEN is Professor of Education at the University of Washington, where she also serves as Director of the Model Preschool Center for Handicapped Children and as Associate Director of the University's Experimental Education Unit. She is the author of many articles, particularly in the areas of early childhood education, Down's syndrome children, and early intervention with the handicapped. Dr. Hayden serves on several publication advisory boards, and is a member of many national organizations whose activities concern the needs of handicapped children and their families.

GAEL D. McGINNESS is a staff member at the Frank Porter Graham Child Development Center, University of North Carolina. She was formerly a member of the staff at the University of Washington's Experimental Education Unit, Child Development and Mental Retardation Center. She was an Educator II and Research Information Specialist at the Unit for the past five years, and was most recently involved in a program for severely handicapped infants.

Early Intervention with Severely/ Profoundly Handicapped Children

DIANE D. BRICKER
RICHARD IACINO

University of Miami

As with many educational practices, there are both active proponents and opponents of early intervention (Bricker, D. D., Bricker, W. A., Iacino, & Dennison, 1976). The critics tend to focus on proliferation of day care facilities as one more blow to the shaky foundation of the American family and to appropriate emotional development during the formative years of children (Moore & Moore, 1972; White, 1975). Although few would disagree that young children need stable and stimulating environments, some might question the assertion that the only appropriate setting for a young child is in the home with the parent. In fact, data suggest that children can thrive in non-home settings (Caldwell, 1970; Karnes & Teska, 1975; Schaefer, 1970). Often the criticism of early intervention programs has focused on the placement of youngsters in crowded, unappealing situations with an untrained staff, and even the advocates of early intervention are dismayed by exposing young children to such environments over extended time periods. For the most part, investigators of preschool educational programs have been concerned with the effects on the normally developing child or children from low-income circumstances; little attention has been focused on early intervention for the handicapped child (Bronfenbrenner, 1974).

Some proponents of early intervention have developed rather thorough rationales for the earliest possible provision of services to the severely handicapped child (Haring & Bricker, 1976). One of the major tenets of such rationales rests on the developmental model. Viewing the evolution of complex human behavior from a developmental perspective has appeal in that it provides the educator with a useful set of strategies to interpret behavioral change and to develop intervention procedures. One of the important assumptions underlying developmental theory is the interactive effect between the child and his environment (Piaget, 1970). Such environmental interaction is apparently necessary for the acquisition of more complex cognitive and social skills (Lewis & Rosenblum, 1974; Piaget & Inhelder, 1969). A second important assumption underlying a developmental approach is that complex response forms develop from the modification and elaboration of simpler forms of behavior. If environmental interaction is necessary for growth, and delays in or absences of prerequisite responses lead to a cumulative deficiency, then intervention should be initiated when a significant handicapping condition is detected. We all tend to be judged by normative standards and, the further a child deviates from given norms, generally the more remediation time and effort will be required to eliminate the deficit. Waiting four or five years before intervening with a severely handicapped child simply delays the chance to deal with the developmental problems when they are least complex. Keeping to a minimum the time interval between detection of serious deficits and the initiation of intervention is essential to efficient remediation

Intervening early with the severely impaired child is also useful in precluding the development of related disabilities and/or undesirable behavior. For example, without proper developmental intervention in the form of positioning and exercising, the spastic child could develop contractures that may interfere with the acquisition of a broad range of important behaviors. If such children are not the recipients of consistent and appropriate exercising, the probabilities are high that non-reversible rigidity could develop.

Not only is early intervention important for inhibiting the development of associated disabilities, but early programming seems equally important in preventing or minimizing the acquisition of undesirable behavior. Most children are institutionalized not because of learning problems but because they emit a variety of either socially unacceptable (e.g., pica, soiling) or aggressive (e.g., biting, hitting, self-mutilating) behaviors. Such behavior is not an unavoidable accompaniment to a severely handicapping condition; rather, it is often the result of improper management during the early years of development. Teachers dealing with older severely handicapped children who were without the benefit of early intervention programs spend a sizable portion of each training day dealing with the elimination of undesirable or inappropriate behavior. Such valuable teaching time could be better spent assisting a child in the acquisition of new and functional behavior.

The potentially disruptive effect of the significantly impaired child on his family argues strongly for the establishment of early intervention programs for this population. It seems both unreasonable and unfair to expect families to cope with the difficulties associated with a severely/profoundly handicapped child without assistance. The problems of this population are multiple and complex, requiring solutions that necessitate the concerted effort of many individuals (Martin, 1976). If we are sincere in our statements that severely/profoundly handicapped children belong in the community, then the proper support resources must be available for parents. To expect parents to cope with a significantly impaired child for five or six years without the continuing assistance of trained professionals invites the development of parental attitudes which will probably result in the child's eventual institutionalization. Consequently, community-based early intervention programs need to be available so that parents can find the necessary educational and support services essential for adequately maintaining their significantly impaired child in the home.

Although expert opinion, convincing rationales, and even a modicum of supportive data can be assembled for both sides of the debate concerning the merits of early intervention, such a debate may be specious. As Bruner (1970) has suggested, the false dichotomy that has been established between home care and day care is a fruitless argument which should be ended and the real issue of providing quality care for young children should be brought into focus. This suggestion has received added impetus from two sources. The first is consumer demand which has evolved from an increasing number of parents, especially those of handicapped children, seeking day care and early educational programming for their children. In response to this, many community agencies have begun to provide day care and intervention services for the preschool child. The second source is the nationwide trend of extending the public school entry age downward, especially for the handicapped child. These current conditions reinforce Bruner's position that arguments for and against early intervention are practically moot. The fact is that early intervention services are being demanded and provided. The development of the necessary provisions to ensure the delivery of quality services to all small children, no matter what the setting or programmatic variables, is now the challenge.

Criteria for Early Detection

As Hobbs (1975) has noted, the most important aspect of a label or definition should be that it assists in the delivery of appropriate services to an individual. Therefore, the primary reason for developing a definition of severely/profoundly handicapped is that it assists in assuring that significantly impaired children are the recipients of appropriate and necessary services. Prerequisite to early intervention is the need for a mechanism or system that can reliably detect young children having severely handicapping conditions. Critical for early detection is the establishment of a definition or criteria that will lead to the identification of appropriate children. Some of the definitions of the severely/profoundly handicapped appearing in the literature do not seem to be useful for the purposes of early detection (Sailor, Guess, & Lavis, 1975; Sontag, Burke, & York, 1973; Stainback, Stainback, & Maurer, 1976). Consequently, we are proposing two criteria specifically for the detection of children needing early intervention services.

> Criterion One: At least two independent observers agree that the child's current behavioral repertoire is significantly deficient or impaired in two or more of the following areas: sensorimotor, language, motor, and social-self help skills.

The difficulty with this criterion is deriving an exacting specification for "significantly deficient or impaired." Obviously, this implies comparisons of behavior which are deficient in relation to normative rates or sequences. Specifically, the problem centers on the extent to which the child must vary from normative standards before he meets the criterion of significant impairment. Until we have more accurate developmental sequences derived from empirically valid and reliable information, the specification of "significantly deficient or impaired" will continue to lack precision. Nonetheless, despite its imprecision, considerable agreement is reached among trained observers in terms of what constitutes a significant deficiency or impairment when this criterion is used.

> Criterion Two: There is a high probability that the presenting condition or observed deficiency is not correctable with episodic intervention but will require longitudinal intervention.

Episodic intervention refers to procedures that are either: a) relatively short-term in nature and have clear initiation and termination points, and/or b) isolated training routines in which little attempt is made to generalize and integrate the target reponse across a wide variety of settings, stimuli, and activities. Removal of a cataract would fit the first type of episodic intervention in that the procedure has a definite beginning and ending and is short term. Such an operation may significantly alter a child's visual impairment but cannot by itself eliminate the developmental deficits of a severely/profoundly handicapped child. An example of the second type of episodic intervention is providing physical therapy twice a week in special therapy sessions apart from classroom teacher or parent and without attempting to assure that the child's newly acquired skills are being used in other settings. As Brown, Nietupski, & Hamre-Nietupski (1976) have suggested, one cannot assume that the profoundly handicapped learner will be able to generalize a newly acquired skill to other materials or use it under novel conditions. Therefore, a teacher who does not include in a training routine systematic procedures for generalizing a new response to appropriate settings and conditions may find that the severely impaired child produces the response only in the specific training session where it was learned. If a child's basic problems can be eliminated through a form of episodic intervention, then the child does not meet these proposed criteria for the severely/profoundly handicapped.

The use of the two criteria discussed above to determine whether a child is severely impaired will necessitate certain changes in typical diagnostic procedures. Traditionally, children are brought to a center for diagnostic testing, which lasts for a few hours at most. During this time the child is often exposed to a variety of professionals who administer a set of standardized measures and interviews. Generally, on the basis of this small sample of behavior and in conjunction with historical data, determinations are made about future intervention strategies for the child. The use of the two criteria suggested above, as an alternative, necessitates a systematic sampling of behavior across several testing and intervention sessions. Although such a procedure is more time-consuming, the validity of the information acquired by such a process should compensate for the greater time expenditure.

We have not specified as inclusion criteria such factors as severe motor impairments, fragile and chronic health problems, or specific forms of aberrant behavior. While there seems to be little doubt that such problems have a high frequency of occurrence in this population, the absence of such problems should not serve to exclude children from the category of severely/profoundly handicapped.

The criteria proposed above, i.e., the existence of significantly deficient or impaired behavior and the necessity for long-term intervention, are potentially effective methods for determining which children are going to need early services specifically designed for the severely impaired. Since these criteria use as a reference the continuing development of the child (which is relative to normal development and the child's potential response to educational programming), they should be useful for selecting the significantly impaired child, no matter how young. The 8-month-old baby who does not track visually, localize to sound, hold his head erect, or make any grasping responses, and who, after a few days of intensive training, gives no evidence of acquiring any of these skills rapidly, is a child who should be a candidate for early intervention. The 15-month-old child with cerebral palsy who has severe spasticity in the trunk and limbs, major food allergies, visual impairments, and gives no evidence of rapid change after short-term intervention, is a child who meets the definitional criteria and should be placed in an longitudinal intervention program. The criteria proposed here are offered as a working definition with the clear understanding that more specification is necessary before the validity of such selection factors can be determined.

Components of an Early Intervention Program

The inclusion of early intervention as an essential part of a comprehensive educational program for the severely impaired child assumes that such programs will be designed to assist the child and his family in the acquisition of appropriate educational goals. In designing an effective early intervention program, the following components need to be considered: a rationale or philosophy that provides the basic structure of, and sets the methodology for, the intervention approach; trained personnel (e.g., direct interventionist, parents, and consultants from other disciplines); appropriate curricula; a managed physical environment that supports and reinforces the necessary intervention strategies; and a mechanism for effective, programmatically usable evaluation. A potentially effective way to elaborate on these components is to detail their actualization in the experimental early intervention program for severely/profoundly handicapped children, birth through five years, developed at the University of Miami's Mailman Center for Child Development.

A Rationale

The relatively new business of planning programs for the severely handicapped young child is prone to a serious pitfall, that of developing and using nonfunctional objectives and procedures. The strategy of model building provides an organizational system for selecting and programming relevant behavioral targets which can circumvent this problem. The number of activities and skills that severely and profoundly handicapped children need to learn in order to make developmental progress are enormous, and therefore selection of training targets on the basis of random choice makes little sense.

Our intervention system for educational programming is based on an approach to complex human behavior recommended by J. McV. Hunt more than a decade ago (1961). Hunt's approach was in turn predicated on over 50 years of research and thought on human behavior by Piaget and his colleagues (Piaget & Inhelder, 1969; Piaget, 1970). The structure of this intervention approach is derived from two major sources. The first is from cognitive formulations about development, which provided the form and organizational patterns of the structures, schemes, or operants as they are developed from the infant's reflexive behavior system. A second source is comprised of the behavioral approaches to human development which emphasize mechanisms for changing behavior and altering patterns of behavioral control exhibited by antecedent stimulus events. Such an integration of developmental and behavioral approaches to intervention has precedents in earlier articles (Lynch & Bricker, 1972; Bricker, W. A., & Bricker, D. D., 1974).

The rationale we use is structured on three basic assumptions:

1. The infant generally comes equipped with a series of reflexive responses. Through subsequent interaction with the environment, the infant modifies his basic reflexive behavior into successively more complex levels of development.
2. Generally speaking, behavioral development seems to follow a developmental hierarchy which is consistent across children.
3. For those children who are not born with the necessary reflexive behavior or who do not subsequently acquire more complex behavior, the environment must be arranged or structured to facilitate the acquisition of such critical responses.

It is not necessary that an intervention program adopt the rationale stated above which has been cited only as an example; rather, the point is that an educational intervention program for the young severely handicapped child must have some rationale which will serve as a superstructure for making decisions.

Trained Personnel

Trained personnel comprise the second component which must be considered in designing an effective early intervention program. Although empirical validation of the competencies necessary to work effectively with this population has yet to be accomplished, some requisite skills have been determined through observation of classroom personnel. These skills fall into five broad categories: knowledge of developmental processes, ability to synthesize transdisciplinary inputs, willingness to serve as a trainer of staff and parents, ability to evaluate effectively all aspects of intervention, and analysis of the teaching/learning interaction.

It is the rare and unusual person who can walk into a class of severely/profoundly handicapped children and develop and implement an effective intervention program without the benefit of prior experience with children in general and handicapped children in particular. Even experienced teachers often indicate dismay and experience failure when first working with significantly impaired children. Consequently, implementation of a successful early intervention program requires that the teaching staff have relevant experience working with the target population. In addition, the direct interventionist needs behavior management skills that can be used in a variety of settings and situations. In this context, the term "behavior management" is used in its broadest sense to indicate a manager of all behavioral skills, both social and academic.

In most cases the nature of the problems presented by the severely/profoundly handicapped child requires input from a variety of disciplines. Most early intervention programs will not be able to support a cadre of full-time specialists necessary for the direct delivery of appropriate services to each child enrolled in every class. The traditional model of removing a child from class for an hour of therapy per week will not produce success with this target population. Rather, those individuals (e.g., teachers and parents) who have repeated or continuous contact with the child should be trained to deliver the necessary special services. If such an approach is to be successful, the teacher must be able to organize the acquisition, evaluation and implementation (in a practical sense) of inputs from disciplines that either are not or cannot be included as daily, integral parts of an intervention program. The teacher becomes an educational synthesizer who is the pivotal force in the overall educational program by seeking and coordinating the necessary resources to produce growth and change in the severely impaired child (Bricker, D. D., 1976).

Training other individuals within the classroom setting, home, or community is another important role of the direct interventionists working with the severely/profoundly handicapped child. Many classroom personnel and parents often have limited skills for working with the target population. The direct interventionist will have to decide what information and skills the staff and parents should have, and then develop procedures for teaching the selected material and strategies. The success of the direct interventionist in this role as a supportive staff trainer will have a great impact upon the effectiveness of the intervention program with young and severely impaired children. Although the effectiveness of one-to-one individual training has been questioned with older and less impaired children (Brown et al., 1976; Bricker, D. D., Dennison, L., & Bricker, W. A., 1976), such an approach seems to be necessary when dealing with young profoundly impaired children. The interventionist cannot provide all the necessary training for each child in the program and, therefore, is forced to rely on others in the child's environment to function in the role of teacher or trainer in both the classroom and home.

If the assumption that assistance is required from multiple sources as well as from supportive personnel in the classroom and home is correct, then cooperation of parents, staff, other professionals, and community agencies is necessary. To coordinate and balance inputs from so many sources, the direct interventionist needs to possess organizational skills. The complex ecological system that needs to be built to properly maintain the severely/profoundly handicapped child requires careful and thoughtful coordination. Without such coordination between the home, school, and various agencies and professional personnel, an inconsistent and perhaps conflicting training program may occur for the child and the families.

In order to assess the various aspects of the intervention program to determine which components are functioning appropriately and which aspects of the program need modification, the direct interventionist needs to have evaluation skills. This is a complex and difficult role and, while the interventionist may have to seek expert assistance, he should nonetheless have enough information to ask the appropriate questions to develop and implement the preferred evaluation strategies. As with the programmatic rationale, it is not necessary for an effective early intervention program to adopt our view of the essential teacher competencies; rather, it is important that some careful thought and attention be given to the selection of the various roles to be filled by the direct interventionist.

Curricula

The importance of an effective curriculum cannot be overstated. As Weikart and Lambie (1970) have suggested, the curriculum should serve as a guide for the teacher rather than as a specific format for the child. Although there are a variety of existing curricular materials for young impaired children, the field is still far from developing comprehensive, empirically validated programs (Baldwin, 1976). We view curricula as tools to assist the teacher in:

1. Isolating the necessary behavioral components to reach a specified terminal state;
2. Sequencing those components according to the best information available on normal acquisition patterns;
3. Generating a variety of activities to train each of the necessary steps in the developmental hierarchy.

The first step in generating an operational curriculum is to construct a map of the milestones that occur during the early developmental period. To build a curricular program based on the developmental model, one has to begin by generating a training model in the form of a developmental behavior lattice. A representative example of a developmental behavior lattice is shown in Figure 1, the motor training lattice, which represents an attempt to map the necessary training components for the motor domain, and represents not only a conceptual framework for development within the motor area but also provides the key content areas for training. The lattice should be read by beginning at the box in the lower left corner and moving both upward and to the right along the horizontal axis. The vertical and horizontal placement of the boxes indicates a theoretical sequence of how children may acquire important motor responses. Each box in the lattice represents a behavioral component we believe necessary for the child to acquire an appropriate motor repertoire. Increasingly more complex behaviors, which are constructed as a function of more and more sophisticated environmental interactions, are represented by the vertical dimension of the lattice.

Once the lattice has been formulated, the next step is to expand each program box into a sequence of training targets and to suggest possible activities which would reach and maintain the established goals. Following a lattice structure helps to ensure that training occurs

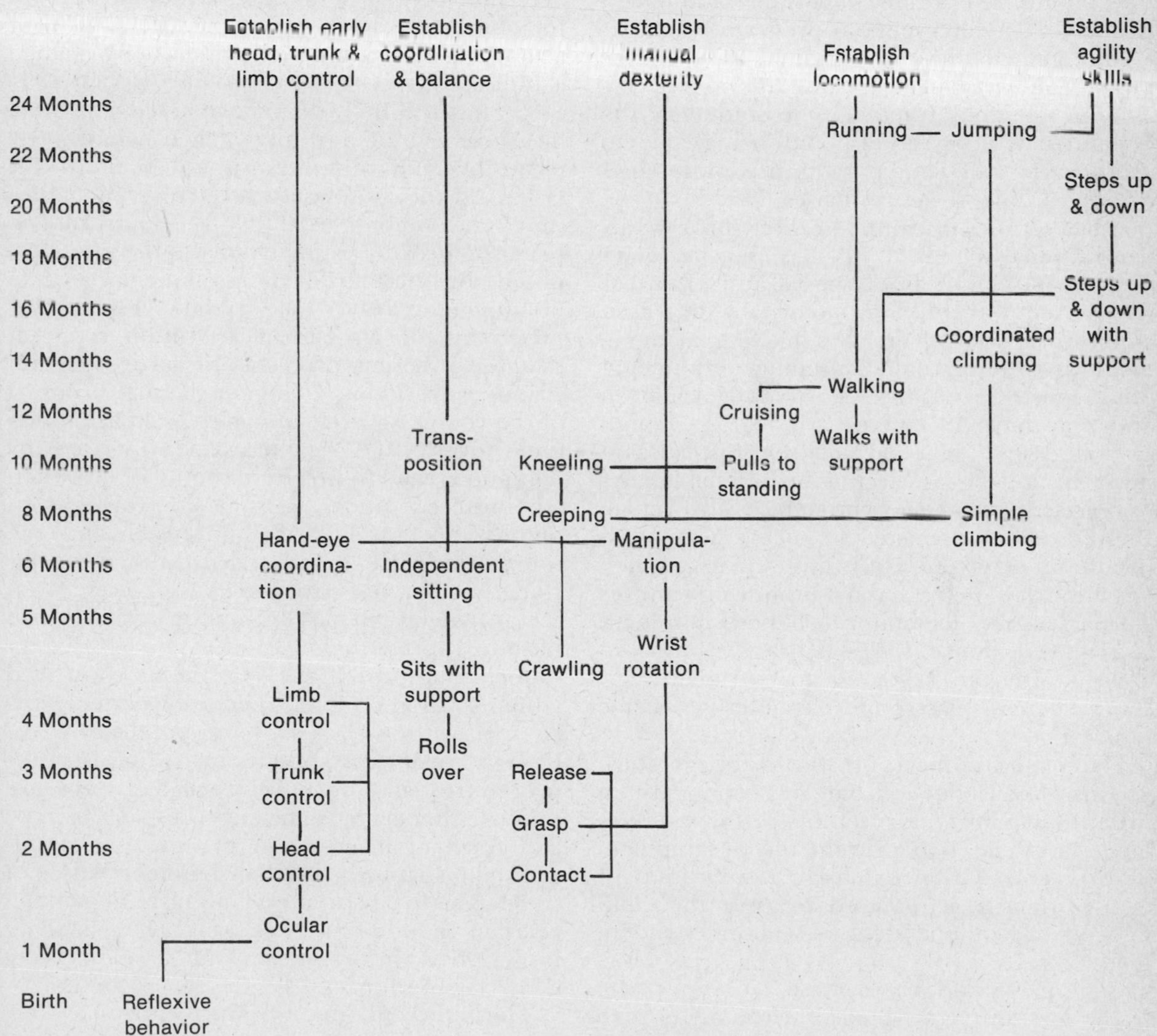

Figure 1. Motor training lattice.

in some developmental order and that the hierarchy between the various training components will be maintained.

Physical Environment

The fourth component we consider essential to a successful early intervention project is the structuring of the physical environment. Often teachers, especially those of young, handicapped children, think of training time only in terms of direct child-teacher interaction. Such an assumption eliminates the potential use of a sizable portion of the day, when the child may not be in direct contact with an adult, to develop and maintain targeted objectives. Clever and thoughtful use of the physical environment can offer a viable teaching mechanism which can be utilized as an important component of an early intervention program. Benefits to be gained through arrangement of the physical environment include increasing the amount of child training time, reducing the dependency upon adults, and being able to use a variety of conditions to assist the child in generalizing target responses.

For a group of young severely/profoundly handicapped children, it may be necessary to assemble a variety of special and often expensive equipment. For motorically impaired children, special chairs and feeding arrangements are often essential. Sleeping accommodations must be available for young children and may have to include cribs large enough to hold 5 or 6 year old children. Special care must be given to selecting manipulable toys or objects. Equipment that can be easily broken, chewed up or damaged in such a way as to produce a safety hazard is unacceptable. Often it is difficult to detect hazard-producing features a priori, so careful monitoring of new equipment is required. Since the significantly impaired child is often ill and/or not toilet-trained, new standards of classroom cleanliness become imperative.

Many children need prosthetic devices which require knowledge of handling and care in order to maximize the usefulness of such equipment, as well as to prevent the development of problems. Often extensive modification of eating utensils is required to assist the child in acquiring independent or semi-independent feeding skills.

Caution should be exercised in replicating traditional nursery school environments with a population of young severely/profoundly handicapped children. Careful planning and arrangement of the physical environment may help significantly in the acquisition of important skills. Such arrangements may involve important modifications in the traditional preschool classroom.

Evaluation

The final component which must be considered in designing an effective early intervention program is a system for evaluating that program. No matter how comprehensive or multifaceted the programmatic support model, the main business of any intervention program must be change in child behavior. Without objective documentation of a child's progress toward established objectives, the results of the interventionist's effort will remain undetermined. Teachers must have a mechanism for objectively determining the effects of programming efforts and evaluating when a change is indicated.

As Stott and Ball (1965) have noted, a reliable measurement of a young child's behavior by means of standardized tests is, at best, a difficult task. Add the complication of a severely handicapping condition to the unreliability of test performance of a young child and the problems posed by standardized assessment become monumental. Nevertheless, the pressures for programmatic assessment are often so great that the inherent problems of using such instruments to monitor the educational progress of the young, severely impaired child are sometimes overlooked. Standardized tests are by definition valid for certain populations when administered under certain controlled conditions, but rarely are children beyond the fourth standard deviation from the norm included in this standardized group. Even given the availability of standardization norms which include representation of the severely handicapped population, the criteria of controlled administration under set conditions can seldom be met with such a deviant population. Although problems posed by administrative procedures and norm-referenced groups are serious, the major deficiency lies in the type and form of information provided by standardized instruments. Such instruments were not developed to assist interventionists in making relevant educational decisions by providing prescriptive information and/or monitoring daily classroom progress.

The interventionist working with a severely impaired population needs a consistent flow of information that will allow for objective monitoring of a child's progress toward an established behavioral target. Not only is data acquisition important but the collection procedures also need to be efficient and should not place unrealistic demands on the teacher's time. The perfect data system, one which will acquire the necessary data efficiently, is yet to be developed, but we are moving toward this goal.

Our major efforts in evaluating child progress have been concentrated on documenting movement through the project's developmental curricula. These curricular materials cover the areas of sensorimotor, language, motor, and social (self-help) skills. As mentioned earlier, a developmental training lattice has been generated for each area. Using the lattice as a guide, a series of training phases can be defined and sequenced, and each training phase is reduced to a series of specific training targets. The teacher's responsibility is to generate a series of activities in order to reach each specific target. These targets and the relevant activities compose the daily classroom program for each of the children.

Recording group data in order to make programmatic decisions on this population is not only difficult but relatively meaningless (White & Liberty, 1976). These difficulties arise from the wide inter and intra subject variation in the multiple problems and existing abilities of the severely/profoundly handicapped population. Although our data collection format is consistent across children, the selection of targets and activities is done on an individualized basis.

The monitoring system is initiated when the teacher fills out a target objective sheet which contains information derived from the assessment procedures for a specific curricular domain. Table 1 contains a target objective sheet focusing on the gross motor area for child EK. The specific target in this case is to have EK hold his head erect for 3 out of 5 minutes. Included on the target objective sheet are the programmed antecedent events, the desired child response, and the potentially effective consequent events. Once such a target has been established and the intervention initiated, the teacher takes data on a daily basis, if possible, or on a probe basis (e.g., once a week). Data were collected on a daily basis in this particular exemplar target, and were charted as shown in Figure 2. An assessment summary data sheet is also helpful for monitoring a child's movement through an entire curricular domain. Each curriculum has been divided into a series of training phases, and probes administered on these phases systematically provide useful information on the child's progress from phase to phase as he adds increasingly more complex target objectives to his behavioral repertoire.

Implementation and evaluation of this programmatic monitoring system in the classrooms over several months has led the staff to believe that such a system has the potential of being useful to direct interventionists. However, validation of this approach will depend upon further implementation with a broad range of children. Determination of whether the information derived is useful longitudinally, as well as on a short-term basis, is also important. The consistent use of this system within demonstration classrooms should provide the necessary information for making intelligent decisions about the efficacy of this particular child-progress monitoring system.

Intervention Process

Rather than presenting a detailed discussion of programmatic content and specific training

TABLE 1

Sample Target Objective Sheet

NAME E.K. DATE BEGUN 2/8/75

AREA Gross Motor DATE ENDED

TARGET OBJECTIVE: When presented with appropriate antecedent events, EK will continuously hold his head erect for at least three minutes of a five minute period.

Antecedent	Response	Consequence
Trainer will sit with EK in a tripod position, supporting him with hands at his waist. Objects which make noise will be held over the head of EK and the trainer will ask him to "Hold up your head."	EK will slowly raise his head to an erect position (i.e., not tilted to either side) and hold it there for the required period of time.	+ Teacher will hold and move about with EK touching him and saying, "good for you." − Teacher will say nothing, wait a few seconds and reinstate command, or, if this is the end of the session, lay EK on his back and say nothing.

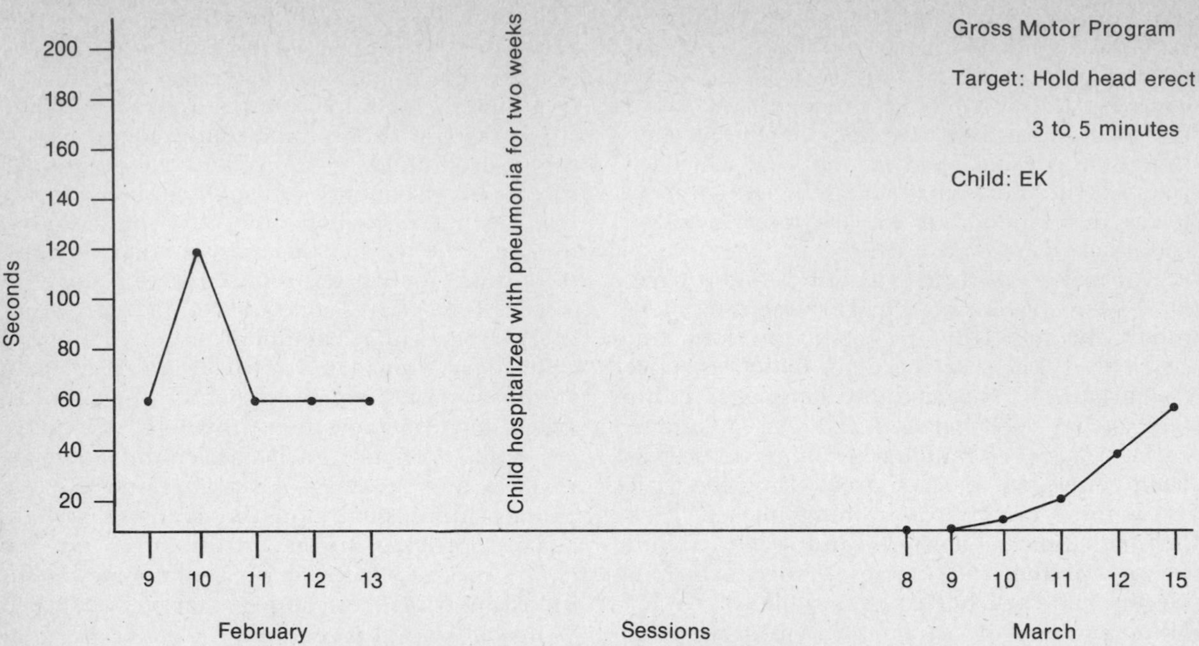

Figure 2. Number of seconds of holding head erect across sessions.

activities, the process of intervention presented in this section will be viewed from a generic perspective. We believe a generic approach facilitates the isolation of the major principles and procedures which transcend daily training activities. Operating from this type of superordinate structure, the intervention process can be conveniently divided into four steps:

1. *Assessment of the child's current functioning level.* This is the process of locating the child in developmental space relative to the target domain.
2. *Development of an intervention strategy.* This strategy should include targeting specific behaviors, selecting potentially effective behavior change strategies and training content, and decision-making as to the most effective means of documenting change.
3. *Implementation of the proposed intervention plan.* Actual implementation should include the use of a wide variety of personnel (including parents), as well as a number of training locations and materials.
4. *Monitoring the effect of intervention on the child's behavior.* The collection and evaluation of data should serve to provide useful programmatic feedback.

The first step in any intervention procedure should be the acquisition of descriptive information necessary for establishing relevant educational objectives. Such information can be obtained through a variety of techniques. Our approach includes administering a developmental test such as The Uniform Performance Assessment System (developed by the Experimental Education Unit at the University of Washington) to assist the teacher in the initial bracketing of the child's developmental level in areas such as communication, preacademic, gross motor, and social-self help skills. Other types of assessment are then employed as may be deemed appropriate (e.g., interview, observations). Once the interventionist has some objective information concerning the child's general functional level, more discrete and detailed information can be obtained by administering assessment instruments linked directly to the curricula. A detailed explanation of this system has been described elsewhere (Bricker, W. A., & Bricker, D. D., 1974; Filler, Robinson, Smith, Vincent-Smith, Bricker & Bricker, 1975). Because our curricula follow a developmental hierarchy, the assumption is that the point at which the child fails in the movement through the assessment phases is the point at which training should be initiated.

After obtaining the necessary information for establishing a series of behavioral targets in each educational domain deemed critical to the child's developmental progress, the next step is to generate a prescriptive program. If one employs a system that relates assessment to the training curriculum, the problem is greatly simplified. The target training objectives become immediately apparent through examination of the child's performance on curricular assessments. How these objectives are to be implemented present the more difficult problems.

Implementation plans should indicate the target, activities to reach established targets, roles of the parent and other adjunctive personnel, and the arrangement of the physical environment. To facilitate the program, the intervention plan needs to be described in sufficient detail both to allow for appropriate execution and to monitor precisely what was done with the child.

Once the plan has been formulated in sufficient detail, the next stage is systematic implementation, which may be largely dependent upon the personnel's knowledge of and skill in using teaching strategies based on behavioral principles. Effective management of the child's behavior by arranging environmental events both on the antecedent and consequence side should facilitate the child's progress toward the established targets. It is important that all trainers use a consistent approach in managing the child's behavior.

Another problem that may arise during the implementation portion of intervention is the coordination of multiple training activities. The interventionist may have to assign priorities to the various behavioral objectives and make sure that activities or objectives are not in competition. With foresight and planning, several objectives can be worked on simultaneously.

The final step in the process of intervention should concentrate on the monitoring of the child's progress toward each of the established behavioral objectives. Procedures for measuring progress have been discussed earlier in this article as well as in other resources (White & Haring, 1976; White & Liberty, 1976). The system that is selected should be functional for the staff, while also providing the necessary information to assist in arriving at sound educational decisions about the child's training program. It is unlikely that a specific evaluation procedure can be applied to an intervention program without modifications that take into account differences in populations, staff, environments, and the educational objectives.

Conclusion

The development of effective early intervention programs for severely handicapped young children means more than assembling interesting materials, exciting people, and imaginative programs. These are artifacts of the more pervasive and more important programmatic components, such as: well-developed rationales, carefully trained staff, adequate developmental curricula, and useful evaluation methods. The goals of the early interventionist should be the development and refinement of these components, as well as thoughtful implementation of sound intervention strategies across various levels of programming. The sobering problems posed by the education of the severely/profoundly handicapped cannot be solved by individuals working in isolation. We must share our information and resources in order to build more effective educational programs for this population.

References

Baldwin, V. An evaluation of curriculum for the severely/profoundly handicapped. In M. A. Thomas (Ed.). *Hey, don't forget about me! Education's investment in the severely, profoundly, and multiply handicapped*. Reston, Virginia: Council for Exceptional Children, 1976.

Bricker, D. D. Educational synthesizer. In M. A. Thomas (Ed.). *Hey, don't forget about me!* Reston, Virginia: Council for Exceptional Children, 1976.

Bricker, D. D., Bricker, W. A., Iacino, R., & Dennison, L. Intervention strategies for profoundly retarded children. In N. Haring and L. Brown (Eds.), *Teaching the severely handicapped: A yearly publication of the American Association for the Education of the Severely/Profoundly Handicapped* (Vol. 1). New York: Grune & Stratton, 1976.

Bricker, W. A., & Bricker, D. D. An early language training strategy. In R. Schiefelbusch and L. Lloyd (Eds.), *Language perspectives: Acquisition, retardation, and intervention* Baltimore: University Park Press, 1974.

Bricker, D. D., Dennison, L., & Bricker, W. A. A language intervention program for developmentally young children. *MCCD Monograph Series #1*, 1976.

Bronfenbrenner, U. Is early intervention effective? *A report on longitudinal evaluations of preschool programs* (Vol. II). DHEW Publication No. (OHD) 74-25, 1974.

Brown, L., Nietupski, J., & Hamre-Neitupski, S. The criterion of ultimate functioning and public school services for severely handicapped students. In M. A. Thomas (Ed.). *Hey, don't forget about me! Education's investment in the severely, profoundly, and multiply handicapped*. Reston, Virginia: Council for Exceptional Children, 1976.

Bruner, J. S. Discussion: Infant education as viewed by a psychologist. In V. H. Denenberg (Ed.), *Education of the infant and young child*. New York: Academic Press, Inc., 1970.

Caldwell, B. The rationale for early intervention. *Exceptional Children*, 1970, *36*(10), 717–726.

Filler, J. W., Jr., Robinson, C. C., Smith, R. A., Vincent-Smith, L., Bricker, D. D., & Bricker, W. A. Evaluation and programming in mental retardation. In N. Hobbs (Ed.). *Issues in the classification of exceptional children*. Vol. I. San Francisco: Jossey-Bass, 1975.

Haring, N., & Bricker, D. Overview of comprehensive services for the severely/profoundly handicapped. In N. Haring (Ed.), *Teaching severely/profoundly handicapped individuals*. New York: Grune & Stratton, 1976.

Hobbs, N. *The futures of children*. San Francisco: Jossey-Bass, 1975.

Hunt, J. McV. *Intelligence and experience*, New York: Ronald Press, 1961.

Karnes, M., & Teska, J. Children's response to intervention programs. In J. Gallapher, (Ed.), *The application of child development research to exceptional children*. Reston, Virginia: The Council for Exceptional Children, 1975

Lewis, M., & Rosenblum, L. (Eds.). *The effect of the infant on its caregiver* (Vol. 1). New York: Wiley-Interscience Publication, John Wiley & Sons, 1974.

Lynch, J., & Bricker, W. Linguisitic theory and operant procedures: Toward an integrated approach to language training for the mentally retarded. *Mental Retardation*, 1972, *10*(2), 12–17.

Martin, E. On education for the severely/profoundly handicapped and Justice Douglas. *The American Association for the Education of the Severely/Profoundly Handicapped*, 1976, *1*, 115–123.

Moore, D., & Moore, R. The dangers of early schooling. *Phi Delta Kappan*, 1972, *53*, 615–621.

Piaget, J. Piaget's Theory. In P. H. Mussen (Ed.), *Carmichael's manual of child psychology* (Vol. 1). New York: John Wiley & Sons, Inc., 1970.

Piaget, J., & Inhelder, B. *The psychology of the child*. New York: Basic Books, 1969.

Sailor, W., Guess, D., & Lavis, L. Training teachers for education of the severely handicapped. *Education and Training of the Mentally Retarded*, 1975, *10*(3), 201–203.

Schaefer, E. S. Need for early and continuing education. In V. H. Denenberg (Ed.), *Education of the infant and young child*. New York: Academic Press, 1970.

Sontag, E., Burke, P. J., & York, R. Considerations for the severely handicapped in public schools. *Education and Training of the Mentally Retarded*, 1973, *8*, 20–26.

Stainback, S., Stainback, W., & Maurer, S. Training teachers for the severely and profoundly handicapped: A new frontier. *Exceptional Children*, 1976, *46*(4), 203–210.

Stott, L. H., & Ball, R. S. Infant and preschool mental tests: Review and evaluation. *Monograph of the Society for Research in Child Development*, 1965, *30*, 1–151.

Weikart, D. P., & Lambie, D. Z. Early enrichment in infants. In V. H. Denenberg (Ed.), *Education of the infant and young child*. New York: Academic Press, 1970.

White, B. L. *The first three years of life*. Englewood Cliffs, New Jersey: Prentice-Hall, 1975.

White, O., & Haring, N. G. *Exceptional teaching*. Columbus, Ohio: Charles Merrill, 1976.

White, O., & Liberty, K. Behavioral assessment and precise educational measurement. In N. Haring & R. Schiefelbusch (Eds.). *Teaching special children*. New York: McGraw Hill, 1976.

DIANE D. BRICKER is an Associate Professor of Pediatrics and Educational Psychology at the University of Miami, where she is associated with the Mailman Center for Child Development. Her duties there include directing an early intervention program for young handicapped children, a model center's program for severely and profoundly handicapped children, and a BEH personnel preparation program for teachers of the severely and profoundly handicapped.

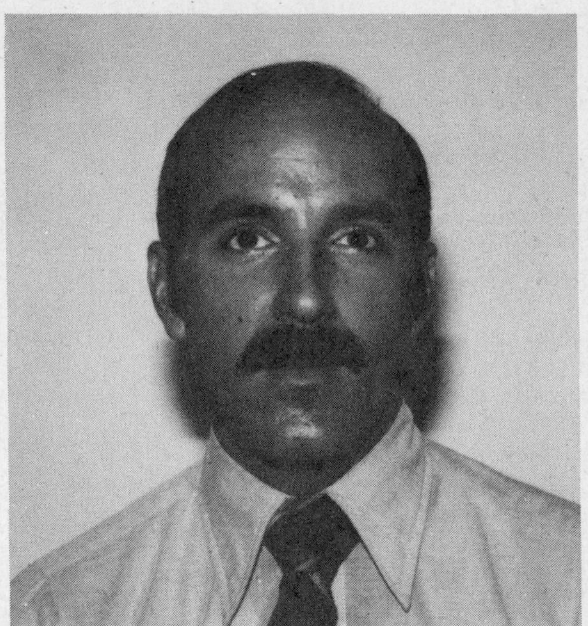

RICHARD IACINO is currently serving as Program Coordinator for the Mailman Center's Debbie School programs at the University of Miami. After receiving a Master's degree in Special Education, he worked at the Kennedy Center Experimental School as classroom coordinator for an early intervention program with developmentally retarded infants. His research interests center on the development of behavioral change monitoring systems for the very young severely impaired.

A Public School Service Delivery Model for Handicapped Children Between Birth and Five Years of Age

LISBETH J. VINCENT
University of Wisconsin-Madison

KAY BROOME
Madison Public Schools

Martin (Note 1) in a policy statement on early childhood education stated that a single agency should assume responsibility for delivering services to preschool-aged handicapped children and that the most logical agency to do this was the public education agency. Presently only 21 states mandate public-school-based programs for handicapped children under five years of age. Of these states, eight require services beginning at birth, one requires services at two years of age, eight at three years of age, and four at four years of age. Even with mandatory legislation, many public school systems are just beginning to develop services. Thus there is need for direction in how to build programs, how to interface these programs into existing public school services, and how to coordinate these programs with existing community services. The purpose of this article is to present one public school system's model for service delivery in the area of early childhood/special education. This school system, Madison Public Schools (MPS), Madison, Wisconsin, has a four-year history of providing early childhood services to at least some handicapped children. In September of 1974, expansion of these services to include all handicapped children three years of age or older was initiated. In September of 1975, these services were expanded downward to include all handicapped children from birth.

The Madison Public Schools Early Childhood Program involves two components, namely services for children birth to three years of age, and services for children three to five years of age. The under-age-three component is funded jointly by funds from the Bureau of Education for the Handicapped and the State of Wisconsin. The three-to-five-year-old component is funded through local public school monies and is consistent with Wisconsin's mandatory education legislation, Chapter 115. The children involved in both components of the program range from severely handicapped to normally functioning and cut across all typical categories used by special education agencies. All classrooms are housed in public school elementary level buildings.

Faculty from various departments at the University of Wisconsin-Madison are affiliated with the project to provide adjunctive services in research, curriculum planning, and undergraduate and graduate student training. This affiliation allows the convergence of maximum expertise on the problems of handicapped and "at risk" children, so as to achieve the goal of creating an educational environment which ensures that each child is receiving the utmost service that educational technology allows us to apply.

One overall goal of early intervention programs should be the smooth transition of all children into traditional kindergartens. This involves building functional/social skills which facilitate blending with peers and adults. While this is not always possible due to factors such as intervention services starting later than birth, or age of diagnosis, or insufficient educational technology, or extreme multihandicapping problems with which regular educators are not trained to deal, this is the goal for each child who enters the Madison Public School Early Childhood Program. The test of whether our system will accomplish this expectation is an evolving one. We, as professionals in the area of early childhood/special education, will need to impact on the systems which serve the children later on. Most certainly, as this evolution takes place, we must be cognizant

This article was supported in part by Grant G007501117 from the Bureau of Education for the Handicapped, USOE, HEW, to Madison Public Schools, Madison, Wisconsin.

of inevitable failures, but we must also recognize that these are results of problems in the system or the professionals' lack of knowledge, and not the children's failures. How often we fail will depend on the speed with which other systems, e.g., educational and medical, evolve. Yet the responsibility for failure must rest with us, the professionals in the area of early childhood/special education, because the accountability for system change is ours more than anyone else's. We must advocate for young handicapped children and demonstrate their potential if other educational, medical, and social systems are to change.

Goals of the Program

In addition to providing direct service of high quality to handicapped children, the MPS early childhood/special education program has four additional goals. These are to: (a) develop a model referral and overall educational service delivery system; (b) continuously develop, validate, and disseminate curriculum and materials for young handicapped children; (c) develop a model system for parent involvement in the program and meeting family needs; and (d) continue to enhance the cooperative arrangement which exists between the public schools, community agencies, and university personnel.

Referral System

If early childhood/special education programs are to be maximally effective, children must be referred as soon as a diagnosis leading to suspected exceptional educational needs is made. Particularly with the more severely handicapped, this is critical. As Beck, Adams, Chandler, and Livingston (1976) point out, 6.8 percent of the potentially handicapped can be identified at or near birth. Most of these children's problems could be considered to fall within the range of severe to profound handicapping conditions. The prime identifiers of these children are personnel from the medical fields. Thus, successful early referral systems are dependent on close ties between educational programs and the medical community. Often these cooperative arrangements have not been established, and consequently children do not receive services as early as they should. This was why we as an educational system set as one of our main goals the development of a model referral system.

During the past year we have learned many valuable lessons about making the referral process work. Presently approximately 85 percent of our children who are referred before they are three years of age are referred by the medical community. A first assumption that people in an educational system needs to make in building a referral system is that it is their responsibility to establish themselves as a credible source of services. Simply announcing that a program is beginning is not sufficient. We have found several strategies effective in this area.

First we made contact with a well respected pediatrician who was supportive of services for the handicapped. We explained to him our program goals, the population we would be serving, the types of services we would offer to children and families. We discussed with him how to make the medical community most aware of these services and asked for his recommendation on strategies which he felt would be most effective in the "saleability" of the project. With his support, we scheduled meetings with various pediatric, family practice, and nursing groups in the city. At these meetings we clearly delineated whom we wished to serve, how we would serve them, and how to refer a family to us. We followed up on this with letters summarizing the presentation to all pediatricians and family practitioners in the city. We also included a referral letter, which they could give to families, explaining the program and how to get involved.

Several additional procedural steps which we have implemented or will be implementing have also proven useful. The first is one of acknowledging a referral. Each time a new medical person or facility refers a child, a letter should be sent which indicates the referral was received, what process will be followed with family, what range of services will be available to the family, and what information the agency or person can expect to receive from the educational system. Then, twice a year the family and child's doctor are sent a summary report which documents present educational goals for the child and educational progress shown. In many instances, the information detailed for physicians is specific to the concerns or treatments they have prescribed. This overcomes the frequent feeling of medical personnel that referring a child to an educational system is like sending him into a big vacuum that never sends information back. An additional strategy that we will begin employing shortly is having parents invite their child's doctor to the school to view the program at a time that is convenient for all of them. Some of our parents have also suggested providing open house sessions when pediatricians/physicians have days off and would be available to visit the project. Additionally, we will also be actively seeking to reach referral sources not presently within our population, e.g., Rheumatoid Arthritis Clinic and School Age Maternity (a Madison Public School program).

Thus, the focus of our referral system is to ensure that the agencies and persons who come in contact with severely/profoundly handicapped children send referrals to us as a standard part of a child's treatment plan. While we have not achieved this with all relevant medical groups in the city, we have made considerable progress. In addition to the medical groups, we have made similar contacts with social service agencies and diagnostic clinics around the city.

Pre-Placement Evaluation System

Each child referred to the public school system as having suspected exceptional educational needs must receive a multi-disciplinary evaluation according to Wisconsin state mandates. The goal of our multi-disciplinary evaluation is to determine whether there is high probability of school failure during kindergarten or first grade without early intervention. This evaluation serves as the first screening and identification of overall needs. Fine-grained assessment which would lead into programming is accomplished after placement in the program.

In order to make this process maximally effective and efficient, we have evolved a concept called the multi-disciplinary diagnostic classroom. When a child is referred, one of the staff family liaison professionals (parent advisor) goes into the home and completes a questionnaire with the parents which covers agencies which would have relevant information on the child, as well as developmental milestone information on the child and areas of parent concern. Once relevant information is gathered from the agencies, the child and parents are scheduled to come into the multi-disciplinary classroom for one afternoon and the following morning. Generally six to eight new children are scheduled for the classroom at the same time. The rationale for scheduling six to eight new children into the classroom has not only been to save staff time, but also to view children in a typical classroom environment and evaluate socialization and interaction skills.

During the first afternoon, one of the program's teachers, who is certified in special education, conducts a standard preschool set of activities, e.g., opening group, fine motor and free play activity ranging from sensorimotor through preacademic domains. During this time, she and the school psychologist isolate areas of concern for each child. These areas are then discussed with personnel from the appropriate disciplines, i.e., speech and language, occupational and physical therapy. The following morning the children come back to the classroom, and these therapy disciplines conduct additional evaluations themselves or direct the teacher in doing so. Following approximately five hours in the classrooms for the children, the discipline representatives sit down and list out areas of exceptional need and program recommendations. These recommendations can vary from a home program with a professional visit once a month to a half-day program four days a week at the center. Also, the recommendations can vary from the involvement of only a special education teacher in developing and implementing the child's plan to four other disciplines being involved, as well. Thus, as a system we do not have a standard program which every child and family receives. We have avoided defining our services on the basis of number of days or hours in school. Rather, we have developed a set of program options for children and parents and attempt to match need to program. Tables 1 and 2 list the various options available for child and family service respectively.

Because of the federal funding which we receive, we are able to serve a small group of children under five years of age who do not have to go through this process. In the infant, toddler, and preschool classrooms, children at risk for developmental problems due to extreme prematurity at birth, extreme environmental neglect, or deprivation factors are also included. While the probability of educational problems when reaching traditional school age is substantial with these children, their early involvement in an interventive system can often circumvent these problems.

Educational Service System

One goal of the classroom-based portion of the MPS early childhood/special education program is to break down the categorical system which results in children's being labeled as one problem type or another (e.g., emotionally disturbed or trainable mentally retarded) early in their educational careers. Other than being identified as displaying exceptional educational needs (EEN), children in the program do not receive typical diagnostic labels. In fact, classrooms contain a wide variety of children with a wide variety of needs. The model

TABLE 1

Program Options for Children

1. Four day per week classroom placement (2¾ hrs. per day).
2. Three day per week classroom placement (2¾ hrs. per day).
3. One day per week classroom placement with parent attending the session and providing transportation.
4. Two one-hour visits to the center per month.
5. One one-hour visit to the center each month.
6. Maintenance check and/or ongoing assessment as needed in another agency setting or in the home.
7. Program consultation to other agency personnel and programming provided in the agency.
8. Home visits by parent advisor and/or other staff members.
9. Other (specified by parents and staff members).

is one of heterogeneous rather than homogeneous classroom groupings. For example, of the 12 children in a classroom, four may be at risk but developmentally normal, four may show mild developmental problems, and four may have moderate to severe developmental problems.

This enables personnel to focus on blending the severely or profoundly handicapped child into the overall classroom environment (blending in the sense that the child will not be immediately identified as different from his peers). In this context social skills become critical and, within the project, appropriate social interaction with adults, other children, and materials is stressed. A child who has severe learning problems can more readily be maintained in a normal environment if his interactive patterns are appropriate. Focusing on social skills does not diminish the learning problems of the children; it does however allow parents to view their child not as someone who is handicapped but rather as someone who has handicapping problems. That is, each child also has strengths—strengths which may mean that inclusion in normal environments is not only possible, but also appropriate.

In order to meet the diverse needs of children grouped in this fashion, professionals from fields other than special education must be involved, and in fact, become an integral part of the educational service system. The concept of interdisciplinary services is not a new one. Many diagnostic clinics are based on an interdisciplinary model, but the model does not usually include the idea of various disciplines training other professionals to perform their functions. This trading of disciplinary skills is the cornerstone of our service delivery model. We call this approach transdisciplinary, implying that the goal of the team is, to the maximum extent possible, to trade skills across disciplines. At present, seven disciplines are involved in providing classroom and home-based educational services to children. These are occupational therapy, physical therapy, psychology, special education, speech and language therapy, social work, and parents. Additional disciplines that we would like to include are adaptive physical education, nutrition, nursing, medicine, art, and music. The dictum of involvement is that all services provided must be in the classroom

TABLE 2

Program Options for Parents

Parents may be involved in one or as many as all of the following.

1. *Classroom Observations and Conferences*: Designed to familiarize parents with ongoing school programming and to allow parents and teachers the opportunity to discuss common goals and concerns.
2. *Classroom Participation*: Designed to provide parents with specific modeling and instruction in programming areas which are being developed in or transitioned to the home.
3. *Telephone Contacts*: Telephone conversations between parents and parent advisor can occur for the following reasons:
    a. Concerns dealing with daily school operation including transportation, illness, changes in the daily schedule, etc.
    b. Specific concerns or questions related to the child's in-class program.
    c. Requests from parents for assistance with behaviors in the home.
    d. Parent advisor may initiate contact to monitor child's home progress.
4. *Notebooks*: A notebook can be sent back and forth between home and school each day in which parents, teachers, therapists, and parent advisors write out noted areas of child progress, and/or problems being encountered.
5. *Home Visits*: Can be requested by parents or arranged by the parent advisor for the purpose of assessing child related programs and development of a plan to deal with them. Staff may be available for further home visits as needed for follow-up.
6. *Involvement with other agencies*: Services offered by the Early Childhood Program will be coordinated with service being offered to the family by other agencies.
7. *Parent Meetings*: All parents are invited to attend meetings on topics such as nutrition, audiology, discipline, etc. The meetings are scheduled as topics are suggested by parents or staff.
8. *Parent Task Forces*: Parents are invited to join and develop task forces which provide information to the project staff itself and the community.

and home environment. Removing a child to a therapy room or testing room is generally prohibited. Forcing service delivery into the classroom enhances trading of skills by the various professionals. Thus, just as we are attempting to break down categorical barriers that result in children's being labeled and then channeled into systems based on the label, we are attempting to break down the disciplinary barriers that result in professionals fighting over children and families.

Of course, simply deciding to develop a transdisciplinary system does not guarantee better service delivery to children and families. Embedding this system in a model which ascribes to accountability and objectivity is necessary. For example, performing physical therapy within the classroom environment does not guarantee that it will be more functional or effective than when performed in a therapy room or clinic. Teaching educators and parents to carry out therapeutic routines across the day does not guarantee greater child progress. However, combining this system with the setting of target objectives, and the systematic evaluation of child progress through data collection, does allow for manipulating level of service to achieve maximal progress. As Sternat, Nietupski, Lyon, Messina, and Brown (1977) have indicated, the transdisciplinary model must be submitted to rigorous evaluation at all times. Such evaluation will enable professionals to individually determine program effectiveness and predict change. Dictating a transdisciplinary team approach does not exclude the many evolutionary stages that must be dealt with.

Building therapeutic services into the classroom environment allows for programming for multiple objectives. Particularly with the more severely involved child, programming for an individual target across a variety of settings, materials, and people is critical (Brown, Nietupski and Hamre-Nietupski, 1976). Within the early childhood project, we are attempting to establish language, motor, social, and cognitive goals for all activities. For example, assessment by the occupational therapist may indicate that the child needs a program in the self-feeding area. Assessment by the speech and language therapist may indicate that the child needs to be programmed in the area of one-word phrases. Assessment by the special education teacher may indicate that the child needs a program in the area of one-to-one correspondence. These three professionals would then meet together to design a set of activities which would involve all these areas. For example, an activity based around snack time which includes facilitative techniques for self-feeding, passing out one cup and napkin to each child, and requesting more of the snack-time foods when desired, or labeling the foods, might be developed. The activity might be conducted by the teacher each time the child is in school and by the parent each afternoon at home. Data collection might be set up on a weekly basis to determine whether the objectives are being met.

In this manner, maximum functionality can be stressed, as can performance across persons, places, and materials. At the same time, systematic examination of data collected can guide the teacher, therapists, and parent in determining program effectiveness and change. Within our public school project, we are attempting to implement this system for at least four activities per day per child. Setting priorities for program areas is a group process involving the whole team and is dependent on the team's meeting together weekly to determine needed changes. Determining needed changes rests on the specific sharing of the team's various areas of expertise. Pragmatically, the system involves careful specification of responsibility for program implementation and data collection, and more complex data collection systems than response-by-response recording.

In addition to the multi-objective system, the classrooms operate on the basis of small group rather than one-to-one instruction, and social rather than tangible reinforcement. This means that the team may be developing an activity for four children, all of whom are at different functional levels. Most often this is accomplished by adapting materials for use at all levels. For example, at one table might be four children who are working on stringing beads. For one child the string might be thick, round, stable plastic and the beads large and round. For another, the string might be thin, plastic, and bendable, the beads small and square. For two others, the string might be very bendable, thin cord and the beads multi-shaped and colored. The first two children could be working individually to get the beads on (fine motor), with the language objective involving verbs (e.g., push and pull) or spatial concepts (e.g., in and through). The other two children might be engaged in a match game, i.e., one child chooses a bead and strings it, and the other child must choose one like it. A cognitive objective of matching color and shape could be operative here, as well as a fine motor objective. For all the children, working independently without adult direction and reinforcement might also be operative.

In summary, the MPS educational system for children under five years of age stresses matching program options with child need. The basic approach is transdisciplinary in nature, involves heterogeneous grouping of children and programming for multiple objectives.

Curriculum Development

As could be interpreted from the preceding discussion, commercially available kits or curricula do not fully meet the model of our early childhood program. In this sense, our service delivery system is an evolving one, our curriculum a changing one. As D. Bricker and W. Bricker (1971) have indicated, bridging together service and research systems is necessary in the area of early childhood/special education if we are to develop maximally effective teaching strategies and procedures for young handicapped children.

Particularly in the area of curriculum development, the cooperation between public school and university personnel is highlighted. In the past year, two dissertations were completed in the program, one in the area of teaching strategy (Certo, Note 2), the other in the area of mother-child interaction (Eheart, Note 3). In addition, two master's theses in the area of parenting skills were undertaken. These research studies, while serving to fulfill degree requirements for the students involved, were directly relevant to the overall classroom and home programs. For example, Certo (Note 2) examined two strategies for teaching preschool children a table-setting task. In one strategy, teacher and setting were varied successively; in the second strategy teacher and setting were varied concurrently. The basic question examined was whether either strategy resulted in the greater learning during acquisition and greater generalization to new teachers and setting. Both strategies were found to be effective during acquisition, and the children involved in each strategy generalized the skills learned to a new teacher and setting. If this finding is replicated across other task situations, it will have significant impact on designing the overall classroom environment. If children learn equally well when teachers and settings are varied during acquisition, greater programming flexibility can be developed.

A new study in which program staff and children will be involved concerns orthopedic needs. In conjunction with a resident in pediatrics at the university, the physical therapist on staff has designed a study to evaluate the effectiveness of foot pointing as a diagnostic tool. Foot pointing was initiated by project staff as a means of evaluating the effectiveness of physical therapy programs to correct gait problems. This effort serves as an example of direct service leading into research.

The development and dissemination of written curriculum products is not only a requirement of our federal funding but a professional obligation and responsibility of educators. Each system must modify and adapt currently available materials and develop new procedures. Exact replication of what other systems or persons have done is not possible and probably not desirable. The key in curriculum development is documentation of effectiveness through rigorous data collection. In this sense, a good service system is a good research system.

Curriculum products which we are currently developing or will be begining in the next year vary from individual programs to overall sequences in an area. Both public school personnel and university students and staff are involved in developing these products. Some examples are a fine motor checklist and curriculum for classroom use based on functional everyday living motor skills, a pragmatic presentation on the operation of a transdisciplinary team, a checklist and curriculum in the area of social/play skills, and a parent manual based on family daily routine. These will be available upon request to other systems, educators, parents, and therapists. Hopefully, they will be used by others as guides, not cookbook answers, in developing service delivery systems.

Family Parent Program

As Hayden (1976) has indicated, early intervention services are greatly needed by parents of young handicapped children. In this sense, including a parent component in a program is one way that the system provides help to families. However, in addition to parents needing help from the system, the system needs help from the parents if it is to be maximally effective. As indicated earlier, parents are one of the disciplines which comprise our team. By this we mean that, like professional disciplines, parents have a set of skills and expertise which they bring to the educational environment. As with other disciplines, these skills are used in determining child needs and program recommendations. In this respect, parent training takes place within the context of one discipline teaching another its skills. Parents train other disciplinary members on the team, and the team members also train parents. Some parents can provide the educational system more valuable information than others, but then so can some speech and language therapists provide more information than others. Just as special education teachers will vary in terms of the amount of inservice or preservice training they will need to work effectively with young handicapped children, so will parents. The only difference between parents and these other disciplines is in staff selection and hiring.

While with paid staff we carefully interview and select persons who have highly developed skills and appropriate interaction patterns with young handicapped children, with parents this process is not possible. Every family referred to the project is accepted if the child displays exceptional educational needs. This means that our service system for parents must have many options. Just as there is no standard program for children, there is no standard program for parents. Rather, the staff and parents themselves attempt to match family needs with the options outlined in Table 2. One overall goal set up for all families, however, is that a mechanism for their ongoing input and involvement with the program be developed. If the parents do not become involved in the program through one of these options, we attempt to develop other options. Overall, the program staff assumes that there is no such thing as an uncooperative parent. "Uncooperative" in this context means that the parent will not do what the educator wants. In children, we term this behavior noncompliance and then develop programs to change it. We are attempting to take a similar approach to parents with the additional point that parents will be involved in developing the change program themselves.

Particularly in families with severely/profoundly handicapped young children, services other than educational programs for the child are often necessary, e.g., medical, social services, and respite care. Thus, part of our parent program involves helping families obtain the services necessary to maintain their child at home in a fashion that is as unobtrusive for the family fashion as possible. In order to achieve this goal, we have placed the responsibility for the parent program not with the classroom teacher but with persons we call parent advisors.

Parent advisors assume responsibility for helping parents to carry classroom programs into the home and also for helping parents to obtain other needed resources and to become involved in the program in ways other than their child's educational program. Recently the parents and parent advisors formed seven task forces to tackle issues and problems ranging from changing legislation to obtaining materials needed in the classroom. These task forces are: (a) information dissemination; (b) record keeping; (c) public legislation; (d) parent touring of visitors; (e) finding materials; (f) referral; (g) parent-developed questionnaire to evaluate the project. Each task force will be chaired by a parent and the chairperson will sit on the project's overall parent advisory panel.

Parents have requested group meetings to discuss issues such as nutrition and behavior management at home. Parents and staff have conducted group meetings on educational topics, such as language development. In addition, parents may choose to come into their child's classroom as observers, data recorders, or teachers on a weekly or monthly basis.

The cornerstone of the parent component is multiple options and flexibility. In order to participate in the project, all parents do not have to do the same thing or commit themselves to a standard set of activities. As indicated earlier, we have hired separate staff members to handle the parent component. Parent advisors must have a wide range of skills in order to carry out this type of parent program. Presently, no one discipline trains personnel to fill this role. That is, we have not found a social work, school psychology, or special education program which trains their graduates to be developers of educational programs for handicapped children, developers and finders of community resources, and support counselors. Therefore, we have chosen to fill our parent advisor positions with representatives from each of these disciplines. Within the context of our transdisciplinary model, these disciplines are responsible for training each other.

As with the transdisciplinary approach in the classroom, this does not inherently guarantee better service delivery to families. It only allows maximal flexibility in allocating resources to potentially meet family needs. Ongoing evaluation of effectiveness is still necessary. It was out of this concern that the task force on evaluating the parent program grew. The traditional means of evaluation, such as determining whether the child's behavior changed after training the parent, or whether the parent's attitude changed after being involved in the parent group, are not sufficient. In the first case, with the severely/profoundly handicapped child the parent could be carrying out a program exactly as we specified and the child might not change because our educational technology is not sufficient. In the second case, the parent could have a better attitude toward their child but still choose to institutionalize because the demands and disruption on the family are too great to maintain the child at home. We do not have a solution to evaluating program effectiveness at this point. Hopefully, out of the task force will come some initial solutions.

Forming the task force is in some ways a solution itself for it says we, as an educational system, do not have all the answers to measuring whether we have helped parents achieve the best possible resources for themselves or their child. As the persons receiving the resources, we would like the parents to help us decide how to evaluate them, rather than deciding what will be evaluated ourselves. This approach recognizes that the parent is an integral discipline with a set of skills and expertise that they bring to the educational system.

Resource Allocation

From reading the previous description of our public schools program, it would be easy to assume that we are an extremely resource-rich system, much richer than other systems. After all, we have teachers and therapists and parent advisors, while many systems have only teachers. We want to point out that we are probably no richer in resources than most early childhood/special education programs. We have only allocated our resources differently. For example, in June of 1976 we were serving 105 children. In many systems this would mean 10–12 special education teachers. Instead, we had five teachers, three parent advisors, one speech and language therapist, one occupational therapist, and one physical therapist. Each teacher, in conjunction with the rest of the team, handled programming for approximately 20 children. Our staff/child ratio, including classroom aides, secretary, and curriculum specialist, is about 6 to 1 which is similar to many early childhood/special education programs around the country.

Conclusion

As a system, we are not extremely resource rich, but we have allocated our resources in a way that we believe will prove maximally beneficial to the children. We must emphasize that we do not believe that we have the answer to ameliorating the problems of young, developmentally disabled children. Rather, we are combining flexible service delivery to children and families with data collection as a way of developing answers. Through a combination of public school, university, and community services, we hope to develop solutions quickly.

The transdisciplinary approach, in conjunction with heterogeneous groupings of children and programming for multiple objectives, seems to offer the most promising direction, particularly in terms of severely/profoundly handicapped young children. Direction is, however, only useful to the extent that it is grounded in rigorous data collection and accountability for child and family change. Direction is only valid to the extent that we, as educators, upset the predictions for future progress that are made about the young severely/profoundly handicapped children with whom we work.

Reference Notes

1. Martin, E. Public policy and early childhood education: A Buddhist garden. Paper presented at the Education Commission of the States national symposium. Boston, Mass., August, 1974.
2. Certo, N. *A systematic comparison of the relative effectiveness of inducing generalization through the utilization of a concurrent vs. successive procedure during initial skill acquisition with handicapped students*. Unpublished doctoral dissertation. Madison, Wis: University of Wisconsin, 1976.
3. Eheart, B. *An observational study of mother-child and mother-mentally retarded child interactions*. Unpublished doctoral dissertation. Madison, Wis: University of Wisconsin, 1976.

References

Beck, R., Adams, G., Chandler, L., & Livingston, S. The need for adjunctive services in management of severely and profoundly handicapped individuals: A view from primary care. In N. G. Haring & L. Brown (Eds.). *Teaching the severely handicapped: A yearly publication of the American Association for the Education of the Severely/Profoundly Handicapped, Volume I*. New York: Grune & Stratton, 1976.

Bricker, D., & Bricker, W. *Toddler research and intervention project report: Year 1*. IMRID Behavioral Science Monograph No. 20. Nashville, Tenn: George Peabody College, 1971.

Brown, L., Nietupski, J., & Hamre-Nietupski, S. The criterion of ultimate functioning and public school services for severely handicapped students. In M. A. Thomas (Ed.). *Hey! Don't forget about me: New directions for serving the severely handicapped*. Reston, Va: Council for Exceptional Children, 1976.

Hayden, A., & McGinness, G. Bases for early intervention. In E. Sontag, J. Smith, and N. Certo (Eds.). *Educational programming for the severely and profoundly handicapped*. Reston, Va: Division on Mental Retardation of the Council for Exceptional Children, 1977.

Sternat, J., Nietupski, J., Lyon, S., Messina, R., & Brown, L. Occupational and physical therapy services for severely handicapped students: Toward a naturalized public school service delivery model. In E. Sontag, J. Smith, and N. Certo (Eds.). *Educational programming for the severely and profoundly handicapped*. Reston, Va: Division on Mental Retardation of the Council for Exceptional Children, 1977.

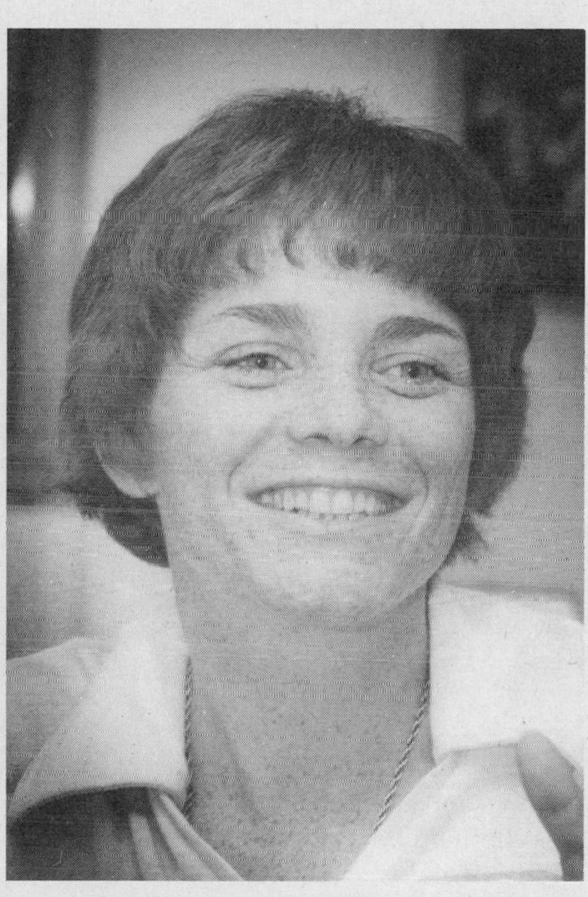

LISBETH J. VINCENT received her doctoral degree in developmental psychology from George Peabody College, Nashville, Tennessee, in 1975. Presently, she is an Assistant Professor in the Department of Studies in Behavioral Disabilities at the University of Wisconsin, Madison, Wisconsin, and Project Director with the Madison Public Schools Early Childhood Program.

KAY BROOME received her master's degree in special education from the University of Wisconsin, Madison, Wisconsin, in 1974. Presently she is the Project Coordinator of the Infant, Toddler and Preschool Project, a part of the Madison Public Schools Early Childhood Program.

VII Teaching Strategies: Measurement and Management

If there is a stereotype of the severely handicapped person, it is that of an individual who cannot do much of anything. While it is true that the severely handicapped person is by definition one who has extreme behavioral deficits, our work with these people has led us to the conclusion that they are capable of doing many worthwhile things—more useful and enjoyable things, in fact, than many casual observers would believe. However, the severely handicapped are often impeded by their behavioral excesses, and this makes it necessary to help them stop doing things that are maladaptive.

James M. Kauffman and Martha E. Snell

Measurement and Evaluation Procedures for Programming with the Severely and Profoundly Handicapped

NORRIS G. HARING

University of Washington

Teaching exceptional children requires exceptional programming techniques. These techniques include careful assessment of each pupil's level of functioning in all areas of development, formation of precise educational programs, careful sequencing of steps within each program to ensure successful progress, professional use of the principles of applied behavior analysis, and appropriate use of measurement tools which will accurately measure pupil progress through each phase of the program.

All of these components are necessary to help handicapped children learn. When the child is severely or multiply handicapped, each of these components becomes vital. Without careful adherence to all of these techniques, the chance of a severely handicapped child's making continued progress toward the goal of eventual self-sufficiency becomes a matter of sheer luck.

A recent survey queried professionals and students in the field of special education who work with severely handicapped pupils (Lynch, Shoemaker, & White, 1976). They were asked to indicate which training materials they needed most, and 76% expressed a need for further training in measurement and evaluation techniques. This area was given high priority for materials development. Without precise measurement tools to monitor child progress, the best-designed programs may be unsuccessful. Without effective evaluation techniques to determine when a child should move to the next phase or program, severely handicapped pupils and their teachers may waste weeks or months on programs that lead nowhere.

General Rules for Measurement of the Severely/Profoundly Handicapped

When steps are small, measurement is more sensitive to behavior changes. Because severely handicapped pupils learn with more difficulty and at a slower rate than less handicapped or normal children, programs to teach such skills as teeth-brushing or independent toileting must be broken down into small increments, or "slices." Then, as the child progresses through each program slice, his proficiency is carefully measured, so that he is moved to the next step only when he has satisfactorily mastered the one preceding it, neither too quickly (before mastery), nor too slowly (after the child becomes bored with the task).

Though group teaching programs are often effective for certain types of learning situations, in general this paper advocates individualized instruction. When programs are designed for individuals, each pupil can progress at his own speed, and measurement can precisely reflect his progress.

Definitions

Measurement, assessment, and evaluation are terms that will be used over and over in this paper. Here are the definitions that will be used for these three processes:

Measurement. A dynamic measure of behavior which charts performance, its rate, quality, or quantity over time, preferably *daily.*

Assessment. Measurement of an individual's performance at any one time to determine his status in cumulative skill or knowledge.

Evaluation. Measurement of an entire sequence or program after it has been completed, in order to assess its effectiveness.

Measuring Observable Behaviors

Deciding *what* to measure is the bridge between program design and measurement technique. First, measure only directly observable behaviors. That is, measure "times pupil looks at ball, pats ball, or rolls ball," not "times pupil plays with ball." These behaviors can be observed by anyone taking data, and this method removes the subjective bias that could occur if the teacher were measuring a vague behavior, such as "seems sad."

Reliable Measures

Another criterion for measurement is reliability. Can an observer achieve consistent marking of a behavior across time? Can two independent observers come up with the same behavior count? If they cannot, then perhaps the behavior selected for measurement is not directly measurable, or perhaps the teacher has not adequately specified what elements constitute the behavior in the first place. Measurement is wasted when inaccuracies occur too frequently, making the data unreliable.

Frequent Measurement

Behavioral change cannot always be detected from one observation or one day of measurement. Often, data must be taken over several observation periods before any clear picture of performance becomes visible. Moreover, data collected frequently, preferably daily, gives the teacher a more accurate picture of the child's actual progress. The more times a behavior is observed and measured, the sooner the teacher knows when it is time to change the program, either because the pupil has mastered the task, or because the data show that the particular teaching intervention is not producing the desired change.

Seeing Change

White and Liberty (1976) have identified various types of changes in behavior. They have broken down, in chart form, the dimensions of observable behavior change. What they have to say about the types of changes that can occur in a child's behavior is worth quoting:

> It is not enough to see behavior. As educators we must see *change* in behaviors. A description of an observable behavior must include a description of the part of the behavior to be changed.
>
> Change in behavior may take many forms. A *topographical* change involves the muscular or skeletal part of the behavior. An answer may be either oral or written (using different muscles). A hand may be raised or lowered (using a different sequence of the same muscles).
>
> Behavior may change in *force*. Does a child whisper, or shout? When writing, is the pencil mark so light that the words are illegible, or is the mark made with such force that the pencil lead breaks? In each case, the general topography (i.e., the muscles and sequence of muscle actions) remains about the same, but the energy or force is changed.
>
> Behaviors with the same force may still vary in *locus*—their direction or target. Does the child shout at the teacher, or at one of his peers? Is the answer written at the base of the problem, or on an answer sheet? In order to change locus, some part of the topography must also change. Have you ever tried to look at a different part of the room without moving a muscle?
>
> These first three types of changes are usually classed under the general reading of "physical." They all deal with the behavior itself. Behavior does not occur in a vacuum, however; behavior occurs in time. There are three "temporal" dimensions of behavior which must also be considered:
>
> First, the *duration* of a behavior may change. A shout may last for two seconds, or drag on for a whole minute. A child might take five minutes to read a short story, or an hour. The behaviors are more or less the same, but they take different amounts of time to complete.
>
> Second, the *latency* between a behavior and some event may change. That is, the delay between some stimulus, or cue, and the time when a behavior is finally emitted may get longer or shorter. A child, for example, who comes to his mother within a minute when called is considerably different than one who takes 30 minutes to arrive after the first call. They both arrive, so the behaviors per se are the same, but the relationship between the behavior and some other event in the environment (in this case, calling) changes.
>
> Lastly, the *frequency*, or *rate*, of a behavior, the number of times a behavior occurs within a specified period of time, may change. Words may be read orally at 10 words per minute or 100 words per minute. In each case the behaviors (words read) remain the same, but are occurring more or less rapidly. The change is not between the behavior and the general environment, but rather between two or more substances of the same behavior. In this sense, behavior may create part of its own environment. (pp. 234–236)

Measures Related To the Program Objectives/Goals

Whatever type of measurement technique the teacher decides to use, he must keep in mind the intended outcome of the task. If the task is "sorts bolts," then the teacher might want simply to measure the number of times the pupil responds correctly. But if he wants the child to begin to sort bolts within a certain time limit (latency), then the measurement tool used must be appropriate for that program. In this case, the teacher might use a measure of responses per minute (how many bolts the pupil can sort in one minute). Such a measure is valuable for preparing a handicapped individual for a work situation.

To review the general rules for measurement, a measurement technique should:

1. Measure small increments of a program (program slices).
2. Be individualized for each pupil on each task.
3. Measure directly observable behaviors.
4. Be reliable over time or between observers.
5. Measure behavior frequently, preferably daily.
6. Relate to the intended performance objective.

One final rule: measurement must be usable by classroom teachers. It looks impressive to design a program that involves measuring correct and error behaviors by frequency, percentage, and latency, but, if the teacher cannot understand the charting procedure, or does not have the manpower or time to measure so many factors, then he will not measure. Measurement must be carried out if a program is to be effective. The best measure, as will be discussed again later in this paper, is the one that is *used*.

Types of Measurement Techniques

The type of measurement tactic to be used in any program must depend on the individual pupil's response characteristics and the nature of each task. Severely and profoundly handicapped individuals learn so slowly that great care must be taken to ensure an effective measure of performance, so that pupils can progress in the most expeditious manner possible toward long-range goals.

There are several forms of measurement commonly used with this population. They range from checklists which measure simply whether or not a child displays a behavior, to percentage of correct and/or error responses made during skill acquisition, to various frequency measures which take into account time spent in the learning process, to trials to criterion. Each of these forms of measurement needs to be examined with respect to its effectiveness in programs for both children and adults.

Binary Checklists

The easiest measurement technique to employ is the checklist, which requires only a "yes" or "no" answer about a pupil's behavior. Can Ted speak his name when asked to say it? Was Mary dry when she came to school this morning? Either she was or she was not dry. Checklists are useful when measuring only whether behaviors occurred or not.

Assessment batteries most often use such checklists. A teacher assessing toileting skills marks "yes" if the child can toilet independently. But think how many actual skills a child must have in order to master this important task: he must know when to enter the bathroom, must know how and in what order to pull down and up his pants, perform, cleanse himself, flush the toilet, and return to whatever he was doing before. To say simply that a child cannot toilet independently may mean anything from "he cannot recognize when to approach the toilet" to "he forgets to wash his hands after toileting." Both individuals still need help in correct toileting procedures, but the former pupil obviously needs more teaching than the latter does. Checklists are most effective when they measure small increments of behaviors, such as "pulls down pants," rather than a gross measure of "toilets independently."

It is easy to look at a cerebral palsied teenager confined to a wheelchair and mark "no" beside the activity "walks independently." However, this tells the teacher nothing about how long the individual has been unable to walk, or how close he can come to walking now, or whether he will ever be able to walk. All the teacher knows is that on that day, that person could not walk. This example points up the major flaws of checklists: (a) they only measure ability after a skill has been learned; (b) they allow no fine distinctions in present ability level; (c) they cannot be used to predict future capabilities; and (d) they measure ability at one observation only, which may be misleading if the individual can perform the task sometimes, but not consistently, an important fact to know in programming for learning. Only when it is used periodically can a checklist reflect behavior changes with any sensitivity.

One drawback of checklists, that of performance measurement over time, can be obviated by periodic application of the same assessment battery. In this way, teachers can at least have a very general evaluation of pupil progress. If, from academic quarter to quarter, a child still cannot button his jacket, then the teacher should initiate a different program to teach this skill. At the Experimental Education Unit, we have devised a computerized information system which employs the checklist form to measure individual child progress in four major skill areas.

The Uniform Performance Assessment System, or UPAS, is designed to measure performance in handicapped individuals from birth to the age of marketable vocational skill abilities.

At this time, level A (birth to age 6) has undergone two field tests. Eventually, academic, physical fitness, vocational, and independent living skill levels will be added to UPAS.

The Level A behavioral checklist contains approximately 247 items in four skill areas: gross motor, pre-academic, social/self-help, and communication. Accompanying it are instructions on exactly what conditions must be observed when measuring each behavior. Behaviors are checked either "yes" or "no" for most items; for some skills, such as sorting by color or shape, fluency or accuracy measures are used. These indicate the number of behaviors emitted within a certain time period. Each skill is assessed by several items, not just one, to give a clear picture of actual functioning level in a certain area, such as ability to match, which is tested by colors, shapes, quantities, and lotto cards.

UPAS is administered by the teacher to every pupil in the program once during each academic quarter. While the UPAS is a checklist, administering it four times a year offsets one of the major problems with checklists, which is measurement over time. By evaluating the change in ability from one quarter to the next, the teacher can locate the areas in which the child continues to lag developmentally, and can design specific programs to help him meet item objectives. Though UPAS follows the general sequence of normal development, it is designed to assess handicapped children, and thus is less concerned with measuring growth against what is normal for an age level than with measuring child performance against an ultimate functioning goal—self-sufficiency within the community.

Assessment checklists like UPAS do have certain advantages. They take little teacher time or special knowledge to administer. In the case of UPAS, which is a computer checklist, the data are easy to enter, store, and analyze. Such checklists can be used to guide general program planning. They are useful if teachers are careful not to rely on checklists of gross skill ability to measure pupil progress on more specific programs. General checklists should be used only for initial measurement of gross behavioral characteristics. Once a teacher discovers lags in development, he can plan programs which employ more sophisticated forms of measurement.

Gentry and Haring (1976) discuss a similar measure called "item data." When programs are sliced, binary data can be collected on each step of the sequence. Thus, if the behavior discussed earlier—independent toileting—were subjected to task analysis (dividing a task into its component parts), the teacher could check "yes" or "no" for each step. This would enable the teacher to see exactly where the pupil needed instruction to master the entire skill. Item data more precisely measure ability and are more responsive to behavioral changes than some other checklist measures.

Time-ruled checklists, which include time as a condition of measurement, are effective because teachers can measure how many times a behavior occurs over a certain period of time. White and Liberty (1976) describe a detailed process of time-ruled measurement, in which codes are used to record behavioral incidents every minute, or during some other predetermined time frame. The teacher observes a pupil's behavior for a set amount of time each day, and codes his actions as they occur. Though the time-ruled checklists provide a detailed account of behaviors emitted over time, they are quite difficult to record, because of the memorization of codes and the teacher time which must be devoted to recording. A simpler way to measure the occurrence of behavior over time is to use percent.

Percent

Of all forms of measurement which require computation of raw data, percent is the easiest for teachers to use and interpret. Percent data measure the number of times a behavior occurs out of the total number of opportunities for it to occur. The formula for finding percent correct (or in error) of a behavior is:

$$\text{Percent} = \frac{\text{number of correct behaviors}}{\text{number of possible occurrences}} \times 100$$

Because so many everyday measurements are expressed in percentages, such as the probability of rain or the proportion of fat in skim milk, we are all familiar with its interpretation. Ninety percent of anything still means most of it, just as two percent means very little.

Percent is sometimes a more accurate measure of performance than binary checklists or item data. It standardizes behavior counts from day to day by keeping the number of correct responses in perspective at all times. Thus, if a child correctly placed a block on a box 8 out of 10 times one day, and 16 out of 32 times the following day, he still decreased from 80% correct to 50% over that time period, even though in terms of raw data he was correct twice as often on day two. When the pupil has many opportunities to respond, generally at least 10, then percentage is a good measure. If the behavior such as tantrumming occurs only four or five times a day, then another measure, such as a simple count of occurrences, might be more effective. The study described next is a good example of the use of percent to measure behavior change.

Self-stimulation among autistic children is often viewed as an obstacle to learning more productive behaviors. Decreasing such behavior is a necessary first step for many teachers. Koegel, Firestone, Kramme, and Dunlap (1974) attempted to increase appropriate play with toys while decreasing the percentages of self-stimulatory behaviors. The method they used was an A-B-A, or reversal, design. During all conditions, the two children involved in the study were seated in a room with three toys placed in front of them for five minutes at a time, several times a day. During the first condition, A or baseline, the children were allowed to self-stimulate at will. One child emitted these behaviors 100% of the time; the other child ranged from 97% to 100%. Play with toys during the phase averaged 2% for the first child and 13% for the second. During the experimental phase (B), an experimenter shouted "no" every time the child began to engage in self-stimulatory behaviors and either held the part of the child's body with which he was emitting the behavior or delivered a mild slap to that part. The percentage of time sample intervals during which unwanted behavior occurred decreased to below 10% and 13% respectively, while the percent of time spent playing with toys increased to above 65% and 85%. When the design was returned to condition A, the unwanted self-stimulation increased rapidly to pre-intervention levels, demonstrating that a mild form of punishment could be effective in suppressing unwanted behaviors that interfered with desirable ones.

This study shows how effective percentage can be in measuring behaviors. Because the number of self-stimulatory behaviors emitted by both children was so high, a simple count would have been an ineffective method of measuring the behavior, so a time-sample count was recorded for the first 3 seconds of each 10-second interval of each session. Measurement by percentage allowed the authors to analyze and replay great numbers of behavioral occurrences in manageable form. The readers of the journal article have a clear understanding of the change in behavior because the data are represented in narrative and graph form in a measure easily understood—percentage.

However, this study, as constructed, could not have shown the possible change in the quality of appropriate play in either child. The data showed that the percentage of appropriate play increased under the experimental condition, while the percent of self-stimulatory behavior decreased, but did either child develop greater intricacy in the level of appropriate play? Did the study measure the amount of time that elapsed between appropriate behaviors (latency)? And what was the duration of each behavior?

This study, after all, was designed to measure the effectiveness of a particular intervention, a mild aversive consequence, on a behavior that seriously interfered with learning. Percent proved to be an effective method of measuring and presenting the data. But if the authors of this study had wished to measure any of the elements mentioned above, they would have found percent to be an ineffective measurement tool. When preparing a severely retarded teenager for vocational placement, the percentage of correctly assembled brake systems he can produce is important, but so is the speed with which he works. Even if he correctly assembles 100% of his brakes, if he completes only one per hour, he is not ready for placement. For such a task, frequency, rather than percentage, is the most effective measure.

Frequency, Duration, and Latency

While a criterion measure or simple percent of total items measured will tell a teacher what fraction of a total number of items a child performed correctly, and a simple checklist will give "yes-no" information about performance, a frequency measure will tell the teacher not only *whether* a child performed, but *how often* the behavior occurred during a given interval. Thus, a checklist indicates that a child did scratch his arms that day, and a percent measure will tell the teacher that Bobby passed 70% of his self-help tasks that day. However, until the teacher knows that the child scratched his arms 198 times each hour during that day, or that Bobby took four hours to perform seven of those ten self-help tasks, that teacher lacks an important item of information about the child's behavior.

The frequency with which a behavior occurs will give that information. For certain types of programs for the severely and profoundly handicapped, such as vocational training, how many times per unit measure the behavior occurs or does not occur is important. Especially when undesirable or dangerous behaviors are involved (for example, the frequency with which a child bangs his head against a sharp desk corner), the amount of behavior emitted over time is a useful measure. Two related measures involving a time dimension are latency and duration.

Latency. The elapsed time between a stimulus and its response is called latency. How long after a severely retarded child is called to "come here" does he actually come? If it takes 10 minutes from stimulus to response, then obviously the teacher will not have many opportunities to shape the behavior. Nor, incidentally, will he be positively reinforced by the child, and this can lead to frustration, avoidance, or even hostility toward the pupil.

Duration. It is often as important to measure the length of time during which a behavior occurs, as it is to measure whether it occurs, or how many times it occurs. Percent measurement could tell a teacher that the number of times Teddy tantrummed decreased by 50%, but percent will not reveal that each tantrum was becoming longer, though occurring less frequently.

Some people question whether frequency is a good measure when the behavior occurs only four or five times a day. In some cases, a simple behavior count might be just as effective. The literature on treatment of ruminating or chronic vomiting offers several examples of such a relatively low-rate behavior which might be measured in another way. Watkins (1972) reports a study in which electric shock was administered to a severely retarded boy who weighed only 45 pounds at the outset of the study, and whose very survival demanded a rapid deceleration of vomiting. During the week-long baseline period, the boy vomited 27 times; during the intervention phase, the vomiting declined gradually, and by the fifth through seventh weeks (when the intervention phase ended), it occurred no more than twice each week. A simple tally of behavior that is emitted at so low a frequency (averaging less than four times daily) might have been sufficient to give a manager a fair picture of its relative increase or decrease. However, if one of the reasons for charting is to increase or decrease the frequency of response, the teacher should know exactly what the frequency was before program intervention. If frequency is taken during baseline, then even though the number of emitted behaviors is low, it will be easier to measure change after intervention. The advantage which frequency offers in comparing behaviors that occur at widely different frequencies is another reason for using this form of measurement. Even where a tally is used, there is often an *implicit* frequency aspect to the measure. In the Watkins study, even though a simple tally might have been used, some similar time dimension (in that case, one week) was necessary in order to have a comparable "denominator" for the data. Where a teacher in a classroom setting uses a tally sheet, the denominator is usually one day. Where a very high-frequency behavior (such as self-stimulation) is the question, plotting on a frequency-per-minute basis may be best.

Apart from ensuring ultimate comparability of data taken in different circumstances, and on behaviors of differing frequencies, frequency affords one additional advantage over other time-based measures, such as duration or percent of time. That advantage shows up in the charting phase, when the behavior is recorded on a semi-logarithmic chart. Such a display of performance shows greatest "growth" in the initial phases. This sort of picture is most encouraging to the teacher and the pupil, who see dramatic change in performance as soon as the program begins to have an effect.

The early stages of learning, in fact, represent the most sweeping changes in skill; learning to sort bolts correctly, even at the rate of five per minute, is a quantum leap in independence over the time when one cannot sort bolts at all. Once a skill has been acquired, the frequency of occurrence is much more difficult to see, as when a gifted student advances from reading at 400 words per minute to reading at 450. The view of behavior given by the frequency chart is a *pyramidal* one that corresponds to what we observe when looking at performance in everyday situations.

Moreover, growth is not measured against some standard norm of functioning, as it is in percent measures or even checklists, but against the individual's own previous performance. A related benefit of frequency is the lack of 'ceiling' on the behavior. Under a percent form of measurement, the pupil can achieve only 100% of whatever task he is learning. Because frequency is open-ended at the top, an individual can continue to increase his proficiency over time in certain skills, with no final or maximum level to bump against. This is especially true of academic and vocational tasks, where a child can increase his frequency of words read aloud or bolts sorted without an upper limit on his performance which would limit further behavior. It is not enough to say that an individual reached 100% criterion because he sorted 10 bolts per minute, if he could have sorted 15 bolts in the same amount of time without a ceiling.

In a study of the effects of contingent shock in reducing body rocking in severe retardates (body rocking being the most common stereotype observed in severely retarded clients), Baumeister and Forehand (1972) used a frequency-per-minute measure, counting each rock as one movement cycle. Because the rocking occurred at such a high frequency initially (22.7, 35.3, and 35.9 times per minute for each of the three subjects during baseline, and down to 1.6, 5.1, and .1 during the contingent shock intervention), the experimenters might have elected to use a duration or a percent-of-time-spent-rocking measure. Once the intervention phase began, however, the frequency-per-minute measure was clearly superior. With the ability to foresee eventual reduction to a low frequency, a manager might choose the frequency-per-minute measure from the outset, so as to have later comparability of data. Perhaps because almost all reduction of behavior studies do aim for achievement of a very low frequency after an initially high one, this frequency-per-minute measure is the most popular one used in deceleration experiments (Liberty, 1976). The dramatic advantage which the measure offers in comparing behaviors that occur at widely different frequency is the obvious reason for its choice.

Percent and other simpler-than-frequency measures have their simplicity as a strong selling point. Even in research studies with the severely handicapped, simplicity (among the fairly sophisticated experimenters doing the work) was apparently a governing factor in the choice of a measure. Liberty (in press) reports that the three most often used measures were, first, checklist of tally, then percent, and only then rate or frequency. Charting frequency does involve special equipment (six-cycle logarithmic graph paper), and it requires special instruction on how to chart the behavior after it occurs. One of the best explanations of how to use these charting conventions is found in White and Liberty (1976). Besides the initial difficulty in learning how to measure via frequency, the time involved in plotting data may be a drawback to its practical use. A busy teacher may not want to take the time to plot data on a large number of programs each afternoon.

Trials to Criterion

Percentage and frequency are excellent measures of some academic and vocational performances and are useful for measuring increase or decrease in the number or frequency of behaviors. However, for many severely and profoundly handicapped pupils, especially young children or those who have never had any programs, simple inducement of very basic behaviors must be the teacher's first consideration.

Trials to criterion is a measurement technique which has recently been used very successfully in programming for the severely handicapped. The teacher sets a desired performance level and then records the number of trials a pupil takes to reach that criterion. For instance, the Experimental Education Unit has developed a buttoning sequence for severely handicapped children which employs a trials-to-criterion measure to chart progress through the program (Edgar, Maser, & Haring, 1974). The child is first taught to pull the large, flat button the last half of the way through the buttonhole, where it has been placed by the teacher or aide. When the child can successfully pinch and pull three consecutive buttons through the buttonholes, he moves on to the next stage, holding the cloth near the buttonhole in one hand and pulling it down and away from the hand that is pinching and pulling the button the last half of the way through the buttonhole. At each stage, the child must perform more of the buttoning task, and as the number of stages the child performs in the sequence increases, the checklist measurement grows, so that teachers have an accurate picture of how many of the steps and which ones the child is performing correctly. When the child can correctly complete all the steps involved in buttoning at any particular stage of the program, he is moved to the next stage.

In several respects, trials-to-criterion measures are similar to checklists: neither requires manipulation of the data, as do percentage and frequency measures; both rely on simple count; and both have as their goal checking off a skill in a skill hierarchy. Latency and duration are not as important as skill acquisition.

Hamre (1974) used a checklist form of measurement for trials to criterion. She developed home-living and self-help skill sequences for severely and profoundly handicapped individuals which were measured by correct or incorrect performance of a sequence of behaviors. First, a task analysis on each skill, such as hairbrushing, was performed. Once the series of steps necessary to successfully complete the task was ordered, a checklist was designed to measure correct response, performance error, and order error. Once criterion was reached on each step, the pupil was moved to a new program. Generally, criterion meant a certain number of errorless trials over an entire sequence of from 6 to 12 steps.

Tawney, et al. (1974), developed curricula for errorless learning which measure pupil performance through a trials-to-criterion format. Severely retarded pupils were taught increasingly difficult discrimination tasks, using a method of incremental learning which allowed them a great deal of success on each level. This was done by very fine program slicing, so that generally high correct rates of responding resulted. To display the data, the steps of each program stage were plotted on the ordinate of a chart, and the number of days needed to reach criterion were plotted along the abscissa. Connected dots showed the pupil's progress in reaching the program stage. Some data were represented as frequency (responses per minute) over days per program. Percent was used to set minimum limits of performance on each step (such as 89% percent of all steps in a sequence accurately performed), but no limits were set on the number of trials to criterion or the time to criterion.

"Individualized" Measurement

No known measurement system by itself is adequate for all children in all programs. Checklists are sometimes too general; percent has a ceiling and does not measure time factors; frequency is difficult to teach and measure; and trials to criterion measurement does not always reflect latency or duration. Perhaps the best procedure in any case is to decide first which measure will give the best picture of performance (effectiveness) and will give both a good approximation to that ideal picture and yet be fairly easy to implement (economics or feasibility). This will yield an *efficiency* answer. Such an answer may be the best one can do in a situation, given all considerations. It may even act as a check on an overzealous supervisor. Too often, we tend to insist on the pristine precision of performance readout that a frequency measure can give, when a simpler measure would really suffice. Such insistence may have the undesirable effect of causing a total rebellion wherein *no* measure of performance that can be trusted will be taken. Better some measure than none. Some performances cannot be as well measured by percent, and therefore must be observed with a simple checklist; with others, latency plus trials to criterion are best. The most important consideration is fitting the best measure to the individual child and to the particular circumstances under which the intervention is carried out.

Application of Measurement and Assessment Tactics

Often, the chronological age range of a child may determine his program and thus influence the assessment and measurement tactics used to discern his abilities and progress. Teaching a severely handicapped infant to turn his head to a sound stimulus may be appropriate, but a child of five needs a receptive language program on a higher level (e.g., "turns to look at teacher when she calls child's name"), even though the child may not have been able to turn his head to sounds when he was first assessed. By age five, it is less important that the child turn to an undifferentiated sound than to more specific, meaningful words.

Often, handicapped children are grouped into four general chronological categories—infant, preschool, school-aged, and vocational. Children within these groups are then placed in classrooms according to the type or severity of the handicapping condition. This section describes various assessment and measurement tactics that have been used successfully with each of these groups of children at the Experimental Education Unit and at other institutions that teach the severely handicapped.

Infant Assessment Tactics

The more we learn about child development, the more we come to realize that what happens to a child before birth and within the critical first few months of life can have a tremendous effect on his later development. Procedures such as amniocentesis alert the physician and the mother to possible handicapping conditions before birth, but neonatal assessments are even more effective measurement tools for early assessment of possible handicapping conditions.

Two of the best-known infant assessments are the Apgar, and the Neonatal Behavior Assessment Scale developed by Brazelton. The Apgar, designed by Virginia Apgar, a pediatrician, is administered to every infant at one minute after birth. It measures five important areas: heart rate, respiration, color, muscle tone, and responsiveness. The infant receives a score of zero, one, or two on each test, two being the best possible response. A score of less than four out of a possible ten on the Apgar scale signals potential defects and should alert the obstetrician and the pediatrician that the child may be at risk for some handicapping conditions. The Brazelton scale evaluates infants from about one week to one month of age. The assessment includes observation of elicited reflexes, a descriptive paragraph on the infant by the doctor, and scores for infant responses to a variety of environmental situations.

Both of these neonatal assessment tactics are in checklist format, though the Apgar measures responses on a scale of 0–2 and the Brazelton on a 9-point scale. The Brazelton has the advantage of more detailed assessment; infant responses are measured within the first week or two on finely broken down responses, including fixing, tracking, and calming.

The Infant Learning Program at the Experimental Education Unit is designed for high-risk infants from two months to two years of age. The children have either scored low on tests such as those listed above, or have been recommended for early intervention by concerned pediatricians or other specialists.

The first evaluation of each child is the Bayley Scale of Infant Development, which is a test of motor and cognitive functions, administered by a psychologist. This test is quite lengthy; members of the team that will eventually work with the infant usually observe parts of the test as it is being given.

Next, the team (composed of an education specialist, psychologist, occupational therapist, pediatrician, nurse, and other professionals) pinpoints areas of concern and discusses its findings with the parents. Together, the team and parents design programs to help the child meet developmental objectives.

The programs are set up according to behavior pinpoints. If the ultimate goal of a program is "child will turn head to the sound of a bell," then various steps along the continuum from "no reaction to sound of bell" to the goal might be as follows:

0. No change in behavior.
1. "Stilling" or startle response.
2. Turn only eyes toward sound.
3. Partially turn head, eyes, toward sound.
4. Turn head and eyes toward sound and focus on object.

The numbers 0 to 4 indicate the code number assigned to each behavioral response. The child is given six tries to respond to the bell. Each trial is coded 0–4, according to the infant's response. Thus, for a given day, an infant's scores on this program might be 1, 3, 0, 4, 4, and 4.

The scores are charted on five different graphs, one for each of the five levels of possible response. The day is plotted along the abscissa and the number of times the infant scores that code per day is plotted along the ordinate. If the aim for the program is a score of 4 on all 6 trials for one session, then the graphs showing the number of times the infant scored a 0, 1, 2, or 3 should decrease during the intervention, and the graph which shows the number of code 4 responses will increase until the aim is reached. Plotting all five charts simultaneously helps the teacher and parents see the child's progress at a glance. If a child does not seem to be progressing toward the stated aim fast enough, then the program can be changed, perhaps by slicing more finely the possible responses that the infant can make.

When the infant reaches the age of two or three, his development can be measured on a wider range of assessment tools.

Measurement of Early Childhood Development

While some handicapping conditions, such as spina bifida, can be identified at birth, many others do not become apparent until the child's preschool years. A measure of child progress over time helps the educator and other professionals plan programs to help remediate handicapping conditions as they appear.

Most of the measures for assessing possible preschool handicapping conditions are based on normal sequential development. A normal child learns to raise his head, sit, crawl, creep, cruise, and finally walk. A handicapped child may either have gaps in his ability sequence or may lag two or more years behind his chronological peers in one or more developmental areas. Assessing child development on a variety of skills over time provides the parent, pediatrician, and educator with a clear measure of child progress. Such measurement also facilitates program planning.

The Uniform Performance Assessment System (UPAS), the assessment program discussed in the preceding section, is a good tool for measuring child progress if it is administered periodically, preferably four times a year. The checklist becomes a measure of child development over time when teachers assess children quarterly and use the results of UPAS to plan programs for skills the pupil does not have.

Another assessment tool devised and employed by the Experimental Education Unit is the Down's Syndrome Performance Inventory, devised by Model Preschool Center staff (1975). Although the Inventory was designed for children with Down's syndrome, it can be used with many other types of handicapped children. The Inventory is a checklist of "sequentially arranged milestones" in four areas of development—motor, cognitive, communications, and social.

The milestones are based on normal child development. Like UPAS, its effectiveness as a measurement tool depends upon periodic application. The Inventory is arranged in levels which are determined by developmental age ranges of between 12 and 18 months. As the child masters all the skills in one area with 80–100% competency, he advances to the next, or more complex, group of skills. For instance, if a severely retarded four-year-old can pass all the gross motor items for Level 1 (developmental age range 0–18 months), he is then assessed on the gross motor items for Level 2 (developmental age range 18 months to 3 years). Because the four skill areas within each level are separate from one another, a child could be at Level 2 on gross motor tasks, yet still be well within Level 1 for communication skills. This breakdown helps the teacher to plan individualized programs for the child, based on his assessed skill level in each developmental area. Thus, a four-year-old severely retarded girl may have programs to respond to "look," to imitate simple speech sounds like "mama," and to walk backwards—quite different levels of functioning, depending on the skill area.

An even more finely sequenced assessment tool is the Pennsylvania Training Model's *Individual Assessment Guide* (Sommerton & Turner, 1975). Divided into sections, the guide first has checklists that provide "gross screening" in major areas of sensory development, activities of daily living, communication, perceptual-cognitive, and social and emotional development. Competency checklists in the next section allow teachers to pinpoint exactly where, in each skill, the individual child has competency and at what point he must be aided to complete the task. A competency criterion of 0 (no competency—0%), 1 (moderate competency—25%), 2 (adequate competency—75%), or 3 (complete competency—100%), instead of a binary measurement, gives a finer focus to each of 30 or more items per checklist. The Individual Prescriptive Planning Sheets which follow in the guide demonstrate how to plan programs to meet the assessed deficits of each child, according to an antecedent-behavior-consequence format. The *Individual Assessment Guide* also includes a section on charting, which shows how to plot the number of correct responses per day.

The Pennsylvania Model is a complete assessment tool, containing checklists of finely sequenced behaviors, a measurement system, and a guide to charting. The pattern of assessment batteries for preschool handicapped children usually follows normal child development in general areas, such as motor and communication skills. While some employ checklists, as does UPAS, other batteries follow a careful sequence of behaviors on a task (e.g., the Pennsylvania Model). Percentage measurement of ability, rather than a "yes-no" answer, provides more information on a one-time basis, but periodic measurement of child growth, both on individual programs and general skill development, is more valuable to the teacher because it gives a measure of ability over time. And when progress must be measured in weeks or months, not days, it is well for teachers to have a measure of the child's increasing skills in a realistic time frame.

Pupils in the classrooms of the Model Preschool Center for Handicapped Children learn gross and fine motor skills, pre-academics, communication skills, and social and self-help skills. In the preschool classroom for children with severe developmental delays, each child undergoes an initial assessment based on UPAS, other standardized checklists, and the teacher's observation of the child's abilities as he plays with a variety of toys and performs (or fails to perform) certain tasks. Children in this classroom have been referred by a pediatrician who has identified severe lags in at least one, and usually more, areas of development, such as communication and fine motor skills, with attendant behavior problems.

Once strengths and needs have been identified for each child, the teacher draws up tentative quarterly objectives and yearly goals for the parent to confirm or change. Once the parent and teacher have decided on short and long range goals for the child, the teacher begins programming for the child, based on areas of identified needs. The programs follow normal child development. Thus, a girl whose walking was stiff and whose balance was very poor was started back on crawling. All the children in this class have severe communication deficits; programs teach simple receptive language such as "take," "look," or "show me," combined with familiar nouns and verbs, and expressive sounds which the child first imitates and then initiates.

Daily measurement helps the teacher to see where a program is working according to plan or better, and which programs need to be changed in order to help the child meet the stated objective.

Measurement Tactics with School-Aged Severely Handicapped Pupils

When most children are in classrooms learning spelling, math, and geography, severely handicapped children are also in school, learning self-help skills, such as handwashing, and pre-academic tasks like sorting and matching. At the Experimental Education Unit's classroom for intermediate-aged children with severe emotional disturbances and accompanying physical or mental deficiencies, each pupil has a specially designed program to help him learn a variety of tasks. The general method of measurement for each program is trials to criterion, combined with *levels of assistance.*

Each program is task-analyzed into steps. For instance, a program to teach hand-washing is broken down into 12 steps. At each level, the pupil may require one of five levels of assistance:

1. Independent
2. Verbal cue
3. Physical prompt
4. Demonstration (not often used because of the limited ability of these children to follow a teacher's model)
5. Physical assistance

The first step of the hand-washing program is "moves to the sink." The teacher directs the pupil, "It's time to wash your hands." The child may need to be physically moved to the sink and from there through the rest of the sequence. Physical assistance is gradually faded to physical prompting, then to verbal cue alone, and, finally, the child should be able to respond independently to the suggestion, "It's time to wash your hands." A criterion of 80% is generally set. If the pupil can achieve 80% of the task at a certain level of assistance for three consecutive days, he is moved on to the next higher level.

In this classroom, trials-to-criterion is used on most self-help tasks, and frequency data are usually taken on behavior. Percent data are most commonly used on group programs and for pre-academics. Much of the pre-academic work learned in this class involves matching, sorting, and sequencing. One example is a simple spelling program. Augie is learning to spell by sequencing three letters to form such words as D-O-G. First, he is taught to match each letter with its double on cards. Then, he matches the same three letters with one distractor (the letter M, for instance). Then, he matches D-O-___, filling in the G, then D-___-___, and, finally, he responds correctly when asked to spell D-O-G without cues. Augie gets one trial per word per day, and is learning six words at a time. When he can perform at 80% correct for three consecutive days, he is moved on to the next phase. Again, as in the hand-washing example, Augie is learning to spell, using the five levels of assistance on each step of the program.

When planning programs for children like Augie, the teacher often has no existing programs, and must sequence tasks, establish measurement techniques, and monitor progress toward a teacher-set goal. There are few texts or published sequences on teaching a severely emotionally disturbed ten-year-old how to spell. In such cases, measurement of child performance over time and evaluation of child progress assume increased importance in helping the teacher provide continuing learning experiences for each child.

Measurement of Vocational Education Programs

Progress through the school years should lead toward a realistic goal. For the severely handicapped, that ultimate function may be a sheltered workshop or other vocational placement. To prepare him for as much independence as possible, the severely handicapped teenager and young adult must have special training in the skills that will serve this end.

Students in the Prevocational Education Classroom at the Experimental Education Unit are learning basic skills that will help them to hold a job and enable them to care for some of their personal needs—skills such as collating booklets, assembling boxes, and washing their hair. Each task is first sliced into small steps; collating booklets may have twelve separate behaviors, from touching the book cover, to opening it, to stacking the completed booklets in a pile to one side of the table.

The whole task is taught at once, but progress on only the first step is measured at the beginning of the program. Percent data are taken. When the student reaches 85% correct on the step being measured, either the next step or one slightly farther along the sequence is measured, while he continues to learn the entire skill. As the student masters the sequence, it takes less and less time to reach criterion on the remaining steps, because the whole task has been practiced from the beginning of the program. Once the criterion of 85% correct is reached on the last step of the sequence, data are taken on the whole task to ensure adequate skill acquisition.

Frequency data are taken to measure the proficiency of the learner when he performs under conditions more like those of an eventual job placement. Yet another form of measurement over time, latency, is used to measure length of time between a request and response. Frequency data are taken on behavior problems by program or day, or by manager.

A recent case study (Mithaug & Hanawalt, 1976) demonstrates the use of both percent and frequency data in this classroom. A nineteen-year-old severely mentally retarded girl was taught to initiate the collating of booklets, while simultaneously her self-biting and aggressive hitting were decreased dramatically. Pressure exerted by the manager on the girl's upper arm proved to be a more effective negative reinforcement to increase the number of booklets collated than either verbal cues or tapping the girl's hand. The manager counted the number of booklets the girl collated during the ten-minute session and then divided that number into the accumulated time required to begin each collating task at step one—touching the booklet cover—of the collating sequence. These data were plotted by touch-booklet responses per minute along the ordinate, and by days along the abscissa. The girls' response rate jumped from 15 responses per minute to about 65 per minute over an 18-day period.

The percent-of-time measure for the girl's inappropriate behaviors was calculated by dividing the number of ten-second intervals during which such a behavior occurred, by the total number of ten-second intervals per work session. Data for aggressive hitting were plotted by percent of time spent hitting over days. This percent dropped to zero and stayed there once pressure was applied to the girl's upper arm. Likewise, the percent of time spent biting hands dropped from 50% to zero within 15 days.

Frequency (in this case, the number of responses per minute) was used to monitor correct responses. Percent was the measurement tactic used to follow the decrease in inappropriate behaviors.

Combining measurement techniques in the Mithaug and Hanawalt (1976) study enabled the experimenters to monitor two kinds of behavior simultaneously. Evaluation of the program to increase the girl's collating behaviors and to decrease her inappropriate behaviors was simplified by the fact that direct and daily measurement was taken and each segment of the total program had a measurement design most appropriate to the study.

Evaluation of Program Measurement

Eventually the teacher comes to the point in his program when he must evaluate the child's progress and plan for the next learning experience. Measurement is itself an ongoing form of evaluation. Especially when employing frequency as the measurement technique, the teacher can make evaluations about pupil performance and begin planning for the next phase of acquisition. In all the measurement types discussed earlier, evaluation is either ongoing (percent, frequency, latency, duration) or can be employed after certain skills are completely learned (checklists, trials to criterion). Adequate and appropriate measurement of pupil progress is essential for evaluation of both individual programs and eventual child proficiency in all skill areas.

Acquisition and Proficiency

It is not enough to teach a severely handicapped person to correctly follow all the steps involved in independent toileting, if the only setting in which he is called upon to perform is the special classroom. If the ultimate goal of teaching is to prepare the individual for life in a community, then he will need to transfer many of the skills learned in the classroom to more normal environments. A person must know how to toilet himself in a variety of places, such as department stores, as well as in his own home or classroom. A teacher could effectively employ trials to criterion to teach a severely retarded person to make change, but if that individual cannot generalize the ability to make change to the local supermarket, he is not ready for community placement. Acquiring a skill is an important first step, but it is only the first one. The handicapped individual must become proficient in using that skill across many settings before we can truly say that he has learned the task.

Evaluation of measurement during skill acquisition helps the teacher determine when the skill has been mastered well enough to begin programming for proficiency. Careful evaluation of an individual's proficiency is necessary to eventually place the person in an environment outside the rarified atmosphere of the classroom.

Community Reintegration

The goal of all programs for the severely and profoundly handicapped must be as near normal functioning in a community setting as is possible for the individual. The 1974 President's Commission on Mental Retardation advocates three interrelated aspects of community reintegration of the severely handicapped: deinstitutionalization of the handicapped; prevention of institutionalization; and establishment and maintenance of responsive residential environments which respect human rights and dignity and hasten more normal community living.

Reavis, Morrey, and Hamel (1976) have designed a three-phase assessment and prescription system to reintegrate the severely and profoundly handicapped into the community. They are:

Screening Level. Obtain specific measures of the level of functioning in basic skill areas necessary for community living (e.g., self help, cooking, emergency reading).

Programming Level. Design a detailed skill assessment instrument to determine individual entry skills into specific programs and to monitor skill acquisition.

Community Entry Level. Design skill assessment instrument and employ it to identify skills necessary for transfer into the community.

Such a criterion-referenced measurement system allows direct sampling of criterion behaviors necessary to enter a less restrictive programming environment. This type of system helps to identify skills at all levels, from initial programming for skill acquisition to eventual community placement. The first two levels of their program have been formatively validated; the third is still being tested.

Conclusion

Increasing pressure to provide appropriate education for *all* children has led to the establishment of classrooms to help severely and profoundly handicapped children and young adults learn basic skills in areas of self-help and vocational training. This handicapped population requires special programming to learn even simple skills like hand-washing, which must be broken down into small increments. Knowing when a handicapped child has successfully acquired a certain behavior is essential in order to keep him moving with continued success through increasingly difficult learning situations. Measurement thus assumes added importance in the teaching process.

There are several types of measurement currently being used with handicapped children which can be used with more severely involved individuals. These include checklists, percent, frequency, latency, duration, and trials to criterion. Each has proved effective for certain types of programs for individual children. The final decision about which measurement technique or combination to use should include consideration of:

1. The individual child's ability to perform the task.
2. The performance objective of the task.
3. The ultimate performance goal of each handicapped individual.

References

Baumeister, A., & Forehand, R. Effects of contingent shock and verbal command on body rocking of retardates. *Journal of Clinical Psychology*, 1972, *16*, 586–590.

Bendersky, M., Edgar, E., & White, O. *Uniform Performance Assessment System (UPAS).* Working paper #65, Experimental Education Unit, Child Development and Mental Retardation Center. Seattle: University of Washington, 1976.

Downs's Syndrome Performance Inventory, Levels 1–7. Experimental Education Unit, Child Development and Mental Retardation Center. Seattle: University of Washington, 1975.

Edgar, E., Maser, J., & Haring, N. G. *The clothes fastening program.* Experimental Education Unit, Child Development and Mental Retardation Center. Seattle: University of Washington, 1975.

Gentry, N. D., & Haring, N. G. Essentials of performance measurement. In N. G. Haring & L. Brown (Eds.), *Teaching the severely handicapped: A yearly publication of the American Association for the Education of the Severely/Profoundly Handicapped.* New York: Grune and Stratton, 1976.

Hamre, S. An approximation of an instructional model for developing home living skills in severely handicapped students. *The American Association for the Education of the Severely/Profoundly Handicapped Review*, March, 1974.

Koegel, J., Firestone, P., Kramme, K., & Dunlap, G. Increasing spontaneous play by suppressing self-stimulation in autistic children. *Journal of Applied Behavioral Analysis*, 1974, 7(4), 521–528.

Liberty, K. A. Data dilemma: Response and measurement units for teachers of the severely handicapped. *American Association for the Education of the Severely/Profoundly Handicapped Review*, May, 1976.

Lynch, V., Shoemaker, S., & White, O. Training needs survey. *American Association for the Education of the Severely/Profoundly Handicapped Review*, 1976, *1*(4), 1–16.

Mithaug, D., & Hanawalt, D. Employing negative reinforcement to establish and transfer control of a severely retarded and aggressive nineteen year old girl. Seattle: Experimental Education Unit, Child Development and Mental Retardation Center, University of Washington, 1976.

Reavis, H., Morrey, J., & Hamel, K. Behavioral assessment procedures for community reintegration. *American Association for the Education of the Severely/Profoundly Handicapped Review*, 1976, *1*(4), 37–46.

Sommerton, E., & Turner, K. *Pennsylvania training model: Individual assessment guide.* Harrisburg, Pa: Pennsylvania Department of Education, 1975.

Tawney, J., Allen, M., O'Reilly, C., Cobb, P., & Aeschleman, S. Developing curricula for errorless learning: A search for order in an unorderly world. Seattle: *The American Association for the Education of the Severely/Profoundly Handicapped Review*, November, 1974.

Watkins, J. T. Treatment of chronic vomiting and extreme emaciation by an aversive stimulus: Case study. *Psychological Reports*, 1972, *31*, 803–805.
White, O., & Liberty, K. Behavioral assessment and precise educational measurement. In N. G. Haring & R. Schiefelbusch (Eds.), *Teaching special children.* New York: McGraw-Hill, 1976.

NORRIS G. HARING is a Professor in the College of Education at the University of Washington, where he also serves as Director of the Experimental Education Unit, Child Development and Mental Retardation Center, and as an Adjunct Professor in the Department of Pediatrics. A widely published author in the field of exceptional children, Dr. Haring is a member of the Washington State Developmental Disabilities Planning and Advisory Council and the state committee for the White House Conference on Handicapped Individuals.

Managing the Behavior of Severely Handicapped Persons

JAMES M. KAUFFMAN
MARTHA E. SNELL

University of Virginia

If there is a stereotype of the severly handicapped person, it is that of an individual who cannot do much of anything. While it is true that the severely handicapped person is by definition one who has extreme behavioral deficits, our work with these people has led us to the conclusion that they are capable of doing many worthwhile things—more useful and enjoyable things, in fact, than many casual observers would believe. However, the severely handicapped are often impeded by their behavioral excesses, and this makes it necessary to help them stop doing things that are maladaptive. In addition, there can be a problem in maintaining behavioral improvement, once progress has been achieved by the severely handicapped. There seems to be little point in working to achieve a goal if what has been taught cannot be retained over a reasonable period of time. Management of the behavior of the severely handicapped, then, presents three major problems:

1. How to train them to do what they can for themselves.
2. How to train them to stop inappropriate behavior.
3. How to ensure that they will continue behaving appropriately after they are taught the appropriate behavior.

The basic problems listed here are exactly the same as the problems one would list for ordinary people. The behavior of the severely handicapped is not so different from our own normal behavior; a whole new set of rules is not required. The principles of learning apply to us all, and the problems presented by the severely handicapped simply demand that we pay particularly careful attention to what and how to teach. There is less room for error in teaching the severely handicapped, less chance for our errors to correct themselves or for chance learning to make up for sloppy teaching.

Implicit in all of the discussion that follows is the assumption that the teacher of severely handicapped persons will measure behavior. It is our view that failure to measure behavior will impede desired changes, especially when one is dealing with severe handicaps.

Applied Behavior Analysis

Behavior modification refers to a learning process whereby the strength or frequency of a behavior is changed by the purposeful arranging of environmental events which are antecedent or consequent to the behavior. A basic assumption is that behavior is a product of its consequences and may also come under the control of antecedent events which set the occasion for its occurrence. A teacher employing behavior modification must follow at least the basic essentials of analyzing the problem or targeted behavior in the applied setting. The steps involved in applied behavior analysis include: (a) selection of the target behavior(s), (b) definition of that behavior in observable terms, (c) some form of direct observational measurement of the behavior, and graphic display of behavioral data, (d) antecedent-behavior-consequence (ABC) analysis and construction of the behavior change program, (e) consistent implementation of the behavior change program, and analysis of actual behavior change.

Selection of the Target Behavior

First the teacher must focus upon the behaviors which need to be changed (*increased* in frequency because the behavior is appropriate but occurs too infrequently, or *decreased* because the behavior is inappropriate and occurs too often). These questions need to be answered:

1. What do you want the child to stop doing? (Behaviors to decrease, e.g., hitting others, biting self, running out of classroom.)
2. What do you want the child to do? (Behaviors to increase, e.g., play cooperatively with others, look at teacher or materials when asked, label colors.)
3. How often do you want these behaviors to occur (targeted level)?

Later sections of this article explain more fully

some examples of appropriate and inappropriate behaviors of the severely handicapped.

Defining the Behavior

The behavior definition should identify in observable terms exactly which characteristics of the child's behavior are of concern to the teacher. Exact definitions can assist a teacher by providing a convenient set of criteria which can be used to make quick judgments within the context of the classroom. Consistent application of behavior modification techniques is one of the key ingredients for successful behavior change, and clear definitions are the first step in the consistent implementation of a technique.

One way to check the clarity of a definition is to see whether two or more observers agree on the presence and the absence of the behavior: when the behavior begins, when it stops, and how long it has lasted. For example, if a teacher defined a child's attentive behavior merely as on-task, not only would the teacher observe responses that would be difficult to judge, but disagreement between observers probably would be frequent. Instead, the behavioral definition must state the specific observable event: "Within approximately five seconds of a teacher's verbal request to look at a particular person or material, the child's eyes are directed toward that person or material." In this example, frequency of visual attention is the primary concern of the teacher. However, at a later point in intervention, duration or length of visual attention also may be in need of improvement (e.g., the child may learn to look quickly in the requested direction, but then his attention may wander).

Observation Procedures and Graphing

A wide variety of observation procedures allow the teacher to estimate the frequency and duration of a behavior during given periods. Target behaviors should be measured over a period of days before any attempt is made to change the behavior (the *baseline* period). After a behavior change program is formulated and put into operation, the continuous measurement of the behavior before and during implementation serves as a barometer by which to judge the program's effectiveness. Do the target behaviors change in the desired direction? Do they reach an appropriate percentage of occurrence? The answers to these questions can be determined by examining the average measurement over a period of days in comparison to the baseline observation, as well as by observing the direction of the change when the behavior is plotted in graphic form.

Cooper (1974), Hall (1971), Hall, Hawkins, and Axelrod (1975), and White and Liberty (1976) detail the observation procedures which will be outlined briefly here. In general, two types of behavior measurement exist: observation involving the measurement of a behavior's lasting products or results, and measurement through the direct observation of an ongoing behavior.

Lasting Products. In the first case, a teacher counts and judges the quality of the tangible products of various academic, vocational, or social behaviors. Therefore, a teacher might measure the number of beads strung, the number of pictures sorted into correct categories, or the number of toys put away after a child's free time. Although counting the by-products of a behavior is often easier than counting occurrences of ongoing behavior, inaccuracies may result if the tangible products are destroyed, removed, or undone before the measurement is completed. Intervention programs which purport to improve academic and vocational behaviors are most easily and naturally evaluated by the measurement of their products.

Direct Observation. When behaviors are measured by direct observation, a teacher will observe during the periods *when* and in the settings *where* the behavior is of most concern. In general, the longer each observation period and the greater the number of observation periods, the more closely the measurement describes the actual behavior. However, since teachers have many demands on their time, it is essential to determine a realistic observation period when the teacher's attention may be directed toward a single behavior.

Measurement of behavior duration (how long the behavior occurs in a given period of time) is most easily done with a stopwatch. When the target behavior begins, the stopwatch is started and left to run until the behavior is terminated. During each additional instance of the behavior, the watch is started and then stopped when the behavior ceases; this results in a recording of the accumulation of time that the behavior was occurring during the total observation period. When such data is graphed, percentages most clearly display the proportion of time a given behavior occurred during an observation period.

Simple measurement of a behavior's frequency involves counting the number of times the behavior occurs during an observation period. A simple tally sheet or a wrist-worn golf counter facilitates accurate counting. If the total possible number of behaviors is fixed or predictable in advance by the teacher, percentages may be graphed (e.g., number of times teeth were brushed, classroom jobs were completed, the child imitated correctly on a ten-item sound-imitation test). However, if there are no constraints on the total number of behaviors that may be performed, then frequency (number of instances) is graphed. In Figure 1 the rate with which a severely retarded child ate soup is graphed as the number of spoonfuls eaten during each 20-minute observation session. Note that the behavior (percentage, number of times counted, amount of time observed, etc.) is displayed along the horizontal axis while the observation periods (days, weeks, etc.) are placed along the vertical axis of the graph. In this particular graph, the eating rate was decreased somewhat by reprimands. Then reprimands were withdrawn (baseline$_2$) and replaced by the teacher's imitation of the child's sloppy, rapid eating (imitate$_1$ and imitate$_2$). The consequence of teacher imitation tended to decrease the eating rate more effectively than simple reprimands.

If the teacher is unable to devote undivided attention, a time sampling procedure is the better method to use. The observation period is divided into a given number of equal segments, and the teacher observes briefly at the termination of each interval. If the child is engaging in the

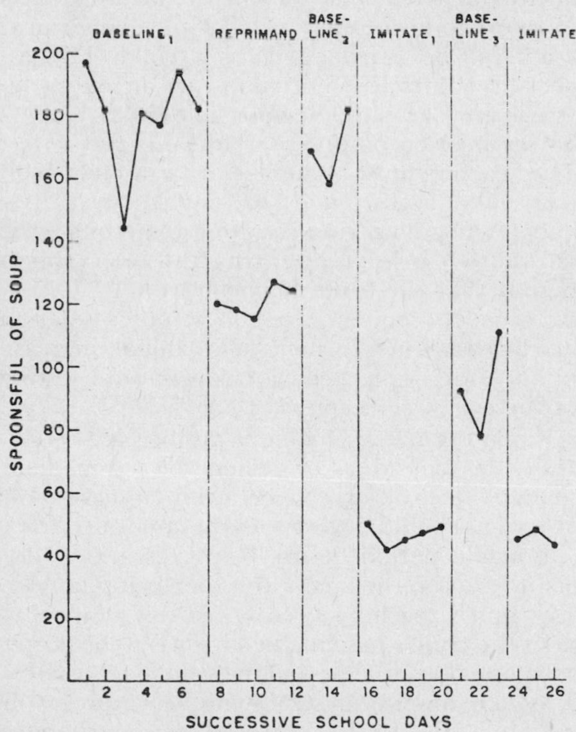

Figure 1. Spoonsful of soup eaten by a severely retarded girl during 20-min. sessions on successive school days.

Source: Kauffman, J. M., LaFleur, N. K., Hallahan, D. P., and Chanes, C. M. Imitation as a consequence for children's behavior: Two experimental case studies. *Behavior Therapy*, 1975, *6*, 537.

behavior at the time of observation, a check is made on the recording form. Any other instances of the behavior are not recorded. In both methods, a clock with a second hand, a stopwatch, or an interval signalling timer is needed when intervals shorter than a minute are being used. With a longer interval, muffled kitchen timers or egg timers enable one to keep track of the passage of intervals.

ABC Analysis

Limiting and defining the problem behavior and measuring its baseline level at the time and in the situation where it is the most troublesome comprise the first steps in an ABC (antecedent-behavior-consequence) analysis. The remaining steps in this analysis enable a teacher to set behavioral goals and devise suitable behavior change strategies which will ensure the accomplishment of these goals (Worell & Nelson, 1974).

Preceding and during baseline observations, the teacher needs to determine the following:

1. What events occur immediately after the behavior (e.g., teacher gives attention, aide provides assistance, child is ignored)?

2. How often do these consequences occur and how consistent are they?

3. How aware is the child of the consequences (could the child verbalize these contingencies; does the child appear to anticipate the consequences)?

4. What apparent effect do the consequences have on the child's resulting behavior (e.g., undesirable behavior decreases initially, then reappears; behavior seems unaffected, etc.)?

Because behavior is viewed primarily as a product of its consequences, it is essential to delineate events which may maintain, increase, or decrease the behavior. This information will be utilized when a behavior change strategy is formulated.

Determining Reinforcers and Punishers. During his stage of the analysis, the teacher must determine what the child likes and does not like. These positive and negative events or tangible items will be employed as consequences to reinforce desirable behavior and its successive approximations and, at times, to punish undesirable behavior.

1. What does the child like, i.e., what events act as reinforcers for the child? Reinforcers may be determined in a number of ways. If the child is verbal, he can be shown actual objects or pictures and asked to select those he likes. Also, the child's choice of activities, toys, or foods might be observed during the normal school day. A more structured observation of the

child's preferences for foods or toys can be made by providing brief samples of three to six items, then allowing free access to the whole group of items and recording choice frequency. Finally, persons knowing the child (parents, peers, siblings, aides) might be asked what the child seems to like. Reinforcers should be arranged hierarchically from most to least liked.

2. What does the child dislike (punishers)? The removal of a positive reinforcer constitutes punishment. Punishers of the type which are presented to an individual (e.g., having to perform an unliked activity) may be determined by asking the child, observing what the child avoids or shows dislike for, or asking others who know the child. Punishers also should be arranged in order, from most effective to least effective.

3. Which reinforcers and punishers are appropriate for use in the classroom (may be applied easily, quickly, without harming the child, without administrative or ethical complications)? The effective reinforcers and punishers on the lists will be used to reinforce the desirable behaviors and, if necessary, to punish the undesirable behaviors.

All the information collected during the ABC analysis is relevant to the formulation of a behavior change program which is a specification of the things that will be done differently in the classroom to change the behavior from its present level to the desired level.

Implementing and Evaluating Behavior Change Programs

Once the specific behavior modification plan has been devised, it is put into action. To increase the probability of success, some essential steps must be taken and certain cautions must be heeded.

Essentials. Behavior modification consists of a process whereby a child learns to perform a new behavior in a situation where he formerly was allowed to abstain from that behavior or to perform another behavior. The child must learn new contingencies ("When I do this, the teacher does that."). This learning process takes time, especially when the child doing the learning is severely handicapped. Also, this process is most likely to occur if the teacher is consistent (every time a child initially engages in the desired behavior a reinforcing consequence is presented). When more than one teacher works with the child, consistency across persons becomes important. Finally, learning is facilitated when the number of opportunities to perform are increased. The more a child performs a given behavior in a particular situation, and the behavior results in the same consequence, the sooner the child will come to understand the contingencies operating.

Sometimes, no matter how carefully an ABC analysis is performed or how consistently it is applied, a behavior change program will not result in the desired change. A teacher cannot determine objectively whether a behavior modification program is successful or unsuccessful unless the behavior is measured throughout the implementation period. Thus, ongoing measurement of the target behaviors by means of the same measurement procedure employed during the baseline period is another essential step for the teacher.

Cautions. Since the evaluation of a behavior change program rests upon accurate measurement, a teacher must try to eliminate sources of error. The best way to ensure confidence in a measurement procedure is to check interobserver reliability; how close are two measurements of the same behavior observed by two people independently (Cooper, 1974; Worell & Nelson, 1974)?

A second caution concerns the observed fluctuations in a behavior during the initial days of intervention. Often a behavior change program will be "challenged" by a child. This especially occurs when attempts are made to decrease undesirable behaviors. The child's bad behavior may become worse before it get better. The teacher must remember that a child who was very accustomed to particular consequences (e.g., tantrum resulting in getting what he wanted) is learning durng the intervention period that the same behavior results in very different consequences (e.g., 3 minutes isolation in the time-out corner). The initial increase in an undesirable behavior is a natural testing of these new consequences.

When the initial change is an increase in undesirable behavior or when no immediate changes are observed, behavior intervention programs should nevertheless be continued for a reasonable period before being discarded, depending upon the target behavior being taught, how much teaching occurs per day, and how close the child's baseline behavior is to be target behavior. This trial period may range from a few days to a few weeks. Once the behavior graph indicates slope in the desired direction, changes need not be made in the program unless: (a) goal has been achieved, (b) the behavior is changing too slowly, (c) undesirable behaviors seem to be increasing as a side effect of the program, or (d) the intervention procedures are so tedious that they are interfering significantly with the rest of the classroom instruction. In the first case, another target may be selected while the first target behavior is placed on a maintenance program. In the second and third cases, the elements of the program are re-examined (reliability, reinforcers, consistency, etc.) and changes are made. In the last case, the intervention program is simplified or the assistance of another individual is sought (aide, parent, regular classroom student, peer).

Planning and carrying out sensible modifications of behavior in the classroom setting requires diligent effort by the teacher. The rewards, however, are evidenced through the observable changes in the child.

Increasing Appropriate Behavior

Although severely handicapped individuals are frequently described by their obvious excesses of inappropriate behavior (e.g., aggressive behavior, nonfunctional repetitive movements), such excesses are almost invariably accompanied by deficiencies in appropriate or adaptive behavior. These deficiencies may include: little or no language; lack of independence in toileting, dressing, and basic grooming skills; inability to match identical objects; lack of competence in such skills as rote counting, color naming, playing with others, ball throwing and catching, and crossing streets.

These deficiencies may often precede and contribute to the development of inappropriate behavior. The converse is also true: when a severely handicapped individual possesses a balance of appropriate behaviors, it is less likely that inappropriate behaviors will be learned. When a person can express wants, is listened to, and has the basic social skills which make one likeable (smiles, social greetings for others, eye contact), that individual is less apt to withdraw from others or to resort to aggressive behavior to satisfy his needs. Although space does not permit description of the wide range of behaviors appropriate for severely handicapped individuals, several major groupings will be discussed.

Characteristics of Appropriate Behavior

At any point in a severely handicapped individual's development, teaching targets may need to be selected in all the following areas: self care, social interaction, pre-academics (early thinking and reasoning skills), language, and fine and gross motor skills. Although the choice and sequencing of such targets is not a totally arbitrary decision, the development of appropriate behaviors will probably always span these diverse areas for a severely handicapped student. As the severely handicapped child grows older and has mastered the basic components of these skill areas, two additional areas of teaching become relevant: daily living and prevocational skills.

All these areas overlap somewhat and cannot be neatly separated from each other. For instance, the receptive language skills (understanding another's gestures or spoken words) are a facet of all the skill areas. Likewise, buttoning, using a fork, and toothbrushing rely upon an individual's fine motor skills of finger and wrist manipulation.

Each skill area may be mapped out in a developmental sequence. For example, when an individual first learns to eat with a spoon, it is held in a palm-down or fist-grasp position and later in a palm-up or finger-grasp position. Also, spoon usage is mastered after one can eat finger foods but before learning to use a fork and before mastering most dressing skills. Each specific behavior in these developmental sequences may be subdivided into *small teaching steps* which are ordered from the easiest or first taught to the hardest or the target behavior. Some steps in teaching spoon usage may include: holds spoon in palm-down position (no eating); holds and uses spoon when given total manual guidance; puts filled spoon into open mouth unaided, when given manual guidance for dipping food; dipping, lifting, and directing spoon. These ordered teaching steps may be used as informal checklists to determine how much of the skill an individul possesses before teaching, where to begin teaching that individual, and how much an individual has learned after teaching

After assessing an individual's present or baseline level of behavior against such a checklist, the teacher will observe one of the following in the individual:

1. He is not able to perform even the simplest behavior.
2. He is able to perform only the simpler behaviors on the list.
3. He is able to perform many or even all of the behaviors *but* (a) does not perform these behaviors frequently enough or without help (e.g., will label body parts about half the time), or (b) performs the behaviors in one place but not in others (e.g., brushes teeth at school but not at home).
4. He is able to perform the target behavior whenever appropriate without assistance, and in a number of different places.

Several different teaching techniques will be described next which may be differentially applied to improve the first three types of outcomes. When a teacher discovers the fourth outcome (complete mastery of a skill), it is important to maintain these behavioral gains and also to select more advanced instructional targets from the same skill area.

Positive and Negative Reinforcement

When an individual's behavior is immediately followed by events that are enjoyed by or reinforcing to that individual, the behavior is more apt to recur. This arrangement is called *positive reinforcement*. To state this another way, positive reinforcement consists of an arrangement in which a behavior is consequated by the presentation of a positive reinforcer or rewarding event. When reinforcers are repeatedly made dependent or contingent upon an individual's performance of a certain behavior, the increase in that behavior will be quite noticeable. We believe that positive reinforcement is the most powerful instructional tool a teacher may apply; it can be used to teach an individual to do something he cannot already do, can do only partially, or can do but refuses to perform. The success of positive reinforcement depends upon at least two teacher characteristics: the ability to determine those events which, when presented, are reinforcing to a child; and the ability to provide those reinforcing events without fail after the behavior has occurred (to reinforce the child contingent upon the desired behavior). (The scheduling of reinforcement is discussed in the following section of this article.)

Another arrangement of events, often confused with punishment, is called *negative reinforcement*. Although it is not often useful as a teaching tool, negative reinforcement can operate without our awareness and, predictably, results in the increase of certain behaviors that are frequently undesirable. Negative reinforcement occurs in the midst of an unpleasant situation. The behavior that is reinforced acts to reduce or remove the unpleasant, painful, or discomforting aspects of the situation. To state this another way, negative reinforcement consists of an arrangement in which a behavior is consequated by a reduction or removal of negative reinforcers (aversive or punishing events). For example, an individual quickly learns to leave a painfully noisy room or to cover his ears; a child learns to complete an assignment to avoid the teacher's disapproval; and a mother may unintentionally learn to grant her child his requests to avoid his anger, crying, or tantruming.

Negative and positive reinforcement are similar in two ways: both lead to an increase in the reinforced behavior, and both may be applied accidentally (without our realization), as well as intentionally, to modify behavior.

Schedules and Immediacy of Reinforcement

When the behavior of an individual being positively reinforced begins to increase, the individual has learned the contingency that is in operation ("If I perform this behavior, then that event will occur."). If the reinforcer is given immediately after the behavior occurs, and before another behavior intervenes, learning will occur more quickly because the cause-and-effect relationship is emphasized and no intervening behaviors are accidentally reinforced. Also, if every instance of the targeted behavior is reinforced (a continuous reinforcement schedule), the individual will have more opportunities to learn the contingency and have no exposure to exceptions (no nonreinforced instances of behavior). Therefore, when positive reinforcement is first being applied to a behavior, it is essential that reinforcement be immediate and continuous.

After the teacher observes an increase in the behavior, the continuous reinforcement schedule should be changed gradually to a partial or intermittent schedule. This means that reinforcers should be presented intermittently or after only *some* instances of the behavior (after every second, every fourth, on the average of every fourth behavior, etc.) but no longer after every instance. The reasons for using an intermittent schedule become clearer when one considers the individual's view of the situation. With continuous reinforcement, the individual learns the behavior quickly but, because every behavior is reinforced, he does not learn to be persistent in situations where no reward is forthcoming. We may say that this behavior is not very "resistent to extinction"or that it is not very strong in the absence of reinforcement. Since no one can realistically expect continuous rewards, we believe it is the teacher's responsibility to gradually replace continuous schedules of reinforcement with intermittent schedules. Furthermore, intermittent schedules reduce the time and effort required of the teacher by allowing the teacher to attend directly to only a portion of the child's appropriate performance.

It is possible for a teacher to schedule reinforcement either according to the number of behaviors (*ratio schedules*: every nth behavior is reinforced) or by the amount of time passing in relation to the behavior (*interval schedules*: the first behavior occurring after the passage of *n* minutes or days is reinforced). When behaviors are discrete (separate and easily counted), ratio schedules may be applied (e.g., labelling objects when asked during language training time, putting on one's jacket). With fleeting or less visible behaviors, or when reinforcing one or more individuals while simultaneously managing a large group, a teacher is advised to use interval schedules. Large wall clocks with second hands, egg timers, and muffled kitchen timers serve to alert the busy teacher of the passage of time. When using interval schedules, it is important to remember that reinforcement is not simply given at the interval's end, but following the first behavior that occurs after the interval is completed.

With both ratio and interval schedules, a teacher does *not* need to be mindful of *exact* behavior counting or interval timing (Hall, Hawkins, & Axelrod, 1975). If an individual has mastered a behavior fairly well, and the teacher decides to replace continuous reinforcement with a ratio schedule of one reinforcer for every three behaviors, the teacher may merely approximate this schedule by reinforcing on the average of every third behavior. Averaged (variable) schedules produce greater persistence than constant (fixed) schedules for the same reason that intermittent schedules result in more persistent behaviors than do continuous schedules—it is harder for the student to figure out whether the absence of reinforcement following a response is just part of the schedule or whether there will in fact be no more reinforcement.

Shaping and Chaining

It is seldom that new behavior is performed perfectly the first time it is taught, and this is especially true with severely retarded individuals. It is more likely that, during the early stages of teaching, a small fraction of the behavior is perfectly performed, and over time more and more of the behavior is performed with increasing perfection. When a teacher provides reinforcement for successively better approximations of the target behavior, until eventually reinforcement is contingent upon exact performance of the target behavior, the teaching process is called *shaping*.

In the section of this article which described characteristics of appropriate behavior, mention was made of analyzing the targeted behavior into smaller, ordered teaching steps. It was suggested that these steps be used as checklists to determine where to begin teaching a skill. If these steps are ordered from simple to complex, they may also be regarded as levels of successive approximation and used to guide the shaping process. However, the first instance of the target behavior may be brief, largely inadequate, and therefore difficult to recognize. In fact, the first instance may be of markedly lower quality than the first teaching step. When this is the case, a teacher should *not* wait for a better approximation but immediately reinforce that beginning level of the behavior, thereby strengthening its frequency and increasing the probability that better approximations will be performed. Since it is not always obvious when a given behavior is better or worse than the behavior which was reinforced earlier, a teacher must attend carefully to approximations while not losing track of the targeted behavior. The art involved in shaping behavior is especially obvious when one attempts to shape random vocalizations into comprehensible speech.

Many behaviors actually consist of a chain of smaller component behaviors performed in a certain sequence. Toothbrushing, for example, was divided into 12 behaviors by Horner and Keilitz (1975), ranging from picking up and holding the toothbrush to putting the equipment away and discarding the disposables. Most self-care skills and other fine and gross motor movements, as well as speech and gestures, may be regarded as behavior chains. When a skill involves a performance chain, the teacher may use a specific teaching procedure called forward or backward *chaining*. Both methods involve the linking of one learned behavior in the chain to the next behavior. In forward chaining, the individual is taught to perform the first step at the beginning of the chain (e.g., pick up toothbrush, pick up spoon) and, as learning occurs, teaching proceeds forward:

1. The individual attempts the first step and receives reinforcement.
2. The individual performs the first step perfectly and receives reinforcement.
3. The individual performs the first step perfectly, attempts the second step, and receives reinforcement.
4. The individual performs first and second steps perfectly and receives reinforcement; and so on.

Depending upon the type and length of the task, the teacher may guide the individual through the remainder of the chain after providing reinforcement at each teaching level.

In backward chaining, teaching begins with the last step and proceeds backwards towards the beginning of the chain as each step is mastered.

However, the teacher generally helps the learner through all the preceding steps until the instructional step is reached. At this point, guidance is withheld and the first approximation of that step performed by the learner is followed by either: (a) reinforcement, when the instructional step is the last step in the chain, or, during later stages of teaching, (b) independent performance by the learner of all the remaining steps in the chain, after which reinforcement is immediately given.

Backward chaining has the advantage of associating teacher-applied reinforcement with the natural reinforcement of task completion. Therefore, when teaching eating and dressing, backward chaining generally is preferred over forward chaining. When a teacher is uncertain in which direction to shape, it is helpful to examine the learner's current performance and teach at the end of the chain where the larger number of steps are approximated.

Secondary and Token Reinforcement

Unlike food and other primary, unlearned reinforcers, the most common reinforcers (praise, smiles, pats on the back, money) rely upon an awareness by the reinforced individual of the reinforcer's value. These are called *secondary reinforcers* and depend upon certain prior learnings and earlier associations with other reinforcers. For instance, if a certain behavior is to be modified by contingently applied teacher praise, the individual must understand the words and their relation to the behavior and must be comfortable in the teacher's presence. With the severely handicapped student, the teacher cannot assume that all commonly mentioned secondary reinforcers actually have reinforcing value for a particular child. Instead, the value that secondary reinforcers have for certain individuals needs to be determined by the observation of their effect on a behavior and, when lacking, this value needs to be taught.

How does one teach another individual to value an event such as praise, smiles, or money? The best method involves learning by association—the pairing of known reinforcers with events which are not reinforcing. For example, prior to giving a snack the teacher might smile and praise the child for sitting. Over time, praise and smiling would take on reinforcing qualities by their association with food. It is best to present the potential secondary reinforcer immediately preceding the primary reinforcer. As the individual begins to show some appreciation for the secondary reinforcer (smiles back, reaches for a handshake, etc.), the teacher may put the primary reinforcer on a more intermittent schedule while continually providing the secondary reinforcer.

It is important to assess the cognitive prerequisites upon which certain reinforcers depend and to match secondary reinforcers to the individual's level of comprehension. Reinforcing with praise demands an awareness of the vocabulary and the complexity of language used. When using money as a reinforcer, one must be sensitive to the mathematical skills involved in preferring a dime over a nickel or five pennies over three.

Another class of secondary reinforcers includes token reinforcement. Tokens may be any concrete item (poker chip, washer, penny, checkmark, star) that is provided as a result of certain behaviors and exchangeable for primary or back-up reinforcers (trinkets, food, beverages). By their association with other reinforcers, tokens acquire a reinforcing value. Tokens have advantages over primary reinforcers in that they can be given more easily and are less apt to diminish in their reinforcing power, since each is exchangeable for one of many back-up reinforcers. Also, tokens serve as a transition stage between edible and other tangible reinforcers and the more abstract reinforcers such as praise, smiles, self-satisfaction.

Money is a token system with which we all are quite familiar and to which most of us are quite responsive. The coins in our money (token) system have specific values which must be known in order to use the system. Specific-value token systems have been successfully used to treat moderately and severely retarded and disturbed individuals (Kazdin & Bootzin, 1972), to increase various academic skills (Baker, Stanish, & Fraser, 1972; Dalton, Rubino, & Hislop, 1973), to teach language skills (Baer & Guess, 1973), and to decrease inappropriate behavior (Hislop, Moore, & Stanish, 1973).

Many severely handicapped individuals will not be able to count or associate specific exchange values with tokens, although this may be learned later. For these students, a varying-value token system is more immediately appropriate. In this type of system, tokens are not assigned an exchange value but are merely awarded contingent upon certain behaviors and are exchanged in varying amounts whenever the teacher decides that the back-up reinforcers are necessary.

Initially, when an individual is trained to associate tokens with reinforcers, the teacher selects a behavior that is easily performed by the student (e.g., imitating movements, pointing to objects upon request). The teacher directs the individual to perform, and each occurrence of this behavior is reinforced with a token. The token is immediately exchanged for the student's choice of a single back-up reinforcer. This process continues until the student shows signs of associating tokens with the reinforcer, signs such as reaching for the tokens or anticipating an exchange by handing the tokens back to the teacher. At this point, the teacher gradually shifts the exchange schedule from continuous to intermittent. When the student is able to collect four or five tokens, a token container is introduced. Teaching the student to lift and empty the container facilitates the collection and exchange procedure. An individual's exchange schedule may be gradually shifted in proportion to his performance; some individuals will easily learn to exchange after every 15 to 20 minutes of continuous performance with tokens and praise, while others may need to exchange every few minutes after perhaps only ten performances. We have found that many minimally skilled, nonverbal individuals have responded to token reinforcement after token training sessions lasting from 10 to 15 minutes.

Antecedents: Stimulus Control

Until now, the techniques described to increase appropriate behavior have been concerned with consequences, what the teacher may do after a desirable behavior occurs. In addition to consequences, there are a number of teaching procedures which are applied before the occurrence of the appropriate behavior and which serve to encourage its performance by creating opportunities for reinforcement. These antecedent events include: instructions to the learner, modeling, response priming (prompting), and the complimentary process of fading. Each technique facilitates a discrimination learning process called stimulus control (learning to perform a certain behavior in the presence of specific visual, auditory, kinesthetic, and/or tactual stimuli). For example, when a child learns to wash his hands, get his lunchbox, and sit at a given place for the noon meal, we could say he has discriminated certain critical antecedent stimuli or cues in the presence of which handwashing, getting lunch, and sitting at a certain place are reinforced by praise and the opportunity to eat. These antecedent stimuli probably include stomach contractions, the teacher's request to prepare for lunch, and the sight of others getting ready. The bulk of all learning actually involves various stimulus discriminations. Instruction, modeling, and prompting will be discussed next as methods to expedite discrimination and stimulus control of certain behaviors.

Instructions. Verbal directions, adjusted to the learner's level of comprehension, are valuable in helping some learners to perform desired behaviors. After the individual's attention is gained, directions should be simply stated and may provide various cues concerning the behavior the individual should be, but is not readily, performing (e.g., "Look at me.") For individuals with fewer comprehension skills, instructions may be accompanied by gestures (e.g., the teacher says, "Sit here," and points to a chair). When instructions alone are not sufficient to encourage the behavior, they may be paired with modeling or with prompting.

Modeling. Modeling or demonstrating the desired behavior for the learner is a common teaching method used by teachers at all grade levels. Modeling is useful because it provides more specific assistance to the learner than do instructions alone. When modeling is employed with the severely handicapped, the teacher should make certain adjustments. After getting the learner's attention, the behavior or a small portion of the behavior is slowly performed from a position *alongside* the learner. Often, the individual may be requested to imitate ("Do this,") before the model is presented. As when using a shaping procedure, the teacher need not expect a perfect imitation initially but should reinforce successively better copies of the model. In general, the model should not be repeated more than once if the individual does not begin to imitate. Instead of providing additional repetitions, the teacher should prompt the learner to imitate the model.

Response Priming, Prompting, and Fading. Often a learner will not respond to directions, models, appealing teaching materials, or even the presence of reinforcers. In these situations where no behavior occurs, shaping cannot be used. Skinner (1968) called this frustrating point in teaching "the problem of the first instance" (p. 206). At these times the learner's response may be primed or prompted with cues (e.g., pointing to or tapping near the correct choice) or with manual guidance (e.g., moving the learner through part or all of the desired behavior). Prompts may be partial or complete in the amount of assistance they provide to the learner. Initially, a teacher may need to prompt a nonperforming learner with a *complete* prompt such that the teacher physically assists the learner in performing the entire response and gives reinforcement for passive cooperation. However, in order for complete learning (stimulus discrimination) to take place, this assistance needs to be faded or gradually eliminated, thereby requiring the learner to perform more on his own. Therefore, during fading, partial prompts are used by the teacher and eventually eliminated completely. It is also true that models and instructions serve to prompt a behavior. Models and instructions must also be faded so that the individual learns to attend to the relevant stimuli and does not become dependent upon the teacher's assistance.

Horner and Keilitz (1975) used all three levels of assistance (instruction, modeling, and prompting) to teach severely handicapped individuals to brush their teeth. These authors faded assistance by decreasing the amount and level of assistance—from all three, to modeling with instructions, to instructions alone, and finally to no instructions. In addition, these teaching techniques have had wide application with the severely handicapped in teaching other self-care skills (Nelson, Cone, & Hanson, 1975; O'Brien & Azrin, 1972; O'Brien, Bugle, & Azrin, 1972), imitation skills (Baer, Peterson, & Sherman, 1965; Striefel & Phelan, 1972) motor skills (O'Brien, Azrin, & Bugle, 1972; Peterson & McIntosh, 1973), language skills (Ausman & Gaddy, 1974; Baer & Guess, 1973; Garcia, 1974; Guess & Baer, 1973), functional academic tasks (Bellamy & Buttars, 1975; Dorry & Zeaman, 1975), and vocational skills (Crosson, 1969; Gold, 1972; Karen, Eisner, & Endres, 1975).

Decreasing Inappropriate Behavior

There are severely handicapped individuals who exhibit little behavior that needs to be stopped, but they are the exception rather than the rule. Historical and contemporary accounts make it clear that many of the severely handicapped are characterized by multiple problems, including disorderly, inappropriate, irritating, and destructive behavior (cf. Balthazaar & Steven, 1975; Kauffman, in press-a, in press-b). The unfortunate teacher who expects students to be tractible merely because they are not labeled "emotionally disturbed," "psychotic," or something else associated with socio-behavioral deviance is in for an abrupt awakening. Although all of the undesirable acts that severely handicapped individuals might perform cannot be listed here, we will describe several major classes of behavior that frequently create problems.

Undesirable Behavioral Characteristics

Many of the undesirable behaviors of the severely handicapped involve basic biological processes, such as eating and elimination. Soiling (encopresis) and wetting (enuresis) are frequently problems. Eating may present problems not only because the individual is sloppy or throws food, but also because the severely handicapped often grab or steal food from others (especially in institutional settings) or eat trash or other inappropriate substances. Aggressive behavior, such as hitting, biting, scratching, poking, is commonly encountered and may be directed toward others or performed on oneself. It is very disconcerting to see one individual maul another or to be the target of aggressive attacks, but it is also disquieting to see a person viciously attack his own body. Bachman (1972) and Frankel and Simmons (1976) have reviewed data indicating that 5 or 6% of severely handicapped institutional residents exhibit self-injurious behavior in which they endanger their own health or life. Another problem is self-stimulation—excessive activity that is socially inappropriate, seems to serve only to provide sensory feedback, and interferes with other adaptive behavior. Finally, the severely handicapped are prone to a variety of other objectionable responses that are common among normal and mildly disturbed individuals (tantrums, arguments, lewd talk or gestures, negativism, and so on). We will describe several strategies for reducing or eliminating such unwanted activity.

Instructions

We believe that one should always try to find the simplest effective solution for the problem of disordered behavior, and there is nothing simpler than telling a person how you want him to behave. Setting up an elaborate system of rewards and punishments is pointless if simple instructions will suffice. Of course, instructions to stop a misbehavior are in many cases ineffective, but giving instructions requires so little effort and is so natural that one is foolish not to make it the first technique to try. Two points are particularly important to remember when giving instructions. First, to have the best chance of success, instructions must be given when the child is paying attention and must be direct, simple, clear, and consistent. Many times instructions fail because they are given while the child is not paying attention, they are too complicated, they are not given with sufficient clarity and directness, or they are not consistent over time and congruent with nonverbal behavior. In the case of misbehavior, good instructions will mean that the severely handicapped student is oriented toward the teacher and has eye contact, and that the teacher will give a simple, loud, clear, and direct command ("No!" or "Stop!"), rather than, "Randy, please don't hit Susan; it hurts when you hit." The teacher's facial expression and other nonverbal communication must be consistent with the verbal instruction (indicative of displeasure), and the instruction must be given consistently for the inappropriate response. Second, instructions ultimately derive their effectiveness from the consequences of behavior. The consequences of following instructions to stop a misbehavior should be pleasant (in this case, *negatively* reinforcing because the student escapes or avoids unpleasantness), and the consequences of disregarding such instructions should be unpleasant. In short, the instructions to stop a misbehavior should themselves be unpleasant for the student; compliance with the instructions should be reinforced and noncompliance should be punished. If the consequences are consistent, instructions to stop inappropriate behavior will become an effective warning.

Reinforcement of Appropriate Behavior

One strategy for decreasing undesirable behavior is to provide positive reinforcement for responses that are *incompatible* with (cannot happen at the same time as) the undesirable response. For example, a child's eye poking might be reduced by providing reinforcement when his hands are away from his face.

Reinforcing incompatible reponses may be a good strategy to use, but a more important consideration is simply that *reinforcement must be provided for appropriate behavior or the behavior management program will fail*. That is, regardless, of what other techniques are employed in attempts to reduce problem behaviors, the success of a behavior management program hinges on making the performance of appropriate behavior rewarding for the severely handicapped person. It has frequently been our experience that, once the individual is provided with something appropriate to do and is reinforced for doing it, the inappropriate behavior vanishes. The reinforcement of appropriate behavior is particularly applicable to institutions providing custodial care, but it applies also to the classroom where pupils are not kept engaged in appropriate tasks (cf. Repp & Deitz, 1974; Vukelich & Hake, 1971).

Extinction

One of the principles of behavior is that, if a response is not reinforced, it will occur less and less frequently and will eventually disappear. The procedure of cutting off the reinforcement that serves to maintain an inappropriate behavior (extinction) has been found to be a most useful tool, as long as positive reinforcement is provided for appropriate responses as well. Extinction can be used effectively only if one can identify the reinforcers maintaining the undesirable behavior and keep them from being obtained in the wrong way. Two factors are important: first, unless *all* reinforcement for the undesirable behavior can be withheld, the extinction procedure will be counterproductive; second, extinction is a relatively slow procedure, and it is likely that there will be an initial increase in the inappropriate behavior before it begins to wane, even if all reinforcement is stopped.

Extinction, especially when combined with other techniques, has proven to be very useful in working with the severely handicapped. The classic case reports of Wolf, Birnbrauer, Williams, & Lawler (1965) and Zimmerman & Zimmerman (1962) illustrate the therapeutic use of extinction procedures with the severely handicapped. Zimmerman and Zimmerman found that temper tantrums and refusal to do academic tasks could be controlled by removing adult attention, the apparent reinforcer, for these trying behaviors. Wolf and his colleagues found that frequent vomiting ceased to be a problem when adult attention and opportunity to leave the classroom were withheld.

Punishment

Many people have a negative reaction to the idea of punishing children, especially severely handicapped children. Yet, in some cases, punishment is the most effective and humane way of decreasing inappropriate behavior (MacMillan, Forness, & Trumbull, 1973). Punishment refers to presenting aversive stimuli or withdrawing positive reinforcers contingent on a response. That is, punishment may be of two basic types: *aversive conditioning*, in which one presents aversive stimuli (electric shock, slaps), or *response cost*, in which one takes away positive reinforcers (points, tokens, food). Punishment need not involve pain or humiliation, but by definition punishment does decrease the rate of the punished response.

In order to be used humanely and effectively, punishment must not be the focus of behavior management. Furthermore, it should always be easy for the individual to escape or avoid punishment altogether—there should always be an obvious way to behave appropriately and obtain rewards, and rewards for appropriate behavior should be the focus. When punishment is required there are several alternative methods to consider.

Aversive Conditioning. Aversive conditioning is most clearly justified in cases of self-injurious or other dangerous behavior. Contingent electric shock has been used, for example, to eliminate self-injurious behavior in severely disturbed and severely retarded children (cf. Frankel & Simmons, 1976). Milder forms of aversive stimuli have been used successfully to resolve other types of behavior problems. Hall, Axelrod, Foundopulos, Shellman, Campbell, and Cranston (1971), for example, found that a child's biting and pinching could be diminished by the teacher's pointing at the child and shouting, "No!". Koegel, Firestone, Kramme, and Dunlap (1974) were able to lower the level of autistic children's self-stimulation by sharply saying, "No!", and briskly slapping or briefly holding (immobilizing) the part of the child's body involved. Salzberg and Napolitan (1974) found that holding a child's hands on a table for two minutes, contingent on his playing with doors and staring out of windows, quickly reduced his inappropriate object contact. Kauffman, LaFleur, Hallahan, and Chanes (1975) reported a case in which the teacher's imitation of a severely retarded child's inappropriate eating was highly aversive. It is important to recognize that, when aversive conditioning is used appropriately, the aversive stimuli are applied only for a specific undesirable response, that all punishment or threat is removed as soon as the undesirable behavior stops, and that ample positive reinforcement is provided for desirable behavior. The key is to make sure that negative consequences consistently follow undesirable behavior and *only* undesirable behavior.

Response Cost. Response-cost punishment can be used only if the individual being punished has previously been given rewards. One cannot take away what someone does not have. The important thing to remember about response-cost punishment is that a reasonable amount of a positive reinforcer must be taken from the individual contingent on a response. That is, an inappropriate response must cost the misbehaving person something; he must experience a fine. The fine may consist of taking away tokens, food, play time (Sulzbacher & Houser, 1968), or even colored slips of paper with the child's name written on them (Hall et al., 1971). There is no point in fining someone who has no valued commodity to take away, who does not understand the relationship between his behavior and loss of rewards, or who does not value what is being taken from him. However, in a predominantly positive behavior management program where the person is earning positive reinforcers, response cost is often a highly effective punishment technique.

Time Out. One of the most useful techniques for decreasing undesirable behavior is time out from positive reinforcement (an aversive or punishing event). Time out implies that there is an on-going program of positive reinforcement from which one can take a break. In the absence of positive reinforcement, one cannot have an effective time out. A time-out procedure means that, contingent on a specific undesirable response (hitting, throwing a temper tantrum), the person will not be able to obtain positive reinforcement. Typically, time out means social isolation; for a brief period of time the person has no opportunity for social interaction and no opportunity to experience rewarding consequences. Time out may mean isolation in a separate area, or it may mean simply that the teacher turns away and refuses to interact with the miscreant.

Like all other consequences used to modify behavior, time out must be applied immediately and consistently in order to be effective. The effectiveness of time out is likely to be greater, too, if a minimum of anger or upset is shown by the teacher when the child is placed in time out. Distress signals on the part of the teacher are likely to be social reinforcers for misbehavior, so maintaining a firm but matter-of-fact demeanor is important. Short time-out periods (5–10 minutes) are usually as effective as long ones (30–60 minutes) if they are applied consistently (White, Nielsen, & Johnson, 1972), and short time-out periods have the advantage of letting the individual spend more time in situations where appropriate behavior can be rewarded. However, it is inadvisable to release the child from time out while tantrums or other inappropriate behaviors are being exhibited, even if the time-out interval has passed.

Time out has been used successfully to modify a wide variety of troublesome behaviors of severely handicapped persons (Sachs, 1973). Aggressive and disruptive behavior (Bostow & Bailey, 1969), inappropriate mealtime behavior (Barton, Guess, Garcia, & Baer, 1970), self-injurious behavior (Lucero, Frieman, Spoering, & Fehrenbacher, 1976), and other inappropriate acts have been reduced or eliminated by using time out in one form or another.

Overcorrection. There are two basic forms of overcorrection: *restitution*, or restoring the environment to a condition better than its condition before the misbehavior occurred, and *positive practice*, or practicing a more correct form of behavior contingent on a maladaptive response. Overcorrecting the deviant behavior of severely handicapped persons, techniques pioneered by Nathan Azrin, Richard Foxx, and their co-workers, has been found highly effective with a wide array of problems, including garbage-eating (Foxx & Martin, 1975), theft (Azrin & Wesolowski, 1974), aggression (Foxx & Azrin, 1972; Webster & Azrin, 1973), self-stimulation (Azrin, Kaplan, & Foxx, 1973; Epstein, Doke, Sajwaj, Sorrell, & Rimmer, 1974; Foxx & Azrin, 1973), and self-injurious behavior (Azrin, Gottlieb, Hughart, Wesolowski, & Rahn, 1975).

Overcorrection techniques have been designed with the characteristics of particular behaviors and individuals in mind, but the principles of making restitution or practicing appropriate behavior have guided intervention. For example, in overcorrecting theft, Azrin and Wesolowski (1974) required retarded persons who stole food from others not only to return the stolen item but to make restitution by purchasing an identical new item and giving that to their victims, too. In overcorrecting self-stimulation, Foxx and Azrin (1973) required children to practice a more correct or appropriate form of behavior for a specified period of time contingent on self-stimulatory responses. For example, a child who engaged in hand-flapping might be required to practice functional hand exercises on command from the teacher for a period of 15 minutes.

Maintaining and Generalizing Behavioral Gains

Every teacher hopes that what has been taught will not be quickly forgotten—that there will be response maintenance. Most teachers hope also for transfer of training, or generalization; that is, they like to think that what they have taught will be practiced in situations other than the classroom or specific setting in which the learner's new skill was acquired; that there will be stimulus generalization; and that the person they have taught will learn some related behaviors in addition to the specific skills for which instruction was given, that there will be response generalization. For example, a teacher who teaches a child how to answer the telephone in the classroom in May will be especially happy to find that the child still answers appropriately in September, that the child answers the phone properly at home, and that related skills, such as responding to instructions given via telephone, have been learned without special instruction.

In truth, there is relatively little research indicating how response maintenance and transfer of training (generalization) can best be facilitated. It does seem rather clear that responses are unlikely to be maintained and training is not likely to transfer to new settings and responses unless specific procedures are used. Unless the teacher goes beyond wishful thinking and deliberately devises a program to make these desirable outcomes occur, maintenance and transfer are not likely to happen (Kazdin, 1975). Several procedures for facilitating maintenance and generalization have been suggested, but the use of these procedures is today supported more by appeals to common sense and extrapolation from laboratory research than by research with humans. The following techniques are suggested as those consistent with the best current thinking (see Kazdin, 1975, for more complete discussion).

Gradually Fading Out Contingencies

In a sound behavior management program, reinforcement and punishment are contingent on specific performances, as we have discussed previously. If contingencies are suddenly dropped, and performance is no longer followed by reinforcement or punishment as in the past, then the individual is likely to perform poorly. The normal individual who finds that a certain desirable response no longer pays off will soon stop performing that response, and the person who no longer suffers negative consequences for inappropriate behavior is likely to regress rather quickly. Of course, there are ways to make behavior resistant to extinction (durable in the absence of frequent consequences), and we will discuss some of them. The point here is simply that removing all the supports (contingencies) for behavior at once is an unintelligent way of managing behavior if one wants it to endure. It makes better sense to withdraw contingencies gradually. If one has devised contingencies that apply to ten behaviors, then it would be advisable to remove the contingencies one at a time, allowing the person to adjust to the absence of one contingency before withdrawing the next. Or if a contingency is in effect 12 hours per day, then it would be prudent to withdraw the contingency for an hour at first and later for longer periods, but only for as much time as the individual will tolerate without losing behavioral gains.

Gradually Increasing Delay of Consequences

An axiom of behavior modification is that behavior is most responsive to its immediate consequences. To some extent, however, it is advantageous to teach individuals to work for delayed rewards or to behave well in order to avoid delayed punishment. In our society, delayed rewards (or the promise of them), often maintain behavior over a long period of time. (Consider the person working for years to obtain an academic degree or saving money for years to purchase a house.) It is unreasonable to expect the severely handicapped, who typically require immediate consequences for learning, suddenly to tolerate long delays in being rewarded for appropriate performance. One must be careful to begin with very slight delays in administering consequences and then gradually lengthen the response-consequence interval. For example, if token reinforcers are being given, they initially may be redeemable for back-up reinforcers immediately after 5 minutes of work, but exchanging them may be put off for gradually longer intervals until eventually they are cashed in at the end of the day.

Gradually "Leaning" the Schedule of Reinforcement

Continuous reinforcement, reinforcement of every proper response, usually is necessary in order to establish a skill that is being learned. Once a response is established, however, it can be maintained more efficiently, in most cases, through an intermittent schedule in which only a fraction of the responses are reinforced. The greater the number of responses and/or the more time that must pass before reinforcement is given, the leaner or thinner the schedule. Responses are unlikely to be maintained if suddenly a rich (continuous or nearly continuous) schedule becomes very *lean* (thin). The astute teacher will gradually wean students by thinning out reinforcement in small steps.

Shifting to Natural Reinforcers

Some reinforcers are considered to be contrived or artificial because they do not ordinarily or naturally occur in the person's environment. Tokens, points, and certain activities that can be used as reinforcers are not natural or automatic consequences for behavior in an unmanaged environment. It is reasonable to expect that responses will have a better chance of being maintained and generalized to new settings if the reinforcers supporting those responses are automatic (e.g., food in the mouth for self-feeding) or part of normal social intercourse (e.g., praise and attention). It is often necessary to use artificial reinforcers to establish responses in the severely handicapped, but it is wise to pair natural reinforcers (e.g., praise) with contrived rewards (e.g., tokens) and to work toward reliance on consequences that are likely to occur in the child's everyday life without a teacher's being there to program them.

Varying the Training Setting

A common complaint about training the severely handicapped is that they learn a skill in one setting, perhaps the classroom, but cannot perform the task in another setting, perhaps on the job or at home. Certainly, it is true that training cannot be expected to generalize across different settings by magic. One way of increasing the chances of accomplishing generalization across settings is to provide training in a variety of situations and under a variety of conditions, with the situations and conditions being as close as possible to the real life settings to which it is hoped generalization will occur. A pragmatic view is that, whenever possible, training should be given in the settings where performance will actually be called for.

Training the Person's Caretakers

The teacher usually is not in a position to follow a learner's progress over a period of many years or to see to the student's care after school hours. Therefore, it is advisable to train parents, siblings, or others who manage the individual's behavior outside the classroom. In fact, if response maintenance and generalization are to be realities, training the person's caretakers in methods of behavior management is usually essential. Training programs for parents and nonprofessionals are readily available (cf. Baldwin & Fredericks, 1973; Larsen & Bricker, 1968).

Teaching Self-Control

Persons who are not severely handicapped have been taught a variety of self-control techniques, including counting and graphing their own behavior, giving themselves instructions, and applying consequences for their own behavior. Self-control techniques may facilitate maintenance of behavior because there is less reliance on external sources of motivation. The extent to which severely handicapped individuals can be taught to be self-controlled has not been researched extensively, but it seems a worthy goal for every person to develop self-control to the greatest extent possible.

The seven techniques suggested here are not mutually exclusive. In fact, many of the techniques are complementary. For example, consequences may be gradually delayed at the same time that contingencies of reinforcement are being faded out. The task of the teacher of the severely handicapped is to employ these seven techniques, and perhaps others as well, to ensure maintenance and generalization of learning, rather than leaving the outcome to chance.

References

Ausman, J. O., & Gaddy, M. R. Reinforcement training for echolalia: Developing a repertoire of appropriate verbal responses in an echolalic girl. *Mental Retardation*, 1974, *12*(1), 20–21.

Azrin, N. H., Gottlieb, L., Hughart, L., Wesolowski, M. D., & Rahn, T. Eliminating self-injurious behavior by educative procedures. *Behaviour Research and Therapy*, 1975, *13*, 101–111.

Azrin, N. H., Kaplan, S. J., & Foxx, R. M. Autism reversal: Eliminating stereotyped self-stimulation of retarded individuals. *American Journal of Mental Deficiency*, 1973, *78*, 241–248.

Azrin, N. H. & Wesolowski, M. D. Theft reversal: An overcorrection procedure for eliminating stealing by retarded persons. *Journal of Applied Behavior Analysis*, 1974, *7*, 577–581.

Bachman, J. A. Self-injurious behavior: A behavioral analysis. *Journal of Abnormal Psychology*, 1972, *80*, 211–224.

Baer, D. M., & Guess, D. Teaching productive noun suffixes to severely retarded children. *American Journal of Mental Deficiency*, 1973, *77*, 498–505.

Baer, D. M., Peterson, R. F., & Sherman, J. A. *Building on imitative repertoire by programming similarity between child and model as discriminative for reinforcement.* Paper presented at the biennial meeting of the Society for Research in Child Development, Minneapolis, Minn., March 1965.

Baker, J. G., Stanish, B., & Fraser, B. Comparative effects of a token economy in nursery school. *Mental Retardation*, 1972, *10*(4), 16–19.

Baldwin, V. L. & Fredericks, H. D. *Isn't it time he outgrew this? Or a training program for parents of retarded children.* Springfield, Ill.: Charles C. Thomas, 1973.

Balthazaar, E., & Stevens, H. *The emotionally disturbed mentally retarded*. Englewood Cliffs, N.J.: Prentice-Hall, 1975.

Barton, E. S., Guess, D., Garcia, E., & Baer, D. M. Improvement of retardates' mealtime behaviors by timeout procedures using multiple baseline techniques. *Journal of Applied Behavior Analysis*, 1970, *3*, 77–84.

Bellamy, T., & Buttars, K. L. Teaching trainable level retarded students to count money: Toward personal independence through academic instruction. *Education and Training of the Mentally Retarded*, 1975, *10*, 18–26.

Bostow, D. E., & Bailey, J. B. Modification of severe disruptive and aggressive behavior using brief timeout and reinforcement procedures. *Journal of Applied Behavior Analysis*, 1969, *2*, 31–37.

Cooper, J. O. *Measurement and analysis of behavior techniques*. Columbus, Ohio: Charles E. Merrill, 1974.

Crosson, J. E. A technique for programming sheltered workshop environments for training severely retarded workers. *American Journal of Mental Deficiency*, 1969, *73*, 814–818.

Dalton, A. J., Rubino, C. A., & Hislop, M. W. Some effects of token rewards on school achievement of children with Down's syndrome. *Journal of Applied Behavior Analysis*, 1973, *6*, 251–259.

Dorry, G. W., & Zeaman, D. Teaching a simple reading vocabulary to retarded children: Effectiveness of fading and nonfading procedures. *American Journal of Mental Deficiency*, 1975, *79*, 711–716.

Epstein, L. H., Doke, L. A., Sajwaj, T. E., Sorrell, S., & Rimmer, B. Generality and side effects of overcorrection. *Journal of Applied Behavior Analysis*, 1974, *7*, 385–390.

Foxx, R. M., & Azrin, N. H. The elimination of autistic self-stimulatory behavior by overcorrection. *Journal of Applied Behavior Analysis*, 1973, *6*, 1–14.

Foxx, R. M., & Azrin, N. H. Restitution: A method of eliminating aggressive-disruptive behavior of retarded and brain damaged patients. *Behaviour Research and Therapy*, 1972, *10*, 15–27.

Foxx, R. M., & Martin, E. D. Treatment of scavenging behavior (coprophagy and pica) by overcorrection. *Behaviour Research and Therapy*, 1975, *13*, 151–162.

Frankel, F., & Simmons, J. Q. Self-injurious behavior in schizophrenic and retarded children. *American Journal of Mental Deficiency*, 1976, *80*, 512–522.

Garcia, E. The training and generalization of a conversational speech form in nonverbal retardates. *Journal of Applied Behavior Analysis*, 1974, *7*, 137–149.

Gold, M. W. Stimulus factors in skill training of the retarded on a complex assembly task: Acquisition, transfer, and retention. *American Journal of Mental Deficiency*, 1972, *76*, 517–526.

Guess, D., & Baer, D. M. An analysis of individual differences in generalization between receptive and productive language in retarded children. *Journal of Applied Behavior Analysis*, 1973, *6*, 311–329.

Hall, R. V. *Managing behavior*. Part I. Behavior modification: The *measurement of behavior*. Lawrence, Kansas: H & H Enterprises, 1971.

Hall, R. V., Axelrod, S., Foundopulos, M., Shellman, J., Campbell, R. A., & Cranston, S. S. The effective use of punishment to modify behavior in the classroom. *Educational Technology*, 1971, *11*(4), 24–26.

Hall, R. V., Hawkins, R. P., & Axelrod, S. Measuring and recording student behavior: A behavior analysis approach. In R. A. Weinberg & F. H. Wood (Eds.), *Observation of pupils and teachers in mainstream and special education settings: alternate strategies*. Minneapolis, Minn.: Leadership Training Institute, University of Minnesota, 1975.

Hislop, M. W., Moore, C., & Stanish, B. Remedial classroom programming: Long-term transfer effects from a token economy system. *Mental Retardation*, 1973, *11*(2), 18–20.

Horner, R. D., & Keilitz, I. Training mentally retarded adolescents to brush their teeth. *Journal of Applied Behavior Analysis*, 1975, *8*, 301–319.

Karen, R. L., Eisner, M., & Endres, R. W. Behavior modification in a sheltered workshop for severely retarded students. *American Journal of Mental Deficiency*, 1975, *79*, 338–347.

Kauffman, J. M. Nineteenth century views of children's behavior disorders: Historical contributions and continuing issues. *Journal of Special Education*, in press. (a)

Kauffman, J. M. *Characteristics of behavior disorders in children.* Columbus, Ohio: Charles E. Merrill, in press. (b)

Kauffman, J. M., LaFleur, N. K., Hallahan, D. P., & Chanes, C. M. Imitation as a consequence for children's behavior: Two experimental case studies. *Behavior Therapy*, 1975, *6*, 535–542.

Kazdin, A. E. *Behavior modification in applied settings*. Homewood, Ill.: Dorsey Press, 1975.

Kazdin, A. E., & Bootzin, R. R. The token economy: An evaluative review. *Journal of Applied Behavior Analysis*, 1972, *5*, 343–372.

Koegel, R. L., Firestone, P. B., Kramme, K. W., & Dunlap, G. Increasing spontaneous play by suppressing self-stimulation in autistic children. *Journal of Applied Behavior Analysis*, 1974, *7*, 521–528.

Larsen, L. A., & Bricker, W. A. *A manual for parents and teachers of severely and moderately retarded children*. Nashville, Tenn.: Institute on Mental Retardation and Intellectual Development IMRID Papers and Reports, *5*(22), 1968.

Lucero, W. J., Frieman, J., Spoering, K., & Fehrenbacher, J. Comparison of three procedures in reducing self-injurious behavior. *American Journal of Mental Deficiency*, 1976, *80*, 548–554.

MacMillan, D. L., Forness, S. R., & Trumbull, B. M. The role of punishment in the classroom. *Exceptional Children*, 1973, *40*, 85–96.

Nelson, G. L., Cone, J. E., & Hanson, C. R. Training correct utensil use in retarded children: Modeling vs. physical guidance. *American Journal of Mental Deficiency*. 1975, *80*, 114–122.

O'Brien, F., & Azrin, N. H. Developing proper mealtime behaviors of the institutionalized retarded. *Journal of Applied Behavior Analysis*, 1972, *5*, 389–399.

O'Brien, F., Azrin, N. H., & Bugle, C. Training profoundly retarded children to stop crawling. *Journal of Applied Behavior Analysis*, 1972, *5*, 131–137.

O'Brien, F., Bugle, C., & Azrin, N. H. Training and maintaining a retarded child's proper eating. *Journal of Applied Behavior Analysis*, 1972, *5*, 67–72.

Peterson, R. A., & McIntosh, E. I. Teaching tricycle riding. *Mental Retardation*, 1973, *11*(5), 32–34.

Repp, A. C., & Deitz, S. M. Reducing aggressive and self-injurious behavior of institutionalized retarded children through reinforcement of other behaviors. *Journal of Applied Behavior Analysis*, 1974, 7, 313–325.

Sachs, D. A., The efficacy of time-out procedures in a variety of behavior problems. *Journal of Behavior Therapy and Experimental Psychiatry*, 1973, *4*, 237–242.

Salzberg, B., & Napolitan, J. Holding a retarded boy at a table for 2 minutes to reduce inappropriate object contact. *American Journal of Mental Deficiency*, 1974, *78*, 748–751.

Skinner, B. F. *The technology of teaching*. New York: Appleton, 1968.

Streifel, J. A., & Phelan, J. G. Use of reinforcement of behavioral similarity to establish imitative behavior in young mentally retarded children. *American Journal of Mental Deficiency*, 1972, 77, 239–341.

Sulzbacher, S. I., & Houser, J. E. A tactic to eliminate disruptive behaviors in the classroom: Group contingent consequences. *American Journal of Mental Deficiency*, 1968, *73*, 88–90.

Vukelich, R., & Hake, D. F. Reduction of dangerously aggressive behavior in a severely retarded resident through a combination of positive reinforcement procedures. *Journal of Applied Behavior Analysis*, 1971, *4*, 215–225.

Webster, D. R., & Azrin, N. H. Required relaxation: A method of inhibiting agitative-disruptive behavior of retardates. *Behaviour Research and Therapy*, 1973, *11*, 67–78.

White, O. R., & Liberty, K. A. Behavioral assessment and precise educational measurement. In N. G. Haring and R. L. Schiefelbusch (Eds.), *Teaching Special Children*. New York: McGraw-Hill, 1976.

White, G. D., Nielsen, G., & Johnson, S. M. Timeout duration and the suppression of deviant behavior in children. *Journal of Applied Behavior Analysis*, 1972, *5*, 111–120.

Wolf, M. M., Birnbrauer, J. S., Williams, T., & Lawler, J. A note on apparent extinction of the vomiting of a retarded child. In L. P. Ullmann & L. Krasner (Eds.), *Case studies in behavior modification*. New York: Holt, Reinhart, & Winston, 1965.

Worell, J. & Nelson, C. M. *Managing instructional problems: A case study workbook*. New York: McGraw-Hill, 1974.

Zimmerman, J. & Zimmerman, E. The alteration of behavior in a special classroom situation. *Journal of the Experimental Analysis of Behavior*, 1962, *5*, 59–60.

JAMES M. KAUFFMAN is Associate Professor of Education at the University of Virginia, where he has taught since 1970. He received his doctorate in special education from the University of Kansas.

MARTHA E. SNELL is Assistant Professor of Education at the University of Virginia, where she has taught since 1973. She also serves as coordinator of the undergraduate program in special education. She received her doctorate in special education from Michigan State University.

VIII Teaching Strategies: Selected Approaches to Curriculum and Instruction

A curriculum that is designed by one service program is rarely adopted in its entirety by other service programs. Each service program appears to feel dissatisfied with the curricula of others and attempts to develop its own. Our first reaction may be to charge that service programs are re-inventing the wheel and wasting their efforts. They may be re-inventing the wheel, but perhaps they are not wasting time and energy, since curriculum development may be used in inservice programs to train teachers in the process of individualizing instruction. Through participation in the development, adaptation, implementation, evaluation, and refinement of curriculum, teachers may learn about language development, motor development, cognitive development, and so forth. In addition, they may learn how to devise, implement, evaluate, and adapt instructional programs to meet the special needs of their students.

Wes Williams and Ernest A. Gotts

Selected Considerations on Developing Curriculum for Severely Handicapped Students

WES WILLIAMS

University of Vermont

ERNEST A. GOTTS

University of Texas-Dallas

The development of educational and habilitative programs for severely handicapped students requires active problem-solving efforts on the part of special educators. One problematic issue that confronts us is curriculum development. As described here, curricula provide the framework of sequential goals within which specific instructional procedures, measurement procedures, and task presentation sequences are developed.

Curriculum development for the severely and profoundly handicapped is currently an art rather than a science. Little empirical evidence exists for determining answers to the kinds of problems teachers are experiencing in service settings. If teachers and support personnel in emerging programs for the severely handicapped are to be effective, they will need options, guidelines, and systematic procedures for solving the problems posed by curriculum development.

The Nature of the Severely Handicapped Population

Individuals across chronological age levels, with various constellations of handicapping conditions, of varying intensities, are classified as severely handicapped. The customary public school response to heterogeneity is to group students for instruction, a practice that enhances administrative convenience and relative ease of lesson planning. However, the stereotyping of group members and the distancing of groups from each other, which may result from homogenous grouping, are counter to principles of normalization. Furthermore, conditions which cause a severe level of handicap occur at a low incidence. Even when we cluster severely handicapped individuals in institutions or in regional centers for services, it is difficult to achieve relatively homogenous groupings.

Because severely handicapped populations served in particular programs will tend to be quite heterogenous, one criterion for an effective curriculum must be its capability to deal with the variety of sensory and physical deficits and the range of developmental levels likely to be encountered. The position of this paper is that there are basic principles, ideas, and program development frameworks that are generally applicable across various types and intensities of handicapping conditions. The specific focus of this discussion will be on the role of skill sequences, together with task analysis, in organizing our instructional interventions sequentially; assessing students' current functioning levels; selecting, developing, and ordering learning tasks; and evaluating instructional success.

Skill Sequences

A skill sequence is delineated to provide a framework of tasks or objectives within which many types of instructional programs may be organized. A sequence is not a statement of how to teach but rather a statement of what is to be taught and in what order. A precise delineation of what is to be taught is an obvious prerequisite to developing instructional programs. Articulation of a sequence is also essential to assessing students' performance levels, in that a sequence delineates what should be assessed, and in what order. Skill sequences are the framework around which curricula may be developed.

Precise sequences are more likely to be successful than casual or unplanned task presentation sequences. However, delineating finer re-

This paper was supported in part by Special Projects Training Grant PR# 451AH6 from the United States Office of Education, Bureau of Education for the Handicapped, to the University of Vermont.

ductions of component skills, adding overlooked component skills, and eliminating unnecessary component skills are part of the process of using and constructing sequences. The construction of sequences should progress from the basis of logical analyses, human development, and commercially available curriculum packages, to the basis of systematic observations of student performance. This process involves a progression from sequences derived through armchair analyses to sequences derived through empirical verification. Using and constructing sequences is a dynamic process in which it is likely that any given sequence will be modified according to student performance.

Skill sequences should never be considered finished products. Our present imperfect knowledge dictates that current skill sequences should continually be refined and revised, on the basis of student performance, our growing knowledge of human development and learning, and the changing values and expectations of society.

In the past, many documented reports of programs that were effective in teaching severely handicapped individuals were concerned with isolated skills, such as naming objects and tying shoes, not with skill sequences. The programs did not explicitly delineate that skills were components of a sequence, nor did they show how the skills were related to other components of a sequence or, ultimately, to adult competency. Longitudinal public education and a more effective instructional technology make it possible for us to delineate longitudinal skill sequences. Furthermore, the goals of deinstitutionalization and child advocacy make it mandatory for instruction of skills to be justified as a cumulative component of longitudinal skill sequences, designed to lead students from their current levels of functioning to functioning in the least restrictive environment possible.

The use of longitudinal sequences offers at least four advantages.

1. Use of longitudinal sequences should help minimize the potentially deleterious effects of personnel turnover (teachers and administrators) on long-term programming.

2. In a skill sequence model which delineates sequences of skills which progress from zero ability level to adult competency, readiness consists of mastery of the prerequisite component skills which facilitate the student in learning more advanced skills. Within this model, a teacher does not simply wait for a student to be ready to learn a skill but teaches the requisite skills.

3. Sequences can facilitate the development of more efficient curricula. If teachers carefully monitor student performance, they can obtain data which indicate the order in which skills are most readily acquired and which skills must be further refined into sequences of component skills. A cycle of constructing a skill sequence, monitoring student performance, reconstructing the skill sequence, and monitoring student performance should lead to more efficient and valid curricula. It is only through such research that we can progress from normal developmental sequences, logically derived notions of sequences, and psychological laboratory research to valid curricula.

4. Use of sequences facilitates the individualization of instruction, e.g., tests or observational procedures can be designed for each component skill in a sequence. Students' mastery of various component skills can be assessed before instruction, and they need only be instructed on component skills they lack and for which they have mastered the prerequisites. Grouping of students for instruction can be done on the basis of the skills students have mastered and the skills they should be taught next. Students to be instructed on the same component skill of a sequence can be grouped. A precise delineation of the current functional level of a student in a variety of educationally important sequences is more relevant for grouping purposes and for developing viable instructional services than is the use of such diagnostic categories as autistic, severely retarded, trainable, psychotic, emotionally disturbed, and low mental age.

Selected Underlying Constructs

Terminology in the education and habilitation of the severely handicapped can be confusing. Many disciplines have made contributions, and professionals from various backgrounds continue to use their specialized vocabularies. The same terms are sometimes used in slightly different ways, and many theoretical frames of reference have been used to analyze similar issues. The differing viewpoints which result may offer us a great deal by helping to conceptualize the problems and to develop strategies for dealing with them. Because the potential for faulty communication and confusion is great, subsequent sections of this paper will include definitions of the way terms are used here.

Tasks. A task is a specified situation in which a particular directly observable behavior should occur. For example, placing pegs in a board and tracking a slowly moving rattle are tasks, in that they are specified situations which require a directly observable response. A distinction should be made between tasks and instructional materials; a task or specified response situation can involve many different materials. For instance, the task of placing a peg in a board can be accomplished with pegs and boards of different colors, sizes, and shapes.

Concepts and Operations. Through tasks, individuals may learn concepts: classifications of objects on the basis of function, form, color, size, and so on. Individuals may also learn operations or classifying actions, such as push and pull, through tasks. Teaching focuses upon tasks. Individuals' mastery of concepts or operations is inferred on the basis of their performances on a number of tasks. For instance, if individuals have been taught to respond to various types of balls in a manner that identifies them as members of the class "ball" across a series of tasks (such as putting away balls, rolling balls, and throwing balls), we may infer that they have learned the concept of "ball." Similarly, after individuals have been taught to "touch" across a number of tasks (e.g., touch ball, touch book, touch blue), we infer that they know the operation (response class) of touch.

Before we can legitimately infer that individuals know a particular concept or operation, they must perform selected behaviors across many tasks. If the tasks used for teaching the concept or operation are relatively nonfunctional to individuals' life spaces, then the concept or operation may be nonfunctional. For instance, the concept of "cup" could be taught through tasks which require individuals to touch various cups. Tasks involving touch responses may be relatively nonfunctional in individuals' life spaces. On the other hand, if the tasks used for teaching the concept are functional to the individuals' life spaces, then the concept should be functional. The concept "cup" could be taught through teaching individuals to sort cups from other items while putting away dishes, sort cups from noncups while setting the table, drink from a cup, and so on.

Skills. A skill consists of discriminating between objects on the basis of form, color, and size (classifying or sorting: concepts) and/or discriminating between responses such as pulling or pushing (classifying responses: operations). For example, for a student to pull up his pants, he must discriminate pants from non-pants (concept) and discriminate between pulling up and pushing down (operation). To demonstrate that he has mastered the skill of pulling up his pants, the student would have to pull up his pants across functional tasks, such as pulling up his jeans while dressing and pulling up his slacks after toileting.

Coordinated Use of Skills: Generalized Plans. As used here, a generalized plan involves the coordinated use of several skills. For example, individuals may exhibit such skills as visually attending to and tracking events (for example, objects and their hands), moving their hands directly to an object in view, grasping it, and shaping their hands to the physical dimensions of an object before grasping it. We may infer that individuals have mastered each skill after we observe them perform each skill across tasks. We may infer that individuals have learned a generalized plan after we observe them coordinating the use of several skills across tasks. That is, if we observe individuals attending to or tracking an object, shaping their hands to the dimensions of the object while moving their hands directly to the object, and grasping an object across tasks (such as grasping blocks, rattles, cups, washcloths), we may infer that they have a generalized plan which may be called top-level reaching. It is essential that we ensure that students have generalized plans or that they can coordinate the use of skills.

Perhaps because of our training or lack of training when we observe or teach students, we often focus only on behaviors in one area, such as motor, language, or mobility. However, skills are rarely learned or performed in isolation. There are several notions on teaching coordinated use of skills: one task, many skills; many tasks, one skill; and functionally related skills.

1. *One Task, Many Skills*. Task analysis may be used to break down a task into components that students must perform to complete the task successfully. For example, the task of building a three-block tower may be logically, though arbitrarily, broken into at least the following components.

a. Gross motor: Students should be able to support themselves in a sitting position and should be able to control their arm and hand movements.
b. Fine motor: Students should be able to grasp blocks and both pick them up and release them.

c. Eye-hand coordination: Students should exhibit top-level reaching, e.g., they should move their hands directly to the object in view as opposed to swiping at it. The hand should be shaped for grasping before it arrives to grasp the object.

Any task (e.g., self-help, vocational, recreational) may be reduced to components ranging from cognitive to motor. Different regimes of child rearing and different focuses in instructional programs may influence the acquisition rate of each component (Uzgiris and Hunt, 1975), but, no matter how far ahead experience pushes the acquisition rate of one component, coordination cannot occur until all the components are acquired.

2. *One Skill, Many Tasks*. For the purpose of clarity, curricula and sequences sometimes provide a specific example of a task individuals should perform in order to demonstrate a skill. For instance, performance of the skill of bringing the hands together at midline may be demonstrated through the task of touching a rattle with both hands at midline. Although instructors sometimes assess and instruct individuals on the specific tasks delineated by a curriculum or sequence, individuals should learn and demonstrate performance of the skill of bringing their hands together at midline across a number of tasks, such as clapping hands, banging sticks, banging rattles, holding a ball with two hands, and so on. Performance of a skill on one specific task is not as important as their performance of the skill across a number of functional tasks which frequently occur in the individuals' life spaces. When assessing performance and teaching, we should not get locked into one specific task but should think in terms of performance across functional tasks. For each skill delineated by a sequence, multiple functional tasks should be devised. The format shown in Table 1 may be helpful in fostering thinking in terms of performance across tasks.

3. *Functionally Related Skills*. For economy of format, instructional objectives are usually categorized into areas, with a sequence for each area. The skills in each sequence typically progress from easy to difficult. For instance, there may be sequences in such areas as gross motor, fine motor, perceptual-motor, receptive language, dressing, feeding/eating, and vocational skills. A potential misuse of sequences occurs when instructors select skills for teaching from a number of areas, and then devise separate tasks for teaching each skill. For example, a separate task could be devised for a gross motor skill (sits unsupported), a fine motor skill (uses thumb in opposition with finger grasp), a perceptual motor skill (takes objects out of containers), and a language skill (points to or places objects in and out on verbal cue). Five separate programs or tasks could derived for teaching the skills.

However, a skill is more functional and more likely to maintain and generalize if it is taught and used in relation to other skills. For example, individuals could be taught the functional use of a spoon (to scoop food) and the functional use of a bowl (to hold food) through separate programs or tasks. However, only when individuals learn the functional relationship between spoons and bowls can they effectively use a spoon to eat from a bowl.

TABLE 1

Multiple Tasks

Skill	Tasks		
Radial palmar grasp	Grasps rattle	Grasps block	Grasps crib rung
Pincer grasp	Grasps bead	Picks up coins	Buttons shirt
Aligning objects in 1-to-1 correspondence	Gives each place a knife, fork, and spoon when setting table	Gives each classmate a cookie when passing out snacks	Places a paper cup in each hole of a cupcake tin when making cupcakes
Labeling balls	Asks for red ball at recess	Asks for yellow ball while playing at home	Asks for medicine ball in gym class
Putting pants on	Puts pants on while dressing in morning	Puts pants on after toileting	Puts pants on after showering

Similarly, students can be taught to grasp and to track visually. These skills become more functional when they are used together to reach for and grasp an object.

The skills in the above example (sitting unsupported, using thumb in opposition with finger grasp, taking an object out of a container, and placing objects in and out on verbal cue) could be taught through separate tasks. However, they would be better taught together through one task. One problem with teaching several skills at the same time through one task is that some teachers, particularly novices, find it difficult to teach and evaluate several skills concurrently. However, with training and practice, the simultaneous teaching and evaluation of several skills is not difficult.

One procedure for teaching and evaluating several skills simultaneously begins with assessing students' performances in several skill areas. On the basis of their performances, we can delineate behavioral objectives for each skill area. Using the skills from the example, we first organize the skills in a chart (Table 2). Next, we design a functional task through which to teach all four skills. An example of such a task is having the student sit on the floor next to the teacher and, on verbal cue, put pegs in and take pegs out of a pegboard, using a thumb in opposition with finger grasp. (The teacher may partially support sitting when necessary.) The task may be presented in a play or game format. Several variations of the task (e.g., putting pieces in puzzles, dropping marbles in a can) should be devised so that the student may be offered a choice of tasks to engage in. If appropriate, several sessions and variations of the task can be presented in one day.

To evaluate the student's acquisition of the skills, a separate data collection system is devised for each objective. For example, the number of minutes the student sits unsupported could be sampled, the number of tries or trials when the student uses his thumb in opposition with finger grasp can be counted, and the number of trials when the student puts objects in and out on verbal cue can be determined. Each day, the data from each instructional session may be summed and recorded on the data sheet (Table 2).

To make recording easier, data may initially be collected on only one skill per session. As instructors become more efficient, data can be collected on two, three, or more skills per session. Data may be collected on performance of the skills across tasks throughout the day.

Students have not mastered a skill until they can independently demonstrate its coordinated use with other skills in the performance of many functional tasks which frequently occur in their life space. To assess skill mastery, a data sheet similar to the one depicted in Table 3 may be used. Each time students independently perform the skill in coordination with other skills in a different functional task, the date and task should be recorded. When students coordinate the use of a skill with other skills across tasks and time, we may consider them to have mastered that skill and proceed to the next skill in that sequence.

Many educational programs are evaluated in terms of how quickly they advance students vertically from lower level skills to higher level skills. However, the effectiveness of a program should be evaluated in terms of whether students perform skills *and* whether they can perform the skills in coordination with other skills across functional tasks, control figures, cues to respond, and settings. This emphasis requires that both rate of skill acquisition and utility of the skill be assessed in determining the efficacy of a program.

Use of Skill Sequences to Evaluate Program Effectiveness

In addition to determining an individual's functioning level and ordering task pre-

TABLE 2

Many Skills, One Task

Task. Place pegs in and out of a hole on verbal cue, using thumb in opposition to finger grasp, while sitting on floor.

OBJECTIVES

	Gross Motor	Fine Motor	Perceptual Motor	Language
STUDENT	Sitting unsupported	Thumb in opposition with finger grasp	Taking object out of container	Pointing or taking in and out on verbal cue

TABLE 3

Task Performance Record

Targeted Skill	Task Setting: School	Home	Other
Pincer grasp			
Tasks			
Cues			
Dates			
Labeling balls			
Tasks			
Cues			
Dates			
Put pants on			
Tasks			
Cues			
Dates			

sentations, sequences may also be used to assess program effectiveness in the sense that instructional programs may be evaluated in terms of the students' rates of progress through sequences. While an educational program for nonhandicapped individuals can be assessed in relation to the rate of normal child development, a basic problem in evaluating the effectiveness of educational programs for the severely handicapped is that there are no established standards against which we may judge severely handicapped students' rates of progress through sequences.

Due to lack of standards, and in some cases the expectation that little can be done, the learning of any skill at whatever rate is sometimes seen as significant. As a result, some educational programs have simply summed the number of component skills a student has learned in selected areas and then reported that this year Johnny learned five gross motor skills and three self-care skills, and so on. Although the educational program has demonstrated that it is effective, and its approach to evaluation is a step in the right direction, there are at least two problems with this summation-of-skills approach.

First, if each skill area were reduced to more component skills, this would increase the number of skills that Johnny might have learned. For instance, if walking unassisted is reduced to ten component skills, it might have been reported that Johnny learned eight component skills. On the other hand, if walking unassisted had been broken into twenty component skills it might have been reported that Johnny learned sixteen component skills. The apparent amount of learning is related to the fineness of our task analysis.

A second related problem in the summation-of-skills approach is that each skill is assigned equal value or weight. The performance of such skills as drinking from a cup, putting pants on, searching for hidden objects, immediate imitation of behaviors, and delayed imitation of behaviors are assigned equal value. Uzgiris and Hunt (1975) suggest that performance of some skills has more significance than does performance of other skills. Performance of such skills as searching for hidden objects and delayed imitation may be better predictors of students' future learning and functioning than performance of such skills as drinking from a cup and putting pants on. If performances of all skills are not equally significant, on what basis do we assign different values or weights to skills?

There are at least two non-mutually exclusive, potential solutions to the problem of evaluating program effectiveness. To begin with, if a standard evaluation system could be agreed upon, we could establish a system for collecting data on severely handicapped individuals on a national basis. With a nationwide data collection system, it might be possible to establish rates of development for individuals with various types, degrees, and constellations of handicapping conditions. The data could be used to compare the effectiveness of different educational approaches.

A second strategy for evaluating program effectiveness is to assess it in relation to selected minimal objectives (Christie and McKenzie, 1974). One way to do this is to carefully delineate the skills needed to function in specified life spaces such as apartments, group homes, nursing homes, competitive employment, and sheltered workshop employment. Task analysis and available sequences could be used to generate developmentally based sequencies of skills (minimal objectives), which lead from zero skills and zero ability level, to the skills necessary to function in a specified life space. When possible, skills (minimal objectives) could be assigned weights. The goal should be to provide each student with the skills necessary to function in the least restrictive life space. However, our current lack of knowledge and technology makes it impossible for this goal to be attainable by each and every severely handicapped student; therefore, a range of potential life spaces should be delineated, and the individuals should be taught to live in the least restrictive life space possible.

This alternative leaves us with a sequence of skills, but without a means for determining how rapidly any particular severely handicapped student should advance through it. There may also be some arbitrary time constraints. For example, if the goal of a preschool program is to provide severely handicapped students with the skills to function at home and in a specific school program at age five, the time period to move students through the sequence of skills is limited. If the goal is independent community living, a school program may have an arbitrary time limit, age 21. Such a system of minimum objectives may be represented as in Figure 1. If students' progressions stay on or above the line on the graph, they will potentially meet the goal of functioning in a given life space. If their rates of progression fall below the line, there should be more intensive instructional intervention, rethinking in regard to the appropriateness of the potential life space, and/or a structuring of the potential life space so that students who do not perform certain skills may function in them. For example, a life space may be structured so that students who cannot walk may use a wheelchair for locomotion and students who cannot see can use tactile input to locate themselves in space.

Selected Principles or Assumptions Underlying Sequences

A major issue in curriculum development is that of sequence or order. Learning should proceed in an incremental or stepwise fashion; each new acquisition may build on the previous ones. Various principles or assumptions may underlie the order of skills in a sequence.

As described here, cognitive sequences are sequences of skills which lead to the development of generalized plans for information processing or actions (i.e., inferred internal processes). For example, the following sequence of skills building toward a generalized plan for relating to objects is reported by Uzgiris and Hunt (1975).

1. Incidental use of objects in the exercise of a scheme (situation: mouthing).
2. Appearance of momentary attention to the object involved in the exercise of a scheme (visual inspection).
3. Systematic use of objects in the exercise of schemes (hitting).
4. Beginning of differentiation of schemes as a result of interaction with different objects (shaking).
5. Shift of attention from the exercise of schemes to investigation of the properties of objects (examining).
6. Selective application of schemes depending on the properties of objects (differentiated schemes).
7. Acquisition of new schemes as a result of studying various properties of objects (dropping and throwing).
8. Beginning of appreciation of the social uses of objects (socially instigated behaviors).
9. Beginning of the representation of objects is implied by reference to them in a shared interaction (showing).
10. Representation of objects in a symbolic system is indicated by verbal expressions of recognition (naming). (p. 123)

Difficulty and complexity increase as we move down the sequence. In this sequence, we see increasingly complex skills for relating to objects which are components of a generalized plan for relating symbolically to objects. In such a cognitive sequence, to infer that students have developed a generalized plan, their performance of directly observable skills (such as mouthing, visual inspection, and hitting) across a variety of tasks would have to be observed. Students' development of a generalized plan cannot be directly observed; it is inferred on the basis of their performance of specified observable skills across a variety of tasks.

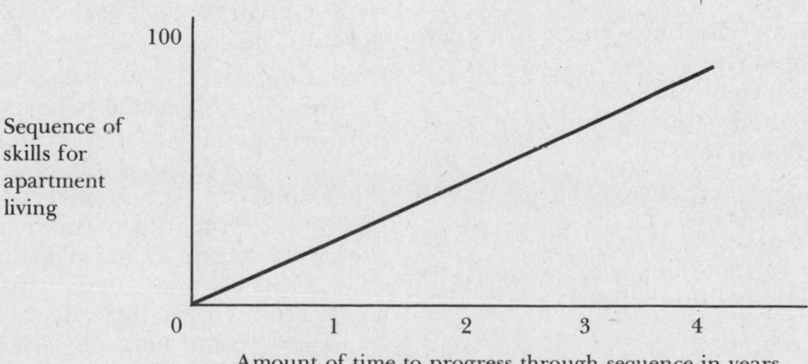

Figure 1. Minimal objective sequence

Skill sequences are sequences of directly observable behaviors. The sequence of behaviors for developing dressing skills progresses from zero skills, zero ability level, to a level of adult functioning. The steps described by the Behavioral Characteristics Progression (BCP) (1973) are:

1. Cooperates passively when being dressed.
2. Moves limbs to aid in dressing (e.g., holds out foot for shoe, arm for sleeves).
3. Assists in getting dressed by passing or holding clothing.
4. Identifies own clothing.
5. Partially closes one of the three front fasteners (e.g., pushes button halfway into hole, zips halfway up or pushes snaps together).
6. Pulls t-shirt, undershirt and other pull-over garments down over chest after head and arms put in by adult.
7. Puts one arm into sleeve of t-shirt and pulls over chest.
8. Puts both arms into sleeves of t-shirt and pulls over chest.
9. Pulls t-shirt down over head, puts arms in sleeves and pulls over chest.
10. Places head into neckhole and puts t-shirt on completely.
11. Closes one of three front fasteners—either buttons, zips, or snaps.
12. Pulls pants, briefs, and other pull-down garments up from hips to waist after pants pulled up to that point by adult.
13. Pulls pants up from knees to waist.
14. Pulls pants up from ankles to waist.
15. Pulls pants up completely from floor to waist.

.
.
.
.

45. Dresses daily at designated times without being reminded (e.g., in the morning, after shower).
46. Selects clean clothing, changes underclothes regularly.
47. Selects and uses protective clothing according to the weather, location, etc. (e.g., raincoat, boots, hat).
48. Selects clothing for different occasions and locations.
49. Polishes shoes.
50. Attempts to maintain a clean, neat appearance throughout the day. (pp. 16–18).

Most of the skills in this sequence are simple behaviors which may be directly observed. Students' mastery of one skill in the sequence, such as pulling up pants, may be verified by observing students' performances of the skill across such tasks as pulling up pants while dressing and after toileting. On the basis of students' performance of specified behaviors across tasks, we may infer that they have mastered a simple skill.

Comparison of the two examples from Uzgiris and Hunt and the BCP highlights some relevant considerations. The Uzgiris-Hunt sequence is at the level of major developmental steps that lead toward a generalized plan for symbolically relating to objects. The sequence is constructed within a Piagetian theoretical framework. In contrast, most of the Behavioral Characteristics Progression items are at a very specific directly observable level, span the time potentially covered from early childhood to adulthood, and are not constructed around a cognitive theoretical framework. In neither sequence is there a direct relationship between the hierarchical level of the items in the sequences and chronological age (CA). That is, neither sequence specifies at what CA a specific task should be learned. They suggest only an order in which tasks may be presented.

The distinction we have made between cognitive sequences and skill sequences is arbitrary. The basic difference is that cognitive sequences are constructed on the basis of some cognitive theoretical framework and skill sequences are usually constructed on the basis of a logical analysis of the complexity of the skills (simple skills typically precede more complex skills), without reference to theory which provides a rationale for the significance of specific behaviors involved.

There are relative advantages and disadvantages in building curricula around cognitive sequences and skill sequences.

1. Cognitive sequences focus on generalized plans or the coordinated use of skills, whereas skill sequences may not focus on the coordinated use of skills.

2. Cognitive sequences may not precisely specify the observable behaviors students must perform across tasks to demonstrate development of generalized plans. Thus, a student's development of a generalized plan is somewhat open to varying interpretations. A skill sequence precisely specifies the skills and tasks a student should perform to demonstrate mastery of a skill. However, a high degree of specification may not foster teaching students to perform skills across functional tasks that occur in their life spaces.

3. Skill sequences will almost always assist us in determining how to construct tasks. Cognitive sequences usually include fewer direct implications for task design.

An arbitrary distinction has been made between cognitive and skill sequences to illustrate that different kinds of sequences may be derived on the basis of different underlying principles and that there are advantages and disadvantages to different approaches. Additional selected non-mutually exclusive principles underlying sequences are:

1. *Developmentally based sequences or sequences with logically built-in order*. Sequences have a logically built-in order when early skills in the sequence are components of later skills. For example, the skills of visually tracking an object through arcs of 45 degrees, 90 degrees, and 120 degrees are component skills of tracking an object through an arc of 180 degrees.

2. *Maturation of the nervous system*. The sequential order of early skills in visual, auditory, and motor sequences may be dependent on the maturation of the nervous system.

3. *Complexity*. Skills in a sequence may be ordered on the basis of complexity, e.g., lower skills in the sequence may be less complex than higher skills.

4. *Normal development or order*. Skills in a sequence may be ordered as they generally occur in normal development.

5. *Socialization*. Such skills as self-feeding, toileting, visual attending, and following simple directives may be more important in the socialization process than other skills, such as labeling colors. That is, the performance of certain skills makes an individual more socially acceptable to parents, educators, and others. Such skills may be given priority and so may occur earlier in a sequence.

6. *Normalization*. One goal should be to teach students, within the limits of their abilities, so that their behaviors approach those considered normal of their chronological age. In some cases, students may be taught to perform specific skills at a given time so that their behavior approaches that of their normal peers.

The preceding list of underlying principles is far from exhaustive. The order of skills in a sequence may be determined on the basis of one or all of these ordering principles. Sequences generally delineate key skills and the order in which they may be taught. However, a sequence provides only a basic framework for assessing individual performance and ordering instruction. It does not provide a precise recipe. The ordering principles listed above may be used in conjunction with task analysis to adapt sequences (e.g., reorder skills, add new skills, delete skills) and to derive new sequences to meet individual students' needs. An understanding of the principles used to derive a sequence facilitates the appropriate use and adaptation of the sequence.

It has been our experience that teachers of severely handicapped students can rarely use commercially available or normal child development sequences without substantial adaptation. From a training perspective, it is essential to provide teachers with the skills involved in task analysis so that in practical situations they can adapt available sequences or create new sequences to fit the developmental functioning levels and needs of their students.

Task Analysis: A Problem Solving Strategy for Developing Curriculum

After it has been determined that it is important for students to perform the skills required by a particular objective, task analysis may be used as a problem-solving strategy for determining what to teach and for developing the proper sequence that will enhance student mastery of the objective. The product of task analysis is a skill sequence, i.e., a precise delineation of a behavioral objective, the objective's component skills, and an appropriate sequencing of the component skills. The sequence of component skills should lead from responses in the student's repertoire to mastery of the objective. The product of task analysis is *not* a statement of how to teach or assess but rather a statement of what is to be taught and assessed. As a problem-solving strategy, task analysis involves a cycle of constructing a sequence, monitoring student performance, reconstructing the sequence based upon student performance, monitoring student performance, and so on. It is only through such a process that the instructor can progress from logically derived notions of sequences to valid sequences.

A task analysis can usually be accomplished in seven steps.

1. Delineate the behavioral objective.
2. Review instructionally relevant resources.
3. Derive and sequence the component skills of the objective.
4. Eliminate unnecessary component skills.
5. Eliminate redundant component skills.
6. Determine prerequisite skills.
7. Monitor student performance and revise the sequence accordingly.

(See Williams, 1975, for additional information and examples of how to perform task analysis).

Delineating Behavioral Ojectives

Preliminary to task analysis is the determination of appropriate behavioral objectives for the students. Through formal and informal evaluations, the students' performance levels should be determined in such areas as self-help, motor, communication, and social skills. A number of available assessment resources are appropriate for the severely and profoundly handicapped. (For example, the BCP provides an assessment framework for 52 skill areas.) After determining the students' functioning levels in selected areas and delineating the skills the students will need to function in their immediate and future life spaces, the instructor can state behavioral objectives for each student.

Behavioral objectives are statements describing the skills students should perform under specified conditions. The first step in establishing a behavioral objective is to describe the observable skills the students should be able to perform when they have mastered the objective. Observable skills have definite beginnings and endings and so objectives should include expressions such as "point," "write," "name," "list," "pick up," "match," and not expressions such as "appreciate," "understand," "realize," or "comprehend." Although we are concerned with what students understand, believe, feel, know, or appreciate, we can only make inferences concerning students' knowledge, understanding, or appreciation by assessing the overt and measurable behaviors the students perform. We can only make statements about students' understanding of a concept such as "cup" by stating the behaviors the students perform in relation to cups. A *behavioral* objective could be to label specified concepts: in the presence of specified objects (e.g., cups), when asked, "What is this?", the students should say "cup."

The second step in establishing a behavioral objective is specifying under what conditions (givens) the students are to perform the skills. Precise statements of conditions are necessary if we are to agree on which students have mastered an objective. What if four students presented various cups and given the cue, "What is this?", can correctly label only white coffee cups, while two other students can correctly label a variety of cups which differ in size and color? It might be difficult to agree on which students had mastered the objective. A better objective would be: presented specified objects (blue, white, big, or little cups) and asked, "What is this?", the students will say, "Cup."

Even after precisely specifying the conditions, it might still be difficult to agree on which students had mastered the objective. What if four students correctly label 85% of the cups and two students correctly label 90% of the cups? If objectives are to be useful, they must state desired performance levels, as well as desired performance conditions.

An objective can be defined and refined until it becomes absurdly long and detailed. However, it is only necessary to write objectives in sufficient detail to enable any outside observers to concur as to which students had mastered objectives.

Although the importance of precisely formulating instructional objectives cannot be overemphasized, as Goodstein (1975) points out, precisely formulated instructional objectives can impose limitations in the development of instructional programs for handicapped students. For instance, if an objective states that students should verbally label items, an alternative objective may have to be formulated for nonverbal students. Alternative objectives may also have to be formulated for motorically impaired students, deaf students, blind students, and others.

> As instructional objectives become more precisely formulated, there exists a parallel need to formulate more alternative objectives. As listings of alternative objectives become more numerous, the ability of the teacher to use the listings of objectives to make sequencing decisions for curriculum planning becomes more limited. (Goodstein, 1975, p. 2)

Goodstein's (1974) Matrix Teaching System is useful in formulating instructional objectives for handicapped students. Table 4 is a cursory description of this system.

The interactive units (matrices) focus independently upon teacher and student behaviors. Interactive units are composed of five dimensions: interactive mode of teacher, interactive mode of student, means of student response, cognitive level of material, and instructional content (the component skill of the sequence). These dimensions are composed of alternative teacher and student interactive modes, alternative means of student response, and alternative cognitive levels of material. The instructional content may be subdivided into as many component skills as the teacher demands or students' learning characteristics dictate.

The five dimensions and the alternatives delineated in each dimension form a matrix of unique combinations of instructional interactions. The interactive units or matrices facilitate the precise formulation of alternative objectives (tasks) to meet the individual needs of handicapped students. Teachers may select alternatives from such matrices in formulating objectives or tasks which are tailored to the motor, visual,

TABLE 4

Sample Matrices

Teacher Interactive Mode
Physical Manipulations
Visual stimuli presentation, e.g., gesture, sign language, pointing
Auditory stimulus presentation

Student Interactive Mode
Physical Manipulations
Visual stimuli, e.g., gestures, drawing, pointing
Auditory stimuli

	Student Responses
Verbal	Imitate (copy), Identify
Non-verbal	Manipulate, imitate (copy), gesture, point, draw, use communication board, etc.

	Cognitive level of Materials
Enactive	Three-dimensional stimuli, e.g., objects
Iconic	Pictures, line drawings
Symbolic	Words, numbers, gestures

Content
Break down a skill into as many component skills as necessary to facilitate skill acquisition.

auditory, and speech impairments of individual students.

Reviewing Instructionally Relevant Resources

Generally, the more information about the skill area brought to the task analysis, the better the task analysis. Curriculum guides, textbooks, commercially available materials, references on normal child development, and other teachers' task analyses offer information on the component skills other people have delineated and how they have sequenced them.

One might review concepts of task analysis through reading such sources as *Teaching: A Course in Applied Psychology* (Becker, Engelmann, and Thomas; 1969). Commercially available language materials may be examined to determine how they analyze and teach concepts. A review of developmental literature, such as Uzgiris and Hunt (1975), may be performed to determine what children typically master before they learn to label objects. If a commercially available instructional program or sequence which precisely fits students' needs is found, it should be used. If a program or sequence which fits our students' needs is not available, a task analysis will help to adapt available sequences or devise new sequences.

Obviously, the opportunity to research an objective before performing a task analysis depends on the availability of references, the ability to select directly relevant references without first sorting through reams of nonpertinent literature, and the amount of time available. In conjunction with any school program, there should be a professional library of relevant source materials. Instructional Material Centers and Area Learning Resource Centers are excellent information sources, and one of the best resources is the task analyses of other teachers.

Deriving and Sequencing the Component Skills of the Objective

After the essential reference work has been completed, the necessary component skills of the target behavioral objective are derived through three processes: (a) listing the component skills suggested by commercial materials and relevant developmental literature; (b) asking the question, "To master this objective what component skills must the student be able to perform?" (This question is asked until further component skills cannot be derived); and (c) performing the skills indicated by the objective, watching others perform the skills, and imagining oneself performing the skills while noting the necessary component skills and their order of occurrence.

It is not always appropriate to teach skills in the order in which students are ultimately to perform them. For example, in teaching students to eat independently with a spoon, the first skill is filling a spoon, the second is moving the spoon from plate to mouth, and the last is inserting the spoon into the mouth. If the first skill of the sequence is taught first, the students have their spoons filled but they cannot get the spoons to their mouths. Thus, they do not enjoy the natural reward of placing a full spoonful of food into their mouths. It would be necessary to reward the students (with a toy or praise) for filling their spoons and then physically help them move the spoons to their mouths and insert them. On the other hand, inserting the spoon could be taught first. The reward for learning to insert the spoon independently would be the food. This is a naturally occurring reward that should ultimately maintain the students' self-feeding. Next, the students could be taught to move their spoons independently from their plates to their mouths. Finally, the students would learn to fill their spoons independently. In this case, teaching the last component skill of the sequence first is advantageous because students are always rewarded with food for correct performance of the final skill in the sequence. Similarly, it is efficient to teach the last component skill of many self-help, home living, and vocational objectives first. For such objectives, the task analysis process involves first delineating the component skills students should perform first, second, and so on. However, the sequence of skills for such objectives is presented in reverse order.

A skill sequence may be depicted as a lattice. In a lattice, a step format is used. That is, the first component skill of a skill sequence is placed in the lower left hand corner of the page and each sequential component skill is placed in boxes connected by a line with a 90-degree angle.

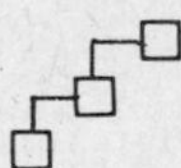

This lattice convention indicates that a lower level skill may facilitate the acquisition of higher skills, but mastery of the lower skill is not necessary before the student can begin to learn higher skills. The terminal objective is always placed in the upper right-hand box and each component skill hangs from that box. The teacher must be sure to sequence the component skills from easiest (far left box) to hardest (far right box). If one skill must be learned before another skill, hang the boxes directly underneath one another with a connecting straight line.

A possible lattice is:

In the foregoing example, our objective was to teach students to label cups. Figure 2 displays a lattice of skills which could be generated by task analysis. We will briefly describe how we derived the lattice. If the students are to learn to label cups, they should be able to discriminate between cups and noncups. Thus, they should be able to discriminate visual cues. Discriminating visual cues is our first component skill (prerequisite skills, Box 1). Blind students can use other sense modalities to discriminate between cups and noncups (prerequisite skills, Box 2). Literature on child development indicates that children use objects functionally before they learn to associate labels with objects. An additional component skill is functional object use (prerequisite skills, Box 3). Non-motorically impaired students may be taught functional object use through manipulating objects and observing others manipulate objects. Motorically impaired students may learn functional object use through observing others manipulating objects. (Of course, functional object use can be broken into further components).

Children can usually match an object to an identical object by using visual cues before they can associate a label with an object. Thus, another component skill could be, "When presented a cup, students should be able to find (match) an identical cup from an array of one cup and several non-cups," (Phase 1, Box 1). Many instructional materials present tasks in which the students draw lines between like objects. Sighted students may be taught to use visual cues to match to sample. Blind students may be taught to use other cues.

Students should know that cups can be different sizes, shapes, and colors and still be cups. We must translate the notion of knowing into a behavioral objective. Students should be able to match a cup to a similar cup (nonexact match) from an array of objects (Phase II, Box 1) either on the basis of visual cues or tactile cues.

Receptive comprehension of object labels is another component skill (Phase III, Box 1). Children can usually identify objects before they can name them. For example, when presented a directive such as, "Show me a cup," children can identify which object is a cup before they can label objects, when asked a question such as, "What is this?". If students are to demonstrate receptive comprehension of object labels, they should be able to discriminate auditory cues (prerequisite skills, Box 4). Deaf students may demonstrate receptive comprehension of visual cues, such as the sign language symbol for cup (prerequisite skills, Box 5). Furthermore, deaf-blind students may use tactile cues.

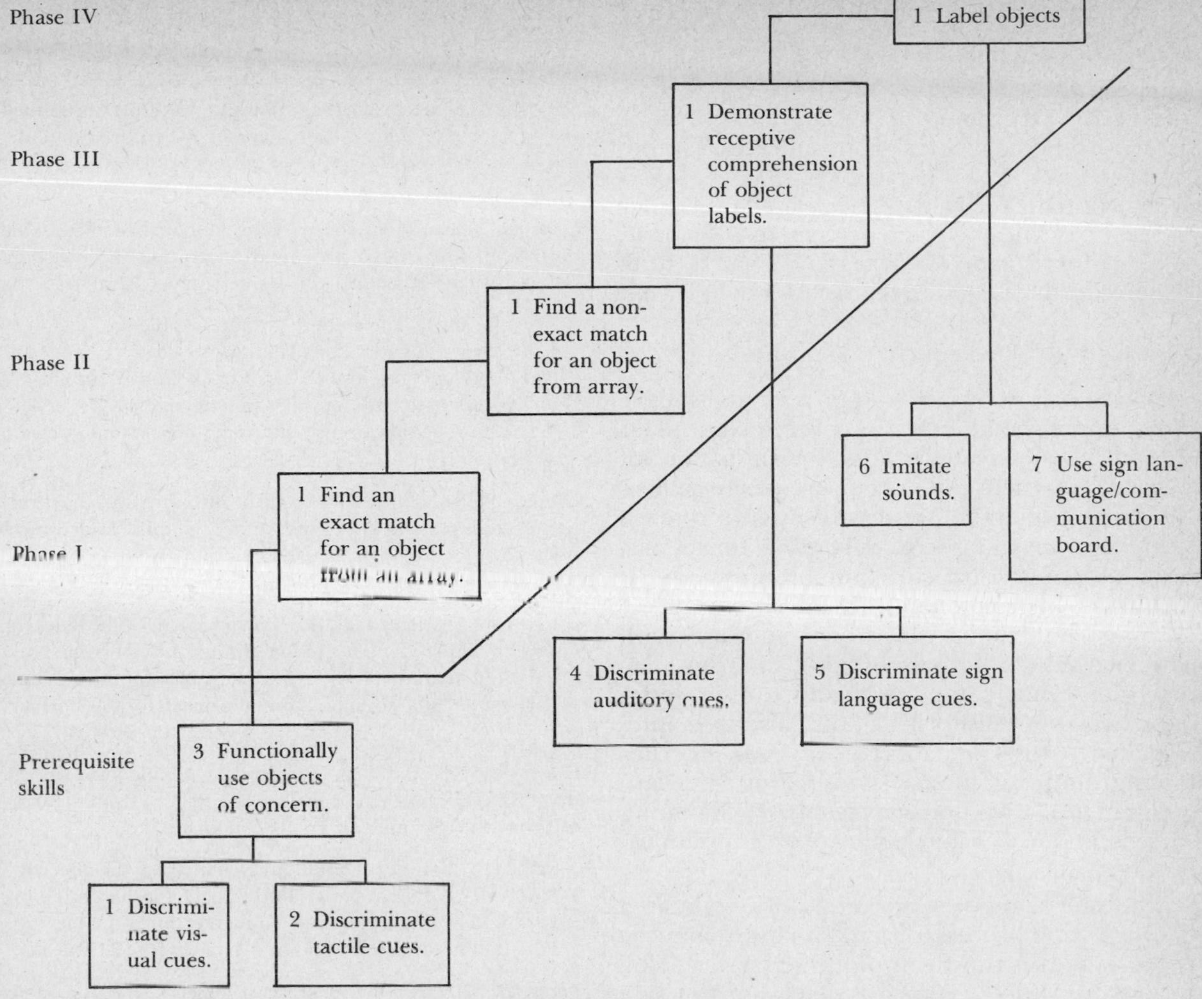
Phase IV
Phase III
Phase II
Phase I
Prerequisite skills
1 Label objects
1 Demonstrate receptive comprehension of object labels.
1 Find a non-exact match for an object from array.
1 Find an exact match for an object from an array.
6 Imitate sounds.
7 Use sign language/communication board.
4 Discriminate auditory cues.
5 Discriminate sign language cues.
3 Functionally use objects of concern.
1 Discriminate visual cues.
2 Discriminate tactile cues.

Figure 2. Lattice for labeling objects.

To teach students to label objects, they should be able to imitate sounds (prerequisite skills, Box 6). Imitation itself can be broken into many component skills. Nonverbal students may use sign language or communication boards to label objects (prerequisite skills, Box 7).

This simplified task analysis suggests that the objective has at least the following component skills:

1. Can discriminate visual or tactile cues.
2. Can discriminate auditory cues or sign language cues.
3. Can functionally use the objects of concern.
4. Given an object, can find (match) an identical object from an array of objects.
5. Given an object, can match a similar object (nonexact match) from an array of objects.
6. Match identical objects by drawing lines between objects.
7. Demonstrate receptive comprehension of object labels.
8. Imitate sounds or use sign language/communication boards.

(See Smith, D. D., Smith, J. O., and Haring, N. G. The modified lattice system: An approach to the analysis and sequence of instruction and objectives. Experimental Education Unit, Child Development and Mental Retardation Center, University of Washington, Seattle, Washington, undated, for details on constructing lattices.)

Eliminating Unnecessary Component Skills

The word "necessary" is a key word when deriving component skills for the objective. Many common classroom tasks are closely related to valid objectives, and it is easy to mistake these related tasks for necessary tasks. For example, the task of indicating objects which are identical by drawing a line between them is a related task, not a necessary one. Because this task is not necessary to the learning of skills required by the objective, we could eliminate it. However, because a task is not included in our task analysis does not mean that it is not instructionally relevant. Many related tasks, such as drawing lines between objects, may facilitate skill generalization or transfer. That is, they require students to use a skill across related tasks.

Determining Prerequisite Skills

When the necessary component skills have been established, entry or prerequisite skills should be delineated. The determination of which component skills are prerequisite skills is arbitrary. Generally, we do not intend to teach students everything (e.g., functional object use, discriminating visual cues, imitation of sounds) within one instructional program, such as object labeling. Functional object use and imitation could be taught as part of a self-help or play program. Some component skills can be designated as prerequisite skills (e.g., discriminating visual cues, discriminating tactile cues, discriminating auditory cues, discriminating sign language cues, functional object use, imitating sounds, and use of sign language or communication board).

The skill sequences or hierarchies generated through the process of task analysis may be represented in the form of either vertical skill listings or lattices. Figure 2 displayed the skill sequence in a lattice format. Table 5 displays the skill sequence in a vertical list format.

There are advantages to both the lattice format and the list format. The lattice clearly portrays an overview of all the component skills of the sequence and their inter-relationships, but it does not formulate precise behavioral objectives and these will have to be precisely formulated to make them instructionally useful. The list format precisely formulates behavioral objectives which may have to be reformulated to meet the needs of some students.

It must be emphasized that task analysis should not be used for reinventing readily available sequences. Task analysis should be used to further refine or adapt available skill sequences (add or delete component skills) or to create new sequences to fit the functioning level and particular needs of students.

TABLE 5

Object Labeling Sequence

Objective: To teach labeling of noun concepts. Presented selected objects (blue, white, big, or little cups) and the question, "What is this?"/"What do you want?", the student should say, "Cup."

Criterion: The student should label the cups correctly nine out of ten times he is presented a cup and the question, "What is this?"/"What do you want?".

Prerequisite Skills: The student should be able to:

1. Discriminate visual or tactile cues.
2. Functionally use the objects (drink from a cup).
3. Discriminate auditory or sign language cues.
4. Imitate sounds or use sign language/communication board.

Phase I: Given a blue, white, big, or little cup and the directive, "Show me the cup," the student should find (touch, point to, pick up) its exact match from an array of three objects (one cup and two noncups).

Part 1: The student should find the match for the blue cup.
Part 2: The student should find the match for the white cup.
Part 3: The student should find the match for the big cup.
Part 4: The student should find the match for the little cup.

Phase II: Given a blue, white, big, or little cup and the directive, "Show me the cup," the student should find (touch, point to, pick up) a cup (not an exact match) from an array of three objects (one cup and two noncups).

Part 1: The student should find a match for the blue cup.
Part 2: The student should find a match for the white cup.
Part 3: The student should find a match for the big cup.
Part 4: The student should find a match for the little cup.

Phase III: Given an array of three objects, one cup (blue, white, big, or little) and two noncups and the directive, "Show me cup," the student should find (touch, point to, pick up) the cup.

Part 1: The student should find the blue cup.
Part 2: The student should find the white cup.
Part 3: The student should find the big cup.
Part 4: The student should find the little cup.

Phase IV: Presented a blue, white, big, or little cup and the question, "What is this?", the student should say, "Cup," make the sign for cup, or point to cup on a communication board.

Part 1: The student should label the blue cup.
Part 2: The student should label the white cup.
Part 3: The student should label the big cup.
Part 4: The student should label the little cup.

Longitudinal Skill Sequences

As articulated previously, we need to delineate longitudinal skill sequences which progress from zero skills, zero ability level, to skills necessary to function in the least restrictive life space possible. Any time a task analysis is performed, portions of long-term skill sequences are delineated. For instance, the task analysis of concepts presented above delineated a sequence which started with functional object use, progressed through matching objects to similar objects, and terminated with labeling noun concepts. If we had started with a much broader objective, such as providing students with the skills necessary to function independently in an apartment and in competitive employment, the task analysis would have delineated longitudinal skill sequences in many skill areas which progress from zero skills to adult functioning. The longitude of a skill sequence derived through task analysis depends on the behavioral objectives formulated and the extent to which we delineate all the component skills.

Conclusion

Curriculum development for the severely and profoundly handicapped is currently an art rather than a science. At this time, it is not possible to articulate a precise formula for developing curriculum nor to suggest which of the currently available curricula may be most viable.

A curriculum that is designed by one service program is rarely adopted in its entirety by other service programs. Each service program appears to feel dissatisfied with the curricula of others and attempts to develop its own. Our first reaction may be to charge that service programs are re-inventing the wheel and wasting their efforts. They may be re-inventing the wheel, but perhaps they are not wasting time and energy, since curriculum development may be used in inservice programs to train teachers in the process of individualizing instruction. Through participating in the development, adaptation, implementation, evaluation, and refinement of curriculum, teachers may learn about language development, motor development, cognitive development, and so forth. In addition, they may learn how to devise, implement, evaluate, and adapt instructional programs to meet the special needs of their students.

Some of the components of developing a curriculum and training teachers to implement and adapt it appropriately may be:

1. Analyze your students' current and potential future community life spaces (home, vocational, recreational). (You may find that your community lacks some viable life spaces for severely handicapped individuals, such as group homes.) Attempt to delineate the skills needed to function in these life spaces.
2. Review available curricula and evaluate them in terms of whether they teach the skills students must perform to function in the community life spaces. Do the curricula lead from zero skills to functioning in the least restrictive community life space possible?
3. Select curricula which appear to fit your needs most closely.
4. Develop a strategy for adapting these curricula to your system and using them as a base for developing your own curriculum.
5. Develop a strategy for involving teachers, parents, and the community in the development, implementation, and evaluation of the curriculum.
6. Delineate task forces charged with developing various components of the curriculum. Teachers should be intensively involved in this aspect. One person (preferably not a classroom teacher) per each task force should be charged with incorporating the ideas of the teachers into a curriculum, checking the curriculum devised against accepted developmental sequences, ensuring that the curriculum is designed to provide students with the skills they must perform in the community life spaces, and writing the final curriculum.

Curriculum development is a huge task. If not tackled in small components, it may appear too overwhelming to accomplish. It might be appropriate to select a small component of your program where you think curriculum development efforts will be the most successful. Assign this component a small curriculum development task. Use this small project to work out the problems of the curriculum development process and then slowly expand. Map out the entire territory you need to cover and begin to fill in the uncompleted parts. Your enthusiasm will grow as you see progress.

Curriculum is only one component of providing appropriate instructional services for severely handicapped students. Teachers' abilities to implement and adapt the curriculum to the special needs of students either make or break a program. In fact, well trained teachers can often make a program work despite the undeveloped state of the curriculum.

We need preservice training programs that incorporate a heavy emphasis on the processes of developing, adapting, and individualizing curriculum. To the extent that teacher education programs fail to provide such experiences, on-the-job training in curriculum development for the severely handicapped will remain our only viable approach to improving educational services. As a field we need to rise to this challenge and ensure that appropriate technical assistance and resources are available to those who are seeking to upgrade their programs.

References

Becker, W. C., Engelmann, S., & Thomas, D. R. *Teaching: A course in applied psychology*. Chicago: Science Research Associates, 1971.

Behavioral characteristics progression, Palo Alto, California: Vort Corporation, 1973.

Christie, L. S., & McKenzie, H. S. Minimum objectives: A measurement system to provide evaluation of special education in regular classrooms. An unpublished manuscript. Special Education Area, College of Education and Social Services, University of Vermont, Burlington, Vermont, Spring, 1974.

Goodstein, H. A. Solving the verbal mathematics problems: Visual aids and teacher planning equals the answer. *Teaching Exceptional Children*, 1974, *6*, 178–186.

Goodstein, H. A. Assessment and programming in mathematics for the handicapped. *Focus on Exceptional Children*, 1975, 7 (7), December.

Uzgiris, I. C., & Hunt, J. McV. *Assessment in infancy*. Chicago: University of Illinois Press, 1975.

Williams, W. Procedures of task analysis as related to developing instructional programs for the severely handicapped. In L. Brown, T. Crowner, W. Williams, & R. York (Eds.) *Madison's alternative for zero exclusion: A book of readings*. Madison, Wisc: University of Wisconsin, 1975.

WES WILLIAMS is Coordinator of Development and Evaluation of Pupil Training Programs for the Center for Special Education, and Assistant Professor, Special Education Program Area, College of Education and Social Services, University of Vermont in Burlington.

ERNEST A. GOTTS is an Associate Professor of Special Education at The University of Texas at Dallas. He is presently active in research and teaching in the area of the moderately and severely handicapped in early childhood. Dr. Gotts participates in various professional societies, writing, and has served as a consultant to state and Federal governments. He is currently Governor for the Division for Early Childhood in the Council for Exceptional Children.

A Piagetian Approach to Curriculum Development for the Severely, Profoundly and Multiply Handicapped

BETH STEPHENS

The University of Texas at Dallas

Traditionally, the goals, objectives, or competencies to be achieved by an educational program are listed first and then a curriculum is designed which makes it possible for the pupil to attain these competencies. Because the levels of development or learning that can be achieved when individually appropriate instruction is given over time to severely or profoundly handicapped pupils presently are undetermined, long-term objectives cannot be established with certainty. However, there is general agreement that the establishment of certain self-help skills is a valid goal for some of these persons. Others may transcend these basic abilities and go on to acquire rudimentary vocational skills. In both cases, task analyses of desired competencies readily reveal that the abilities normally acquired in infancy and early childhood (e.g., eye-hand coordination, memory for and anticipation of recurring events) are prerequisites for self-help or vocational activities. Therefore, programming should initially offer the opportunity to establish basic abilities. To trace the emergence of these skills, and then to seek to establish them in those who have not achieved them in the more or less incidental way that normal children do, requires knowledge of development on the part of the programmer.

The search for a mapping of the pathways of early development leads to the work of Jean Piaget, a Swiss psychologist, who has traced the genesis of cognitive development from the infant's first visual tracking of an object, through purposeful manipulation of objects, on to the development of logical thought. While he has worked to outline the stages of cognitive development, special educators have sought to incorporate his findings into intervention programs.

In the effort to apply Piaget's theory of cognitive development to curriculum design for the severely and profoundly impaired, two of his tenets have been emphasized: (a) a person may be impervious to experiences designed to promote cognitive development if the experiences demand thought processes that are more advanced than his current level of functioning; (b) cognitive development proceeds as a person interacts with his environment, i.e., with surrounding people and things.

One implication of these tenets is that knowledge of a person's present level of cognitive development is a prerequisite to individualized curriculum planning, i.e., curriculum activities should be developed which require performance slightly in advance of his current level of functioning. Ideally, the activity should be sufficiently ahead of present developmental levels to be motivating, but not so far in advance as to be frustrating. To achieve an appropriate match requires: (a) skill in appraising cognitive development; (b) skill in devising and implementing developmentally equivalent activities; and (c) appraisal of their appropriateness and effectiveness.

The second tenet—that cognitive development requires interaction rather than passivity—is realized through activities in which the pupil is the experimenter-doer, rather than the listener-observer. The teacher may provide the opportunity for an experience, but the pupil has to do the experiencing.

When one works with severely and profoundly impaired persons, their responses to ongoing events serve to indicate their current functioning level. Piaget's four-stage theory of cognitive development provides a background for the interpretation of their behavior—behavior which may appear inappropriate or even bizarre in terms of their chronological age—but yet is quite appropriate for their developmental stage. Therefore, curriculum planners should be aware of these Piagetian stages and of means for assessing them.

Appraisal of and Programming for Cognitive Development

Discussion of Piagetian assessments that may be used to diagnose cognitive development in the severely and profoundly impaired should be preceded by an overview of their theoretical framework.

Cognitive development, as viewed by Piaget, is an ongoing, sequential process which continues from birth to maturity. Emphasis is on adaptation as intelligence develops from the continuous interaction between an individual and his environment. This interaction prompts outward adaptive coping and inward mental organization. The adaptation-organization process results in constant reorganization of the structures of the mind. Two complementary processes are involved in this reorganization:

1. *Assimilation*, which corresponds to inner organization, and occurs when an organism incorporates something from its environment into its mental structures.

2. *Accommodation*, or outer adaptation, which occurs when environmental conditions require coping which necessitates a modification, revision, or rearrangment of existing mental structures or "schemas."

As the child grows, inwardly organizing or assimilating, and outwardly coping or accommodating to environmental experience, he becomes more capable in his adaptations. Thought is elaborated and organized. Each child has his own pace or rhythm of intellectual development which, like physiological development, has an organismic regulation. Through equilibrium, a mechanism of change and continuity, a state of balance is maintained (Gardner, 1974). Thus, there is the generation of the mind (Stephens, 1971).

As Piaget traced the origins of intelligence, he described four major stages of intellectual development which occur between the neonate's simple reflex activity and the adult's ability to engage in abstract thought. These stages are presented in Table 1. Normally, the stages are achieved in a hierarchical sequence; however, a blocking of certain developmental areas frequently results in irregularities or decalages in development, particularly in profoundly or multiply impaired persons.

TABLE 1

Piaget's Stages of Intellectual Development

Stage and Approximate Age	Characteristic Behavior
I. Sensory-Motor Operations	
A. Reflexive (0–1 month)	Simple reflex activity; example: kicking.
B. Primary Circular Reactions (1–4.5 months)	Reflexive behavior becomes elaborated and coordinated; example: eye follows hand movements.
C. Secondary Circular Reactions (4.5–9 months)	Repeats chance actions to reproduce an interesting change or effect; example: kicks crib, doll shakes, so kicks crib again.
D. Coordination of Secondary Schema (9–12 months)	Acts become clearly intentional; example: reaches behind cushion for ball.
E. Tertiary Circular Reactions (12–18 months)	Discovers new ways to obtain desired goal; example: pulls pillow nearer in order to get toy resting on it.
F. Invention of New Means through Mental Combinations (18–24 months)	Invents new ways and means; example: uses stick to reach desired object.
II Pre-Operational	
A. Preconceptual (2–4 years)	Capable of verbal expression, but speech is repetitious; frequent egocentric monologues.
B. Intuitive (4–7 years)	Speech becomes socialized; reasoning is egocentric; "to the right" has one meaning—to his right.
III. Concrete Operations (7–11 years)	Mobile and systematic thought organizes and classifies information; is capable of concrete problem-solving
IV. Formal Operations (11 years upward)	Can think abstractly, formulate hypotheses, engage in deductive reasoning, and check solutions.

(Stephens, 1971, p. 48)

Because the severely and profoundly handicapped frequently do not proceed beyond the second stage, a major portion of this discussion will center on the substages of the first, or sensory motor, stage and the second, or pre-operational, stage.

Stage I—Sensory Motor Operations

Normally, this initial stage is achieved during the child's first 24 to 30 months; however, profoundly impaired persons may remain at this level for life. Behavior during this period is characterized initially by a collection of reflex actions, e.g., arm-waving, kicking, crying, sucking, and swallowing; later, these actions become coordinated and generalized. An object's permanence is discovered. There is increasing realization that things outside the field of vision can be returned to it. Relationships are established between objects that are similar and between objects that are dissimilar. Discussion of the six substages of the sensory motor stages and examples of activities which appropriately occur within each follows:

1. *Reflexive*. A shift occurs in the neonate's ready-made reflexive schemata. Active groping replaces passive release and is most noticeable in the sucking schema. *Sucking* becomes generalized and may include the edge of the blanket. Later in the substage, if sucking is not followed by swallowing, rooting starts again.

Initially, grasping is done reflexively, as the infant closes his hand around any object that touches his palm. Later, his interest widens to things that come within his grasp; objects that pass before the neonate's eyes are tracked visually. However, if the infant is motorically impaired, he may not engage successfully in reflexive grasping; if he is visually impaired, he may not track objects with his eyes. The following are examples of intervention activities which may be used to assist a person in moving from early reflexive movements to variation and extension of these movements. If motor involvement is noted, a medical examination and report, followed by a physical therapist's appraisal and recommendations, should precede attempts to promote reflex activity.

(a) To strengthen palmar grasp, curl the person's fingers around an object, e.g., a dumbbell rattler. While he is grasping the object, tug at it; if he does not resist the tug, place your hand over his in a manner which insures continued closure of his palm around the object as you introduce a movement of resistance.

(b) Promote rooting behavior by tickling the infant's face near the mouth with a feather or with light strokes of your finger; as rooting occurs in that direction, transfer the tickling to the other side of the face.

(c) To engage the infant in visual tracking, hold a bright moving object approximately 10 inches in front of his eyes and move it slowly across his field of vision. If he loses focus, return the object to his field of vision and again pull it slowly to the right or left; continue until a moving object is tracked first with irregular, and then with smooth, accommodations. For visually impaired persons, substitute auditory for visual tracking of objects. As tracking is generalized, the person should spontaneously turn his head in the direction of light or sound.

(d) If there is marginal reflexive kicking, engage the person in adduction and flexion of the legs; if arm-waving does not occur, engage his arms in sweeping movements.

2. *Primary Circular Reactions*. As new associations are formed, experience begins to dictate types of action. The first acquired adaptations are noted in variations of reflexive actions. As hand movements become something to look at, and something heard becomes something to see, reciprocal coordination appears. Hunt (1961) comments that, although the eye follows what the hand does, the hand does not realize that the eye sees it. Interest is in the movement itself, and not in the effect that movement produces. As hand-waving behavior becomes coordinated with hand-watching behavior, the infant spends extended periods of time observing his own hands. When an object comes in contact with the waving hand and an interesting sound or movement results, the hand-waving occurs again, i.e., if a chance action proves interesting or satisfying, it is repeated. As the infant sucks, saliva collects on his tongue; he enjoys playing with it, so he lets it accumulate again and repeats the process. When these responses become repetitious, they are termed "circular reactions." At this substage, imitation will occur only if the model starts by imitating the child. Constant repetition of a behavior pattern occurs as it is being mastered by the infant and it is used later in an entirely different and frequently inappropriate context. A description of intervention activities designed for this substage follows:

(a) Hold a colorful sound-making object directly in front of the infant; as eye contact and hand extension occur, move the object from one side to the other, from the infant's shoulder level to waist level. The infant's eye contact and touching of hand to object should follow the path of the object's movement. A motorically or visually impaired child's hand should be guided through the desired action.

(b) Place the infant's hand in his field of vision;

then put crumpled aluminum foil in his hand and fold your hand around his. As he clasps the foil, engage his hand in a waving motion. After repeating the action several times, release the infant's hand and encourage him to continue the activity without physical guidance.

(c) During bathtime, use a string to attach a floating toy to the child's wrist. Guide him through wrist movements which cause the toy to sink and bob in the water.

(d) When the infant has become proficient in activities similar to the three above, an activity which requires slightly more advanced skills should be introduced. For example, hold two brightly colored, sound-producing objects approximately 8 inches apart and 10 inches from the infant's eyes. Move the objects alternately. Guide the infant's head in visual and auditory tracking of the two objects and in alternate touching of hands to the objects.

3. *Secondary Circular Reactions*. During this period, there is a limited anticipation of effect. Chance movements which produce an effect on an object are intentionally repeated. The infant may shake his legs and, in so doing, move a bassinet; as the bassinet moves, the doll on the hood swings; the infant sees the doll swing, so he repeats the kicking action. Also, the meaning of an object becomes assimilated. A rattle is shaken, producing a noise, so repeated shakings occur. Although there is awareness that the means (shaking) beget the end (noise), the differentiation between the two is not understood. Inappropriate means are frequently applied to a situation (Hunt, 1961). The child waves paper and it rattles; later, he may grasp a spoon in his hand and wave it, and expect it to rattle also. Objects acquire permanence, as limited but active search is made for things absent; when this occurs, it is evidence that the infant has memory for past events. A spatial field is constructed, as looking becomes coordinated with grasping, and arm movements become coordinated with sucking.

The eye-hand coordination which is accomplished at this stage frequently remains beyond the capacity of the profoundly impaired. Efforts to promote visual tracking of objects may be successful, and hand-waving behavior may be accorded visual regard. Yet, when it becomes necessary to relate eye movements to hand movements in order to grasp objects, simultaneous coordination of the two frequently is beyond the abilities of the profoundly impaired. Whether or not extensive training in promoting coordination will lead to its accomplishment over time has yet to be determined. However, extended effort is warranted, since eye-hand coordination is a prerequisite for most self-help skills.

Imitation during this stage is limited to sounds and movements which are a part of the child's repertoire and which are visually or auditorily perceptible to him. Activities at this stage continue to involve the repetition and mastery of intent; there is desire and effort to preserve and continue interesting experiences. At this stage, an infant who is engrossed in an activity may look up briefly as a person enters the room and then return to the activity. Such behavior may be regarded as a precursor to recognition of persons and to sustained directed attention.

Behavior characteristic of this substage occurs in the following activities:

(a) After a squeeze-and-squeak toy is demonstrated and then handed to the infant, he should engage spontaneously in manipulative behavior until he too elicits a squeak and then repeats the procedure. If he does not, he should be guided through appropriate movements and their repetition.

(b) Interest the infant in a noise-making toy; allow him to explore it tactually and then, as he observes, place the object behind a larger object; he should engage spontaneously in the action required to retrieve the first object. If he does not, demonstrate retrieval; if he still does not initiate retrieval behavior, guide him through the appropriate physical motions.

(c) Clap your hands in view of the infant; repeat, and then take the infant's hands and guide them in a clap. Following this, demonstrate clapping and then pause for his spontaneous clapping; if it does not occur, guide him again through the appropriate actions. (Note: Meeting of hands in space may require coordination which has not been learned by severely impaired infants; if so, clapping one hand against a stationary object would be an appropriate adaptation.)

(d) Demonstrate the sound that occurs when two blocks of wood, covered with sandpaper, are rubbed together. Place the blocks in front of the child; if he does not repeat the action, guide his hands through the appropriate motions.

4. *Coordination of Secondary Schemata*. Observation of a child's behavior during this phase of the stage indicates that means are definitely differentiated from ends. Discovery of an independent universe is made, i.e., the "me" is discriminated from the "not-me" (Hunt, 1961). Clear demarcation of adaptive behavior occurs. The child will immediately remove an undesired object (hand) that stands in the way of a desired one (bottle). Attempts are made to dupli-

cate speech sounds and to imitate movements observed in others. New models are included in imitative actions, although imitation may be inaccurate, e.g., the child may open and close his mouth as he attempts to replicate another person's eye-wink.

Extensive exploration of new objects is a characteristic behavior, as earlier schemas are adapted or combined and applied to new situations. The separation of means and ends is completed. Activities which involve these distinctions and coordinations are described below:

(a) Demonstrate the movement necessary to activate a whirligig. Following this, present the object to the child; if he does not initiate the hand movement necessary to activate the whirligig, guide his hands through the necessary motions.

(b) After the child observes the splash an object makes when dropped into a basin of water, hand the object to him; if he does not spontaneously drop it in the water, guide him through the activity. Repeat until he drops the object into the basin of water unguided. Thus the means (releasing the object) accomplish the end (splash of object into the water).

(c) When provided with a strange object, such as a loose-leaf notebook, the child should engage in manipulative behavior which involves his repertoire of exploratory actions, e.g., rubbing, scratching, patting, banging, and shaking, as he studies the effect each activity has on the object.

(d) Set an immobile object on a table in front of the child. He should make an effort to view the object from various angles, as well as from full front. If he does not, place him in positions that provide varying perspectives.

5. *Tertiary Circular Reactions*. Action is no longer merely repetitious or made by chance. Objects are of interest in themselves, and are the cause of active experimentation. If things fall accidentally, the child purposefully lets them fall again, in order to watch the act. Interest is not only in the object, but in what can happen to it; there will be active pursuit of a ball which has rolled under or behind something. There also is a subordination of means to an end, and a display of the constructive elements which characterize intelligence. If a toy is placed on a cushion, the child will grasp the cushion and pull it toward him, in order to grasp the object. Assimilation and accommodation become clearly differentiated, and imitative behavior closely approximates the model.

As Hunt (1961) notes, transition to the substage of tertiary curricular reactions is marked by the child's shift of attention from a moving object to what he does to create the movement; the deliberate variation of movement that follows leads to what Piaget describes as "a discovery of new means through active experimentation." Imitative behavior is extended to manipulation of portions of the head invisible to the child, e.g., imitative touching of his front lock of hair. Object permanence is widened as intensive search is made for hidden objects. Search behavior is highly significant because it demonstrates the possession of mental imagery and memory, i.e., you have to maintain a mental image of an object as you hunt for it, and the recognition which accompanies finding requires both memory and mental imagery. Persons who have severe motor impairment may have difficulty in engaging in the manipulative behavior that characterizes this stage, yet may give evidence of approximately normal memory and mental imagery, through their gross attempts to engage in search behavior. Activities characteristic of this stage follow:

(a) Let the child observe placement of a piece of candy in a box; close the flap top and hand the box to the child. Through active experimentation, the child should manage to open the box and secure the candy.

(b) Let the child observe as several blocks are poured from a large cylindrical container. Hand him the empty container; his refilling it with the blocks indicates distinction between the container and the contained.

(c) Pat one hand with another hand; guide the child's hand as he imitates the activity. When imitative behavior is established, pat mouth; pause for child to imitate; repeat procedure as nose, forehead, ear, and top of head are patted in that order. The child should display an ability to respond with gestures that are invisible to him.

(d) Place an object on the floor, out of the child's reach, and give him a stick. Through exploratory behavior, the child should discover ways of moving and returning the object with the stick.

6. *Invention of New Means through Mental Combinations*. Awareness of relationships is at a sufficiently advanced level to permit deductions. Piaget's classic example concerns a child's attempt to extract a watch chain from a slightly opened matchbox. After initial trials to obtain the end of the chain, the child stops and looks attentively at the slit in the matchbox as she opens her mouth wide, wider, then still wider; following this, she slowly enlarges the drawer opening—wider, wider, and still wider—until she can put her finger in the matchbox drawer and pull out the chain (Piaget, 1963). Prob-

lem-solving is accomplished through internal or mental coordinations. When placed in a problem situation, the child will pause and appear to consider alternatives before initiating attempts to achieve desired ends, i.e., the act is imitated internally before it is initiated physically. Deferred imitation (imitation of absent persons, etc.) presages symbolism during this period.

Object permanence (or the understanding that objects continue to exist, even if out of sight), is initiated during earlier periods of the sensory-motor stage, but generally is not completely established until the sixth substage. Development of the object concept which is embedded in sensory-motor intelligence provides the basis for a new level of reasoning. At this level, problems need not be solved by physical activity; instead, the solution can be obtained through mental operations (Gardner, 1974).

Four activities are presented which are indicative of reasoning at the sixth substage:

(a) Present the child with a box which has small and large circular openings on the top. Also present small and large discs which correspond in size to the openings. As the child observes, push one disc through a corresponding opening. Supply the child with small and large discs. Examination of objects and forethought should precede attempts to push appropriate sized objects through holes in the box.

(b) As the child watches, push a desired toy far under a large, low chair. Encourage retrieval; after unsuccessful trials to reach it from the front of the chair, the child should move to a position near the back of the chair which will allow him to retrieve it.

(c) Say a word familiar to the child and have him repeat it. When this is accomplished, introduce a word unfamiliar to him, display the object it signifies, and have him repeat the word.

(d) Wind an alarm clock and let the child observe the turning key as the alarm sounds. As the sound ceases, hand the clock to the child. If he does not spontaneously attempt to turn the key, guide him in the activity. Let him observe the results, and then hand him the clock again and indicate that he is to wind the key.

Origins of intelligence lie in the sensory-motor period, which Hunt (1961) likens to a slow-motion film in which pictures are viewed in succession, but without the continuous vision necessary for understanding the whole. Although sensory-motor intelligence is intelligence in action, it is not reflective. There are three essential conditions for transition from the sensory-motor to the reflective level:

1. Increase in speed which allows knowledge of successive phases of an action to be integrated into a simultaneous whole.

2. Awareness of the mechanisms of an action; awareness of the nature of a problem helps in reaching a solution.

3. Increase in conceptual distances, which permits actions to go beyond the limits of near space and time.

Throughout life, the perceptions and practical sets of sensory-motor intelligence lie at the source of thought (Stephens, 1971). Analysis of the six substages that comprise the sensory-motor stage results in the derivation of Piagetian principles which can be applied to curriculum planning (Hunt, 1961).

Stage II — Pre-Operational

1. *Preconceptual*. Following initial symbolic functioning which makes language acquisition possible, a period begins in which symbolic and preconceptual thought develops. The child becomes capable of educing a signifier (a word or image) which serves as a symbol for the significate (some perceptually absent object or event). Through the use of symbols, it becomes possible for thought to classify separate past, present, and future events. Also, at this level, the child initiates imitative play. Piaget views imitation as a form of accommodation. As the child becomes more adept at imitation, it is possible for him to engage in internal, as well as external, imitations. A mental image, which is internal imitation, constitutes the signifier or word. At this level, the child who earlier opened her mouth wider and wider in imitation of the possible widening of the matchbox drawer, would reduce this imitation to a schematized image from which use of the signifier or word would arise. Through symbol or language usage, thought becomes socialized, and from socialization arises the need to justify egocentric reasoning. The child attempts to think about his own thinking (Flavell, 1963). As a child at this level of development views an object or event, he tends to concentrate on one outstanding feature at the expense of others; thus, error in logical reasoning occurs. The weight of two balls of clay may be compared and found equal, yet when the child sees one of the balls rolled into a long sausage shape, he tends to say the long object weighs more. He fails to decenter — to consider width as well as length. Stable equilibrium between assimilation and accommodation has not been achieved.

The primitive reasoning characteristic of the preconceptual child is termed "transductive"; it is neither inductive nor deductive, but proceeds from particular to particular. At this age, a child may attempt to smoke a piece of white chalk because it resembles a cigarette. He addresses his attention only to the physical appearance of the object, neglecting to classify one as a writing instrument, the other as something to smoke. Another characteristic of this period is the inability to distinguish play and reality as separate realms, possessing different rules.

Play is an important contributor to preoperational thought. Assimilation predominates in play as real objects are subjected to, and often distorted by, playful action. By contrast, imitation is accommodation. When behavior is assimilated, it becomes incorporated into a person's habitual responses; it is not imitation. In imitation, a child accommodates to the behavior of another. During successive developmental stages, three types of games progressively appear. *Practice games*, which involve playful repetition of a physical skill, emerge during the sensory motor period. *Symbolic "let's pretend" games* are engaged in at the preconceptual stage, as one object is used to suggest another (e.g., a stick becomes a horse, or a large box becomes a house). Later, but not until the concrete stage, *games with rules* are engaged in successfully. Still later, construction games demand processes which are transitory between concrete and abstract thought. Thus practice (sensory-motor level), and later, symbolic and imitative (preconceptual level), games generally are the types most appropriate for severely and profoundly impaired persons.

Preconceptual confusions (e.g., when traveling through a strange town, a person declares a swimming pool which he is viewing for the first time is the same one he swam in last week), although amusing in young children, serve to call attention to the inadequate thought structures of the severely impaired person. Errors in classification occur when objects are used inappropriately (e.g., the person attempts to drink from a bottomless cylinder because it is the size and color of a cup).

Examples of activities appropriately engaged in by persons at the preconceptual level follow:

(a) Provide the child with four nested cylinders (cans); encourage him to separate them and place them randomly on the table. Then have him insert them one inside the other. If the seriation of four proves too difficult, reduce the task to two cylinders with marked difference in size and build to a task involving four. Later, nested blocks may be used; because the corners of blocks have to be aligned before they can be nested, this task is more advanced than the seriation of cylinders.

(b) Simultaneously present a familiar concrete object and a colored photograph of it, as you repeat its name aloud. Have the pupil point first to the object and then to the pictorial symbol, as you both repeat the name. Follow the same procedure with a second object and its pictorial symbol. Then, repeat randomly the name of first one object, and then the other, as the child points to either the correct concrete object or its pictorial symbol. Severely and profoundly impaired persons often require extensive experience before they can successfully make the transition from the concrete object to its pictorial (symbolic) representation.

(c) Introduce symbolic play by putting a dog collar on a toy dog and pulling him along as you make barking sounds; place the dog's face in a bowl of food as you make eating sounds. Encourage the child to repeat and extend the symbolic play. Generally, lower functioning persons have to be introduced to symbolic play through demonstration.

(d) As you wear a man's hat, engage in play indicative of a father's role as the child observes; then reverse roles and have the child imitate the father. Extend the play to include a variety of roles, e.g., mother, teacher, fireman, etc.

2. *Intuitive Thinking*. A gradual coordination of relations leads the child from a preconceptual or symbol acquisition stage to one in which these symbols or words can be manipulated in operational thought. Although the processes are often rapid, the intelligence remains prelogical. Reasoning is intuitive. Even though the child observes two small glasses, A and B, identical in size and shape, and each filled with an equal number of beads, and in turn observes as the beads from glass A are emptied into another glass A_1 which is taller and narrower, he tends to conclude that the quantity of beads has changed. A_1 contains more than B because "it is higher." Concomitant with this statement may be the admission that no beads have been added or removed.

Error is perceptual in nature. Thinking is influenced by what is seen at a given moment. Attention is centered on height relations, and width is ignored. The ability to "decenter"—or give regard to two aspects, height and width, rather than centering on height alone—becomes possible only when reasoning gives simultaneous regard to both relations.

Appropriate activities for persons functioning at the intuitive stage are those in school readiness curricula which include experiences involving concepts of time, space, number, casuality, classification, mental imagery, and memory. Lavatelli (1973) has applied Piaget's theory to an early childhood curriculum by extending and adapting activities that were used by the Geneva School to assess reasoning. Examples follow:

(a) Present a simple pattern of strung beads (e.g., red, blue, red, blue, red, blue) and have the pupil duplicate it. When this color and sequence discrimination is mastered, increase the difficulty of the task, either by adding a third color, or by alternating the sequence of the beads (e.g., one red, one blue, one red, one blue, four red, four blue, one red, one blue, one red, one blue).

(b) Place three groups of objects on the table, with five objects in each group (e.g., five blocks, five sticks, five balls). Request the pupil to hand you "a block"; after he responds, request "a stick" and "a ball" successively. Increase the request to "two blocks," "two sticks," "two balls." The pupil should pick up and move the two objects, so that he actively experiences and assigns meaning to "twoness."

(c) Present: five big black dogs
five little black dogs
five big white dogs
five little white dogs.

Instruct the child to put all the big dogs together; when this is done, request that all the little dogs be put together. Then request that all the black dogs be placed together, and then all the white dogs. Experiences are needed which demonstrate that objects can be grouped into a variety of categories.

(d) Have child observe as you use eight blocks to build a form:

(1) One block wide and eight blocks long; hand him the blocks and ask him to repeat the design from memory.
(2) Two blocks wide and four blocks long; hand him the blocks and ask him to repeat the design from memory.
(3) Four blocks wide and two blocks long; hand him the blocks and have him repeat the design from memory.
(4) Vary the task to include two blocks wide and four blocks high, etc.

Correct performance on this task involves understanding of space, sequencing, number, memory, and mental imagery.

Because cognitive impairment is usually a major factor in the functioning of severely, profoundly, and multiply impaired persons, a Piagetian approach to curriculum development would give high priority to programming for sensory-motor and pre-operational development. For this reason, the following discussion of the third and fourth stages of cognitive development is an overview (although it is acknowledged that some profoundly handicapped persons may develop beyond the first two stages). For an extended discussion of the last two stages, see the detailed analysis in Ginsburg's and Opper's (1969) introduction to the theory.

Stage III—Concrete Operations

From infancy onward, objects or events are classified, compared for similarities or differences, located in space or time, evaluated or counted. These cognitive classifications, seriations, or systems of explanation are termed "groupings," and they last throughout life. As reality is assimilated into existing thought structures, equilibrium of the assimilatory framework is maintained by grouping.

The integrated, intellectual system achieved through grouping is used by the child in organizing and manipulating the surrounding world. Thought structure makes possible such intellectual operations as arithmetic; comparison of classes and relations of objects and events; measurement of time and space; and operations that involve systems of values and interpersonal interaction. The distinguishing characteristic of the mobile equilibrium that promotes grouping is that thought is no longer centered on a particular state of an object, but can follow successive changes through various detours and reversals.

Because the operations involved here are constantly tied to action, they are concrete, rather than formal. Children at this stage may be unable to develop such processes if there is no manipulation of concrete objects, that is, if reasoning involves only verbal propositions.

Stage IV—Formal Operations

Achieved in most persons between the ages of 12 and 18, formal operations are a stage of intellectual equilibrium which has been evolving since infancy. As the transition is completed, observation no longer directs thought, as it did in the concrete period; instead, thought directs observation. With abstract thought, the adolescent extends consideration beyond the present, and forms theories. He becomes capable of hypotheses and deductive reasoning. Reasoning with reality involves concrete groupings. Formal thought invokes reflection on these groupings and is, therefore, operating on operations (Stephens, 1971).

Assessment of Cognitive Functioning

It is now realized that one of 20th-century psychology's most important contributions has been Piaget's demonstration that cognitive development proceeds through a series of hierarchical stages. His concern has been with the sequence of cognitive development and the definition of criteria for classifying behavior (Woodward, 1971). Inhelder (1968) extended Piaget's findings to the diagnosis of reasoning in the retarded and later Woodward demonstrated uses of Piagetian stages in assessing cognitive development in the severely subnormal. Stephens, Miller, and McLaughlin (1969) and Stephens (1972) analyzed differences which occur when the development of reasoning in normal individuals is compared with that of retardates. The Piagetian diagnostic method is particularly useful in assessing lower-functioning retardates. The interest here is not in a two-digit IQ figure, but in determining the individual's stage of cognitive development, so that appropriate activities can be designed to assist him toward the next higher level of functioning.

Through the use of Piaget's hierarchical scale, individuals who had previously been viewed as an undifferentiated group, whose performance is more than −3 standard deviations (SD's) from the mean, can be differentiated. Uzgiris and Hunt's measure, *An Instrument for Assessing Infant Psychological Development* (1964), can be adapted for use with older severely retarded subjects who appear to be functioning at the sensory-motor level. For criteria, Uzgiris and Hunt have selected situations which are easily elicitable and measurable (described by Piaget in his writings on the sensory-motor period), and which can be reliably observed by different people. The six series of behavioral schemata which comprise the instrument are:

Series I. *Visual Pursuit and Permanence of Objects*. This series begins with the ready-made schema of looking. The first accommodations of this schemata are manifest in the pursuit of slowly moving objects held at a constant distance from the infant's eye. This is followed by "lingers with glance at the point where a slowly moving object disappeared" (Uzgiris and Hunt, 1964, p. 56). Later the infant "obtains a partially hidden object" (Uzgiris and Hunt, 1964, p. 56); still later, he may obtain an object hidden under one or two layers of material or paper.

Series II. *Development of Means for Achieving Desired Environmental Events*. The second series begins with commonly observed "hand-watching behavior." Piaget described the development of hand-watching as an assimilation of the manual schema by the visual schema. With coordination comes the ability to grasp. The development of intention comes out of the feeling of effort in reaching for desired objects. From this development, the series proceeds to clearer evidence of intention in the differentiation of means and ends. The series starts with observed hand-watching behavior and proceeds to "grasps objects when both hand and object are in view," to "grasps without hand being in view," on through a series of accomplishments to such actions as "uses string as means to obtain object (pull toy) after demonstration," and later "without demonstration," and on to "uses stick to reach object."

Series III. *Development of Schemas in Relation to Objects*. The series begins with the appearance of coordinations between the schema ready-made at birth, such as sucking, to coordination between the manual schema and sucking (hand-mouth coordination or thumb-sucking) to the schema of bringing objects in front of the eyes in order to look at them. Later, such schemas as hitting, patting, and shaking develop. Attending to objects leads to examining them, which provokes interest in novelty; then social interaction is seen, as the schema of showing becomes evident. Later, there is recognition of objects, expressed in naming.

Series IV. *The Development of Causality*. Development begins with the infant's attempts to hold on to desired inputs and may be viewed as branching from Series II. Initially, the infant engages in hand-watching behavior; later, he keeps an object active by means of secondary circular reactions. Several steps later, he seeks to continue an interesting performance by touching the performing agent; still later, he "recognizes another person as an independent causal agent by giving back an object to have it activated again" (for example, a musical top). At an even later stage, he "activates a mechanically operated object after demonstration."

Series V. *The Construction of the Object in Space*. As the infant coordinates the schemata of looking and listening, he begins to localize sounds and their sources; things he has heard become things he can find and look at. Later, he begins to reconstruct the trajectory of objects. Items on the scale include "localizes the source of sound"; "follows the trajectory of a rapidly moving object"; "recognizes the reverse side of objects"; "shows understanding of gravity by permitting an object to roll down an incline"; and "makes detours in order to retrieve objects from behind obstacles."

Series VI. *Development of Imitation.* The series consists of two sections, one pertaining to vocal, and the other to gestural, imitation. The vocal series begins with the ready-made schemata of vocalizing. As he develops an interest in novelty, the infant also starts to imitate unfamiliar sound patterns, at first by gradual approximation, and later by direct imitation. He progresses to imitate words that are within his vocabulary, and then systematically repeats practically all new words.

The gestural series follows a similar progression. The infant begins to imitate simple gestures (hand-waving), and later progresses to the imitation of unfamiliar gestures that he can watch himself perform (stretching his leg out straight), and to gestures which he cannot watch himself perform (facial gestures, such as winking his eye) (Stephens, 1971).

An assessment comparable to the Uzgiris and Hunt measure has yet to be devised for the pre-operational stage, a stage which normally occurs from approximately two to seven years. Those who work in the field of mental retardation are acutely aware of the needs for instruments to assess this stage, because the severely and moderately retarded generally do not develop beyond it. Although Educational Testing Service has announced the development of procedures —*Cognitive Growth in Pre-School Children* (Melton, Charlesworth, Tanaka, Rothenberg, Busis, Pike, & Gollin, 1968)—which measure areas previously identified by Genevan research as prime contributors to the intellectual development of the pre-operational child, there is no reported effort to extend the use of these procedures to persons who are mentally retarded. A listing of the areas of pre-operational thought which are covered by the instrument and of the methods used in their appraisal follows:

1. *Classification Skills* are measured by a series of tasks designed to tap preferential sorting; ability to abstract a common property of two objects; and ability to sort when presented with a verbal clue.

2. *Time* is assessed by a time sequence task, designed to measure the young child's understanding of time, as represented in a pictorial sequence.

3. *Distance* understanding is assessed through the use of a pegboard frame on which are taped two paths to a three-dimensional model of a schoolhouse. One path is straight, the other crooked and the child predicts which of the two routes involves more traveling.

4. *Number Conservation.* A set of objects is placed in a row before the child (A). Then an equivalent parallel row is constructed (B). Each element of set A is directly in line with the corresponding element of set B. The child is asked if there are as many objects in row B as in row A. Next, the visual cues to the one-to-one correspondence of elements are destroyed, by either compressing or expanding one of the rows. The child is again questioned on the numerical equivalence of the sets.

5. *Basic Language Structure* is measured by two tasks. In the Language Comprehension Task (LCT), there are 20 cards containing pairs of stimulus pictures, but they depict different relationships between the elements. The child's job is to distinguish which relationship a particular word implies and then to point to the corresponding picture. The other measure is the Verbal Instruction Task (VIT), a task which requires the child to indicate his understanding of verbal symbols by manipulating various materials (Stephens, 1971).

During the preconceptual stage, both play and imitation have major roles. Reality is adapted to the self (assimilation) in play; the self is adapted to reality (accommodation) in imitation (Flavell, 1963). For the severely retarded, successful performance at the pre-operational period generally represents optimum development.

For children who perform at levels achieved by average children between the ages of two and six, an instrument designed by Haeussermann (1958) and later revised by Jedrysek, Klapper, Pope, and Wortis (1972), is available. Here, the goal is to determine potential for development

> . . . through circumvention of certain assessment obstacles—visual, auditory, or motor impairment—which may be present. For example, in assessing a child with auditory impairment, effort is made to determine if his memory has served to compensate for the insufficiency of his auditory perception. Effort is made to sample the child's intactness as the nature and extent of the impairment are determined.
>
> Areas included in the assessment are:
>
> 1. Recognition of concrete familiar life-size objects
> 2. Recall of missing picture from memory
> 3. Orientation in time
> 4. Recognition of symbols and forms
> 5. Color discrimination
> 6. Form discrimination
> 7. Multiple-choice/color-form sorting
> 8. Manipulative ability
> 9. Amount recognition
> 10. Eye motion and gross vision

> Since Haeussermann's evaluation was based on tasks which are sequential in development, the child's performance level indicates what is to be accomplished next. . . . Because the moderately retarded frequently are multiply-handicapped, Haeussermann's techniques are particularly appropriate in their assessment . . . (Stephens, 1971).

When consideration is given to the pre-vocational training of severely, profoundly, and multiply impaired persons, it becomes evident that information on the sequence of abilities assessed by Haeussermann can be used as a basis for planning habitation programs. Such skills as color-matching, form discrimination, and classification, measured in Haeussermann's developmental appraisal, are basic to the tasks generally performed by these persons in sheltered work environments (Ferrara, 1976).

> As emphasis on the early diagnosis of abilities or disabilities has increased; there has been demand for measures which identify motor, perceptual, or cognitive deficits, and which can be quickly and easily administered, preferably by the classroom teacher. The Valett Developmental Survey of Basic Learning Abilities (Valett, 1966), for use with children two to seven years old, was designed to meet these needs. (Stephens, 1971).

Assessments which measure Piagetian reasoning at the concrete and formal levels, and which are listed in writings by Inhelder (1968) and Stephens (1972), have demonstrated usefulness in assessing the thought processes of the educable mentally retarded. These studies indicate that mentally retarded persons do not achieve formal thought. Since severely, profoundly, and multiply impaired persons are a heterogeneous group, measures are needed which will assess cognitive development from the sensory-motor to the formal thought stage. The instruments cited in this discussion can be used for this purpose.

Programming

A Piagetian approach to curriculum development is one that emphasizes the process of learning, rather than the product. It is one that emphasizes the need for the pupil to be actively involved in the learning situation; the need for him to proceed at his own tempo; and the need for him to explore and to manipulate, to question and to seek—in short, to learn to reason. What is sought is a comprehensive curriculum that extends horizontally, to provide the repetition or variety of experiences generally required by the severely and multiply handicapped for the mastery of a skill. Yet, it must also extend vertically, through closely sequenced activities that are designed to lead the pupil, slight achievement by slight achievement, up the developmental scale. To date, there is not one program which has both sequentially related and branching activities plus the adaptations which are necessary if they are to be used with a variety of handicapped individuals (e.g., deaf-blind, cerebral palsied-mentally retarded, etc.). Therefore, the programmer will of necessity draw from a variety of existing resources, identify lacunae, and then set about adapting or devising individually appropriate activities. As one proceeds it is evident that, at the sensory-motor and pre-operational levels, activities labeled "motor" and "social" also include elements of reasoning or cognitive development.

Materials which are available, and which can be adapted for use in a Piagetian curriculum for the severely, profoundly, and multiply impaired, include the *Vision Up* program, which was devised at the Idaho State School for the Blind (Robinson and Croft, 1975). This program contains developmentally sequenced activities, designed to provide the intervention experiences required by blind children as they proceed through the various developmental areas (including cognition). A treatment program, devised for severely retarded persons by McCarthy, Stevens and Billingsley (1969), contains sequential decks of treatment cards in areas including sensory-motor development.

Although not designed for severely or profoundly handicapped pupils, the *Portage Guide to Early Education* (Shearer & Shearer, 1972) contains developmentally sequenced behavioral checklists and accompanying activity cards for children whose mental ages are birth to five years. The cards define and describe the activity, the criterion for success, and the required materials.

The contribution of play to the development of reasoning during the pre-operational period has long been recognized by Piaget (1962). Persons seeking guidelines for intervention-play programs can utilize activities designed by Corrado and Reed (1969) which involve interaction with a variety of sensory training and manipulative materials.

Activities which are characteristic of preschool Montessori programs (Montessori, 1964) are consonant with an interactionist's notion of development, i.e., that "developmental experience is experience through activities, not simply stimulation undergone" (Hess & Bear, 1968). Montessori emphasized free activity, but the activity contains order and control which comes from a well-organized environment, rather than being directly imposed by the teacher. Her writings suggest activities which promote abilities to distinguish, classify, catalogue, and order—abilities that are basic to reasoning at the pre-operational level. However, the approach should be extended from activities which center on sensory materials to those which involve a wide variety of significant objects.

Pre-operational-level activities which are designed to promote intellectual development also are found in Connor and Talbot's (1966) curriculum for pre-school mentally retarded children, and in Lavatelli's (1970) Piagetian-based early childhood curriculum. Although designated for early childhood, minor changes in the materials used in the activities can make them appropriate for older individuals who function at these levels.

As the search continues for developmentally appropriate activities, it is clear that sequentially arranged test items can become sequentially arranged activities. The Developmental Activities Screening Inventory or DASI (Du Bose & Langley, 1976), which was designed to assess severely and multiply impaired children, contains many items (or activities), which involve basic reasoning and which are intended for persons who function in the six to sixty month range. Haeussermann's *Developmental Potential of Pre-School Children* (1958) has sequentially related test activities which can be converted to program activities. Such activities are devised to circumvent impairment and reach the level of intact functioning which occurs in normal children between the years of two and six.

If assessment indicates cognitive development has proceeded beyond the pre-operational level, activities which are designed to promote reasoning in blind pupils (Stephens, in press), and in socially maladjusted-mentally retarded pupils (Stephens and Sower, in press) who function at the concrete and formal stages of reasoning, could be used, particularly if adapted to varying combinations of handicaps. Two years of intervention-type research have produced modules which contain sequentially related activities, designed to offer experience in factorially defined Piagetian reasoning areas, plus data indicating that their use does promote development in these areas.

Conclusion

This paper is entitled "A *Piagetian* Approach . . ," rather than "*Piaget's* Approach to Curriculum Development for the Severely/Profoundly or Multiply Handicapped." For over half a century, Piaget has worked to delineate, describe, and document cognitive development from the reflex activity present at birth to the reflective thought of adulthood. He has not delineated and described a curriculum which would be appropriately applied during these stages of development. We, the trainers who work with severely, profoundly, and multiply impaired persons, have this as our charge. We do have his dictums:

1. Activities should be *appropriate* for the person's present level of development.
2. Cognitive development proceeds as a person *interacts* with the people and things which surround him.
3. Rates or tempos of development *vary* from person to person.
4. The structures of thought are *general* and apply across a variety of objects and concepts.
5. A person must *know* what it is that is being programmed for, what it is that is being promoted. Otherwise, he will not prepare for it correctly and will not recognize its importance when it occurs. A belated and indecisive movement of hand toward an object may appear insignificant, but it is an important forerunner to the handgrasping that is involved in self-help and vocational skills.

References

Connor, F. P., and Talbott, M. *An experimental curriculum for young mentally retarded children.* New York: Teachers College Press, 1966.

Corrada, J., and Reed, J. *Play with a difference.* New York: Play School Associations, 1969.

Du Bose, R. F., and Langley, M. B. *Developmental activities screening inventory.* Nashville: George Peabody College for Teachers, 1976.

Ferrara, D. *Determination of pre-vocational skills in severely, profoundly and/or multiply impaired persons.* Philadelphia: Philadelphia Association for Retarded Citizens (Personal communication 1976).

Flavell, J. H. *The developmental psychology of Jean Piaget.* Princeton, New Jersey: Van Nostrand, 1963.

Gardner, Howard. *The quest for the mind.* New York: Random House, 1974.

Ginsburg, H., and Opper, S. *Piaget's theory of intellectual development.* Englewood Cliffs, New Jersey: Prentice-Hall, 1969.

Haeussermann, Elsa. *The developmental potential of preschool children.* New York: Grune and Stratton, 1958.

Hess, R. D., and Bear, R. M. *Early education.* Chicago: Aldine Publishing Company, 1968.

Hunt, J. McV. *Intelligence and experience.* New York: The Ronald Press, 1961.

Inhelder, B. *The diagnosis of reasoning in the mentally retarded.* New York: John Day Company, 1968.

Jedrysek, E., Klapper, Z., Pope, L., and Wortis, J. *Psychoeducational evaluation of the preschool child.* New York: Grune and Stratton, 1972.

Lavatelli, C. S. *Teacher's guide: Early childhood curriculum—a Piaget program.* Boston: American Science and Engineering Company, 1970.

Lavatelli, C. S. *Teacher's guide: Early childhood curriculum.* New York: American Science and Engineering Company, 1973.

McCarthy, James J., Stevens, Harvey A., and Billingsley, James F. *Program development for severely retarded institutionalized children.* Madison: The University of Wisconsin, 1969.

Melton, R. S., Charlesworth, R., Tanaka, M. N., Rothenberg, B. B., Busis, A. M., Pike, L., and Gollin, E. S. *Cognitive growth in preschool children.* Princeton, New Jersey: Educational Testing Service, 1968.

Montessori, Maria. *The Montessori method.* New York: Schocken Books, 1964.

Piaget, J. *Play, dreams and imitation.* New York: W. Norton and Company, 1962.

Piaget, J. *The origins of intelligence in children.* New York: W. W. Norton, 1963.

Robinson, Lee, and Croft, Noel. *Vision up.* Gooding: Idaho State School for the Blind, 1975.

Shearer, M. S., and Shearer, D. E. *Portage project checklist.* Portage, Wisconsin: Cooperative Educational Service Agency #12, 1972.

Stephens, B. The appraisal of cognitive development. In Beth Stephens (Ed.). *Training the developmentally young.* New York. The John Day Company, 1971, 45–67.

Stephens, B. *The development of reasoning, moral judgment, and moral conduct in retardates and normals.* Final Report, Phase II, Cooperative Project #15-P-55121/3-02. Philadelphia: Temple University, 1972.

Stephens, B. *Remediation of reasoning in congenitally blind pupils,* Dallas: The University of Texas at Dallas (in press).

Stephens, B., Miller, C., and McLaughlin, J. *The development of reasoning, moral judgment, and moral conduct in retardates and normals.* Final Report, Phase I, Cooperative Project #RD 2382-P. Philadelphia: Temple University, 1969.

Stephens, B., and Sower, R. *Remediation of reasoning in mentally retarded-socially maladjusted pupils.* Dallas: The University of Texas at Dallas (in press).

Uzgiris, I., and Hunt, J. McV. *Instrument for assessing infant psychological development.* Urbana, Illinois: The University of Illinois, 1966.

Valett, R. E. *The Valett developmental survey of basic learning abilities.* Palo Alto: Consulting Psychologists Press, 1966.

Woodward, W. Mary. *The development of behavior.* Middlesex, England: Penguin Books, 1971.

BETH STEPHENS received her Ph.D. in Special Education at The University of Texas and did post doctoral work with Jean Piaget and Barbel Inhelder at the University of Geneva. She has been a faculty member at the University of Illinois and Temple University. Currently she heads the Special Education Program at The University of Texas at Dallas and serves as a member of the President's Committee on Mental Retardation. She is immediate past president of the Division of Mental Retardation, Council for Exceptional Children. Her research efforts center on the analysis and remediation of Piagetian reasoning in handicapped persons.

Music Instructional Programs for the Severely Handicapped

JUDITH ANNE JELLISON

University of Minnesota

The idea of music for and by the handicapped is not new. What is new is the formal recognition and support now given by the recently formed National Committee, Arts for the Handicapped (NCAH), as well as by the Department of Health, Education, and Welfare and the United States Congress. NCAH states that it is a "moral, civil, and legal right" for handicapped persons to receive a level of services in the arts equal to that of the non-handicapped. The statistics presented by NCAH dramatically point to the disparity of these services. While approximately 75% of non-handicapped children have access to the arts in their educational program, only 10% of their handicapped peers receive such programs (NCAH, 1975).

One might then ask the question: of this 10%, how many severely handicapped students receive these services and what percentage is music? Although these data were not reported by NCAH, one may safely speculate that the percentages are quite low. The Committee report goes on to suggest that arts programs can contribute to the general education of the handicapped in three important ways: (a) arts experience can play a role in the education of all children, not just the talented; (b) the arts, if they are infused in the basic curriculum, can be valuable tools for learning; and (c) an emphasis on process, rather than product, in the arts builds a positive attitude towards learning and develops basic skills (NCAH, 1975).

Music has long been an integral part of society and community life. It is associated with personal expression, enjoyment, and relaxation. We respond to its sociological, psychological, religious, or political overtones. If the primary longitudinal objective for the severely handicapped is to teach those skills necessary for community functioning, then music skills and experiences should be integrated into the curriculum.

While, philosophically, there is no disagreement with this proposal and its moral and ethical implications, the low statistics indicate a lack of behavior toward this goal. Music has not received attention in program development for the handicapped, primarily because of (a) an "exclusiveness model" associated with the purpose of music, as well as with performers and teachers, and (b) a lack of appropriate examples demonstrating the structuring of music and music materials within an effective instructional technology.

While several examples will be included in this manuscript, it is not the intent here to provide numerous activities for immediate application. Many such activities are available; however, their usefulness is limited because of the lack of a cohesive and practical working model, to give direction and flexibility to teachers in instructional programming. The purpose of this article is to propose an approach to music within a behavioral model, in order to facilitate its integration into an emerging instructional technology—a technology that proves its applicability in the teaching of the severely retarded. It is intended that teachers will be able to use this model as a frame of reference for analyzing, selecting, modifying, developing, and implementing music activities in instructional programming.

Questioning The Exclusiveness Model

Music as Art

Objective thinking leads us to recognize and value music as art—to value composers, performers, teachers, and researchers in music. Their endeavors have resulted in expanding our alternatives for happiness. The attitude that music (as aesthetics) should best be in the hands of skilled musicians is probably quite rational. However, this attitude of exclusiveness is limiting and is only partially correct. With such an attitude, we are restricted to associate music only with complex phenomena, aesthetic experiences, and aestheticians. A much broader analysis and study of music describes music as behavior and as an environment in time. When music is described in this manner, the exclusiveness model starts to disappear. All professionals involved with the study of behavior and behavior change can then work more easily with music and integrate it within instructional models to meet both music and non-music objectives. This approach is summarized in the three major premises of this manuscript:

1. Music can be described as behavior.
2. Music can be structured as a contemporary environmental determinant of behavior.
3. Music can be structured within an integrated delivery model, using well established teaching principles, to teach both music and non-music objectives.

Music as Behavior

A generally accepted definition of music focuses on the physical properties of music. Music has been described as organized sound and silence in time (Madsen & Madsen, 1970). Sound (generally pitch) and silence in spatial relationships result in rhythm. Pitches vary in quality (complexity) because of the distinguishing characteristic of the transmitting source (i.e., oboe, voice, piano), as well as their being heard simultaneously with other pitches. Loudness can also influence the quality of pitches. The relationship between organized sound and silence in time (physical properties of music) and behavior is activity—observable movements through space. To observe a person involved in any music activity is to observe behavior and more specifically, music behavior. Music behaviors are generally classified in the following music activities: (a) performance, (b) composition, (c) listening, (d) conceptualization, and (e) verbalization. Although teachers comment that students are listening or "thinking" (conceptualizing), these two behaviors need to be externalized by observable behaviors in order to be effectively taught and reinforced.

A general overview of learning skill areas (i.e., motor, perceptual, language, symbolic, social) and these general music activities identifies parallels and similarities between the two. For example, similarities of music activities to general learning skills are suggested in Table 1.

TABLE 1

General Music Activity	General Learning Skills
Composition	Symbolic
Performance	Motor, perceptual motor, social
Listening	Perceptual
Verbalizing	Language, social
Conceptualizing (verbal, motor)	Perceptual motor, language, symbolic

The parallels are by no means exclusive, but reflect general relationships. More specific parallels are apparent when specific observable behaviors are delineated. (See Table 2.)

Only a few examples have been listed. Teachers may select many other music behaviors to parallel non-music behaviors. It will become apparent that the majority of music behaviors are associated with performance or listening. By taking advantage of simple rhythm instruments for activities, a music reinforcer (playing the instrument) is readily available, in addition to the social reinforcement given by the teacher for correct responses. As demonstrated by the examples, the parallel music behavior should be closely related to the physical properties of the non-music behavior, the temporal properties of the non-music behavior, and the effect the non-music behavior is to have on the environment. A teacher should no more assume that social skills are being acquired by two or more students singing together than if they were standing beside one another. Also, teaching or singing songs about "large" and "small" may be entertaining, but it is not necessarily instructive. Music cues and music responses must parallel closely the non-music instructional program objectives.

Music as an Environmental Determinant of Behavior

Music can be described as art, as sound and silence in time, and as behavior. Music can also be described as events that occur in time. While music events occur in time throughout life, the function of these events is generally unknown to us. Listening to music during dinner and playing the guitar in the evening seem to exist as activities isolated in time. Generally, we are not aware of the effects that a particular music event has on our responses before, during, or after it takes place. However, these music events occur as environmental events which may affect a person, whether or not this effect is immediate or known. The occurrence of any behavior is determined by environmental events which change after, or as a consequence of, the behavior. The occurrence is also determined by environmental conditions and events before or during the behavior.

Music can be structured as an environmental event to influence behavior—to teach non-music skills to the severely retarded. To structure music for these purposes is to suggest music as a therapeutic environment. A therapeutic environment, by definition, requires that the be-

TABLE 2

Specific Observable Skills Related to Music Activities

SKILL AREA	PARALLEL BEHAVIORS	MUSIC/ NON-MUSIC
I. MOTOR		
Left/right orientation	1. Puts out right (left) foot upon cue.	Non-music
	2. Marches right and left upon cue.	Music-performing
Gross muscle endurance	1. Holds heavy objects in outstretched arms—brings together.	Non-music
	2. Holds medium sized cymbals in outstretched arms—plays.	Music-performing
II. PERCEPTUAL-MOTOR		
Eye-hand coordination	1. Hits nails with hammer.	Non-music
	2. Hits xylophone bars with mallet.	Music-performing
III. PERCEPTUAL		
Visual tracking	1. Follows light beam moving in varying directions.	Non-music
	2. Follows hand of conductor or lighted baton conducting live or recorded music (faces students—can use students as conductors).	Music-performing
Auditory sequential memory	1. Repeats names spoken by children in correct sequence.	Non-music
	2. Identifies familiar instruments played in correct sequence.	Music-listening
IV. LANGUAGE		
Object discrimination	1. Discriminates objects by answering "yes" or "no."	Non-music
	2. Discriminates simple music instruments by answering "yes" or "no."	Music-verbalizing
Concept formation—(large and small)	1. Points to small (large) object upon cue.	Non-music
	2. Plays small (large) resonator bell upon cue.	Music-performing
V. SOCIAL		
Name recognition	1. Identifies self upon name cue by raising hand, verbalization, standing, etc.	Non-music
	2. Identifies self upon name cue by playing instrument.	Music-performing
VI. SYMBOLIC		
Match to sample	1. Matches letter of alphabet to sample by pointing.	Non-music
	2. Matches letter (A–G) attached to keyboard on mallet instrument by playing "letter."	Music-performing

havior generated be maintained after the therapeutic agent or environment (music) is removed. Empirical evidence supports the use of music as a therapeutic environment to influence changes in non-music behaviors. It has been structured in laboratories and in applied settings as a stimulus to precede, accompany, and follow behavior. Thus, music can be described as an event in time. Within this framework, much of the research and clinical data suggests that music generally functions as a discriminative stimulus, a kind of structural prompt, and a reinforcer.

Music as a Discriminative Stimulus

Music that gets our attention constitutes a class of stimuli that has probably been paired in the past with either positive or negative experiences. These stimuli may vary from person to person. The teacher can identify music stimuli that have been paired with positive experiences by observing the student in various music activities and by presenting various music sounds to the student. It can be assumed that if the teacher observes a high occurrence of attending, smiling, clapping, positive vocalizations, rocking, swaying, or other body movement immediately following the first few sounds of a song, record, or music instrument, these music stimuli are discriminative stimuli (S^D's) for the behavioral responses. Whether the music has been paired with reinforcing persons, places, or things, or whether listening to or producing music is intrinsically reinforcing, the teacher can structure music activity or sound to help teach non-music instructional objectives. The strength and existence of music as a discriminative stimulus was demonstrated by Cotter and Toombs (1966) and Steele (1967), when specific listening preferences were observed and continued over time with mentally retarded children, even when social reinforcement was not available.

Clinical evidence indicates that music as an S^D is useful to get the response going. These data have implications for instructional programming. For example, if a recording of children's music acts as an S^D for hand clapping or vocalizations, the teacher may use this music immediately before an instructional session for motor/verbal imitation. Social approval can be given for appropriate behavior to music, as well as for imitation. Responses may be overt (i.e., handclapping or vocalizations) or covert (i.e., listening or attending). Music stimuli, such as the sound of a resonator bell or tuning fork, paired with the verbal cue, "Look at me," may act as a practical S^D to teach appropriate attending skills (i.e., eye contact, head and body position). Music stimuli paired with verbal cues may offer more flexibility for the teacher in relation to teacher location in the classroom. Maintenance of attending skills, regardless of teacher position, is certainly an instructional objective for all students. With music and appropriate verbal cues as S^D's, the physical proximity of the teacher to the student or class may vary. Reliance on physical prompting with verbal cues may restrict teacher position and necessitate more extensive fading. Of course, music stimulus is not being suggested to replace physical prompting, but is suggested as an alternative, if music proves to be a discriminative stimulus for the appropriate behaviors.

One of the more frequent uses of music as an S^D is the singing of songs or the playing of records for singing. In this writer's opinion, the use of singing activities, with or without records, is one of the most misunderstood and misused tools of instructional programs. Generally, it has been assumed that the concepts being sung are being learned. It is crucial that the teacher decide *how* the activities are to be structured and for what purpose, if they are to facilitate the learning of non-music behaviors. If the intention is to structure these activities to set the occasion for the occurrence of non-music behavior, then the non-music behaviors must be emitted during the music activity with no additional prompting. For example, listening to a record or singing a song about colors does *not* necessarily teach this concept. However, this activity may be useful to set the occasion for attending, which is necessary for the teacher to proceed with the teaching of color discrimination. These attending behaviors should be observed during the music activity. The lyrics of the music may be completely irrelevant to using music for this purpose. For example, an instrumental record or a song about the weather may be more successful as an S^D for attending behavior. If singing *anything* acts as an S^D, then it is appropriate to include verbal cues in the song that will continue to be used when music is faded. The objectives for using music as an S^D must be kept clearly in mind, remembering that: (a) the appropriate responses must occur during the activity, if music is to act as an S^D; (b) music, if it is an S^D, is an S^D for those behaviors being observed; and (c) the music will eventually be removed, with the responses being maintained under non-music classroom conditions (i.e., teacher's verbal/non-verbal cues).

Music as a Structural Prompt

If music is structured in time concurrent with the behavior, it is generally being used as a structural prompt. Madsen, Madsen, and Michel (1975) demonstrated that simple tonal pairings with Wepman word-pairs, as well as stories-plus-melodies using these word-pairs, improved language discrimination of the pairs, when compared to other treatments and the contact-control group. Recall has been facilitated for nonsense syllables (Staples, 1968) and digit spans (Jellison, in press), when paired with melodies. Harrison and Lecrone (1966) used taped sung instructions and demonstrated significant improvement in self-help skills, psychomotor skills, and instruction-following skills, when compared to spoken instructions given to severely retarded children. It has also been demonstrated that forgetting (retroactive inhibition) is not the same for melodies as it is for words. That melodies are more easily remembered (Madsen, Collings, McLeod, & Madsen, 1969) and that a child seems to demonstrate a high auditory discrimination for tones and melodies may provide an explanation for experimental results. While these conjectures, as well as those related to possible hemispheric functioning for verbal and non-verbal stimuli (music) are not within the scope of this paper, they are mentioned briefly to indicate that theories and data continually appear in the literature to suggest the use of music as a successful structural prompt to teach non-music behaviors.

Although empirical evidence exists for this functional use of music, it would be erroneous to assume that so-called educational music records and music-based activities increase the probability of the student's learning the non-music skill. Since this type of activity is so common, specific suggestions to assist the teacher in selecting, modifying, and developing these music activities will be presented in another section of this paper.

Music as a Positive Reinforcer

Birnbrauer, Wolf, Kidder, and Tague (1965) briefly review recommendations that are generally suggested to maintain student motivation: (a) prepare materials that are intrinsically reinforcing (interesting and meaningful); (b) provide high-interest materials, combined with established teaching procedures, to increase the probabilities of success; and (c) present social and symbolic reinforcers (i.e., teacher approval, grades, and stars) for appropriate behavior. Music can well serve to maintain motivation, since it can be intrinsically reinforcing, combined with well established teaching principles, and presented as a reinforcer.

An initial study by Madsen, Wolfe, and Madsen (1969) led to such speculations which were later empirically demonstrated by Greer, Randall, and Timberlake (1971), Greer, Dorow, and Harrison (1975), and Forsythe (1975). Research indicates that music can be structured as a reinforcer for the teaching of arithmetic and mathematics (Madsen & Forsythe, 1973; Miller, Dorow & Greer, 1974); speech (Hewett, 1965); vocational skills (Bellamy & Sontag, 1973); motor skills (Hill, et al., 1974) and reading (Steele, 1971). Music can also be used to decrease behaviors that interfere with learning (Jorgenson 1974; Hanser, 1974). It is important to point out that, in most studies, teacher approval was also used with contingent music. The use of music *with* social reinforcement increases the effectiveness of the teaching and increases the probability of the behavior's being maintained as the music contingency is faded from the environment.

If nothing but primary reinforcers (food, liquids) are identified for some children, new reinforcers must be developed—reinforcers that are most often used in the ordinary classroom. In a recent study (1975), Dorow demonstrated that verbal approval and verbal approval plus music could be conditioned as secondary reinforcers, when paired with food. The newly conditioned reinforcers were effective in teaching imitative behaviors to severely retarded children when food was removed, verbal approval *plus* music being more effective than verbal approval alone.

The results of the preceding studies can assist the teacher in the structuring of music as a reinforcer to increase appropriate non-music behaviors. The teacher may determine potential music reinforcers by observation. Considering those music behaviors (listening and performing) and sound sources (records, music instruments) that are generally found to be high-interest activities and materials, the teacher may include these in procedures to arrive at the student's music reinforcement program. The teacher should define potential music reinforcers that can be presented to individuals and groups. More than one student may enjoy listening to records and may complete tasks for this reward. To earn minutes of listening by meeting changing task criteria is an effective use of music as a reinforcer. By devising a listening station with several headphones, the teacher can use one record player very efficiently for several students. A student may purchase listening time by using pennies or he may earn time slips for this activity. In addition, non-music behaviors, such as counting or paying the appropriate amount for a purchase, may be reinforced with additional listening time. Individual time to learn to play the autoharp, color-coded chord organ, or drums, may also be earned. Students can earn their choice of music on cassettes or records by meeting task criterion. To increase interpersonal and group social skills, the contingent listening time may be shared with a friend. The operation of a chord organ or autoharp can also be structured for two players. Music activities which require group interactions can be reinforcers, and can also serve as structural prompts with teacher approval for socialization and following directions (i.e., folk dancing, passing objects in music games, or creating melodies for name recognition). These examples illustrate the structuring of music as a reinforcer to teach non-music behaviors. The creative teacher can generate and implement many procedures for individual, group, and situational variables.

Structuring the Music Environment for the Teaching of Music and Non-Music Skills

The Basic Instructional Model

To observe music as behavior and to structure music as a determinant of behavior suggests some form of instructional technology that utilizes learning theory research. Many texts are available that present elementary principles of behavior and the utilization of these principles in applied settings (Hamblin, Buckholdt, Ferriton, Kozlov, & Blackwell, 1971; Hanley, 1970; Reynolds, 1958; Whaley & Malott, 1969). Application of learning theory research to music education and music therapy is a relatively new phenomenon and at present, few texts are available. (The reader is referred to Madsen, Greer, & Madsen, 1975, as an excellent source of detailed descriptions of research in music behavior.)

An instructional technology has emerged which uses a form of behavioristic task analysis and the systematic application of empirically derived principles of learning for teaching severely handicapped students (Brown, Bellamy, & Sontag, 1971). However, the development of music skills and the structuring of music within this technology has not, as yet, been presented in the literature. Because of the lack of literature in this area, the purpose of the remaining section is to discuss music and music materials as related to the research and the basic components of a behavioristic task analysis. Only those components will be discussed that may present unique problems as the teacher implements music within this instructional technology.

Specifying Music and Non-music Objectives

The first component of a behavioristic task analysis is the specification of instructional objectives and the conversion of those objectives into observable, measurable behaviors. The purpose here is not to discuss this procedure, which has been elucidated elsewhere (Mager, 1962; Wheeler & Fox, 1972), but to discuss music and non-music objectives in relation to priorities and to the teacher as model.

To assure the acquisition of functional skills for community living, the teacher of the handicapped generally establishes skill clusters (i.e., functional academic skills, vocational skills, sensorimotor skills, etc.) as a method of specifying the major instructional areas. A question arises as to priorities—how much time should be spent teaching what skills. The teacher, faced with a formidable task, is now asked to include music in the curriculum. A reasonable solution may be the addition to the staff of a music therapist, to assist in structuring music within an integrated delivery model. However, what *should be* and what *is* often are two different situations and alternatives for the present should be considered.

Two approaches to the teaching of music can be delineated: (a) the direct teaching of music skills, using an instructional technology comprised of some form of behavioristic task analysis and teaching principles, and (b) the indirect teaching of music skills, by teaching for transfer effects as music is structured to teach non-music objectives. In the former, the music objective takes precedence, with the continuing reinforcement of appropriate music and non-music behaviors; and in the latter, the non-music objective takes precedence, with the continuing reinforcement of appropriate non-music and music behaviors. These approaches may be illustrated by referring to examples using music and non-music objectives. (See Table 3.)

Music and non-music objectives are determined in a similar manner. Functional behaviors that we observe in community living are generally those marked by society as good and those that serve some positive use for the individual and society, now or in the future. These behaviors are valued as they occur at an acceptable level in the behavior repertoire of most children and adults. In order to determine the most appropriate music objectives for functional community living and to identify potential music reinforcers, the teacher may begin as follows:

1. List the community resources that promote or provide music materials and activities (community choruses/orchestras, concert halls, school vocal and instrumental concerts, music stores, listening record libraries, record stores, industries associated with the making of instruments or records).
2. Observe students in various music environments.
3. Observe adults and children in the community and schools in various music environments.
4. Ask adults and children to identify preferred and desired music activities.

5. Identify times when children and adults prefer music and use music for a purpose.
6. Identify personal music behaviors in relation to preferences, skills, desired behaviors, and occurrences throughout the week and on weekends.

TABLE 3

TEACHING MUSIC BEHAVIORS THROUGH MUSIC/NON-MUSIC OBJECTIVES	SOME SUGGESTIONS FOR CONTINUING REINFORCEMENT OF MUSIC/NON-MUSIC BEHAVIORS
Music	*Music*
Plays small (large) resonator bell upon cue.	1. Teacher approval—performance. "Good! You played music on the small (large) bell."
Appropriate music behavior (listening)	2. Music as reinforcer—"Good! Now I'll play a song on the bells for you." "I like the way you're listening to the song."
	Non-Music
Appropriate classroom behavior	1. Teacher approval for "following directions," "working hard," "taking turns," etc.
Non-music	*Non-music*
Points to small (large) toy animal upon cue.	1. Teacher approval. "Good! You pointed to the small (large) toy."
Appropriate use of materials	2. Object as reinforcer. "Good! You may hold the small toy." "You are being very careful with the toy and I like that."
	Music
Appropriate use of leisure time (music listening)	1. (After a number of trials/objects) "You did so well pointing to small and large that you may listen to some music for fun."
Appropriate music behavior (listening)	2. "You're listening so well." "You must like music."

It is suggested that the teacher identify his own music skills, as a vehicle to help identify music objectives for the severely retarded. By so doing, the teacher also identifies those music behaviors that he will be able to model (primarily singing and playing rhythms on unpitched instruments). Although the effect of modeling music behaviors on imitation training for non-imitative students has not been conclusively determined, Luckey (1966) reports significant increases in rhythmic body movements, singing, marching, and verbal interactions during music activities in which the teacher modeled the responses for imitative retarded adults.

The potential problems in modeling music behaviors may be: (a) the teacher has learned acceptable music skills, but is reluctant to demonstrate or model these behaviors in front of an audience, or (b) the teacher has learned poor music skills and inadvertently models these behaviors as music is structured for the teaching of non-music skills. While the teacher should objectively evaluate his own music skills, it is crucial that the teacher determine the relevance of the music model to the instructional objective. For example, if the objective is for the student to sing a melody in tune (correct pitches), then the teacher must be able to sing in tune, or find another model. However, if the objective is for the student to "sing" a sentence, watch the teacher while singing, or enjoy singing, then the teacher must be able to model these responses.

In the first situation, this writer has observed that many teachers, if they are reluctant to sing, resort to records as substitutes. An overdependence on records restricts the teacher's flexibility to divide complex responses into less complex responses, and also restricts the appropriate sequencing of those responses. Also, the record, rather than the teacher, often determines the instructional objectives. Generally, if the teacher is able to imitate consistently a melody and rhythm pattern of a familiar song at a level at which it is recognizable, he will serve as an acceptable model for singing and playing musical instruments. While the development of non-music skills may be the primary objective in the second situation, the teacher should be careful to provide the best music models possible, when music is structured in the program. Music skills may be learned inadvertently, and the student who imitates a poor model and develops poor music skills, has little chance to be included in extracurricular music activities, or in church or community performing groups.

Selecting/Modifying and Developing Materials

The sheer numbers of music books, instructional texts, and records that are published each year for use in the ordinary classroom are overwhelming. Just as remarkable is the heavy emphasis upon the development of music instructional materials for the exceptional student. Many of these materials should be considered for music instructional programs for the severely retarded student. To search for a text or collection of activities specifying "severely handicapped" in the title is a fruitless endeavor at this time. To use the available materials, it is clear that the teacher will have to modify the activities or develop new ones. In selecting, modifying, or developing activities, the following components of a behavioristic task analysis should be met before teaching or structuring the activity:

1. Specify the instructional objective(s) for the music/non-music skills to be taught.
2. Break down complex tasks into a series of less complex, connected tasks.
3. List prerequisite skills for each task.
4. Sequence tasks to be taught for easy to hard discriminations.

These procedures will be considered basic to the teaching of non-music and music skills. They should also be considered as music is modified to occur as a structural prompt for the learning of non-music skills. Music structured as an S^D or reinforcer does not need to follow this analysis. Therefore, the following will focus on modifying songs and records of songs and writing new songs to facilitate the learning of music and non-music skills.

In modifying songs, the familiar song, "Head and Shoulders, Knees and Toes" will serve as an example. The words for this song are:

"Head and shoulders, knees and toes,
  Knees and toes,
  Knees and toes,
Head and shoulders, knees and toes,
  My fair lady."

A way of modifying this song, using components of a behavioristic task analysis, is suggested below:

Skill Area: Motor development (body awareness).

Prerequisite Skills: (a) Hears and follows directions; (b) has imitative skills; (c) is visually able to observe actions of others; and (d) is physiologically able to touch all body parts.

Terminal Objective: Given one and two component verbal and sung directives, the student will be able to identify any combination of body parts by touching at a criterion of three consecutive correct responses per directive.

Secondary Objective: Given the singing of the song, "Head and Shoulders," the student will identify head, shoulders, knees, and toes by touching at the appropriate time when these body parts are cued in the singing. (It is assumed that a basic teacher objective for all music-related objectives is to reinforce students for appropriate facial and bodily expressions of enjoyment.)

Measurement: Baseline, followed by continuous recording of correct and incorrect responses, as well as responses to model and responses with priming. (For measurement procedures, see Hall, 1971.)

Materials/Equipment: None.

Procedures: With a small group seated in a semicircle in front of the teacher, the teacher will say, "I am going to sing a song for you. In this song I will ask you to touch your head, touch your shoulders, touch your knees, and touch your toes." The teacher will then look at each student and sing, "*Student's name*, touch your head." (The teacher will use the first part of the melody of the first line of the song.) If the student responds correctly, the teacher says, "Good," records the response, and proceeds to the next student with the sung directive, "*Student's name*, touch your shoulders." Each student will be given the opportunity to respond to each one-component directive. If a student does not respond correctly, a student in the group will be asked to model the correct response. Physical guidance (priming) will be used on those few occasions when a student fails to imitate the model.

The teacher will then say, "Everyone did so well, I'm going to sing some more of the song for you. This time I will ask you to do two things." The teacher sings the melody of the first line of the song, "*Student's name*, touch your head and touch your shoulders." Procedures will be similar to the first example, giving each student the opportunity to respond to the sung directives, "Touch your head and touch your shoulders," and "Touch your shoulders and touch your head."

The teacher will then proceed with (a) knees, (b) knees and toes, and (c) toes and knees.

The teacher will say at this point, "You have been working so hard, I'm going to sing the whole song for you." The teacher will sing the entire song, modeling the correct responses. When the song is completed, the teacher will say, "Everybody—do it with me," and sing:

"Everybody touch your head,
Everybody touch your shoulders,
  Touch your knees,
  Touch your toes,
Everybody touch your head,

Everybody touch your shoulders,
Good for you!"
(The above can then be repeated, varying the order of the four body parts.)

The teacher will then give spoken one and two component directives to each student to touch head, shoulders, knees, and toes. The teacher will continue to record all responses.

Variations can include additional body parts sung and spoken and the use of three-component directives. Additional variations, to teach receptive language skills and social skills, can include directives that vary possessive pronouns—"Touch my (your, his, her) head," and directives that replace possessive pronouns with students' names.

If a teacher wishes to use educational records in the program as structural prompts to teach non-music objectives, he should follow procedures similar to those suggested for songs. Using the basic components of a behavioristic task analysis, the teacher may also:

1. Tape easier sections of phrases for use as cues and proceed to more complex sections.
2. Use taped complex sections (some have instrumental sections) to play as possible music listening reinforcers to reinforce attending.
3. While taping, turn down the volume control to delete words or phrases not relevant to initial instruction.
4. Sing phrases from the record with the addition of student names or "everyone."
5. Sing with the recorded phrases selected for instruction, keeping the recorded music as background.
6. Sing particular concept words louder than other words. Also, sing over other words, replacing them with the specific content word (i.e., if teaching "red," tape the phrases, turning down the volume when other colors are sung). Sing "red" to replace the other colors, gradually introducing more colors, as included in the original lyrics.
7. Use additional stimulus and response prompts when necessary.
8. Reinforce correct responses by offering students simple instruments to play along with the music. (It is better to begin with one instrument, i.e., tambourine, and to circulate this among the students as correct responses are observed.)
9. Do not play the entire record for the students until all students have learned the correct responses, or unless the music is to be used as a listening reinforcer.

In developing new songs for students, the teacher has the flexibility to write lyrics which are less complex and which can be sequenced properly. Melodically, some preliminary research suggests that the probability of recall of words sung is inversely related to the number of words emphasized by pitch and decibel level (Renner, Jellison, & Day, 1973). These results suggest that the teacher should construct a melody line that places only a few key words at a higher pitch than all other words in that phrase. Also, the results suggest that these words be sung louder than the words preceding or following them. While this research is exploratory, it appears that emphasis in singing may be related to parallel speaking variables of loudness and pitch in determining which words will be recalled, as well as the number of words recalled. In addition, it would seem appropriate that rhythm patterns for newly written songs parallel as closely as possible those of the parallel spoken directive. Composing songs to increase the probability of the occurrence of correct responses to sung directives is a crucial area for investigation. It is expected that research will give us further direction in determining how to construct the melody line for educational songs.

Conclusion

As a result of the increasing efforts of parents, teachers, researchers, and local and national agencies that support the arts, music is being considered one of the components in the building of a relevant community-based curriculum for the handicapped. The inclusion of music within an integrated delivery model provides opportunities for the teaching of music skills for leisure, as well as the structuring of music to teach academic and social skills.

Recognizing that exciting and effective music activities have been proposed that reflect other viewpoints, we hope that future efforts will lead to empirically verified procedures that will ultimately result in superior services for the severely handicapped.

References

Bellamy, T., & Sontag, E. Use of group contingent music to increase assembly line production rates of retarded students in a simulated workshop. *Journal of Music Therapy*, 1973, *10*, 125–136.

Birnbrauer, J. S., Wolf, M. M., Kidder, J. D., & Tague, C. Classroom behavior of retarded pupils with token reinforcement. In H. W. Sloane, Jr. & B. D. MacAulay (Eds.). *Operant Procedures in Remedial Speech and Language Training*. New York: Houghton Mifflin, 1968.

Brown, L., Bellamy, T., & Sontag, E. The development and implementation of a public school prevocational training program for trainable retarded and severely disturbed children. Madison, Wis: Madison Public Schools, 1971.

Cotter, V. W., & Toombs, S. A procedure for determining the music preferences of mental retardates. *Journal of Music Therapy*, *3*, 57–64.

Dorow, L. G. Conditioning music and approval as new reinforcers for imitative behavior with the severely retarded. *Journal of Music Therapy*, 1975, *12*, 30–39.

Forsythe, J. The effect of teacher approval, disapproval, and errors on student attentiveness: Music versus classroom teachers. In C. K. Madsen, R. D. Greer, & C. H. Madsen, Jr. (Eds.). *Research in Music Behavior*. New York: Teachers College Press, 1975.

Greer, R. D., Dorow, L., & Harrison, L. Aural discrimination instruction and the preferences of sixth grade children for music listening, story listening and candy. In C. K. Madsen, R. D. Greer, & C. H. Madsen, Jr. (Eds.). *Research in Music Behavior*. New York: Teachers College Press, 1975.

Greer, R. D., Randall, A., & Timberlake, C. The discriminate use of music listening as a contingency for improvement in vocal pitch accuracy and attending behavior. *Council for Research in Music Education*, 1971, *26*, 10–18.

Hall, R. V. *Managing behavior: The measurement of behavior*. (Vol. 1). Lawrence, Kansas: H & H Enterprises, 1971.

Hamblin, R. L., Buckholdt, D., Ferriton, D., Kozloff, M., & Blackwell, L. *The humanization processes*. New York: Wiley-Interscience, 1971.

Hanley, E. M. Review of research involving applied behavior analysis in the classroom. *Review of Educational Research*, 1970, *40*, 597–626.

Hanser, S. B. Group-contingent music listening with emotionally disturbed boys. *Journal of Music Therapy*, 1974, *11*, 220–225.

Harrison, W., & Lecrone, H. The effect of music and exercise upon the self-help skills of non-verbal retardates. *American Journal of Mental Deficiency*, 1966, *71*, 279–282.

Hewett, F. M. Teaching speech to an autistic child through operant conditioning. *American Journal of Orthopsychiatry*, 1965, *35*, 927–936.

Hill, B., Montegar, C., Rawers, R., & Reid, D. The use of contingent music in teaching social skills to a nonverbal, hyperactive boy. *Journal of Consulting and Clinical Psychology*, 1974, *42*, 656–661.

Jellison, J. Accuracy of temporal order recall for verbal and song digit-spans presented to right and left ears. *Journal of Music Therapy*, in press.

Jorgenson, H. The use of a contingent music activity to modify behaviors which interfere with learning. *Journal of Music Therapy*, 1974, *11*, 41–46.

Luckey, R. E. Adult retarded responsiveness to recordings as a function of the music therapist participation. *American Journal of Mental Deficiency*, 1966, *71*, 109–111.

Madsen, C. K., Collings, D., McLeod, B., & Madsen, C. H., Jr. *Music and language arts*. Paper presented at the regional convention of the National Association for Music Therapy, Atlanta, Spring 1969.

Madsen, C. K. & Forsythe, J. L. The effect of contingent music listening on increases of mathematical responses. *Journal of Research in Music Education*, 1973, *21*, 176–181.

Madsen, C. K., Greer R. D., & Madsen, C. H., Jr. (Eds.). *Research in Music Behavior*. New York: Teachers College Press, 1975.

Madsen, C. K., & Madsen, C. H., Jr. *Experimental research in music*. Englewood Cliffs, N.J.: Prentice-Hall, 1970.

Madsen, C. K., Madsen, C. H., Jr., & Michel, D. E. The use of music stimuli in teaching language discrimination. In C. K. Madsen, R. D. Greer, & C. H. Madsen, Jr. (Eds.). *Research in music behavior*. New York: Teachers College Press, 1975.

Madsen, C. K., Wolfe, D. E. & Madsen, C. H., Jr. The effect of reinforcement and directional scalar methodology on intonational improvement. *Council for Research in Music Education*, 1969, *18*, 22–34.

Mager, R. F. *Preparing instructional objectives*. Palo Alto, Cal.: Fearson, 1962.

Miller, D. M., Dorow, L. G., & Greer, R. D. The contingent use of music and art for improving arithmetic scores. *Journal of Music Therapy*, 1974, *11*, 57–64.

National Committee, Arts for the Handicapped. Information sheet. Unpublished manuscript, Washington, D.C., 1975.

National Committee, Arts for the Handicapped. Arts for the handicapped program. Unpublished manuscript, Washington, D.C., 1975.

Renner, E., Jellison, J., & Day, S. B. Emphasis in music as a prompt for verbal imitation. In S. B. Day, E. S. Benson, R. A. Good (Eds.). *Miscellaneous Papers of the Bell Museum of Pathobiology*. Minneapolis: University of Minnesota Medical School, 1973.

Reynolds, G. S. *A primer of operant conditioning*. Palo Alto, Cal.: Scott, Foresman, 1968.

Staples, S. M. A paired-associate learning task utilizing music as the mediator: An exploratory study. *Journal of Music Therapy*, 1968, *5*, 53–57.

Steele, A. L. Effects of social reinforcement on the music preference of mentally retarded children. *Journal of Music Therapy*, 1967, *4*, 57–62.

Steele, A. L. Contingent socio-music listening periods in a preschool setting. *Journal of Music Therapy*, 1971, *8*, 131–139.

Whaley, D. L. & Malott, R. W. *Elementary principles of behavior*. New York: Appleton-Century Crofts, 1971.

Wheeler, A. H., & Fox, W. L. *Managing behavior: A teacher's guide to writing instructional objectives* (Vol. 5). Lawrence, Kansas: H & H Enterprises, 1972.

JUDITH JELLISON is Director of Music Therapy in the Department of Curriculum and Instruction of the University of Minnesota. She has also taught vocal and instrumental music in public schools and has been a music therapist for handicapped children and adults. Dr. Jellison's research interests include the psychophysiological measurement of music behavior and the use of music in language development. She is currently studying verbal recall resulting from the dichotic presentation of song and speech stimuli.

EASTERN NEBRASKA COMMUNITY OFFICE OF RETARDATION
Central Office
116 South 42nd Street
Omaha, Nebraska 68131

Mental Retardation Region VI

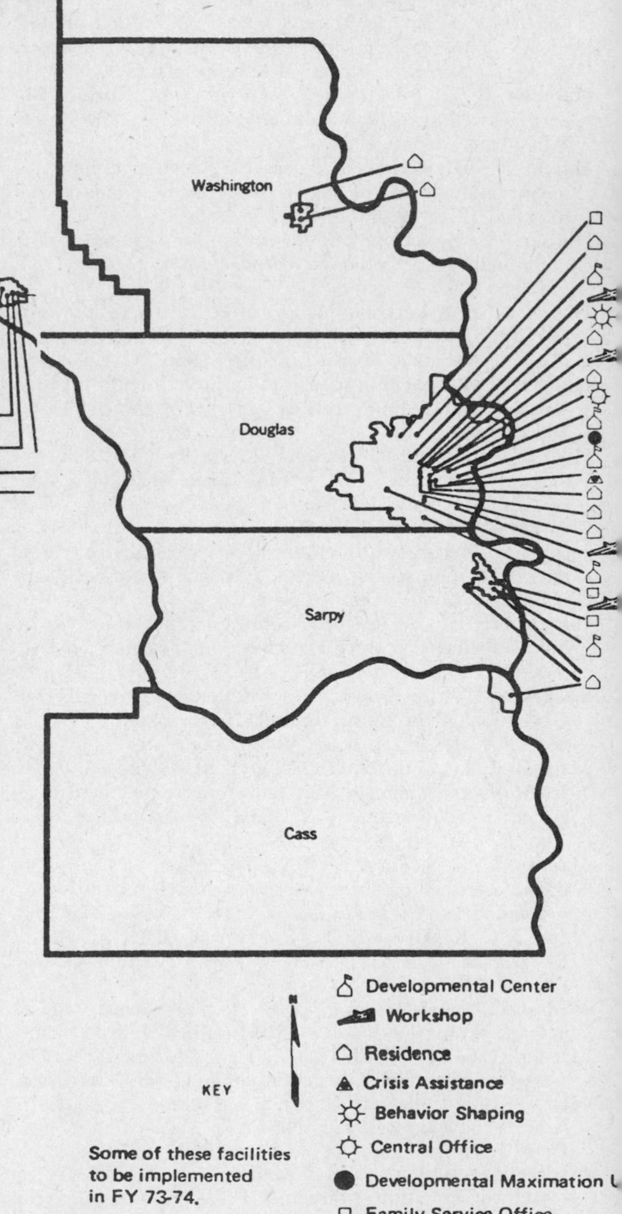

BACKGROUND

The Eastern Nebraska Community Office of Retardation (ENCOR) is a unique agency established July 1, 1970 as a joint venture among the five counties in eastern Nebraska as seen on the adjoining pages.

By means of the Nebraska Inter-local Cooperation Act, the counties of Cass, Dodge, Douglas, Sarpy, and Washington have legally designated ENCOR as the Regional Mental Retardation Service Agency for this five-county region, with the responsibility of "providing mental retardation services to individuals residing in the region included within the physical limits of the counties, signatory to the agreement."

ENCOR operates under the philosophy of NORMALIZATION and as such provides programs and/or services only when existing service agencies are unable or unwilling to include the mentally retarded in their programs. Through this method of maximizing the use of existing programs, ENCOR has accomplished two things: 1) helped to eliminate duplication of services; and 2) freed federal, state, and local monies for the development of needed, but heretofore undelivered, programs and services for the mentally retarded.

IX Teaching Strategies: Approaches with Motorically Involved Students

All children face developmental roadblocks in growing up, and overcoming these obstacles is a difficult process for any youngster. The development of children is a process of emerging from the mother's arms to the diversity of the neighborhood and the increasing complexities of the classroom. Most parents spontaneously provide their offspring with opportunities for growth, expecting them to learn, and they do. For children who are mentally and/or physically handicapped, however, this process often works in reverse. The label "normal" signals an open road to growing and learning. The label "handicapped" is a dead end.

Philippa H. Campbell, Karen M. Green, and Linda M. Carlson

Occupational and Physical Therapy Services for Severely Handicapped Students: Toward a Naturalized Public School Service Delivery Model

Part I. Integrated Versus Isolated Therapy Models

JANET STERNAT
ROSALIE MESSINA
Madison Public Schools

JOHN NIETUPSKI
STEVE LYON
LOU BROWN
University of Wisconsin-Madison

Recent judicial and legislative actions have affirmed the right of all children to a public school education. Public school officials throughout the nation are engaged in activities designed to culminate in the best possible educational services for students with substantial impairments in academic, motor, self-help, and social skills. In Part I of this paper, we shall describe selected aspects of two service delivery models (isolated and integrated) that have been, or are being, used by physical and occupational therapists in public school settings for severely handicapped students. In the isolated therapy model, the therapy is given in a segregated environment, away from the home and schoolroom where the student generally functions. In the integrated model, the therapy becomes part of the student's total developmental life space, because it takes place in the school, the community, and the home.

The models share certain characteristics, and thus are not mutually exclusive. However, for purposes of illustration and communication, examples of the sequence of treatment within the two models will be given. These examples lie at opposite ends of a continuum. Such an artificial dichotomy should make several basic issues clearer and, consequently, allow for an open approach to the development of exemplary physical and occupational therapy service delivery models for severely handicapped students.

The Isolated Therapy Model

Assume that the teacher of a severely handicapped student (Billy) thought he needed physical or occupational therapy and referred him for services. With an isolated therapy model, the following sequence of events might occur:

1. Billy is removed from his classroom by the therapy staff and transported to the therapy room.
2. Through formal and informal testing, the therapist obtains diagnostic information, presumably related to Billy's current level of developmental motoric functioning.
3. From the diagnostic information gathered, it is hypothesized that Billy is operating motorically at approximately a four-month developmental level. The therapist, together with a physician, prescribes a program designed to induce progression through a normal developmental motor

This paper was supported in part by Madison Public Schools Federal Contract No. OEC-74-7993, and in part by Grant No. OEG-0-73-6137 to the University of Wisconsin-Madison, from the Department of HEW, USOE, Bureau of Education for the Handicapped, Division of Personnel Preparation, Washington, D.C. A revision of this paper will be published in *Education and Training of the Mentally Retarded*.

Appreciation is expressed to Nancy Dodd for her valuable contributions to Part I and Part II of this article.

sequence. That is, the therapist will attempt to teach motor skills in the order of their appearance in normal motor development, beginning with the skills that typically appear at the four-month level.

4. Billy is brought to the therapy room twice each week. During therapy, the therapist attempts to develop "pull to sitting" and "roll to side," two motor skills which typically surface at the four-month level.
5. After therapy, Billy is returned to his classroom. Often, the therapist has another student scheduled for therapy immediately after Billy. The time necessary to consult with Billy's teacher or parents about the structure and content of the developmental motor program, and his progress within it, is therefore unavailable. Efforts by the teacher or the therapist to ensure that skills taught in the therapy room are maintained and absorbed into classroom or home curricula are consequently unsuccessful. The teacher and the parents may not be aware of Billy's motor needs and, therefore, may not allow for, or may even inhibit, the acquisition of the motor skills the therapist is attempting to teach.
6. After six months of therapy, Billy demonstrates little progress. (When pulled to sit, he exhibits slight head lag, but has not yet learned to roll to side.) Although the therapist may want to continue working with Billy, his limited progress may lead to a reduction in therapy to weekly or bimonthly checks. Billy's time may be given to another student who shows "more potential."

This hypothetical situation exemplifies a type of therapy service a severely handicapped student might receive under the isolated therapy model.

Assumptions of the Isolated Therapy Model

At least four basic assumptions underlie the isolated therapy model:

1. The information related to motor skills, which is secured in an isolated therapy room, will yield information that validly represents *general* motoric functioning. The isolated therapy model assumes that the level of motor skills observed in the therapy room reflects the level that is manifested by the severely handicapped student in the home, classroom, lunchroom, and on the playground.
2. Knowledge of the sequence in which motor skills are typically acquired by normal children makes it possible to determine the order in which motor skills should be taught to a severely handicapped child. That is, once the therapist has assessed the motor skills of a severely handicapped student, the developmental relationship to a typical normal sequence can be determined. The therapist then can teach the absent skills in the same order as they appear in the normal motor development sequence.
3. Episodic therapy (i.e., therapy conducted once or twice a week for 20 to 30 minutes a session) will result in substantial general motor skill development.
4. Skills acquired in one environment will be performed in other environments. For example, it is assumed that, if a student performs the pincer grasp in the therapy room in the presence of the therapist, he will perform the same skill in the classroom in the presence of the teacher, and in the home in the presence of his parents. While this assumption of skill generalization may be valid for normal and mildly handicapped students, it is highly inferential and often unacceptable when applied to the severely handicapped.

The isolated therapy model has been effective with a variety of physical-motor problems in normal and mildly handicapped persons, so it is understandable that it is being used with severely handicapped students in the public schools. However, the general or exclusive use of the isolated therapy model with severely handicapped students should receive careful scrutiny and, in most instances, be rejected. More efficacious alternatives are available.

The Integrated Therapy Model

Assume that the same severely handicapped student, Billy, is referred by his teacher for physical or occupational therapy in a setting that emphasizes an integrated therapy model.

1. The therapist comes to the classroom and home and observes Billy while he engages in various activities (e.g., during play time, feeding, toileting, and group activities) and administers range-of-motion tests in the presence of the teacher and the parents.
2. From the information derived from observations and various informal tests, the therapist concludes that Billy's primary motoric needs are in the area of head control. That is, Billy rarely maintained his head

in an upright position, or turned his head to view objects or people to his right or left.

3. The therapist, the teacher, and the parents jointly design an instructional program that can be implemented at school and at home to develop head control skills. The program is also structured to develop a number of movement patterns which incorporate clusters of developmental skills.
4. The therapist provides direct service to Billy only twice a week.
5. In addition to direct therapy, the therapist trains Billy's teachers and parents to implement the program both in the classroom and at home, during as many activities as possible. So, in addition to direct therapy, Billy is taught head control during feeding, art class, instructional materials center activities, and while watching television, or riding the school bus, or playing at school or at home.
6. After two months, Billy demonstrates slight progress. The teacher, the therapist, and the parents continue therapy and meet regularly to design changes to make the program more effective.

Asumptions of the Integrated Therapy Model

There are at least four basic assumptions underlying the integrated therapy model:

1. Assessment of motor abilities can be best conducted in natural environments, e.g., classrooms, homes, buses. Certainly, selected range-of-motion assessments might be administered in isolated therapy rooms where necessary equipment is more readily available. If the therapist observes the students' motoric functioning in natural environments, he will be able to assess motor performance across many different everyday settings, materials, cues, and persons. This allows a more valid representation of general motoric functioning. The integrated model also assumes that, if the teacher, the therapist, and the parents *jointly* devise the program, it can be incorporated into daily living and educational activities, and will directly relate to immediate, as well as to long-term, developmental needs. Thus, most significant others will be included in the therapy program. Educational activities can be arranged so that performance of target skills can be encouraged (or required) across a variety of settings, materials, cues, and persons.
2. Students should be taught *clusters* of developmental motor skills through functional and game activities, for at least three reasons. First, normal children appear to develop motor skills in clusters (i.e., while refining the ability to sit, the child is also learning to climb and to achieve greater proficiency in crawling activities). Functional and game activities which incorporate clusters of developmental motor skills might, therefore, approximate the normal developmental process. Second, it is believed that incorporating clusters of developmental motor skills into functional and game activities will result in more rapid skill acquisition. Third, functional and game activities can be incorporated into other aspects of a student's life.
3. In order for motor skill training to be effective, therapy must be longitudinal and naturalized. Therefore, therapy should be given throughout each day, in all the environments in which the student functions.
4. For skills to be useful, they must be taught and empirically verified in the environments in which they naturally occur. The integrated therapy model assumes that, when attempting to teach skills which will be used in classrooms, homes, and play settings, those skills should be taught or verified in classrooms, homes, and play settings.

Summary

The integrated therapy model advocates certain strategies based on these assumptions and, consequently, rejects the parallel assumptions of the isolated therapy model. The integrated therapy model advocates four basic approaches:

1. Motoric functioning should be assessed in the student's natural environments. The integrated therapy model rejects the assumption that general motoric functioning can be validly assessed outside natural environments by a therapist who is unfamiliar with the student and lacks stimulus control.
2. Clusters of skills, rather than isolated developmental motor skills, should be taught. Increasingly great discrepancies will result, since it often requires many months to teach a severely handicapped student an isolated motor skill that a normal child would acquire in a few weeks. Although the normal developmental strategy often will result in substantial gains

for other populations, it is rejected as an effective strategy for use with severely handicapped students.

3. Therapy should be incorporated continuously and naturally into the student's daily activities because the integrated therapy model rejects the assumption that skills taught in short episodes once or twice a week will result in significant gains.
4. Skills should be taught in the student's natural environments with a variety of instructional materials, persons, and cues because skills taught in one environment by one therapist, utilizing one set of instructional materials, will not necessarily generalize to the student's natural environments.

It is suggested that physical and occupational therapists working with severely handicapped students utilize an integrated therapy model that meets the following seven criteria:

1. Assessment of motoric functioning must be conducted in *several* natural settings.
2. Parents, teachers, and therapists should design motor skill programs *jointly*.
3. Motor skill programs should be designed to teach *clusters* of developmental motor skills.
4. Clusters of developmental motor skills should be taught through *functional and game activities*.
5. Motor skill training should occur *throughout the day, every day, and in all settings* in which students function.
6. Program revisions should be based upon *student progress* and implemented by parents, teachers, and therapists.
7. The teaching strategies utilized in developmental motor skill programs should rely upon basic principles of neurophysiological functioning. (Several basic neurophysiological principles are presented in Part II.)

Part II. Neurophysiological Principles: Considerations for the Development of Educational Curricula for Severely Handicapped Students

JANET STERNAT
ROSALIE MESSINA

Madison Public Schools

The changes in a skill or a cluster of skills along a continuum from unsophisticated to complex levels are generally called "the developmental process." Development occurs within a context of sensory input and is integrated with motor output through contact and experience with external environments. This process is especially critical in the first 24 months of life. Piaget (1952) has called this period "the sensorimotor stage of development." During this time, the rudiments of many critical concepts are established. The developmental skills an individual acquires from interactions with external environments seem to be a function of at least three basic factors:

1. Accurate sensory intake with continual feedback from resultant motor responses.
2. The number and variety of experiences resulting from interactions in different environments.
3. Continued maturation of the central nervous system (CNS) with integration (incorporation of lower-center activity into a coordinated system) at higher centers, along with inhibition (gradual decrease in effect) of primitive reflexive behavior. (See McGraw, 1975.)

If any of these factors is not operative or is limited, problems will occur in the acquisition and maintenance of concepts and their behavioral referents. This section will delineate several of the underlying neurophysiological factors that may account for *delays* in normal developmental processes, *distortions* of those processes as seen in severely handicapped children's actions, and *deficits* related to organic functioning. Visible actions which are functionally related to the more-difficult-to-observe central nervous system (CNS) functioning, but which may be amenable to remediation, will be discussed. In addition, suggestions for expanding the number of factors typically considered when teaching severely handicapped students will be offered to teachers and other direct service personnel.

Accurate Sensory Intake

Accurate sensory intake is influenced by:

1. The inhibition of irrelevant stimuli at external receptors and various centers within the CNS through complex chemical coding;
2. The ability to accommodate (adapt to) changing stimuli;
3. The feedback from sensory systems within the muscle fibers;
4. The maintenance of arousal levels necessary to perceive information. (See Bach-y-Rita, 1972.)

If the CNS is fragmented, high-intensity stimulation may be channeled without inhibition. This can result in withdrawal or defensive actions (Stockmeyer, 1972). Inconsistency in the expression of socially appropriate emotional responses and hyperdistractability are two other possibilities. A situation might arise in which a student is viewed as noncompliant, when, in fact, distortions of sensory input make it difficult for him to maintain interaction with materials or surfaces.

The inability to maintain contact with surfaces or objects, or to grasp, or to keep feet flat while in contact with varied textures, may also be viewed as overstimulation at CNS levels, when the situation requires inhibition. If the teacher *forces* a student to keep his foot in contact with a surface, without adequately preparing the CNS to accept the input, the spiraling of distractability and the heightening of avoidance and escape actions may result. If the accommodation process is impaired, each presentation of a stimulus may be interpreted differently. Therefore, the teacher must consider the effect of change itself, within stimulus dimensions, on student responses.

The actions described above can occur in reaction to changes in sensory input from many sources, including persons, foods, textures, temperatures, and changes in body position. Students may exhibit action sequences which avoid sudden changes in routine or emit other maladaptive responses, on encountering different intensities of common or novel environmental variables. Programmatic considerations should include a focus on the accommodation process by systematically varying persons, materials, positions, and surroundings to avoid excessive reliance on a limited number of cues. Such systematic variation can prepare the child to handle varying degrees of sensory stimulation.

Although motor responses are observable, they have internal effects which are fed back directly to the CNS through a sensory system specific to muscle fibers (Rood, 1962). The feedback system allows for automatic adjustments by the CNS and, thus, the control of motor planning. If accurate feedback from muscle systems is lacking, students may appear clumsy and may display discrepancies in the rate and precision of movement. Implications for programming include accurate functional motion analysis of required rate, force (e.g., acceleration/deceleration of muscle movements related to strength), and timing of coordinated muscle groups. This analysis should be followed by repeated practice to establish coded neural pathways and efficient patterns of movement. A student who is unable to achieve an accurate hand-to-mouth pattern necessary for eating illustrates the importance of an adequately functioning motor feedback system. The student is required to scoop the food and bring the utensil to his mouth. Successful completion of the hand-to-mouth pattern depends upon feedback from length changes within the muscles and joint receptor feedback throughout the movement. Over time and trials, the number of external cues provided during instruction should be faded, if automatic patterns are to develop and students are to acquire the ability to perform the skills independently.

The CNS also monitors states of arousal at specific centers. Essentially, this means that specific centers need to be chemically primed to accept sensory inputs. Medication, seizure activity, and lack of higher-level cognitive feedback may disturb the functioning of arousal centers, resulting in heightened or suppressed arousal states that are incompatible with attending and responding to relevant aspects of the stimulus environment. Attempts should be made to obtain accurate information about appropriate medications, dosages, and possible seizure activity related to states of arousal.

Number and variety of experiences

Delayed motor development (e.g., when a child is not rolling over at six months or sitting at one year) curtails environmental interactions. If development is delayed and there is a resulting lack of independent functioning, the variety of experiences is reduced further, and CNS functioning may be maintained at reflexive and primitive levels. Low rates of self-initiated movement and exploration, combined with repeated attempts that fail, have the effect of decreasing motivation and, thus, subsequent action. Stated another way, the world is perceived by the child as being too risky or failure-ridden.

There is evidence to support the existence of an innate drive or motivation that is not necessarily connected to reinforcement from the environment (Dudlah, Note 1). The developing process of CNS growth continually initiates practice and repetition of movements, leading to the establishment of neural growth and efficient neural pathways (McGraw, 1975). Many severely handicapped students display low rates of movement and high rates of repetitious practice or irrelevant (stereotypic) motor actions. Low rates of movement and high rates of stereotypic actions can limit the subsequent acquisition and use of higher-level skills outside of highly structured settings. Programming should focus on these critical aspects of the CNS developmental process, which underlie present behaviors. Those behaviors which are not at maximum efficiency or not demonstrating integration should be determined and given sufficient repetition and practice for refinement. Motoric components absent from the student's repertoire, which are catalysts for the emergence of higher-level skills, should be developed to the highest possible level of efficiency.

The child's delayed and limited motor development also may have an effect on adults who are interacting with him. General parent-child interactions often change in response to manifested growth patterns. For example, as a normal child acquires skills, parental handling may be faded. However, parents of delayed children often do not fade their assistance. If fading of parental support does not occur, or if parents do not attempt to direct the child's development, the child's active experiences again deviate from those of a normal child. For example, parents who always provide support for their child's head may be preventing the development of necessary independent head control skills.

Continued Physiological Maturation

Organic defects within the CNS, such as the absence of specific brain areas or tumors or lesions, resulting in non-functional neural centers, are factors that cannot be overlooked. These defects may cause actions that are unrelated to environmental stimuli. Those neurological areas which are functioning may be maturing at grossly different rates, leaving cognitive and motor aspects of learning out of synchronization, and interfering with the child's skill acquisition and his interactions with the external world.

As a result of degenerative diseases such as San Fillipo's disease, tuberous sclerosis, and sickle cell anemia, development may follow normal progressions for a time. However, when degenerative processes occur, some higher-level skills may be maintained, while others deteriorate in apparently unpredictable patterns. If one or more of those interfering factors exist, development may be unique, delayed, or totally arrested. Unless teachers and therapists recognize and program for these possibilities, teaching methods may fail to allow students to function in accordance with their capacities.

Part III. Curricular Suggestions for Teaching Severely Handicapped Students Selected Clusters of Head Control Skills

JANET STERNAT
ROSALIE MESSINA

Madison Public Schools

STEVE LYON
JOHN NIETUPSKI

University of Wisconsin-Madison

This section presents a suggested head control program which is designed to meet the criteria of the integrated therapy model. During the 1976–1977 school year, this program or a facsimile will be implemented with several severely handicapped students in the Madison (Wisconsin) Public Schools.

Head control skills, such as the ability to *move* (rotate, flex, and extend), *balance*, and *right* are vital to human growth and development. (Head righting is referred to here as movement of the head: (a) to the right when the trunk is moved to the left; (b) to the left when the trunk is moved to the right; (c) raised (extended) when the trunk is moved forward; and (d) lowered (flexed) when the trunk is moved backward.) Without such skills, even primitive scanning, selection, inspection, retrieval, and manipulation of objects would be extremely difficult. Close observation of severely handicapped students of different ages and functioning levels often reveals substantial deficits in head control skill clusters. Even such rudimentary skills as independent head and eye movements may not be in their functional repertoires.

Because head control skills are crucial to almost all developmental domains, it is imperative that teachers of severely handicapped students:

1. Assess functioning for the presence of crucial head control skills;
2. Teach students to perform the required skills; or
3. Arrange for adaptive or prosthetic assistance to compensate for the student's inability to learn independent performance of the necessary skill.

The following curricular recommendations are made to facilitate the student's acquisition of three head control skill clusters: *head rotating*, *head balancing*, and *head righting*. These skill clusters are considered prerequisites for many developmental motor skills. (This instructional program is not recommended for use with students less than one to two years old. For such students, it is recommended that teachers attempt to induce progressions through normal developmental motor sequences.)

Instructional Sequence and Task Analysis

Instructional Sequence

The Schemata of Instructional Sequences Chart (Figure 1) illustrates the order in which clusters of head control skills may be taught. The skill clusters referred to in Figure 1 are described below:

I. *Horizontal head movement (rotation)*. Teaching a student to rotate his head horizontally away from and toward the midline position.

II. *Head balancing*. Teaching a student to stop his head to the right and left of midline and above and below the level head position.

III. *Head balancing (after a rotation)*. Teaching a student to stop his head and hold it in a fixed position after a horizontal rotation.

IV-A. *Head righting*. Teaching a student to rotate his head in order to right the trunk after a side-to-side trunk movement.

IV-B. *Initiation of rotation*. Teaching a student to initiate a smooth and continuous head rotation.

V. *Head balancing*. Teaching a student to balance his head when the head is placed in any position within 45° to the right or left of midline, and 10° above or below a level head position.

VI-A. *Initiation of extension*. Teaching a student to initiate a smooth and continuous extension (a vertical head movement against gravity).

VI-B. *Stopping the head (after movement)*. Teaching a student to stop his head appropriately after a movement.

VII. *Head righting (extension)*. Teaching a student to extend his head in order to right the head with the trunk after a frontward movement of the trunk.

VIII. *Returning the head*. Teaching a student to return his head (by rotation, flexion, or extension) to a midline and level position after a head movement.

IX. *Head righting (flexion)*. Teaching a student to flex his head, in order to right the head with the trunk after a backward movement of the trunk. (Though lowering the head below the level head position is referred to here as flexion, the action results from using extensor muscles to decelerate downward head movement.)

Task Analysis of Selected Head Control Skill Clusters

The following is a suggested task analysis of the head control skill clusters delineated in Figure 1. Those phases numbered IV-A and IV-B, or VI-A or VI-B, indicate that the skill clusters might be taught concurrently.

Phase 1: Teaching students to perform basic head rotation skills.

Program Objectives: To teach a student to rotate his head through 45° both from: midline to the right and to the left; and from 90° to the right or to the left of midline toward midline. (For those students whose heads are

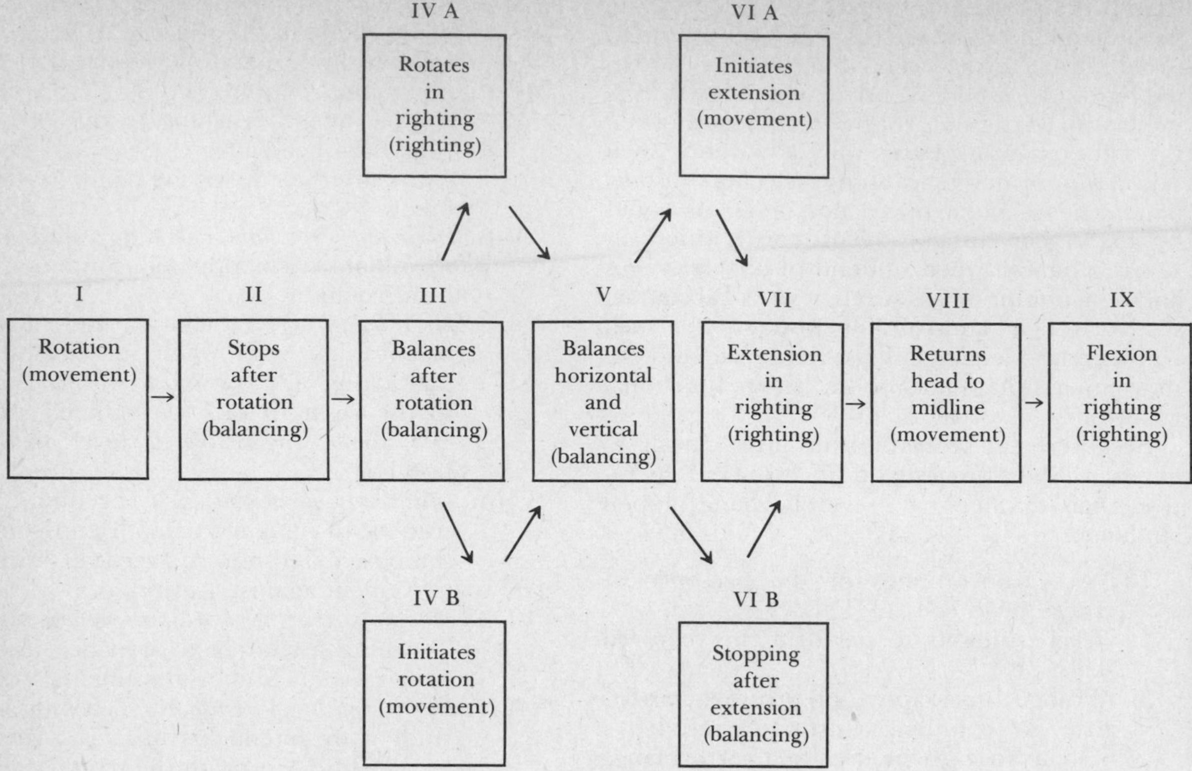

Figure 1. Schemata of instructional sequences.

fixed at 90° to the right or left of midline, an additional part may first be required to teach rotating their heads through 45° *toward* midline. Teaching should then proceed to Part 2 and then Part 1.)

Part 1: Teaching a student to rotate his head through 45° from midline to the right and to the left of midline.

Step 1: Teaching a student to rotate his head through 15° to the right and to the left of midline.

Step 2: Teaching a student to rotate his head through 30° to the right and to the left of midline.

Step 3: Teaching a student to rotate his head through 45° to the right and to the left of midline.

Part 2: Teaching a student to rotate his head through 45° from 45° to the right and to the left of midline toward midline.

Step 1: Teaching a student to rotate his head through 15° toward midline from 45° to the right and to the left of midline.

Step 2: Teaching a student to rotate his head through 30° toward midline from 45° to the right and to the left of midline.

Step 3: Teaching a student to rotate his head through 45° to midline from 45° to the right and to the left of midline.

Phase II: Teaching students to perform basic head balancing skills: Stopping the head, following head rotation.

Program Objectives: To teach a student to stop his head in any required position within 90° to the right or left of midline and 10° above or below a level head position after a rotation of the head.

Step 1: Teaching a student to stop his head at a midline and level head position.

Step 2: Teaching a student to stop his head 10° above a level head position.

Step 3: Teaching a student to stop his head 10° below a level head position.

Step 4: Teaching a student to stop his head above level and 45° to the right or left of midline.

Step 5: Teaching a student to stop his head in any required position within 90° to the right or left of midline and 10° above or below level position.

Phase III: Teaching students to perform head balancing skills, following a rotation of the head.

Program Objective: To teach a student to balance (hold in a fixed position) his head for 5 seconds after a horizontal rotation of 45° toward or away from midline.

Part 1: Teaching a student to balance his

head for 3 seconds after a 15° rotation from midline to the right or to the left of midline.

Step 1: Teaching a student to balance his head for 3 seconds after a 15° rotation to right or left of midline from midline.

Step 2: Teaching a student to balance his head for 3 seconds after a 30° rotation to right or left of midline from midline.

Step 3: Teaching a student to balance his head for 3 seconds after a 45° rotation to right or left of midline from midline.

Part 2: Teaching a student to balance his head for 3 seconds after a rotation toward midline.

Step 1: Teaching a student to balance his head for 3 seconds after a 15° rotation from the right or left of midline toward midline.

Step 2: Teaching a student to balance his head for 3 seconds after a 30° rotation from the right or left of midline toward midline.

Part 3: Teaching a student to balance his head for 3 seconds after a horizontal rotation of 45° toward or away from midline.

Step 1: Teaching a student to balance his head for 3 seconds after a 45° rotation away from midline to the right or to the left.

Step 2: Teaching a student to balance his head for 3 seconds after a 45° rotation from the right or left of midline toward midline.

Part 4: Teaching a student to balance his head for 5 seconds after a rotation of 45° toward or away from midline.

Step 1: Teaching a student to balance his head for 5 seconds after a rotation of 45° from midline to the right or to the left.

Step 2: Teaching a student to balance his head for 5 seconds after a rotation of 45° from the right or left of midline toward midline.

Phase IV-A: Teaching students to perform basic head righting skills by rotating the head following a trunk movement to the right or left. (Trunk movement refers to moving the trunk at the shoulders while maintaining the buttocks stationary.)

Program Objective: To teach a student to rotate his head 45° in order to right the head with the trunk after a lateral movement of the trunk to the right or left a distance of 18 inches.

Part 1: Teaching a student to rotate his head 15° to the right or left, in order to right the head with the trunk after a lateral trunk movement of 6 inches (e.g., after a lateral trunk movement to the right, the head rotates to the left, and vice versa).

Part 2: Teaching a student to rotate his head 30° to the right or to the left, in order to right the head with the trunk after a lateral trunk movement of 12 inches.

Part 3: Teaching a student to rotate his head 45° to the right or to the left, in order to right the head with the trunk after a lateral trunk movement of 18 inches.

Phase IV-B: Teaching students to initiate head rotation.

Program Objective: To teach a student to initiate a smooth and continuous rotation of his head.

Part 1: Teaching a student to initiate a rotation to the right or to the left of midline.

Part 2: Teaching a student to initiate a rotation from the left or from the right of midline toward midline.

Phase V: Teaching students to balance their heads when the head is placed in any position within 45° to the right or left of midline and 10° above or below a level head position.

Program Objective: To teach a student to hold his head in a fixed position (balance) 45° to the left or to the right of midline and 10° above or below level for at least 5 seconds.

Part 1: Teaching a student to balance his head at a level midline head position for 3 seconds.

Part 2: Teaching a student to balance his head level and 15° to the right or left of midline for 3 seconds.

Part 3: Teaching a student to balance his head level and 30° to the right or left of midline for 3 seconds.

Part 4: Teaching a student to balance his head level and 45° to the right or left of midline for 3 seconds.

Part 5: Teaching a student to balance his head at 45° to the right or left of midline and 5° above or below level for 3 seconds.

Part 6: Teaching a student to balance his head at 45° to the right or left of midline and 10° above or below level for 3 seconds.

Parts 7–12: Repeat Parts 1–6 for 5 seconds.

Phase VI-A: Teaching students to initiate a smooth and continuous extension (vertical head movement against gravity).

Program Objective: To teach a student to initiate a smooth and continuous extension (vertical movement against gravity) when his head is placed in any position.

Part 1: Teaching a student to initiate a head

extension when his head is placed below level head position at midline.

Part 2: Teaching a student to initiate a head extension when his head is placed in a midline and level position.

Part 3: Teaching a student to initiate a head extension when his head is placed above a level position and at midline.

Part 4: Teaching a student to initiate a head extension when his head is placed below level and to the right or to the left of midline.

Part 5: Teaching a student to initiate a head extension when his head is placed at a level head position and to the right or to the left of midline.

Part 6: Teaching a student to initiate a head extension when his head is placed above a level head position and to the right or the left of midline.

Phase VI-B: Teaching students to stop their heads after a vertical head movement but before the end of a range of motion.

Program Objective: To teach a student to stop his head after an extension of 10°:

1. From below level toward level when the head is:
   a. Within 45° to the right of midline;
   b. Within 45° to the left of midline;
   c. At midline.
2. From level toward above level when the head is:
   a. Within 45° to the right of midline;
   b. Within 45° to the left of midline;
   c. At midline.

Part 1: Teaching a student to stop his head after an extension of 5° from midline and below level toward a level head position.

Part 2: Teaching a student to stop his head after an extension of 5° from midline and level above and away from level.

Part 3: Teaching a student to stop his head after an extension of 5° from midline and above level.

Part 4: Teaching a student to stop his head after an extension of 5° from the right or left of midline and below level toward a level head position.

Part 5: Teaching a student to stop his head after a 5° extension from the right or left of midline and at level.

Part 6: Teaching a student to stop his head after a 5° extension from the right or left of midline and above level.

Parts 7–12: The same as parts 1–6, except after extensions of 10°.

Phase VII: Teaching students to extend their heads in order to right the head with the trunk after a forward movement of the trunk.

Program Objective: To teach a student to extend his head 45°, in order to right the head with the trunk after his trunk is moved forward a distance of 18 inches.

Part 1: Teaching a student to extend his head 15°, in order to right the head with the trunk after a forward trunk movement of 6 inches.

Part 2: Teaching a student to extend his head 30°, in order to right the head with the trunk after a forward trunk movement of 12 inches.

Part 3: Teaching a student to extend his head 45°, in order to right the head with the trunk after a forward trunk movement of 18 inches.

Phase VIII: Teaching students to return (by rotation, flexion, or extension) their heads to a midline and level head position after a movement.

Program Objective: To teach a student to return his head to a midline and level head position after any two component (horizontal and vertical) head movements.

Part 1: Teaching a student to return his head to a midline and level position after a rotation to the right of midline.

Part 2: Teaching a student to return his head to a midline and level position after a rotation to the left of midline.

Part 3: Teaching a student to return his head to a midline and level position after a flexion down and away from midline.

Part 4: Teaching a student to return his head to a midline and level position after a rotation and a flexion away from midline and level.

Part 5: Teaching a student to return his head to a midline and level position after a rotation and an extension away from midline.

Part 6: Teaching a student to return his head to a midline and level position after any two component (horizontal and vertical) head movements.

Phase IX: Teaching students to flex their heads in order to right the head with the trunk after a backward movement of the trunk.

Program Objective: To teach a student to flex his head 45°, in order to right the head with the trunk after his trunk is moved backwards a distance of 18 inches.

Part 1: Teaching a student to flex his head 15°, in order to right the head with the trunk after a backward trunk movement of 6 inches. *Part 2*: Teaching a student to flex his head 30°, in order to right the head with the trunk after a backward trunk movement of 12 inches.

Suggested Instructional Strategies

Instructional Considerations

Before engaging a student in a motor skill instructional program, it is essential that the effects of general muscle tone on functional activity level be given careful consideration. The arms and legs are the major indicators of the state of general muscle tone, and the trunk and head are the critical points of control that effect changes in overall tonal quality. Only after an analysis of general muscle tone should facilitatory and inhibitory events and specific handling procedures be determined.

Traditionally, tonal states have been organized into the following categories:

1. *Hypotonia*: Too little muscle tone or an inability to maintain postures against gravity.
2. *Hypertonia*: Excessive muscle tone with resistance to passive or repeated movement, or an inability to isolate movements from fixed postures.
3. *Hypokinesis*: Too little purposeful movement and slow movements, with slowness not necessarily related to muscle tone.
4. *Hyperkinesis*: Excessive non-purposeful movement, not necessarily related to muscle tone.

These tonal status categories are partially accurate descriptions of general tonal actions. However, they fail to provide a useful method of determining individualized handling procedures for the following reasons:

1. Traditional categories give only static descriptions of muscle tone which do not account for the constantly changing tonal states that students may demonstrate across environments and time.
2. Classification on the basis of general muscle tone obscures the fact that specific muscle groups often exhibit tones different from general tone.
3. Traditional categories offer one way of determining individualized handling procedures. However, the same handling procedure may be either facilitatory or inhibitory, depending on the muscle groups involved.

In summary, it is doubtful that any single method or criterion can be used to determine appropriate handling procedures without the specification of: (a) changes in muscle tone; (b) the specific movement desired; and (c) the muscle group involved in the desired movement.

Suggested Strategies for the Assessment of Student Progress

To determine existing head control skills related to head movement, head balancing, and head righting, the following general strategies are suggested:

First, students should be observed in natural settings by teachers, parents, and other adults during such activities as eating and bathing, in order to determine general levels of head control skills. Second, students should then be observed in structured settings (see the later section on instructional settings), where more precise measurements (e.g., duration, distance, and degree) can be made. In both structured and natural settings, students should be assessed in prone, supine, and upright sitting positions. During these initial assessment activities, attempts should be made to determine the level of head control skills demonstrated without prompting or priming from the teacher. (A physical prime refers to providing the minimum physical assistance necessary for a student to perform a desired action. At least two types of physical primes can be utilized: a complete physical prime is physically guiding a student through all portions of an action sequence; and a partial physical prime is physically guiding a student through selected portions of an action sequence.)

The structured initial assessment also should include screening for individual deformities, general tonal patterns, and individual sensitivities to various types of sensory stimulation. Third, following observations in natural and structured settings, instructional baselines can be determined for each student in relation to each skill cluster. Fourth, probes can be conducted to assess the student's progress over time.

Suggested Teaching Procedures

When teaching head control skills, the following instructional procedures are suggested:

Step 1: The student can be placed in a structured setting where the performance of specific skills is required. If the student performs the required skills in this structured setting and in at least two natural settings, in the presence of three different persons, and when placed in three different body positions, and without performance cues, the teacher could proceed to the next phase of the task analysis. If the student does not perform the required skills, the teacher might implement Step 2.

Step 2: The teacher could repeat the procedures described in Step 1, providing the student with verbal and gestural cues. If the desired skills still are not performed, the teacher might implement Step 3.

Step 3: The teacher could provide repeated demonstrations (models) of the desired actions and also provide verbal and gestural cues when the student is placed in the different settings described in Steps 1 and 2. If students still do not demonstrate the desired actions, the teacher might implement Step 4.

Step 4: The teacher could present an additional sensory stimulus, e.g., a sound-producing toy, in an attempt to prompt the desired response. In addition, commands and demonstrations could be presented. If the correct actions still are not performed, the teacher might proceed to Step 5.

Step 5: The teacher could place the student in different settings; give commands; model demonstrations; provide additional sensory stimulation; and physically prime the student through the desired actions. If correct actions are still not performed, the teacher might implement Step 6.

Step 6: The teacher could place the student in a setting which is designed to maximize the probability of the performance of the desired actions and maximize the inhibition of inappropriate actions. The teacher then may present inhibitory/facilitatory events which are designed to bring about the desired actions. (See the following section on facilitatory/inhibitory events.) Placing the student prone on a scooter board, and rapidly pulling the student by the arms around the room to facilitate raising the head to a vertical position, is an example of a potentially facilitating event. If the desired actions are still not performed, the teacher should proceed to Step 7.

Step 7: The procedure for Step 6 could be repeated and the teacher could physically prime the student through the correct actions. As the level of performance more closely approximates the correct actions, the teacher may proceed through Steps 8 through 12.

Step 8: The teacher could fade the amount of physical priming.

Step 9: The teacher could decrease the frequency, intensity, and duration of the facilitatory/inhibitory events.

Step 10: The teacher could fade the partial physical prompts.

Step 11: The teacher could decrease the frequency, intensity, and duration of the presentation of additional sensory stimulation.

Step 12: The teacher could fade verbal and gestural cues.

Steps 1 through 12 may be implemented until the student demonstrates the required skills in the settings described in Step 1 on three consecutive occasions in each setting, in three body positions, and in the presence of three different persons.

Facilitatory/Inhibitory Events

Because the tonal patterns of individuals often require considerable changes before actions can be performed, some inhibitory/facilitatory events may be more effective when used *prior* to engaging a student in the actions. When less tonal change is required, some inhibitory/facilitatory events may be more effective when used *while* engaging a student in the actions. The following inhibitory/facilitatory events, when used before or during instructional activities, will assist in the instruction of head movement, balancing, and righting. Therapists, teachers, and others working with severely handicapped students are encouraged to use available inhibitory/facilitatory events and to continually create new ones that meet the student's needs.

Suggested Inhibitory/Facilitory Events.

Skill: Teaching a student to rotate his head to the right, or left, of midline.

1. *Suggested events for use prior to head rotation*
   a. *An inhibitory event*: Rotate the trunk while the student is prone or supine.
   b. *A facilitatory event*: Place the student in a supine position on a large soft pillow or mat and press down on his side.
2. *Suggested events for use during head extension*
   a. *An inhibitory event*: Maintain joint compression on the neck.
   b. *A facilitatory event*: Exert firm down-

TABLE 1

Structural Teaching Setting 1 (Vertical Surface)

Students are placed 12 inches away from the front of a solid room divider. Objects are fastened to the divider and arranged at points both horizontally and vertically from midline and level head position.

Suggested Natural Teaching Settings

Description of Setting	Location(s)	Adult(s)	Materials	Body Positions	Other Concurrent Training
Bedtime (in crib)	1. Rest period at school 2. Home (bedroom) 3. Relative's home	1. Therapist 2. Parent 3. Relative	1. Mirror 2. Bubbles 3. Mobile	1. Supine 2. Sidelying 3. Sitting 4. Ringsitting	1. Eye contact 2. Body awareness 3. Relaxation training
Play at toybar*	1. Classroom 2. Gymnasium 3. Home (playroom)	1. Older students 2. Phys ed teacher 3. Siblings	1. Instructional materials 2. Gym class materials 3. Toys	1. Kneel/standing 2. Seated 3. Standing	1. Play skills 2. Fine motor skills 3. Motor planning
Mealtime	1. School 2. Home 3. Restaurants	1. Student teacher 2. Babysitter 3. Therapist	1. Mealtime equipment 2. Foods	1. Held semi-reclining 2. Prone 3. Sitting upright	1. Mealtime skills 2. Language 3. Social skills

* A toybar may be constructed by suspending objects from a fixed horizontal bar or rope at an appropriate height.

ward pressure on the lower part of the back on both sides of the spinal cord.

Skill: Teaching a student to flex his head downward toward a level head position from above a level head position.

1. *Suggested events used prior to head flexion*
   a. *An inhibitory event*: Stimulate the student to flex his entire body.
   b. *A facilitatory event*: Place the student prone over an inflated ball and accelerate rapidly from side to side.
2. *Suggested events used during head flexion*
   a. *An inhibitory event*: Maintain pressure on the sternum.
   b. *A facilitatory event*: Place a vibrator on the student's sterno-cleidomastoid muscles (large muscles in the sides of the neck).

Instructional Settings

There are three types of instructional settings where student performance can be measured in precise units of distance, degree, and time. In Setting 1, objects are arranged on a vertical surface, such as a standard room divider. In Setting 2, objects are arranged on a horizontal surface, such as a table top. In Setting 3, objects are suspended from a wooden grid at varying lengths in front of the student, at varying distances from the floor, and at varying distances from left to right of midline.

Natural settings at home and in school correspond to the structured settings. They involve different materials, persons, and body positions. The three types of structured and natural settings, and suggested activities that are relevant to natural settings are presented in Tables 1, 2, and 3.

Conclusion

Traditionally, severely handicapped students have received physical and occupational therapy services under what has been termed an isolated therapy model. An isolated therapy model involves assessment and instruction of isolated, vertically arranged developmental motor skills, in artificial settings, in the presence of the therapist. Following instruction, an inference is made that the student will integrate and perform those motor skills across a variety of functional tasks, natural settings, language cues, and persons. Unfortunately, it has been our experience that such inferences are rarely

TABLE 2

Structured Teaching Setting 2 (Horizontal Surface)

Students are seated in the center of a hollow horseshoe table. Objects are placed at varying points from a midline and level head position of the student.

Suggested Natural Teaching Settings

Description	Location(s)	Adult(s)	Materials/ Stimuli	Body Position	Other Concurrent Training
Table setting or mealtime preparation	1. Home 2. School 3. Picnics	1 .Parent 2. Sibling 3. Teacher aide	1. Mealtime equipment a. Silverware b. Plates, cups, bowls 3. Foods	1. Sitting 2. Standing 3. Sidelying	1. Object function 2. Object discrimination 3. Home living skills
Swimming	1. School 2. Neighborhood beach 3. YMCA	1. Phys ed teacher 2. Parent 3. Sibling 4. Swimming instructor	1. Water toys a. balls b. animals c. innertubes d. raft e. other persons	(Floating positions) 1. Prone 2. Supine 3. Upright	1. Swimming skills 2. Language 3. Gross motor training
Placement in suspension with head halter	1. School (during instructional activity) 2. Home (family room) 3. Music class	1. Teacher 2. Babysitter 3. Music teacher	1. Materials related to instructional activity 2. Toys at home 3. Musical instruments	1. Sitting upright 2. Standing 3. Sidesitting	1. Tracking 2. Scanning 3. Object manipulation

TABLE 3

Structured Teaching Setting 3 (Objects Suspended in Space)

Students are seated under a grid (36″ × 36″) from which objects are suspended in space at varying distances from a midline and level head position of the student.

Suggested Natural Teaching Settings

Description	Location(s)	Adult(s)	Materials	Body Positions	Other Concurrent Training
Bathtime	1. Home 2. School	1. Teacher 2. Parent 3. Other relative	1. Towel, washcloth, soap 2. Clothes 3. Favorite water toys	1. Sidelying 2. Sitting 3. Supine	1. Self-care skills 2. Language 3. Fine motor skills
Dressing	1. Home (bedroom) 2. School (bathroom) 3. Swimming pool	1. Respite care worker 2. Teacher 3. Phys ed teacher	1. Clothing 2. Adaptive devices for teaching dressing skills	1. Long sitting 2. Sitting in corner 3. Sitting in box or barrel	1. Self-care skills 2. Fine motor skills 3. Body awareness
Transporting or positioning*	1. School 2. Home 3. Community	1. Busdriver 2. Sibling 3. Day care center worker	1. Transporting device (wheelchair or walker)	1. Inverted 2. Prone 3. Supine	1. Gross motor training 2. Social skills 3. Community living skills

* Many severely handicapped students need either extensive assistance or are totally dependent upon others for transportation. Because much of their day is spent being transported, it is crucial that this time be used productively by teachers, parents, and other persons.

tenable. Therefore, the contention made in this paper is that the general or exclusive use of an isolated therapy model should be rejected. As an alternative to an isolated therapy model, an integrated therapy model is proposed. An integrated therapy model requires assessment and instruction of clusters of developmental motor skills across a variety of functional tasks, natural settings, language cues, and persons. Under the integrated therapy model, no inference is made that skills acquired under one set of conditions will be performed under other sets of conditions.

The integrated therapy model described here is by no means complete. Undoubtedly, it will undergo revision as we learn from our mistakes. Hopefully, with continued improvement in the integrated therapy model we will begin to meet the motor needs of severely handicapped students more fully.

Reference Note

1. Dudlah, A. M. A motor development checklist. Unpublished manuscript. Madison, Wis: Central Wisconsin Colony and Training School, 1976.

References

Bach-y-Rita, P. *Brain mechanisms in sensory substitution*. New York: Academic Press, 1972.

McGraw, M. B. *The neuromuscular maturation of the human infant*. New York: Hofner Press, 1975.

Piaget, J. *The origins of intelligence in children*. New York: International Universities Press, 1952.

Rood, M. S. The use of sensory receptors to activate, facilitate, and inhibit motor response, autonomic and somatic, in developmental sequence. In C. Sattely (Ed.). *Approaches to treatment of patients with neuromuscular dysfunction*. Study course VI, Third International Congress, World Federation of Occupational Therapists. Dubuque, Iowa: W. C. Brown, 1962.

Stockmeyer, S. A. A sensorimotor approach to treatment. In P. H. Pearson and C. E. Williams (Eds.). *Physical therapy services in the developmental disabilities*. Springfield, Ill: Charles C. Thomas, 1972.

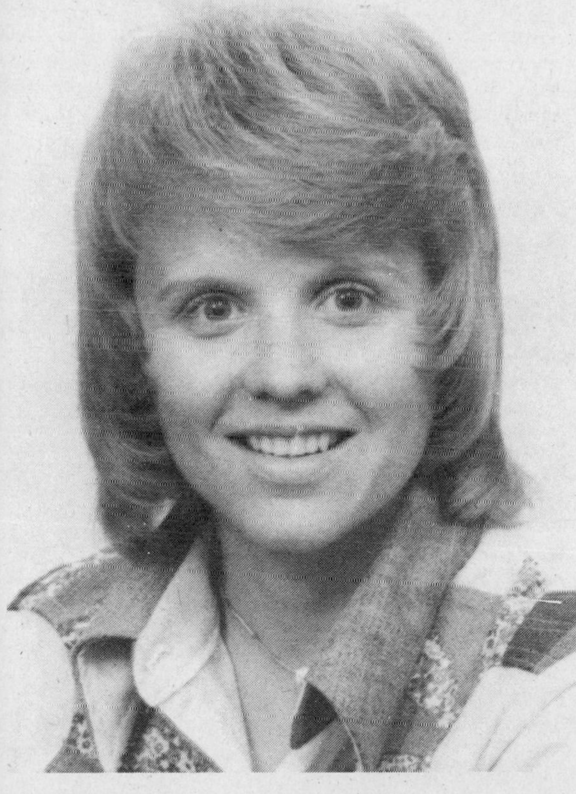

JANET STERNAT is a registered Physical Therapist with the Madison Public Schools and Project MAZE (The Madison Alternative for Zero Exclusion). Her activities include curriculum development in the area of gross and fine motor and mealtime skills with severely handicapped students.

ROSALIE MESSINA, OTR, has since 1972 been an Occupational Staff Therapist in the Madison, Wisconsin, public school system. For the past two years, she has participated in its MAZE Project, a USOE-BEH demonstration project for severely handicapped students. The project involves efforts with parents, teachers, and university students in the design and implementation of feeding and motor skill programs for the severely and profoundly handicapped.

JOHN NIETUPSKI is a research assistant and doctoral candidate in the Department of Studies in Behavioral Disabilities at the University of Wisconsin, Madison, and is also program consultant to Project MAZE (The Madison Alternative for Zero Exclusion), a BEH/USOE funded demonstration project.

LOU BROWN is a Professor in the Department of Studies in Behavioral Disabilities at the University of Wisconsin, Madison. His professional career has been concentrated on developing public school service for severely handicapped students from birth through young adulthood.

STEVE LYON is a doctoral student and research assistant with the Department of Studies in Behavioral Disabilities at the University of Wisconsin, Madison.

Handling, Positioning, and Feeding the Physically Handicapped

BONNIE L. UTLEY
JENNIFER F. HOLVOET
KARIN BARNES

Kansas Neurological Institute

The severely or profoundly retarded student whose limited performance in the classroom is compounded by the presence of physically handicapping conditions presents additional problems to classroom personnel. Even small children with severe physical impairment are difficult to carry, feed, and program within traditional classroom routine, due to abnormal posture and movement. For these children to achieve functional skills, the manner in which they are positioned and handled throughout the school day should be consistent, in order to decrease abnormal posture and movement and to increase the potential for development of early and basic motor patterns. Some of these early desirable patterns are head control, arm support, and equilibrium reactions.

Students who are physically impaired usually exhibit one or more of the following characteristics:

1. Spasticity (increased muscle tone), as evidenced in overall patterns of flexion (bending) or extension (straightening). The student with flexor spasticity displays sharply bent joints, with the elbows, wrists, hips, and knees held at angles of 90 degrees or less and the spine rounded forward. Attempts by classroom personnel to straighten a bent arm or leg are met by resistance and occasionally increased joint flexion. The other common manifestation of spasticity is that of overall extension. The student's head pushes back, the back arches, the arms are either stiff, thrown out and up, or flexed; the legs are straight, rotate in at the hips and knees and often "scissor" across one another. The feet are pointed and are also rotated toward the midline of the body.

2. Athetosis (fluctuating muscle tone), as shown in almost continuous uncontrolled movement of the head and extremities. In some students the movements are in a circular or rotary pattern; in others, the movements are random. Both spasticity and athetosis often increase if the student becomes excited or attempts to grasp or localize his movements.

3. Hypotonia (decreased muscle tone), the opposite of spasticity and less common than either spasticity or athetosis. These students are flaccid and appear to have little muscular strength.

None of these characteristics of muscular involvement is mutually exclusive. For instance, an individual student may display characteristics of both spasticity and athetosis. The distribution of involvement will also vary according to individual, with either the upper or lower extremities being more involved or involvement limited primarily to one side of the body.

In addition to the overall characteristics of too little, too much, or constantly fluctuating levels of muscle tone, most physically handicapped individuals have abnormal posture, and movement is difficult. Voluntary movement requires that overall body posture adapt constantly before and during movement. For example, in standing we transfer our weight automatically on to one leg before taking a step (Bobath, B., 1963). Changes in posture are made possible by the presence of righting and equilibrium reactions. These are automatic reactions and develop in a definite sequence in normal individuals. They are absent or delayed in many physically handicapped students. (For a more detailed explanation of these automatic reactions and their function, see Table 1.)

The final characteristic of these individuals is the presence of abnormal reflexes. Some of these reflexes are present in normal infants at various ages (primarily before 1 year), but

This paper was supported in part by the Division of Training Programs, Bureau of Education for the Handicapped, USOE Grant Number OEG-0-74-2766 (principal investigators: Doug Guess, Wayne Sailor and Leonard Lavis), and by the Division of Health, Education, and Welfare, Office of Education, Grants in Procurement Management Division/SSB Grant Number OEC-300-75-0308 (principal investigators: Doug Guess, Wayne Sailor and Phyllis Kelly).

TABLE 1

Righting and Equilibrium Reactions

Reflexes and reactions	Age of appearance and inhibition in normal development	Stimulus that elicits reflex	Description
Neck righting reflex	Present from birth to 4 months, then gradually diminishes.	Place the student on his back and turn the head to one side.	The body rotates as a whole toward the side to which the head is turned.
Body righting reflex acting on the body	Emerges between 6 to 8 months and is present until 3 years of age.	Place the student on his back and turn the head to one side.	This reflex modifies neck righting by the addition of rotation of the trunk between the shoulders and pelvis. (Rather than the body turning as a whole unit, the head turns to one side, then the shoulder girdle and finally the pelvis.)
Body righting reflex acting on the head	Emerges between 4 to 6 months and inhibited between 1 to 5 years.	Place the student's feet on the ground or lay the student on either side on a hard surface.	This reflex "rights" the head in space by bringing it into alignment with the trunk of the body.
Equilibrium reaction in lying on abdomen and back	On abdomen, this response emerges between 4 to 6 months; on the back, between 7 to 10 months. Normal throughout life.	Place the student on a tilt board on the abdomen or back and tilt to one side.	The head bends and the body arches toward the raised side. The arms and legs straighten and come out from the midline of the body.
Quadrupedal equilibrium reaction	Appears between 10 to 12 months. Normal throughout life.	Place the student on hands and knees and tip gently to one side.	The arm and leg on the raised side straighten out from the midline; the opposite arm also extends out from the midline as a protective reaction.
Sitting equilibrium reaction	Appears between 12 to 14 months. Normal throughout life.	1) Place the student in a sitting position and push gently to one side.	The head moves to the raised side; the arm and leg of the raised side straighten out from the midline of the body as do the opposite arm and leg.
		2) Push the student backward from a sitting position.	The head, shoulders, and arms move forward and the legs straighten
		3) Push the student forward.	The legs flex, the spine and neck extend and the arms move backward.
Standing equilibrium reaction	Appears between 12 to 18 months. Normal throughout life.	1) Place the student in a standing position, straighten and pull outward on either arm.	The opposite arm and leg straighten outward and the head "rights" itself to maintain the normal position in space.
		2) Hold the student under the armpits and tip him backward.	The head, shoulders, and arms move forward and the feet point upward bending at the ankles.

they are suppressed and replaced by more voluntary forms of muscle coordination as the child develops. In many physically handicapped individuals, these reflexes persist long after the normal age of inhibition, causing abnormal movements and making more advanced forms of movement impossible. (See Table 2 for a more detailed explanation of these reflexes.)

The theoretical basis underlying this article is that of Karel and Berta Bobath (1962; 1964). Their neurodevelopmental approach enables severely involved students to learn functional skills without relying on abnormal patterns of posture and movement. The three aims of the Bobath approach are to (a) normalize muscle tone: proper positioning and handling can minimize abnormality of tone; (b) inhibit abnormal reflexes: positioning and handling can help minimize the occurrence of abnormal reflex patterns; and (c) facilitate active move-

TABLE 2

Postural Reflexes

Reflex	Age of appearance and inhibition in normal development	Stimulus that elicits reflex	Description	Detrimental effects
Asymmetrical tonic neck reflex	Birth to 4 months, then gradually diminishes.	Turning the head to either side while student is lying on his back.	When the head is turned to the side, there is extension of the arm and leg on the face side and flexion of the arm and leg on the opposite side.	1) Makes rolling over difficult or impossible. 2) Causes the student to collapse while in all fours position if the face turns to either side. 3) May prevent child from getting both hands to mid-line for hand activities. 4) Makes establishment of self-feeding and ambulation difficult because of alternative flexor and extensor tone.
Symmetrical tonic neck reflex	2 to 4 months, gradually diminishes.	Raising and lowering of the head while the student is held over the knees or in an all fours position.	When the head is extended (raised up) extensor tone in the arms and flexor tone in the hips and legs increase. Lowering (bending toward the chest) of the head produces increased flexion in the arms and extension in the hips and legs.	Interferes with normal posture while sitting. Bending the head forward to look at an object increases extension of the hips causing the student to sit with rounded back, the hips sliding forward in the chair.
Tonic labyrinthine reflex	Appears during 1st and 2nd months and is normal up to 4 months of age.	Place the student: 1) On his stomach. 2) On his back.	1) On back—extensor tone becomes dominant throughout the body (back arches, legs and arms straightened, head pushes back). 2) On stomach—flexor tone becomes dominant throughout the body (arms, legs and hips bend, head is tucked to chest).	1) On back—difficult to raise the head, roll over or move from this position due to the inability of the student to flex. 2) On stomach—difficult to raise the head or maintain an all fours position due to overall flexion.
Startle reflex	Normal from birth.	Place the student in supported sitting and push him backwards past the balance point or make a loud noise.	The arms are straightened and are thrown out and up.	Interferes with use of the arms for support in sitting.

ment along the normal developmental sequence: after normal muscle tone is established, the student can more freely engage in voluntary movements.

Consistently incorporating these aims and other elements of careful programming into the school day can at best improve the motor skill functioning of the students and at least help minimize the development of contractures and make the child easier to handle. Accordingly, this article addresses the following areas:

1. *Assessment and measurement:* Assessment of the student's current performance level gives classroom personnel a sequence of behaviors for programming. Knowledge of ways to measure the target behaviors identified through assessment ensures a continuous and accurate record of progress.

2. *Proper positioning:* Positioning of both individual students and the materials presented helps to normalize tone and decrease the occurrence of abnormal reflex patterns (Bobath, B., 1969).

3. *Task analysis:* Breaking down and training

target behaviors in the gross and fine motor domains give classroom personnel an active role in programming for these students.

4. *Feeding techniques:* Proper feeding of students who exhibit abnormal oral reflex patterns can improve the student's nutrition, make mealtime more relaxing, help decrease drooling, and improve speech potential.

5. *Precautions:* Knowing what to avoid helps decrease abnormal tone and ensures the student's safety.

6. *Sources of additional information:* An awareness of resources for more technical and extensive information allows classroom personnel to take initiative in expanding their expertise regarding physically handicapped individuals.

It is hoped that no member of a classroom team will attempt to work with physically involved children without the direct supervision and training of a physical and occupational therapist. The availability of specialized occupational and physical therapy services is on the increase but, realistically, for the majority of teachers, such services are available on a consultant basis or not at all. This article is designed to provide teachers with a place to start effective programming for their physically involved students.

Assessment

The services of occupational, physical, and speech therapists are needed for accurate assessments. The terminology associated with determining gross and fine motor developmental level, and positions for reflex testing, are two technical areas requiring background in the allied health professions. If the local school system does not provide diagnostic services, it would be advisable to locate professional assessment through a hospital outpatient clinic, United Cerebral Palsy clinic, university affiliated facility, a student's family doctor, or private physical therapist. For those personnel working in areas with no available assessment services, some tests intended for overall evaluation of severely handicapped individuals include sections on gross and fine motor development. These tests and their sources are listed in "Sources of Additional Information" at the conclusion of this article.

General Positioning and Handling

To help normalize tone by decreasing abnormal patterns, support should be given consistently at several key points on the student's body. These key points are the neck and spine, the shoulder girdle, and the pelvic area (Bobath, B., 1969). These points, because of their location on the trunk of the body, control the amount of muscle tone present in the extremities. It is ineffective, for example, to work on the target behavior of grasp release if the student is in total extension (back arched, arms stiff and thrown out). Too much force must be exerted to make bending of the elbow or release of the tight fist possible while the student is extended. Instead, giving support at a key point (e.g., flexing and holding the student at the hips and shoulders) will decrease overall spasticity and enable the student's arms and hands to relax.

Avoid attempts to control all the extremities but rely on giving support at the key points and then ask the student for voluntary movements. For example, the extended spastic student can be held with his hips and knees bent and his scissored legs separated over one of the trainer's legs. In addition, placing the trainer's hands on the shoulders and applying slight downward pressure, while rotating the shoulders in a forward direction, will permit the student to more readily engage in motor imitation.

In supported sitting, the child's pushing back of his head can be reversed by giving support at the neck. Place the forearm around the student's neck and shoulders, applying gentle pressure to round the shoulders slightly forward and in toward the midline of the body (Finnie, 1975). This should enable the student to hold his head in a more normal position.

To counteract flexor spasticity, a different type of control is exerted at the same key points. Position the student facing outward on your lap, separating the legs around one of your legs. Do *not* bend but gently straighten the legs downward at the hips, if possible. Press the upper body against your chest so the spine is straight and rotate the shoulders back and down. Maintain gentle pressure with one of your hands extended high across the student's chest and placed against one of his shoulders. This will help keep the spine straight and allow the student to hold his head up. Place the materials to be worked with close enough for the student to reach easily, yet far enough away that voluntary extension of the usually flexed arms is facilitated.

In addition to controlling the key points, restraint is sometimes used successfully with athetoid individuals whose arms and legs flail. For work on grasping, self-feeding, and simple self-care skills requiring use of the upper extremities, restraining the feet by strapping them to wheelchair footrests and using weights on the arm not being used helps to decrease involuntary movements. The use of restraints and weights should be limited to those situations in which one is working with the student on a one-to-one basis, as their prolonged or unsupervised use may prove detrimental to the student. An alternative to the use of restraint is to stand behind the student, place your hands on his shoulders, and press firmly in and down. This stability at a key point of control is sufficient to enable some athetoid students to localize their hand movements.

In summary, if the hips and knees are usually extended, gently flex at the hip; if the legs scissor, rotate outward and separate. For flexion, extend the spine and neck. Work to achieve the opposite of whatever abnormal patterns are typical for each student.

Lifting and Carrying

Carrying should be kept to a minimum, replaced by a focus on independent mobility; mobility devices should be used for those students who can neither walk nor crawl. When classroom routine requires that a student be carried, the following pointers are helpful. Control of the shoulders, head, and hips is important before carrying and while carrying the child. For those students who are primarily extended, bring them to a sitting position with the hips and knees flexed before lifting. Stand in front of the student, place his arms around your neck and his legs around your waist. Make sure the hips and knees remain bent by allowing the weight of the student to rest on one of your forearms. The trainer supports the student's trunk by placing the other hand on the upper back between the shoulder blades. As the student develops sufficient head and trunk control to balance himself, move your hand down his back. When the student is placed on the mat, floor, or chair to which he has been carried, slowly remove your overall support, keeping the student in a flexed position, and maintain control at the key points. Larger spastic students can be carried in the same manner; keep their hips high on your body and extend their arms downward over one of your shoulders.

Another way to carry small students starts with the student seated. Stand behind the student and extend one arm around each side of his body, giving trunk support at waist level. Lift and separate the legs, keeping the hips and knees bent, and rest the child on your hip bone. One-arm or two-arm support can be given to the trunk area, again moving your control down as head and trunk control improve. This type of carrying allows the student to see where he is going and is suitable for both spastic and athetoid individuals.

A third way to carry a small student involves placing him in a sitting position and lifting from behind. The trainer places his arms under the student's arms and grasps the inside of each thigh directly above the knee, exerting slight outward pressure as he does so. The student's back is braced against the trainer's chest, giving maximum head and trunk control. This keeps the hips and knees flexed, and also allows the student to see where he is going.

If the student is lying down and is difficult to bend to a sitting position, roll him to a side-lying position first. To do this, bring his arms close to his body, either at the sides or across the chest, then push simultaneously at the hips and shoulders. Gently flex the student's hips and knees, place one of your arms around his shoulders to rotate them forward and down, then roll the student up to a sitting position to be lifted.

For the spastic student who is primarily flexed with his chin tucked to the chest and spine rounded, start with him in a sitting position. Stand behind the student, reach under him and place one of your hands on his pelvic area from between his legs. Place your other arm under one of the student's arms, across the upper trunk and position to put slight pressure against the rounded shoulders. The student's back will be straight and braced firmly against your chest as you lift and carry. The hypotonic or flaccid child can be carried in any of these positions; give adequate support to the key points and give no more head and trunk control than is necessary to keep the student upright.

Finally, keep the following suggestions in mind to avoid muscle strain during lifting and carrying:

1. Keep your back straight and bend at the knees rather than at the waist.
2. Keep the student's body as close to yours as possible.
3. Do not carry a student any farther than is necessary (place the student or the surface to be transferred to as close to each other as possible).
4. If a student is large, avoid carrying him by yourself.
5. When moving a child from a wheelchair, *always* lock the brakes and slide the stu-

dent forward to the edge of the chair before you lift.

6. Talk to the student; tell him where and why you are moving him, and require him to do as much as possible for himself.

Relaxation

To promote relaxation in handling both spastic and athetoid students, avoid quick movements since this tends to increase muscle tone.

For students who spend the majority of their school day in wheelchairs, the following exercise is beneficial. Place the student on a mat in a side-lying position. For extended students, flex at the key points and, for flexed students, extend the neck and spine. Kneel on the mat so your knees are at the student's waist, and place one hand on the shoulder and one on the hips. Pull the shoulders slowly toward you while simultaneously pushing the hips in the opposite direction. Alternate the pushing and pulling movements several times. The distance moved at either the hips or shoulders should be no more than 3 to 5 inches to avoid rolling the student completely over. If the distance is more than 3 to 5 inches, the student may feel his weight shift and attempt to catch himself, thereby increasing muscle tone. This exercise should be done for five minutes several times a day, and it is especially recommended following intensive one-to-one programs during which the student may have exerted himself. It is also useful to relax the student's whole body before feeding.

Another technique to promote relaxation is to hold the student in one of the positions recommended for carrying, and slowly rock him by shifting your body weight from side to side. Hold the student securely at the key points and keep him close to your body to give him trunk support and to avoid muscle strain on your part.

Simply placing and holding an extended student in a flexed side-lying position on a mat for a few minutes will help him relax. If the legs typically scissor, place a pillow between the knees and make sure the lower arm is not under the body. This position is especially recommended for those students whose chests are flat or whose spine curves to either side. For those students with sideways curvature of the spine, place them on the side which makes their spines as straight as possible.

Gross Motor

Most assessment scales measure small increments of development in the gross and fine motor areas. There are several broad areas of gross motor development that affect the physically handicapped student's performance during the school day. The following are broad areas with some suggested positions and techniques for their facilitation.

Head Control

Head control can be encouraged by placing a student in the following position. Lay the student on his stomach with arms flexed at the elbow and tucked under the chest, palms down. The head should be lifted, for a few seconds initially and then for longer and longer periods of time. Programs for visual tracking and eye contact can be conducted with the student in this position, particularly if the student is placed on an incline mat.

For facilitating head control in sitting, place the student astride one or both of the trainer's knees, facing him. Place one hand on each shoulder, rotating the shoulders in and down. This helps the student lift his head and hold it erect (Finnie, 1975). As head control becomes possible in this upright position, the trainer may begin to tilt the student backward very slowly until the head begins to drop backward. At this point, pause for a few seconds and bring the student forward to an upright sitting position again. These same techniques may be accomplished with a student who is too large to be held on the lap, by placing him on a stool (Bobath, K., and Bobath, B., 1964).

Rolling Over

To develop or improve a student's ability to roll over from a position of lying on his back, flex the student slightly at the hips and knees and place his feet on the floor. Extend one of the student's arms over his head. Flex his other arm at the elbow, then place it across his chest. Kneel at the upper part of the student's body, placing one hand on each side of the student's head. Lift his head slowly to a height of 2 to 3 inches, gently turning the head to one side as you do so. The student may be able to roll over at this point. "Segmental" rolling may occur, with the body rolling over first at the shoulders and the hips, then at the knees and feet in a progression, or the student's body may flip over as a single unit, but the latter is abnormal (neck righting reflex). If neither segmental nor total body rotation occurs with turning the student's head, flex the top leg to a full 90-degree angle at the hip, push the knee so it touches the mat, and extend the other leg. Apply a gentle push at the shoulders, then at the hips and knees, going as far down the body as necessary for the student to roll completely over to his tummy. To complete the roll so the student is again on his back, turn the face to the side opposite the direction turned to from lying on his back, extend the leg opposite to the face, and flex the other leg. Apply a gentle push at the shoulders and hips if necessary.

Rolling over can be detrimental to some students. Refer to available diagnostic information to determine whether the child has an asymmetrical tonic neck reflex (see Table 2) and/or a neck righting reflex. If he does, do not work on this skill without specific instructions from an occupational or physical therapist. The positions described may elicit these abnormal patterns. In some athetoid students, attempts to perform this behavior will increase flailing of the extremities; if this occurs do not utilize these techniques.

Moving From a Lying to a Sitting Position

Many physically handicapped students are unable to move when placed on their backs due to the extension elicited by this position. Classroom personnel should avoid pulling a student to a sitting position by grasping his elbows or hands and pulling forward. This typically results in the extended student's back arching and his head pushing back, whereas the flexed student will flex more if stretch is applied in this manner. To increase trunk and neck strength to make sitting possible, position the student against a pillow so his back is leaning 3 to 5 inches back from an upright position. Kneel at the student's feet, which are flat on the floor, and make sure the hips and knees are well flexed. Place the student's hands palm down on the floor within a few inches of the hips, if possible. Ask the student to sit up and slowly bring his shoulders forward, if necessary, until they are upright. As the student's ability to sit up improves at this angle, move the pillow a few inches at a time so he is leaning farther back. This procedure requires good head control. (For a more detailed explanation of another way to teach this skill, refer to Trudy's program later in the text.)

Sitting

Sitting "tailor" fashion (Indian style) provides stability and a broad base of support for athetoid and flaccid students. It is not, however, recommended as the only sitting position for either flexor or extensor spastics. Tailor sitting can increase flexor tone because the hips and knees are sharply bent; pressure is also exerted on the outside surfaces of the feet, reinforcing the inward rotation seen in many extended spastic students.

A position to alternate with tailor sitting for spastic students is "long" (straight leg) sitting. This can be done by placing the student on his buttocks, grasping each leg at the knee and simultaneously rotating and separating the legs outward. If this is done from behind, the student can lean against the trainer, and support for the student's back can be gradually decreased as trunk control improves. For students with some trunk control, this procedure can be done from the front.

Sitting balance for the flaccid student can be brought about by placing the trainer's hands on the student's lower back with the thumbs at each side of the spine. Push down firmly to facilitate head-raising and straightening of the spine. This can be done either on a stool or on the trainer's lap (Finnie, 1975).

Crawling

Crawling can be detrimental to the spastic child because pulling himself across a mat on his stomach strengthens abnormal patterns. The chin may tuck to the chest and head-lifting may become impossible. The hips become stiff and straight and the toes point. Athetoid students often are unable to crawl due to the inability to lift the head or bear any weight on the arms. An alternative to crawling is the use of a scooter board for those students who also lack good head control.

Standing

Prior to working on standing as a target behavior, consult with a physical or occupational therapist or a physician. This is necessary for two reasons. First, dislocated hips are not uncommon among physically handicapped students and to bear weight with this deformity can further injure the joints as well as cause pain. Second, an abnormal walking reflex can be elicited by pressure to the ball of the foot. Standing a student with this reflex results in an alternating high-stepping pattern, thereby preventing the acquisition of balance on both feet, which is a prerequisite to walking.

For students who have been approved for positioning in standing, the use of a standing table is recommended for short periods of time during the school day. (For procedures to improve standing ability, refer to Jack's standing program later in the text.)

Walking

For students who have achieved standing balance and protective extension of the arms (ability to catch themselves if they fall), the following position can help to facilitate walking. Stand behind the student and grasp each of his arms at the elbows. Straighten and turn out the arms, pushing the shoulders up and forward (Finnie, 1975). Avoid holding the student under the arms and leaning him forward to encourage walking, because he usually falls forward and tries to catch himself in an alternating pointed stepping response. This elicits scissoring due to increased stiffening of the legs.

Sample Programs for Gross Motor Development

The following sample programs for specific behaviors include procedures and suggested data recording systems for accurate measurement of progress. The programs included in this paper are designed for specific students with particular combinations of problems, and they represent only one way of approaching these problems. They are provided to demonstrate how to design a program and how to systematically apply knowledge gained from relevant readings and from consultation with allied health professionals.

Michael: Head Control Program

Michael is a 3-year-old hypotonic student with some involuntary movements. His head lags when he is pulled to a supported sitting position from his back. The longest recorded length of time he has held his head up is 3 seconds.

Positioning

1. Place Michael on his back on a mat.
2. Kneel at his feet.
3. Flex and slightly separate his legs and bring his knees close to his abdomen.
4. Cross his arms across his chest.
5. Place your hands palm up underneath each of his shoulder blades.
6. Extend your thumbs around his upper arms.

Procedures

1. Rotate the shoulders forward and down.
2. Slowly lift Michael to the point where his spine and the mat form an angle of 45°, and pause. See if his head is in alignment with his spine or if it has lagged. Wait 3 to 5 seconds to see if his head will come up.
3. Continue to lift to a full upright sitting position (Michael's spine and the mat form an angle of 90°), and again see if his head is in alignment or if it will come up in 3 to 5 seconds.
4. Slowly return Michael to lying on his back without changing the position of your hands on his shoulders.
5. Repeat for 10 trials per session, one or two sessions per day.

Data

1. Attach a large piece of paper to the wall next to the mat where the program is conducted. Draw a right angle on the paper with approximately 18-inch lines at 0°, 45°, and 90°. When Michael's back is in line with the 45° line, record whether or not his head is in alignment with his spine. Record the same information at 90°.
2. Start a stopwatch when you begin to elevate Michael from the mat. Systematize the length of time it takes for you to do so: 30 seconds, for example. For each trial, record how many seconds pass before Michael's head lags.

Trudy: Moving From a Lying to a Sitting Position

Trudy is an 8-year-old spastic student with no abnormal reflexes. She is primarily extended, with her upper extremities more involved than the lower. She has good head and trunk control and can roll over.

Positioning

1. Place Trudy on her back with her knees and hips flexed.
2. Place her arms straight with hands palm down 3 to 5 inches from her sides.
3. Kneel slightly to one side of Trudy.

Procedures: Part A

1. Place your hands on Trudy's knees.
2. Push the knees to one side until the lower knee touches the mat. This should bring her to a side-lying position; if not, place one hand under the shoulder opposite the lower knee and rotate the shoulder in the same direction as the

knees until she is completely on her side.
3. Place your hand just below the elbow of the arm resting on the mat.
4. Place your other hand and forearm around Trudy's shoulders.
5. Lift to half the distance between side lying and resting on elbow.
6. Ask Trudy to sit up. When Trudy can consistently lift herself from halfway between the mat and an elbow leaning position, begin lifting her a fewer number of inches until she can raise herself from the floor.

Procedures: Part B

1. Move the support on Trudy's arm down to the hand by placing your hand on top of hers.
2. Place your other hand and forearm around Trudy's shoulders.
3. Lift to half the distance between leaning on elbow and side-sitting.
4. Ask Trudy to sit up.
5. When Trudy can consistently lift herself from halfway between resting on elbow and side-sitting, begin lifting her a fewer number of inches until she can raise herself from her elbow to a completely upright side-sitting position.

Data

1. Again, draw a right angle on a piece of paper. Attach the paper to the wall next to the mat. Calibrate it in degrees. Record from how many degrees Trudy can sit up.
2. Attach a piece of paper calibrated in inches on the wall. Record from how many inches above the mat Trudy can raise herself to sitting.

Jack: Standing Program

Jack is an 8-year-old athetoid student who demonstrates good head control and fair trunk control. Flailing motions of the extremities are present. However, it is felt that he is a good candidate for a standing program because he can momentarily bear weight with his legs straight and his feet flat on the floor.

Positioning

1. Stand Jack in front of a sturdy box or surface that is of midchest height. The box should be 4 to 6 inches in front of his chest.
2. Place both his arms on the box so that his elbows and hands are resting on the surface. Jack may lean slightly forward. Do not allow him to lean his head or trunk backward or to the side since such actions might cause undesirable reflexes.
3. Position a small roll (approximately 7 inches in diameter) between his feet. His feet should be pointing forward and slightly outward.
4. Sit behind Jack. Place your knees or legs around Jack's to give him support and place your hands on top of his hips.

Procedures

1. Push down on Jack's hips with a firm but gentle pressure. This should be done in an alternating manner—push, relax, push, relax, push, relax.
2. Allow Jack to stand for a given length of time, giving support by holding his legs with your legs and his hips with your hands.
3. Placing a toy on top of the box may give him incentive to stand longer. However, do not allow Jack to raise his elbows from the surface to play with the toy. The elbows resting on the box provide stability and decrease flailing.
4. If Jack's body begins to deviate forward, to the side, or backward, straighten him back to the correct position by pulling his hips back to midline.
5. When Jack's legs buckle under him, remove him from the standing position and let him lie on a mat for 1 minute to rest.
6. After resting, return him to the starting position. Repeat the above procedures.

Note: This procedure is difficult for the student. Repeat the procedure only one to three times for the first few sessions. As Jack's strength improves, increase the number (or length) of the trials.

Data

Measure length of standing time on straight legs within a given time in the following progression:

1. With total support.
2. With trainer's hands removed.
3. With trainer's legs removed.
4. With box removed.

Roger: Walking Program

Roger is a 10-year-old male who demonstrates spastic characteristics in all extremities. Some flailing movements are also present. He was considered for a walking program because he is able to bear partial weight on his legs, and can alternately lift his feet from the floor. Roger stands with his feet together, legs stiffly extended, and knees turned inward.

Prerequisite Programs

Before actual walking training can begin, Roger must be trained in:

1. Weight transfer. The trainer pushes the student's hips from side to side. This transfers body weight alternately from foot to foot.
2. Protective extension. When pushed quickly forward or to the sides, his arms should move out toward the direction of the fall in order to protect him from falling. The trainer will catch the student to prevent an actual fall.

Equipment

A 6-foot-long board that is 2 inches wide and 6 inches high, nailed or secured to the floor.

Procedures

1. Stand Roger so that he is straddling the board. The board helps keep his feet apart and increases stability. His feet should be pointing forward. Do not allow the toes to point inward. The feet must be flat on the floor to prevent abnormal toe walking.
2. Stand close behind Roger. The trainer's legs will also have to straddle the board.
3. Grasp the inside of Roger's elbows from behind.
4. Raise both arms to a horizontal position so that the arms are straight out from the sides.
5. At the same time, rotate the arms so the palms are facing upward. This arm position (horizontal abduction and external rotation) inhibits scissoring of the legs and allows him to place the feet more normally on the floor (Semans, 1967). This position should be maintained throughout the entire procedure.
6. The first step is taken with the left leg. The trainer's knee may tap the back of this leg to encourage bending and forward movement.
7. At the same time, the student's body weight must be shifted to the right leg. Do this by tilting his whole body to the right while keeping the arms in the outward position.
8. The left foot should return to the floor ahead of the right foot.
9. Lean Roger to the left side so that his weight is now resting on the left foot.
10. The student will take a step with the right leg. Again, the trainer can tap his knee against the back of the student's right knee to bend it forward.
11. The right foot returns to the floor ahead of the left foot.
12. Repeat the above procedures, taking as many steps as the student can tolerate.

Data

1. Record the number of steps taken in a session.
2. Fade out the assistance and score how much assistance was needed on each of the first 10 steps.
3. Record the amount of time it takes Roger to walk a given number of steps.
4. Record how many steps were taken in a given period of time.

Fine Motor

The importance of developing a student's fine motor control is seen in the areas of self-help, play, communication, and academic work. When a student's arms and hands cannot move in front of his body and manipulate objects, he is greatly handicapped. The trainer should understand basic ways in which to manipulate the arms and hands, including the following aspects of fine motor development: reaching, grasping, grasp release, and midline positioning.

Reaching

The spastic student may have his arms flexed next to his body. The trainer can bring the arms forward by holding both arms over the outside of the elbows and tops of the arms. Then, with one smooth movement, lift and turn his arms out and forward (Finnie, 1975). While doing this, instruct him to reach for a toy that is placed in front of him. Encourage him to assist actively in the reaching.

The typical position of the athetoid student's arms is turned up and outward at the shoulders, with the elbows bent. The trainer should hold both arms on the outside of the elbows and upper arm. With one movement, turn the shoulders in and slightly down. Bring him forward and then gradually lift the arms up.

Straighten the elbows during this same movement (Finnie, 1975). Place a toy in front of the student to encourage active participation.

If a spastic or athetoid student demonstrates reaching difficulty, the trainer may want to place him on his stomach over a wedge. The student's arms should be placed over the higher edge. Place a toy within reaching distance and use the above appropriate methods to assist reaching.

Grasp

Active grasp for the student with weak and open hands may be developed by using resisted activities such as pop beads, squeezing and rolling clay, and tug-of-war. When working with the student's hand, keep the wrist bent back to help curl the fingers. A quick, firm push into the student's palm with the trainer's thumb will encourage finger closure. A detailed grasping program for the student with no grasp is outlined in Cathy's program, described later in the text.

If the student's hand is tightly fisted, first follow the procedure for release discussed below. Then place a hard object into his hand. Instruct him to close his fingers actively over the object. Do not press down into the palm or handle the hand excessively, since this will tighten the fist. Work in a sequence of release-grasp and always finish with release.

Release

Methods to release a tight fist are: (a) shaking the hand gently from the wrist, (b) bending the wrist down, (c) gently pulling the base of the thumb out of the palm, (d) wrapping a towel around the fisted hand for 20 minutes, (e) positioning the student's body out of a flexed posture (see section on positioning). To avoid increasing the tightness of the fist: never force the hand open, avoid handling the palm side of the hand and wrist, and do not put the student in a stressful situation. Do not attempt to splint the hand open, because splinting may cause increased tightness or may damage the hand. If, on a rare occasion, splinting is required, it should be prescribed by a physician and constructed by an occupational therapist.

The student whose hand usually remains open may not have an active release. This can be developed by closing the hand into a fist and instructing the student to open his hands. The trainer can make a game out of this exercise by placing the student's fingers over the edge of a table on which his arm is resting, hanging a preferred toy a few inches above the finger tips. Instruct the student to touch the toy with his fingers. As the student learns to move his fingers back actively, the trainer may place his hand over the student's closed fingers and press down as he tries to open his hand.

Midline

One of the important considerations of fine motor development is hand activity at the midline and across the midline. When the student's arms and hands are brought together in front of his body, the two sides of the body have a chance to develop the ability to work together. If both arms are working together, the more able arm may help improve the more involved arm. Activities for this include rolling pin, stacking rings, and standing blocks, or any activity that requires both hands working together at midline.

Some students avoid putting one or both hands across the midline of the body because of a developmental lag or disability on one side of the body. Activities for this problem include transferring blocks from one hand to the other, and placing toys on one side and instructing the student to pick them up with the opposite hand. The trainer may have to hold the other hand down during this activity. Be careful that the student does not turn his body to one side when reaching.

Sample Programs for Fine Motor Development

Cathy: Grasping Program

Cathy is a 7-year-old student whose arms and hands have little strength and flail randomly. She does not demonstrate an active grasp. Occasionally, however, her fingers will move toward the palm. This movement is not strong enough to grasp an object.

Positioning

1. Sit Cathy so that she is in an upright position and her trunk is well supported.
2. Place her close to a table high enough that she can rest her elbows on it without having to lean forward.
3. Sit directly in front of her table so that the student's hands can be easily manipulated.

Procedures

1. Use a brightly colored peg or dowel rod that is ½ inch in diameter and 3 to 4 inches long.

2. Place Cathy's right elbow on the table in front of her body. The forearm should be placed so that her right hand, palm up, is 8 inches from her face.
3. Use your left hand to support the back of her right hand. Cathy's wrist should be bent slightly back by the trainer's hand.
4. Place your right thumb across her right palm. Press your thumb down quickly into her palm five times and release. This procedure will cause the fingers to close. This procedure should take only 5–6 seconds.
5. With the trainer's right hand, place the peg across her palm between the thumb and fingers.
6. Continue to hold her right hand in the described position. Using your right hand, quickly push the fingers away from the peg. This will facilitate finger closure.
7. Instruct the student to grip the peg at the same time.
8. Cathy should touch the peg with all four fingers.
9. If she does not grip the peg, the trainer should curl her fingers around the peg and hold them for several seconds.
10. Repeat the procedure five times with the right hand. Do the same procedure five times with the left hand.
11. Place smaller objects in her palm as her grasp improves.

Data

Measure (+) or (−) if all four fingers actively touch the peg.

AMY—REACHING PROGRAM

Amy is a 10-year-old athetoid student. She exhibits a typical extension pattern in which her arms are turned out and up at the shoulders, her elbows are bent and her wrists are bent down. She has an asymmetrical tonic neck reflex (ATNR) to the right side; i.e., when her face is turned to the right, her right arm straightens and her left arm bends more.

Positioning

1. Place Amy in a secure sitting position on a mat with her trunk bent slightly forward.
2. Sit directly in front and slightly to the left of Amy. Do not sit to the right side of her body as this would encourage her to turn to the right, thus eliciting the ATNR.
3. Place a large ball in front of Amy.

Procedures: Part A

1. Grasp her around the outside of each arm, slightly above and on the elbows.
2. While pulling the arms forward, rotate the shoulders in and slightly down. The arms will then be straight forward, elbows straight, and the palm side of the hands will be facing the mat.
3. While pulling the arms forward, encourage Amy to touch the large ball.
4. Return her arms close to her body.
5. Repeat this procedure 5 to 10 times.

Procedures: Part B

As Amy begins to assist in the reaching, add more steps to the program:

1. Use a heavier object to push against to provide more resistance. Pushing against a heavier object will help improve strength and stability in the arms.
2. Practice bringing the ball back closer to her body after she has reached forward.
3. If Amy's wrist continues to bend downward, she should reach forward with only one hand so the trainer can use both hands to manipulate one arm. Use the same procedure with her elbow as above. With the trainer's other hand, bend the wrist up by placing your thumb against the back of her hand and your fingers under her fingers. Move the arm forward.

Data

Record the number of times she is able to reach for the ball with the trainer's assistance and without his assistance.

Feeding

Many severely and profoundly mentally retarded students have extensive and, in some cases, life-threatening feeding problems. Some of these problems are the result of developmental delay while others are due to neurological involvement. Persons involved in the training of these students need techniques for improving or developing feeding patterns.

PREFEEDING EVALUATION

In order to determine the type(s) of intervention needed, a thorough prefeeding evaluation is needed. If the services of a physical therapist, occupational therapist, or speech clinician can be obtained for this evaluation, the trainer will be better able to serve the student's particular needs. When such services are unavailable, the following are some important landmarks to help the trainer evaluate the student.

Look at the whole student.

1. Determine the student's muscular status in order to determine optimum positioning.
   a. Hypotonia (less than normal muscle tone): flaccid student.
   b. Hypertonia (more than normal): stiff student.
   c. Involuntary muscle actions: flailing student.
   d. Limited muscle action: contractures
2. Determine whether pathological or primitive reflexes are present. Such reflexes will result in postures which make eating difficult. If present, they must be inhibited during feeding training. Some reflexes of particular concern are:
   a. Symmetrical tonic neck reflex (TNR)
   b. Asymmetrical tonic neck reflex (ATNR)
   c. Tonic labyrinthine reflex
   d. Rooting reflex
   e. Sucking reflex

   Methods of evaluating these reflexes are described in detail by Karel and Berta Bobath (1962, 1964), Lewis, Foshage, and Breeden (1975) and Pennucci (undated).
3. Determine the degree of head control displayed by the student by observing:
   a. Whether the student can raise his head when placed on his stomach.
   b. Whether his head hangs back when pulled (from the shoulders) to a sitting position.
   c. Whether his head falls forward or to either side when held in a sitting position.

   Special assistive devices or positions will be needed for those students who lack head control.
4. Grasp and release: Observe the student to see if he can grasp and release a spoon (palmar grasp) and/or a smaller piece of candy between the thumb and index finger (pincer grasp). Then observe whether he can let it go or whether it just falls out of his hand. (Be sure to test both hands.) Extensive physical guidance will be necessary to teach self-feeding to a student without grasp and release.
5. Hand to mouth: Observe the student to see if he spontaneously puts his hand (with or without objects in it) to his mouth. If he does not, it is recommended that finger feeding be eliminated when beginning self-feeding training.
6. Sitting balance: Place the student in a sitting position, if possible. Observe whether the student sits freely, or needs one or both hands to prop himself. If the student is unable to sit without using his arms for support, special positioning (or special chairs) will be needed.

Look at mouth function.

1. Tongue movements: Observe the student at rest and when active. By the time a student is 6 months old, he should be able to pull his tongue back, stick it out, raise it to the top of his mouth, move it to both sides, press it down, and keep it in his mouth (Farber, 1974).
2. Sucking reflex: Look for this when giving student pureed food. It is a rhythmical movement. The tongue moves from the lips to the gums or roof of the mouth. It is pathological after 6 months of age if the student has not developed true sucking, which involves a negative pressure in the mouth and a reasonably nonmoving tongue (the tongue does not come forward).
3. Bite reflex: Test for this reflex by placing a plastic-covered metal spoon in the student's mouth and using a very slight pressure on the student's teeth or gums. If he has a positive bite reaction, he will clamp his jaws together. If this interferes with feeding, it is pathological.

   NOTE: Plastic or wooden utensils and fingers should not be used to test students, since the bite reaction is very strong and damage or injury could occur (Farber, 1974).
4. Gag reflex: This reflex is protective and is present throughout life. The presence of a gag reflex can be tested by using a swizzle stick. Place the swizzle stick on the front of the tongue in the midline and press down slightly. The examiner should be able to apply pressure along the midline of the tongue, progressing in toward the back of the tongue at least ¼ of an inch or ⅓ of the tongue before the student gags. If gagging occurs with light pressure on the tongue tip or if it interferes with feeding, it can be considered hyperactive and should be inhibited. If it does not occur, it should be facilitated (Farber, 1974), since the gag reflex is a normal protective mechanism.
5. Swallowing: Many multiply handicapped

students exhibit pathological swallowing patterns. The most common of these is "chugging," i.e., letting liquids and soft foods slide down the throat without swallowing. Check for this by observing whether the student throws his head back when given liquid. It can also be tested by holding the student's head upright, presenting him with a liquid, and feeling the student's upper throat and neck to determine whether swallowing is occurring.
6. Drooling and lip closure: Note whether the students' lips close over his teeth.

Sample Feeding Programs

After assessing the student, it is important to write a feeding program which details positioning for the student, any pre-feeding exercises done to relax the child or to facilitate tongue movement and mouth closure, and an explanation of feeding techniques. A data system should also be instituted in order to determine the effectiveness of the training.

Janie—Swallowing Program

Janie is a 14-year-old female with severe retardation and spastic quadraplegia. She is in an adapted wheelchair (Macey, 1974). She manifests a severe ATNR, has no sitting balance, or hand-to-mouth activity. She has a sucking reflex present with tongue thrust, and manifests what appears to be an occasional bite reflex. Her gag reflex is normal, and she does not demonstrate lip closure, tongue movements, or true swallowing. She has previously been fed lying down and is on a strained food diet.

Positioning

1. Adjust the wheelchair back to be upright, as close to 90° as possible. It is very difficult to swallow in a reclining position, which increases the dangers of choking and inhalation pneumonia. Furthermore, positioning the student in an upright position helps break the spastic extension pattern, making it easier for Janie to control her arm and mouth movements.
2. Remove the head supports. This is done in order to give lip and jaw control.
3. Roll up one or two towels and place them behind Janie's neck. This flexes her head and helps further break up the spastic extension pattern that maintains her tongue thrusting and prevents swallowing. It is very important that the back of the spastic student's head is not touched by the towels, the teacher's arm, or the back of the chair, since pressure on the head facilitates the extension pattern (Farber, 1974).
4. Make sure Janie is facing straight ahead as each bite is presented. This is a feeding technique rule that is applicable to all students.

Prefeeding Procedures: Part A (for lip closure)

1. Stand next to wheelchair.
2. Place index finger above lips.
3. Place middle finger below lips.
4. Separate lips gently with quick movements in opposite directions five times. (See Figure 1.)

Prefeeding Procedures: Part B (for jaw closure) and to stimulate salivation)

1. Stand in front of wheelchair.
2. Place thumb and index finger on opposite corners of the mouth just below cheekbones.
3. Stroke downward firmly five times. (See Figure 2.)
4. Allow 30 seconds and watch for lip closure.
5. Repeat the two procedures three times in a row.

Feeding Techniques

1. Stand next to the left side of wheelchair.
2. Place right arm around the back of Janie's neck, making sure the arm does not press on the back of the head. Push with forearm until Janie's head is no longer in ATNR, but is facing straight ahead.

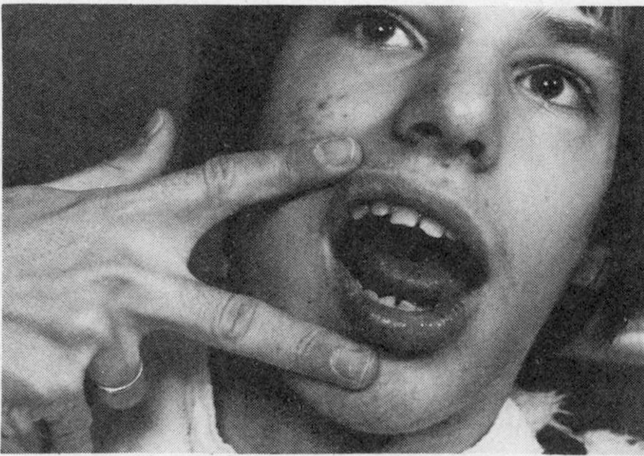

Figure 1. Prefeeding procedure for lip closure.

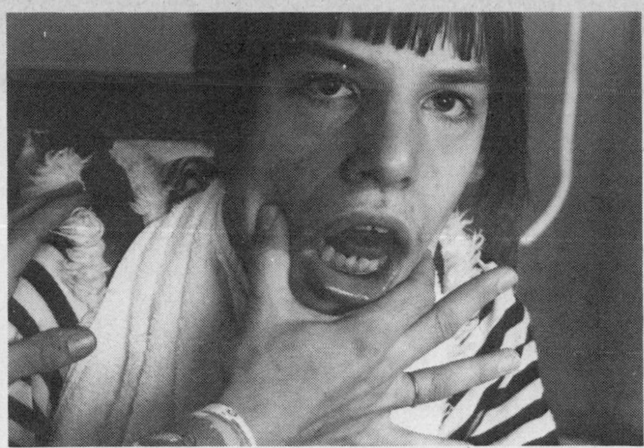

Figure 2. Prefeeding procedure for jaw closure and to stimulate salivation.

3. Place the index finger of right hand above upper lip, and middle finger below lip. This is the position for controlling the lips. (See Figure 3.)
4. Bend third finger and place below chin in the indentation behind jawbone. Extend one little finger downward along throat. This is the position for jaw control (Farber, 1974; Mueller, 1972).
5. Using left hand, fill spoon half-full with food (food should be on the tip of the spoon). If the mouth is too full, the student cannot swallow.
6. Present food to Janie, approaching her mouth from the front directly in midline. Always present food from the front to prevent the student from leaning to the side.
7. With right third finger press upward underneath the chin with a quick *firm* movement. This is the correct way to get the student to open her mouth.

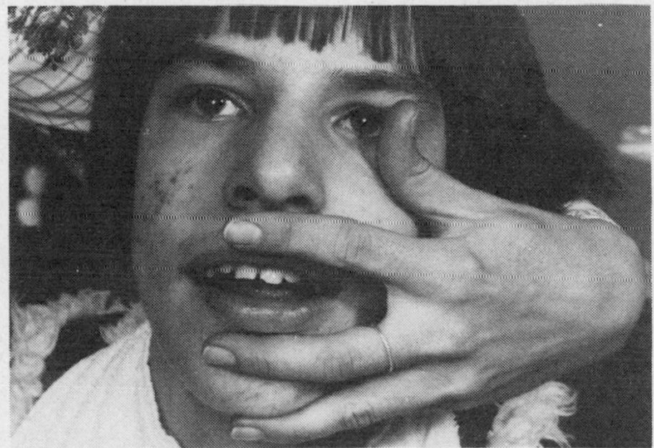

Figure 3. Feeding technique; position for controlling the lips.

8. Wait a few seconds to see if her mouth opens; if not, repeat every few seconds until mouth opens.
9. Place spoonful of food in mouth and place spoon on tongue halfway back. If the food is placed on the tip of the tongue, tongue thrusting will increase; if placed too far back, the student may gag.
10. Press downward *firmly* with the tip of the spoon on surface of the tongue. This causes the tongue to retract and carry the food to the back of the mouth. A very firm pressure is necessary (Eddington, 1971a).
11. Begin to withdraw spoon, making sure not to pull spoon along the roof of her mouth or against her teeth. Scraping the teeth facilitates the abnormal bite reflex, which, in turn, prevents normal swallowing (Eddington, 1971a).
12. As spoon is withdrawn from mouth, press lips together gently with right index and middle finger on the surface of spoon.
13. Withdraw spoon completely, allowing lips to remove food from the spoon (Holser-Buehler, 1966).
14. Push jaw up with third finger. This will keep the student's mouth shut and at least some of the food in her mouth. It is probable that some of the food will run out over the trainer's fingers. Do *not* use the spoon, fingers, or towel to remove this food from the child's chin. Dabbing or scraping the child's chin facilitates mouth opening and will undo all the foregoing work (Holser-Bueler, 1966).
15. Hold mouth shut in this position and stroke the throat around the Adam's apple, either in an upward or downward direction, with your little finger. This facilitates swallowing.
16. Continue this position until Janie swallows, watching her throat carefully to detect swallowing action (this may take up to 60 seconds or more).
17. Repeat this procedure for 15–20 minutes. If the student has not taken an adequate amount of food for nutrition, the rest of the meal may be given in a less-structured manner.

Data

One can measure either the number of bites swallowed in a given amount of time, the amount of food swallowed (if there is any method for recovering spilled food), or the time needed to feed a given number of bites. Other measures could include weight gain of the subject (especially good for infants) or amount of soiled linen.

Sam: Sucking and Swallowing Program

Sam is a 12-year-old multiply handicapped student who demonstrates a hyperactive gag reflex, drooling, and no sucking or swallowing of liquids. A sucking program was initiated to strengthen his lips and tongue and to give him a means of drinking without choking.

Positioning

1. Seat Sam in an upright and symmetrical position. He should be placed in a chair with a high back and arms. A seat belt and chest retainer should be used. This keeps him from falling forward due to lack of muscle control (Farber, 1974).
2. Hold his head upright and in the midline with one hand.
3. The trainer should stand in front of Sam.

Prefeeding Procedures to Reduce Gagging and Promote Lip Closure

1. About one hour before feeding, position Sam correctly. The following procedure will usually upset the student and should therefore not occur just prior to feeding. He should be allowed time to calm down between this procedure and the remaining prefeeding exercises.
2. Use the area between the knuckles of the first two fingers and press upward underneath the chin with a quick firm movement to open the mouth.
3. Wait a few seconds to see if his mouth opens; if it does not, repeat step 2 every few seconds until mouth opens.
4. Use your non-dominant hand to keep the head straight and to keep the mouth open. This is done by placing the thumb close to one of the student's jaw joints, covering the chin with the area between the thumb and fingers, and placing the fingers as close as possible to the student's other jaw joint and exerting downward pressure.
5. Take a swizzle stick in the other hand and place it on the tip of the tongue.
6. Press down on the stick, then move it back about 1/16 of an inch and press down again. Continue until the tongue "humps up." (Do not go more than halfway back.) This is called "walking the tongue" and reduces a hyperactive gag reflex. It is not a pleasant or easy exercise for the trainer or the student, but it can make the difference between a student who can eat solids and one who cannot (Farber, 1974).
7. Close mouth for swallow.
8. Repeat above procedure 5 to 7 times.
9. Let student rest.
10. Just before feeding, position Sam correctly.

Feeding Techniques

1. Do not use milk or any sweet substance for this training. Use Gatorade®, unsweetened orange juice, or meat broths. Milk thickens the saliva and makes drinking difficult, whereas sweet fluids increase drooling.
2. Make sure the fluid is only moderately warm or cool. Food that is either cold or hot facilitates oral pathology, particularly in the hypersensitive student.
3. Present the straw or tube in the midline. Dip plastic or rubber tubing (¼ inch in diameter, 4 to 5 inches long) in the fluid, then place index finger over the end of the tubing, thus filling 2 to 3 inches of the tube with the fluid. A plastic straw can be used for a student who does not bite or collapse the straw.
4. Place the filled tubing in Sam's mouth. Close his lips around the tubing, using index and middle finger, and give jaw control. Release the end of the tubing, allowing the liquid to flow into his mouth. Repeat this 3–4 times.
5. Again, place the filled tubing in Sam's mouth and close his lips. Hold the tube horizontally. Whenever Sam sticks his tongue into the end of the tubing or sucks, allow the liquid to run into his mouth.
6. When Sam can suck with the tube horizontal for five trials, the tube should be lowered gradually (reaching criterion for five trials at each step). When the tube is nearly vertical, it should be placed directly into the liquid.
7. When sucking is well established (all liquid consumed for 2 to 3 weeks), substitute a short plastic or aluminum straw. When this is established, gradually increase the length of the straw (Eddington, 1971a; Palmer, 1947).

Data

One can measure the length of time it takes the student to drink 1 teaspoon, 1 ounce, a 4-ounce glass of liquid, etc., the number of ounces consumed in a given time (10 minutes, 5 minutes, 1 minute), the number of sucks in succession, the length of the straw (which measures the power of the suck).

Billy: Chewing Program

Billy is an 8-year-old male with severe retardation and spastic quadriplegia. He has oral hypersensitivity. He has been fed pureed food all his life and has good sucking and swallowing patterns.

Positioning

1. Adjust the wheelchair back to be upright, as close to 90° as possible.
2. Roll up one or two towels and place them behind Billy's neck.
3. Position his hands in the midline and make sure he is facing straight ahead as each bite is presented.

Prefeeding Procedures (To Reduce Hypersensitivity)

1. Use the index fingers to stroke the area between the upper lip and nose. Use quick downward strokes and do not touch the lip.
2. Use the index finger to stroke the corners of the mouth. Use quick inward strokes.
3. Use the index finger to stroke the area between the chin and lower lip. Use quick upward strokes (Zelle, 1974).
4. Wrap one thickness of a clean, dry washcloth (preferably terrycloth) around the index finger and stroke the inside of both cheeks. Then close the mouth by pulling down on the chin. This will give the student a chance to swallow.
5. Stroke the outside surfaces of the upper and lower gums, using firm *horizontal* strokes. Close the student's mouth and allow him to swallow. Stroke the inside surfaces of the upper and lower gums, using horizontal strokes. Close the student's mouth and allow him to swallow. If Billy resists by clenching his teeth, stop the session and continue at another time (Zelle, 1974).

Feeding Techniques

1. Stand or sit in front of the wheelchair.
2. Place your thumb on the student's chin, third finger under the jaw, and index finger on the side of the jaw. This is a position for lip control in a student who has good head control. (See Figure 4.)

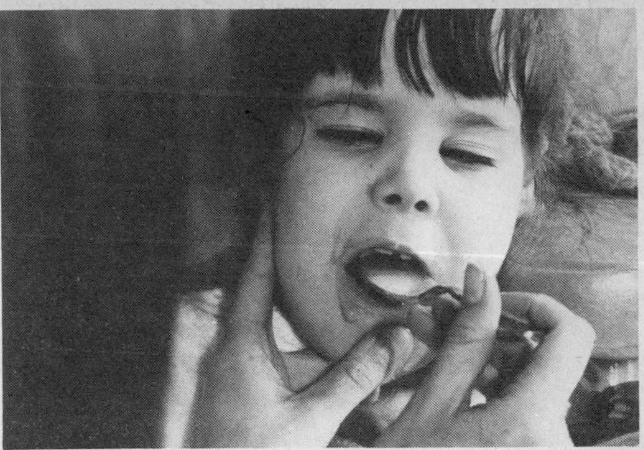

Figure 4. Feeding technique; position for lip control in a student who has good head control.

3. With third finger, press upward on the chin with a quick firm movement. Repeat until mouth opens.
4. Place a finger-shaped piece of dry bread, melba toast, licorice, Bit-O-Honey®, or beef jerky on his molars on one side.
5. Allow his mouth to close; use jaw control if necessary.
6. Gently tug on the food. This often stimulates a chewing action (Farber, 1975).
7. Then move his jaw in an up, down, sideways pattern using your hand that holds the chin and jaw. Hold on to the food with the other hand and continue to tug on it.
8. Do this 1 or 2 times, then begin the meal.
9. Begin feeding with almost pureed soft food (junior baby food texture), such as mashed potato, bologna or braunschweiger, fish, skinless weiners, applesauce.
10. Place the food between the molar and the outer cheek. This causes the tongue to pick up the food. Do most of the work on the weakest side of the mouth, but occasionally alternate sides.
11. Withdraw the spoon from the mouth and pull the student's chin down rapidly. This facilitates mouth closure.
12. Hold the student's mouth closed and assist Billy in making up, down, and sideways movements of the jaw. Pause intermittently to allow him an opportunity to chew independently.
13. Wait until he swallows.
14. Repeat this procedure for 15 to 20 minutes. If student has not taken in an adequate amount of food for nutrition, the rest of the meal can be given using more pureed foods.

15. Increase the texture of the foods gradually as student shows more tolerance, by decreasing blending time about 1 second per week.

ANN: DRINKING FROM A CUP

Ann is a 2-year-old female with athetoid cerebral palsy and severe mental retardation. Her head control is relatively good, but she has achieved no trunk control. It was felt that Ann could benefit from a cup drinking program, since her spoon feeding program was going well.

Positioning

1. Cross your legs at the knee.
2. Place Ann across your lap in such a manner that your higher leg is under her knees. This lowers her bottom and flexes her hips and knees. This position is recommended only for young students who can easily be controlled in your lap. This lap position inhibits the extensor pattern which would prevent swallowing. This position should not be used with a student who has an asymmetrical tonic neck reflex.
3. It is important not to face Ann the same way each time. Place her with her left side next to your body at some meals and her right side next to your body at others.
4. Stabilize her head and trunk by placing one arm around the base of her skull and rolling her shoulders forward with your forearm. Her other shoulder should be held forward by the pressure from your chest. This position gives good support and helps keep the head in midline. Your hand should be free to give lip control (Farber, 1974; Finnie, 1975)
5. Use weighted cuffs on her left arm to keep it still. This also helps stabilize her head and trunk and reduces the danger of her hitting the cup (Zinkus, 1971).

Prefeeding Procedures (To Facilitate Lip Closure)

1. Do Prefeeding Procedure, Part A (Janie's program).
2. Do Prefeeding Procedure, Part B (Janie's program).

Drinking Techniques

1. Use a plastic or paper cup (preferably a transparent one) with a semicircle cut out of the rim, so that when the cup is tipped, Ann's nose is not covered. This will considerably reduce her fighting the cup. A transparent cup makes it easier for you to position the cup correctly.
2. Do not use milk or any sweet substance for this training. Use Gatorade®, unsweetened orange juice, or meat broths. (See Sam's program.)
3. Make sure the fluid is only moderately warm or cool.
4. Never allow the student to grasp the cup between her teeth or tilt her head back when drinking. This causes abnormal swallowing.
5. Fill the cup fairly full so it is not necessary to tip it up over Ann's nose.
6. Use supporting hand to give lip and jaw control. Place thumb on upper lip, index finger on chin, and third finger under her jaw.
7. Push up gently with third finger to encourage mouth opening. Hold the jaw so the mouth opening is small.
8. Using free hand, place the rim of the cup gently against Ann's lower lip.
9. Tilt the cup until a little liquid touches the tongue. (See Figure 5.)
10. Leave the rim of the cup on lower lip, but do not push down. This teaches a more normal drinking pattern where several swallows are taken before the cup is removed.
11. Using index finger, firmly place the upper lip against the inside rim of the cup. The teeth should not hit the cup (particularly if the student has a bite reflex). Simultaneously, apply upward pressure to the jaw and lower lip.
12. Hold the lips closed until swallowing occurs.

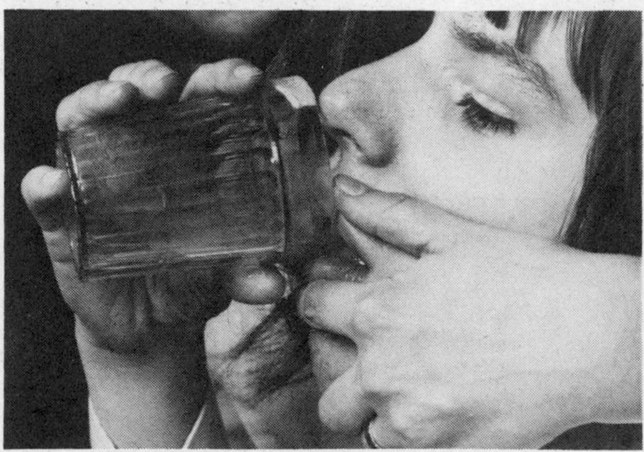

Figure 5. Drinking technique.

13. Repeat until Ann has drunk two or three mouthfuls of liquid, then remove the cup and jaw control and let her rest.
14. Feed the rest of the liquid from a bottle at first. Gradually increase the amount of liquid given from the cup (resting after each two or three swallows).
15. The steps should be eliminated in the following order:
    a. Holding the lips shut for swallowing.
    b. Holding the upper lip in contact with inner rim.
    c. Drawing the lower lip over the teeth.
    d. Holding the cup (if appropriate assistive device can be found).

Data

One can measure number of ounces drunk in a given period of time, the number of swallows in succession, or the amount of assistance necessary to drink two swallows.

Precautions

The general methods of handling and positioning outlined in this article are suggested management techniques for the physically handicapped. Individual students differ in the severity and distribution of involvement necessitating careful and continuous observation of the effectiveness of any of these techniques. Modify them as necessary to bring about more normal muscle tone throughout the body.

In addition to the *do's* described, here are several *don't's*. Some of these have been mentioned previously but, because of their importance, are repeated. **Do not:**

1. Allow the student to lie on his back for dressing, sleeping, or playing.
2. Allow the student to remain in any one position for more than 60 minutes at a time.
3. Pull an extended student's head to an upright position by placing your hand on the back of his head.
4. Pull any physically handicapped student by his feet or hands; use the key points to change position.
5. Allow the feet to dangle while in a sitting position.
6. Allow "bunny hopping" (from hands and knées position, the student first extends the arms forward, then pulls the legs so they are between the arms).
7. Allow sitting "W" style (sitting with buttocks between the feet).
8. Allow one-handed activities.
9. Support the head and all extremities at all times; allow the student to use developing head and trunk control.
10. Bounce the student on his feet, throw him in the air, or tickle him since these actions increase abnormal tone.
11. Stand over the student so he needs to look up to see you.
12. Allow the student to throw his head back during feeding, thereby permitting the food to slide down the throat without active swallowing.
13. Feed the student very large bites.
14. Hit on the back for choking; instead flex the entire body, particularly the chin.
15. Pull out a utensil that a student with a bite reflex has clamped down on; tuck the chin to the chest and wait for the jaws to relax.
16. Use a new feeding technique for the entire meal; begin the meal with the new technique when the student is most hungry and gradually increase the portion of the meal being presented in this way.

Sources of Additional Information

The following sources, as well as those found in the reference list, are recommended to those desiring more complete knowledge of techniques for managing physically handicapped persons.

Ball, T. S., Hendrickson, H., & Clayton, J. A special feeding technique for chronic regurgitation. *American Journal of Mental Deficiency*, 1974, *78* (4), 486–493.

Banus, B. *The developmental therapist: A prototype of the pediatric occupational therapist*. Thorofare, New Jersey: Charles Slack, 1971.

Bobath, B. A neuro-developmental treatment of cerebral palsy. *Physiotherapy*, 1963, *49*, 242–244.

Bobath, B. Treatment principles and planning in cerebral palsy. *Physiotherapy*, 1963, *49*, 122–124.

Bobath, B. The treatment of neuromuscular disorders by improving patterns of coordination. *Physiotherapy*, 1969, *55*, 18–22.

Brunnstrom, S. *Movement therapy in hemiplegia: A neurophysiological approach*. New York, New York: Harper and Row, 1970.

Crickmay, C. *Speech therapy and the Bobath approach to cerebral palsy*. Springfield, Illinois: Charles C. Thomas, 1966.

Feeding the child with a handicap. Washington, D. C: U. S. Department of Health, Education & Welfare (Pamphlet division), Children's Bureau, 1967.

Fiorentino, M. *Reflex testing methods for evaluating CNS development*. Springfield, Illinois: Charles C. Thomas, 1972.

Fiorentino, M. *Normal and abnormal development: The influence of primitive reflexes on motor development*. Springfield, Illinois: Charles C. Thomas, 1972.

Godfrey, A. *Feeding techniques for children with cerebral palsy*. Salt Lake City: State of Utah, Department of Social Services, Division of Health-MCH (undated).

Harklerood, D., & Lohrey, B. Neuro-developmental treatment for cerebral palsy: Some practical application for occupational and physical therapists. In L. Pedretti, *Manual for advanced physical disability procedures*. San Jose, California: San Jose State University, Sparton Book Store, 1973.

Ingram, T. T. S. Clinical signs of infantile feeding reflexes. *Developmental Medicine and Child Neurology*, 1962, *4*, 159–169.

Inservice training manual for State of New York, Department of Mental Hygiene Developmental Centers. New York, NY: United Cerebral Palsy Association of New York State, Inc., 1974.

McCormack, J., Hamlet, C., Dunaway, J., & Vorderer, L. *Educational evaluation and planning package: Volume 1*. Medford, Mass: Massachusetts Center for Program Development and Evaluation, 1976.

Pearson, P. H., & Williams, C. E. (Eds.) *Physical therapy services in the developmental disabilities*. Springfield, Illinois: Charles C. Thomas, 1972.

Schalock, R., Ross, B., & Ross, I. *Basic skills screening test*. Hastings, Nebraska: Mid-Nebraska Mental Retardation Services, 1975.

Shearer, D., Billingsly, J., Frohman, A., Hilliard, J., Johnson, F., & Shearer, M. *The Portage guide to early education: Instructions and checklist*. Portage, Wisconsin, Cooperative Educational Service Agency #12, 1970.

Somerton, M. E., & Turner, K. D. *Pennsylvania training model individual assessment guide*. King of Prussia, Pennsylvania: Regional Resources Center of Eastern Pennsylvania for Special Education/PRISE, 1975.

Stockmeyer, S. An interpretation of the approach of Rood to the treatment of neuromuscular dysfunction. *American Journal of Physical Medicine*, 1967, *46*, 900–956.

References

Bobath, B. Treatment, principles and planning in cerebral palsy. *Physiotherapy*, 1963, *49*, 122–124.

Bobath, B. The treatment of neuromuscular disorders by improving patterns of co-ordination. *Physiotherapy*, 1969, *55*, 18–22.

Bobath, K., & Bobath, B. An analysis of the development of standing and walking patterns in patients with cerebral palsy. *Physiotherapy*, 1962, *48*, 144–153.

Bobath, K., & Bobath, B. The facilitation of normal postural reactions and movements in the treatment of cerebral palsy. *Physiotherapy*, 1964, *50*, 246–262.

Eddington, C. *Spoon feeding your child*. Salt Lake City: State of Utah, Department of Social Services, Division of Health—MCH, 1971a.

Eddington, C. *Teaching your child straw drinking to encourage sucking*. Salt Lake City: State of Utah, Department of Social Services, Division of Health—MCH, 1971b.

Farber, S. *Sensorimotor evaluation and treatment procedures for allied health personnel*. Indianapolis: Indiana University—Purdue University, Indianapolis Medical Center, Occupational Therapy Program, 1974.

Finnie, N. R. *Handling the young cerebral palsied child at home*. New York, N.Y: E. P. Dutton, 1975.

Holser-Buehler, P. The Blanchard method of feeding the cerebral palsied. *American Journal of Occupational Therapy*, 1966, *20*, 31–34.

Lewis, C., Foshage, K., and Breeden, D. *Feeding the handicapped child*. CRU-UAF working paper. Kansas City, Kansas: University of Kansas Medical Center (CRU-UAF), 1975.

Macey, P. G. *Mobilizing multiply-handicapped children: A manual for the design and construction of modified wheelchairs*. Lawrence, Kansas: Division of Continuing Education, University of Kansas, 1974.

Mueller, H. Facilitating feeding and pre-speech. In P. Pearson and C. Williams (Eds.). *Physical therapy services in developmental disabilities*. Springfield, Illinois: Charles C. Thomas, 1972.

Mysak, E. D. *Principles of a reflex therapy approach to cerebral palsy*. New York: Teachers College, Columbia University, 1963.

Palmer, M. F. Studies in clinical techniques: II. Normalization of chewing, sucking, and swallowing reflexes in cerebral palsy: A home program. *Journal of Speech Disorders*, 1947, *12*, 415–418.

Pennucci, J. *Oral reflexes*. Columbus, Ohio: The Ohio State University College of Medicine, School of Allied Medical Professions, Occupational Therapy Division, (undated).

Semans, S. The Bobath concept in treatment of neurological disorders. *American Journal of Physical Medicine*, 1967, *46*, 732–788.

Zelle, R. *Procedure to reduce sensitivity to texture and promote oral hygiene*. Sacramento, California: Alta Regional Center, 1974.

Zinkus, C. Feeding skill training. In: *Feeding the handicapped child*. Nashville, Tennessee: University of Tennessee Child Development Center, 1971.

BONNIE L. UTLEY is a teacher-trainer in the Personnel Preparation Program for the Education of the Severely Handicapped of the Kansas Neurological Institute in Topeka. Her field of specialization is the general care of the physically handicapped.

JENNIFER F. HOLVOET is a Personnel Training Specialist for teachers and paraprofessionals in the Personnel Preparation Program for Education of the Severely Handicapped at the Kansas Neurological Institute in Topeka. Mrs. Holvoet previously worked for Project MORE (Mediated Operational Research in Education).

KARIN J. BARNES is a Registered Occupational Therapist for Project LEARN, Model Education Project for the Orthopedically Impaired and Severely Handicapped, at the Kansas Neurological Institute in Topeka. In this capacity, she is responsible for the care and treatment of the physically handicapped.

Approximating the Norm Through Environmental and Child-Centered Prosthetics and Adaptive Equipment

PHILIPPA H. CAMPBELL

Children's Hospital, Akron, Ohio

KAREN M. GREEN

Eastern Nebraska Community Office of Retardation

LINDA M. CARLSON

Western Wisconsin Cerebral Palsy Evaluation and Treatment Center

All children encounter developmental roadblocks in growing up, and overcoming these obstacles is difficult for any youngster. A child's development is a process of emerging from his mother's arms to the diversity of the neighborhood and the increasing complexities of the classroom. Most parents spontaneously give their offspring opportunities for growth, expecting them to learn—and they do. For children who are mentally or physically handicapped, however, this process often works in reverse. The label "normal" signals an open road to growing and learning. The label "handicapped" signals a dead end.

Because of the quantity of recent legislation mandating the integration of the multiply handicapped into more normal modes of education, the so-called defective children, previously found only in infirmaries and large institutions, now have access to the same open road (public school education) and the same possibilities for personal development as their normal peers. This trend is encouraging, but it may have no beneficial effect if we continue to expect the child who is orthopedically handicapped to succeed in that more normal environment without the necessary support systems to facilitate growth. When he fails, we are apt to place the blame on the child (as not capable), rather than to place the blame on the support system, where it belongs. When the child fails, it is because his teachers have failed to find ways to teach him the necessary skills. To believe otherwise is to reinforce the myth that severely handicapped children cannot succeed.

Philippa H. Campbell contributed the section on adaptive equipment. Karen M. Green and Linda M. Carlson contributed the section on environmental and child-centered prosthetics.

Adaptive equipment can be very useful in helping the profoundly handicapped child succeed, but if it is poorly selected, improperly fitted, or badly designed, that equipment can become a liability. Although many types of adaptive equipment are commercially available, seldom is one type appropriate for all children, and frequently commercial equipment must be modified to fit the age, size, and needs of an individual child. The purpose of this paper is to provide teachers with a rationale for the use of adaptive equipment and prosthetic devices; to present some guidelines that may be helpful in determining when and why to use such equipment; and to demonstrate, through a series of case studies, some of the major applications of this equipment.

Factors to Consider in Selecting Equipment

Equipment can be chosen to prevent or alleviate deformities in the child with neurological or orthopedic problems, or it can be used to enable the child to function more normally in therapy, in the classroom, or at home. The purpose of the equipment, the size and age of the child, and the available space and financial resources should be considered in the selection. Frequently, there are medical contra-indications to the use of equipment that might otherwise be developmentally appropriate. For instance, the child may be developmentally ready to stand but have dislocated hips. Standing a child on dislocated hips might further damage the hip sockets, thus causing greater deformity. Because of such circumstances as this, it is important to check with the child's physician and therapist about the function or appropriateness of a particular piece of equipment.

The purposes of using equipment (*e.g.*, preventing deformity or enabling specific function) can frequently be accomplished without manufactured equipment. This is especially important to remember when financial resources are limited. In such cases, positioning the child may be a workable alternative, or parents or senior citizens may be willing to make specific equipment if plans and diagrams are supplied. For children with severe deformities, hand-designed equipment may be the only solution because it may not be possible to fit the child with readily available devices.

Whether or not a child is supplied with equipment depends greatly on his needs. No one piece of equipment will be fully satisfactory for any child. Rather, each child needs to have a variety of positions (perhaps made possible by equipment), which he can use to function maximally in his environment. Few pieces of equipment will meet the needs of more than one child. In order to achieve maximum function, positioning through equipment must be well planned for the individual child, and in line with his functional abilities.

Positioning

Appropriate positioning is essential to the profoundly handicapped child's ability to perform motor, self-help, language, and cognitive skills. Many profoundly retarded children have abnormal or primitive postural tone, which causes them to move too much or too little and within restricted motor patterns. When his movement is confined to limited patterns, the child may have difficulty learning to move himself in his environment. He may have problems with such gross motor milestones as lifting his head or sitting independently. If he is unable to move his arms well, it may be impossible for him to develop self-feeding skills or to perform classroom activities. Because his movement is limited to stereotyped patterns, the child's arms or legs may tighten and become fixed in certain postures. Proper positioning can help prevent the development of contractures (permanent shortening of muscles, tendons, or scar tissue), and deformities, as well as help normalize the child's postural tone. Normalizing the child's tone means positioning him in ways that will help loosen his muscles if they are too tight and help stabilize his muscles if they are too loose. Placing the child in normalizing positions will help make him more able to perform developmental motor, cognitive, and language skills.

Positioning a child can involve either static (fixed) or dynamic (movable) positions. For the child with less severe motor involvement (such as Down's syndrome or mild cerebral palsy), it is usually better to try dynamic positioning. This approach allows the child to move as much as he is able and can help him learn to move in more normal patterns. A child who has poor independent standing balance, and who is unable to walk unaided, may be allowed to perform classroom activities while standing in front of a table, rather than sitting in a chair. This approach to positioning will help the child to develop better standing balance and to walk with support (cruise along furniture) at the same time that he is participating in cognitive or language activities.

For the child with more severe motor involvement, the only possible type of positioning may be static. In this type of positioning, the child's movement is channeled into more normal patterns. A severely involved, immobile child who lacks head control may be positioned on his stomach over a wedge to help him learn to lift his head. Static positioning, however, should not be a classroom goal in itself but, rather, should be used in conjunction with the cognitive or language goals established for the child. The proper positioning will make it easier for a child to lift his head, but it will not give him a reason to do so. Stimulation from the child's environment makes him want to lift his head; proper positioning makes this response possible.

In his first year of life, a normally developing child learns to prop on his stomach, sit, stand, and walk. Positioning for the handicapped child, whether static or dynamic, usually involves some adaptations of these basic developmental positions. Selection of proper positioning for the handicapped child, however, may be more related to functional than developmental status. For example, a position of supported sitting may be chosen for a child who, developmentally, may never sit independently. The purpose of this positioning is to enable the child to use his arms more appropriately, not to help him learn to sit independently. Before selecting positioning for a particular child, the parent, teacher, or therapist must first identify the functional goals which the positioning is to provide and must assess the current functional-developmental status of the child.

Positioning may be accomplished with or without specific equipment. In some instances, foam rubber or strategically placed pillows may be all the equipment that is needed. Positioning does not necessarily require special equipment and, if money or resources are not available, can still be accomplished by less sophisticated means, materials, and designs.

Lying Positions

Back lying, prone stomach lying, or side lying are the three basic positions in anti-gravity patterns. For most handicapped children, particularly those who tend to stiffen (spasticity) or who are older, back lying is a poor position. When the back of the head is stimulated, this child tends to push back with his head and become stiffer. It then becomes more difficult for the child to reach forward with his arms or to bring his head forward. With older, long-institutionalized children, back lying may be the only possible position, because of severe deformities in the chest, spine, or legs. If back lying must be used, placement of a pillow behind the head helps bring the child's neck into a flexed (bent forward) position which helps to prevent the child from pushing back with his head. (See Figure 1.)

Back lying should not be used unless it is impossible to place a child in any other position. For a profoundly deformed child, in addition to pillows behind the head, blocks of foam rubber may be used to provide support (behind the shoulders, under the knees, or around the head). (See Figure 2.)

Stomach (prone) lying is frequently a good position for a younger child without head control or for an older child who is unable to support himself on his arms. In addition to encouraging head control and arm support, stomach lying tends to normalize extreme extensor tone. Because it is one of the earliest positions a normal infant assumes developmentally, it is frequently used for handicapped infants and children. Stomach lying, however, makes it difficult for an infant or child to use his arms for activities other than support. If the child must fully use his arms to support himself in a stomach-lying position, it will be difficult or impossible for him to use his arms to manipulate toys or to reach out. Because of this, visual stimulation is often best used, in order to encourage the child to hold up his head when prone. If sufficient head control exists in the prone position, a pointer attached to a strap may be placed on the child's head and used to manipulate objects through head movements.

Frequently, support must be provided in stomach lying in order to properly position the child. Support can be provided by a foam rubber wedge (Figure 3) if the child's muscles are stiff, or by a wooden wedge if the child's muscles

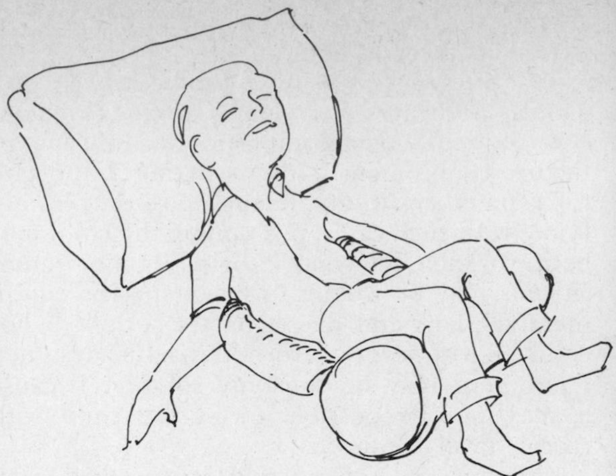

Figure 2. Child properly positioned in back-lying, using pillows and sandbags.

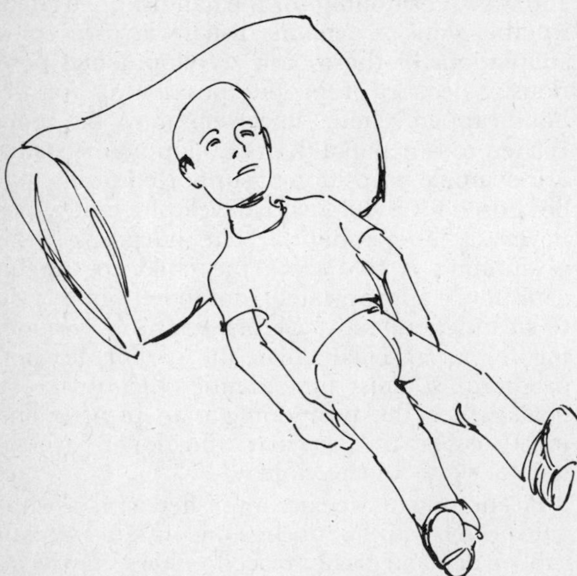

Figure 1. Young child positioned in back-lying, with pillow behind head to inhibit extensor tone.

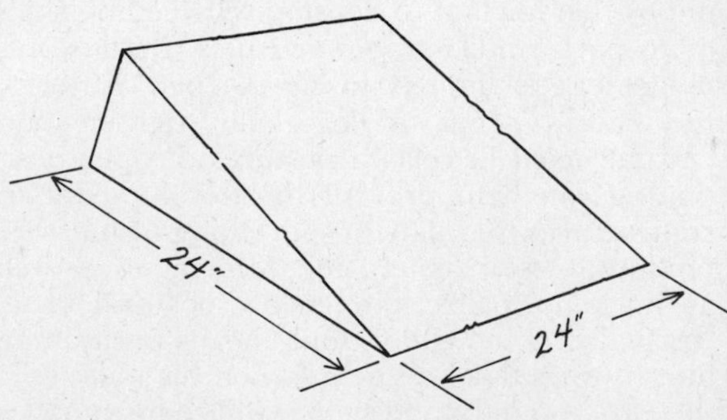

Figure 3. Wedge (may be cut from foam rubber or made of wood covered with padding; height of wedge should be equal to length of child's arms when extended).

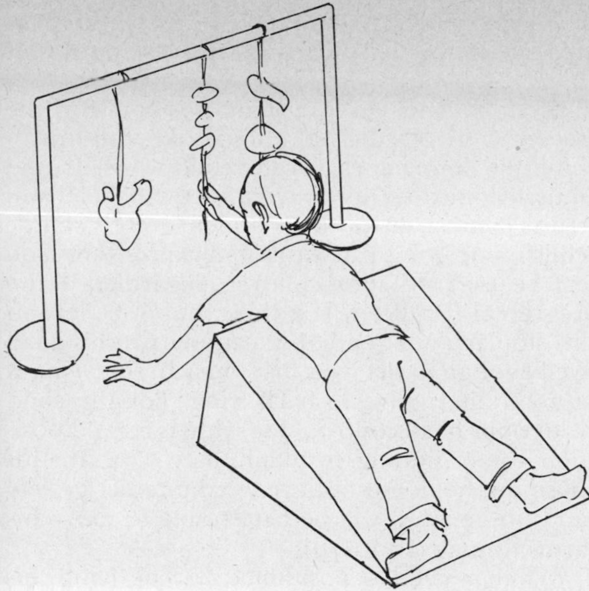

Figure 4. Child properly positioned on wedge.

Figure 6. Child properly positioned on foam rubber roll or rolled up towels or blanket.

are hypotonic. If wedges are unavailable, a blanket or several towels rolled into a long cylinder, and held together by tape or rope, will provide adequate support for some children. The wedge or roll must be the correct size for the child, so that he is able to keep his arms in contact with a hard surface in order to support his weight on them (Figures 4, 5, and 6). Additional rolls, pillows, or sandbags may be needed in order to position the deformed child in more normal alignment.

An alternative to stomach lying on the floor is the use of the prone board, commercially available, or easily made (Figure 7). The prone board can be incorporated with the scooter, in order to provide the moderately physically involved child with total adaptive positioning. Advantages of the prone board are that it is more readily adapted to classroom and family activities, such as eating meals. For an older child, it is a more socially acceptable position than lying on the floor. It is not, however, without its disadvantages. If it is used improperly or for the wrong type of child, the child's motor difficulties may become more severe. Moreover, positioning with the prone board is quite static.

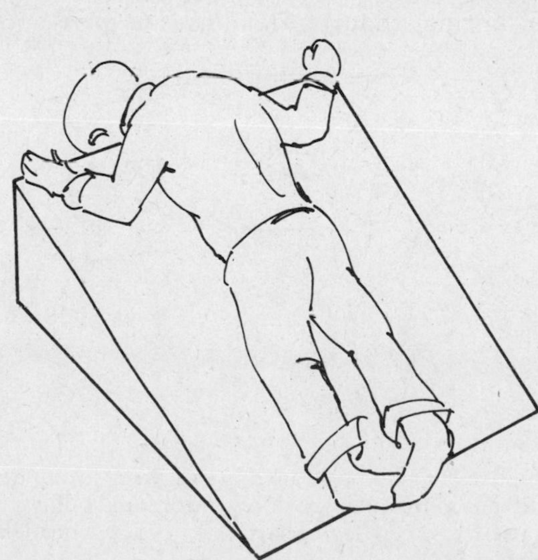

Figure 5. Child improperly positioned on wedge.

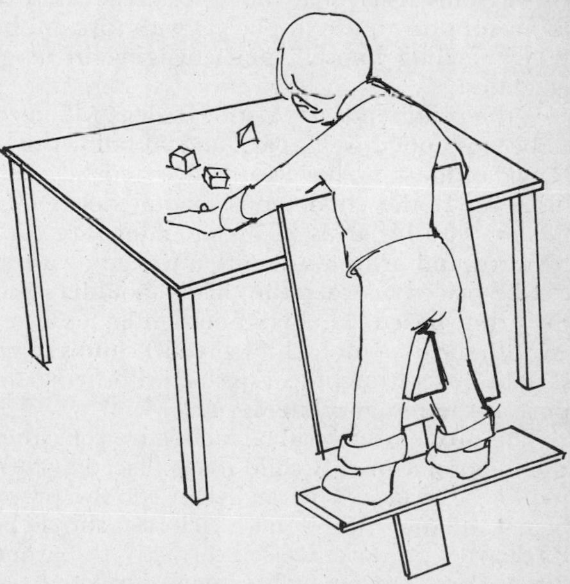

Figure 7. Child properly positioned on prone board.

A child with some mobility may be severely restricted if placed on the board for extensive periods of time. If the prone board is used in situations where most of the other children are not immobile, the safety of the child on the board may be jeopardized. (Very active children may trip over the board.) A final consideration is the positioned child's sense of security. If the child is extremely fearful when placed on the board, he may need to be gradually introduced to it. Fearfulness may cause him to become more stiff, thus negating the positive effects of the positioning. Above all, no child should be placed on the prone board before consultation with his physician or therapist. Although the prone board is popular and readily available, it should not be used indiscriminately.

Positioning of the child on the prone board is done in two steps: (a) placement of the child on the board, and (b) placement of the board in relation to the table. Children whose poor muscle tone gives inadequate support for their skeletal structures must be well supported on the board. The footplate (a footrest attached perpendicularly to the board) should be adjusted so that the child can learn to maintain support from his feet, rather than hanging over the top of the board. The knee plate should provide support so that the child's legs can easily remain straight. His hips should be in contact with a hip support, with straps placed around the hips to keep them as straight as possible. If the child tends to slide to one side, wooden supports may be added to keep the child's back straight; sandbags or pillows may also be used. The child's arms should reach the table so that he can develop support through his arms, or so that he can free one arm from support to use in playing with toys on the table, feeding himself, and engaging in other activities.

If the child tends to be stiff, his legs will need to be positioned well apart, and so pillows or a foam wedge may have to be inserted between his legs. If the child tends to pull down into flexion with his arms (if his shoulders are bent forward and arms also bent), a wedge or a roll can be placed between the child's shoulders and the prone board to help him straighten his arms. As with the hypotonic child, the stiff child's spine should be as straight as possible, with firm support at the hip and knees.

The prone board will be ineffective for either the hypotonic or stiff child if it is placed against too low a surface. The angle between the prone board and the surface on which it rests should be 65 degrees or more. If used correctly, the prone board can help normalize tone, develop head and arm control, prevent deformities, and allow a child to participate easily in classroom and family activities.

Side lying is an excellent position for the severely involved institutionalized child with multiple deformities, for the child whose flaccid muscle tone does not provide adequate head and trunk control, or for the younger severely spastic child. Side lying can easily normalize tone and can be used with most children, regardless of the degree of handicap. If a child cannot be left on his stomach unattended or cannot turn his head well enough to sleep on his stomach, side lying is a good alternative to back lying. For the child with poor head control, side lying is a good position for beginning to manipulate toys. In this position, he does not have to counteract gravity and, in general, will be better able to move his arms to play (Figure 8).

When a child is positioned in side lying, his head should be kept forward with pillows and his legs should be kept apart. Frequently, the child needs to be maintained in this position with sandbags or needs to be positioned against the crib rails with straps or a side-lyer (lateral supports), made of wood. Frequently, positioning the child between sandbags and a wall is adequate if extensor tone is not too poor.

Developmental Skills

Children enrolled in educational programs for the profoundly handicapped often have such severe motor problems that positioning may be used as a goal in itself. If gross motor skills are part of the classroom program, head control or sitting may become an objective. Although this may be appropriate, it is essential for persons working with handicapped children to realize that normal children demonstrate gross motor

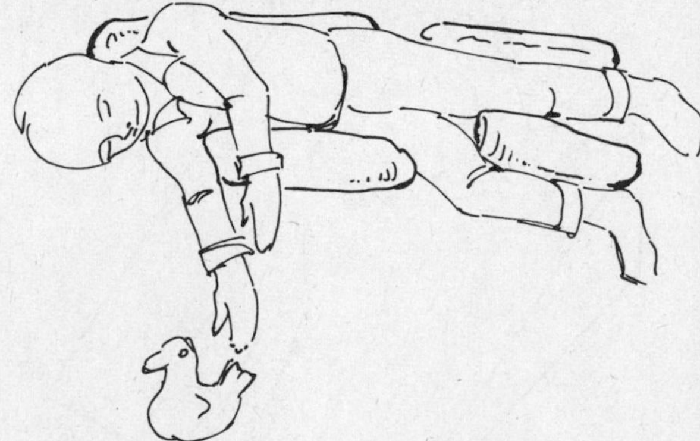

Figure 8. Child positioned in side-lying, using heavy sandbags to maintain position. Additional pillows may be used to keep legs apart and to keep head bent forward.

milestones in connection with learning to adapt more effectively to their environments. When selecting equipment, the child's ability to use the equipment to engage more easily in self-care, feeding, cognitive, and language activities should be linked with positioning considerations. Equipment should be a means of helping the child to demonstrate more adequate skills in all areas of development. It should not simply facilitate motor control, but should extend such control through manipulative environmental applications.

Gross Motor Skills: Mobility

As the normal child becomes mobile in his environment through rolling, creeping, crawling, and finally walking, he learns a great many non-motor skills. His mobility provides access to exploratory and social situations. Most profoundly handicapped children seldom demonstrate independent mobility; even rolling is difficult for many. Subsequently, their environments become limited to what other persons expose them to or make possible for them. The lack of independent mobility may well contribute to the lack of initiative frequently seen in immobile children.

Mobility can be encouraged in children in a variety of ways and, in order to allow the child to explore his environment independently, some form of mobility should be developed as early as possible. The functional abilities of the child will determine the type of equipment chosen to help him develop mobility, and the equipment itself may provide mobility without teaching the child to crawl or to walk. In other words, equipment can be selected to make a child mobile without teaching him a gross motor skill.

Walkers, scooters, crawlers, etc., either commercially available or homemade, can provide mobility (Figure 9). Although selection of these items is best done with the help of a physical or occupational therapist, a scooter is probably the best type of mobility equipment for either the spastic or flaccid child, as well as for the child with severe deformities.

Other types of equipment can help a child develop the gross motor skills of rolling or standing. Placing a child in a sheet or blanket, and slowly moving the child by manipulating the blanket can facilitate learning to roll. Placement of the child in a barrel (Figure 10) if he is not severely deformed can help him learn to turn independently. Rolling should be done in conjunction with activity. A child does not just learn to roll; he learns to roll toward something or out of a position in which he is uncomfortable.

Helping a child to stand can be accomplished in a variety of ways. Some children need only the support of a corner or a table or a wall, in order to develop balance. Generally, these are children without spasticity (or stiffness). When a child needs more support, standing boards (Figure 11) or chimney tables, commercially available, may be used. However, it is often difficult to observe how well the child is standing or whether he is using his arms to hang on to the table, rather than supporting his weight on his feet. The back-support standing board is easier to build by hand, and a positioned child can be easily observed to make sure the equipment is assisting him in standing.

There are many ways in which a child can be helped to learn to sit independently or to sit with support. A younger child without much physical (motor) involvement is likely to learn to sit with minimal modifications to give him support. A child with stiffness (spasticity) may need considerable modification in order to be properly positioned in sitting (Figure 12). It may not be possible to place the older institutionalized child with multiple deformities in a sitting position in good body alignment. Because poor body alignment may contribute to the further development of deformities, the child may not be a candidate for sitting, or the pros and cons of improper positioning with improved functioning may have to be carefully considered.

Many types of wheeled chairs are commercially available for both children and adults. When purchasing commercial sitting equipment, it is important to assess carefully the child and his needs and to match them carefully with the benefits that a particular piece of commercial equipment offers. No one type of commercial equipment is best for all children, although some chairs are more easily modified to fit a number of different children than others. In selecting a wheelchair, the following should be considered: the amount of use inside and outside; ease in putting a child into the chair and removing him from it; the amount of modification which has to be made in order to fit the child properly; the child's potential for wheeling the chair himself; the amount of increased function the chair provides; the durability of the chair and its cost. Help in appropriately fitting a child may be obtained from an occupational or physical therapist or sometimes from the company which supplies the chair. (A list of equipment sources is given at the end of this article.)

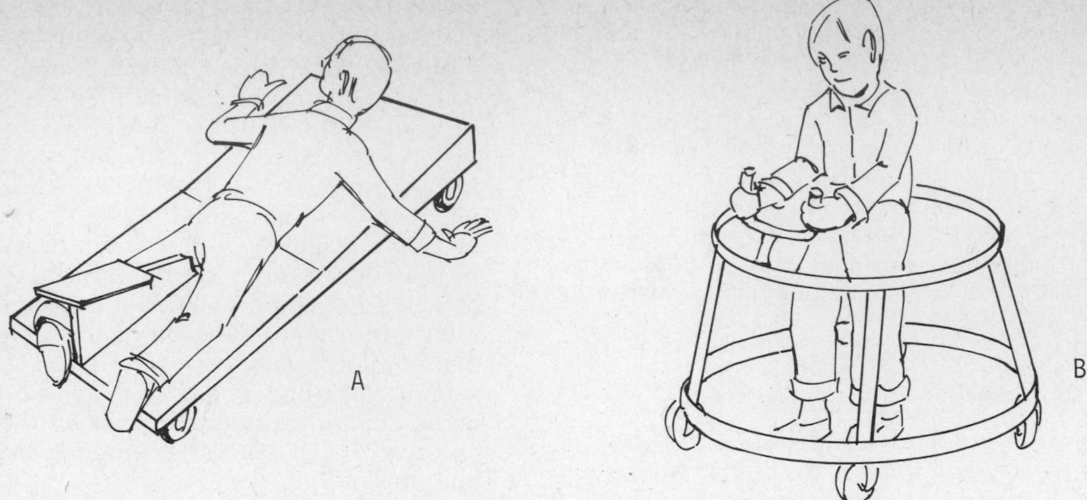

Figure 9. Types of mobility equipment.
A. Scooter adapted for child with bilateral flexion deformities at the knees.
B. Ring walker for use with child without extensor spasticity in the lower extremities.
C. Crawler for younger child.
D. Bike adapted for use by less involved child.

SELF-HELP SKILLS

The child with severe motor involvement may often be penalized in other areas of development because of his physical inabilities. A child with poor balance in sitting may be unable to free his arms from supporting himself when sitting, in order to use them for dressing. If fine motor abilities, such as grasp and release, are impaired by contractures, deformities, or spasticity, fine motor skills in dressing may not be possible. In planning a self-help program for the profoundly retarded child, ways may have to be devised which will either circumvent the amount of

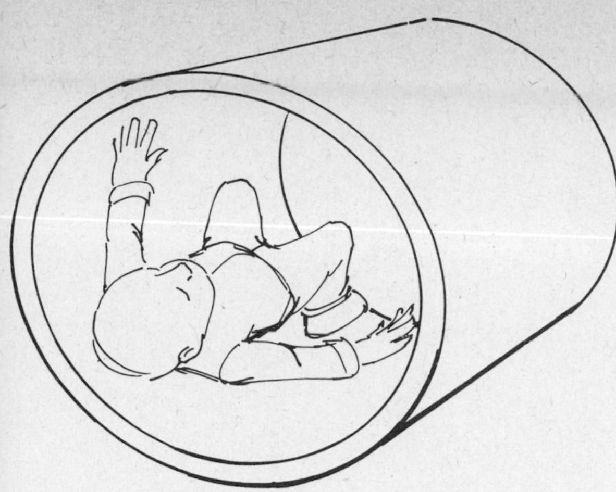

Figure 10. Child rolling in padded barrel.

motor skill required by an activity, or will provide alternate means of performing the motor skills involved. Use of equipment can help a child perform self-help skills which he might be unable to perform on his own. Many types of equipment to assist in dressing, feeding, and self-feeding have been designed, and are available through commercial sources or in several books written about activities of daily living (ADL) equipment. (Sources are listed at the end of this article.)

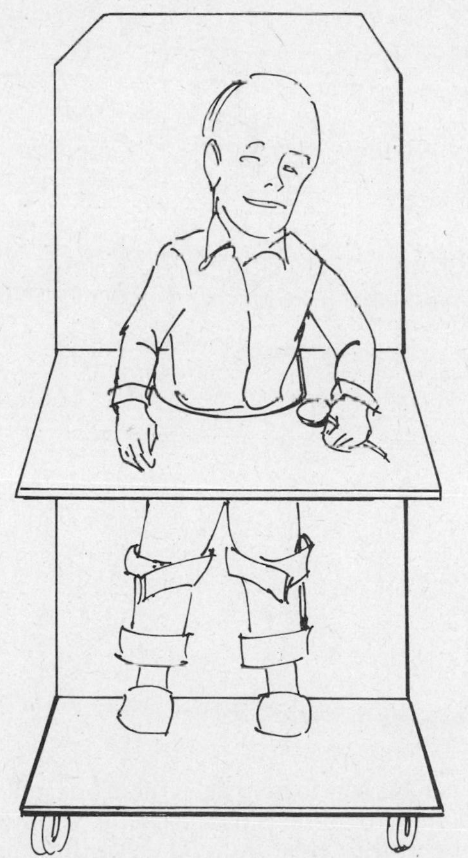

Figure 11. Child in supported standing position, using standing table.

Choosing self-help equipment for a child requires the same careful assessment of his functional-physical-developmental levels as selecting positioning or gross motor equipment. A few guidelines follow:

1. Make sure that the child's position is maximal for performing feeding or dressing skills. Sitting balance should be well developed (either independently or through equipment) to the point that the child is able to free both of his arms to use for activity, rather than for balance.
2. Make sure the child's position is such that tone is normalized. If the child is very stiff or too hypotonic, he will be unable to use his arms for function.
3. Know exactly what function you want the child to perform and exactly what motor action and skill are required. Select equipment to perform or to assist in performing those motor skills the child is unable to do on his own.
4. Equipment will not teach a child how to chew or hold a spoon, or take off his shirt. Equipment will only make it more possible for him to perform the motor skills. He still will have to be taught how to do the activity.

Toileting

Sometimes toilet training is not attempted with the younger profoundly handicapped child because it is too difficult to position him properly on the toilet. Equipment can help a physically handicapped child to sit on the toilet and, if the equipment is properly fit to normalize tone, the child will be physically better able to use the toilet when placed there. When children who are very stiff are positioned improperly on the toilet, their abdominal muscles become very tight, making it physically impossible for them to eliminate. The hypotonic child must be provided with trunk and hip stability to achieve enough tone in the abdominal muscles to eliminate when on the toilet.

Commercial equipment is usually designed for infants, young children, or adults. For the child outside these age ranges, toilet equipment will have to be specially built in order to obtain normalized tone through positioning (Figure 13).

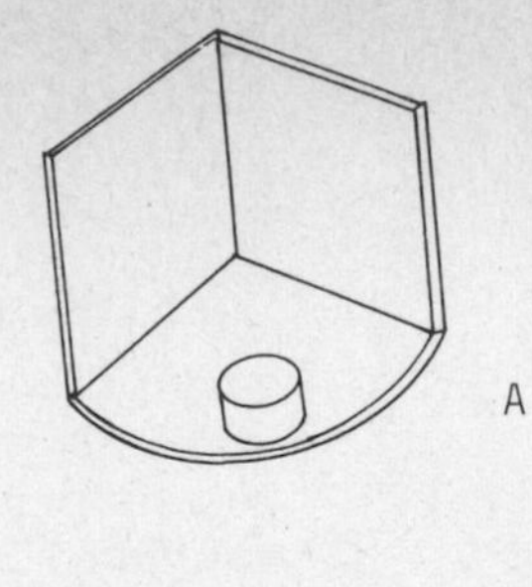

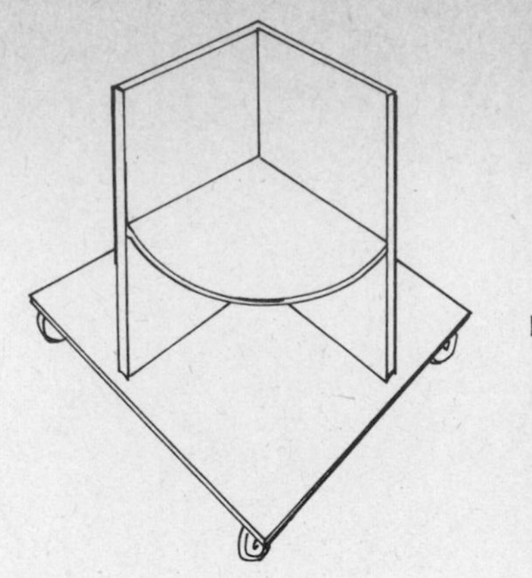

Figure 12. Homemade sitting apparatuses.

A. Corner chair with center post to facilitate leg abduction.
B. Upright corner chair.
C. Tilted corner chair for hydrocephalic child.
D. Sawhorse chair.
E. Pony chair.

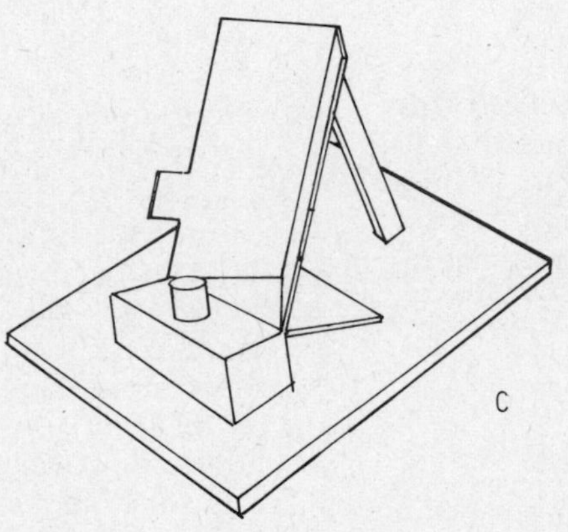

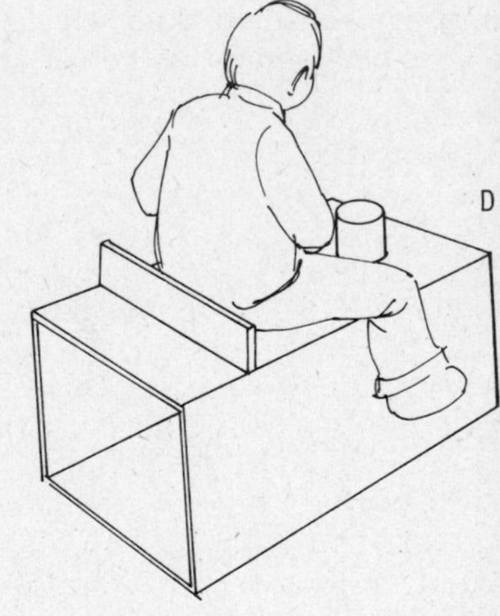

Until a profoundly handicapped child develops the muscle control necessary to be toilet trained, modifications in diapering can be utilized. These can help to prevent deformities and can assist in normalizing tone in the legs. A child with stiffness in the legs should have extra diapers put between his legs to help keep them apart. For the child with "frog" legs (i.e., legs flexed outward), it is helpful to twist the diaper so that the legs are not forced apart by the amount of diaper between them.

For younger infants who are very stiff, diaper-

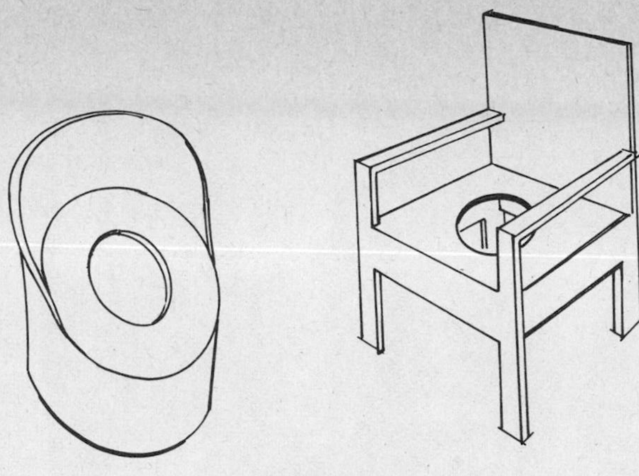

Figure 13. Toileting modifications.

ing can be done with the child lying on his stomach. The diaper then is pinned or taped in the back instead of in the front.

Cognitive Development

The developmental needs of the profoundly handicapped child are often so great that educational programs for these children have emphasized self-help and gross and fine motor skills. Normal children develop motor and cognitive skills in interaction with each other. Although equipment has value in programming for the handicapped child, equipment is only a way of providing the child with a means of interacting with his environment. All equipment should be used for the purpose of helping the child interact more functionally; it should not be used as an end in itself. A properly positioned child will be more easily fed or may learn to feed himself because he is better able to move his arm in a hand-to-mouth pattern. A prone board may give him the stability necessary to enable him to play with toys. Normalized tone may make it possible for him to eliminate when placed on the toilet, or more normal tone may allow the muscles to move so that the child can vocalize or babble. Equipment will not teach him to perform these skills; he still needs to be taught how, through the teaching methods most effective for him.

Recently, specific equipment has been developed to help a child respond in academic-cognitive learning tasks. Head pointers or arm splints have been effective in enabling children, previously unable to respond motorically, to point in response to questioning. Adaptations with both these basic devices have enabled children and adults to feed themselves, type, and write.

Several non-verbal communication systems have been used with profoundly handicapped children in conjunction with head pointers or other equipment, to allow the non-verbal child to communicate. Electronic communication boards can be activated with the slightest motor response and frequently have been combined with electric typewriters to allow a child more sophisticated communication. Such devices must be used with good gross motor positioning (prone board, sitting, or standing) in order for the child to operate them efficiently. The cost of these devices may be prohibitive, but they do demonstrate that much more creative use of equipment with profoundly handicapped children and adults is possible.

With children of lower functioning, a head pointer may be too difficult to operate. Typing may not be relevant. Basic toys and readiness educational materials may then be modified to enable the child to respond more effectively to his environment. When trying to develop cognitive skills in a severely physically handicapped child, the teacher should attempt, through material selection and design, to teach problem-solving skills, however basic, without also requiring significant motoric response. A physically handicapped child may never have sufficiently well controlled grasp and release to stack one-inch cubes; however, he may be able to grasp, stack, and release large foam rubber blocks, or he may learn to manipulate and match bean bag shapes, rather than wooden ones. If the teacher has established well formulated cognitive goals for the child, material selection to match these goals should be possible.

Environmental and Child-Centered Prosthetics

The following three cases are used as examples of the use of environmental and child-centered prosthetics to provide the opportunity for the child to succeed in a normative environment.

Paul: Participator Rather than Spectator

Paul is a multiply handicapped, 16-year-old boy who attends the adolescent education program at Ryan High School in Omaha, Nebraska. Previously, he would have attended school in a totally segregated setting; the present arrangement permits Paul to interact regularly with non-delayed high school students. He is one of 12 severely handicapped youngsters participating in this integrated program sponsored by Region VI, the Eastern Nebraska Community Office of Retardation (ENCOR).

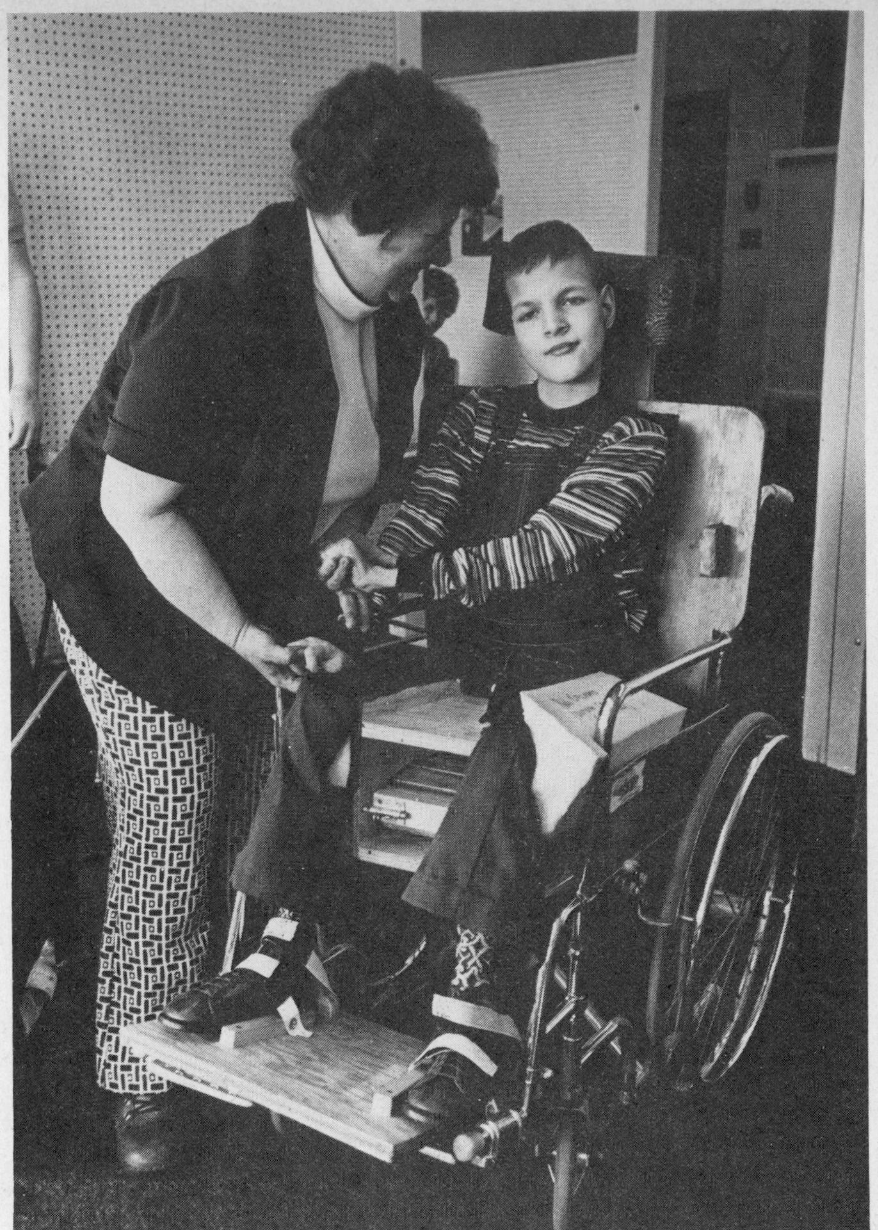

Figure 14.
The adapted chair functions to support Paul in the upright position. Special inserts and devices may be required to fit the special needs of the person.

Paul had never used any adaptive equipment before age 12 because no program was available. As a result, he lost out on a great many opportunities to interact with the environment. He spent all of his time in a horizontal position, from which his only perception of the world was via ceilings. No one had any idea how interested or alert he really was.

Paul's ability to move is severely limited without maximum environmental supports. As a result, he has almost no opportunity to use those skills he does possess without help. To give Paul a chance to sit erect requires adapted special equipment (Figure 14). For instance, a student like Paul may not have the ability to hold his head up and maintain an erect trunk. He requires individually-tailored equipment to assume those postures that most persons assume automatically. If Paul is not well-positioned, such body functions as circulation, respiration, and digestion will also be poor. As discussed earlier, proper feeding procedures, developmental education activities, and other available programs are more readily accessible to Paul in an upright posture. The positioning chair renders him

Photography by Robert Coleman, Nebraska Psychiatric Institute, Omaha, Nebraska.

mobile, so he can become a part of a peer group; his teacher can bring him into his surroundings, rather than leaving him on the floor apart from the others. With the use of an adapted commode, Paul has rapidly completed toilet training.

Usually, candidates for adaptive equipment are positioned so that their hips are maintained at a right angle. This impedes the natural spastic tendencies in some reflex-bound children. It may be necessary to pad the back of the chair with 1-inch foam rubber and naugahyde. Chest supports or side supports can be used if the person has limited head and trunk control. The detachable neck pillow is placed so that the back of the head and neck are supported. A device shaped like a half-circle is placed midway between the ear lobe and the shoulder, with great care to avoid pressure on these body surfaces.

A ventilated wedge seat for the sitting surface is contoured for comfort. The device distributes the body weight along the thigh. Elevation at the knees of ½ to 2 inches helps to control scissoring or frogging. If the child is extremely thin or has severe deformity of the hips, a padded cut-out seat may be used. This seat relieves pressure on the bony portions of the buttocks. A seat belt should be attached to the bottom of all chairs so that, when the belt is fastened around the child, it will cross just at the bend in the hips when he is in a sitting position. With the use of the wedge seat and seat belt, it is possible to hold the child back in the chair, so that the body weight is supported by the thighs and not by the lower back (a poor and uncomfortable posture that is seen in many cerebral palsied persons when these devices are not used). Prolonged periods of weight-bearing on the lower back increase the likelihood of spinal curvature.

Many people need aids to stabilize their feet, legs, arms, and hands. Those with uncontrolled movements (athetosis) need stabilization of three extremities, in order to use the fourth extremity voluntarily. In addition, by stabilizing the upper arms close to the body, with the hands resting on the laptray in front of them, they may be able to support their body trunk in better alignment. Velcro straps are used for stabilization. In cases where there is an undue amount of stress exerted on the feet, wooden foot cut outs with Velcro straps are constructed. The cut-outs should be sufficiently large to allow the shoe to fit snugly in the wooden form. Other adaptive supports may be necessary for isolated cases of severe body deformity.

With his body stability assured by this equipment, Paul is able to control his own head. With

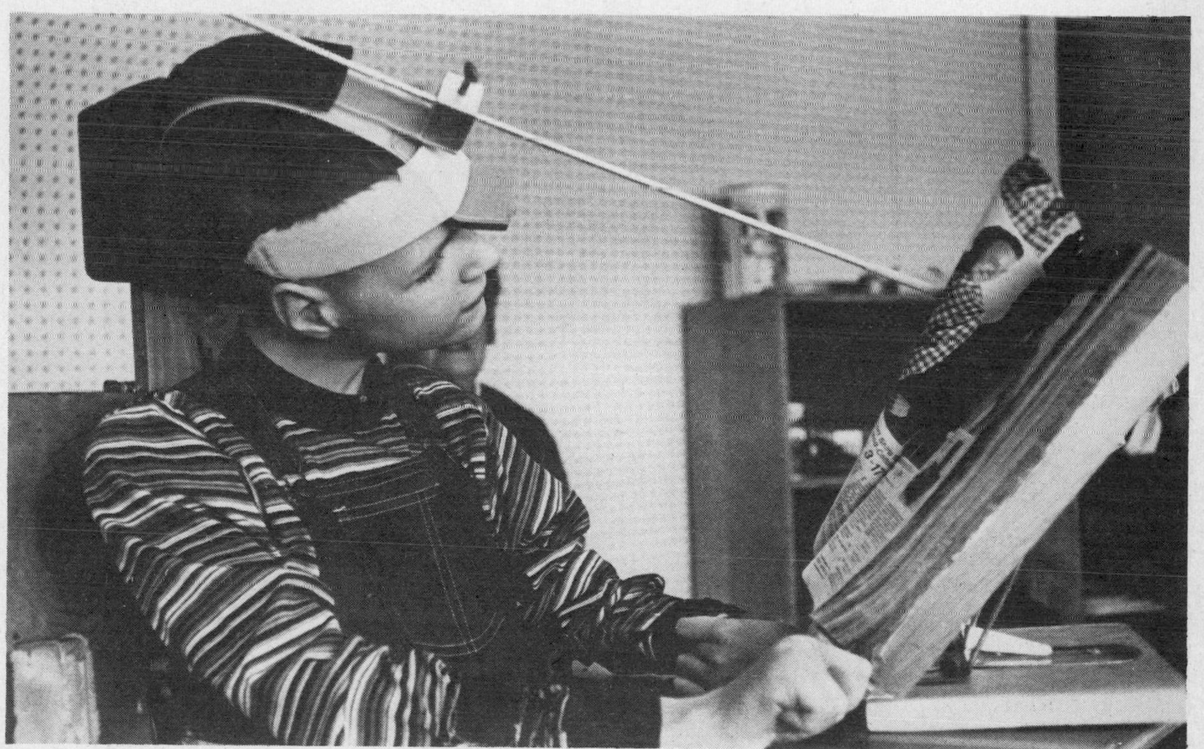

Figure 15. With a "head stylus", Paul is able to work independently. All that is required is the ability to move his head forward, backward, and sideways.

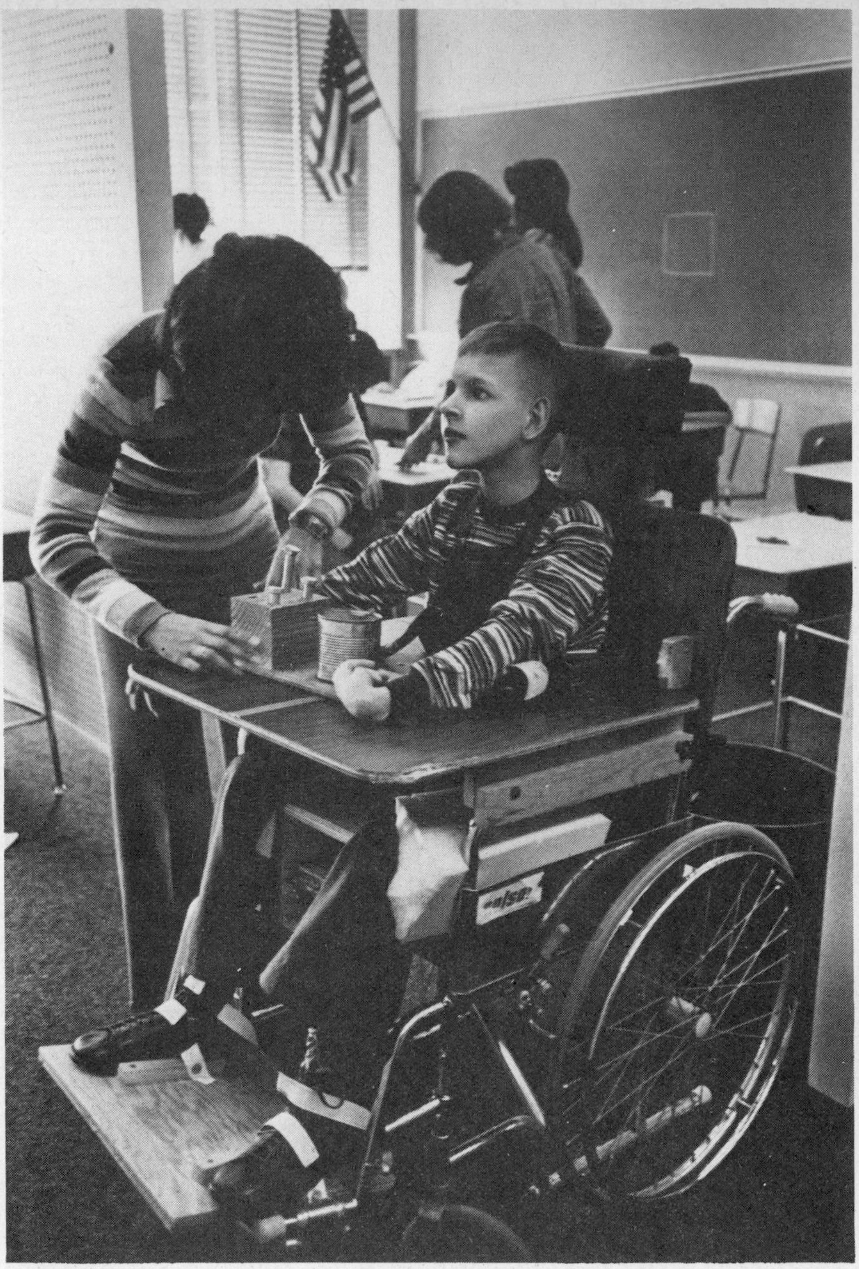

Figure 16.
Paul is able to work on age-appropriate learning tasks in the integrated classroom setting through the assistance of the adapted chair. Stabilizing several extremities renders at least one limb functional. Paul is able to maintain good eye contact with both the teacher and the learning materials in the upright position.

the head stylus, he is able to read and enjoy quiet moments, controlling his environment and life space as he chooses (Figure 15). The stylus can also be used to move cards for matching, sorting, and categorizing. If the situation is properly structured, and allows the individual to experiment with moving the objects, accidental correct movements can be self-reinforcing and rapidly become purposeful. Paul's positioning chair gives him a mobility that would be otherwise impossible. (Figure 16). He can now move from the classroom to the dining room to the outdoors. Because the chair is collapsible and thus, portable, Paul can travel to and from school, on excursions, in fact anywhere that a teacher or his parents will take him. Paul's world, once so small, is now wide and interesting to him.

Ronda: Reading the Readiness

Ronda, aged 10, attends J. P. Lord School for orthopedically handicapped children, which is part of the Omaha public school system, and lives at Hattie B. Munroe Pavillion Residence on the University of Nebraska Medical Center campus with other orthopedically handicapped children. This residence is necessary because there is no school program in her home town which could provide her with the requisite educational/developmental experience.

Ronda is a severely involved youngster, sometimes described as a "wet noodle." Her attempts to tell people her needs, by erratic arm movements, caused her to lose head control and eye contact with those around her. The result was that the total effort to communicate and learn took more energy than she had. With the stability of the positioning chair, and with educational materials raised to eye level when her head was upright, her learning abilities and opportunities were greatly increased. Ronda learned to turn her eyes to the right and left to signify "yes" and "no," and this skill increased her communication considerably. When the staff learned that eye movements were her most potent asset, they began to explore a range of alternatives for capitalizing on this skill.

The teaching staff introduced the Bliss Communication System, a symbol system based on visual units of meaning, rather than on sound or phonetic units like the alphabet. When the Bliss symbols were combined with physical stabilization, eye movements, and the educational materials presented in the angled vertical position (Figure 17), Ronda was able to move away from a laborious process of pointing to a color code system to count or spell. She can now give such messages as: "I went in a car to the lake with my parents to go fishing in a boat," using all noun symbols or pictures from a magazine. She is also using an electronic communication system, through which she can visually track lighted symbols at 2-second intervals, "talking" faster than most of the staff! This is remarkable progression from the early stages when Ronda was perceived by the staff as being severely limited intellectually as a result of her physical disabilities.

Shown this progress, the staff became more inventive and explored alternatives for expanding Ronda's control even further. An overhead pulley feeder (Figure 18) was introduced. By giving her left elbow support with an overhead sling, and by strapping her forearm and hand to the "eater," the staff discovered that, if Ronda was allowed to try to bring food to her mouth, her severe jaw extension and tongue thrust decreased. Although she is not completely independent, her self-esteem, body perceptions, and enthusiasm have skyrocketed as a result of a small extension of self-control. Not only was the process powerfully reinforcing to Ronda, but it was a potent motivator for her teachers as well.

Ronda's chances for independent ambulation are minimal. Ronda, however, enjoys "stomping around" while supported. Because she is naturally a sitting and supine child, the vertical

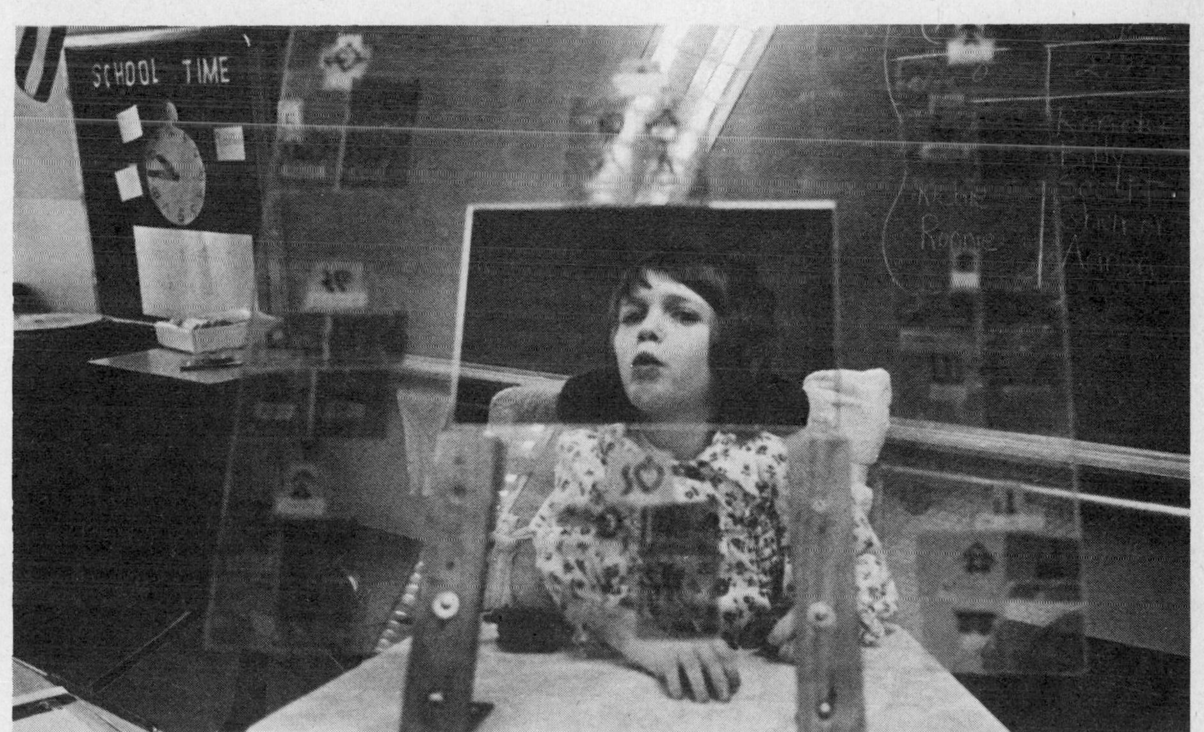

Figure 17. Ronda can communicate very rapidly when materials are presented in the angled, vertical position which allows her to maintain head and eye control.

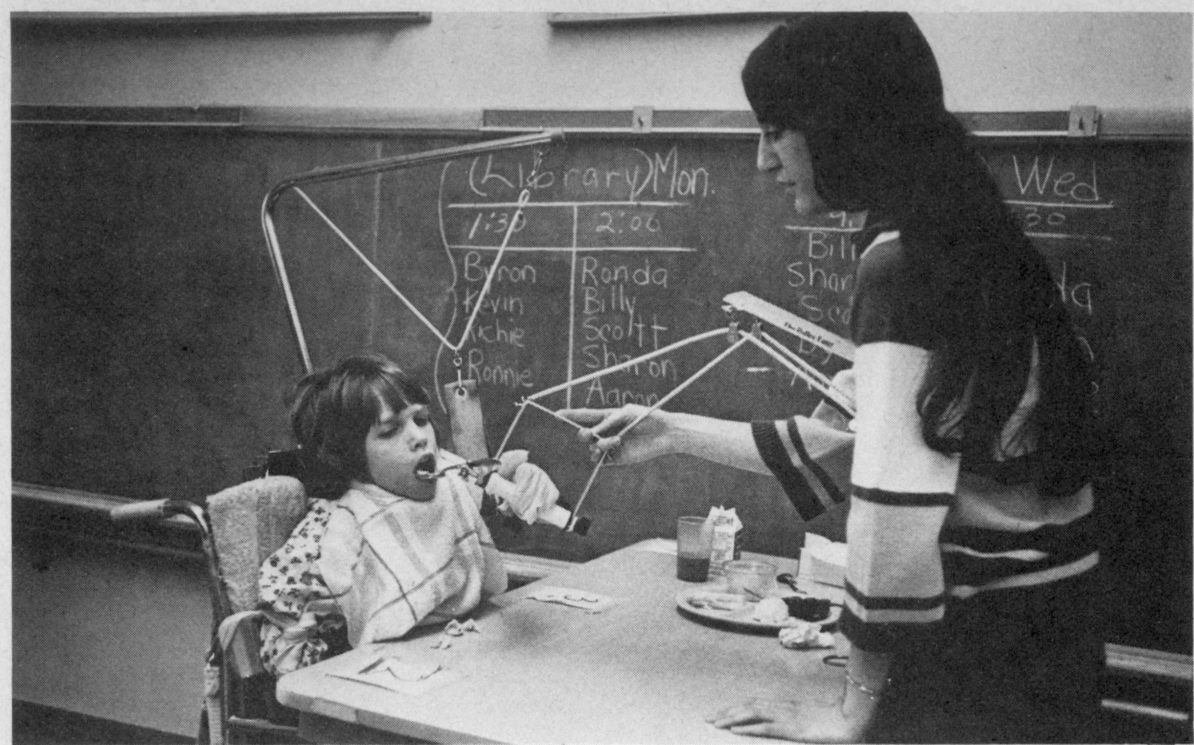

Figure 18. The "overhead feeder" allows Ronda the dignity and control to feed herself with minimal assistance. An added benefit was an obvious decrease in jaw and tongue thrust.

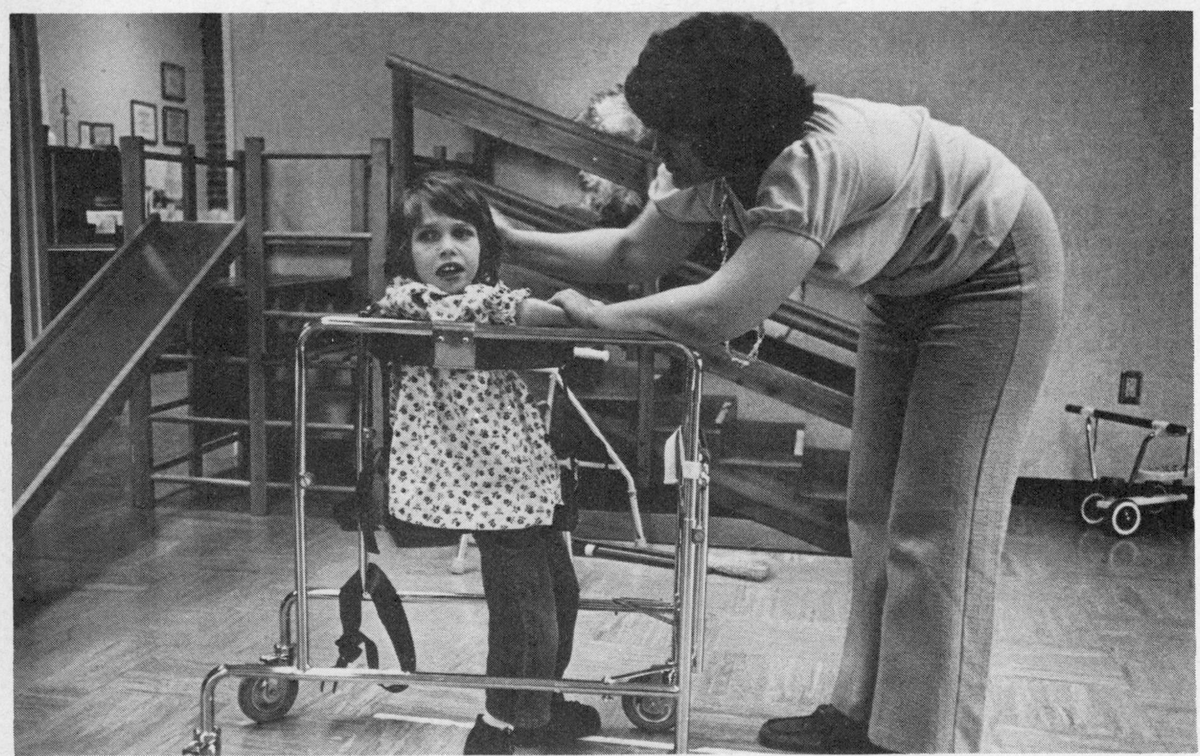

Figure 19. Ronda is allowed to experiment with spatial relationships such as backward, forward, and sideways with supportive equipment.

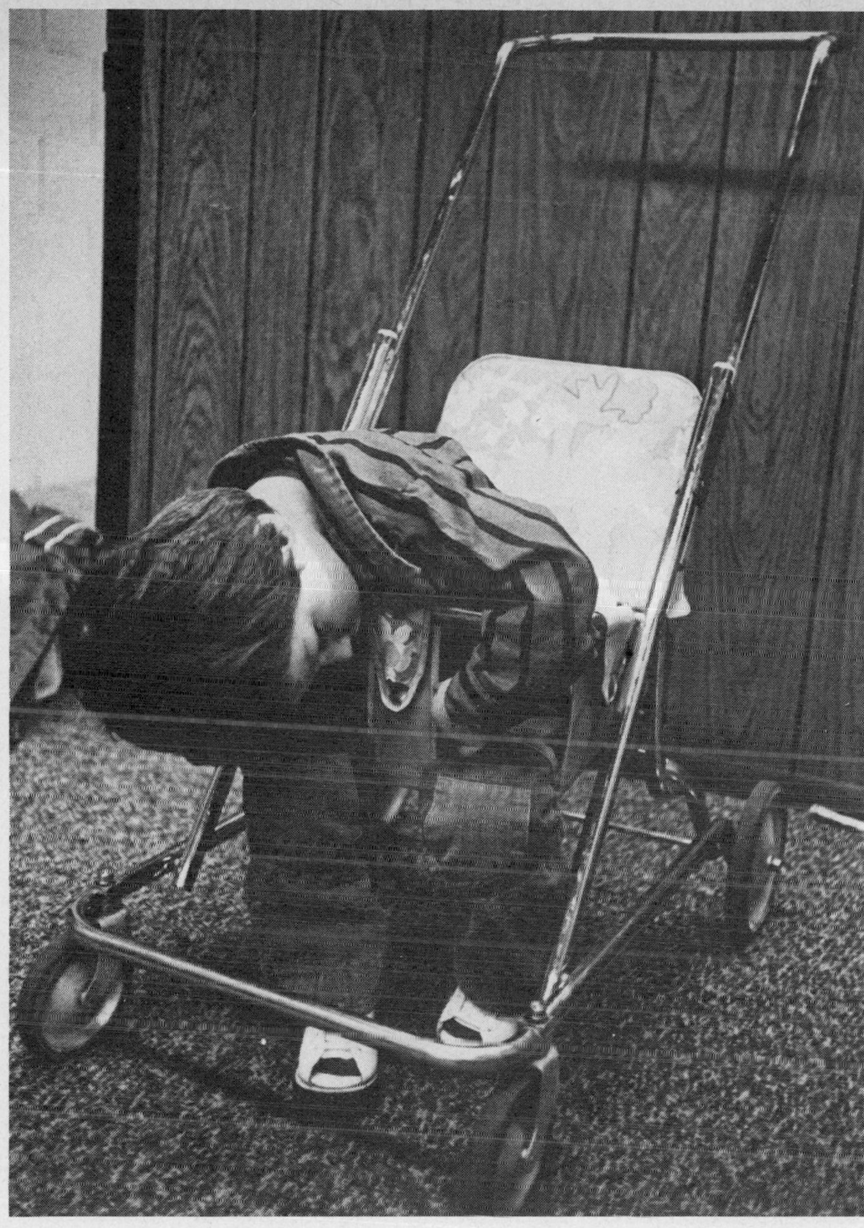

Figure 20.
Without adaptive supports, Chad loses control and is unable to move his body or interact with his environment. Being in positions like this for extended periods promotes irreversible deformities.

position was a refreshing change for her. By introducing a supporting piece of equipment (Figure 19), she could propel herself and explore a whole new world. Such concepts as forward, backwards, and sideways gained a concrete meaning.

The total effect of this process was an astonishing revelation for those who had perceived Ronda as a totally dependent child whose future hinged on the presence of other people to meet her needs.

Chad: Made To Order

Chad is a three-year-old who participates in ENCOR's Coordinated Early Education Program (CEEP) which places developmentally delayed children, regardless of the extent of their handicap, among their age peers in a normal community educational setting.

On the floor, Chad demonstrated the ability to raise his arms to reach an object, but, as the effort and excitement involved in accomplishing the task increased, he became stiff and locked into a deformed position. When placed in a toddler stroller, he was left to his own devices and rolled up into a ball (Figure 20).

Obviously, little learning can occur in either of these positions. There is also danger of physical deformities occurring over time if a child is allowed to remain in these postures. The place to begin with a child like Chad is to assess care-

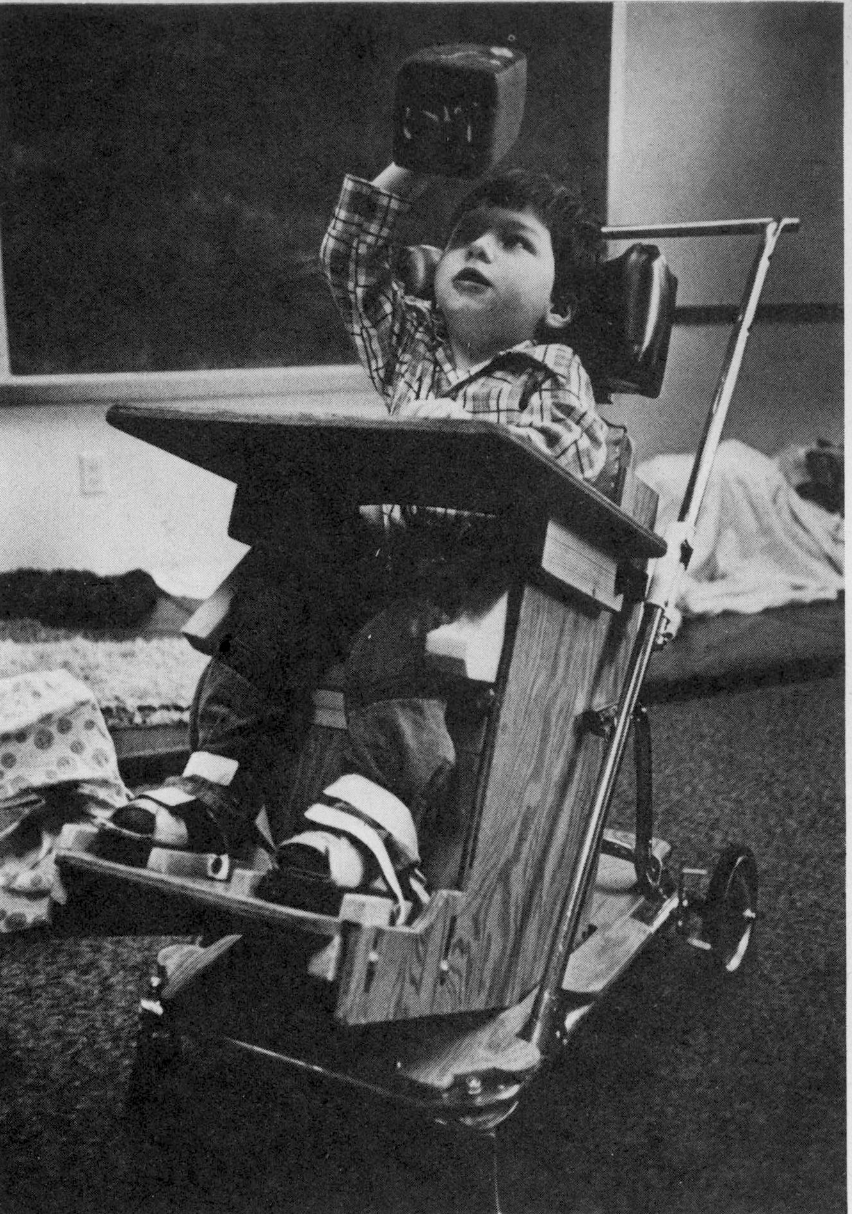

Figure 21.
After individual assessment by a team of developmental therapists, the "positioning stroller" was built to meet Chad's particular needs. He is now able to manipulate objects at eye level.

fully both his strengths and weaknesses. To provide Chad with the wide range of support systems he needs to grow and develop, his parents, classroom teacher, and a number of different specialists need to work together to design a program for him. Obviously, proper positioning was the priority need established by them all: mother (feeding), teacher (playing), specialists (correcting deformities). This required that the developmental therapist assess Chad's reflex patterns, changes in postural tone, visual perceptual status, and movement potential and then establish with the teacher the learning objectives for him. Because each child may combine skills and deficits in each of these areas in different ways, *individual* assessment is essential to planning the curriculum. The need for adaptive equipment to facilitate developmental growth becomes obvious when the results of the assessment are known. In Chad's case, the staff recognized his interest and efforts to reach and bat at objects when he was on the floor, but his posture did not allow him to succeed. They provided Chad with a special seating apparatus to compensate for his postural deficits. Chad was able to use his arms not only to reach for, but actually to grasp objects, bringing them into his visual field (Figure 21). This positioning stroller also converts to a car seat and can be detached from the frame and set in a more upright position on a platform during feeding time. During feeding, when he was more vertical, Chad began

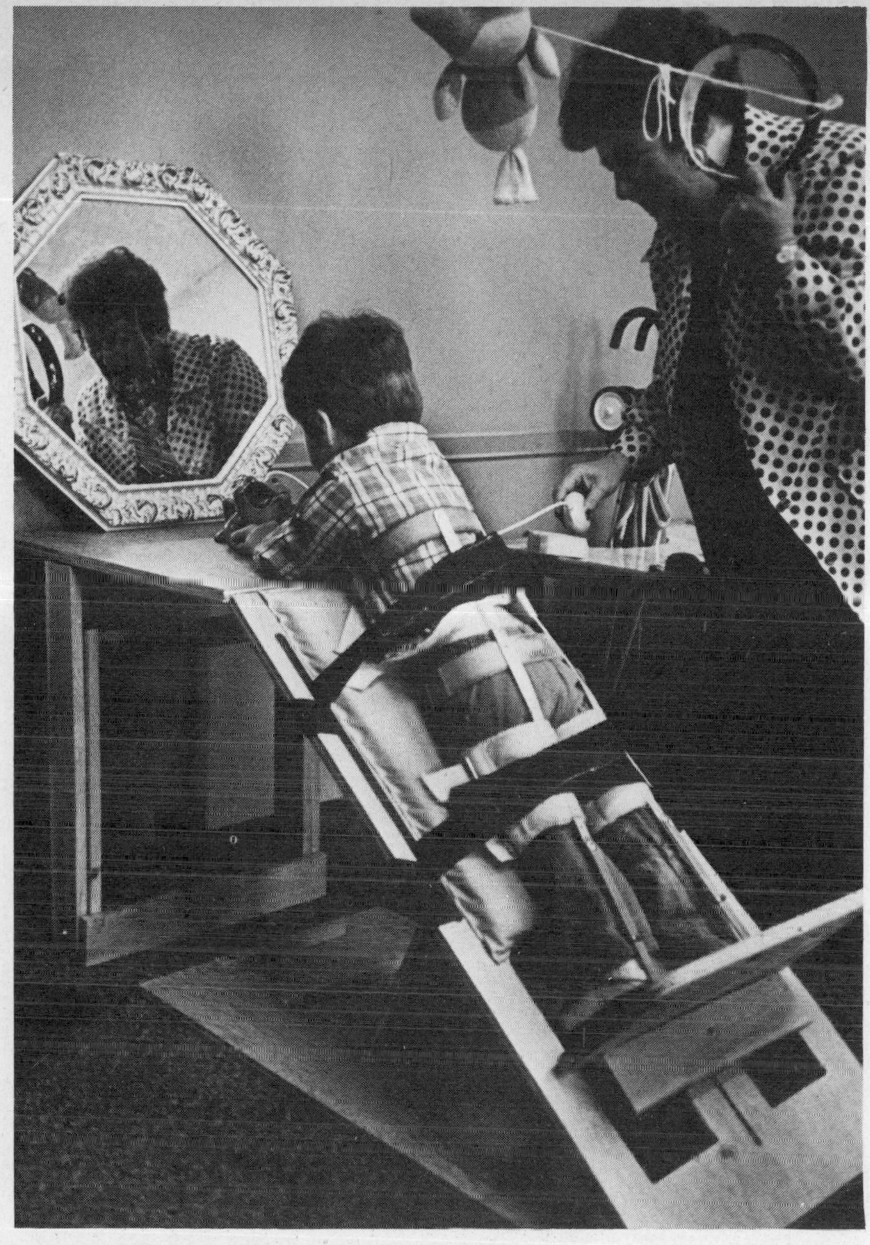

Figure 22.
The prone-tilt table allows Chad to work with his hands in midline while gradually introducing him to the upright position. Regardless of the degree of handicap, all persons need to put body weight on their hip sockets to prevent dislocation.

to show more and more control over his head and trunk and would raise his own head to receive the spoon. When the staff saw this, new program opportunities became apparent, including use of the prone tilt board (Figure 22), an apparatus which gradually introduces the child to the upright vertical position and affords a playing surface to engage hands in exploration. It places hips in alignment so that the joints will develop and, thus, not dislocate from lack of use. As Chad developed even more head and trunk control, the staff introduced him to the stand-up table (Figure 23).

With the routine assessment and progressive equipment changes, Chad's progress in both gross motor and cognitive development were stimulated. Had these and other services not been available to him, he might have remained in an infantile position, facing the possibility of multiple deformities, such as curvature of the spine, joint deformity, frequent respiratory congestion, and, finally, sensory deprivation resulting in total withdrawal.

While we are very cautious not to set the child up for failure, we must also remember not to set *ourselves* up for failure. To add the frustration of not succeeding immediately, the physical coordination and body flexibility of children like Chad change very rapidly according to growth, the kind of day they are having, the effects of their

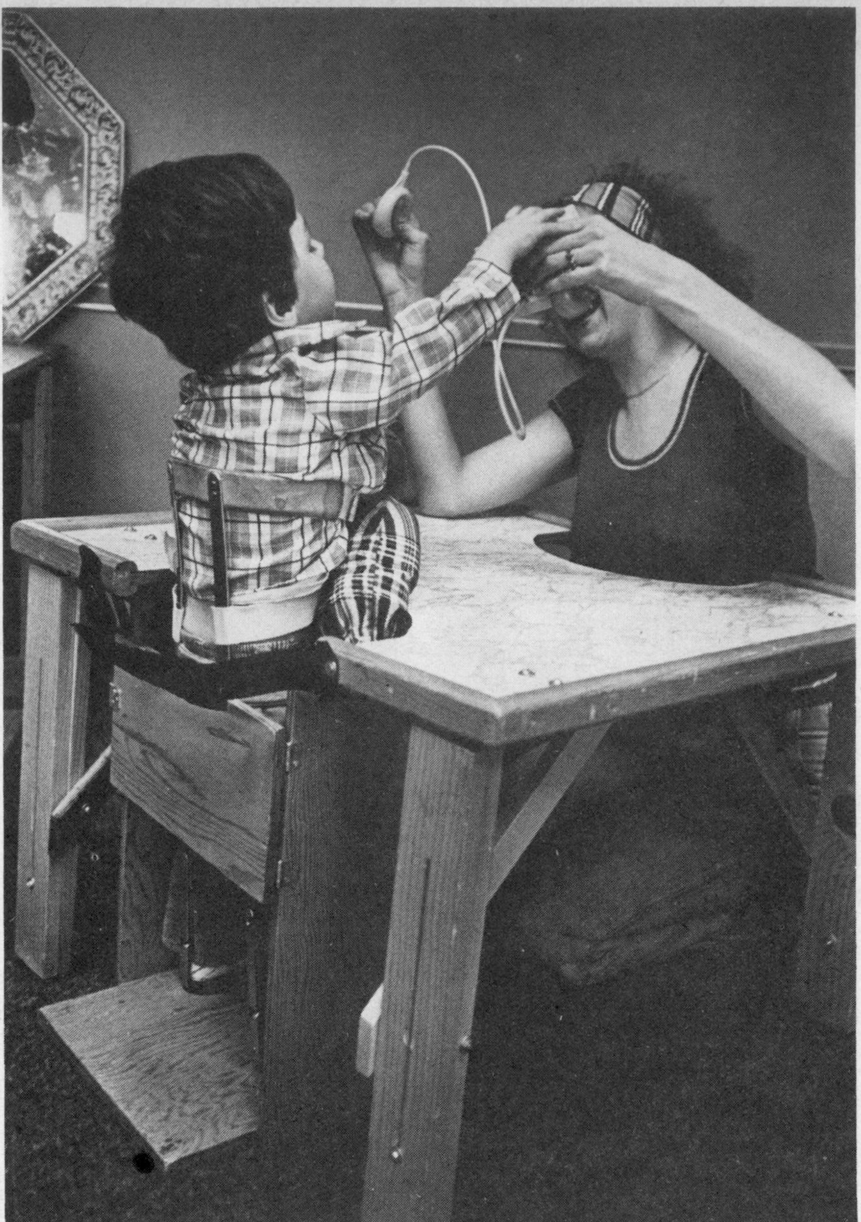

Figure 23.
Therapy and developmental education activities can be combined. Chad is working on head and trunk control, weight bearing, eye-hand perception, and fine motor coordination, all in a single activity.

medication, and other factors. As a result, it is necessary to have different types of equipment for different types of activities. The children do not stay in one piece of equipment all day long. If the child's school day is to be optimally enriching, he needs equipment that enables him to experience a number of activities in a number of different positions.

Conclusion

Even today, people with the potential of Paul, Ronda, and Chad can be seen in large institutions and infirmaries, spending the better part of their lives in cribs in grossly deformed body positions. The full range of options necessary to help these youngsters develop is still not offered. Some of the options we have described here require architectural changes, money, training of parents and staff in special skills, and techniques to support the orthopedically handicapped person in integrated settings. Basic to such programs is the absolute faith that, given the right environments, opportunities and adaptations, people like Paul, Ronda, and Chad can grow and develop. This belief leads to the recognition that labels should not determine one's future. Rather, all persons, regardless of their limitations, can participate, communicate, and determine their roles in life.

Sources of Additional Information

Books on Adaptive Equipment

Finnie, N. *Handling the young cerebral palsied child at home.* New York: E. P. Dutton, 1975.

Robinault, I. (Ed.). *Functional aids for the multiply handicapped.* Hagerstown: Maryland: Harper & Row, 1973. (Available in paper from United Cerebral Palsy Association, Inc., for $3.50.)

Pamphlets on Adaptive Equipment

Aids for the special. (Order from 131 Sayre St., Elizabethtown, N.J. 07208.)

ICTA catalogue. *Aids for children.* (Order from ICTA Information Center, FACK, S-161 03, Bromma 3, Sweden.)

In-Service Training Manual, United Cerebral Palsy Association of New York State. (Order from Department of Mental Hygiene, 815 2nd Avenue, New York, N.Y. 10017.)

Please help us help ourselves. (Order from Indiana University Medical Center, Occupational Therapy Department, Indianapolis, Indiana.)

Selected equipment for pediatric rehabilitation. (Order from Blythedale Children's Hospital, Bradhurst Avenue, Valhalla, N.Y. 10595.)

Selected Companies Which Sell Adaptive Equipment Appropriate for Profoundly Handicapped Children and Adults:

Be-OK Self Help Aids. (Fred Sammons, Inc., Box 32, Brookfield, Ill. 60513).

CLEO Living Aids. (3957 Mayfield Road, Cleveland, Ohio 44121).

Contourpedic Corporation. (1106 Edgewater Ave., Ridgefield, N.J.).

Preston Catalogue (J. A. Preston Corporation, 71 5th Ave., New York, N.Y. 10003).

Adaptive Equipment (and Chair) Companies:

Adaptive Equipment Company. (Mr. Max Sallack, Chesterland, Ohio). Company makes adaptive chairs, prone boards, pony chairs, corner chairs, wheelchair inserts, tricycle pedals, equilibrium boards, etc. Company also will design and make equipment for individuals.

Adaptive Therapeutic Systems. (36 Howe Street, New Haven, Conn. 06511). Company makes a specialized chair, prone boards, feeding and writing equipment, etc.)

Gunnel Manufacturing Company. (7768 Waterman Road, Vassar, Michigan 48768).

L. Mulholland and Associates. (1563 Los Angeles Ave., Ventura, Calif. 93003).

Ortho Kinetics, Inc. (1225 Pearl Street, Waukesha, Wisc. 53186). Gunnel, Mulholland, and Ortho Kinetics manufacture various types of adaptive chairs—appropriate for some multiply handicapped children.

Selected Articles on Adaptive Equipment:

Altschuler, S., Pidcoe, S., & Moss, B. Oral eating device for food placement. *American Journal of Occupational Therapy,* 1975, *29,* 229.

Arcangel, P., & Schoenthal, W. Conversion of ring walker to chair for child with multiple orthopedic deformities. *Physical Therapy,* 1973, *53,* 1296–7.

Colby, J. Portable child-size tilt table. *Physical Therapy,* 1974, *54,* 26.

Cristarella, M. Comparison of straddling and sitting apparatus for the spastic cerebral palsied child. *American Journal of Occupational Therapy,* 1975, *29,* 273–76.

Epling, C. Positioning high chair. *American Journal of Occupational Therapy,* 1974, *28,* 112.

Gilbert, P. Wheelchair insert for hip and trunk support for children with cerebral palsy, Physical Therapy, 1974, *54,* 254–55.

Gmetter, B. S., & Richards, M. Pulley feeding system. *Physical Therapy,* 1973, *53,* 973–74.

Holse-Buehler, P. Wheelchair utility tray. *American Journal of Occupational Therapy,* 1969, *23,* 49–50.

Mathis, J. Adaptive walker for a child with cerebral palsy. *Physical Therapy,* 1975, *55,* 1344.

Munroe, J. Walkers adapted for the handicapped child. *Physical Therapy,* 1973, *53,* 868–870.

Phillpat, R. Head helmet for cerebral palsy. *American Journal of Occupational Therapy,* 1975, *29,* 291.

Riley, M. The effect of an arm restrainer on involuntary movement. *American Journal of Occupational Therapy,* 1969, *23,* 116–18.

White, J. Stimulation box for the profoundly mentally retarded. *American Journal of Occupational Therapy,* 1976, *30,* 167.

Wilbur, F. Foam rubber sidelying support for children with cerebral palsy. *Physical Therapy,* 1975, *55,* 1345.

PHILIPPA H. CAMPBELL, a registered occupational therapist, is Coordinator of Community Outreach Services for Children's Hospital in Akron, Ohio. This program provides physical, occupational, and speech services to multiply handicapped children in ten Ohio counties. Ms. Campbell is a graduate of Susquehanna University and received a Master's degree in Education from the University of Pittsburgh. She is currently a doctoral candidate in Special Education at Kent State University.

KAREN M. GREEN, R.N., is Director of Developmental Training at the Eastern Nebraska Community Office of Retardation (ENCOR) in Omaha. She was formerly Director of the Developmental Maximation Unit and Motor Development Services for ENCOR, and Treatment Team Leader at Glenwood State Hospital School in Glenwood, Iowa. There she supervised the Foster Grandparent Program and acted as Nurse Consultant in Outpatient and Preadmission Evaluation Services.

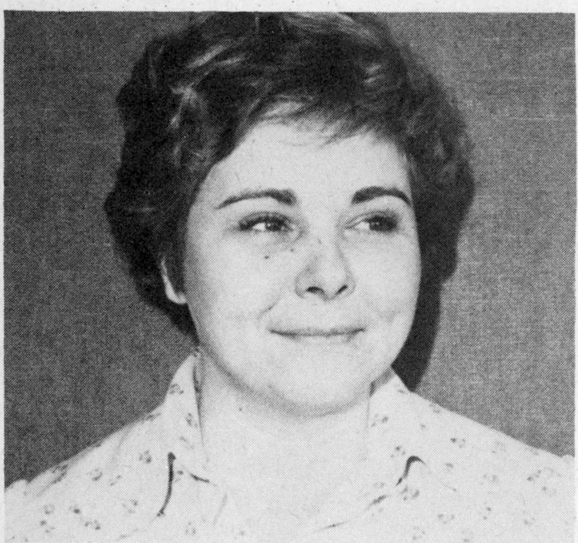

LINDA M. CARLSON, a registered occupational therapist, is Liaison Developmental Therapist between Gunderson Clinic and Home/Community Based Programs for the Western Wisconsin Cerebral Palsy Evaluation and Treatment Center, Gunderson Clinic-Lutheran Hospital, La Crosse, Wisconsin. She previously served as Assistant Instructor, Staff Occupational Therapist, and Consultant for the Meyer Children's Rehabilitation Institute in Omaha, Nebraska.

X Teaching Strategies: Communication and Language

Undeniably, the influence of learning theory has had a major impact on the design of remedial speech and language development programs for children who are speech-deficient or nonverbal. This impact has probably enhanced the practical application of direct service to the severely handicapped population; it has also raised many issues about the very nature of language acquisition in both normal and handicapped children.

Doug Guess, Wayne Sailor, and Donald M. Baer

Basic Considerations in the Development of Communicative and Interactive Skills for Non-Vocal Severely Handicapped Children

DEBERAH HARRIS-VANDERHEIDEN
GREGG C. VANDERHEIDEN

University of Wisconsin

The development of effective educational programs for children with physical, cognitive, and multiple handicaps has recently become a concern of great importance. Clinicians and teachers are increasingly being required to develop appropriate, prescriptive, academic, and prevocational programs for children who may not have been previously enrolled in formal instruction. One group of children and young adults for whom effective learning programming may be particularly difficult includes those children who are non-vocal, non-manipulative, and non-ambulatory. These children are, in most cases, unable to explore and interact motorically with their environment, except on a very limited basis. As a result of this motoric restriction and, even more significantly, as a result of their inability to talk or to communicate with others, they are severely restricted in their ability to interact with other persons. Most children in this population have cerebral palsy or some other type of neurological disorder, and a great many of them are also mentally retarded. However, the degree of retardation and the extent of the influence of motoric restriction on their learning ability and potential is difficult to assess if the child is unable to communicate in a reliable, unambiguous manner. Therefore, an important first step in the development of effective educational intervention for these children is the initiation and development of effective communication and interaction skills. It is only through the child's ability to communicate that his acquisition and development of learning skill can be measured, and effective programs developed. As stated by Hollis, Carrier, and Spradlin (1976), no matter what the "handicapping condition may be, in order for teachers to be effective, they must be able to locate or develop at least one functional communication channel; that is, functional reception (sensory input) and expression (motor output)" (p. 268). Communication skill is especially crucial for this population, as it is the non-vocal severely handicapped (NVSH) child's primary means of interaction and the process through which his educational and communication competence, social adjustment, and vocational potential are measured.

Speech is obviously the most effective and universal means of communication and should be developed in those children who show the potential and have the intact oral mechanism necessary for it. Many NVSH children, however, will never be able to acquire effective, functional communication through speech, and supplementary or augmentative means of communication must be explored. Exploration of augmentative non-speech or non-vocal communication for use with children who are severely motorically impaired is a dynamic, long-range process, one which requires commitment from the team of professionals and parents working with the child, and one which will involve a great deal of initial trial and error. This paper will explore some of the considerations and initial steps involved in developing augmentative non-vocal communication programs for these children.

Information contained in this chapter has been accumulated from research projects carried out in cooperation with the National Science Foundation (EC 40316), the Bureau of Education for the Handicapped, U.S. Office of Education (OEG 0-74-7461, OEG 0-74-9057, OEG 0-74-3321), and the Dane County Developmental Disabilities Services Board.

Considerations in Developing a Communication Program

Basic considerations involved in the development of non-vocal communication programs unfold as a series of factors to evaluate and track at various points in the development of the program. This series involves considerations which require attention prior to selection of a communication aid or technique, considerations in the actual selection of an aid or technique, and considerations subsequent to the selection of an aid or technique (Table 1). Each of these considerations will be described and discussed separately.

Current Communication Ability

It is important to develop a communication program which will utilize and elaborate upon the child's present communication ability and which will incorporate and expand upon those methods which have been successful for him in the past. The amount of functional communication which the child has, in conjunction with an assessment of his current communication needs, will direct the short and long range goals of the communication intervention program.

Functional communication may be defined as the clear, unambiguous transmission of thoughts and ideas from the child to another person, wherein the message received by the listener matches the intended message of the child (Sanders, 1976).

The child's communication ability will, in most cases, be difficult to assess through presently available standardized assessment measures, as most have not been developed or adapted for use with non-vocal, non-writing severely handicapped children. The evaluation team should be prepared to utilize and develop informal assessment procedures which will more accurately evaluate the child's language skill and knowledge. Accurate assessment of the child's cognitive skill level, receptive language or comprehension, expressive language or production, and his use of language for communication purposes is prerequisite to the development of the communication intervention program. For discussions on informal assessment procedures, the reader is referred to Miller (1974).

Current Communication Needs

Once the child's communication ability and amount and extent of his functional communication have been evaluated and documented,

TABLE 1

Basic Considerations in the Development of Communication Programs for Non-Vocal Severely Handicapped Children

Factors to evaluate and track prior to selection of an approach or technique	Factors to evaluate and track during selection of an approach or technique	Factors to evaluate and track subsequent to selection of an approach or technique
Child's current communication ability and amount of functional communication.	Child's visual and hearing ability.	Continual evaluation of:
Child's current and future communication needs.	Child's method of ambulation.	The effectiveness of the physical technique and mode chosen.
Child's motivation to communicate and present and prior attempts at communication.	Child's usual positioning and posture.	The effectiveness and appropriateness of the vocabulary system chosen.
Prognosis for the development of effective oral communication.	Child's physical abilities and availability of a consistent, reliable response mode which may be tapped in the implementation of an augmentative communication mode.	The changing communicative, educational, vocational and environmental needs of the child.
Child's physical and social environments and their role and influence on his communication development.	Child's ability to associate, store and retrieve meaning associated with pictures, words and events & current reading and word recognition skill. (MacDonald 1974)	
Child's primary message receivers or communicative audience and the motivation of others to communicate with him.		
Child's current and future educational and vocational goals and needs.		
Amount and type of professional and parental assistance available.		

his clinicians, teachers, and parents should assess his present and future communication needs. Evaluation may determine that the child's current communication ability is not functional or appropriate for his current needs, and new or augmentative response and communication modes need to be developed. In other cases, the child's present communication may be functional and appropriate for his immediate interaction needs, but may require intervention and further elaboration at a future date.

In those cases where intervention involving the use of an augmentative non-vocal approach will be most beneficial to the child, initial exploration into appropriate augmentative systems should begin with accurate documentation of the child's immediate and long-range communicative needs.

An evaluation of such questions as the following may help to determine those needs.

1. How does the child demonstrate desire to communicate or interact with others?

2. Are his communication attempts recognized and successful?

3. Has an inability to communicate caused frustration or lack of response or passivity in the child?

4. Through what methods does the child communicate (e.g., gestural or signing, attempted vocal, pointing, gross motor, eye movement)?

5. Which of these methods should be improved and are there other potential methods which seem to be within the range of the child's ability?

6. If the child's present method of communication is restrictive, what are possible causes of the restriction?

7. Is communicative interaction expected from the child, i.e., is he required and/or encouraged to make desires and needs known through communication?

8. Does the child use communication to serve functions such as those listed below (Chapman, 1972). If not, why not? Is it because of the child, his environment, or the method used for communication with him?

Functions of Communication

1. To give information.
    a. Reference
    b. Predication
2. To get information.
3. To describe ongoing activity.
4. To get the listener to:
    a. Do something
    b. Believe something
    c. Feel something
5. To express one's own intentions, beliefs or feelings.
6. To indicate a readiness for further communication.
7. To solve problems.
8. To entertain.

The augmentative approach which is implemented (e.g., manual signing, communication board or aid) will effect the quantity, quality, and effectiveness of the child's initial communicative attempts. It is therefore critical that the technique or approach chosen meet the child's communication needs and allow him to express himself in the most efficient and effective manner possible. A successful communication intervention program is one which is based upon and generated by the child's needs.

Motivation to Communicate and Communication Experiences

Of crucial importance in the development of the program is the child's motivation and need to interact in a communicative manner with others. If all the child's needs and wants have been provided by others and he has not been required or given the opportunity to transmit basic wants and feelings through communication, it is likely that there has been a dulling effect on the child's motivation to communicate. The child may have already become a passive observer of others' interaction. In another light, if all the child's experiences with a communication mode or approach have required much effort on his part, with little reward in the way of satisfactory transmission of thought (e.g., through yes/no or twenty-question type of interactions), the child may no longer exhibit a desire or motivation to communicate. Because communication with these children can be time-consuming and painstaking, message receivers often relay feelings of inconvenience or impatience. Children notice this and, as a result, tend to limit their communication to avoid these feelings. If any of these or other combinations of circumstances have prevailed and the child has lost desire or motivation to communicate with others, then providing this motivation will be an important first step in the communication development program.

For some children, particularly those who may have severe cognitive handicaps, lack of motivation to communicate may be the result of lack of knowledge or experience with the meaning or power of communication. Initial steps in communication development programs for these children will involve teaching them the meaning and uses of communication and how it can serve them. A good start toward this might involve initially teaching the child those movements, actions, concepts, or words which, when he uses them, cause an action or reaction on the part of a familiar person in his environment. The child could be taught that, through communication (whether achieved through body or gross movement, gesture, pointing, or words), he can begin to control and affect his environment. Once the child understands that communication can enable him to acquire more control over his interaction with others, and he is allowed and encouraged to display choices and make decisions, his motivation to communicate will, in most cases, markedly improve.

Prognosis for Effective Oral Communication

Since speech is the most efficient and effective mode of communication, if there is any potential for the child to develop speech, this skill should be worked on throughout the communication program. Augmentative techniques may be used for many children as a temporary mode of communication until oral skills are developed to the point of effectiveness (i.e., the child's vocal communication is understood by strangers, and is not laborious or ineffectively slow).

In the past, speech and non-vocal communication techniques have been seen as alternate rather than complementary approaches. This has largely arisen from a concern that the implementation of non-vocal techniques would interfere with or inhibit the child's potential for developing speech. Recent studies by McDonald (Note 1), McNaughton and Kates (Note 2), and Vicker (1974), however, have shown that intervention with non-vocal communication techniques has not hampered the development of speech and, in many cases, has facilitated speech development and improved intelligibility in children who had limited vocalizations. This is an important development and suggests that non-vocal communication techniques or aids should not be thought of as alternatives to speech but as augmentative or supplementary means of communication for children who are not currently able to communicate effectively through speech. It also suggests a second role for non-vocal communication techniques, i.e., as a means to develop basic communication skills and thus facilitate the communication/language/speech development process for the child who may later be able to develop fully functional speech. In either case, the child can be provided with the early means of communication and interaction that are essential to cognitive and linguistic development. Speech therapy should of course be carried out in conjunction with a non-vocal program whenever speech is seen as a possibility for the child.

Role and Influence of Physical and Social Environments

The physical environments in which the child will be communicating also play an important role in the selection of an augmentative aid or technique. The child who resides in a residential facility will have different communication needs from the child who resides in a foster or natural home and attends day school programs. The learning environment will also play an important role; children's communication needs for daily interaction will vary, depending on whether they are enrolled in a primary academic, pre-academic, or pre-vocational or sheltered work setting. The environment in which the child will primarily be communicating will affect both the type of physical aid or technique which is chosen, as well as the type and nature of the content or vocabulary. The environment will also affect the type of communication which will be initiated by the child and the types of individuals with whom the child will be trying to communicate.

Primary Message Receivers

The child's primary message receivers, or communicative audience, and the motivation of others in his environment to communicate with him will be important considerations in the development of the intervention program. When designing a non-vocal program that will require active participation on the part of message receivers, or may require that message receivers learn a new symbol system or response mode, the willingness and commitment on the part of these persons to communicate with the child will play a crucial role in the success of the system. Perhaps even more important is the necessity of providing the child with a system which will allow him to communicate with his peers, as well as with his parents and other adults with whom he may deal. The child needs a system which will allow him to interact with all persons in his environment, and which will foster not only academic, vocational, and linguistic development, but social skills and peer interaction, as well. If the child's peers are unable to read, or put together words for him as he spells them out, then it may be best to give the child a system which also includes pictographic or ideographic symbol modes which his peers can understand, and respond to. This will help foster spontaneous peer interaction and social development, as well as an understanding and use of language that is broader than the academic or need-related communication typical of most adult interaction with a non-vocal child.

Educational and Vocational Goals

The following sections of this paper describe a variety of aids, techniques, and vocabulary systems for developing a non-vocal communication system. With a little forethought as to the child's future educational and/or vocational plans, a developmental system may be implemented to provide the child with functional communication at the early stages in his development and with effective means for communication, writing, and control of other devices that may be necessary to meet his expanding needs as he grows. For instance, if it is anticipated that the child will be able to achieve spelling skill or master sight words and be able to use a wordboard, letter/word board, or letterboard, then it would be to the child's benefit to teach him the alphabet or traditional orthography as early as possible in order to develop his skill in spelling, sentence structuring, and word sequencing. The future physical environment of the child will also be an important early consideration in terms of the physical aid or technique selected. The process of providing the child with effective augmentative communication is a dynamic process, and the more one is able to predict about the child's future needs and environments, the better one will be able to design initial intervention steps and procedures.

Professional and Parent Cooperation Available

Throughout the entire intervention program, the type of professional help available and the amount and type of parental cooperation will play a major role in determining the communication approaches and programs that may be viable for exploration with the child. The communication intervention program should be an interdisciplinary one, with expertise from a variety of sources. The expectations and input which can be expected of the professional team and of the parents is important to consider early in the intervention process. This is especially important if one aspect of the program may need to be implemented by persons who are familiar with that aspect, but who have not been directly trained to implement and incorporate it in a multi-disciplinary program. For example, an occupational or physical therapist may not be available to contribute to the program, and thus the classroom teacher or speech/language clinician will be expected to provide input and guidance as relates to the child's physical skills and abilities. A thorough evaluation of the staff's commitment to and recognition of the need for the development of a non-vocal communication program for the child should be conducted and documented prior to the development and initiation of intervention strategies.

Considerations in Selecting Aids and Techniques

Once the foregoing factors in early programming have been considered, evaluated, and discussed with all persons who will be involved in the communication development program (including the child, when appropriate), the intervention team is ready to move into the series of considerations involved in actual selection of an aid or technique. Among the following factors that should be evaluated and tracked are the child's:

1. Vision and hearing ability;
2. Usual method of mobility;
3. Usual positioning and posture;
4. Physical abilities, and the availability of a consistent and reliable response mode which may be tapped in the implementation of an augmentative communication mode;
5. Ability to associate, store, and retrieve meaning associated with pictures, words, and events (McDonald 1974);
6. Current reading and word recognition skill.

The last three considerations are particularly important in (a) the selection of an appropriate physical response mode which will augment residual oral skills, and (b) the selection of a symbol or vocabulary system through which the child will transmit messages and thoughts. These two particular selection decisions will consume a great deal of the program effort and will be discussed separately, following discussion of the other considerations listed.

Visual and Auditory Skills

Vision, hearing, and other sensory skills become increasingly important in those communication methods which do not primarily involve oral communication. If the child is unable to vocalize, his message elements will most likely be displayed to him and to his message receiver in a visual manner. This would include methods ranging from the gestures of a signing system to the sequentially lit vocabulary elements of an electronic communication aid. When selecting the type of visual display/communication approach to be used, it is important to assess the child's ability to attend to and discriminate visual stimuli, his ability to discriminate figure-ground configurations, his visual color discrimination ability, the optimal distance of display items for visual acuity, and the optimal size for vocabulary/message elements.

Similarly, hearing acuity and discrimination are equally important factors to assess. Much of the child's communication will involve auditory feedback between himself, the message receiver, and, in some instances, the communication aid itself. In most instances, the message he indicates will be vocalized for him by the message receiver, and the child must be able to hear this feedback and confirm the accuracy of the message transmitted. Audition is also the primary source of language input for the child and it is, therefore, essential to establish the integrity of this system. When children are non-vocal and multi-handicapped, a hearing problem can easily be overlooked or mistaken for mental retardation or an inability of the child to understand what is being said. For this reason, special care should be taken to check for hearing problems.

Method of Mobility

A primary concern in the selection of a particular communication method is the child's customary means of mobility. If the child is usually in a wheelchair and is able to utilize a laptray arrangement to support a communication aid of some sort, there are a variety of aids or techniques from which to choose. If the child does not spend much time in a wheelchair, a laptray arrangement for support or incorporation of a communication aid may be useful only in certain environments or situations. The child who is unable to talk or write, and who is physically handicapped yet ambulatory, poses a problem in communication development. It is difficult to provide this child with an augmentative communication system which will be effective for him, yet easy to carry when walking, especially if crutches or other mobility aids are necessary. There are some aids, however, which have been designed for these individuals as well (cf. Vanderheiden & Grilley, 1976).

Usual Positioning and Posture

The child's usual positioning and posture should be carefully evaluated. Seating posture, head control, hand, arm, and leg control are interrelated and the success of a child in using a technique or aid may be directly attributed to proper seating and bracing which will give him maximum control of his arms and torso. The role of posture and stability in a communication system is often overlooked or underestimated but should be emphasized in the communication development program. For further information on this topic, the reader is referred to Finnie (1975), McDonald and Schultz (1973), Vanderheiden and Grilley (1976), and Vicker (1974).

Physical Abilities and the Availability of a Consistent, Reliable Response Mode

Once the child's usual method of mobility, his motor skills, and his coordinative abilities have been evaluated, the availability of a consistent, accurate, voluntarily controlled motor movement which may be used as a physical response mode needs to be assessed. A physical response mode should utilize motor movements which are relatively easy for the child to execute, and which will not easily result in fatigue on the part of the child or the message receiver.

The motor movement (or movements) which the child is able to control accurately and consistently will dictate the augmentative mode or approach which will be of most benefit to him. If, for example, the child is able to point, in a gross or fine manner, he will most likely be able to use a direct selection approach such as a communication board. If the child is unable to point and has consistent voluntary control over one or only a few motor movements (e.g., movement of leg, head, knee,), then a scanning approach will probably be more successful. If the child is unable to point, but has accurate and relatively quick control of a motor movement, an encoding approach may be used. These three approaches will be discussed in detail later; of importance here is that the type of communication system available to the non-vocal child is dependent upon those physical skills which he can control as alternative response or production modes. Evaluation of the child by occupational and physical therapists, and observation of his motor movements in various environments, will be required before a particular approach can be selected.

Ability to Associate, Store, and Retrieve Meaning Associated with Pictures, Words, and Events

Because the augmentative system which will be developed will be primarily a visual one, it is important that the child be able to associate, store, and retrieve meaning associated with visual representations of those objects, persons, and events in his environment about which he will be communicating. If, through evaluation and observation, it is determined that the child is unable to associate meaning with words or pictures, initial steps in the communication program may involve manipulation and communication of meaning associated with objects or persons with whom the child is already familiar. If the child has had no experience associating meaning with any type of visual representation, it may be necessary to begin the program by demonstrating the action of objects or persons to the child so that he may begin to associate meaning with them.

In addition to association and semantic skill and knowledge, the child's reading and word recognition skills are important, particularly in the selection of appropriate symbol and vocabulary systems. If the child is unable to read or spell, then selection of an ideographic or pictographic system, e.g., Rebus (Woodcock, 1965), Blissymbols (Bliss, 1965), may be necessary. Too often, unnecessary restrictions are placed upon the child's early communication attempts if he is required to read or spell before he is able. Children should be provided with a communication system which they can use immediately. For most children this will initially be a picture or symbol system of some type. Once the child has a functional communication system, reading, spelling, and other advanced communication techniques can be taught more easily and with less frustration and more cooperation on the part of the child.

Providing an Effective Augmentative Physical Response Mode

A great many different techniques have been developed that can provide the non-vocal physically handicapped child with a means of indicating the elements of his message. All of these techniques are essentially variations on three basic approaches: direct selection, scanning, and encoding. The range of complexity of these approaches will be discussed briefly in this section, along with examples of aids which have been developed based upon these techniques.

Direct Selection

A direct selection technique is any technique in which the desired output or message element is directly indicated by the message sender (Vanderheiden & Harris-Vanderheiden, 1976). The direct selection technique (Figure 1) is the most straightforward and the simplest of the three techniques mentioned above. The simplest example of the use of a direct selection technique would be a child pointing directly to an object to convey a message: to a glass when he wants a drink, to the door when he wishes to go outside. Another example of the use of a direct selection technique is the use of a letter, word, or pictureboard whereby the child directly points to message elements in a sequential order, in order to relay thoughts and ideas.

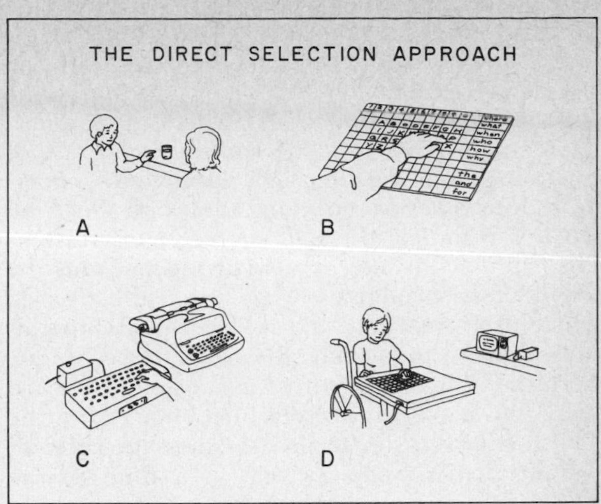

Figure 1

Expanded and/or recessed keyboards are examples of direct selection aids which can provide a child with an independent means of writing (Figure 1, item C); portable direct selection aids have been developed to provide children with pointing ability (even children with very limited and irregular pointing skills) with a portable, independent means of communication (Figure 1, item D).

Scanning Aids or Techniques

Scanning involves the use of any aid or technique in which message elements are offered to the child through a visual display. The child selects the elements of his message by providing some response (e.g., head, eye, hand, or foot movement) to the person or aid presenting the message elements. Depending upon the particular aid used, the child may respond by simply signalling when he sees that the correct element has been selected by the message receiver or the display, or by actively directing an indicator (e.g., a light or arrow) toward the desired message element.

In more general terms, a technique is considered scanning if message elements (pictures, words, letters, symbols) are presented to the child one at a time so that he can indicate the message element he wants by providing some sort of response or signal when the desired element is reached. The simplest example of scanning involves the use of yes/no and twenty-questions types of communication with the child. In this instance, the message receiver presents the child with choices, one at a time, and the child nods, or signals "yes," when the desired element is reached. To add reliability to this technique or to facilitate the use of the technique with the alphabet, a letterboard or pictureboard may be used to present the choices to the child. In this instance also, the message receiver would present choices one at a time to the child, who needs only to be able to make a consistent, reliable, and unambiguous response which acts as a signal of affirmation. Because all message elements need to be scanned until the child's desired element is reached, this technique becomes a very slow one and requires the constant attention of the message receiver. To reduce the amount of time and effort required of the message receiver, and to provide the child with more control, simple electronic or electromechanical aids can be used to implement the scanning approach. (Examples are illustrated in Figure 2.) Pictures, symbols, words, or letters can be used as vocabulary elements, and different switches or input modes can be used with the aid, depending upon the child's physical ability.

The need for constant and undivided attention by a second person can be completely eliminated if the child is using an aid which provides him with the ability to print out his message independently. Figure 2, item D, shows an aid which uses the scanning technique and controls a typewriter. With this aid, the child could prepare his message and then call the attention of the second person. The second person would only need to direct his attention to the work for the brief period of time necessary to read the message instead of having to concentrate on the child's communication during the entire period needed to construct the message. With such an aid, a child would be able to participate in group discussions or interactions without having to monopolize the time of the person with whom he was communicating.

A portable communication aid is a great advantage to the child. This is a problem which is not usually encountered with the simpler aid, but is encountered with aids designed to control typewriters. Special aids have therefore been designed which can print out (or display)

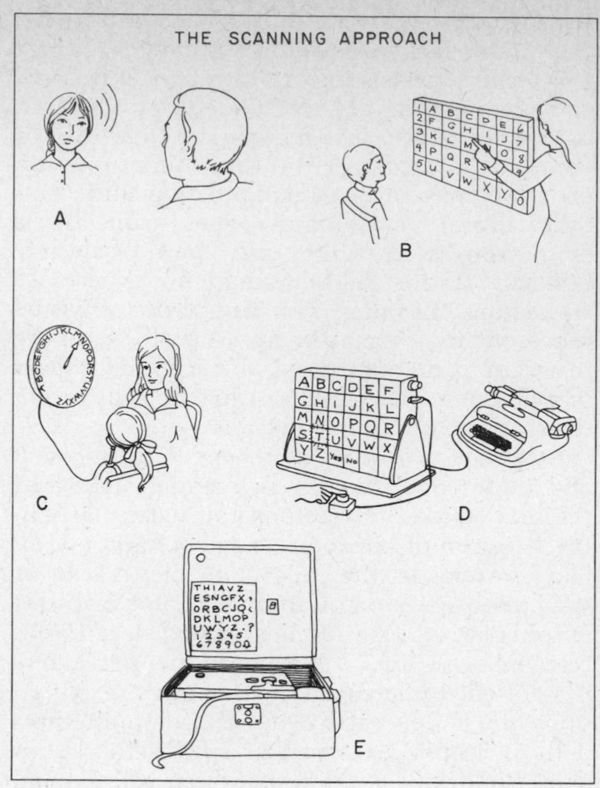

Figure 2

the child's message and are yet compact enough to move around with the child in his wheelchair (Figure 2, item E).

Encoding Techniques

Encoding techniques are those techniques or aids in which the desired character is indicated by a pattern or code of input signals and where the character codes must be memorized or referred to on a chart (Vanderheiden & Harris-Vanderheiden, 1976).

An aid can be used with any number of switches. The code may involve activating the switch(es) sequentially, simultaneously, or in a specific time sequence.

One very simple example of an encoding technique is the arrangement of pictures, symbols, words, or letters on a card with a number pair beside each. The child could direct a second person's attention to any message element by pointing to the two numbers on his number line corresponding to the number pair beside the desired item. In this manner, a child who is able to point to only a small number of items reliably would be able to indicate, by encoding, any one of a large number of items on the chart. For children too young to use a number pairing technique, colors could be used in conjunction with the numbers in a color-number encoding technique. With this method, the chart would be separated into any number of sections, each of a different color. For example, eight pictures, symbols, etc., could be placed within each section next to a single number. The child would then indicate his choice by indicating the color of the section his choice was in, and then the number that was next to his choice.

For the child who cannot point but who does have control over his eyes, the above encoding techniques can be implemented by use of the child's gaze. One method of doing this involves the use of a clear plexiglas panel with the numerals on it (Figure 3, item B), called an ETRAN-N. The child communicates by looking at the numbers (or color and number to indicate the elements of his message on the listing). For advanced children, the letters of the alphabet can be put directly on the plexiglas sheet and a more sophisticated coding system can be used.

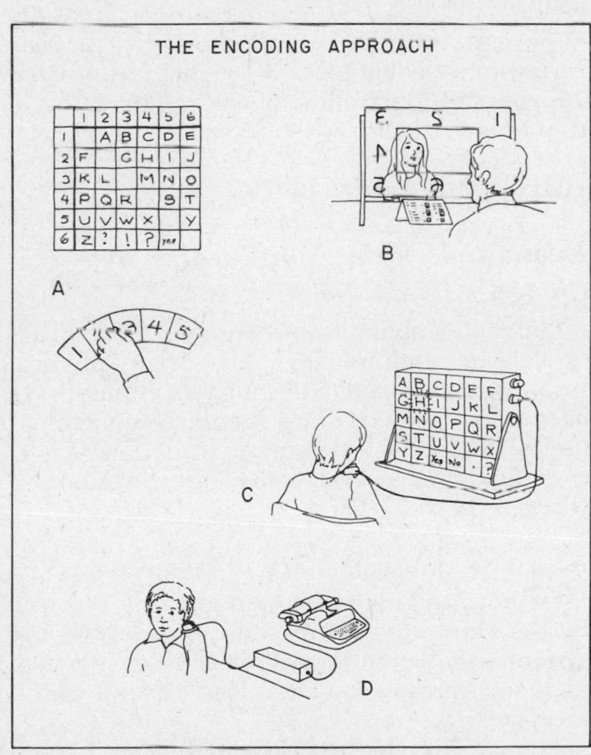

Figure 3

Aids can be used to make encoding systems easier to use by decoding the child's movements for the second person and by directly displaying the child's choice. An aid could, for instance, decode a child's Morse Code and directly display the appropriate letter (Figure 3, item C). As with the scanning and direct selection approaches, there are also encoding aids which can provide the child with a completely independent means of writing in either a stationary form (Figure 3, item D) or a portable form (Figure 3, item E).

Currently, there are a great many different aids and techniques which incorporate any one or a combination of these three approaches for communication by children with severe motor and cognitive handicaps. Only a cursory review has been presented here. A complete review of aids and techniques is available in Vanderheiden and Grilley (1976) and Vanderheiden and Harris-Vanderheiden (1976).

Considerations in Selecting and Developing a Vocabulary System

For non-vocal physically handicapped children, selection and development of an appropriate and effective symbol system and vocabulary may be more important to the effectiveness of the child's overall communication development than the particular physical mode through which he communicates. In the selection and development of a vocabulary system, it should be remembered that the system initially chosen will not usually be the final or only system used by the child. As with the selection and development of an appropriate and effective physical mode, the selection of an appropriate symbol system is a dynamic and long-range process. The vocabulary system will need to change, expand, and allow the child to communicate expressively on a level commensurate with his linguistic and cognitive skill. There may not be one "best" system that will be effective for the child in all of the environments and situations in which he will interact and, therefore, more than one system may be developed for the child.

The selection of an appropriate symbol system will be one of the most difficult initial decisions in the child's communication development program. Even after the initial vocabulary choice has been made, there are still a variety of other choices and decisions, equally as important, that will need to be decided. These involve positioning of vocabulary elements, sequencing of message elements, and so on. In this section, important considerations in the development of a symbol or vocabulary system will be discussed. A complete review of traditional and newly developed graphic systems of communication which may be used with augmentative non-vocal aids and techniques is discussed in Clark and Woodcock (1976) and Vanderheiden and Harris-Vanderheiden (1976).

Selection of a Symbol System

The following considerations should be kept in mind when selecting a symbol vocabulary system for use with particular augmentative aids or techniques, and also when reviewing and developing a particular symbol system which will serve as a non-vocal child's total vehicle for expressive communication. The symbol system chosen should be (Vanderheiden & Harris-Vanderheiden, 1976):

1. Compatible with the aid or technique with which it is to be used.
2. As nonrestrictive of the child's communication as possible.
3. Appropriate to the child's current level of receptive and expressive language ability.
4. Developmental and flexible in order to grow with the child's changing communication needs.
5. Acceptable to the child, his parents and teachers and those with whom he will be communicating.

When selecting a symbol system for use with a particular aid or technique, it is important to consider the communicative needs which the aid is expected to meet, and the functions which it will serve. Symbol systems which may be used with non-vocal aids, including Rebus (Woodcock 1965), Blissymbols (Bliss 1965), pictures, line drawing, words, letters, etc., need to be matched with operational features of the physical aid. For example, pictures or Blissymbolics or Rebus symbols may be used as a vocabulary on aids which allow the teacher or clinician to construct visual displays, but they are not appropriate vocabularies for aids which utilize a mechanical or electronic alphabetic printout (e.g., typewriters or electronic aids). Traditional orthography (the alphabet) can be implemented with virtually any alternate physical display mode.

Whatever vocabulary is provided to the child will be limited and restrictive. If the vocabulary is to be presented to the child through a communication board, eye chart, or other visual display, there will be a finite amount of space, usually between 25 and 600 words, not nearly enough for even a four-year-old child. Symbol systems should, therefore, allow the child to express as much as possible with the fewest symbols so as to best utilize the limited space available. With constraints such as these in mind, a symbol system which allows expression of a wide range of concepts and meaning with a relatively small number of actual symbols may be chosen over a symbol system which is not as flexible. (Blissymbolics may, for this reason, be chosen over pictures, or a wordboard with an alphabet display may be chosen over a wordboard display alone.)

If the communication method chosen for the child is to be effective, it should allow the child to construct utterances which are commensurate with his present expressive ability. If a child is unable to spell, read, or recognize sight words, then pictures, Rebuses, or Blissymbols would be a more appropriate vocabulary choice. It is important to the educational and developmental processes of the child that he be provided with a communication system that is effective for him in his early communicative growth. Above all, the symbol system chosen must be acceptable to the child, his parents, and others with whom he will be communicating.

Development of an appropriate and effective vocabulary system is a difficult task, which will require a considerable amount of trial and error. The considerations mentioned here are important, but equally important is a complete review of available types of symbol systems and appropriate application of each. For study in this area, readers are referred to Clark and Woodcock (1976), and Vanderheiden and Harris-Vanderheiden (1976).

Evaluation of the Non-Vocal System Chosen

Once the above considerations have been dealt with, and initially appropriate physical response mode and vocabulary systems have been implemented, there should be an evaluation of the non-vocal communication system as a whole. Factors to evaluate include the following (Place & Roelike, 1975):

Accessibility/Reliability of the System

Is the communication system easily accessed by the child and the message receiver? Is the system reliable in operational characteristics, and in transmission of clear, unambiguous messages?

Is the child's method of communication available to him *wherever* he goes? (This may require 2 or 3 aids, one for the classroom, one for easy use in transport, for use at home, in public places, on the playground, beach, etc.)

Flexibility

Is the system effective for the child and the message receiver in the types of environments in which the child primarily communicates? Is the system easily adaptable to new constraints or demands placed upon it either in operational or vocabulary components?

Complexity of Message Transmission

Does the system allow the child to construct and express complex thoughts and ideas as well as basic needs and wants? Are message receivers able to clearly decipher and respond to the child's message? Is there any message distortion and, if so, what are some potential causal factors? How might they be eliminated?

Transmission Time

Is the speed or rate of communication commensurate with the child's ability? The message receiver's ability?

Compatibility of the System to the Environment

Is the system compatible with the child's interaction in the home, residential placement, classroom, or vocational placement? Does the size, weight or bulk of the aid interfere with any of the child's activities?

Receptivity of the Child and Message Receivers to Use of the System

Is the system being used by the child, and are the child's communicative attempts being responded to and fostered by individuals in his environment? If not, what are potential causes for lack of communicative interaction? How can this be alleviated?

Once the communication program has been implemented, and parents, professionals, and child are developing interactive communicative skill through use of an augmentative non-vocal method, periodic checks and re-evaluation should be made of the effectiveness of the system.

Continual Evaluation of the Effectiveness of the Physical Technique

In nearly all cases, the child's physical abilities will change as he uses the aid or techniques which have been developed. It is important to evaluate continually the physical response mode and communication method being used by the child in order: (a) to ensure that it is providing him with the ability to communicate at the fastest speed he can handle, (b) to ensure that the system does not fatigue the child or the message receiver, and (c) to ensure that the physical requirements of the child and of the message receiver are appropriate and not impeding successful communication. In addition, it will be necessary, at various points in the child's use of a non-vocal aid or technique, to assess whether the technique itself is still appropriate in the same form for the child. A child who is initially unable to point may develop pointing ability at a later date and may be able to move from a technique such as scanning to a faster technique such as direct selection.

Continual Evaluation of the Vocabulary System

As mentioned previously, some children may begin use of non-vocal communication by using pictures or a symbol system other than traditional orthography. If the child has or can develop spelling or sight word recognition skills, then these should be fostered because they will eventually allow him greater freedom of choice in the type of aid or technique available to him.

Conclusion

The development of a communication program for non-vocal children will be a dynamic process, involving a great deal of trial and error and individualization according to the needs and strengths of the educators, clinicians, and children involved. Depth of discussion related to individual topics has been sacrificed in order to provide a broader overview of the diverse but interrelated factors which will determine the success of the communication program. Of primary concern has been transmission of the necessity for clinicians and educators to evaluate and study the entire process of communication as it relates to the child and to his interaction with others. Some parts of the program may be more important than others at times, but all of the considerations mentioned should be given equal attention and evaluative tracking. Like communication itself, communication programming is a daily, interactive process which must be adaptable to changing situations and needs. It is hoped that the content provided here will help in the initiation of communication and interaction for severely handicapped children.

Reference Notes

1. McDonald, E. T. Development of communication skills in cerebral palsy. Paper presented to the American Academy for Cerebral Palsy, November 18, 1974.
2. McNaughton, S., and Kates, B. Visual symbols: Communication system for the pre-reading physically handicapped child. Paper presented to the American Association on Mental Deficiency. Toronto, Ontario, Canada, June, 1974.

References

Bliss, C. K. *Semantography.* Sydney, Australia: Semantography Publications, 1965.

Chapman, R. S. Some simple ways of talking about normal language and communication. In J. McLean, D. Yoder, & R. Schiefelbusch (Eds.). *Language intervention with the retarded.* Baltimore: University Park Press, 1972.

Clark, C. R., & Woodcock, R. W. Graphic systems of communication. In L. Lloyd (Ed.). *Communication assessment and intervention strategies.* Baltimore: University Park Press, 1976.

Finnie, N. R. *Handling the young cerebral palsied child at home.* New York: E. P. Dutton & Co., 1975.

Hollis, J., Carrier, J., & Spradlin, J. An approach to remediation of communication and learning deficiencies. In L. Lloyd (Ed.). *Communication assessment and intervention strategies.* Baltimore: University Park Press, 1976, 268.

McDonald, E. T., & Schultz, A. R. Communication boards for cerebral palsied children. *Journal of Speech and Hearing Disorders,* 1973 (38), 3–88.

Miller, J. F. *A developmental approach toward assessing communication behavior in children.* Madison, Wisconsin: Waisman Center on Mental Retardation and Human Development, University of Wisconsin, 1974.

Place, L., & Roelike, M. Non-vocal communication techniques and aids for the physically handicapped. Faribault, Minnesota: Faribault State School, 1975.

Sanders, D. A. A model for communication. In L. Lloyd (Ed.). *Communication assessment and intervention strategies.* Baltimore: University Park Press, 1976, 11.

Vanderheiden, G., & Grilley, K. *Non-vocal communication techniques and aids for the severely physically handicapped.* Baltimore: University Park Press, 1976.

Vanderheiden, G., & Harris-Vanderheiden, D. Communication techniques and aids for the non-vocal severely handicapped. In L. Lloyd (Ed.). *Communication assessment and intervention strategies.* Baltimore: University Park Press, 1976.

Vicker, B. *Nonoral communication system project, 1964–73.* Iowa City, Iowa: Campus Stores Publishers, University of Iowa, 1974.

Woodcock, R. W. *The Rebus Reading Series.* Nashville, Tennessee: Institute on Mental Retardation and Intellectual Development, George Peabody College, 1965.

DEBERAH HARRIS-VANDERHEIDEN is the Area Coordinator for both the Language and Communication Research and the Training and Clinical Services Programs at the Trace Research and Development Center for the Severely Communicatively Handicapped, University of Wisconsin, Madison. Her research efforts have included: directorship of a Blissymbol research program for mentally retarded children; field evaluation of independent communication aids; and research into vocabulary development and acquisition of language in non-vocal physically handicapped children.

GREGG C. VANDERHEIDEN is co-founder and director of the Trace Research and Development Center for the Severely Communicatively Handicapped, University of Wisconsin, Madison. He has been principal investigator on grants from the National Science Foundation and the Bureau of Education for the Handicapped, USOE, which dealt with the exploration, development, and evaluation of communication aids and techniques. He has also given presentations at conferences of ASHA, AAMD, CEC, NCC, AAESPH, ACEMB, and AAAS, and has published articles and chapters relating to his research in communication.

Manual Signing as a Language System and as a Speech Initiator for the Non-Verbal Severely Handicapped Student

KATHLEEN STREMEL-CAMPBELL
DEE CANTRELL
JIM HALLE

Project MESH (Model Education for the Severely Handicapped)
Bureau of Child Research
Parsons, Kansas

The critical need for the development of language training tactics for moderately and severely handicapped children has generated a proliferation of ideas, techniques, and programs. Most of these published programs were generated to teach the verbal child more speech. Only recently have there been a variety of programs focusing on the child who is nonverbal due to the severity of his handicap and/or the sterility of his environment. Of the nonverbal populations (retarded, deaf retarded, autistic, and physically handicapped), the physically handicapped probably have the largest arsenal of alternative communication strategies available to them.

One of these, the Bliss Symbol System, is composed of 340 symbols through which word meaning is conveyed. The symbols produce a syntax that differs from English and, thus, meaning is not coded by the same principles. Handwriting, typing, and fingerspelling offer three other potential communication systems for the physically handicapped. Prerequisites for these systems greatly limit their applicability for use with the severely handicapped. All of them require spelling and reading skills, a degree of manual dexterity, and a certain speed of performance.

Communication boards are another system available to the physically handicapped child. Within the area of communication boards and cards, there are many varieties that differ in regard to equipment and content (Vanderheiden, 1975). A restrictive factor of this system is described by Vicker (1974): "as the degree of intellectual deficit increases, the value of the communication board as a substitute expressive system usually decreases" (p. 32). A variation in the use of communication boards to train nonverbal severely handicapped children in language was suggested by Premack (1970) in his work with Sarah, a chimpanzee. His use of a symbol system and his treatment of language from the perspective of its function, rather than its structure, greatly simplify the language training process. Carrier's work (1974) is an attempt to adapt a system for severely retarded children similar to that of Premack. In Carrier's program a nonspeech response mode is substituted for speech. Geometric forms function as linguistic constituents, and the child has only to select and correctly arrange forms appropriate for the meaning to be conveyed. This program is limited in the variety of syntactic structures taught, as well as in its overall portability.

Sign language offers several advantages for the physically handicapped over the previously mentioned systems. Portability is not a consideration. Spelling and reading are not requirements in the acquisition and use of sign language. Speed of communication is enhanced by the fact that each sign corresponds to a word as opposed to a letter, as in handwriting, typing, and fingerspelling. However, signing has several drawbacks that must also be considered. Just as speed may be enhanced by the sign-to-word correspondence, the number of symbols to learn is greatly increased (as opposed to 26 in handwriting, typing, and fingerspelling). In addition, the disadvantage of a limited audience, which occurs with the Bliss symbols and fingerspelling, also applies here. Finally, the most devastating drawback for the physically handicapped is the degree of motor control necessary to form the multitude of gestures.

With populations other than physically handicapped, this last drawback loses some of its

Preparation of this paper was supported by HEW Contract, OEG-0-74-7991, to the Bureau of Child Research, University of Kansas. The authors also wish to thank Shirley Berger for her assistance in preparing this paper.

significance and thus sign language becomes a more viable alternative language system. The populations that have made the most extensive use of sign language are the normal deaf, the deaf retarded, the severely retarded, and the autistic.

Hall and Talkington (1970) evaluated the feasibility and the concomitant language development of the manual approach to programming for the deaf retarded. The majority of their subjects demonstrated rapid comprehension and functional use of the manual sign system, with academic skills and interest developing subsequent to its initiation. The authors made these findings after four hours of daily instruction for six months. In addition to manual communication, five other content areas were trained during this period.

Kopchick, Rombach, and Smilovitz (1975) described another program for an institutionalized deaf retarded population. The authors concluded that the results of their pilot project suggest that a total environment approach, which consistently stimulates and reinforces the use of sign language, can be an effective way of facilitating the development of language skills. In Berger's (1972) work with the deaf retarded, a multimodel approach is utilized. Response modes are programmed to move from gross motor responding through manual signing, fingerspelling, writing, and speaking. Her program places a heavy emphasis on receptive, as well as expressive sign training.

While sign language has been a prevalent means of communication with deaf populations, it has only recently been used with severely retarded individuals (Bricker, 1972; Larson, 1971; Mansfield Training School, 1973; Richardson, 1975; Topper, 1975). Its use with this population has varied greatly. For example, Bricker (1972) focused her investigation on initial word meaning. Her results suggest that imitative sign training facilitated word-object association in retarded children. Larson (1971) stated that her program for the nonverbal retarded child is not intended to replace but to stimulate the development of expressive speech. It utilizes a sequence for the development of sign language that in many ways parallels speech development.

In contrast to Bricker's and Larson's rather specific use of signs, others have generated entire programs that utilize signing as a major method of communication. The Mansfield Training School has created a dictionary comprised of basic signs and vocabulary chosen specifically for the retarded in an attempt to facilitate state-wide standardization. They advocate incorporating signs into every facet of daily living, so that the impact is immediate and functional. Southbury Training School (Richardson, 1975) utilizes a very similar approach of introducing signs as they become relevant to tasks being performed in the classroom. Signing production is demanded only after the student demonstrates an understanding of the meaning of the sign and an ability and willingness to imitate it.

In much the same way as the Mansfield and Southbury programs evolved, Denton State School (Topper, 1975) was searching for a program which would "provide the profoundly and severely retarded residents with maximum communication ability, one which would be meaningful in content and functionally relevant to the residents' environment as well as their personal and physical needs" (p. 30). The gestures used in the Denton program are a combination of Indian sign language and sign language of the deaf. There is more emphasis on gross motor as opposed to fine motor gestures. In this way a more simple and concrete system of gesturing is achieved, one which is as closely related to the natural action as possible.

Sign language has recently been adapted for use with another special population—the autistic. Miller and Miller (1973) developed a language program based on two kinds of training. The first involved the use of connected boards, elevated 3 to 6 feet above the ground, which served as facilitators for the second, which was sign training. Specifically, the authors establish functional activity that makes the use of signs more likely.

> . . . a child poised 5 feet above the ground (standing on two wooden beams) and wishing to get through a box enclosure with doors on each end had to make the sign for open (hands parting) before the teacher would open the door and let the child through. In the same fashion, he had to perform a down sign before a drawbridge would be lowered, or a pick-up sign before an obstacle would be removed from his path. Once children could respond to and use signs effectively above ground, they were trained to generalize this understanding to everyday situations on the ground. [p. 75]

The results of this study demonstrate that for all children, the pairing of signs with spoken words facilitated responding to these words (receptive language). This is similar to what Bricker (1972) demonstrated. Though the children used fewer signs expressively than they did receptively, even the lowest functioning among them could initiate a few signs (e.g., eat, drink, open). Also noteworthy in this study is the finding that the younger children were more likely to achieve success in both expressive signs and words.

The David School staff utilizes a total communication approach in its efforts to treat the nonverbal autistic-psychotic child. Sign language is an important component of this approach, one that allows effective, immediate, and appropriate communication with others in the children's environment to occur. As Smith (1973) stated:

> The language of signs has, in my experience, been the percursor to the appropriate use of speech, if speech is acquired. The ultimate goal is speech used appropriately for communication. However, if speech does not develop, the child has been provided with the language of signs, which also enables him to continue with academic learning and personal growth. [p. 3]

This article details procedures used and the rationale for using them. The initial signs to be trained and approximations of the signs also are discussed.

In general, the previously cited sources were of a clinical nature and as such had as their central focus an entire program capable of transmitting an alternative system of communication to populations not presently engaging in oral speech. Now the focus of this review will turn to animal research that has addressed some very specific questions with far-reaching implications for the teaching of communication systems to severely handicapped populations.

Gardner and Gardner (1969) in their pioneering work adapted American Sign Language for use with a young female chimpanzee named Washoe. They found that, by using a combination of training methods including manual guidance and handshaping, they obtained the following results:

1. The signs acquired earliest were simple demands.
2. Washoe demonstrated the ability to generalize the use of a sign from the original referent to a wide class of appropriate referents.
3. Washoe's rate of acquisition of new signs was continually accelerating.
4. From the time she had eight or ten signs in her repertoire, Washoe began to use them in strings of two or more.

The direct value of the Gardners' work is limited, but its implications for the controlled study of sign language are overwhelming. It would now be possible to answer some very important, clinically-relevant questions. What is the most efficient method of teaching signs? Which signs should be taught first and why? What are some of the considerations to take into account in making these decisions?

Fouts, a colleague of the Gardners, attempted to shed some light on the first question by making a controlled comparison of three training techniques: molding (physical guidance), imitation, and a combination of molding and imitation (1972). Washoe was the only subject involved in these experiments. The results suggest that a combination of first molding and then imitation is the optimal training method. Two additional interesting findings were reported in this article. The first relates to the difficulty Washoe experienced in producing nontouch signs in the first of two experiments. "Touch signs involve a touching action, in which one hand contacts the other hand or another part of the signer's body. Nontouch signs do not have such tactile feedback" (p. 516). The second finding was that the motivational significance of the referent of the sign had an impact upon the ease with which the sign was learned. These discoveries have implications for which signs should be chosen for initial training.

In a later study (1973), Fouts investigated the generality of the previous findings with four more chimpanzees, and looked at the consistency in the ease with which signs are acquired. He found that Washoe was not unique in that the four subjects of the later study also learned sign language. Of greater significance to teachers of special populations of humans is his conclusion that many errors fell into one of three categories:

1. Those related to conceptual similarities (e.g., fruit, food, and drink);
2. Those related to gestural similarities (e.g., signs for listen, look, and key all involve the index finger);
3. Those related to a preference for forming certain signs over other signs.

These could be helpful considerations when one is deciding which signs to teach together or in what order to teach different signs. At the close of this study, Fouts speculates that some signs are apparently easier for a chimpanzee to acquire than others, perhaps because some signs are similar to pre-experimental behaviors in the chimpanzee's repertoire (e.g., sucking thumb is similar to sign for "drink"). Other signs may be absent from the chimpanzee's repertoire or even in opposition to natural tendencies (e.g., the "look" sign involves touching the index finger near the eye, a response that is foreign to the natural tendency to protect the eyes).

Hayes and Hayes (1952) came to similar conclusions. They found that problem-solving ability is a function of past experience. Their cage-raised chimpanzees, which lacked experience with materials and mechanical principles involved in the target problem, performed much more poorly than home-raised chimpanzees which had requisite experiences. Perhaps the chimpanzees in Fouts' study (1973) had not had much experience with fine motor manual manipulations. The Hayes' also concluded that a response cannot be imitated unless its components are in the subject's available repertoire of voluntary acts (e.g., finger-touching near eye may not be a voluntary act).

Manual Signing for the Nonverbal Child

Needs Assessment.

Those involved with establishing language in the nonverbal child must decide initially if the nonoral training approach is appropriate for their population. It is often difficult to determine whether the child is capable of speech, i.e., if the oral-motor mechanism necessary for speech is intact. Since it is possible that speech capabilities may be present in the nonverbal child, many trainers wonder if the use of a nonoral approach will, in fact, hinder speech. Other trainers realize that the speech (oral) approach with the nonverbal child may be a long and laborious task, gaining little speech and an extremely limited language system. Once a decision is made to use a nonoral approach, factors indicating the advantages and disadvantages of the various nonoral methods must be weighed. Possibly the most important factor in program selection is the individual child. Each child comes into training with certain motor, conceptual, and social affective skills. These skills play a part in determining whether a child will succeed in one type of nonoral method as opposed to another.

The severely handicapped population at Project MESH (Model Education for the Severely Handicapped) range from physically handicapped children who demonstrate high receptive language abilities, to severely retarded children who display severely delayed receptive and expressive language skills. This wide range of language skills and deficits necessitated the availability of three nonoral methods. The first nonoral program to be developed was a written-word card system that trained the child to structure word cards into functional sentences. This system consisted of a limited vocabulary until the child could learn to spell and use an orthographic system. Only children displaying fairly high receptive skills have succeeded within the written system. The second nonoral program involved the use of a mechanical, nonoral communicator containing five display windows. Pictures superimposed with written words were presented via slide cards. The child operated the communicator by pressing touch plates and was able to "write out" sentences. The physically handicapped child demonstrating fairly high receptive skills was placed in this program. Obviously, the severely retarded child with low receptive and expressive language functions was not a candidate for the above programs. The needs of many of our severely retarded children necessitated the development of yet another nonoral program, a manual signing program.

Population

The students participating in the development of the manual signing program were residents of the Parsons State Hospital and Training Center, Parsons, Kansas. The nine students included in the signing program were enrolled in an all-day, off-grounds education program (Project MESH). Their ages ranged from 10 to 18 years, with a mean age of 13 years. According to the audiometric assessments by the training center's speech department, seven of the students had hearing within normal limits and the remaining two children had mild losses. The students represented three measured intellectual levels based on the American Association of Mental Deficiency's classification system (Heber, 1958). The students were essentially nonverbal and many displayed additional handicapping conditions. Table I contains the pretest data which gives the percent of correct responses and measured intelligence (MI) levels and adaptive behavior (AB) levels. Seven of the students did not demonstrate noun imitation or noun production. Only five of the students displayed any vowel or consonant imitation. Spontaneous vocalizations for the remaining five children consisted of one or two stereotyped vowel utterances. Four of these nine students were originally placed in a verbal program because they demonstrated some verbal imitation skills; however, after two months within the oral system, they showed very little progress and were placed within the manual signing training program.

Certain advantages and disadvantages were inherent within the manual signing system, just as they were present in other nonoral systems. The primary advantage of the signing program was its feasibility for spontaneous use. Appropri-

TABLE 1

Pretest Scores (Percent Correct), Measured Intelligence Levels, and Adaptive Behavior Levels

Students	C.H.	S.L.	G.L.	R.H.	J.B.	M.G.	C.W.	D.J.	B.W.
Motor Imitation w/Object	90	80	0	100	100	100	90	0	7
Function of Object	90	100	0	90	70	80	90	0	0
Object Discrimination	100	30	20	100	100	60	80	10	10
Vowel Imitation	50	20	0	60	90	65	0	0	0
Consonant Imitation	30	10	0	20	80	30	0	0	0
Noun Imitation	0	0	0	30	50	0	0	0	0
Noun Production	0	10	0	10	0	0	0	0	0
Adaptive Behavior (AB)	III (low)	IV	IV	IV (low)	IV	IV	IV	IV	IV
Measured Intelligence (MI)	III (low)	IV	IV	V	IV	IV	IV	IV	V

ate communicative features, such as facial expressions and eye contact, could be maintained throughout the communication exchange. The transmission time was short, providing an efficient means of communication for student, trainer, and listener. However, to be functional, the receiver had to be familiar with the system, and the response topography had to be available to the student before the system could be utilized in an effective manner. Initially, the need to train teachers, parents, or cottage aides seemed to be a disadvantage but, since the manual sign language functioned as a novel language system for the caretakers, they actually served as better language trainers with the manual signs. Initial observational data collected in our classrooms showed that the teachers attended to the student's signs, prompted the correct signs and expanded the signs significantly more than the oral correlates presented by the verbal students. The teacher became more aware of the student's language and communicated with him at his level of functioning.

The manual signing program was broken down into three components, which functioned as: (a) a language system, (b) a speech initiator, and (c) a language facilitator. The first two components were designed specifically for the severely nonverbal child. The third component, using manual signing as a language facilitator, was utilized primarily with trainable children who have some verbal language. It was used as a prompt to enhance the acquisition of the verbal elements. (Our discussion on program development will concern only the first two components).

Sign Content and Sequence

The content and sequence of the signs were important issues in the development of the signing program. Special considerations were given to the vocabulary and syntactic components, and the following questions were asked:

1. From what signing system should the vocabulary be derived?
2. What type of syntax system should be used?
3. What signs should be selected for initial acquisition?
4. Should a normal language development sequence be used?

Stokoe (1965) stated that the nature of sign language structure is quite similar to the oral language structure. Visible distinct units, called *chereme*, are analogous to the phoneme or sound unit. Sign language also contains an inventory of signs (lexicon) and rules for combining or structuring (syntax). The American Sign Language (ASL) provides a basic lexicon that has in part been used by other manual communication systems. However, the semantic and syntactic systems of ASL are not directly parallel to the English semantics and syntax (Stokoe, 1965). Mayberry (1976) provides some syntactic and semantic differences between ASL and the other systems and offers suggestions for their use in developing manual programs for the severely handicapped. For the most part, lexicon used in the development of our manual sign system for nonverbal children was selected from the ASL and signed English. However, there are sign variations in ASL that may be regional, just as there are dialect variations in the English language, so signs with the same meaning may not be produced in the same way by even deaf signers. Since the ASL syntax is different from the English syntax, it was not selected as the syntax system for our signing program. Each sign was trained as equivalent to a written English gloss of that sign, and sign combinations were constructed as early developing structures. Training signs as a gloss of English was done for two reasons. First, the system often functioned as a speech initiator, and it was felt that training two different syntax systems would be confusing to the child. Second, verbal children who were learning English syntax were exposed to the nonverbal children using signs.

Each sign in the ASL has three aspects or features that distinguish it from all other signs. These features are: the place of the hand(s) in relation to the body (*tabula*), the configuration of the hand(s) (*designator*), and the movement of the hand(s) (*signation*). The signs may also be classified as touch and nontouch and as one-handed or two-handed. In a normal child some sounds and, hence, some words, are acquired before others. Many manual signing programs do not seem to take these variables into consideration in selecting initial signs for training. Although the use of functional or motivational objects is essential in determining which signs to train, it should not be the only factor in initial sign selection. It seems that a child's success within the manual sign system may be related to his success with the initial set of signs that are trained. Observational data with the chimp, Washoe, showed that early touch signs were acquired more rapidly than nontouch signs and that confusions often occurred in signs with meaning similarity (Fouts, 1972).

Only recently have studies on the acquisition of sign language become available (Bellugi & Fischer, 1973). Schlesinger and Meadows (1972) analyzed the sign language of four children whose families made use of the sign system simultaneous with the use of speech. Their initial data indicated that the milestones in sign language acquisition parallel the milestones in spoken language acquisition. Their data on signed constructions are supported by Bloom's (1970) analysis of two-word structures. Utilizing this information, our manual sign training utilizes the normal developmental data provided by Bloom (1970), Brown (1973), and Bowerman (1973). The early two-word syntactic constructions trained within our program are similar to the normal child's utterances which express semantic relations. (Table 2 lists these relations and the sign correlates.)

TABLE 2

Semantic Relations Expressed by Two-Sign Combinations

Action-Object	*play ball*
State-Object	*want cookie*
Agent-Action	*Jeff* (you) *eat*
Action-Location	*go school*
Object-Location	*bus school*
Recurrence	*more pop*
Negation	*no candy*
Possession	*Tim* (point) *shoe*
Demonstrative	*there* (point) *book*
Feature Marker	*dirty shirt*
Recipient of Action	*give comb*

Training Components

The child's success in learning to communicate via signing is not only a function of the training content and sequence; the procedures used in training are equally important. A child learning language must learn the symbolic system being used and must learn to use that system for communication. The signs themselves and the combinations of these signs may be described as symbols. However, the functions of those signs and their combinations serve as communication. The nonverbal students learn a different symbol system from their verbal peers, but their environment is structured to parallel that of their peers. Thus, the communication aspects of the oral and nonoral training programs do not differ.

Assessment

Before a student was placed within the manual sign system, a specific assessment test was given to determine if the child was a candidate for signing. The student's receptive language skills were assessed to see whether he had experience with the objects that were to be trained initially. Other tests were given to determine if the child should be placed in a prerequisite training program before receiving sign training. The students within our program were initially assessed on the use of objects and on the visual-verbal discriminations of objects. The student's motor dexterity with objects in structured settings and in random activities was assessed to determine whether he had the response topography necessary for the initial sign training. Even though a child did not imitate the gross signs, he used various aspects of a sign in spontaneous activity. A sign imitation pretest was given to each child, and, if the student scored above an 80% criterion level, the handshaping phase of training was eliminated. Each test consisted of 10 to 20 items and the scores were plotted on a profile. The pretest data were analyzed in terms of program and training step placement.

Once the student was selected for manual signing training, additional information was obtained. The child's dominant hand or hand preference was assessed, as well as his object preference. Hand dominance with severely handicapped children was assessed by observing (out of 10 trials) which foot led when the student was in an equal-foot, stance position, and observing which hand the student used to reach for objects or for support when both hands were free and in a neutral position (Murphy, 1976). Object preference was assessed by informal tests that were part of the assessment battery.

Training Procedures

A set of basic procedures was utilized in the manual signing program. A number of these procedures served a more useful function during the initial acquisition process even though they were included in the entire training sequence.

A time-delay procedure adapted from Touchette (1971) was used to minimize errors and to determine the transfer from one mode of training to another. In the initial steps of the program, the criterion behavior to be acquired (imitation) and the controlling stimulus (handshaping) were presented simultaneously. Utilizing this procedure in a signing program necessitated a slight delay, since one cannot model and handshape at the same time. Once the child was correctly responding to handshaping (not resisting) at a 90% criterion level, a 1-second delay was given, i.e., the trainer presented the imitation model to the student, inaudibly counted "1001" (approximately 1 second), and handshaped the sign approximation if no response had occurred within that 1-second time period. The child was reinforced for correct imitated responses or handshaped responses. Incorrect responses were handshaped, but no reinforcement was given. If the student made five incorrect responses in a training block, the delay was decreased by 1 second. Thus, the child could wait for the handshaping stimulus and be reinforced or imitate the model and be reinforced. The time delays were increased by 1-second intervals each time the child reached a 90% criterion over two 10-trial training blocks. This procedure of waiting for the controlling stimulus and receiving reinforcement was used only to the 5-second interval and at 5 seconds the student was no longer reinforced for prompted responses. The majority of the students in the signing program began imitating at least one sign in the 2-second interval, and imitated the signs at a 90% criterion level at or before the 4-second delay. This does not mean that the student waited 3 seconds and then responded to the imitative stimulus. Many of the responses had only a 5-second latency. Once the child was able to imitate the initial set of signs, imitation became the controlling stimulus and production (response is under only verbal control) served as the criterion behavior. The time delays in the production phase of training corresponded to those presented in the imitation phase: simultaneous, 1-second, 2-second, 3-second, 4-second, and 5-second (not reinforced) intervals were presented. The data for one student, presented in Figure 1, demonstrate the major feature of the procedures—a relatively errorless method of training. The student naturally received a maximum of social reinforcement when he responded correctly without the controlling model. Once the child was under imitative control on two signs, the second set of training signs was initiated at the 1-second interval. If the child made more than two errors over two training blocks, the simultaneous interval was presented. The method of training followed a handshaping-imitation-production sequence unless the student's pretest indicated no need for one of the components.

Initially, only sign approximations were handshaped and even more gross approximations of signs could be accepted. The student's dominant hand was handshaped as the active hand for two-handed signs and as the signing hand for the one-handed signs. The trainers attempted to model the signs with their dominant hands; however, if the child signed with his nondominant hand, it was not recorded as an error. The approximations occurred mainly within the configuration aspect of the sign. The movement and placement aspects of the signs were given less freedom in varying from the trainer's sign. The trainer provided the correct model as a stimulus and as feedback immediately after reinforcement was delivered. Fading and shaping techniques were used to train more precise sign diction. The signs had to become more exact as more signs were added to the student's lexicon. Therefore, the initial training of the signs with the nonverbal student was similar to the initial training of words with the verbal student.

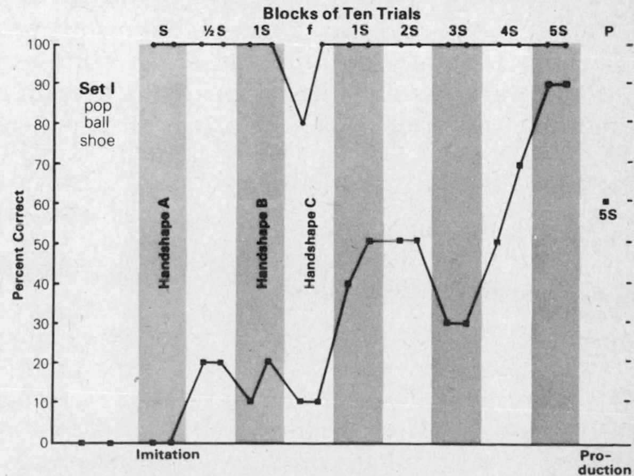

Figure 1. The use of time-delay procedure in the acquisition and maintenance of signs.

The major difference was that the signs could be directly handshaped.

The majority of nonverbal students displayed normal hearing and could profit from the speech input. Unlike the hearing-impaired student, the normally hearing, nonverbal student could utilize speech for receptive functioning while utilizing signing for expressive functioning. In fact, the student could use the manual sign system as a speech initiator and later use speech as his expressive mode. For these reasons, speech was used for giving directives and was always paired with the sign stimuli in manual sign training. The trainer never used a sign without also using the English word as a gloss. Specific words that were functional in reception as well as in expression were often signed to the student before the sign was actually trained. This was done so that the student could become familiar with the sign and pair it with appropriate objects or actions before he was actually using the sign.

Training Model

Now that the procedures basic to our program have been briefly outlined, they will be organized into a more functional framework. During the initial development of our program, various content sequences were trained to different groups of students to determine which signs could be acquired more rapidly. Also, comprehension and production of signs were trained in a multiple baseline design. These research studies were conducted in order to answer specific questions in designing a manual signing program.

During the initial phases of program development, the students were seen for individual training in 1/2-hour sessions, four times a week. (Currently the sign training is conducted in group sessions with two to three students being seen for 1/2-hour to 45-minute sessions.) The student was positioned at an approximate right angle to the trainer (*T*) before each session began. This seating arrangement was assumed to provide an appropriate model for the student (not a mirror-effect model), while allowing the trainer to handshape the response easily.

The stimulus items used in training were actual objects, events, and relations. The signs referring to those objects or actions were presented in training sets. Noun signs were trained within the first two training sets, and one or two verbs were frequently included in the third training set. Set I contained two or three signs, Set II contained three signs, and Set III contained four signs, for an initial sign vocabulary of ten signs. The signs within each set were trained concurrently, with each set being trained in ten trial blocks. Each sign within a set was randomly presented throughout the 10 trials, with no identical sign being presented more than three times in succession. Two or three training blocks (20–30 trials) per student were usually presented during a session. The time remaining in the session was spent training the function of unknown objects. After the student had reached Set I criterion, these signs were placed on review, while Set II training was conducted.

The first step in training involved requiring the child to place his hands in his lap before each trial was presented. Maintaining the student's hands in this position was especially important in signing, because initially the student may tend to develop superstitious movements as a part of the signs if he is allowed to make free hand movements. Later in training, the child must learn to initiate and complete a sign utterance by assuming and resuming a neutral hand position. Once the child was maintaining inactive quiet hands, the training proceeded.

Only one student out of nine demonstrated that he could imitate the signs in Set I. The remaining eight students required the handshaping procedures. Three types of handshaping procedures (A, B, C) were used. Handshaping A, B, and C are generally defined within the following training example. Some form of fading usually took place within handshaping A, B, and C.

Set I Training

A. Block #1: Sign Imitation.
Controlling Stimulus: Handshaping A.
Time Delay: Simultaneous.

Stimulus Items: Ball and Shoe.
Criterion: 90% on two blocks.

Trainer	*Student*
1. Presents object (Trial 1).	Looks at object.
2. Says student's name.	Looks at trainer.
3. a. Says, "What's this?"	
b. Says, "shoe" while signing *shoe*.	

c. Immediately handshapes *S*'s hands.

Trainer	Student
(1) Configuration formed } Handshape A	Student does not resist.
(2) Positioning made } Handshape A	Student does not resist.
(3) Movement guided } Handshape A	Student does not resist.
4. a. Provides verbal reinforcement.	May touch or play w/object.
b. Says, "shoe" while signing *shoe*.	
c. Provides tangible reinforcement.	Accepts reinforcer.
5. Says, "Quiet hands" (initially guiding hands to lap).	Maintains hands in lap.
6. Presents remaining (2 . . . 10) trials in Block #1.	
B. *T* presents second training block. Same as A, 1–6.	Same as A.

When the student has completed two training blocks at a 90% criterion, the training may be described as follows:

Set I Training

Block #1: Sign Imitation.
Controlling Stimulus: Handshaping B.
Time Delay: 1-Second Interval.

Stimulus Items: Ball and shoe.
Criterion: 90% on two blocks.

Trainer	*Student*
1. and 2. Same as A.	Same as A.
3. a. Says, "What's this?"	
b. Says, "ball" while signing *ball*.	
c. Waits 1 second.	a. May correctly imitate T's sign. b. May respond incorrectly. c. May wait for handshaping.
4. a. Reinforces for imitation if a.	
b. Provides correct model and advances to next trial if b.	
c. Immediately handshapes S's hand(s) if c.	
(1) Configuration formed } Handshape B	Does not resist.
(2) Positioning made } Handshape B	Does not resist.
	Completes sign by guiding movement.
d. Provides verbal reinforcement.	May play with object.
e. Says "shoe" while signing *shoe*.	
f. Provides tangible reinforcement.	Accepts reinforcer.
5. Says, "Quiet hands."	Maintains hands in lap.

During the 1-second delay period, the student had the option of: (a) correctly imitating *T*'s sign, (b) making an incorrect response, or (c) waiting for handshaping. If the student made five or more incorrect responses during any one training block or 70% errors on two consecutive training blocks, the time delay was decreased by 1 second. After the student had reached criterion at the handshaping B 1-second delay step, the procedures were repeated with the controlling stimulus becoming handshaping C (only configuration was handshaped) with a 2-second time delay. Handshaping C was faded during the 3-second delay, graduating from a half handshape to a touch. The exact emphasis of the handshaping depended on each individual student; some students needed a prompt that indicated a closed fist, others a prompt that indicated a wrist rotation. The delay procedure allowed the student to bypass parts of the handshaping procedure if he could imitate a sign without it.

An individual sign was considered to be under imitative control when the student correctly imitated five consecutive trials of that sign. A third sign was added at this time, and training with the three signs continued until Set I (three signs) reached the 90% criterion for imitation. Thus, the first and second signs to be acquired remain in the training set for maintenance.

After imitation criterion was met, a pretest for sign production was given. If the child did not meet production criterion (90% across two consecutive blocks), production training was initiated at the 1-second time delay. The procedures during the production phase of training followed those described earlier except that the controlling stimulus was imitation and the criterion behavior was production.

The students learned at least two sets of nouns before verbs were trained. Many of the initial verbs represented motivation signs ("eat") and were trained in direct relation with their referents. That is, later in training, the child was required to sign "eat" during the reinforcement phase before an edible was given. Here the actions themselves were used as stimulus items. At this point, the student was learning a language system. Initially, this training involved a rather structured approach since many of the severely handicapped students did not readily indicate their wants and needs by even nonlinguistic means. In order for communication to develop, the environment had to be structured in such a way that it elicited the use of signs and was conducive to communication. Once the child had acquired a sign, the classroom teacher also provided conditions for this sign to occur.

After the student was producing between five and ten noun signs, he was often able to imitate new signs without handshaping. Once an initial noun and verb vocabulary was established (approximately 20 signs), relation signs indicating recurrence (*more*) and negation (*no*) were trained. Later two-sign constructions expressing various semantic relations (Table 2) were trained. As the student expressed more structure with his signs, he required less structure in training.

Data Systems

Precise recording of each specific signing response and verbal response (if they occurred) was necessary to gear the program for each individual student. Stokoe (1965) has composited a table of symbols used for writing the signs of ASL. An adaption of these symbols was used for recording the specific signing response made by each student. Therefore, the type of approximation or error could be rapidly recorded. Phonetic transcriptions were used to record any verbal response the student made. The trainer recorded the data to show whether the student had made a correct response without the controlling stimulus being presented ⊕, a correct response with the controlling stimulus +, the aspects of the sign that differ from *T*'s model sign, and the verbal approximations.

Results

The initial data collected in the course of the program's development were analyzed to determine whether some signs could be trained in fewer trials than other signs. Although a few individual differences were noted across students, the majority of students showed some general acquisition trends. Not all students received the same training words within the first three training sets. Various content sequences were selected to sort out the object variables and the sign variables.

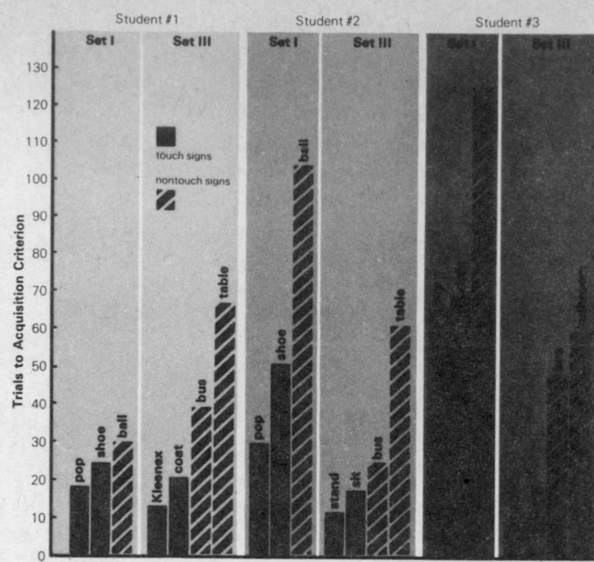

Figure 2. Acquisition of touch versus nontouch signs.

Figure 2 presents the acquisition data from three different students on training Sets I and III. All three children received the same signs in Set I, which consisted of two touch signs (shoe and pop) and one nontouch sign (ball). A variation of the sign for "ball" was selected in which a bouncing action was demonstrated. This variation was selected so as not to interfere with another similar sign to be trained in a later set. Set II was not included since only touch signs were presented. Student #1 showed a small difference between the touch and nontouch signs on Set I; but a touch-nontouch difference was shown in acquiring Set III signs. Students #2 and #3 demonstrated a more rapid acquisition on the touch signs in both Set I and Set III training.

Only Subject #2 acquired the motivational sign ("pop") before the nonmotivation sign ("shoe"). This is not surprising since "pop" did not always directly follow the sign for "pop." The sign ("pop") was trained within the training set and if the student pointed to "pop" after receiving three tokens he was handshaped or given a model for the sign and then given "pop" as a reinforcer. Fewer errors were made by the students when "pop" was directly contingent on the sign during the reinforcement period.

Acquisition data across the first three training sets for the subjects are presented in Figure 3. Students #2 and #3 showed an increased acquisition rate between Set I and the other two sets. Student #1 showed no increased acquisition rates across the three training sets; however, he reached criterion in relatively few training trials.

Individual students showed some interesting patterns during training on the first three sets. A number of the students used two-handed touch signs in place of one-handed touch signs during initial training. One of the signs that prompted a two-handed response for three different students was the iconic (representing the actual object or object action) sign "comb." The relationship of two-handed signs versus one-handed signs is currently being studied more systematically to determine whether two-handed signs are acquired more rapidly than one handed signs.

A few of our students received training on signs with meaning similarity: two words from the same category ("pants" and "shirt") were trained within the same training set. Four out of five students confused these signs for one another early in training. The similarity in movement may have also been a confounding variable. One child acquired the clothing signs only after they were placed in different training sets.

Two-handed signs which were made at the same place in relation to the body ("shoe," "pop," "spoon," "book") produced very few errors, even though all four of these signs were usually trained within the first two training sets.

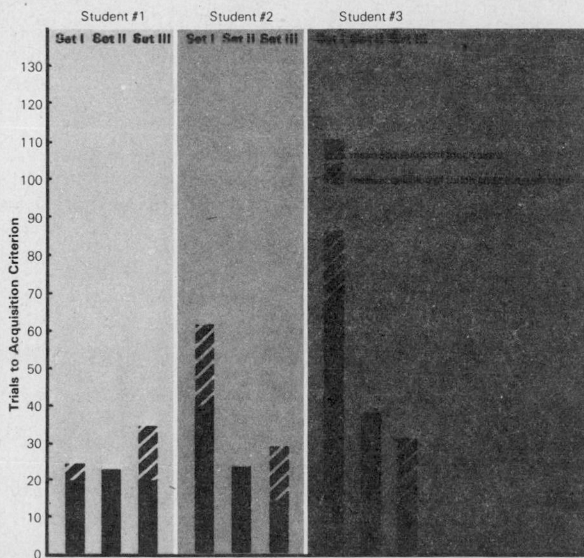

Figure 3. Acquisition of signs across training sets.

The majority of errors for the students were made on the configuration aspect of the sign. These configuration errors were both substitution errors (one sign given for the correct one) and errors in which only very gross approximations were used.

The students in the manual signing program are utilizing many of their signs within the classroom. Not only do the signs serve as a means of communicating, but six of the students are pairing some word-approximations with their signs. One child began approximating two words three weeks after her sign training was initiated. This girl had not previously imitated sounds or words, even though she was originally placed in an oral program. This student has dropped the signs for which she can use word approximations. Another child is pairing word approximations with his signs and uses two words without signs. Therefore, we do not see the signs interfering with speech but, rather, the signs seem to facilitate speech initiation. We should point out here that these verbal pairings are always reinforced.

Discussion

A program for teaching manual signing language to severely retarded persons was developed and successfully implemented with nine students. The manual signing program was discussed in terms of a language system and a speech initiation system. It was proposed that a number of variables be considered when selecting the initial sign content and sequence in order for efficient learning to take place. The syntax of the program was trained as an English sign system.

The procedures basic to the program were as follows:

1. A time-delay procedure was used throughout training.
2. The method of training followed a hand-shaping, imitation, production sequence.
3. Approximations of initial signs were trained and exact models were provided.
4. Shaping and fading procedures were used to train closer sign approximations.
5. The dominant hand or the active hand was used for the sign.
6. Simultaneous speech was used as a gloss for each sign.

Preliminary data on the students showed that touch signs were acquired more rapidly than nontouch signs. The majority of errors were made on the configuration aspect of the sign, even though approximations were trained.

Initial data also showed that signs within the same conceptual class (e.g., "shirt" and "pants") should not be trained within the same training set. The majority of students began to pair speech with their signs during the second training set.

The whole issue of imitation may be relevant both to sign language and speech. Garcia, Baer, and Firestone (1971) found that generalized imitation was restricted to the topographical type of imitation currently being trained or having been previously trained so that when motor imitation was being trained, vocal imitation remained at baseline. The relationship between this finding and that of sign training functioning as a facilitator for speech appears contradictory. However, if we look closely at the typical procedure of sign training, a plausible explanation is evident. It is possible that those who claim that signs are facilitators for speech are in reality training a generalized motor imitation response via sign training and then observing a transfer from the motor response class to a vocal response class due to their pairing of the sign with the spoken word and referent object. The sign is a motor response that has specific meaning and it is paired with a word that has specific meaning. This may account for the motor-verbal transfer observed within the sign training.

Our findings were gathered from data on a relatively small population. Additional data on a larger population are needed and more specific research questions need to be asked before our results can be substantiated. Initial data collected in the course of developing a pilot program have led to some additional questions:

1. At what point in training are touch and nontouch signs acquired at the same rate?
2. Is there a difference in the acquisition of motivational signs directly reinforced with the referent, and motivational signs not directly reinforced with the referent?
3. Are two-handed touch signs easier to acquire than one-handed touch signs?
4. How similar in form do signs have to be before they interfere with acquisition?
5. Do signs trained in one setting with one trainer transfer to other settings and trainers, and how can this transfer be facilitated?
6. Does training sign comprehension facilitate the acquisition of sign production, or do they function independently?

Answers to these questions will enable us to develop a more efficient and effective manual signing program for the severely retarded, nonverbal child.

References

Bellugi, U., & Fischer, S. A comparison of sign language and spoken language. *Cognition,* 1973, *Vol* (No) 187–200.

Berger, S. A clinical program for developing multimedia responses with atypical deaf children. In J. McLean, D. Yoder & R. Schiefelbusch (Eds.). *Language Intervention with the Retarded.* Baltimore: University Park Press, 1972.

Bloom, L. *Language Development: Form and function in emerging grammars.* Cambridge: MIT Press, 1970.

Bowerman, M. *Early syntactic development: A cross-linguistic study with special reference to Finnish.* Cambridge: Cambridge University Press, 1973.

Bricker, D. Imitative sign training as a facilitator of word-object association with low-functioning children. *American Journal of Mental Deficiency,* 1972, *76,* 509–516.

Brown, R. *A first language: The early stages.* Cambridge: Harvard University Press, 1973.

Carrier, J. K. Application of functional analysis and a nonspeech response mode to teaching language. *American Speech and Hearing Association Monograph,* 1974, *18,* 47–95.

Fouts, R. Use of guidance in teaching sign language to a chimpanzee (Pan Troglodytes'). *Journal of Comparative and Physiological Psychology,* 1972, *80,* 515–522.

Fouts, R. Acquisition and testing of gestural signs in four young chimpanzees. *Science,* 1973, *180,* 978–980.

Garcia, E., Baer, D. M., & Firestone, I. The development of generalized imitation within topographically determined boundaries. *Journal of Applied Behavior Analysis,* 1971, *4,* 101–112.

Gardner, R. A. & Gardner, B. T. Teaching sign language to a chimpanzee. *Science,* 1969, *165,* 664–672.

Hall, S. & Talkington, L. W. Evaluation of a manual approach to programming for deaf retarded. *American Journal of Mental Deficiency,* 1970, *75,* 378–380.

Hayes, K. J. & Hayes, C. Imitation in a home-raised chimpanzee. *Journal of Comparative and Physiological Psychology,* 1952, *45,* 450–459.

Heber, R. A manual on terminology and classification in mental retardation. *Monograph Supplement, American Journal of Mental Deficiency,* 1958, 64, No. 2.

Kopchick, G., Rombach, D., & Smilovitz, R. A total communication environment in an institution. *Mental Retardation,* 1975, *13* (3), 22–23.

Larson, T. *Communication for the nonverbal child. Academic Therapy,* 1971, *6*(3), 305–312.

Mansfield Training School. *Manual language dictionary—A functional vocabulary for the retarded.* (Booklets 1–3). Mansfield Depot, Connecticut: Authors, 1973–1975.

Mayberry, R. If a chimp can learn sign language, surely my nonverbal client can too. *American Speech and Hearing Association,* 1976, *18*(4), 223–228.

Miller, A., & Miller, E. Cognitive-developmental training with elevated boards and sign language. *Journal of Autism and Childhood Schizophrenia,* 1973, *3*(1), 65–85.

Murphy, N. Personal communication, *January 22,* 1976.

Premack, D. A. A functional analysis of language. *Journal of Experimental Analysis Behavior,* 1970, *14,* 107–125.

Richardson, T. Sign language for the SMR and PMR. *Mental Retardation,* 1975, *13*(3), 17.

Schlesinger, H. S. Language acquisition in four deaf children. In H. S. Schlesinger, & K. P. Meadow (Eds.). *Sound and Sign.* Berkeley: University of California Press, 1972.

Schlesinger, H. S. & Meadows, K. P. *Sound and Sign.* Berkeley: University of California Press, 1972.
Smith, C. H. Total communication utilizing the simultaneous method. In I. M. Creedon (Ed.). *Appropriate behavior through communication: A new program in simultaneous language.* Chicago, Illinois: Dysfunctioning Child Center Publication, 1973.
Stokoe, W. *A dictionary of American sign language on linguistic principles.* Washington, D.C.: Gallaudet College Press, 1965.
Topper, S. T. Gesture language for a nonverbal severely retarded male. *Mental Retardation,* 1975, *13*(1), 30–31.
Touchette, P. E. Transfer of stimulus control: measuring the moment of transfer. *Journal of Experimental Analysis of Behavior,* 1971, *15,* 347–354.
Vanderheiden, G. Non-speech communication development as a basis for programming for the severely handicapped. Paper presented at the Second Annual Conference of American Association for the Education of the Severely/Profoundly Handicapped, Kansas City, Missouri, 1975.
Vicker, B. The communication process using a normal means. In B. Vicker (Ed.), *Nonoral communication system project.* Iowa City, Iowa: University Hospital School, The University of Iowa, 1974.

DEE CANTRELL is a Research Assistant for the Bureau of Child Research and a Language Technician for Project MESH in Parsons, Kansas.

KATHLEEN STREMEL-CAMPBELL is a Research Assistant for the Bureau of Child Research. She also serves as Director of the Communication Unit for Project MESH in Parsons, Kansas.

JAMES HALLE is a Research Assistant for the Bureau of Child Research and a Language Technician for Project MESH in Parsons, Kansas.

Communication Management for the Non-Responsive Child: A Team Approach

SUSAN F. SOLTMAN
JANE A. RIEKE

University of Washington

Teachers and other professionals who work with severely/profoundly handicapped children are faced with many different problems. The children are difficult to assess. They may have multiple problems which make it difficult to decide on treatment priorities. Many of these children show very slow gains, and staff and parents tend to be easily discouraged. It takes the cooperation of specialists in many disciplines to provide a useful and supportive educational program for severely handicapped children.

The Interdisciplinary Educational Team has proved to be a highly successful approach to meeting the needs of children in programs for the severely/profoundly handicapped at the Experimental Education Unit of the Child Development and Mental Retardation Center, University of Washington, Seattle. In this setting, the Educational Team is made up of the parent, teacher, nurse, occupational therapist, pediatrician, family liaison specialist, and communication disorders specialist (CDS). (The communication disorders specialist is a speech pathologist who is a specialist in verbal and nonverbal communication development, including language, speech, and pre-speech functions.)

During the first Educational Team meetings, the child's deficits in communication are almost always identified as major problems by both parents and teachers. This concern has resulted in an additional and particularly close working relationship between the teacher and the CDS who work with these children. The process of working together, which has been developed by this two-discipline team, will be described in this article, with attention to the responsibilities of each of the team members as they work together to promote communication skills for severely/profoundly handicapped children. (See Rieke, 1974, for additional discussion of this topic.)

The key to the team process is that the CDS views the child in his classroom setting in terms of the variety of activities planned for him and the people he interacts with. Assessment and management decisions are focused on how the child functions on a daily basis. The teacher and CDS decide on the basis of the classroom assessment what types of language or communication programs meet the needs of each child. The CDS makes certain that language and communication goals are both communicatively useful in the child's environment and developmentally appropriate for each child. The teacher and the CDS cooperate totally in designing and implementing the program.

Traditionally, a child who needed help with speech or language problems was taken out of the classroom to work with a clinician in a separate therapy room. Recently, however, some clinicians have been working with children in a corner of the classroom where the children normally spend most of the school day. This shift has helped to open lines of communication and to foster fruitful cooperation between teachers and clinicians; thus, specialists from the two disciplines have worked out many interactive plans that neither could have managed separately. Because the severely/profoundly handicapped child is in need of such interdisciplinary consideration, the new pattern of interaction has been especially promising for work with that child.

In this article we will explain the team process as it was implemented to meet the challenge of the unresponsive child who functions on a very low level. In the population of severely/profoundly handicapped children there are always some who demonstrate little, if any, communicative awareness. Some children appear to be so unresponsive to the people around them that it seems unrealistic to set communication goals for them. In these instances, careful classroom observation and recording by a skilled communication disorders specialist are essential to determine in what subtle ways each child responds and to uncover events or combinations of events that elicit

All names used in this article are pseudonyms.

response. It is usually necessary then for the teacher and CDS to plan a management program which can be carried on throughout the day in the classroom. An explanation of the kind of planning and implementation needed for an in-classroom program will be included later.

This article also suggests an additional dimension for work with severely/profoundly handicapped children, in that management programs can be designed to permeate the child's day and that such programs can affect habit patterns. These programs can be data based; therefore, all performance changes can be measured. The planning of such programs comes about through team efforts. Effective teamwork requires not only a willingness for people from different disciplines to cooperate, but also requires some guidelines—procedures—to facilitate this process. Although useful wherever teamwork is indicated, such interaction has been essential in developing communication programs for non-responsive children.

Procedures in the Team Process

The procedures which have been developed to facilitate the team process serve as guidelines in several areas. First, the procedures delineate the tasks to be addressed to move from the identification of the problem through the management phases. Second, they indicate who is responsible for each step in the procedure and suggest questions that need to be considered. Table 1 outlines the steps in the procedures and indicates who is responsible for implementing them.

TABLE 1

Communication Management Team Procedures

Steps in the Team Procedure	Team Member(s) Responsible
1. *Assessment request* Does (child's name) have any responsive behaviors we can build on?	*Parent-Teacher-CDS*
2. *Observations; systematic recording* What are the environmental situations, people, or actions which elicit responses from the child? What are the responses the child demonstrates?	*CDS*
3. *Sorting information* Which situations draw the most responses? What kind of responses occur most frequently?	*CDS*
4. *Designing the intervention program* What will be the goal? What can the teacher do to facilitate more responses from the child? How often can the teacher intervene?	*Teacher-CDS*
5. *Implementing the all-day program* What kind of data collecting and charting will be done?	*Teacher*
6. *Decisions for changes in the program* What do the data show?	*Teacher-CDS*

1. Assessment Request: Parent-Teacher-CDS

The first step in the procedure is to assess each newly enrolled child to determine how he communicates, when he communicates, and his language developmental level. During the initial meeting with the teacher and the parent, the CDS will want to learn what concerns each has to get an idea of what priorities the parent and teacher have set for communication at home and in the program. They also will indicate what bothers or frustrates them.

Example: Mrs. Burn said that her daughter, Shirley, had no awareness of people, and, in fact, slept most of the time. Mrs. Burn reported she even had to force-feed Shirley. The teaching staff confirmed these statements. It seemed that the child was non-responsive. The teacher and CDS were both unwilling to write off the child, and the teacher requested that the CDS observe Shirley in the classroom to see if she showed any subtle responses to her environment.

2. Observations: Systematic Recording—CDS

The classroom assessment conducted by the CDS involves a systematic recording of the child's communication behaviors. The CDS may record the child's initiated behaviors or the child's responsive behaviors, and the record will include the events both prior to and following the specified behavior. These records are then analyzed for decisions about effective management. A predetermined period of time (10 or 20 minutes) can be established for recording, and arrangements can be made for the CDS to record at different times during the day for a period of several days.

For the non-responsive child, the assessment involves a strategy of recording in detail the communicative interactions between the classroom staff and the child. The CDS must pay special attention to what room conditions or events evoke some response from the child. It is also important to record what kinds of responses the child makes, including subtle postural or facial changes.

Example: Shirley, who is 7 years old, is non-ambulatory. We observed that she could sit with support but had poor head control. It was difficult to know how well she heard or how much she saw. She made no vocal sound other than an occasional soft moaning. The teaching staff had observed that she sometimes looked in the direction of people, and they thought that she was more in touch with her surroundings when they played records.

It was difficult for the CDS to observe and write down all of the antecedent conditions (environmental stimuli). There were so many things happening at one time that required attention: all of the visual, physical-motion, auditory, and tactile events which occurred around Shirley had to be noted. A special form had to be developed. The recording also included documentation of the minute degrees of responses Shirley made, such as closing and reopening her eyes, and lifting her head.

3. Sorting Information: CDS

When the systematic recordings of communicative interactions have been completed, the CDS must sort through the data to find which antecedent events (environmental stimuli) resulted in the largest number of responses from the child. The data will also indicate how the child responded and what led to the highest level of response developmentally; that is, whether the response was non-verbal only or whether there were some sounds of even word approximations from the child.

Example: We will review in detail later the sorting procedure which took place with Shirley's data. However, the results indicated clear patterns of response. With a response rate of 66%, the response that occurred most frequently was that she looked at the adult. This response occurred when Shirley faced an adult and the adult walked toward her and talked to her. In other words, Shirley was most responsive when she had sensory input of seeing movement plus hearing auditory stimuli.

4. Designing the Intervention Program: Teacher-CDS

When the CDS has the information which responds to the concerns of the teacher (or parent or major care provider), he is ready to meet with the teacher to review results and to design an intervention program. Several needs may show in the data, and there probably will be several possible goals to select for the child. There may also be several management possibilities.

It should be made clear that this step in the procedure, designing the intervention program, is a time for team input and cooperative decisions. In some cases, it will be appropriate for the CDS to take the child from the classroom to a therapy room for distraction-free individual work. Sometimes the wiser decision will be to work within the classroom, developing a receptive or expressive language program for a child or a group of children. In still other situations, the decision may be to include the child in the classroom's ongoing language programs or in commercially available programs appropriate for a given child or children. With children who are non-responsive or whose habit patterns we wish to alter as rapidly as possible, the decision to implement an all-day management program may be the best team decision.

If the decision is for an all-day management program, it is up to the teacher, with the help of the CDS, to decide what can be carried out in the classroom. A plan sheet is then written which describes in behavioral terms the goals and procedures for the program.

Example: In the program for Shirley, the teacher and CDS first selected a goal: Shirley was to respond by looking at the adult. The team then discussed what the teacher could do to increase the number of responses from Shirley. The teacher also had to decide how many times she could reasonably expect classroom personnel to take time to approach Shirley to seek a response.

5. Implementing the All-Day Program: Teacher

After the teacher and the CDS have selected a communication behavior and appropriate management strategy, the teacher will be ready to implement the program. It is helpful to post the goal or target in a conspicuous place. This serves not only as a staff reminder, but assures consistency of management. Decisions about the kinds of data to be recorded and the person responsible for them are also made at this time. During the team meeting, a data form and plan sheet will have to be designed. The teacher or aide responsible for the data which monitor the child's progress also will be designated.

Example: For Shirley, the selected goal was: Shirley will look at an adult who approaches her.

The management: The adults will approach and talk to Shirley when they are in her line of vision. If she looks at the adult, the adult will pat her and praise her. If she does not look, the adult will give no reinforcement.

The data: Data were collected 10 times over the course of the day. The correct/error data were marked by the adult at each trial. The data sheet was posted conveniently on the wall with the reminder board.

6. Decisions for Changes in the Program: Teacher-CDS

Both the CDS and the teacher will be interested in following the data to see if the staff can add the intervention strategy to its interaction with the child and to see what changes occur for the child. There are several possible problems which should be mentioned.

As with any teaching or behavior management program, a review of the data can help pinpoint necessary changes in the program. If the child is not having success at a desired rate it may be that the antecedent event (what the teacher says or does to encourage the child to respond) needs to be changed, or the consequent event (what the teacher does after the child responds) needs to be changed.

If the child has progressed to a high level of success in the present program, the CDS and teacher need to plan the next step to keep the child moving toward higher developmental levels of communication. These are basic decision points in making changes within the child's present communication program.

The all-day program dealt with in this article requires staff to be aware of two particular problems, consistency and frequency. All classroom staff members should be alert to the child's communication target and the procedure established to evoke the response from the child. If the procedure is too complicated or if it is not clearly explained on the reminder board, staff members may vary in what they say and do. As a result, the data may show that the child is making little progress in responding consistently. If there is inconsistency in running the program and the inconsistency is adversely affecting the success of the child, this situation should be rectified by the CDS and the teacher.

Frequency of the trials is another problem. Teachers are often comfortable with what we refer to as "sit down" programs, wherein a specific amount of time is scheduled for the teacher or CDS to sit down with the child and run the program. However, the all-day program is designed to be conducted intermittently throughout the day. It provides a procedure for communicating with the child in a consistent manner by which the child will be successfully responsive and the adult can reinforce that success. But because the trials are to be done between the ongoing teaching and caregiving activities, busy teachers and staff sometimes find it difficult to complete the desired number of trials each day. If this happens, the CDS and teacher need to consider ways of handling this problem.

The next section will cover additional ways to work toward consistency and frequency of trials in implementing an all-day communication intervention for the non-responsive child.

The Team Approach in Action

In this section, we will review the steps of setting up a communication intervention program for a particular child (Shirley), and will include examples of the forms, charts, and plan sheets which were used. The purpose of these details is to provide guidance for those who wish to replicate the procedures. The information will undoubtedly also suggest ways of adapting present procedures used in a variety of settings by staff who work with low-functioning, non-responsive children. (It may be helpful to refer to Table 1 throughout this section.)

The Child: The Challenge

When Shirley was enrolled in the program, she was 7 years old. She was a profoundly retarded child whom doctors had described as functioning at the 1-month level of development. She was very small, weighed 47 pounds, and had a history of serious feeding problems. She had been tube fed until she was 5, but was presently being spoon fed. However, she had developed no chewing behaviors. She did not sit without support. She had fair head control in supported sitting, but her basic muscle tone was hypotonic, or floppy. Shirley had been referred to the program at the Experimental Education Unit by the staff of a nearby suburban school district, where she had been in a class for severely handicapped children for one year. Prior to that time, she had been at home with her parents and two older brothers because there were no public school programs for children like Shirley. The referring teacher was concerned because the staff had been able to do no more than feed and diaper her and provide physical therapy through passive exercises.

Assessment Request

When Shirley was enrolled in this school, the Educational Team met to discuss plans for her instruction. Shirley's mother said her greatest concern was that Shirley get enough caloric intake to maintain or gain some weight. Feeding Shirley was still a problem, because she seemed to be hypersensitive to touch around and in the mouth. Feeding at home took an inordinate amount of time. The CDS asked how Shirley communicated her likes, dislikes, or needs. Mrs. Burn replied that Shirley seemed to be unaware of people, but did express her dislikes when food touched her mouth: she would frequently turn her head away from the spoon. Mrs. Burn thought she recalled Shirley looking at people occasionally, but she was not sure if this was a coincidence or was done in response to attention from people around her. Mrs. Burn said, "Actually, we're not sure just how much she can see or hear. She really sleeps much of the time and just doesn't seem to be interested in her environment."

At the conclusion of the conference, the parent, the teacher, and the CDS, along with the other members of the Educational Team, agreed that a communication assessment would be done, but that Shirley's immediate need was in the area of feeding and maintenance of muscle tone.

The first assessment that was attempted was an adaptation of the type of formalized procedure usually administered. The CDS presented a variety of loud sounds, noisemakers, and voice stimuli in the classroom to try to elicit from Shirley some consistent, observable response. Shirley did not show any consistency of response. Only occasionally did she look at the face of the person talking to her.

The teaching staff decided to try a training program to develop in Shirley some consistent turning to sound and some eye contact. These instructional programs were written as structured sit-down programs for specific time periods each day. At the end of 10 weeks, the data showed no progress, even with several changes in reinforcers. It seemed that Shirley was not ready for these direct training programs, and they were dropped. The staff continued with the motor, feeding, and sensory stimulation activities which comprised the rest of Shirley's school day.

Mrs. Burn, the teacher, and the CDS were unwilling to give up on Shirley. What concerned them was that the classroom staff were inadvertently paying very little attention to Shirley except during times when they worked specifically with her. This was understandable. It was easy to forget to communicate socially with a child who gave virtually no response to any of the efforts of the staff. But the CDS did have some information from the questions she had asked during the first meeting. The mother had reported that Shirley turned her head away from foods she didn't like, and that she sometimes looked at people, but no one knew what situations caused her to look. The new concern raised from the classroom situation was how to get some kind of social interaction to occur in the classroom.

At a meeting with the classroom staff, the CDS summed up the assessment questions as follows:

1. How can we get the classroom staff to encourage responses from Shirley at times throughout the day, especially during those times when Shirley is now being left unattended?
2. What kind of social or communicative approach will elicit a response from the child?
3. What level of response is most likely to occur (in other words, what response can the adult expect to get from Shirley that will be possible to reinforce)?

It was clear that recording all of the environmental conditions in a busy classroom of six children and three adults and observing all of the very subtle responses Shirley might make would be a real challenge for the CDS.

Observation: Systematic Recording

There are many kinds of recording forms which are useful when the CDS is observing the communicative behaviors of children. The form described as Table 2 is geared to direct the recorder's attention to two particular aspects of communicative interaction in the classroom: namely, what events in the environment trigger response, and the nature of the response. The form is designed so observations directed to these two questions can be systematically and accurately recorded.

1. *Environmental Antecedents*. Does the child respond to any combinations of visual, tactile, auditory, or kinesthetic input from the communicative environment of adults and children in the classroom?
2. *Pupil Behavior (Responsive)*. If the child does respond, what are the kinds of responses he or she makes?

Another useful form has been the four-column format. In Table 3, the third column

TABLE 2

Communication Behavior Observation and Recording Form

Environmental Antecedents	Pupil Behavior (Responsive)

is used to include any initiating behaviors (what the child does to make his or her needs known or to get attention from others), and the fourth column is used to record observations of what others do to respond to the child when he or she initiates a need or seeks attention. However, for Shirley, a simple two-column form was sufficient.

The CDS checked with the teacher to find out which times would be best for observing (times at which Shirley was not scheduled for teaching activities). In this instance, a mutually agreeable time was arranged on three consecutive days, and data were recorded for 10 minutes each day. The teacher and staff were instructed to try some things they thought might elicit a response from Shirley. The CDS arranged to record what happened. Other than that open request to attempt eliciting a response, the staff was asked to keep the interactions as natural as possible as normal classroom activities were pursued.

The CDS watched Shirley and recorded all attempted interactions in very brief terms (Table 4). The CDS was looking for answers to the following questions:

1. What are the environmental situations, people, and actions that make changes?
2. What are the responses Shirley makes?

It was exciting to see that Shirley did indeed respond at least some of the time by looking or turning her head. After three days of gathering data, it was necessary to sort this running log of interactions so the results could be shared with the classroom staff. The sorting procedure is described in the next section.

Sorting Information

Two basic questions were asked when the recording form was designed: what did the CDS want to learn from the data and how many categories of answers were recorded. In Shirley's situation, the questions were:

1. What types of communicative interactions get the most responses from Shirley (environmental antecedents, Column 1)?
2. What kinds of responses did she give most frequently (pupil behavior, Column 2)?
3. What percentage of the time did Shirley respond?

The types of environmental communicative antecedents from the first column of the systematic sampling data are listed vertically on the left of Table 5 (How to Sort the Data). These antecedent events are grouped into six categories.

TABLE 3

Communication Behavior Observation and Recording Form

Environmental Antecedents	Pupil Behavior (Response)	Pupil Behavior (Initiates)	Adult Response

TABLE 4

Communication Behavior Observation and Recording Form

Pupil: Shirley *Time*: 9:20–9:30 a.m.	*Recorder*: Soltman *Date*: 10/1/75
Environmental Antecedents	Pupil Response
1. Bell to side of pupil.	1. Turns head and looks.
2. Adult talks and approaches.	2. Looks at adult.
3. Adult talks.	3. Looks up at adult.
4. Adult walks away.	4. Looks at adult.
5. Adult says, "Hi, Shirley!" (Stimulus is more than 6′ away from pupil.)	5. Turns head and looks at speaker.
6. Adult says, "Hi, Shirley!" (Stimulus is more than 6′ away from pupil.)	6. No change.
7. Adult approaches.	7. Turns to, looks at adult.
8. Adult talks to pupil.	8. Turns away from speaker.
9. Adult talks and touches pupil.	9. Looks, turns away from adult.
10. Adult says, "Hi, Shirley!"	10. (Head down) no change.
11. Adult says "Hey, Shirley" and touches.	11. Head up.
12. Adult approaches and talks to pupil.	12. (Head down) no change.
13. Adult touches and talks to pupil.	13. Looks at adult.

The data responsive to question 2 (What kinds of responses did she give most frequently?), which were gathered from pupil behavior, Column 2, were listed horizontally across the top of Table 5 and fell into eight types of responses. At this point, information recorded in a running log on Table 4 was sorted onto Table 5 and tallied so it could be more readily analyzed.

When we look at the results of ths data sorting, we find the environmental antecedent which elicited the greatest number of responses (9) from Shirley was when an adult who approached her also talked to her while moving toward her. Shirley was most responsive when she had both auditory stimulation (someome talking to her) and visual stimulation (someone moving toward her). In answer to question 2 (What kinds of responses did she give most frequently?), it is clear that Shirley responded eight times by looking at the adult who was in her line of vision and who was talking to her. It is interesting to note that when adults only talked to Shirley (auditory input only), she was the least responsive: five times she showed no change in her behavior, twice she turned away, and only once did she lift her head and look at the speaker.

It would have been helpful to have had this information before attempting the sitdown program for increasing Shirley's looking behavior. It appears that auditory input, e.g., a voice at close range saying, "Look, Shirley," was not a sufficiently strong stimulus to elicit a looking response from the child. It may, in fact, have been aversive, since twice Shirley turned away from the person talking to her. (At this point, it should be stressed that these conclusions are only areas to probe, since they are based on a small sample of data. The information should be used as a starting point for further investigation.)

In answer to the third question (What percentage of the time does she respond?), the results of the tally show that Shirley responded 66% of the time. This was good news to the people working with her who now had a positive starting point where there previously had been no hope. Since Shirley did have some responding behaviors, it was time to design a communicative intervention program to increase her responding.

Designing the Intervention Program

The CDS and the teacher met to discuss the results of the data which had been recorded. They reviewed Table 5. Since Shirley had not responded well to the earlier training program, which presented consecutive trials, the teacher and the CDS decided that an all-day communication intervention was appropriate for Shirley. Such a program which would distribute the trials over a longer period of the day, would increase the teachers' opportunities for success and the child's opportunities to respond and to be reinforced for responding. For Shirley, who was so unresponsive to the people in her environment, it was important to increase the number of social responses and the consistency of these responding behaviors before a more structured sitdown responding program could be designed and implemented. In short, an all-day program would help staff members to be consistent and would encourage them to interact with Shirley throughout the day. The teacher and CDS hoped that such a plan would result in an increase in Shirley's responses. In time, this increase should build

TABLE 5

How to Sort the Data

Pupil: Shirley
Total time: 30 minutes
Question: What kinds of communicative response behaviors does the pupil have?

Recorder: Soltman
Dates: 9/30, 10/1, 10/2

	Pupil Behavior								
Environment Antecedents	No change	Opens eyes	Head up + looks	*Looks at*	Turns eyes to	Turns head, looks	Turns head away	Makes sound	Total responses
1. *Adult approaches + talks*	2	0	0	*7*	0	2	0	0	*9*
2. Adult approaches	0	0	0	0	0	1	0	0	1
3. Adult talks to	5	0	1	0	0	0	2	0	3
4. Adult talks + touches	1	0	1	1	0	0	1	0	3
5. Adult walks away	1	0	0	0	1	0	0	0	1
6. Adult moves pupil's wheelchair	2	1	0	0	3	0	0	0	4
TOTAL	11	1	2	8	4	3	3	0	21

Results:
Responses: 21 = approximately 66%.
No change: 11 = approximately 34%.

Note: Items in *italic* indicate the most pertinent data to consider in program planning.

toward a higher level of response or a broader variety of responses.

Setting the Goal and the Objectives

The teacher and the CDS decided that the goal would be for Shirley to respond consistently by looking at the adult. This goal was selected because it was the type of response which occurred most frequently on Table 5. With a different child, the data might have revealed two or three types of behaviors from which to select a goal. In that case, the behavior at the highest developmental level would have been chosen. It is, of course, important for the CDS to be knowledgable about the variety of developmental sequences which comprise the area of communication, language, and speech.

The Management Plan

Since the data recorded from classroom observations had been so explicit, it was easy to arrange a management plan. (For a more extended discussion of management planning, see Haring & Gentry, 1976.) The teaching staff was instructed to use those strategies which data analysis showed to be most effective in getting a response from Shirley. Staff members would talk to her as they walked toward her. They would expect her to look at them. The rationale for this strategy appears on Table 5, where we see that the environmental antecedent of an adult walking toward Shirley and talking to her resulted in more responses from her than any other type of situation. This, then, became the plan.

The next step in setting up the program was to plan what to do when Shirley *does* look and what to do if she *does not* respond by looking. These decisions complete the first phase of the basic program plan. In Shirley's case, the teacher wanted to give social praise and friendly touching to Shirley whenever she responded by looking at the adult. If she did not look, the adult would move on and give her no attention. Social praise and attention, including touching, were chosen because they were the easiest and most natural for the busy teaching staff, and the teacher knew that food was not reinforcing. The search for a more powerful reinforcer might be needed, but that decision was deferred pending the outcome of the data to be recorded.

How Often Can the Program Be Run?

The teacher wanted a consistent number of trials given each day. This would make data collection and recording simple for the classroom staff, and it would help the staff remember to perform a specified number of daily trials for Shirley. The plan was designed to help resolve the problem the staff had of forgetting to interact with this non-responsive child.

The teacher felt that, during a 5-hour school day, the adults could easily complete 10 trials among their scheduled activities with all of the children. The trials were to be intermittently presented. With all-day programs, it is important to be realistic about what can be added to the responsibilities of an already busy teaching staff. It is better to maintain a reasonable number of trials and have staff members offer to do more, than it is to overload them.

The decisions for Shirley's all-day communication intervention were recorded on a plan sheet (Table 6), and the first day of the systematic intervention was written.

The plan sheet was part of Shirley's educational program which the teacher kept on the child's clip board. As plan changes were made, the teacher added these changes to the existing plan sheet. This allowed for easy review of the exact steps in the program. The plan sheet should be concrete and brief, but with sufficient detail that any staff member or substitute teacher could read the plan sheet and implement the program.

Implementing the Program

The teacher explained Shirley's program to her aides and parent helpers. A reminder board (Figure 1), which was printed in 3″ letters, was posted on the wall. This described: what Shirley was to do, what staff members were to do, what to do if Shirley responded, what to do if Shirley did not respond, and how many trials were to be completed per day.

A data sheet to keep a record of Shirley's responses was taped to the bottom portion of the reminder board. A percentage graph was posted with the reminder board. The data sheet served not only to keep an accurate record of whether or not Shirley responded, but it also was a visible reminder to the adults of how many trials had been given during the day.

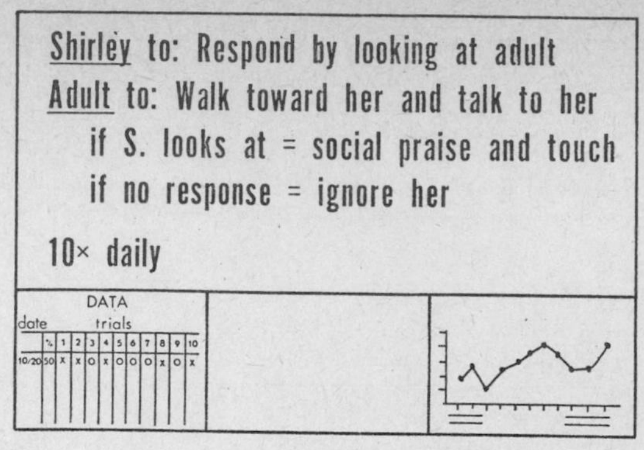

Figure 1. Reminder board.

The teacher and the helpers found it convenient to mark the data sheet after each trial. Ten trials can be converted into a percentage of correct responses very easily. The CDS transferred the results of the daily records to the graph of programs every two weeks preceding the regular Educational Team meeting. During the meeting, Shirley's communication program was studied, along with her other programs, as her progress and that of the other pupils in the class was reviewed. The data indicated progress and the need for changes in the programs.

Decisions for Changes in the Program

The percentage graph and data sheets are helpful tools in making decisions for change. Shirley was responding on an average of 38% during the first two weeks of the program. Over the next two weeks, she increased her looking at people to an average of 60%

TABLE 6

Plan Sheet

Type of movement cycle: *Communication*
Plan sheet #1 Pupil: *Shirley* Date: *October, 1975* Location: *Room 5* Managers: *Foster + staff*
Yearly objective: *To respond to a variety of social stimuli* Quarterly objective: *To respond by looking*

Date	Teacher activity procedure/preparation	Child behavior—Correct—Consequence			Child behavior—Error—Consequence	
10/5	When facing Shirley, *talk* to her as you *walk toward* her. Ten times per day; intermittently through day.	To look at adult.	1:1	Praise her, pat her.	Does not look at adult.	None.
11/10	Same.	Same.	1:1	Praise her, tickle her tummy.	Same.	Same.
3/6	Same, plus reminder: trials are to be done *intermittently* throughout day.	Same.		Same.	Same.	Same.

of the trials presented. However, her responding decreased again, and the graph dropped back to 44.5% rate of response during the following two-week period. What was happening? The teacher wondered if social praise and touching were strong enough reinforcers for Shirley.

The classroom staff had noticed that she seemed to enjoy being tickled, an action that had been used as a reinforcer in another program. The team decided that it was worth trying, and tickling was added to the program plan in hopes that it would serve as a reinforcer for the looking response.

Instructions to the classroom staff which appeared on the plan sheet (11/10) and on the reminder board now included social praise *plus* gentle tickling every time Shirley responded by looking at the adult who approached and talked to her. The change in Shirley's response was soon evident as the percentage of correct resonses began to increase when the tickling was added as a reinforcer.

The Need for Consistency

Those who work with profoundly handicapped children recognize that progress is often slow with these children and that maintaining a 60–70% correct rate of response is considered commendable. We have learned also that children so severely involved often behave inconsistently from day to day. Health-related problems, such as seizure activity or medication management, often make differences in the way the child responds.

The information one gets from a graph can indicate problems in the intervention plan, but sometimes it is the incidental observations made by a teacher or by the CDS which pinpoint the cause or reveal the remedy. This was true at a point later in Shirley's program. During the fifth month of her responding program, the CDS noted that the data showed a marked decline (from the 60–70% correct range down to 35%). The CDS talked to the teacher about the change, but the teacher had no clues. They wondered whether the cause could be related to a health problem. However, when Shirley's other programs were reviewed, she appeared to be doing well in other areas.

Shortly after, when the CDS was working in the class with another child, she noticed that a new helper was hurrying to catch up on the number of trials needed to complete Shirley's communication program. The new aide did five trials consecutively, quickly marked the data (all "no response") and hurried on the next task. Shirley was not ready for consecutive trials. The data was reflecting this. The reminder board was again changed to show: "Trials are to be done *intermittently throughout* the day." This information was also recorded on the plan sheet (date 3/16). Following this change, the mean number of correct responses rose to 75% over the previous month. This problem alerts us to the importance of reviewing the information on the reminder board with all of the staff members from time to time. The review can be done by the teacher or by the CDS. When several people are involved in implementing all-day programs for the children, it is important to check periodically to see that the procedures being used are consistent with the plan. Consistency of program management is important. Such consistency allows us to gather the information we need in order to know what helps these children and what does not help them.

Frequency of Trials

The all-day program for communication intervention provides a plan for communicating with a child when a frequent number of trials is necessary to change a habit pattern, and where consistency of management is also important. When the plan is carefully written, it gives the teachers information about what kind of response can be expected from the child. In the case of Shirley, who seemed not to respond, it was important for her to have success in responding throughout the day, at a response level of looking. The requirement was for sufficient success to begin changing Shirley's non-responding pattern. The data in this case clearly indicated that the number of trials necessary to change the habit pattern needed to be spread throughout the day rather than administered consecutively.

The first important information the classroom staff requires is what response a given child *can* make. Then it needs to know the strategies which will elicit that response from the child. (For Shirley, the response was looking; the strategies were talking as one walked toward her and then tickling her gently and providing social praise.) The other important decision concerns the number of trials necessary to change the behavior—as, in this case, to increase the behavior (looking). This case study demonstrates the importance of an all-day program with intermittent trials for success, as opposed to a sit-down program with successive trials.

It has been our experience that when staff time is heavily committed to other programs, or when there is no visible or regular reminder, busy staff members tend to forget to provide the sufficient number of trials for an all-day program. Without a sufficient number of trials, the reinforcement cannot be given enough times to increase the desired behavior.

At the time this article was written, Shirley had been in the program at the Experimental Education Unit for seven months. She was becoming a responding child. She looked at people when they approached her while talking to her.

Reviewing the Data Again—The Team

The question asked in item 6 of the procedures outlined earlier in this article was, "What do the data show?". The data continued to show success for Shirley in her communication program about 60% to 70% of the time. Shirley's many other needs and the needs of her classmates consumed the time allotted for staffings. Also, as the staff became busier with more children and additional programs planned to meet the many needs of the children, the teacher began to notice a decrease in the *number* of trials given Shirley on this all-day program. There were fewer tallies on the data sheet provided. Again, the teacher contacted the CDS, and they shared their mutual concern. The CDS, who also checked the tally sheet regularly, had noticed that there were many days which could not be charted. At the following Education Team meeting, they discussed this problem and agreed that staff members needed the weekly feedback and praise from the CDS to help them remember Shirley's data and to keep them going. Even though Shirley was responding by looking, this type of response appears somewhat unrewarding in a culture where communicative interaction is usually verbal. Also, when gains are made very slowly, or when it takes continued managment strategies simply to maintain the gains that have been realized, staff members who work closely with severely and profoundly handicapped children need the support of other personnel, such as the CDS, to keep them motivated. This is a factor which needs to be recognized and time for it allotted in the schedule of all staff members. In the case of Shirley, the immediate staff who worked with her day after day needed to know what kind of response they could expect from her, the strategies which would secure this response, the visible reminder from the reminder board, the visual feedback from the daily graph, and the regular sharing with the CDS. When the CDS and the teachers review the data at regular meetings, the review serves as a dynamic vehicle for making changes in programs and for providing feedback to the staff. It is often necessary for the CDS to stop by the classrooms, review the data, and commend the staff. The head teacher frequently makes this request, but it is a good practice, whether requested or not.

Conclusion

We have discussed not only the challenges of the team approach, but also the many advantages of the team concept for those who work with severely/profoundly handicapped persons. We have outlined a process for facilitating team decisions and effective management procedures. With particular reference to very low-functioning, non-responsive persons, the all-day management plan has been a way to effect changes in children.

References

Gentry, N. D., & Haring, N. G. Direct and individualized instructional procedures. In N. G. Haring & R. L. Schiefelbush (Eds.). *Teaching special children*. New York: McGraw-Hill, 1976.

Rieke, J. Communication in early education. In N. G. Haring (Ed.). *Behavior of exceptional children*. Columbus, Ohio: Charles E. Merrill, 1974.

SUSAN F. SOLTMAN is the Communication Disorders Specialist for the Program for Severely/Profoundly Handicapped, Experimental Education Unit, Child Development and Mental Retardation Center, at the University of Washington. She previously served with the Unit's Model Preschool Center for Handicapped Children, Communications Classrooms, and helped develop training strategies for speech pathology students and preschool teachers. She holds a Certificate of Clinical Competence in Speech Pathology from the American Speech and Hearing Association.

JANE A. RIEKE is Coordinator of the Communication Programs at the Experimental Education Unit, Child Development and Mental Retardation Center, of the University of Washington in Seattle. She is responsible for communication and language training for students from the departments of speech pathology and education who are assigned to the Unit. She has provided technical assitance and training to a variety of programs across the country, and is the author of "Communication in early education," a chapter in N. G. Haring (Ed.). *Behavior of Exceptional Children* (Columbus, Ohio: Charles E. Merrill, 1974).

A Behavioral-Remedial Approach to Language Training for the Severely Handicapped

DOUG GUESS

University of Kansas

WAYNE SAILOR

San Francisco State University

DONALD M. BAER

University of Kansas

In recent years, a number of behavioral speech and language curricula for severely handicapped children have appeared in the literature (Drash & Leibowitz, 1973; Kent, 1974; Tawney & Hipsher, 1972; Gray & Ryan, 1973; McKenna-Hartung & Hartung, 1973). Other well known approaches to instruction have combined behavioral techniques and procedures with psycholinguistic theory (Stremel & Waryas, 1974; Miller & Yoder, 1972a, 1972b, 1974) and with Piagetian cognitive theory (Bricker & Bricker, 1970, 1974). Undeniably, the influence of learning theory has had a major impact on the design of remedial speech and language development programs for children who are speech-deficient or nonverbal. This impact has probably enhanced the practical application of direct service to the severely handicapped population; it has also raised many issues about the very nature of language acquisition in both normal and handicapped children. This chapter discusses some of the issues central to a behavioral-remedial approach to language training, and describes a structured curriculum which has evolved directly from this approach.[1]

Remedial Versus Developmental Logic

A consistent area of disagreement evolving from the design of curricula for language training is that of remedial versus developmental logic in constructing a teaching sequence. *Developmental* logic assumes that the best way to teach language to a speech-deficient child is to follow the same sequence by which normal children learn their language. The basic premise is that, if language has a complex structure, then parts of that structure are dependent on components already mastered. Conceivably, there is no alternate sequence in which language can be learned, at least by children learning it at the usual stages of development. This possibility is bolstered by the reported uniformity with which children acquire language. Those adhering to a developmental logic argue that if there were several or more possible sequences, then would not at least some children display different sequences?

By contrast, *remedial* logic supposes that children being taught language later in their lives no longer represent the same collection of abilities and deficits that normal children experience as they acquire language, because such language-delayed children have, by definition, already failed to acquire language adequately in their earlier years. The usual recipient of a language intervention effort is likely to be a retarded child, possessed of certain deviant means of interacting with others, and acquainted with the physical ecology of the world and its mechanics—all of it deficient and likely to be distorted, but none of it any longer representative of the knowledge and ignorance, ability and inability, of the normally developing young child.

---

[1] The preparation of this chapter was supported in part from USOE/BEH Grant OEG-0-74-2766 to Doug Guess, Wayne Sailor, and Leonard Lavis at Kansas Neurological Institute; and in part from USOE/BEH Contract OEC-0-74-9184 to Doug Guess and Wayne Sailor at Kansas Neurological Institute.

The authors are most grateful to Sue Porter, Division of Community Services, Arkansas Mental Retardation and Developmental Disabilities Services, and Hugh Sage, Beatrice (Nebraska) State Home and Training School for their continued assistance and support in the field-testing of the curriculum.

Remedial logic, then, does not ask in what order the retarded child needs to learn language, but, rather, in what order language acquired most quickly will accomplish some improvement in the language-deficient child's ability to communicate. This position is strongly grounded in the success of past studies that taught such children quite arbitrary elements of language, with virtually no regard for their readiness to learn each particular element.

Remedial logic also assumes that language must have the characteristic that linguists call "generative" (Chomsky, 1959), if it is to be taught to an individual who has failed to acquire it naturally. That is, language must be self-generating, so that new elements can be produced by the child, not by the teacher, and these new elements must follow the rules of speech used by the rest of us. A remedial approach cannot assume that the ability to generate language is inherent in the child's genetic endowment. Indeed, these children have already failed to acquire language in an environment that modeled it for them, sometimes as well as the environments in which normal children learn their language. If that failure results from the child's genetic predisposition to learn language, then it has already shown that the predisposition is faulty, and an alternative will be required.

Furthermore, remedial logic is most concerned with motivating the child, not only to learn language from the teaching program, but also to learn it from ongoing structured interactions outside the program. The child must find that newly acquired language is useful in gaining more "power," or control over the environment, than was possible without language. Thus, a program based on remedial logic tries to establish first the most useful elements of language that the child might need. These first elements probably should be labels, but more important, they should be labels of reinforcers for the child, and they should be labels that the child can use as requests that will be granted by those attending him. Thus, remedial programs will supply a child with language responses that maximally enhance control of the environment that the child encounters. The remedial assumption is that, if a child achieves some control, not only of the language teacher but also of much of the environment, through the language responses he has learned, then a motivation is established that could prompt the child to learn to attend to a language-using environment; to learn by observation; to learn the skills of *asking* for language training from language users (e.g., "What's that?"); and to learn the skills of remembering these tactics for later productive use in gaining even more control of the environment.

Reception and Production

Another of the critical problem areas confronting the developers of language training curricula has been, and continues to be, the relationship between reception (understanding), and production (expressive language). Stated very simply, the issue comes down to one of order and position in a training sequence. Should a language curriculum teach comprehension of a given linguistic structure before training expression of that form, or vice versa, or does it matter? Many highly credible proponents of all three positions can be found. This may come as a surprise to those who, unaware of the present controversy, assume that comprehension of linguistic forms necessarily precedes production of those forms. After all, in order to talk about something, you must first understand it. Or must you?

Bloom (1974) has postulated that the relationship between production and reception is multidirectional in development, involving shifts between mutually dependent, but quite different, underlying processes. This analysis represents a significant departure from traditional psycholinguistic theory. Bloom's position is demonstrated, in part, by the case of the young child's first words. Children use words inappropriately as they begin to acquire linguistic skills. They show that they have heard a word but that they did not understand it. Whether the child will come to understand the word may well depend upon what happens *after* he has produced it. A similar phenomenon characterizes the normal child's language acquisition toward the end of the second year, in the period of transition from single-word utterances to longer, sustained, structured speech. The child need not comprehend the syntactic-semantic structure of a sentence in order to be able to respond appropriately, when there is direct reference to the environmental context in which the sentence occurs. According to Bloom, the child does not have to process the syntax in order to respond to relationships among words with immediate identity forms.

Bloom concluded that the comprehension-production issue may hold different results for language training aimed at the development of speech that is largely representational by the immediate environmental context, e.g., Piaget's (1962) stage of concrete operations, than for language training aimed at speech that reaches the level of formal logical operations. The latter theoretically characterizes the linguistic processes of the normal child at about age 12. The critical transition level for the child's language development is the shift to the ability to speak and understand events, relationships, and factors that are independent of external situations or immediate internal states. While language training for the achievement of linguistic skills at the concrete level might well proceed, on the basis of present knowledge, from initial training on production to later training on comprehension, the relationship between the two is less clear at higher stages of development. In short, according to Bloom, there are simply no guideposts to assist the language trainer. There are, however, strong grounds for questioning old assumptions about language development.

Ingram (1974) has updated the traditional thesis that comprehension precedes production in normal language development and, therefore, dictates the preferred directionality of efforts toward the acquisition of linguistic skills in the handicapped. According to Ingram (1974) ". . . *comprehension ahead of production is a linguistic universal of acquisition* . . ." (p. 313). However, differences in the positions taken by Bloom and Ingram seem to dissolve at their various points of juncture regarding specific linguistic forms. For example, to return to the example of "first words," Ingram (1974) stated that his position makes no claim that first words produced must have been "noticed," a possible function of attention, memory, and frequency of exposure. Bloom (1974) treated the issue of "knowing" a word as simply having perceived (heard) the word. At this point, the distinction between Bloom's position and the presumably opposite position taken by Ingram appears to be purely semantic, if it can be said to exist at all.

In analyzing some of the higher or more complex forms of language development, the positions of Bloom and Ingram differ only in polemic. Bloom takes the more conservative position that so little is known about how children move from concrete to logical operations that it is not possible to offer guidance on the training order of comprehension and production. Ingram says that complexities displayed are evidence that comprehension should necessarily precede production in training strategies. Ingram concludes that research on the conceptual issue of reception and production should consist of an effort to shed light on the gap between the two in the acquisition of language, rather than to attempt to determine which precedes the other. Ingram's recognition that receptive and productive language are really much closer together than has been assumed in the past is really not at variance with Bloom's position that research efforts need to be directed toward uncovering the interactive relationship between the two modes at various stages in the attainment of linguistic competence.

Language analysts and program developers working within a behavioral context have approached the issue of comprehension and production somewhat more pragmatically than have the cognitive-developmental analysts. Rather than study the issue from the standpoints of observation and manipulation of language development in young, normal children, proponents of the behavioral model have sought to attack directly the question of which should be trained first when attempting to remediate language deficiencies among handicapped children. In so doing, they have arrived at a theoretical position on the issue inductively, from empirical data to theoretical stance. Interestingly, this current behavioral stance is not at variance with the position taken by Bloom (the two may develop independently) or Ingram (the issue is the gap between the two in various stages of development). Behavioral researchers have used a laboratory analog to analyze the receptive/productive issue, and have isolated the components of the process through direct experimental control and subsequent observation. The results of this research have direct relevance to language training efforts with linguistically deficient children, to the extent that the training methods employed are derived from the procedures which, at least partially, comprised the analog, and which are applied to subjects who resemble those studied in the laboratory situation. This approach assumes, first, that the language-deficient person will acquire language by essentially the same process that the young, normal child acquires it, but much more slowly, and only with intensive sequentially applied training procedures; second, that the relationship between reception and production on linguistic processes can be uncovered by studying the separate process of *generalization* across the two, under specifiable training conditions.

The sequence of studies which used the analogic method to treat the comprehension-production issue was conducted by Guess (1969), Harrelson (Note 1), and Guess and Baer (1973a). These studies have been summarized, with implications for language training efforts (Guess & Baer, 1973b). Within the narrow confines of the content area studied, specifically the acquisition of the plural morpheme, these studies support the position that, with severely handicapped children, the two repertoires (reception and production) may indeed be functionally independent. That is, training in one mode does not necessarily generalize to the other and, ultimately, both must be trained. These results would seem to support Bloom's (1974) position, that reception and production represent functionally independent processes at early stages in either the language development of normal children, or language acquisition in response to training efforts with language-deficient children. Also, corresponding to Bloom's analysis, the results of these studies shed little, if any, light on the relationship of the two processes in later stages of more advanced language use.

The implication of the behavioral analysis for training, as well as for Bloom's observations, is quite simply stated: train both modalities simultaneously or in rapid succession, but do not necessarily expect that the development of one, through training, will automatically enhance the development of the other, without direct training.

Generalization

Of all the unsolved problems confronting those engaged in efforts to train communication skills in nonverbal or speech-deficient children, the issue of generalization is certainly the most current and pressing. The technology for language assessment and training is in its initial growth years. Curricula are available with which to begin the communication training process with children who have no language system. These curricula are of such a quality as to lead to modest predictions of success over time. At issue is whether this newly trained complex set of behaviors can and will extend beyond the confines of the particular setting, persons, materials, and so on, that produced the new skills. The critical question is: what is needed in the way of supplemental child training to produce generalization of the new language by the child?

Harris (1975) has provided an excellent review of the recent literature on speech intervention with nonverbal children, using operant techniques. This review focused on a number of component areas of language training, including attention training, nonverbal imitation, verbal imitation, and functional speech and language, with the generalization of training effects as the issue. Harris found that in all the studies reviewed to date in all component areas, generalization of responses to conditions that contained some, but not all, of the cues present during training, either failed to be demonstrated to occur or was neither programmed to occur nor measured where it might have occurred.

Harris speculated from her review that: (a) based on a study by Garcia (1974), generalization may be accomplished by utilizing more than one person to train subjects from the outset; and (b) one of the important factors in facilitating generalization should be repeated training in a wide number of settings. She concluded that language training must focus upon the natural environment rather than upon the classroom.

Within the behavioral approach, the concept of generalization has, for more than two decades, been viewed as a *passive* and somewhat insignificant process. This may well account for past failures on the part of the operant language program developers to program actively for language extension, or generalization. Generalization was simply regarded as a failure of discrimination. Discrimination was the active process and an improved technology for the production of discrimination learning was felt to lead to the process of generalization by artifact. If a child was taught a sufficient number of discriminations, generalization would occur without a specific technology of its own.

Stokes and Baer (in press) recently reviewed some 200 studies that might be construed as contributing to a separate technology of generalization, e.g., generalization viewed as an active process apart from corresponding or earlier developments in discrimination learning. The reader is referred to this review, which describes seven hypothetical tactics that, taken together or in part, may lead to the development of a strategy for the production (or training) of generalization in language-deficient children. In actuality, the technology for producing generalization is fairly advanced, although little has been demonstrated that prescriptively leads the language trainer to program for generalization from language instruction settings to nontraining settings. It is certain, however, that further research on the problem will be forthcoming; there is already a firm basis for a cogent attack on the problem. Studies must focus on organismic variables (what must the child know in order to generalize?), as well as ecological variables (what must take place in the child's nontraining world?) to produce the combination of events leading to reliable linguistic generalization.

There are other central issues that should be considered in discussing an approach to language program development for severely handicapped children. The issues of content sequencing and response generalization were briefly mentioned in the discussion of developmental versus remedial logic. A more thorough discussion of these areas can be found in Guess, Sailor, and Baer (1976a). Nevertheless, the chapter thus far has identified several critical issues for an operant approach to language intervention for the severely handicapped—issues which have had a direct impact on the design and construction of the language development curriculum presented in the next section.

Functional Language Training Program for the Severely Handicapped

The curriculum described in this section has evolved from a combination of specific laboratory experiments and intensive field-test studies over the past five years. The experiments were conducted at Kansas Neurological Institute and the University of Kansas in an attempt to analyze the extent to which severely handicapped children could respond to systematic language instruction. These investigations have dealt with an array of linguistic skills pertaining to morphological grammar, syntax, and the relationship between productive speech and receptive language (cf. Guess and Baer, 1973b, for a partial review of these studies). The cumulative results of these investigations strongly indicate that severely handicapped children can be taught a variety of rule-governed speech skills, and that the techniques used in training can be effective for a large number of the linguistic deficits found in the severely handicapped population. As a result, these studies have engendered the optimism to embark on the development of a comprehensive speech and language training curriculum for this population—a curriculum which systematically moves severely handicapped children through a sequence of training steps and phases, with the ultimate goal of achieving at least a modest degree of functional, spontaneous, conversational speech.

The curriculum has necessarily undergone, and continues to undergo, continual change as a result of both experimental and field-test application. An earlier version was described in Sailor, Guess, and Baer (1973) and Guess, Sailor, and Baer (1974). A still later version was presented in Guess, Sailor, Keogh, and Baer (1976). The very logic of the curriculum dictates ongoing revision, especially with respect to the sequencing of the training steps. The curriculum is based on remedial logic. As such, the training sequence is heavily dependent on acquisition data from children undergoing training. In essence, we depend extensively on the performance of severely handicapped children to tell us what should be taught, the order in which it should be taught, and the most effective and efficient procedures to use in training. The initial content of the program was designed after making some judgment of what these children should learn. The initial ordering of the linguistic skills to be taught was determined by giving consideration to identified developmental norms for normal children. Nevertheless, we have made no assumptions that the development of certain linguistic skills is necessarily dependent on the prior existence of other prerequisite behavior. Only data from a large number of children undergoing training will be utilized to resequence training components inductively.

The research model used to develop the curriculum has combined an experimental speech and language unit at Kansas Neurological Institute with field-test sites in day care centers and other institutional facilities located in Nebraska and Arkansas. The specific training procedures for various components have been developed in the laboratory at Kansas Neurological Institute where an initial application was conducted with a small group of severely handicapped children. The experimental modules developed in this laboratory were sent to field-test sites for more extensive application under less controlled conditions. Problems arising in application of the curricula are referred back to the laboratory for further study and analysis. This arrangement has allowed us to revise the curriculum continually, on the basis of direct feedback from the practitioner under more normal and quite varied practical situations; at the same time, the technical problems of the curriculum can be evaluated under more controlled experimental conditions.

Prerequisite Skills

The initial design provided only for the development of oral speech. Accordingly, prerequisite skills included the physical ability to produce speech sounds, adequate vision, and sufficiently normal hearing. Additionally, entrance into training required that the student be able to imitate words verbally, although perfect articulation was not required (nor was it generally expected). However, pilot work is now being done to adapt the program content and sequence to an exact English signing system for children with severe hearing losses or for children for whom speech sound production is particularly difficult. In addition, the curriculum is being adapted to communication boards for children who are both incapable of speech production and also physically impaired to the extent that signing is not possible. These adaptations are discussed more fully in a later section.

Verbal imitation remains, however, the most important criterion for entrance into the *oral* version of the program. We are fully aware that the establishment of verbal imitation is a most difficult undertaking for many severely handicapped children. Our own results with a large field-test population would indicate that about 30 to 40% of the severely handicapped children in training fail to develop verbal imitation, even with the best current training procedures available. We have outlined elsewhere (Guess, Sailor, & Baer, 1976b) some issues and possible new directions in the further development of a technology for teaching verbal imitation to "difficult-to-teach" children. As one final comment, a few nonimitative children have nevertheless done quite well in the functional language training sequence. These children, however, gave indication that their poor performance in imitation training was more of a motivational problem than a lack of imitative ability.

Dimensions

The complete instructional curriculum includes 60 individual training steps, subsumed under five dimensions. The dimensions represent a basic framework in accordance with the particular training emphasis and theoretical underpinnings of the program. These dimensions are *reference*, *control*, *self-extended control*, *integration*, and *reception*.

Reference. This dimension represents a basic function of language learning: that certain sounds (words) represent objects and events in our environment, or attributes of these objects or events. For example, the word "ball" represents a specific object of finite size, color, and texture. The word "eat" represents an activity describing the process of delivering food to one's mouth. "Red" is used to symbolize a color which can vary in hue, and which can be an attribute of an infinite number of objects; "big" is used to describe relative size. In the program, *reference* is used in many contexts, including basic labeling of objects, description of actions, ownership (my, your), attribution of colors and relationships between objects (size, position, location).

Control. This dimension introduces children to the power of language by teaching them various forms of requesting behavior, such as "I want (object) or (action)"; "I want (action-with-object)"; and "I want you to (action-with-object)." The purpose of including the forms of requesting is to emphasize to children the importance of language in managing their environments, and to give them the skills to initiate speech for making their needs known. Explicitness about the controlling function of language is then added by including possessive, descriptive, or relational and locational properties that further identify the object or event appropriate to the request.

Self-Extended Control. Reference and *control* dimensions are useful for children to manage their environment within the limitations of the referents known to them. However, speech-deficient children often have only a meager number of referents at their disposal (i.e., they simply do not know the necessary labels for all of the objects, actions, and action-with-objects that they wish). Thus, a *self-extended control* dimension is included in the curriculum, designed to teach children to request more specific information based upon their own determination of what they do not know from what they already know. *Self-extended control* is developed by teaching children to ask such questions as, "What is that?" in response to unknown objects; "What are you doing?" in response to unknown actions; "Whose (object)?" when identifying ownership of objects; "What size?" to inquire about the largeness or smallness of objects; "What color?" when confronted with novel color stimuli; and "Where (object or location)?" to establish or identify the relationship between objects or the location of either objects or persons.

Integration. Language skills taught in *reference*, *control*, and *self-extended control* are put together in such a manner that skills previously taught are integrated with skills currently being taught to maximize appropriate interaction with the environment. *Integration* presents training steps that teach children to discriminate as to when to seek appropriate information via questions, and when to respond with appropriate referents when the information already exists in their language repertoires. A second function of *integration* is "dialogue" which, conceptually, provides a teaching format requiring the children to chain together all or some of the previously learned skills, so that they can carry on a simple but appropriate conversation centered around a functional activity or theme.

Reception. Corresponding to specific attainments in productive speech, concepts are also taught at the receptive level, to complete the children's ability to speak and understand. In this curriculum, however, a productive skill is taught before the corresponding skill is taught at the receptive level. For example, children are trained to label objects before they are taught to receptively identify these same objects. The training of productive skills in the program, followed by receptive training (if necessary) of the same skill, is not intended to minimize the importance of receptive training, but to emphasize the productive nature of the program, which, by design, has the purpose of bringing the children rapidly into the speaking community (as contrasted to the mute instruction-following community).

Content of the Curriculum Sequence

The 60-step training sequence is divided into six content areas: Persons and Things, Action with Persons and Things, Possession, Color, Size, and Relation/Location. The number of steps in each of these content areas is presented in Table 1. The content areas are grouped into four separate parts, which represent the training order.

Persons and Things.[2] The initial nine steps in this content area teach the student to label common objects; to identify the same objects receptively; to request objects using a two-word utterance, "want (object)" in Step 2, and later, "I want (object)" in Step 8. In this part of the training sequence, the student is also taught to ask, "What's that?" when confronted with unknown objects; to discriminate between asking "What's that?" and labeling objects; and to remember the labels of novel items given in response to the question. In addition, the student is trained to use "yes" and "no" as receptive indicators for understanding object labels (Step 7) and to chain two previously learned responses together (in Step 9).

Not unexpectedly, our results show that the initial nine steps in the program are quite difficult for many children learning to speak. One should expect a child to require several hundreds of trials to reach criterion for many of the steps in the content area. The yes/no concept taught in Step 7 is especially difficult for severely handicapped children. Some fail to meet criterion at all, and must be returned to the step at a later point in training. Nevertheless, our data indicate that acquisition in learning accelerates as the child progresses through the program. Subsequent sections of the curriculum are mastered at a much faster rate, even though the concepts taught become more complex and the utterances increase in length.

Action with Persons and Things. This content area includes 19 individual teaching steps that center around the expressive and receptive use of verb actions. In the sequence, the student is taught both to express and to identify a large number of common verb actions. The verb actions are first trained separately (e.g., "I play") and then in combination with the objects of the action (e.g., "I play ball").

The teaching of the second-person pronoun "you" is interwoven in the training sequence together with the appropriate discrimination between the first and second person pronouns (I/you). At a later point in the sequence, children are taught to expand their own repertoires by asking questions in order to identify actions which are novel to them (e.g., "What are you doing?"). Also, there is further expansion of

TABLE 1

Content Categories in the Training Sequence

Part	Content Area	Steps
I	PERSONS AND THINGS	1– 9
II	ACTION WITH PERSONS AND THINGS	10–29
III	POSSESSION COLOR	30–35 36–42
IV	SIZE RELATION AND LOCATION	43–49 50–60

[2] Part I of the training curriculum (Persons and Things) is now available from H & H Enterprises, Inc., Box 3342, Lawrence, Kansas, 66044.

concepts and skills taught in the Persons and Things sequence, including increases in object labels, extension of the "yes/no" concept to identify actions, and more varied uses of requests. Action with Persons and Things systematically increases the length of response utterances required, and integrates these utterances into new and different response chains as parts of trained conversational units.

Data analysis suggests that most children will acquire the skills in the Action with Persons and Things sequence more rapidly than in the previously taught Persons and Things sequence. Indeed, it is not unusual for a child to reach criterion performance in one session, with many of the steps in the Actions with Persons and Things sequence. More significant, however, many children show a rapid increase in the general use of speech while undergoing training in this sequence; new and novel speech responses not specifically trained begin to emerge.

Possession. Steps 30 through 35 are concerned with teaching the concept of possession appropriate to the pronouns "my" and "your." In this six-step sequence, students are taught to identify the ownership of objects, using the productive pronouns "my" and "your"; to identify ownership receptively using "yes/no" as indicators of their understanding; to request objects, using the correct possessive pronoun (e.g., "I want my/your (object)."); to ask the question, "Whose (object)?", when ownership is unknown; and to use the possessive pronouns appropriately in the context of a simple conversation that involves requests and the description of actions. In the last instance, "my" and "your" are integrated with previously taught responses, thus expanding the length of students' utterances and systematically adding possessive pronoun usage to previously learned concepts.

The data base for this training sequence, as well as for the remaining sequences, includes considerably fewer children at this stage of the field-test effort. Ongoing data analysis from children who have gone through this and the remaining sequences indicates, however, a maintenance of the acquisition rate previously described. While some steps take longer for criterion performance to be reached, the overall acquisition remains consistent with previous sequences. Nevertheless, some modification in the procedures for some of the steps will most likely be made as more field-test data become available.

Color. In Steps 36 through 42, students are trained to use color descriptors. Initially, they are taught to label common colors, and then to label objects using the correct color descriptors. Students are next taught to identify objects of various colors receptively, by a pointing response. The other steps in the sequence teach students to make requests to open boxes of various colors; to then identify the same action at the receptive level, using "yes/no" as indicators for correct responses; to ask the question, "What color?", when presented with unknown color labels; and to integrate color in conversation that centers around the activity of coloring. This final step combines a number of previously learned responses and concepts to accentuate the use of color descriptors.

Size. Steps 43 through 49 teach students to use the size descriptors "big" and "little." In this sequence, students are taught "big/little" as referent labels; to identify big and little objects with the appropriate size descriptors; to state the location of objects placed in big or little boxes; to identify receptively the location of items placed in big or little boxes, using "yes/no" responses; to ask, "What size?", when given a request for objects; to identify receptively the size of objects given to them, using the "yes/no" response; and to engage in a brief conversation that integrates both color and size descriptors.

Location/Relation. The last sequence in the program (Steps 50 through 59) pertains to the functional use of position descriptors ("on/under") and location descriptors ("inside/outside"). Students are taught to use "on/under" and "inside/outside" as reference labels; to identify receptively the position and location of objects and persons using the "yes/no" response; to request objects placed in the "on/under" position; to request a person to go inside/outside of various locations (e.g., "I want you to go outside the room."); and to ask the questions, "Where is my (object)?", and "Where are you going?". The position/location concepts are integrated in a brief conversation in Step 59.

Step (60) concludes the curriculum. Step 60 provides an integration and review of the skills and concepts trained in all the concept areas. This step integrates the concepts of verb actions, possession, color, size, position, and location in a rather lengthy interaction between students and their language trainer.

Integration of Steps in the Curriculum

The entire 60-step curriculum is divided into six content areas, each containing its own sequence of instruction. Nevertheless, it is important to realize that the design of the program sequence emphasizes the gradual introduction of new skills prefaced by more fundamental concepts. Thus, the 60-step sequence is interlocking, so that new skills are introduced as soon as possible, in the context of previously learned skills, so that students are not abruptly faced with concepts for which adequate training has not been given. In addition, the length of the response utterances required is increased gradually across the training sequence. For example, the mean response length of utterances required in the productive training steps in the initial Persons and Things category is 1.9 words; the longest verbal response type in that same category is three words. By the time the students reach the final content area of the program (Location/Relation), the mean response length has been expanded to 4.4 words and the the longest sentence type is seven words. Similarly, the trainer's response length in presenting instructions and questions also increases, and more rapidly, across the 60-step sequence.

Structure of the Training Steps

Each individual training step in the curriculum follows a similar outline, which includes the Training Goal, Training Items, Procedures, Training Instructions, Scoring Form, a Summary Form, and a section entitled Programming for Generalization.

Training Goal. This section describes the specific skill or concept to be trained in the step, a brief statement as to how the step is integrated with previous steps, and the identification of the step with whichever of the five dimensions (Reference, Control, Self-Extended Control, Integration, Reception) it embodies.

Training Items. This section describes the specific type of materials or objects needed for the step. The stimulus items and props required for each step are frequently left to the discretion of the teacher or trainer, whose selections can be made through knowledge of the students and their living environments. For the most part, however, the training stimuli include common, readily available, and functional items. The use of objects, rather than pictures, is preferred, to increase the authenticity of the training environment.

Procedures. For each trial in a session, the trainer provides the student with a stimulus, which can be a question, a command, or the presentation of an object or modeling of an action. The student, in turn, may give a correct response, a partially correct response, a wrong response, or no response at all. The trainer must respond accordingly. When correct responses are given, the student is usually reinforced and praised. Trainers select the types and amounts of reinforcers dispensed for correct responses. However, considerable effort has been made to construct many steps so that a correct response is *intrinsically* reinforcing for the student, especially in the later steps.

Obviously, students will not respond correctly on every trial. Indeed, some students may require lengthy periods of training before correct responses, or even partially correct responses, are made. Thus, the trainer must be prepared to deal with partially correct responses, incorrect responses, and no responses. The various steps in the program use one of two basic procedures when correct responses are not given on the first presentation of a trial. These are the Training and Correction Procedure and the Two-Trainer Training and Correction Procedure.

The Training and Correction Procedure describes how language trainers should use prompts, put-throughs, and shaping techniques to correct errors made by the student. The Training and Correction Procedure allows for flexibility in reacting to idiosyncratic responses made by the student, yet provides a systematic framework that allows the trainer to be consistent when correcting errors.

There are certain skills and concepts for which a second trainer can best serve as a model for the correct response, following an error or no-response by the student. These situations occur when the concept to be taught involves a reversed or conditional discrimination that depends on the person who originated the response. The concept of "I/you" serves as a case in point. The first person singular pronoun "I" is used by a speaker, whereas the second person singular pronoun "you" generally refers to the person spoken to. In teaching the "I/you" discrimination, a second trainer is helpful, since that person (whether he is another adult or, usually, another child who has already mastered the concept) can provide the correctly modeled answer by assuming the same speaker-listener role as the student. Accordingly, a Two-Trainer Training and Correction Procedure is used in those steps in the curriculum in which a reversed or conditional discrimination is taught.

Training Instructions. Each step includes instructions to the trainer describing the order in which items and trials are to be presented, what the trainer says to the student, and what the student is expected to reply. The trainer's instructions to the student are always printed in capital letters (e.g., WHAT IS THAT?). The expected response from the student is printed in small letters with quotation marks (e.g., "ball"). When appropriate, the instructions also explain the arrangement of training items for the session, and the position or location of the student in the room. For some steps, the instructions also describe a skill test which allows the student either to skip a particular step altogether, or to exit from the step without having to undergo further training.

Scoring Forms and Summary Sheets. Each step includes a scoring form (data sheet) specifically designed for the skill being trained. These forms also provide descriptive information for the trainer to assist in correctly following the instructions. The scoring form includes space for the student's name, the name of the trainer, the date, and session number. Each form also includes a summary table for tabulating percentages of correct responses for every session. Percentage conversion tables are provided for the trainer to assist in the rapid and accurate tabulation of correct responses.

Summary sheets are also provided for each step to record program progress across sessions. Additional space on the summary sheet is used to indicate the date when training was started for that step, the date when criterion performance was reached, and the total number of sessions required to achieve that criterion performance. Also, the program includes instructions for graphing data from the summary sheets for those trainers wishing to have a visual display of progress of their students.

Programming for Generalization. Many of the steps in the curriculum have an additional section that describes extending a newly learned skill to the student's natural environment. Ordinarily, the generalization training procedures are to be administered by the student's parents, parent surrogates, teachers, or other significant persons who have daily contact with him. The purpose of the generalization procedure is to increase the use of a newly taught skill with persons different from the trainer, and in environments different from the student's training setting. Additionally, the generalization training procedures help to keep other persons aware of the student's progress across time. Thus, the student's parents or parent surrogates become familiar with the skills available to the student as he advances through the program so that such skills can be attended to (and reinforced) when they occur spontaneously.

An Illustration

The following reproduction of a training step serves to demonstrate how each step is organized in accordance with the structure described in the preceding section. Step 3 from the Persons and Things Category of the program is presented. This particular step is designed to teach the student to request things, using a two-word response, "Want (object)."

Step 3

Requesting Items

Training Goal. To train the student to request items, using a two-word response ("Want [item]"). This step initiates training in the *control* dimension of language (i.e., saying things that require another person to do something).

Training Items. Ten items (food, liquids, toys, etc.) that are reinforcing to the student. The most important thing in making your selection of items for the step is that the student *wants* them. It is also important that the student be able to label the items. Thus, items for Step 1 should be used if they are important to the student. If new items are used, you should make sure that the student can label them.

Procedures. Use the Training and Correction Procedure (from Part I Training Manual: Guess, Sailor and Baer, 1976a), realizing that considerable shaping may be required.

Step 3

Training Instructions

1. Hold up each item, one at a time, and ask WHAT WANT? A correct response must include the word "want" plus the correct label for the item (e.g., "want car"). The student is given the item for a correct response. For example, if you hold up a cookie and ask WHAT WANT? and the student responds, "want cookie," then you give the student the cookie (or a portion of it). If the item is nonconsumable, let the student play with it before asking that it be given back for

use in further trials. When you ask for the item back, extend your hand and say, I WANT (ITEM). Partial responses by the student are of particular importance in the step. If partial responses are given (e.g., labeling the item without first saying "want"), you should emphasize the missing component when modeling the correct response (e.g., *WANT* [ITEM]). Some examples of typical trials, using the Training and Correction Procedure are presented in Table 2. These examples are keyed to the first six trials in the sample Scoring Form for Step 3, Figure 1.

2. Present the ten items three times each in a session (for a total of 30 trials), as indicated on the Scoring Form for Step 3.

3. Count the number of correct (+), incorrect (−), shaped (S), and no-response (NR). Refer to 30-Trial Session in Appendix A (from the Part I, Training Manual) for converting these numbers to percents, and enter percent on the bottom of the Scoring Form.

4. Record percent correct response for each session on Summary Form for Step 3. (See sample summary for Step 3, Figure 2.) Continue training until criterion performance is

TABLE 2

Example Trials for Step 3 Training

Trainer	Student
Trial 1	
(Holds up cookie)	
WHAT WANT?	"Cookie"
THAT'S CLOSE, DICK. LET'S TRY AGAIN. SAY, *WANT* COOKIE.	"Wa cookie"
THAT IS MUCH BETTER, *WANT* COOKIE. (Gives portion of cookie to student for coming close and scores [−] on Scoring Form for the first response, "cookie." Here the trainer chose to reinforce the student for a good attempt, "wa cookie," following the correction procedure. This would not be done in later trials if the word "want" is being correctly articulated.)	
Trial 2	
(Holds up cup of Coke)	
WHAT WANT?	"Wa Coke"
GOOD! YOU *WANT* COKE. (Gives cup with small portion of Coke to student and scores [S] on Scoring Form for shaped response.)	
Trial 3	
(Holds up piece of candy)	
WHAT WANT?	"Want candy"
VERY GOOD TALKING, DICK! (Gives piece of candy to student and scores [+] on Scoring Form.)	
Trial 4	
(Holds up toy car)	
WHAT WANT?	"Car"
NO DICK, YOU *WANT* CAR. (Scores [−] on Scoring Form.)	
WHAT WANT?	"Want car"
THAT'S RIGHT. *WANT* CAR.	
Trial 5	
(Holds up milk)	
WHAT WANT?	(No response)
(Scores [NR] on Scoring Form.)	
DICK, SAY *WANT MILK*. WHAT WANT? (Note the trainer provided the correct model [WANT MILK] and quickly asked the question, [WHAT WANT?])	"Milk"
(Says nothing and goes to next trial; trainer should consider whether student really wants the milk.)	
Trial 6	
(Holds up ball)	
WHAT WANT?	"Want ball"
THAT IS REALLY GOOD! (Gives ball to student, scores [+] on Scoring Form.)	
(Lets student play with ball for a short while, then holds hand out.)	
I WANT BALL.	(Gives ball to trainer)
THANK YOU.	

Student Dick Date April 3, 1975 Session #1
Trainer Bill

List items used:

(1) Cookie (2) Coke (3) Candy (4) Car (5) Milk
(6) Ball (7) Apple (8) Drum (9) Book (10) Gun

Present this item: Ask, WHAT WANT?	Expected Response: "Want (item)" (Score)	Present this item: Ask, WHAT WANT?	Expected Response: "Want (item)" (Score)	Present this item: Ask, WHAT WANT?	Expected Response: "Want (item)" (Score)
(1)	−	(1)	−	(1)	−
(2)	S	(2)	S	(2)	−
(3)	+	(3)	+	(3)	+
(4)	−	(4)	NR	(4)	−
(5)	NR	(5)	−	(5)	+
(6)	+	(6)	S	(6)	+
(7)	+	(7)	+	(7)	+
(8)	S	(8)	+	(8)	−
(9)	S	(9)	S	(9)	+
(10)	−	(10)	S	(10)	+

Score trials as correct (+); incorrect (−); shape (S); or no response (NR)

"want + (label)" Percent Summary for Session

	+	−	S	NR
Score	12	9	7	2
Percent	40	30	23	7

Figure 1. Scoring form for step 3.

reached (80 percent correct in one session or 12 in a row correct in one session).

5. Advance the student to Step 4 when criterion performance is reached and initiate generalization training for Step 3.

Note: Use only items that the student really wants for this step, and make sure to give the item to the student for correct responses. Training on this step will be difficult and nonfunctional if these two considerations are not met.

Programming for Generalization

When the student has reached criterion performance on the step, parents and parent surrogates should periodically present the trained items to the student and ask, "WHAT WANT?". The item and verbal praise are given for correct responses. Additional, nontrained items should be included if the student maintains a high level of performance. Parents and parent surrogates should be especially sensitive to spontaneous requests by the student which include the newly trained response. Such spontaneous (or self-initiated) requests should be heavily reinforced.

A Case Example

A more complete description of results from the program is detailed elsewhere. Guess, Sailor, Keogh, and Baer (1976) have presented group data for the first nine steps, showing mean number of sessions to criterion for each step. More recent group data depicting mean number of sessions for Steps 1 through 35 are presented in Guess, Sailor, and Baer (1976b). Additionally, Firling (Note 2) has

Student________________________ Trainer________________________

Date Training Started April 3, 1975 Date Training Ended April 12, 1975 Total Sessions to Criterion 8

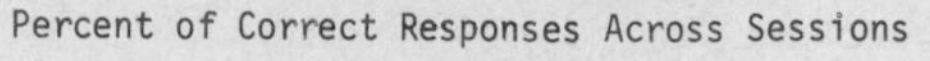

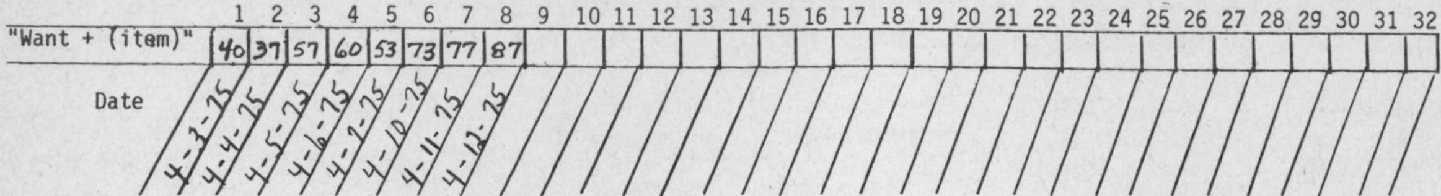

	1	2	3	4	5	6	7	8	9	10	11	12	13	14	15	16	17	18	19	20	21	22	23	24	25	26	27	28	29	30	31	32
"Want + (item)"	40	37	57	60	53	73	77	87																								
Date	4-3-75	4-4-75	4-5-75	4-6-75	4-7-75	4-10-75	4-11-75	4-12-75																								

Figure 2. Summary form for step 3.

described the progress of an autistic boy through the first 48 steps in the program. Data were presented for each step, as well as discussion of how the program effectively established speech in this previously nonverbal child.

All results available to date indicate that progress through the training sequence varies widely among students. Nevertheless, a general finding indicates that acquisition of the steps accelerates as the students progress through the program, e.g., the further the students advance in the program, the easier it is for them to master the concepts and skills taught, even though the responses required are increasing both in complexity and length.

The following abbreviated case study describes the progress of a profoundly retarded boy who has advanced through the entire 60-step sequence. At the time training was started, the student, Larry, had measured IQ scores ranging from 11 to 20. He was 12 years old, having spent most of his life in an institution for the mentally retarded. Larry was diagnosed as a Down's Syndrome case and, by normal standards, was physically undersized for his age. Larry had well developed verbal and motor imitation skills when functional language training was begun. Previously, he had been in an imitation training program where he had progressed quite rapidly. Occasionally, Larry produced isolated words which, for the most part, were poorly articulated, even though they were appropriate to the situation.

Larry entered Step 1 on July 27, 1972, and completed Step 60 on October 3, 1975. During this 39-month period, he was provided approximately 279 training sessions. Since each session lasts approximately 15 minutes, it is estimated that about 59 hours of direct training were required to advance Larry through the 60-step sequence. This estimate is conservative, however, since Larry needed about 40 sessions to complete an earlier version of Step 7 (the initial training of "yes/no"). This step was later revised several times to improve its efficiency in teaching the "yes/no" concept. Other steps, early in the sequence, were also revised, subsequent to the time period when Larry received training on them.

At the conclusion of the curriculum, Larry had developed oral speech to the extent that he willingly engaged in appropriate conversational speech. He was subsequently enrolled in a special education class in a school outside of the institution, where he is progressing quite well. Larry relates verbally to his classmates and teacher, and he is now learning to read. Articulation remains a problem, although substantial improvement has been noted without the benefit of articulation therapy. A more recent intelligence test showed an IQ score of 34. While this improvement is not dramatic, Larry has now moved out of the profoundly retarded range. With continued educational opportunities, further gains in both adaptive behavior and intellectual performance can be expected. The provocative question, however, remains: Where might Larry be now if the 59 hours of speech and language training had been invested ten years earlier when he was two years old?

Adaptation of the Curriculum to Nonoral Language Systems

For some children, the absence of certain prerequisite skills and other severe physically impairing motor and sensory conditions are such that the development of preferred oral speech is unlikely under even the best training circumstances. The time consumed in training speech skills (i.e., articulatory control and accuracy, respiratory control, voice and pitch quality) is so prohibitive that other nonspeech forms of communication must be considered as alternatives. Still other children have no specific severe motor or sensory impairment in their diagnosis, and yet show expressive speech skills that lag far behind their understanding levels. Extensive articulation and verbal imitation training may produce only modest results in these children. They continue to be only minimally imitative and display but a few sounds and syllables in their spontaneous vocalizations. A few children have highly defined intonation patterns in their speech, suggesting that they are using some system of rules in their effort to communicate. However, the exact rules or system cannot be determined because of unintelligibility.

Obviously, methods to develop communication and facilitate speech acquisition are needed for the types of children described. Pilot research is now being done to adapt the oral speech version of the functional language training curriculum to alternative nonoral language systems, specifically communication boards and exact English signing.

Communication Boards

Lois Waldo, Speech Pathologist at the Kansas Neurological Institute, has been responsible for adapting the curriculum to the communication board system. This adaptation, for the initial sequence of the curriculum (Persons and Things), is being prepared by her for further testing and analysis in selected field-test situations.[3]

Apparatus and Materials. The communication boards used in training consist of 18″ × 24″ paint canvasses placed inside an envelope of clear heavy plastic. For wheelchair students, the boards are placed on their lap trays so that students may have their communication system available during most hours of the day. For ambulatory students, several boards are placed in critical areas of the living environment.

Noun symbols used for the individual steps in the curriculum consist of black, felt-tipped outline drawings on white cards. The verbs and "yes/no" symbols were selected from the *Peabody Rebus Reading Program* (Woodcock, Clark, and Davies, 1969). The remaining symbols have been originally drawn to meet specific needs of the students and to correspond to material in the oral speech version of the curriculum. Regardless of where the students begin in the program, their initial training is conducted with 3″ × 5″ symbol cards. As the students' responding is established, and their pointing behavior is refined, the cards are reduced to 1″ × 1″ in size. With the exception of one of the symbol cards, one card represents one word. To communicate with a multi-word response, the student must point to more than one symbol card. The exception, to be discussed later, is the symbol for "no card." The symbols are placed on the board only as needed in training. Once the symbol is used in training, it remains on the board in the approximate location.

Adaptation of the Steps in the Oral Speech Curriculum. Attempts to adapt the first nine steps (Persons and Things) of the curriculum are in the initial development stage. Some changes have been made in most of the steps, and procedures for adapting the three steps (4, 5, and 6) that involve asking questions have yet to be worked out.

In Step 1 (Labeling), the only change required was that of response definition. The following definitions are used to record responses:

Correct Response: Student points to the symbol card representing the object-label requested;

Incorrect Response: Student points to more than one card, points to the object, points to an incorrect symbol, touches the board but not on the symbol, or resists a prompt;

No Response: Student does not point within a 10-second period;

Shaped Response: Student requires additional cues or prompts to complete an accurate point.

Instructions were also added for this step (as well as other steps) describing where the symbol cards would be displayed on the communication board.

Step 2 (Object Recognition) required no changes since the communication board (i.e.,

[3] Field-test adaptation of the program to communication boards can be obtained from Lois Waldo, Speech and Audiology Department, Kansas Neurological Institute, Topeka, Kansas, 66604.

the expressive mode of communication) is not required in the response, and the student is instructed to point directly to the objects, rather than to a symbol representation.

Step 3 (Requesting Objects) has required only that the response mode be changed. In responding, the student points first to the symbol for "want," and then to the picture-symbol for the object desired. As is true for the oral speech training procedures for this step, it is most important that symbols be used to represent objects that the student actually does want, rather than objects selected for convenience.

Step 4 (Asking, "What's that?"), Step 5 (Acquiring New Object Labels), and Step 6 (Memory for New Object Labels) have all been omitted at present from the communication board sequence because each of these steps includes a question-asking response, as well as discriminated question-asking and labeling responses. Procedural problems associated with this type of response are being worked out so that this important self-extending communication skill can be taught. In the meantime, it was considered important for the students to realize that they could not respond to every stimulus in their environment with the few symbols available on their boards. Therefore, a training step was included in the curriculum to teach students to reply "no card" when confronted with items that they did not have available as a label symbol. The symbol used to present "no card" is an outlined square with a red slash through it. This symbol is placed in the upper left-hand border of the communication board. This added training step helps prepare the student for the "yes/no" training in Step 7.

Step 7 ("Yes/No") is done exactly as written in the oral program except for the response mode. The symbols for "yes" and "no" are again taken from the *Peabody Rebus Reading Program*. Procedural changes for Steps 8 and 9 have yet to be developed.

Preliminary Evaluation and Observations. The progress of six children currently in the pilot curriculum has been steady and rapid. These children had few functional speech and communication skills prior to training. They can now request objects and materials of importance to them. Nonvocal communication is being established at a rate which is probably much faster than that for oral speech, based upon a history of failure for most of these children in oral speech training. Even those children who were not pointing well in initial training are improving in the development of this response. Developing a good pointing response has taken considerably less time than have prior attempts to teach vocal imitation or articulation.

There are numerous problems in need of attention. Different methods of making the communication boards more portable for ambulatory children need to be found. Also, there are many children with such severe motor impairments that a board display using the number of symbols required in the present method is not realistic. A system of coding the board for as few separate response areas as possible needs to be researched and developed.

Exact English Signing

Most recently, pilot work has begun to adapt the oral version of the curriculum to an exact English signing system with children and adolescents who are hearing-impaired or children who have not progressed in extensive oral speech training and yet have the fine motor coordination necessary for producing finger signs. Galen Berry, Speech Pathologist/Audiologist at Kansas Neurological Institute, has assumed primary responsibility for adapting the program to the signing system.[4]

Some children with severe hearing losses or severe speech impairment are being trained to use signs only. Other children with less severe hearing losses (usually assisted by hearing aids) are being trained to attempt oral speech simultaneous with the appropriate signs. At this point, however, response accuracy is required only for the correct use of signs. Thus far, adaptation of the program to a signing system has been much easier when compared to the communication board system. Notably, the *self-extended control* (question-asking) steps in the Persons and Things sequence have been easily adapted to the signing system, a problem area for adapting the program to communication boards.

The major disadvantage of the signing system is, of course, the limited audience available to the child for communication. The use of the signing system with simultaneous attempts

[4] Information on adapting the program to the exact English signing system can be obtained from Galen Berry at the Kansas Neurological Institute in Topeka, Kansas.

to elicit oral speech warrants close observation with low-functioning children in the program. The real possibility that the signing system may serve as a mediator for the production of oral speech among these children is a promising area for future research. This holds true for even those children who have good potential for oral speech development.

Selection of a Communication System

Persons attempting to develop some form of communication system with severely handicapped children are faced with the selection of appropriate content material (a curriculum), as well as the decision about a mode of expression (oral or nonoral) that is best suited to the particular physical and behavioral abilities and skills of the child. A current technology is, unfortunately, not available for making precise and accurate decisions regarding either of these areas.

The adaptations currently being tested with our 60-step training sequence have added important new contributions to the development of communication skills among the severely handicapped population. Some fairly rough guidelines for the potential language teacher using the curriculum with a severely and multihandicapped population are presented.

Oral Speech Development

This obviously preferred mode should be used with children capable of articulating words (even though perfect articulation is not required). The child may or may not be verbally imitative. For the nonimitative child, progress in imitation training should be a determining factor for switching to a nonoral system. Younger children should be given a more extensive opportunity to develop verbal imitation skills before changing to an alternative language system. Adequate hearing is another condition important for oral speech development. It is usually present in children capable of at least fairly accurate word articulation. The importance of adequate vision for the oral version of the curriculum remains unknown. Children who have definite visual problems, but not to the extent that they cannot identify the objects and actions used in the various training steps, are still suitable candidates for speech training. An oral adaptation of the program may be constructed for children with severe visual defects, who possess normal hearing and can articulate words. Fine motor coordination is not required for the oral speech mode if severe impairment to the speech mechanisms is not present. Currently, there are cerebral palsied students in the oral field-test version of the curriculum who have quite severe motor impairments in their arms and legs.

Exact English Signing

Children assigned to an exact English signing adaptation of the curriculum should have adequate vision and the fine motor coordination necessary for finger signs. Neither normal hearing nor the ability to articulate words is necessary for this mode of expression.

Communication Boards

Children selected for this adapted system of the program need not be able to articulate words, nor have the fine motor coordination necessary for signing. Only a simple pointing response to the symbol card is required. Children with gross physical impairment of their arms can be equipped with headsticks to make the pointing response. Use of the communication boards does require, however, both adequate vision and hearing. It is conceivable that some children with both severe hearing and motor impairments could be taught to understand signing (as an input system) and to use the communication board for expression (output).

As a final note, the curriculum may also be adapted for children who have severe impairments to both their vision and hearing input modalities. This adaptation should probably include a three-dimensional symbol system, so that the tactual modality can be used for stimulus input, and a simplified motor response can be used for response output. The three-dimensional symbol system described by Hollis, Carrier, and Spradlin (1976) for deaf/blind mentally retarded children represents the initial technology toward such a system.

Reference Notes

1. Harrelson, A. *Effects of productive speech training on receptive language*. Unpublished master's thesis. Lawrence, Kansas: University of Kansas, 1969.
2. Firling, J. Functional language for a severely handicapped child: A case study. Unpublished manuscript. Manhattan, Kansas: Kansas State University Speech and Hearing Center, 1976.

References

Bloom, L. Talking, understanding, and thinking. In R. L. Schiefelbusch and L. Lloyd (Eds.). *Language perspectives: Acquisition, retardation, and intervention*. Baltimore: University Park Press, 1974, 285–311.

Bricker, W. A., & Bricker, D. D. A program of language training for the severely handicapped child. *Exceptional Children*, 1970, *37*, 101–111.

Bricker, W. A., & Bricker, D. D. An early language training strategy. In R. L. Schiefelbusch and L. Lloyd (Eds.). *Language perspectives: Acquisition, retardation, and intervention*. Baltimore: University Park Press, 1974, 431–468.

Chomsky, N. Review of B. F. Skinner. *Verbal behavior. Language*, 1959, *35*, 26–58.

Drash, P. W., & Leibowitz, J. M.: Operant conditioning of speech and language in the nonverbal child: Recent advances. *Pediatric Clinic of North America*, 1973, *20*, 233–243.

Garcia, E. The training and generalization of a conversational speech form in nonverbal retardates. *Journal of Applied Behavior Analysis*, 1974, *7*, 137–149.

Gray, B., & Ryan, B. *A language program for the non-language child*. Champaign, Illinois: Research Press, 1973.

Guess, D. A functional analysis of receptive language and productive speech: Acquisition of the plural morpheme. *Journal of Applied Behavior Analysis*, 1969, *2*, 55–67.

Guess, D., & Baer, D. M. An analysis of individual differences in generalization between receptive and productive language in retarded children. *Journal of Applied Behavior Analysis*, 1973a, *6*, 311–329.

Guess, D., & Baer, D. M. Some experimental analyses of linguistic development in institutionalized retarded children. In B. Lahey (Ed.). *The modification of language behavior*. Springfield, Illinois: Charles C Thomas, 1973b, 3–60.

Guess, D., Sailor, W., & Baer, D. M. To teach language to retarded children. In R. L. Schiefelbusch and L. Lloyd (Eds.). *Language perspectives: Acquisition, retardation, and intervention.* Baltimore: University Park Press, 1974, 529–563.

Guess, D., Sailor, W., & Baer, D. M. *Functional speech and language training for the severely handicapped. Part I: Persons and things.* Lawrence, Kansas: H & H Enterprises, Inc., 1976a.

Guess, D., Sailor, W., & Baer, D. M. Intervention program for children with limited language. In R. L. Schiefelbusch (Ed.). *Bases of language intervention*. Baltimore: University Park Press, 1976b.

Guess, D., Sailor, W., Keogh, W., & Baer, D. M. Language development programs for severely handicapped children. In N. Haring and L. Brown (Eds.). *Teaching severely and profoundly multihandicapped children*. New York: Grune and Stratton, 1976.

Harris, S. L. Teaching language to nonverbal children—with emphasis on problems of generalization. *Psychological Bulletin*, 1975, *82:4*, 565–580.

Hollis, J. H., Carrier, J. K., & Spradlin, J. E. Intervention strategies for nonspeech children. In R. L. Schiefelbusch (Ed.). *Bases of language intervention*. Baltimore: University Park Press, 1976.

Ingram, D. The relationship between comprehension and production. In R. L. Schiefelbusch and L. Lloyd (Eds.). *Language perspectives: Acquisition, retardation, and intervention.* Baltimore: University Park Press, 1974, 313–334.

Kent, L. *Language acquisition program for the severely retarded*. Champaign, Illinois: Research Press, 1974.

McKenna-Hartung, S., & Hartung, J. R. Establishing verbal imitation skills and functional speech in autistic children. In B. Lahey (Ed.). *The modification of language behavior*. Springfield, Illinois: Charles C Thomas, 1973, 61–90.

Miller, J., & Yoder, D. A syntax teaching program. In J. McLean, D. Yoder, & R. L. Schiefelbusch (Eds.). *Language intervention with the retarded: Developing strategies*. Baltimore: University Park Press, 1972a, 191–211.

Miller, J., & Yoder, D. On developing the content for a language teaching program. *Mental Retardation*, 1972b, April, 9–11.

Miller, J., & Yoder, D. An ontogenetic language teaching strategy for retarded children. In R. L. Schiefelbusch and L. Lloyd (Eds.). *Language perspectives: Acquisition, retardation, and intervention*. Baltimore: University Park Press, 1974, 505–528.

Piaget, J. *The language and thought of the child*. New York: World Publishing Co., 1962.

Sailor, W., Guess, D., & Baer, D. M. An experimental program for teaching functional language to verbally deficient children. *Mental Retardation*, 1973, *11*, 27–35.

Stremel, K., & Waryas, C. A behavioral-psycholinguistic approach to language training. *American Speech and Hearing Monographs*, 1974, *18*, 96–124.

Stokes, T. F., & Baer, D. M. An implicit technology of generalization. *Journal of Applied Behavioral Analysis*, in press.

Tawney, J. W., & Hipsher, L. W. *Systematic instruction for retarded children: The Illinois program. Experimental edition: Part II. Systematic language instruction*. Danville, Illinois: The Interstate Printers and Publishers, 1972.

Woodcock, R. W., Clark, C. R., & Davies, C. O. *Peabody Rebus Reading Program*. Circle Pines, Minnesota. American Guidance Service, 1969.

DOUG GUESS is Associate Professor, Department of Special Education, University of Kansas. He was formerly Director of Psychology and Research at Kansas Neurological Institute. Dr. Guess is a member of the Board of Editors for the *Journal of Applied Behavior Analysis*, and a member of the Board of Directors of the American Association for the Education of the Severely and Profoundly Handicapped. He has published widely on the subject of speech and language training for severely handicapped children.

WAYNE SAILOR is Associate Professor, Department of Special Education, San Francisco State University. He was formerly Project Director for the Personnel Training Program, Education of the Severely Handicapped, at the Kansas Neurological Institute in Topeka, and a Research Associate of the Bureau of Child Research at the University of Kansas. He is a member of the Board of Directors of the American Association for the Education of the Severely and Profoundly Handicapped.

DONALD M. BAER is the Roy A. Roberts Professor of Human Development, and a Research Associate with the Bureau of Child Research, University of Kansas. He is past editor of the *Journal of Applied Behavior Analysis*, and co-author (with Sidney Bijou) of two volumes entitled *Child Development*. He has worked in the areas of social development, language, imitation, and behavior analysis.

On Specifying What to Teach: The Movement from Structure, to Structure and Meaning, to Structure and Meaning and Knowing

JON F. MILLER

University of Wisconsin, Madison

Many children do not acquire language at an appropriate rate or of sufficient quality to be considered normal for their age and language community. They may fail to do so for a number of reasons, many of which are still unspecified by basic research on communication deficits.

Language teaching programs developed prior to 1969 seemed to be based on two general assumptions about these children. The first was that the child was not able to use those processes employed by normal children to acquire language. This assumption led to the development of teaching programs whose content differs both in sequence and in complexity from the language acquisition of the normal child over time. The second assumption was that the child had not learned language because he had not had sufficient language stimulation or exposure. Resulting programs bombarded the child with concentrated verbal stimulation, giving little, if any, thought to the content.

These two assumptions led directly to the development of teaching programs or technologies for training language which have been successful for specific populations. Our experience in implementing these approaches with mentally retarded children was, in general, unsuccessful. Our conclusion, early in 1970, was that existing programs ignored the essential characteristics of language itself—its structure and its creative, displaceable nature—resulting in a lack of specificity of what was to be taught. We felt that one avenue for the improvement of teaching strategies would be to concentrate on the content, or what is to be taught, and to seek soundly based methods of selecting and sequencing the content for teaching. Our goal then was to develop the content for teaching that would provide minimal steps for learning and provide the basis for moving from one level of complexity to the next in a logical progression.

In order to facilitate language acquisition in the retarded child, it is necessary to choose the content of the language training program so as to provide the child with the salient features of the language system and maximum communication ability. Where can information be found on which to base these decisions? The data available in the development literature constitute such a source. Normal children learn some structures of the language system earlier than others. For example, noun phrase expansion occurs before verb phrase expansion; attribution or adjectives appear before auxiliary verbs in active declarative sentences; negative sentences are appropriately produced before questions; yes/no questions are appropriately produced before "wh" questions; the present progressive /ing/, expressing ongoing action, appears before past tense /ed/, noting past events; both of these are expressed before future events are expressed. Active, negative, and question sentences appear before passive sentences and embedded sentences. Development occurs in all of these structures simultaneously, some progressing more rapidly than others. Children progress through a number of developmental stages on each construction before they achieve adult mastery.

There is a developmental hierarchy of structures to be learned. The order may be determined within the child, either by complexity of form (linguistic structure), or by complexity of function (meaning) which reflects his cognitive capacity. The language acquired by the child is a system which has specific structure or form, allowing him to talk about a wide variety of objects, events, and relationships (functions) of which he is cognitively and perceptually aware. Every utterance, then, has both a form and a function. These can be discussed as separate entities, but rarely, if ever, do they exist separately in the natural language.

Form and function appear to interact in a very specific way for children acquiring the language system: "New forms first express old functions, and new functions are first expressed by old forms" (Slobin, 1973, p. 184). As new forms are acquired by the child, they first express old functions, those already known by the child. Throughout the acquisition process, there is a definite trade-off between the cognitive-perceptual system and the linguistic system.

These facts about language acquisition in children formed the basis for our first language program, which was completed in 1970 (Miller & Yoder, 1972a). The focus of the program was the development of the teaching content, applying the general principles and data uncovered in studying the normal child's acquisition of language. Although there was some awareness at that time of the semantic and cognitive components in language acquisition, the program's major focus was on the acquisition of syntax, which reflected the major emphasis of the language acquisition literature at that time. It should be noted, however, that the framework was constructed to allow for further exploration of meaning (semantics) and knowledge (cognition) as their importance continued to emerge in the literature.

The principles and data derived from normal language development studies seemed particularly important to content development of teaching programs for mentally retarded populations. A review of the literature related to the language behavior of mentally retarded children, completed in 1970 (Yoder & Miller, 1972a), concluded that retarded children develop the language code in a manner similar to children without intellectual deficits, but at a slower rate. This conclusion, however, was equivocal, in that there were few developmental studies and no longitudinal studies of language development in retarded children. It was assumed, however, that the retarded child acquired language in a manner similar to that of non-retardates, except for a rate difference. This assumption supported the application of normal developmental data in content selection for teaching programs designed for retarded children.

The result of this initial attempt to apply normal developmental data can be found in a syntax teaching program (Miller & Yoder, 1972a). The following is a summary of the basic points expressed in that program:

1. Before the child becomes a language user, he needs to have something to say (concepts) and a reason for saying it (semantic intent), as well as a way of saying it (linguistic structure).
2. There are four critical developmental stages:
   a. Single words
   b. Word strings (topic-comment)
   c. Syntactic constructions
   d. Three-word sentences
3. Throughout the entire program, the clinician works from comprehension to production.
4. New words and syntactic relationships are established by supplying the underlying concepts through environmental manipulation and experience. That is, manipulating the child's environment allows him to experience the underlying concepts necessary for the comprehension and expression of words and syntactic relationships.
5. The following techniques are used to facilitate comprehension and production at the four program stages:
   a. Reinforcement of correct response
   b. Imitation for stimulus control
   c. Expansion of verbal responses
   d. Modeling of verbal responses
6. The clinician's initial input to the child should be "telegraphic speech." Later, the clinician will use full grammatical sentences, as shown in the expansion and modeling techniques.
7. This program is limited in scope because we lack a detailed description of children's language development which incorporates cognitive, linguistic, and nonlinguistic components. As additional developmental information becomes available, the program can be expanded accordingly. (p. 210)

Through the implementation of this program, the success of the teaching strategy of applying developmental data in content selection became apparent. In a further discussion of content selection in language teaching programs (Miller & Yoder, 1972b), the following operating principle was proposed:

> The content for language training for retarded children should be taken from the data available on language development in normal children. This content should be taught in the same sequence that it is acquired by the normal child. (p. 9)

It should be recognized that the assumption underlying this operating principle is still a working hypothesis about the language behavior of retarded children. The data base is primarily syntactic, indicating that the form of the language expressed by retarded children is similar to that of the normal child at the same stage in development, though the retarded child is much older. The operating principle has, however, provided a logical basis for selecting the grammatical structures to be taught and a map of the relevant structures through the development period. Language training studies evoking this procedure for content selection have demonstrated its effectiveness (Stremel, 1972; Rabush, Note 1).

The Shift From a Syntactic Basis for Language Learning to a Semantic Basis

As studies on normal language development have emerged since 1970, there have been rapidly changing views (and new insights) regarding the basic elements acquired in initial language learning. These changing views represent a shift from viewing acquisition as based on syntactic units to a recognition that acquisition is probably based on semantic units, at least in the early stages of development.

In attempting to apply these insights in developing content for language teaching programs, we drew the following conclusions regarding what a child is learning when he is acquiring his language in the early stages (Miller & Yoder, 1974).

1. Semantic functions provide the basis for early language acquisition.
2. Semantic functions are derived directly from the child's experience, both linguistic and nonlinguistic. Through experience with objects and events around him, the child begins to conceptualize particular objects and relationships. At that same time, he is experiencing the linguistic code of his community spoken around him. Through frequent experiences with particular objects and relations, accompanied by linguistic marking of environmental events, the child begins to mark linguistically those objects and relationships he can conceptualize. When perceived objects and relationships are marked (that is, spoken), they become semantic functions and the child has begun to map aspects of his experience linguistically.
3. The functions expressed at the single-word level then become expressed by two words. Relatively few new functions are expressed as the child moves to two-word forms. This phenomenon tends to support Bowerman's (1973a; 1973b) notion that early structural relationships are based on simple order strategies that are semantically based and intended to express a specific function. Children express similar semantic functions all the way through the earliest stage of development, though their utterance increases in length from one to seven morphemes (Brown, 1973a; 1973b).
4. Within this framework, syntax can be thought of as a general abstract organizational structure which allows the child to use the numerous semantic functions acquired in comprehension and production in a manner consistent with his linguistic community.

   The need for syntax arises in order for the child to make his expression of semantic functions understood by others in his community. That is, a consistent form for utterances is necessary for communication to take place. This form, syntax, allows the expression of semantic functions in a variety of ways that may be unique but are fully comprehensible. It appears that the development of syntax may begin at the time the child uses two-word utterances consistently, or later, and continues for quite a few years (Chomsky, 1969; Epstein, Note 2).
5. The things that children talk about in their first utterances are remarkably consistent across languages (Bowerman, 1973a, 1973b; Brown, 1973; Slobin, 1973). This consistency across language further supports the notion that semantic functions are the basis for language development. The similarity of functions expressed in early development is the result of perceptual-cognitive development which is universally consistent for all human beings. Although all languages can be described syntactically, children acquire syntax over time as a means of mapping the semantic functions acquired for communication needs in their linguistic community.

In considering the content to be taught in the early stages of language training (single words to three-word utterances) in the light of recent developmental data, we concluded that the basis of early language development is the semantic function. Semantic functions, then, are the basic elements of a teaching program directed toward this early developmental period (Miller & Yoder, 1974).

The program completed in early 1973 proposed a set of operating principles which could be applied individually, to take advantage of each child's language-learning environment. This individualistic approach to language teaching emphasizes the content to be taught, while recognizing individual differences among children. As such, it offers a strategy for constructing teaching programs which include operating principles for decision-making about critical issues.

This program is based on the notion that semantic functions form the basis of what is learned by children acquiring language. Through evoking the following principles within the context of a behavior modification paradigm, the teacher can direct the child toward the acquisition of a functional and creative communication system.

Operating Principle 1. The content for language training of retarded children should be taken from the data available on language development in normal children.

Operating Principle 2. Semantic functions should be ordered for teaching on the basis of frequency of occurrence, and the selection of the form of utterance should be determined by the sequence of forms acquired by normal children.

Operating Principle 3. A single, frequently occurring experience, demonstrating a particular semantic relationship should be selected and paired with an appropriate word. After the child demonstrates mastery, he should move to multiple experiences which express the same function.

Operating Principle 4. First expansions of single-word utterances should be of relational functions previously expressed.

This program specifies the relationship between form, function, and experience, and provides for the shaping of attending behavior and increasing motivation in retarded children. It also provides a method for testing the relative contribution of programmed experience and linguistic marking in enhancing cognitive-perceptual awareness of objects and events in the child's environment that are the basis of language development (Miller & Yoder, 1974).

The question remains: is precise specification of content and sequence of linguistic behaviors within a teaching program sufficient to maximize the child's development of a functional communication system?

Allowing a child to develop a system to communicate basic needs, wants, and ideas may require more than the mere acquisition of linguistic features taught in specified ways and places. Mittler (1974), Morehead (1972), Morehead and Ingram (1973), Miller and Yoder (1974), and others have suggested that imaginative and representational play, along with appropriate stimulation within living environments, form an important foundation for cognitive and linguistic development. The ability to play, or to cope in such a way as to make one object or activity stand for another, is one precursor of learning that things have names, and that language can be used creatively and generatively. We concluded: to the extent that language development is related to general representational skills and is dependent upon conceptual development, it may be necessary to assess and attempt to develop certain conceptual functions as an integral part of a communication development program.

Current Trends in Considering the Major Components of Semantic-Based Teaching Programs

A careful, detailed reconsideration of the relationship between semantics and cognition is the steppingstone for a re-examination of the basis for content selection in teaching programs whose focus is the development of meaning. The inextricable relationship between semantics and cognition (Furth, 1970; Johnston, Note 3) signifies that when we consider semantics as part of the content of a language treatment program, we must be concerned with more than just the development of meaning expressed through language itself. We must also be concerned with the development of cognitive behaviors and with the environmental input relative to the child's general experiences, as well as specifically relative to the child's linguistic stimulation. Although these factors are clearly not independent of the child's learning and acquiring both cognitive structures and language, it is helpful to try to demonstrate the increased complexity of our problem.

Figure 1 expresses the major components to be considered and their potential interactions. As can be seen in Figure 1, our original characterization of meaning in the early period of development is expressed in terms of semantic relations and derives primarily from the work of Lois Bloom, Roger Brown, and Melissa Bowerman, as reported in numerous publications. These semantic relations characterize initial meanings expressed in child language from single words through two and three term relations. The most frequently recurring relations through the first two stages of language development have provided the content for the semantic-based program of Miller and Yoder (1974) for that early period of development.

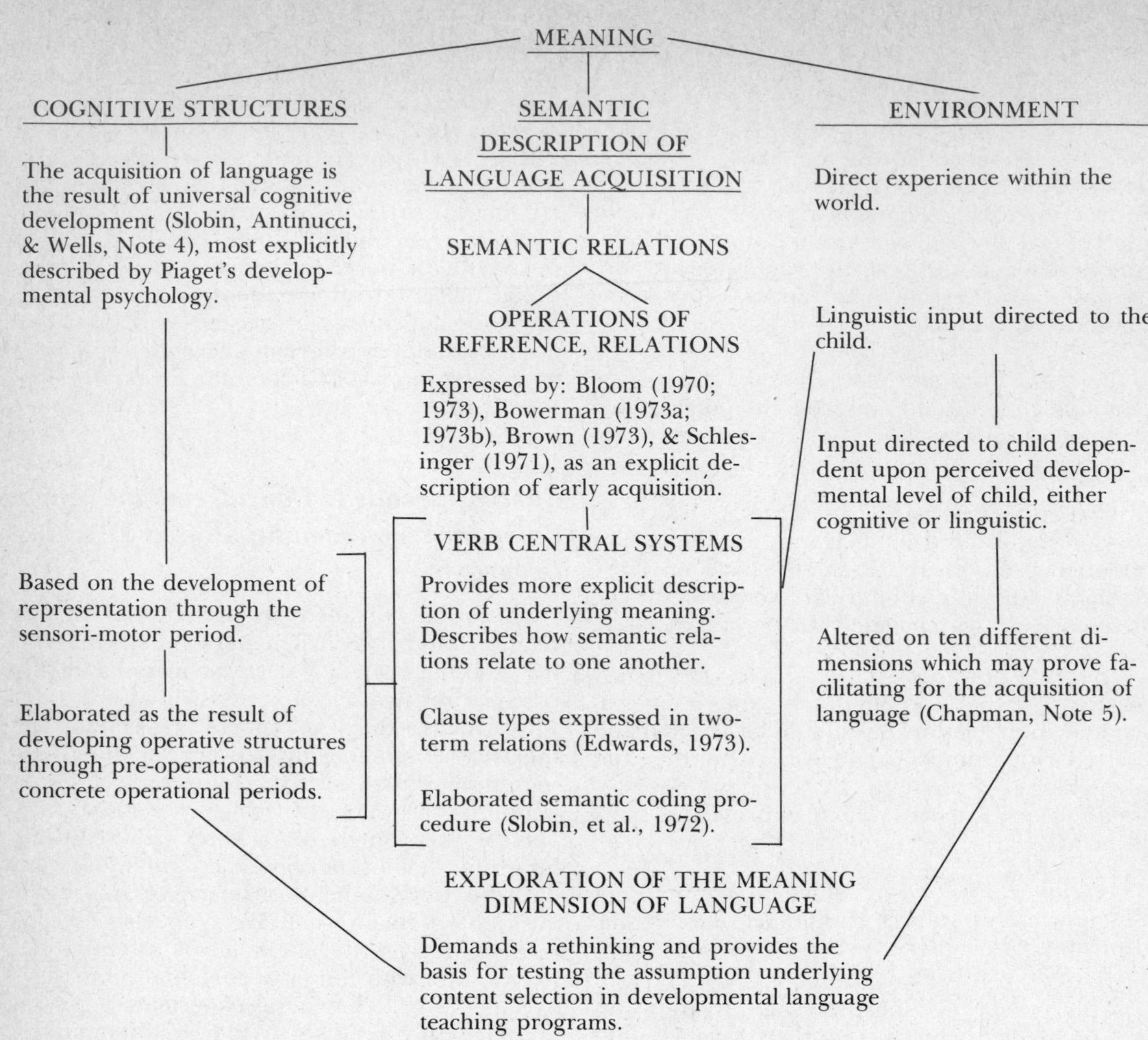

MEANING
COGNITIVE STRUCTURES
SEMANTIC DESCRIPTION OF LANGUAGE ACQUISITION
ENVIRONMENT
The acquisition of language is the result of universal cognitive development (Slobin, Antinucci, & Wells, Note 4), most explicitly described by Piaget's developmental psychology.
Direct experience within the world.
SEMANTIC RELATIONS
OPERATIONS OF REFERENCE, RELATIONS
Linguistic input directed to the child.
Expressed by: Bloom (1970; 1973), Bowerman (1973a; 1973b), Brown (1973), & Schlesinger (1971), as an explicit description of early acquisition.
Input directed to child dependent upon perceived developmental level of child, either cognitive or linguistic.
VERB CENTRAL SYSTEMS
Based on the development of representation through the sensori-motor period.
Provides more explicit description of underlying meaning. Describes how semantic relations relate to one another.
Altered on ten different dimensions which may prove facilitating for the acquisition of language (Chapman, Note 5).
Elaborated as the result of developing operative structures through pre-operational and concrete operational periods.
Clause types expressed in two-term relations (Edwards, 1973).
Elaborated semantic coding procedure (Slobin, et al., 1972).
EXPLORATION OF THE MEANING DIMENSION OF LANGUAGE
Demands a rethinking and provides the basis for testing the assumption underlying content selection in developmental language teaching programs.

Figure 1. Major components of semantic-based teaching programs.

Methods for Describing Semantic Development

The specificity of the semantic relations used in the Miller and Yoder program (1974) to capture the meanings expressed by children has been questioned by Melissa Bowerman (1974). Her arguments, from a strictly linguistic point of view, basically deal with what the child means by what he says and whether the meaning he expresses is adequately characterized by these semantic relations. Indeed, are notions such as agent action and object location specific enough to characterize the child's meaning and do they, in fact, have psychological reality for the child? Brown (1973) has cautioned that these semantic relations may be nothing more than convenient categories for data reduction, analysis, and comparison and may or may not actually correspond to aspects of the structural knowledge which enables children to produce and to comprehend sentences.

Recent semantic analysis systems (Edwards, 1973; Slobin, Antinucci & Wells, 1972; Wells, 1975) have sought to overcome the problems of the early semantic relations discussed by Brown (1973). These newly emerging procedures are based on verb-central semantic theories, such as Chafe's (1970). The Edwards procedure, for example, provides a way of organizing verbs and cases (Fillmore, 1968) into a set of deep semantic clause types. Compare the specificity of description and the relationship between clause types and semantic relations described in Table 1

TABLE 1

Brown's (1973) Semantic Classification of Two-Word Utterances

Basic Operations of Reference

1. *Nomination* (simple naming function) has two prototypical situations.
   - A. Pure nomination operation: child names, usually in response to questions (what's that?) R—the, a that, it + book, car, baby, etc., or (where's x?) R—this, that, him, there + ball, pig, shoe, etc.
   - B. Demonstrative—Entity: Child initiates utterance by pointing as he names ("See boy, here bed, there wall, there book, here more").
2. *Recurrence*: Request for (imperative) or comment on (declarative) the recurrence of a person, entity, or process ("More write, more raisin, more milk").
3. Nonexistence: Objects or actions specified did not exist or occur although they were expected to exist or occur ("All gone, or no, or no more") + dog, juice, book, etc.

Basic Semantic Relations

1. Agent—Action	"Adam sleep," "Eve drive," etc.
2. Action—Object	"Bite finger," "Hit ball," etc.
3. Agent—Object	"Mommy sock," "Horsie flower," etc.
4. Entity—Locative	"Lady home," "Lotion tummy," "Car garage," "Sweater chair," etc.
5. Action—Locative	"Sit bed," "Go home," "Go there."
6. Possessor—Possession	"Daddy chair," "Dolly hat," "Dog tail," "Mommy nose," etc.
7. Entity—Attribute	"Yellow block," "Little fish," "Pepper not," etc.

(Brown's semantic relations) and Table 2 (Edwards' clause types). (These two tables represent the complexity of recent semantic systems developed to describe primarily two-word utterances.)

The increased specificity of verb-central semantic analysis systems provides the necessary methodology for describing the acquisition of meaning through the developmental period. Ongoing studies by Derek Edwards and Gorden Wells in England, and Dan Slobin in the United States, will give detailed descriptions of children's semantic achievements. Such descriptions could provide the content, extending through the developmental period, for language teaching programs of the type described by Miller and Yoder (1974).

The primacy of cognition in language development and the direct relationship between meaning (semantics) and knowing (cognition) discussed by Furth (1970) and Johnston (1974), call into question the efficacy of the direct application of the semantic achievements of normal children as program content for mentally retarded children, as well as for other children with language deficits.

There are two primary considerations in selecting semantic content for teaching. The first is the child's experiential history and present environmental situation. This point was discussed by Miller and Yoder (1974), and provided the sole basis for determining the semantic content of that program. The second necessary consideration is the cognitive behavior of the child. If Piaget's developmental psychology is used as the descriptive base for cognitive behavior, the meanings expressed in language reside in the operative structures of the speaker. The meanings expressed through language and the knowledge of operative cognitive structures are synonymous (Furth, 1970).

The direct application of the meanings expressed by normal children as content for teaching children with language deficits necessarily assumes that children with language deficits have normal cognitive structures. The order of acquisition of major meanings expressed in language by normal children has relevance for children with language deficits only if similar cognitive performance can be demonstrated. Such an order of semantic achievements through the developmental period directly reflects the development of operative cognitive structures. The resulting order of semantic clause types expressed reflects the complexity of developing operative structures or knowledge, rather than the complexity of the semantic component of language. Meaning resides in the speaker/hearer, not in the language (Furth, 1970). Let us examine the small number of research reports on cognitive behavior from the Piagetian view of mentally retarded children. The retarded child is of particular interest because of the multiple etiologies which may lead to his behavioral classification. Additionally, retarded children constitute a substantial population with demonstrated problems in acquiring language. Studies by Woodward (1959, 1963), Sinclair (1969), Das (1973), Inhelder (1966), Wohlhueter and Sindberg (1975), and Kahn (1975) cover a range of developmental achievements which demonstrate potential cognitive deficits of differences at particular stages of development, compared to normal children. The data, although not

TABLE 2

Some Basic Clause Types (Edwards, 1973)

Notation:
(x) = x is optional
(x) (y) = either x or y or both
$\frac{x}{y}$ = either x or y but not both

		Static	*Dynamic*	*Causative*
Actional	1-Directed Action		I + O + V. DIR. ACT. (The brick hit the floor.)	(Ag) + I + O + V. DIR. ACT. (John hit Bill with a brick.)
	2-Movement		O + VDYN. MOV (The wheel turned.)	(Ag) (I) + O + VCAUS. MOV. (Bill turned the wheel with his elbow.)
Relational	3-Locative	O + VSTAT. LOC + L (The book is on the chair.)	O + VDYN. LOC S G (The book fell off table/on the floor.)	(Ag) (I) + O + VCAUS. LOC + S G (John took the book off the shelf/put it on the shelf.)
Stative	4-Possessive	O + VSTAT. POSS + P (The book belongs to Bill.)	O + VDYN. POSS + B (Bill got a present.)	(Ag) (I) + O + VCAUS. POSS + B (John gave Bill a present.)
Character-izing	5-Experiential	E + VSTAT. ATTR (John likes opera.)	E + VDYN. EXP + (Ph) (John got interested in opera.)	(Ag) (I) + E + VCAUS. EXP + (Ph) (Mary interested John in opera.)
	6-Attributive	O + VSTAT. ATTR (The jar is broken.)	O + VDYN. ATTR (The jar broke.)	(Ag) (I) + O + VCAUS. ATTR (Bill broke the jar with his fist.)

Cases: Ag = Agent; O = Object; I = Instrument; L = Location; G = Goal; S = Source; — = Possessor; B = Beneficiary; E = Experiencer; Ph = Phenomenon.

Table 2 shows a way of organizing verbs and cases into a set of deep semantic clause-types. The clause-types are divided into two major groups, Actional and Stative, and they have the same names as the verb-types which are their central relational element. Each clause contains a single verb and the cases it selects, and all verbs are either actional or stative.

compelling, certainly support further exploration of cognitive behavior and its relationship to semantic aspects of language acquisition and to the development of language teaching programs for children with language deficits.

Projections and Predictions for Future Research on the Role of Cognitive Behavior in Language Development

Furth (1970) relates Piaget's developmental psychology to language at two levels—figurative and operative. First, language is a system of conventional symbols and, therefore, representational in nature. Representation is figurative in nature, the making present of a concrete reality. Figurative knowing stresses that kind of knowledge which focuses on static configuration or content of sensory input. The matter of symbols (language) is then dependent upon, and explained by, specific learning from the environment. The learning of a specific representational system or language is dependent upon, and explained by, specific learning from the environment. Figurative development may be operationalized in early development as the development of representational behaviors, as evidenced in play, imitation, and language itself.

Second, the meanings expressed through language are equivalent to the operative knowing of the individual. Operative structures are knowledge, and correspond to the person's actual stage of knowing and understanding. When operative structures are applied to symbolic representations, they are the actual meaning of the symbolic situation (Furth, 1970). Operative development can be operationalized as the emergence of knowledge of space, time, causality, and object permanency in the sensori-motor period. Achievements on operative cognitive dimensions reflect the meanings available for expression, while figurative achievements are basic and necessary for the acquisition and use of a language system to express available knowledge. Obviously, the two systems are interdependent and interactive. They may, however, have independent developmental bases, thus forming a potentially useful distinction for studying emerging cognitive and linguistic processes. Deficits on either dimension have consequences for the child's acquisition and use of a language system.

At the present time, it appears productive to consider potential cognitive differences as being primarily of two types: (a) figurative—dealing primarily with perception, including representational skills, language, and play drawings as the expression of knowledge; and (b) operative knowledge itself as manifested in operative structures. The problem remains for us to devise methods to differentiate between operative and figurative deficits as they relate to language. Specifically, we must delineate deficits in knowledge and deficits in the expression of available knowledge. Evaluation of the child's verbal language behavior, by careful analysis of semantic clause types, can potentially provide an index of what he knows of the world, since the meanings expressed through language reflect operative structures of the child. The language structures (phonological and syntactical) used to express meaning are the result of direct environmental learning and, as a representational system, has its basis in figurative cognitive dimensions. Analyzing the structure of a child's language could test the integrity of the general figurative cognitive dimensions necessary for language learning.

The direct analysis, i.e., non-language-related procedures, of the cognitive behaviors exhibited by children with language deficits is likely to yield a number of possible results, as listed in Table 3. The descriptions listed in Table 3 are, to some extent, predictions derived from observational experience at the Waisman Center. The list is general and not intended to be exhaustive. Future research will probably result in several subgroups within each of the five categories, each with a distinct performance protocol on figurative and operative cognitive dimensions.

There is another developmental dimension that is not expressed in Table 3. The five categories listed may not all be present throughout the sensory-motor, pre-operational, and concrete operational stages of development. Some may be limited to certain periods of development. Others, because of the cognitive dimensions affected, may prevent further elaboration into later developmental stages. The important point here is not only that different configurations on figurative and operative dimensions may exist in children with deviant language, but that the child's achievements on operative dimensions reflect the meanings he is capable of expressing, and his figurative achievements

TABLE 3

Possible Cognitive Findings on Figurative and Operative Dimensions with Language-Deviant Populations

1. *Same operative achievements as normal children of same age (CA); figurative deficits on language-related concepts due to lack of auditory perceptual experience*. Deaf children (Furth, 1971).
2. *Same figurative and operative achievements as normal children but acquired at a slower rate*. Rate difference.
   A. Children exhibiting a general developmental delay, including language, who may or may not be classified as retarded.
   B. Mentally retarded children—mild and moderate levels.
3. *Specific figurative and operative deficits*.
   A. General representational skills—aphasic children (Morehead and Ingram, 1973).
   B. Relations, space, time, movement, causality—mentally retarded children.
4. *Uneven development across figurative and operative dimensions which may cross developmental stage boundaries*. Vertical peaking on specific dimensions. For example: Object performance V S-M level, imitation and play at Stage III S M level of development.
   A. Mentally retarded children.
   B. Multiply handicapped children.
5. *Lack of horizontal development on figurative and operative dimensions within cognitive stage of development*.
   A. Failure to recognize new instances without direct prior experience—mentally retarded children.
   B. Inability to infer relationships to new instance—mentally retarded children.
   C. Partial achievements within stage with possible vertical extension into the next stage as in number 4 above. Mentally retarded children.
   D. Failure to achieve some notions within a stage. Mentally retarded children, aphasic children.

reflect his ability to acquire and use a language system to express his knowledge throughout the developmental period. Level of development on figurative and operative cognitive dimensions provides a two-dimensional matrix through which we may begin to study the developmental relationship between language and cognitive behavior in deviant populations.

In reviewing Table 3, it is apparent that the meanings expressed by a child reflect at least the level of operative structure development. The development of operative structures may, however, exceed their expression through verbal language, as discussed by Morehead and Ingram (1973) with aphasic children and by Furth (1971) with deaf children. Morehead and Ingram propose a general representational deficit as the basic problem of their aphasic children. Furth's deaf children, on the other hand, lack the primary perceptual process through which verbal language is acquired and, therefore, lack experience with verbal language as a representational system.

Both the Morehead and Ingram (1973) and Furth (1971) studies support Cromer's (1974) notion that cognition is a necessary, but not a sufficient, condition for language development. With both aphasic and deaf children, the problem resides within the child and what he brings to the language-learning situation. In addition, however, the environment must be considered relative to Cromer's statement (see Figure 1). Furth (1971) has pointed out that language is acquired through direct experience in the environment. A language spoken around the child and to the child is essential for its acquisition as a representational system. Studies show that the speech directed to children by their parents is different from adult-to-adult speech. Chapman's (Note 5) recent review of these studies reveals the alteration of ten different dimensions which she contends may facilitate the language acquisition process. In general, these alterations are toward simplification and explicitness as the language relates to situational context. Such alterations appear to be important in facilitating cognitive growth on figurative dimensions related to the development of representational skills generally, and verbal language as a representational system specifically. Deficiencies on the environmental dimensions affecting the language addressed to him, and his direct experience with the language, will influence the child's ability to acquire the language as a means of expressing his knowledge, despite his level of cognitive growth on operative dimensions.

Potential cognitive differences (figurative and operative, or both) with populations exhibiting deviant language (Table 3) increase the complexity of selecting appropriate content in treatment program development. When meaning—semantics—is the central focus, it increases the complexity of the relationship between (a) syntax, semantics, language in general, and its use in communicaiton, and (b) the underlying conceptual basis necessary for its acquisition. Future research focusing directly on cognitive—linguistic behaviors of children with language problems will result in improved methodologies, clear decision-making procedures for individualized treatment program development, and an improved understanding of the important cognitive-language dimensions necessary for language growth.

Conclusions

1. Emerging semantic development data from normal children will probably not be directly relevant to specific content selection because it assumes an intact conceptual system in the deviant child.
2. Four factors emerge as primary in selecting initial semantic notions as content for teaching at the present time. These factors must be considered in relation to the individual child's development on cognitive dimensions and language use through comprehension and production.
   A. Level of cognitive development on figurative (imitation, play) and operative (space, time, causality, object permanency) dimensions.
   B. The child's experiential history and usual environmental interactions (Miller & Yoder, 1974).
   C. The child's requirements for functional communication within the environment.
   D. The child's communicative intentions as shown by gestures, vocal behavior, and body posture or position.
3. With the implementation of Slobin's (1972) operating principle—new forms first express old functions (meanings) and new functions are first expressed by old forms—both form and function, syntax and semantics can be logically integrated with a teaching program in a functional way. Indeed, Slobin's operating principle points out the inseparability of the two components within a sentence. For any utterance or sentence to be taught, we can select the form and the meaning(s) to be expressed. To do so in a careful, well motivated way will increase our chances of leading the child to acquire appropriate communication skills.

Sources of Additional Information

Anderson, J. *The grammar of case.* Cambridge, England: Cambridge University Press, 1971.

Antinucci, F., & Parisi, D. Early language acquisition: A model and some development. In C. A. Ferguson & D. I. Slobin (Eds.). *Studies of child language development.* New York: Holt, Rinehart, & Winston, 1973.

Halliday, M. A. K. Notes on transitivity and theme in English (Part I). *Journal of Linguistics*, 1967, *3*, 27–81.

Halliday, M. A. K. Notes on transitivity and theme in English (Part II). *Journal of Linguistics*, 1967, *3*, 199–244.

Halliday, M. A. K. Notes on transitivity and theme in English (Part III). *Journal of Linguistics*, 1968, *4*, 178–215.

Ingram, D. Therapeutic approaches III: Establishing and developing language in congenitally aphasic children. In J. Eisenson (Ed.). *Aphasia in children.* New York: Harper & Row, 1972.

Lee, L. R., Koenigsknecht, R., & Mulhern, S. *Interactive language development teaching*. Evanston, Ill: Northwestern University Press, 1975.

Ruder, K., & Smith, M. Issues in language training. In R. Schiefelbusch & L. Lloyd (Eds.). *Language perspectives: Acquisition, retardation, and intervention*. Baltimore: University Park Press, 1974.

Stremel, K., & Waryas, C. A behavioral-psycholinguistic approach to language training. In L. McReynolds (Ed.). Developing systematic procedures for training children's language. *ASHA Monographs*, 1974, *18*, 96–130.

Tyack, D., & Gottsleben, R. *Language sampling, analysis and training*. Palo Alto: Consulting Psychologists Press, 1974.

Reference Notes

1. Rabush, D. Language development for trainable children: A comparison of two treatment programs. Unpublished doctoral dissertation, University of Denver, 1973.
2. Epstein, H. The child's understanding of causal connectives. A paper presented at the Fifth Annual Child Language Research Forum, Stanford University, April, 1973.
3. Johnston, J. What the hell is semantics? Unpublished paper, University of California, Berkeley, 1974.
4. Slobin, D. I., Antinucci, F., & Wells, C. G. Semantics of child speech. Unpublished paper, Institute of Human Learning, University of California-Berkeley, 1972.
5. Chapman, R. Mothers' speech to children. Paper presented at the Wisconsin Speech and Hearing Association Meeting, Madison, Wisconsin, October, 1974.

References

Anderson, J. Ergative and nominative in English. *Journal of Linguistics*, *1*, 1–32.

Bloom, L. Language development: *Form and function in emerging grammars*. Cambridge, Mass: M.I.T. Press, 1970.

Bloom, L. *One word at a time*. The Hague, Netherlands: Mouton, 1973.

Bowerman, M. *Early syntactic development: A cross-linguistic study with special reference to Finnish*. Cambridge, England: Cambridge University Press, 1973a.

Bowerman, M. Structural relationships in children's utterances: Syntactic or semantic? In T. E. Moore (Ed.). *Cognitive development and the acquisition of language*. New York: Academic Press, 1973b.

Bowerman, M. Discussion summary—Development of concepts underlying language. In R. Schiefelbusch & L. Lloyd (Eds.). *Language perspectives: Acquisition, retardation and intervention*. Baltimore: University Park Press, 1974.

Brown, R. *A first language: The early stages*. Cambridge, Mass: Harvard University Press, 1973.

Chafe, W. *Meaning and the structure of language*. Chicago: University of Chicago Press, 1973.

Chomsky, C. *The acquisition of syntax in children from five to ten*. Cambridge, Mass: M.I.T. Press, 1969.

Cromer, R. Receptive language in the mentally retarded: Processes and diagnostic distinctions. In R. Schiefelbusch & L. Lloyd (Eds.). *Language perspectives: Acquisition, retardation*, and *intervention*. Baltimore: University Park Press, 1974.

Das, J. Patterns of cognitive ability in nonretarded and retarded children. *American Journal of Mental Deficiency*, 1972, 77, 6–12.

Edwards, D. Sensori-motor intelligence and semantic relations in early child grammar. *Cognition*, 1973, *2*, 395–434.

Fillmore, C. The case for case. In E. Bach & T. Harms (Eds.). *Universals in linguistic theory*. New York: Holt, Rinehart, & Winston, 1968.

Furth, H. On language and knowing in Piaget's developmental theory. *Human Development*, 1970, *13*, 241–257.

Furth, H. Linguistic deficiency and thinking: Research with deaf subjects, 1964–1969. *Psychological Bulletin*, 1971, *71*, 83.

Halliday, M. A. K. Language structure and language function. In J. Lyons (Ed.), *New Horizons in Linguistics*. Harmondsworth, England: Penguin, 1970.

Inhelder, B. Cognitive development and its contribution to the diagnosis of some phenomena of mental deficiency. *Merrill-Palmer Quarterly*, 1969, *12*, 299–319.

Kahn, J. V. Relationship of Piaget's sensori-motor period to language acquisition of profoundly retarded children. *American Journal on Mental Deficiency*, 1975, *79*(6), 640–643.

Miller, J., & Yoder, D. A syntax teaching program. In J. McLean, D. Yoder, & R. Schiefelbusch (Eds.). *Language intervention with the retarded*. Baltimore: University Park Press, 1972a.

Miller, J., & Yoder, D. On developing the content for a language teaching program. *Mental Retardation*, 1972b, *10*, 9–11.

Miller, J., & Yoder, D. An ontogenetic language teaching strategy for retarded children. In R. Schiefelbusch & L. Lloyd (Eds.). *Language perspectives. Acquisition, retardation, and intervention*. Baltimore: University Park Press, 1974.

Mittler, P. Language and communication. In N. Clarke and A. Clarke (Eds.). *Mental deficiency: The changing outlook*. London: Methuen Manual of Modern Psychology, 1974.

Morehead, D., & Ingram, C. The development of basc syntax in normal and deviant children. *Journal of Speech and Hearing Research*, 1973, *16*, 330–352.

Morehead, D., & Morehead, A. From signal to sign: A Piagetian view of thought and language during the first two years. In R. Schiefelbusch & L. Lloyd (Eds.). *Language perspectives: Acquisition, retardation, and intervention*. Baltimore: University Park Press, 1974

Schlesinger, I. M. Production of utterances and language acquisition. In D. I. Slobin (Ed.). *The ontogenesis of language*. New York: Academic Press, 1971.

Sinclair de Zwart, H. Developmental psycholinguistics. In D. Elkind & J. Flavell (Eds.). *Studies in cognitive development*. New York: Oxford University Press, 1969.

Sinclair de Zwart, H. Sensori-motor action patterns as a condition for the acquisition of syntax. In R. Huxley & E. Ingram (Eds.). *Language acquisition: Models and methods*. New York: Academic Press, 1971.

Sinclair de Zwart, H. Language acquisition and cognitive development. In T. E. Moore (Ed.). *Cognitive development and the development of language*. New York: Academic Press, 1973a.

Sinclair de Zwart, H. Some remarks on the Genevan point of view on learning with special reference to language learning. In L. Hinde & C. Hinde (Eds.). *Constraints on learning*. New York: Academic Press, 1973b.

Slobin, D. Cognitive prerequisites for the development of grammar. In C. Ferguson & D. Slobin (Eds.). *Studies in child language development*. New York: Holt, Rinehart, & Winston, 1973.

Stremel, K. Language training: A program for retarded children. *Mental Retardation*, 1972, *10*, 47–49.

Wells, G. Learning to code experience through language. *Journal of Child Language*, 1975, *1*, 243–269.

Wohlhueter, M. J., & Sindberg, R. Longitudinal development of object permanence in mentally retarded children: An exploratory study. *American Journal on Mental deficiency*, 1975, *79*(5), 513–518.

Woodward, M. The behavior of idiots interpreted by Piaget's theory of sensori-motor development. *British Journal of Educational Psychology*, 1959, *29*, 60–71.

Woodward, M. The application of Piaget's theory to research in mental deficiency. In N. Ellis (Ed.). *Handbook of Mental Deficiency*. New York: McGraw-Hill, 1963.

Yoder, D. E., and Miller, J. F. What we may know and what we can do: Input toward a system. In J. E. McLean, D. Yoder, and R. Schiefelbusch (Eds.). *Language intervention with the retarded: Developing strategies.* Baltimore: University Park Press, 1972.

JON F. MILLER is an Associate Professor in the Department of Communicative Disorders, University of Wisconsin, and Section Head, Communicative Disorders, for the Waisman Center on Mental Retardation and Human Development. He is also Associate Editor of the *Journal of Speech and Hearing Research*. A researcher in the areas of normal and deviant language development and language programming, he is currently developing informal assessment procedures for evaluating comprehension and production of language of mentally retarded children.

Prevalence of Other Handicaps (%) in Mentally Retarded Persons

Function	No Handicap	Partial Handicap	Severe Handicap	Description of Severe Handicap
Ambulation	57.8	32.4	9.9	Able to take few steps with help or totally unable to walk
Upper limbs, gross motor control	57.5	34.2	8.2	Unable to hold large objects or complete lack of muscle control
Upper limbs, fine motor control	56.1	34.9	9.0	Minimal use of hands, cannot use eating utensils
Speech	45.1	33.4	21.5	Can possibly communicate needs or wants, but uses few or no words
Hearing	85.0	11.5	3.4	Functionally or totally deaf, hearing aid partial or no help
Vision	73.3	20.9	5.9	Minimally sighted (uncorrectable) or legally blind
Seizures (epilepsy, convulsions)	82.3	15.1	2.7	Severe seizures partially controlled or uncontrollable
Behavior, emotional disorders	58.1	35.7	6.3	Adjustment not possible in home environment, abnormal behavior, dangerous to self or others
Toilet training	77.5	10.2	12.3	Dependent on others, slightly toilet trained, or not trained

Percentages may not add to 100 due to rounding.

Adapted from: Conroy, J.W., and Derr, K.E. *Survey and analysis of the habilitation and rehabilitation status of the mentally retarded with associated handicapping conditions*. Washington, D.C: Department of Health, Education, and Welfare, 1971.

XI The Educational Team: Roles and Training

The use of a technological approach to serving the needs of the severely handicapped requires the joint participation of many individuals, including the classroom teacher, the teacher aide, the child's parents, and others who provide direct services for the child. To be effective, all contributing members must be trained, although to differing degrees, to implement and maintain the often rigorous teaching programs for individual children. The trained teacher must know both how to apply existing programs appropriate to the area of training, and how to develop his own programs or program variations based upon the idiosyncratic needs of different children. Additionally, the trained teacher must know how to train others, in turn, to follow the instructions and procedures inherent in the application of these programs.

Dennis J. Tucker and R. Don Horner

The Use of Many Disciplines with the Severely and Profoundly Handicapped

VERNA HART

University of Pittsburgh

The use of multi-disciplinary approaches in work with the handicapped has been advocated for many years, but never has it been as critical as in the current work with severely and profoundly handicapped children. The need for a variety of professionals has been recognized because of the complexities of the children who are now being educated and because of their age range. Teachers have traditionally dealt with children of elementary, junior high, and high school age, and then only with children who were, for the most part, mildly handicapped. To work with severely and profoundly involved infants, pre-schoolers, and adults has sent most of those teachers who have been educated in the traditional training programs to outside sources for support and for verification of policies.

The work of a multi-disciplinary team, the exact roles of the team members, and the application of the data that has evolved from the team have never been specifically defined. What has evolved in most multi-disciplinary teams is a number of individuals working independently and without much interaction between members. Thus, the team concept and the role that can be played in involving team members in the education of the severely and profoundly handicapped needs to be examined.

The Multi-Disciplinary Approach

This approach has evolved from the medical model where various persons with expertise in diverse areas bring their particular knowledge to bear in dealing with a particular patient. The primary way in which it has been used in special education is in the initial evaluation of the exceptional child. The child is examined by a team of people whose areas of expertise are thought to contribute to the total functioning of the child. The use of the team has been particularly advocated by those who are interested in educating the "whole child," and who feel that knowledge of the various aspects of the child must be integrated in order that he may achieve maximum educational gains.

A problem often evolves when various professionals attempt to deal with the whole child. In the determination to examine all of the many aspects, an evaluation is often made without coordinating those aspects, or parts of the child, and relating them to the whole. An examination of hearing may reveal whether a child hears, but, in the case of the severely and profoundly handicapped, whether or how the child performs during the audiological evaluation is often determined by the degree of retardation, prior conditioning to hearing tests, and the over-all ability of the child to respond in a test situation. The child whose muscles are so severely contracted that he is unable to reach is certainly penalized by the audiologist whose response pattern demands raising the hand or reaching out to place an object. Means are often missing within an evaluation system to prevent the fragmentation of the child and to view the results as part of the whole and as influenced by the other parts.

The relative degree of importance attached to the information gained from the contributing team members is often determined by the type of setting in which the child is placed. If placement is in a medical setting, then medical information receives the most emphasis. If the setting is a psychotherapeutic one, a psychological or psychiatric emphasis will be given. If the setting is strictly educational, primary importance is attached to that data which is thought to bear on the level of intellectual functioning.

Another factor that determines the emphasis given to the data collected is the particular person who collects the information from the various disciplines and collates it into a working prescription. The background of that person will usually determine the relative emphasis to be given to the information. The manner in which data are shared also determines the degree of emphasis that will be given to different reports. Sometimes the information found during multi-disciplinary examinations is reported in a staffing where the various members who have examined the child report their findings in light of their expertise and experience. Some type of decision is then made, usually in relation to the particular type of setting that is anticipated for the child.

Too often, however, the multi-disciplinary approach results in a child's being seen by a number of professionals and the data being sent to and collected by one member of the team. Each professional has viewed the child in the light of a particular discipline and has made recommendations accordingly. Thus, a medical, audiological, psychological, and educational report may all be sent to a school nurse, psychologist, or teacher without a group decision being made as to the best procedures to be followed with the child. The chance of opposing recommendations is great, as those who have worked in this type of setting can testify. There is potential that important data will be overlooked because the person receiving it may not recognize the implications of some of the recommendations that have been made in the reports. Thus, the value of all the reports depends on the expertise and values of the person receiving the information. It is also possible that all the information received will be examined only as it relates to the major discipline of the person making the decision, or as it applies to the philosophy of the facility where the child is currently enrolled.

The Inter-Disciplinary Approach

To prevent some of the abuses of the multi-disciplinary approach, many programs have adapted an inter-disciplinary approach. This design involves the use of the same team members that are used in a multi-disciplinary approach, with an attempt to control the fragmentization of their findings. Again, the child is seen by various members of the team and evaluated according to their expertise. However, the child is evaluated by team members independently and then discussed by these team members. A group decision is made regarding recommendations for the child. Thus, each team member offers input to the total programming for the child by group consensus.

There are several similarities between the multi-disciplinary and inter-disciplinary approaches. In each, the approach itself focuses responsibility for the diagnosis of various aspects of the child on the individual team member involved. The value of each member's contribution depends upon that member's ability to deal with the type of child being evaluated and to report the findings. With the severely and profoundly handicapped, much depends upon the member's ability to deal with very involved children. If the team member has seen several of these children and believes they can and should be educated, the contribution to the evaluation process would, of course, be much greater than it would be if the member was totally unfamiliar or resistive to working with the type of child involved.

The recommendations of the multi-disciplinary and inter-disciplinary approaches are usually recommendations for intervention. These recommendations may or may not consider the various resources available for their implementation. In other words, it is often the ideal, rather than the manageable. A problem that evolves from this type of recommendation is that the child may never have the opportunity to be enrolled in an ideal intervention program. A recommendation for a one-to-one type of program in a state that allows a staff ratio of one to five is unrealistic, if other resources are not available. However, the team members often end their responsibilities by only making recommendations. Actual implementation is not considered, and is dismissed as not being part of their responsibility. Implementation then falls to the person often the least able to carry it out because of lack of power, the classroom teacher. If the responsibility for implementing recommendations falls to that teacher, he may not be able to make major administrative changes that will affect staffing, the type of services available, or the number of hours that additional services may be available. Thus, the greatest value of having a multi-disciplinary or inter-disciplinary team—the numbers of expert members contributing to the decision—becomes the greatest weakness because responsibility is diffused among the various members and the ultimate responsibility often rests with the person with the least authority to carry out the recommendations.

Another great weakness is that the multi-disciplinary and inter-disciplinary approaches themselves often lack an important step in their models: immediate and ongoing feedback with responsible follow-up of the recommendations. Often the only follow-up consists of observing state guidelines for the numbers and types of evaluations that a child will have within a multi-year time frame. This weakness is particularly glaring in the case of severely and profoundly handicapped children when the intensity of their multiple problems is so acute. The necessity for more frequent interaction with team members can be verified by anyone who has been involved with this particular population.

The Transdisciplinary Approach

The transdisciplinary approach has evolved in an attempt to deal with some of the problems inherent in the other two approaches. A primary therapist is designated to deal with individual children. In an attempt to reduce the compartmentalization and fragmentizing of services to the child, one person is appointed for direct contact. This reduces the number of professionals involved in direct care of the child. The approach may be similar to the preceding two in the initial evaluation and may use an interdisciplinary approach in making the initial plan for implementation. However, implementation is carried out by only one of the members in cooperation with the others. Each discipline then depends upon the others, supporting the efforts of the others, although being neither dominant nor parasitic. This plan attempts to cover more aspects of interdisciplinary teamwork than the others.

This approach, advocated by Dorothy Hutchinson and Una Haynes, has been recommended in the United Cerebral Palsy Collaborative Infant Program, supported by the U.S. Office of Education, Bureau of Education for the Handicapped and the Division of Developmental Disabilities, Social Rehabilitation Services. Hutchinson (1974), in discussing the model, feels that the composition of the team depends upon the needs of the clientele. Occupational therapy, physical therapy, speech therapy, audiology, nursing, medical, social work, psychology, education, and child development are all areas from which this model draws its resources. Although this model does not differ from the composition of team members used in the inter-disciplinary and multi-disciplinary approaches, the actual implementation, and therefore the ultimate responsibility, takes a different form. Each team member assumes some of the responsibilities of the other team members. Thus, one person represents more than one discipline and is able to deliver services based on multiple disciplines. Hutchinson (1974) states that the transdisciplinary approach does not come automatically, but must be well planned. She discusses Tuckman's four stages of group cohesiveness and states that the groups will go through them in working out a team relationship. The stages (forming, storming, norming, and performing) relate how the team goes through the levels of testing and dependence to intragroup conflict, the development of group cohesion, and on to functional role relatedness and productivity. Hutchinson notes Parker's (1956) twelve operational principles as helpful in producing this team action. In developing a viable transdisciplinary approach, Hutchinson believes that role transitions take place between team members, placing demands on each member as both a learner and a teacher in releasing some of his role to other team members.

Hutchinson lists several steps necessary for a member to become a meaningful transdisciplinary team member. The primary prerequisite is that the individual team member have depth in his own discipline. Only by having this extensive knowledge can that member pass information and decisions on to the other team members. The individual's role must then be continuously enriched. Expansion of the knowledge of each member is gained as new learnings are applied under the directed supervision of others in the multi-disciplinary team who are deemed appropriate. For this to happen, there must be role release by the appropriate team member or authorization by the appropriate discipline to disseminate expanded knowledge. In some instances, this authorization is given to parents to carry out a program originally designed by professionals. As the parents or parent surrogates become more knowledgeable in their process of expansion and enrichment, they assume more responsibility. Throughout the program, there is consultative backup by members of the original team. Each discipline contributes to problem solving and to the complex decisions that might be demanded because of the need for intensive interdisciplinary expertise. During this phase, some new information might need to be tested by an appropriate team member before it is transmitted to the team. Throughout the endeavor, then, each team member remains accountable for what he teaches, how well the individual person responsible for the program facilitation has learned, and for the benefits to the client. This degree of accountability for the outcome of the recommended program is missing in the other two delivery systems.

Uses of the Team Approach

Various names have been given to the multiple models providing services to the handicapped child. A newer nomenclature is *ancillary services*. The name "ancillary" merely means "helping," and help can be provided by many sources. Ancillary services can be provided by the community, by professionals, by related programs, by peers, and by parents. In the case of severely and profoundly handicapped children, the team might have a slightly different composition from the more traditional models which have evolved from the medical prototype. A lawyer might be an appropriate person to have on the team of a child who is being denied appropriate education. Child advocates are assuming more of a role. Parents are being recognized for the part they can play in educating their own children to maximum potential. Foster grandparents are also to be considered part of the services available to the children.

Although any team's composition depends upon the needs of the child, it has been traditional to use team members only during the evaluation process. Multi-disciplinary participation has historically been linked mainly to the assessment-diagnostic function. Andrews (1957) points out that there is usually a multidisciplinary approach used during the assessment-diagnostic phase, but that only the educational approach is used during the prescription, intervention, and evaluation phases. Andrews (1957) states that use of the team only in the initial phase is ineffective because the children need a comprehensive therapeutic program with intensive and long-term cross-disciplinary input. If each discipline is to influence the therapeutic core of special education, special education should become a partnership of disciplines.

No matter what theoretical approach is used in setting up the team, all disciplines must be involved in setting the goals for the child. Setting objectives must be accomplished by members functioning as a team to achieve the most effective relationship between disciplines. Merely having input from various members is not enough for accountability measures. There must be integration and coordination of information from all disciplines involved. Each team member must also be involved in some measure in the intervention and evaluation phases.

The needs of the severely and profoundly handicapped are so great that input from many sources is needed. Until more teachers are trained in a transdisciplinary manner, there will need to be almost daily input from other disciplines into the regular teaching program. Responsibility and accountability need to be shared by all of the members involved with the child. Implementation cannot remain the responsibility of one person. With the staffing needs of profoundly involved children, implementation is carried out by numerous people. All must be involved in the educational process, with each sharing in the accountability.

Information to be Gained from a Team Approach

For classroom teachers dealing with severely and profoundly handicapped children, different problems will be encountered with different children. The use of a team in working with a child is necessary. However, many teachers cannot deal effectively with much of the information offered to them because they lack the background to interpret data received. Other teachers are so overwhelmed with the problems of the children that they are not even able to question team members effectively and so cannot make adequate use of the team involved. However, all team members must be involved in determining goals, writing prescriptions, intervening, and evaluating.

Different data can be gathered from diverse professionals. In the case of profoundly involved children, medical problems loom large. It is important, then, to obtain specific information from the medical team member. Is the child medically restricted from certain activities? Are there behaviors that have particular medical significance? Are any of the behaviors noted a result of a medical problem? Are visual and hearing problems acuity losses or are they a result of the child's never learning to use his vision and hearing? If medications are prescribed for the child, who should be responsible for seeing that the child receives the appropriate dosage at the right time? When should the child be re-examined? Are there seizures? What data do medical personnel need to have gathered on seizure activity in the classroom? Helpful data can sometimes be gathered in the classroom throughout the day, not only on the number of seizures but on their duration, the events preceeding them, and how the seizures were handled. In this manner, seizure activity as an avoidance mechanism can be examined, as well as information obtained for medication control.

In working with severely and profoundly handicapped children, teachers often suspect vision and hearing losses because of lack of response on the part of the child. Frequently, there is an acuity problem, but sometimes the degree of retardation is such that the child is functioning at a level where he makes no use of his vision and hearing. Often medical people will term a case where there appears to be no observable reason to account for the visual or hearing loss a "cortical deafness" or "cortical blindness." This may mean that the child, through training, may learn to use either his vision, his hearing, or both. A frank and open discussion with the medical people in this regard can often help in adequately planning for the child to learn to use both vision and hearing.

Psychological information is also of importance. The psychologist on the team can be used to obtain specific information about the functioning level of the child. Since most states demand some type of appropriate psychological test, it is important for the teacher to know that the tests are appropriate. What implications for the educational program can be drawn from the tests? How valid is the type of test for this type of child? When should the child be retested? Was the testing situation one in which the child could perform to his capacity? Is there particular data that the teacher can furnish to the psychologist? Is the psychologist aware of learning potential in particular areas? Was the child penalized because of some particular physical problem so that he could not give the proper response?

An audiologist who is experienced in working with severely and profoundly handicapped children can often be of assistance in helping plan appropriately for the child. Is is important to know whether the child responds to pure tones, to speech, to the noises of toys. Does he respond to any type of sound? Are special tests needed to determine the type of loss the child demonstrates? What kind of training is recommended for the use of residual hearing?

Information useful to the teacher in working to develop the use of hearing is whether or not the child demonstrates a startle reflex. If a child is able to tune out noises to the degree that he is not even aware of a loud burst of noise and does not startle in reaction to it, he will also be able to tune out such things as sounds in the environment, verbal commands, and verbal reinforcements. Whether or not responses to these can be conditioned is something that needs to be discussed when developing a cross-disciplinary program for the child.

Social work is another area that can contribute to the total programming for the child. Family dynamics, the degree of acceptance and willingness to carry out programs begun in the educational setting, family involvement with the child, rewards and punishment systems within the family, what the family responds to in terms of reinforcement, and prior experiences of the child that have been both reinforcing and aversive can all be obtained in a good social history. A social worker, working with the family, can often complement the school program of the child. It is important for future progress of the child that the family be involved with the total program throughout the evaluation, prescription, and intervention stages.

A team member who is familiar with language development can be a valuable member if the teacher lacks that training during his preparation. Those with an adequate background can offer alternatives in language development. Will some type of adaptive device work? Should manual communication be taught? Does the child have the ability for speech? Is there potential for symbolic behavior? What steps are to be taken in establishing some means of communication with the child?

Occupational and physical therapy are areas that can contribute to programming for the severely and profoundly handicapped. Using neurodevelopmental techniques, a trained developmental therapist can aid considerably in feeding, dressing, positioning, and carrying. Team members can contribute to programming by offering activities appropriate for the neurodevelopmental level of the child. Means to facilitate feeding and speech can also be used. Proper positioning for the child in the classroom will allow carryover from the physical therapy into the child's total environment, and will not negate the work that is spent in physical therapy. Knowledge of contractures and how to carry, hold, and position the child can aid in that child being able to make the most of his limited motor functioning. Activities that lead to further abnormal reflex patterns can be eliminated.

Too often a considerable part of the day is spent in various types of therapies and the total program may be overlooked. So much time is involved in a one to one relationship with therapists that the child does not have the opportunity to develop group or peer relationships. These facts need to be considered when planning for the very involved child. Team members who are willing to carry out their therapy in the classroom where the teacher and aides have the opportunity to observe and to learn proper techniques cannot help but contribute to greater progress. If a child is involved in a part-day program, he should not be removed from the classroom during that part of the day to undergo therapies or examinations that could be offered during the remainder of the day. By establishing a team approach where all members are involved in assessment, prescription, intervention, and evaluation, the total child can be considered and such factors can be discussed.

Because of the great amount of knowledge needed to deal adequately with the many needs of the severely and profoundly handicapped, no one person can be expected to have all the necessary skills and information. Consequently, there will always be a need for some type of team approach. The better and more efficient the team, the better the services offered to the child. No matter what approach used or the type of team involved, the better the expertise and the greater the willingness of the team members to share their information, the greater the benefits for the child.

References

Andrews, R. Multi-disciplinary models in special education? *The Slow Learning Child*, 1975, *32*(1), 45–55.

Hutchinson, D. A model for transdisciplinary staff development. *A nationally organized collaborative project to provide comprehensive services to atypical infants and their families* (Technical Report #8). New York: United Cerebral Palsy Associations, 1974.

Parker, J. C. Guidelines for in-service education. *In-service education*. Fixty-sixth yearbook of the National Society for the Study of Education. Chicago: University of Chicago Press, 1957.

VERNA HART has long been interested in children with multiple handicaps, completing her doctorate in this area in 1967. She has investigated team teaching with severely and profoundly handicapped children and has been involved in work with handicapped infants and preschoolers. Dr. Hart has coordinated an evaluation program for severely handicapped children, and is currently on the faculty at the University of Pittsburgh, engaged in teacher preparation for those working with the pre-academic child.

Interdisciplinary Model: Planning Distribution and Ancillary Input to Classrooms for the Severely/ Profoundly Handicapped

ROBIN BECK

University of Washington

This paper will begin with a brief interpretation of the history of many individuals' involvement in the delivery of services to the handicapped. This is done because the author intends to take an untraditional view which, hopefully, will become operational for the educator of handicapped individuals, as well as useful to the child advocate, whether parent, teacher, physician, school administrator, lawyer, or other interested person.

It is not without bias that a medical model of service delivery is a focus of this review. This is not only because a medical diagnostic model was imposed by national policy decisions made in the early 1960's, but also because the model is relevant to the current change in policy direction for the comprehensive management of severely/profoundly handicapped persons in the mid '70's.

The medical model—more as it is popularized than as it actually exists—has been one in which practitioners are solely responsible to a patient for the management of his specific health care needs. This responsibility, perhaps defined as appropriate diagnostic and therapeutic responses, is contingent on fee for service (accountability), and something even more prominent in the field today—liability. These contingencies, accountability and liability, can be operationally or legally defined. They are not often presented as determinants of professional behavior, but whether or not you agree that they *are* determinants, mentioning them here will be useful for later discussion.

The aspect of the medical model that will be emphasized is the increasing dependency of physicians on an ever-expanding number of specialists and direct ancillary services in making decisions about patient management. Nevertheless, the two factors that have remained constant are the physician's ultimate accountability and liability. (In the recent epidemic of malpractice lawsuits, both physicians *and* ancillary services specialists have been sued.)

With increased nationwide concern for the mentally and physically handicapped in the 1960's, there began a concerted effort to assist this heterogenous population, within what can be described as a medical framework, i.e., diagnosis and therapeutic intervention (and, in the case of physical handicaps, prevention). The results of this effort have been remarkable, but their impact on the numbers of mentally retarded or physically handicapped individuals has been frustratingly slight. Moreover, as an immediate and foreseeable consequence, the medical model with emphasis on prevention has raised moral issues which have not yet been resolved.

One aspect of this approach has been the gathering together of formerly disparate disciplines under the same roof for a more organized attack on the diagnosis of mental retardation. These teams have traditionally been multidisciplinary and their product has been comprehensive diagnostic evaluations. Their weaknesses have been many, including their costs in time and money, and, until recently, the lack of an appropriate follow-up resource for comprehensive diagnostic evaluation. These evaluations have always included recommendations for intervention, but the resources for implementing them have been unavailable in most communities.

The medical model that has relevance to educational intervention for the severely/profoundly handicapped population is not the multidisciplinary model, which diffuses responsibility, but an interdisciplinary approach which places responsibility on the individual practitioner. Where accountability and liability are specified, service follows. So too, the educator of the severely/profoundly handicapped

The author would like to thank Ms. Connie Pious for her editorial comments.

infant or child is now accountable and liable for educational intervention.

While there is precedence for interdisciplinary efforts by teachers, the management problems posed by the severely/profoundly handicapped population will expose educators to some new situations which will require new responses. We have only the briefest experience to guide us in the rather dramatic changes we will face in the next few years as we educate teachers for the severely/profoundly handicapped, and plan the timing and type of interdisciplinary input that will be required in the classrooms. The purpose of this paper is to present an approach that may prove useful in planning the distribution of classrooms and of the interdisciplinary personnel who will provide direct input to the teachers and parents within those classrooms.

A Model for Planning Classroom and Ancillary Service Distribution

Factors Influencing the Geographic Distribution of Classrooms

Of the many issues which must be considered in the process of developing services for this population, this paper will concentrate on the types and distribution of services which are directly relevant to teachers' competencies in providing effective intervention. In relation to these concerns, there are assumptions about intervention for the severely/profoundly handicapped which must be stated at the outset, since they have influenced the model developed below.

First, educational intervention should begin immediately after identification of an infant or child as severely/profoundly handicapped, or at risk of becoming so. This has implications for the intake process of an educational intervention program, as well as for the numbers of infants and children served by that program. This paper will deal primarily with the population from birth to age 6 which may require these services. This group is the focus because, at the present time, it appears that early identification is possible and that, in the near future, public schools will become the community-based resource for these individuals from birth onward.

Second, for severely handicapped individuals within a school program, most of the behaviors which require systematic programming will fall within the range of behaviors displayed by their normal peers within the age group of birth to age 6. This does not imply that intervention programs should be locked into normal developmental models, but it does reflect the fact that, at the present time, most infant programs (birth to 3 years of age) are utilizing this tactic, and this has influenced the types of interdisciplinary input required by the teachers in such programs.

Third, the severely/profoundly handicapped population, including those labeled "educationally high risk," have multiple problems. In the past quarter century, the medical intervention models have led to the establishment of large, expensive, multidisciplinary clinics to meet the special needs of this population. Most, if not all, of the students in a classroom for the severely/profoundly handicapped will be receiving periodic services from such programs. Since the service from clinics includes manipulation of medications, including seizure medications, or surgical intervention for specific handicapping conditions, both of which may have an impact on the performance of an infant or a child in the classroom, the teacher must have access to information related to these procedures. But information must go both ways: the classroom-based intervention program must have the capacity of generating information needed for appropriate medical decisions, formerly made in isolation by physicians who treated seizures or orthopedic deformities, or who did *not* treat them because of a child's severe retardation and inadequate prognostic data. If, indeed, "getting to a standing position" becomes a classroom objective for a child, talipes equinovarus (club feet) must be corrected, if possible. If complete seizure control interferes with academic performance, then a compromise must be made which involves input from the teacher, the family, and the physician. Community-based comprehensive educational intervention for the severely/profoundly handicapped must include medical input and provide information for appropriate medical management of the multiple problems found in this population.

Finally, it seems important that classrooms for these infants and children should be as close to their homes as possible. This is not only because transportation for this population is expensive, but because, at present, there appears to be no advantage whatever in centralization of services. Perhaps this is most evident in the infant programs. These classrooms involve the infant, the parents, the teacher, and ancillary classroom staff who provide periodic input. Classroom time is at least one hour weekly, with the teacher responsible for 15 to 20 infants and their parents on a completely individualized basis. Transportation is usually provided by parents. These assumptions have influenced this model, in that the ancillary services have been centralized, but not the classrooms. The classroom-based management program is seen as a service that should be available at a minimal distance from the homes of the population being served.

Ancillary Services for the Classroom

Several types of classrooms are available for children from birth to 6 years. An infant classroom (in which the parents and infant are with the teacher for at least one hour weekly) is one in which maximum emphasis is placed on the parents' carrying out classroom-based intervention at home. The teacher-to-student ratio for the infant classroom (here, for simplicity, including children from birth to age 3) is approximately one to 20.

A more traditional classroom can be envisioned for the preschool-age group (here, for simplicity, the 3 to 6 year olds). Washington state policy makes busing feasible and the length of time in the classroom each week can be extended. Typically, classrooms for the preschool-aged child operate two hours daily for four or five days weekly. Each teacher is responsible for two classes each school day. The teacher-to-student ratio in each class may vary from one to six or one to ten, depending on the availability of volunteers and aides.

The individual classroom based in a community requires at least 15 to 20 infants from birth to age 3 who are either severely/profoundly handicapped or educationally at risk. By the time these students reach age 3, two to four teachers will be required to meet their educational needs until they reach an age where the public schools are no longer legally responsible for their educational programs.

With these basic units in mind, it is possible to begin to plan the types of ancillary services which must be provided to these classrooms. In Table 1, these service specialists are listed, along with a brief description of their special training and areas of expertise. In the second column are listed the number of unit classrooms for which these individuals can provide direct service to the teacher.

There are obviously many variables which could change these ratios. At the present time, they appear reasonable and are based on experimental programs for severely/profoundly handicapped children in this age group. Services from nurses or social workers are not shown; inclusion of these individuals is optional with each program.

TABLE 1

Service Specialists

Ancillary service	Ratio Individual/Classroom Unit
1. DEVELOPMENTAL THERAPIST (Trained in occupational or physical therapy with special training in the age range from birth onward, with emphasis on S/P handicapped).	1:2 Infant classrooms. 1:4 Preschool classrooms and elementary school classrooms.
2. SPEECH-COMMUNICATION DISORDERS SPECIALIST	1:4 Infant, preschool, and elementary classrooms.
3. SPECIAL EDUCATION CONSULTANT OR PSYCHOLOGIST (Special training in curriculum, programming for S/P handicapped, and assessment).	1:8 Infant, preschool, and elementary classrooms.
4. MEDICAL CONSULTANT (General medical, child development, medical, and educational intervention.) Part-time consultant on a fee basis.	1:8 Infant, preschool, and elementary classrooms.

Other Resources Available to the Classroom

The multidisciplinary clinics involved in the management of the complex, multiple medical problems of the severely/profoundly handicapped are always in urban areas, usually at medical training facilities, and may be remote from the community-based classroom. These are birth defect types of clinics; coordinating their periodic care and intervention with long-term educational intervention is part of the function of the interdisciplinary classroom unit.

Also, at any point in the classroom intervention program, the multidisciplinary assessment and periodic follow-up available at child development centers or at university-affiliated facilities could prove invaluable. Ongoing research at such centers may offer future intervention tactics applicable in classroom settings. These centers can also centralize data on the types and numbers of individuals within each diagnostic category of severely/profoundly handicapping conditions receiving services over a wide geographic area.

Planning the Distribution of Classrooms and Ancillary Personnel: The Christaller Model

All of the above information will now be applied to a hypothetical situation, with the imaginary goal of adequately serving the educational needs of all severely/profoundly handicapped and educationally high-risk infants and children in the age range of birth to 12 years. Classrooms will be located within a prescribed geographic area and centers for the ancillary disciplines providing services to those classrooms will be identified. If the model is to be operational, it is also necessary to make fairly accurate cost projections for the particular service delivery described.

Although several models could be used to describe service delivery, Christaller's Center Place Theory will be presented here. Walter Christaller's Center Place Theory is described in a most interesting article in *Scientific American*: "Rural Market Networks," by Stuart Plattner (May, 1975, *5*, 66–79). In this article, Dr. Plattner does a comparative study of two complex geographic marketing communities and uses the theory (or model) to analyze such factors as the flow of goods and services. Not only is this model simple and geometrically pleasing, it is easily reversible, i.e., instead of describing here a complex service or a market community, it is possible to *design* one, using the geometric solution the theory provides. There are many variations in the possible solutions offered by this theory. The K = 3 model is used here because it fits the assumptions discussed at the beginning of this section.

The service area selected to depict the model is Region I of the Seattle public school system, chosen primarily because good maps are available, showing the location of elementary schools. While this service area is a real geographic entity, this proposal concerns a hypothetical model, and the actual numbers used in the calculations for the model were chosen for simplicity. In this region, there are 53 elementary schools with a mean population of 341 children in each school, and an estimated total population, from birth to age 6, of 18,000 children. To calculate the number of severely/profoundly handicapped children in this age group, a fairly accurate percentage of .005 can be used, giving a total of 90 children requiring educational intervention. If high-risk infants and children in this age range are included, we should utilize a higher percentage (for example, .015), since entry into the program should have a high false positive rate. This is justifiable, due to the inaccuracy of periodic infant assessment tools currently available. The latter percentage yields a total of 135 children who will require the services of our infant program.

For the preschool program, a slightly smaller percentage will be utilized, approximately .0075, which gives a total of 67 preschool children requiring services. For the remainder of the elementary school population, the .005 percentage can be used, which gives a total of 90 children in the age range 6 to 12. Therefore, the total population served will be 292 children.

Obviously, as the children grow older, the number included in the severely/profoundly handicapped program will approach the .005% number. This will occur for at least three reasons: first, greater accuracy of classroom-based assessment over time; second, the results of educational intervention itself; third, the higher morbidity and mortality faced by this population.

In Figure 1 is a simplified map (no streets), showing the distribution of elementary schools in the service area. The first step is to place this array on a featureless plane (a plain piece of white paper will do). Next, the points in

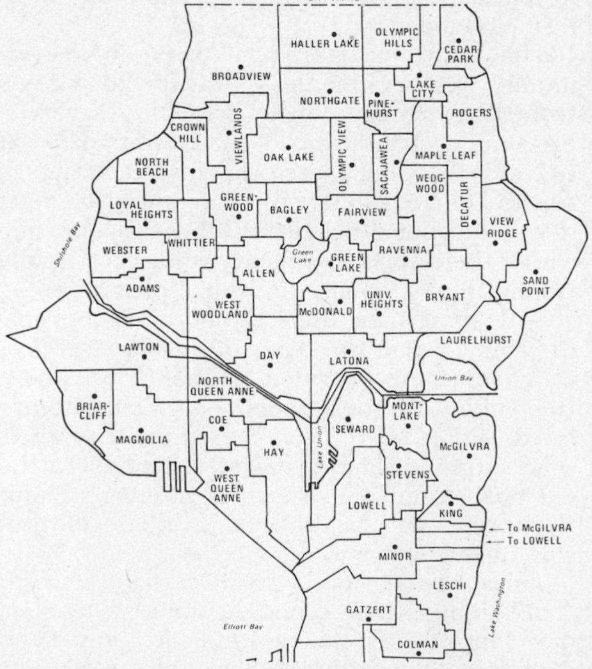

Figure 1. First step: Plot elementary schools in the service area.

this array are connected with line segments. (See Figure 2.) For this example, it was easiest to begin with lines in an east-west orientation. The number of dots on each line, signifying the number of schools, gave that line and its name these were transferred to a final approximation where the lines were made equal; equilateral triangles were then constructed. The final result is a plane, covered with triangles, which approximates the distribution of elementary schools in this geographic area (Figure 3). In the next figure, the center of each hexagon has been circled (Figure 4). This designates a school which serves an array of other schools, and a geographic area sufficiently large to warrant placement of a program for severely/profoundly handicapped children. These will be designated B-centers, of which there are 13 in the present example. Each B-center must provide service for 10 students in an infant program, five students in a preschool program, and seven students in an elementary school program for the severely/profoundly handicapped or educationally high-risk. Given the classroom teacher-to-pupil ratio above, this means each B-center needs one-half of an infant classroom, approximately one-half of a preschool classroom, and approximately one elementary classroom for the severely/profoundly handicapped population in this example.

In the present model, an administrative decision must be made. Two options are open:

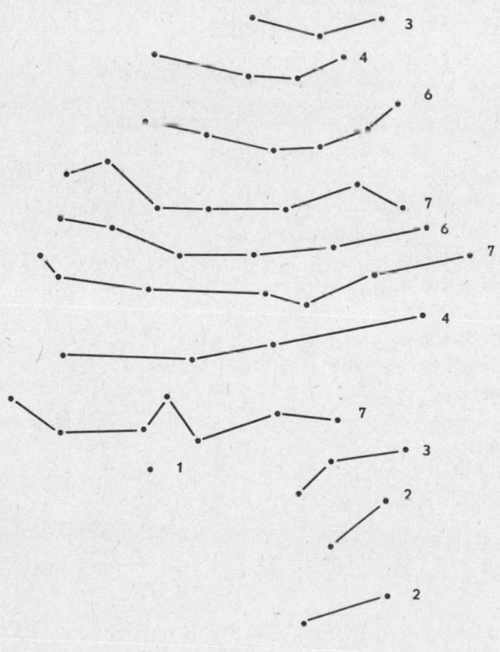

Figure 2. Second step: Connect points indicating elementary schools with line segments.

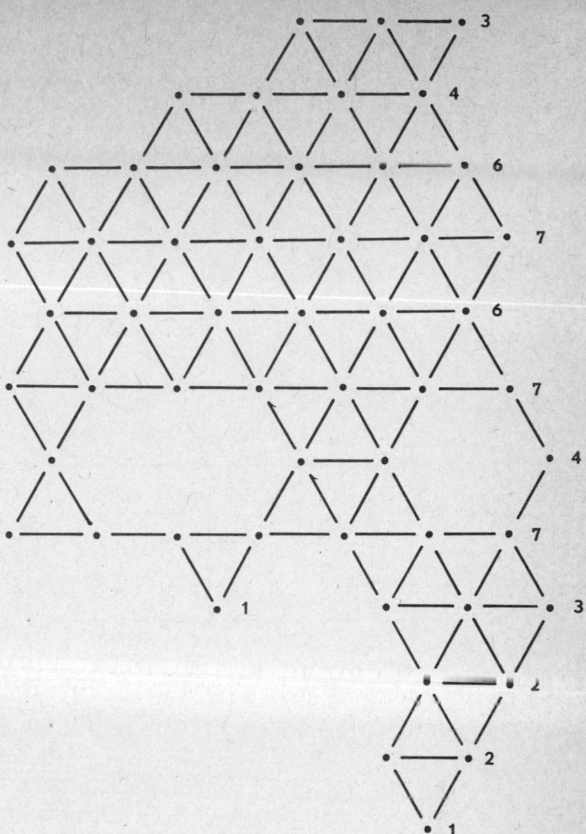

Figure 3. Third step: Construct equilateral triangles from approximations of points indicating elementary schools.

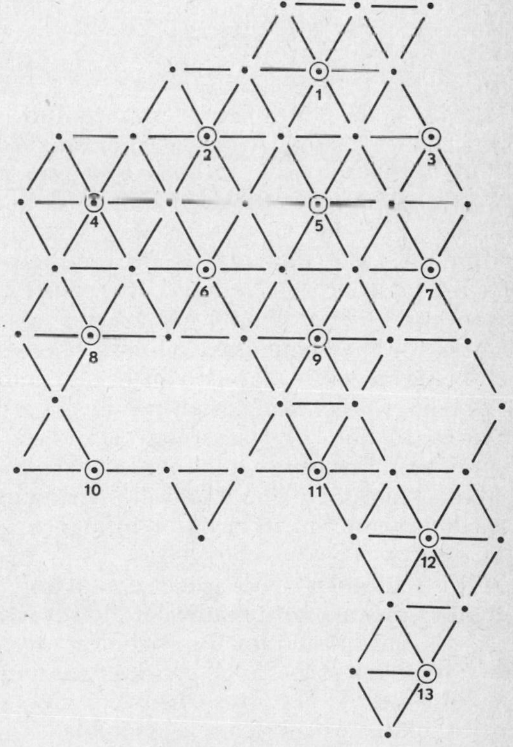

Figure 4. B-centers.

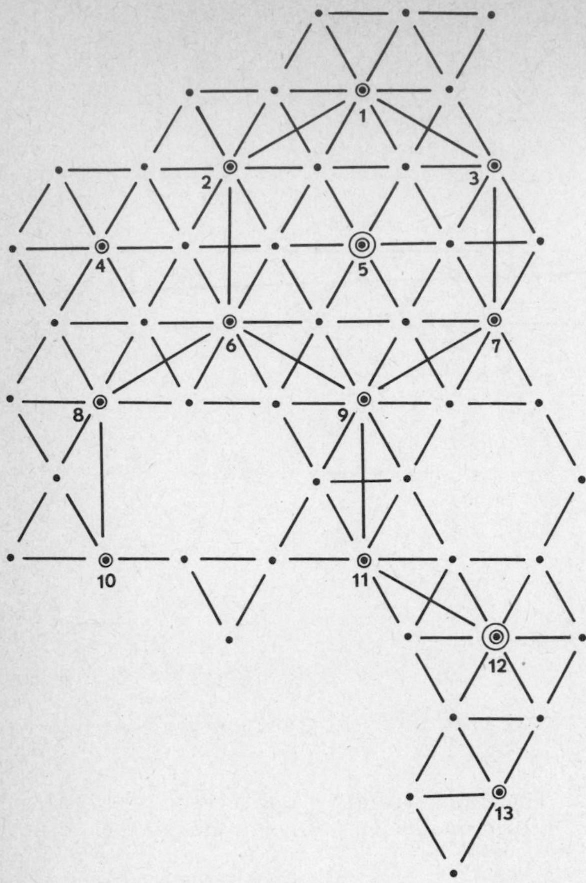

Figure 5. A-centers.

either halve the number of infant and preschool programs, or let one teacher spend half of the time each day with a preschool class and the other half working with infants and parents. The latter option was chosen in planning service delivery in this model. For each B-center, 13 teachers will be required for the infant and preschool programs, and 13 teachers for the elementary school program.

Drawing larger hexagons, a different center—an A-center—is designated, which not only provides B-center services, but also becomes a site for bringing together the interdisciplinary team members who will provide input to each B-center in its area of influence. (See Figure 5.)

In this particular geographic region, only one A-center appears automatically; however, because of the distribution of B-centers, we can cast symmetry aside and provide another to meet our needs. For these two A-centers, the interdisciplinary teams can be assembled. In the first A-center (school #5), there are a total of seven B-centers, plus two outside, making a total of nine. Nine B-centers are the equivalent of 4.5 infant classes, 4.5 preschool classes, and 9 elementary classes. For this area, five developmental therapists are needed, four speech-communication specialists, two special education consultant psychologists, and two medical consultants.

For school 12, the second A-center in this example, only four B-centers are served. This is equivalent to two infant classrooms, two preschool classrooms, and four elementary classrooms. The personnel required at the second A-center are two developmental therapists, one speech-communication specialist, one special education specialist or psychologist, and one half-time medical consultant.

To calculate total costs for this model program, refer to Table 2. Costs and salaries are consistent with those current in the geographic area.

Providing services from birth to age 3 is optional. Therefore, the costs of the infant program have been calculated separately. (See Table 3.) The program for infants actually accounts for only 23% of the total cost, the savings accomplished primarily by not providing transportation. For parents to be able to participate, the resource must be close to the home, thereby offering savings in both time and money for the families of these children.

TABLE 2

Costs of Model Program

	Number	Salary	Total
Teachers	26	$ 9,000	234,000
Developmental Therapists	7	10,000	70,000
Speech-Communication Specialists	5	10,000	50,000
Special Education Consultants (master's level) or Psychologists	3	12,000	36,000
Medical Consultant Service	2	20,000	40,000
Salaries			430,000
Employee benefits			80,000
Administrative costs			50,000
			560,000
Add 50% for other line items			280,000
			840,000
Transportation (2 minibuses for B-center)			351,000
TOTAL COSTS			1,191,000
Cost per child—$4,079			

Factors Influencing Successful Educational Intervention

We have planned our service delivery model for the severely/profoundly handicapped and educational high-risk population in our service area. Certain factors will determine the success or failure of such a model. The first and most important will be appropriate referral to the program by "first contact" individuals and agencies in the community, including physicians, nurses, health departments, child protective services, etc. Along with the institution of such a service delivery model must go a community-wide educational program, giving direct input to local medical societies and other organizations, as well as tapping extant information systems. An example of the latter is the planned special education referral system now being coupled to a medical consultant hot-line at the University of Washington School of Medicine. Local physicians will be able to obtain information on programs and services available in their community or region merely by picking up the telephone.

Shaping the community at large—particularly the medical community—to consider educational intervention for the severely/profoundly handicapped or educationally high-risk individuals will be a major challenge for all of us in the next few years. While early identification (diagnosis) of these infants and children is part of the curriculum for primary care physicians, referral to an educational resource is not part of the management procedure usually presented to physicians in training. Indeed, classroom-based management of the severely/profoundly handicapped infant or child will be a completely new experience for most physicians. Certainly, when implementing a service delivery model for educational intervention, we must consider that there will be many changes required in the behavioral patterns of many individuals, and that this will require *time*. Sadly, at present, there are no economic contingencies at all to facilitate the involvement of physicians in the classroom-based management of these infants and children.

Finally, while planning ancillary services for the infant, preschool, and elementary school classrooms for the severely/profoundly handicapped in the model, there has purposely been no discussion of the dynamics of an interdisciplinary team. In fact, most of the current literature on team diagnosis or intervention is about "how the team works," rather than "what the team does." In most instances, the teams will function in variable ways, as varied as the individuals who make up the team and as variable as the individual student on whom these efforts focus. The types of ancillary services available to the teacher are identifiable, however, and a thorough background in each must be part of the teacher's training if ancillary disciplines are to be appropriately utilized in the classroom. This training allows the teacher to request appropriate input and to carry out specific intervention tactics suggested by the ancillary specialists. These tactics, coupled with periodic review of each child's progress within the classroom by the teacher and the interdisciplinary team, would maximize the chance for successful educational intervention.

TABLE 3

Costs of Infant Program

Teacher salaries: 9,000 × 6.5	58,500
Developmental Therapists: 10,000 × 3	30,000
Speech Communications: 10,000 × 3	30,000
Special Educators/Psychologists: 12,000 × 1	12,000
Medical Consultants: 15,000 × 1	15,000
Salaries	135,500
Benefits	27,100
Administrative costs	20,000
	182,600
50% for line costs	91,300
TOTAL COSTS	273,900
Cost per child: $2,029	

ROBIN BECK, M.D., is Director of the Pediatrics Clinic at the University of Washington and a staff member of its Experimental Education Unit. His work in ambulatory pediatrics and in community-based intervention with severely handicapped children has been described in many publications. Dr. Beck also works with teachers in the classroom-based management of severely and profoundly handicapped children. His professional interests have been directed to improving physician training in ambulatory pediatric care, including school-related problems.

Competency-Based Training of Paraprofessional Teaching Associates for Education of the Severely and Profoundly Handicapped

DENNIS J. TUCKER

Kansas Neurological Institute

R. DON HORNER

University of Kansas

Sontag, Burke, and York (1973) have stated: "In our view, there is a direct relationship between the level of the students' disability and the competencies of the teachers, i.e., the more pronounced the level of disability, the more specific and precise are the competencies required of the teachers" (p. 23). Thus, providing education and training services for the severely handicapped should necessarily require the bringing together of all factual information currently available in the area of programmed human learning, including knowledge of basic learning principles, techniques for precise measurement, and the application of a problem-oriented, objective task-analysis approach. Programming for the severely handicapped should include a developmentally planned sequence of instruction, a rapid time schedule under optimally motivating conditions in application of the programs, and a continuous data feedback system for accurately charting progress across time. The severity of the behavioral deficits manifested by these children, in addition to the physical and sensory disabilities which complicate the learning process, demand that their education and training experiences not be left to unattended "natural" development, but instead should be precisely programmed through the systematic manipulation of organism-environment relationships. Thus, a technological approach to the education and training of the severely handicapped must encompass empirical findings from previous and ongoing research efforts in the field, and must include the collection and application of sound training programs which have evolved from these efforts. Although there is, fortunately, a vast amount of new information pertaining to the training of the severely handicapped, the task remains of bringing this information together in training packages that can be used by direct service personnel to aid the severely handicapped.

The use of a technological approach to serving the needs of the severely handicapped requires the joint participation of many individuals, including the classroom teacher, the teacher aide, the child's parents, and others who provide direct services for the child. To be effective, all contributing members must be trained, although to differing degrees, to implement and maintain the often rigorous teaching programs for individual children. The trained teacher must know both how to apply existing programs appropriate to the area of training, and how to develop his own programs or program variations based upon the idiosyncratic needs of different children. Additionally, the trained teacher must know how to train others, in turn, to follow the instructions and procedures inherent in the application of these programs.

Training Paraprofessionals of the Severely Handicapped

The utilization, roles, and duties of paraprofessionals in special education have been subject to controversy for many years (Blessing, 1967; Cruickshank & Haring, 1957; Esbensen, 1966). Reid and Reid (1974) have sum-

This paper was supported in part by Division of Personnel Preparation, Bureau of Education for the Handicapped, U.S.O.E. Grant number OEG-0-74-2766 (principal investigators: Doug Guess, Wayne Sailor, and Leonard Lavis of Kansas Neurological Institute, Topeka, Kansas).

marized the literature and classified paraprofessional duties into four major categories: clerical, housekeeping, noninstructional, and instruction-related duties. With regard to instruction-related duties (Reid & Reid, 1974), the tasks include the following: observe children and write reports; assist in preparing instructional materials; reinforce learning with small groups; read and tell stories. Implicit in these tasks is that teachers will do the teaching and paraprofessionals will prepare materials and manage the children while the teacher teaches. Perhaps with normal children and mildly and moderately handicapped children, where teaching can take place in relatively large groups, these duties are feasible for paraprofessionals. However, this is not the case in classrooms for the severely, profoundly, and multiply handicapped. Fredericks, Baldwin, Grove, Riggs, Furey, Moore, Jordan, Gage, Levik, Alrik, and Wadlow (1975), appropriately stated: "Because of the wide range of individual differences in the severely handicapped population and oftentimes their unmanageability because of previous ineffective home training, effective instruction can oftentimes only be achieved in a one-to-one relationship. Therefore, the utilization of paraprofessionals to provide individualized instruction in the classroom is considered mandatory" (p. 2).

Therefore, the paraprofessional must know basic learning principles and teaching methods to the degree that they can be applied effectively in accordance with the procedures of a training program. Similarly, the child's parents (or parent surrogates) must be trained to maintain and monitor various training programs which extend into the home (or agency) environment. In essence, any major endeavor to provide direct education and training services for the severely handicapped must materially extend to all significant adults who come in contact with the child on a daily basis. To do less would serve only to delay and possibly sidetrack the progress made by the child.

Paraprofessional: Definition

The term "educational paraprofessional" is used to refer to any salaried or nonsalaried person, other than a teacher, who is providing educational opportunities for children (e.g., parents who are involved in educational programs for their handicapped children, direct care staff in state institutions for the mentally retarded, physical therapy aides, vocational specialists in sheltered workshops, and houseparents in sheltered group homes).

The program described here is designed to train a particular kind of educational paraprofessional, a teaching associate (formerly called a teacher aide) who works directly with a teacher in providing educational opportunities for severely handicapped individuals. The major emphasis of this article is on the training of teaching associates to work in educating severely handicapped children through the use of behavioral procedures (Clark & Macrae, 1976; Fredericks, et al., 1975; Gardner, 1972; Hursh, Schumaker, Fawcett, & Sherman, 1973; Panyan, Boozer, & Morris, 1970; Panyan & Patterson, 1974). The article also provides an overall model for a generic competency-based training program for special education personnel, which could, in fact, include the training of teachers.

Teacher and Teaching Associate Relationship

In order to be effective in supplementing the educational opportunities for severely handicapped students, the educational teaching associate must have acquired the informational and performance competencies that are directly related to changing the behavior of these students. The teaching associates will be directly supervised by the teacher and will carry out educational programs developed and implemented by the teacher. Thus, the teacher becomes a classroom manager or coordinator instead of just a teacher (Fredericks, et al., 1975). In order to promote the implementation of educational programs, both the teacher and the teaching associate should receive similar training in those competencies which are directly related to the education of severely handicapped students. This approach suggests that during training the teacher should be provided with practicum training in supervising paraprofessional personnel who work with children.

Teaching Associate Preparation Model

The Kansas program (Sailor, Guess, & Lavis, 1975) is designed to furnish performance-based preservice curricula for the preparation of both teachers and teaching associates, in accordance with the national mandate for equal access to education for all handicapped children and youth.

The competencies specified in this program provide both teachers and teaching associates with the requisite performance skills to develop functional educational programs for individuals who are severely and profoundly handicapped, including those with severe or profound orthopedic impairments, behavior disorders, perceptual, psychomotor, or medical disorders. The competency-based curriculum model was developed around two training components: informational competencies and performance competencies. The identified competencies have been organized into training modules. Each training module has a format which includes the specification of the criteria required to demonstrate successfully the acquisition of the informational and performance competencies.

Academic Courses

The training modules are subsumed under a sequence of courses leading to college credit hours (Table 1). The general curriculum requirements, or core curriculum, for the Paraprofessional Multiphy/Severely Handicapped Program consist of 11 courses, including practica, sequenced across five semesters of training (approximately two years). This core program comprises about 24 of the approximate total of 60 credit hours for an Associate of Arts degree.

The primary purpose of the academic courses is to furnish the teaching associate trainee with the informational competencies necessary to increase the generality of the requisite skills for the education of the severely and profoundly handicapped. A secondary purpose is

TABLE 1

General Curriculum Requirements: Paraprofessional Multiply/Severely Handicapped Program

Semester	Course	Title	Module	
Fall semester	Course 1, 2 hours	Introduction to Mental Retardation and Behavior Management	Module A: Right to Education	A
			Module B: Introduction to Operant Behavior	A
	Course 2, 1 hour	Classroom Participation with Exceptional Children	Module D: Basic Classroom Participation: Practicum I	P
Spring semester	Course 3, 2 hours	Methods in Classroom Measurement and Evaluation	Module E: Measuring Operant Behavior	A
			Module F: Evaluation of Operant Procedures	A
	Course 4, 3 hours	Methods in Classroom Management and Programming	Module G: Strengthening Operant Behavior	A
			Module H: Weakening Operant Behavior	A
			Module I: Schedules of Reinforcement	A
			Module J: Generalization and Discrimination	A
	Course 5, 2 hours	Classroom Participation with Exceptional Children	Module O: Intermediate Classroom Participation: Practicum II	P
Summer semester	Course 6, 2 hours	Techniques in Programming Learning Environments	Module L: Programming Prosthetic Environments	A
			Module M: Programming Engaging Environments	A
Fall semester	Course 7, 3 hours	Curriculum Development for Exceptional Children	Module P: Assessment Scales	A
			Module Q: Writing Instructional Objectives	A
			Module R: Curriculum Planning	A
			Module S: Task Analysis	A
	Course 8, 2 hours	Laboratory in Developing Instructional Programs	Module Y_1: Advanced Classroom Participation 1: Practicum III	P
	Course 9, 2 hours	Seminar in Basic Skills Program for Exceptional Children	Module T: Motor Programs	A
			Module U: Self-Help Programs	A
Spring semester	Course 10, 2 hours	Seminar in Advanced Skills Programs for Exceptional Children	Module V: Language Programs	A
			Module W: Socialization Programs	A
			Module X: Pre-Academic Programs	A
	Course 11, 3 hours	Advanced Practicum with Exceptional Children	Module Y_2: Advanced Classroom Participation 2: Practicum IV	P

Notes: 1) A—Academic Skills, P—Practicum or Applied Skills.
2) Modules C, K, N, Teacher Training Program, not applicable to Paraprofessional Training Program.
3) Course titles are examples and are not intended to be exclusive.
4) Approximately 24 total credit hours.

to lay the groundwork for a common and more professional language system to be used with the teacher, psychologist, counselor, and others.

Practicum Courses

The practicum courses offer the teaching associate trainee a structured program by which to acquire the performance competencies necessary for teaching the severely and profoundly handicapped. These courses are scheduled throughout the training program to provide the trainee with a gradual increase in the amount of time spent in the classroom working directly with children as he acquires more informational competencies. In the first practicum, the trainee spends about one hour per day per week, or the equivalent, in the classroom. In the last practicum, he spends about three hours per day per week, or the equivalent, working with children in the classroom. The number of credit hours assigned to each practicum course may be determined by the local educational agency according to its own guidelines. Nevertheless, the practicum courses remain the most important and functional aspect of the training program, regardless of the credit hours awarded for successful completion of the course.

Curriculum Content Specification

Competency Blocks. Three basic blocks of teaching competencies have been identified: those competencies that are directly related to changing student behavior (e.g., measuring behavior, strengthening behavior, weakening behavior); those competencies that are indirectly related to changing student behavior (e.g., written instructional objectives, curriculum planning, task analysis); and those competencies that have an unknown relationship to changing student behavior (e.g., issues in "right to education," normalization, parent counseling).

Training Modules. Twenty-five modules covering the three basic blocks of instructional competencies for teacher training have been targeted for initial development. The project has developed a module production lattice which illustrates the sequential procedure for developing each individual module. The procedure consists of four basic phases of development: the development of the instructional competencies, the development of the prototype module, the revision and production of the final module, and the publication and dissemination of the final module.

The content of each training module was analyzed and the informational and performance competencies were identified (Horner, Holvoet, & Rinne, 1976). The informational and performance competencies for teaching associates were specified by determining on an a priori basis which competencies would provide functional classroom teaching assistance to teachers. (Table 2 illustrates the relationship of the teacher and teaching associate training modules.)

It was determined that the teaching associate should receive rigorous training in those competency areas that are directly related to changing student behaviors (i.e., concentration on competencies related to actual teaching skills); training in some component parts of the areas indirectly related to changing student behaviors; and minimal exposure to those areas that have an unknown relationship to changing student behaviors. (See Table 3.)

Informational and Performance Competencies. An example of the relationship between teachers and teaching associates with respect to informational competencies for a module is presented in Table 4.

Module A (Right to Education) represents a competency area that falls into Block 3, since its relationship to teaching students is unknown. Out of 20 informational competencies for teachers, only six apply to teaching associates. In addition, Module A contains four performance competencies for teachers, and none for teaching associates. On the other hand, Module B (Introduction to Operant Behavior), in the Block 1 competency area, contains 20 informational competencies for teachers, all of which are applicable to teaching associates. The informational competencies are accompanied by ten performance competencies for teachers, eight of which apply to teaching associates. (See Table 5.)

With respect to Block 2, areas indirectly related to teaching students, Module P (Assessment Scales) serves as an example. A teacher is expected not only to administer assessment scales, but also to interpret the results in order to formulate instructional objectives and plan the curriculum. The teaching associate, on the other hand, is trained only in the mechanics of administering the assessment scale.

In addition to the informational and performance competencies, each module contains a reading list (academic modules only) which corresponds to the informational competencies

TABLE 2

General Competency Area Curriculum Requirements: Teacher and Teaching Associate Multiply/Severely Handicapped Program

Module	Title	Teacher	Teaching Associate
Module A:	Right to Education	X	X
Module B:	Introduction to Operant Behavior	X	X
Module C:	Behavioral Approach to Special Education	X	
Module D:*	Basic Classroom Participation: Practicum I	X	X
Module E:	Measuring Operant Behavior	X	X
Module F:	Evaluation of Operant Procedures	X	X
Module G:	Strengthening Operant Behavior	X	X
Module H:	Weakening Operant Behavior	X	X
Module I:	Schedules of Reinforcement	X	X
Module J:	Generalization and Discrimination	X	X
Module K:	Programming for Normalization	X	
Module L:	Programming Prosthetic Environments	X	X
Module M:	Programming Engaging Environments	X	X
Module N:	Training Teacher Aides and Parents	X	
Module O:*	Intermediate Classroom Participation: Practicum II	X	X
Module P:	Assessment Scales	X	X
Module Q:	Writing Instructional Objectives	X	X
Module R:	Curriculum Planning	X	X
Module S:	Task Analysis	X	X
Module T:	Motor Programs	X	X
Module U:	Self-Help Programs	X	X
Module V:	Language Programs	X	X
Module W:	Socialization Programs	X	X
Module X:	Pre-Academic Programs	X	X
Module Y:*	Advanced Classroom Participation: Practicum III	X	X

* Practicum Modules consist of exercises designed to evaluate performance competencies.

and a system for evaluation. Both of the training programs utilize written examinations for evaluating informational competencies.

Practicum Modules. As illustrated in Table 3, the program contains four practicum modules. Three of the modules pertain directly to the training of children, and the fourth module (Module Y_1) consists of instructional program development. The purpose of the practicum modules is to provide specific applied exercises which allow the trainee to demonstrate the performance competencies identified in the preceding academic modules. For example, the second performance competency in Module B (Introduction to Operant Behavior) states: "A teaching associate of the severely and profoundly handicapped should apply the information acquired through the readings of the Introduction to Operant Behavior Module by . . . 2) engaging in a procedure leading to the identification of conditioned and/or unconditioned stimuli which may serve as reinforcers when made contingent upon and presented immediately after a target behavior" (Tucker, Horner, & Hollis, 1975, p. 1). The teaching associate trainee is then given the opportunity and trained, if necessary, to follow the procedure of identifying potential reinforcers, specified by Striefel (1974), with a child in the classroom. Since effective reinforcers for severely handicapped children are often transitory, the procedure is generally a relevant and functional task for the practicum site classroom, as well as for the trainee.

The practicum exercises guide the trainee across the five-semester training program through a series of activities based partly on a continuum of task complexity. The first practicum module concentrates on instructing the trainee to teach one specific child one specific skill. The second practicum module expands the trainee's responsibilities and skills across different skill domains (e.g., motor development, self-help development, language development). The third practicum module instructs the trainee to teach several children one particular skill as a function of testing the instructional program assigned for development. The fourth and last practicum module essentially confronts the trainee with realistic on-the-job responsibilities and duties. These

TABLE 3

Relationship of Modules to Competency Blocks

Module	Title	Direct	Indirect	Unknown
Module A:	Right to Education			X
Module B:	Introduction to Operant Behavior	X		
Module D:	Basic Classroom Participation: Practicum I	X		
Module E:	Measuring Operant Behavior	X		
Module F:	Evaluation of Operant Procedures		X	
Module G:	Strengthening Operant Behavior	X		
Module H:	Weakening Operant Behavior	X		
Module I:	Schedules of Reinforcement	X		
Module J:	Generalization and Discrimination	X		
Module O:	Intermediate Classroom Participation: Practicum II	X		
Module L:	Programming Prosthetic Environments	X		
Module M:	Programming Engaging Environments		X	
Module P:	Assessment Scales		X	
Module Q:	Curriculum Planning		X	
Module R:	Writing Instructional Objectives		X	
Module S:	Task Analysis		X	
Module Y_1:	Advanced Classroom Participation 1: Practicum III (Laboratory)		X	
Module T:	Motor Programs	X		
Module U:	Self-Help Programs	X		
Module V:	Language Programs	X		
Module W:	Socialization Programs	X		
Module X:	Pre-Academic Programs	X		
Module Y_2:	Advanced Classroom Participation 2: Practicum IV	X		

duties test the trainee's competence in instructing severely handicapped children across several skill programs. In addition to specific structured programmed sessions with the children, the trainee is given experience in unstructured free operant activities with the children, such as snack time, holding activities, and recess. Thus, the practicum exercises offer the teaching associate trainee an array of skills and experiences, ranging from simple to more complex, in a functional classroom setting.

Training Methods

Since there are two basic kinds of competencies identified for training teaching associates, two separate training methods are needed: a set of procedures for training informational competencies, and a set of procedures for training performance competencies.

Academic Course Procedures. Each informational module contains a list of primary and supplemental readings, accompanied by a chart identifying the competencies included in each reading and the sequence in which the readings should be covered. The procedure for completing a module is self-explanatory within the module. Thus, the teaching associate could, in fact, proceed through each module independently at his own rate. However, the possibility exists that the readings might not be adequate for the trainee to acquire the competencies without additional or remedial assistance.

Project personnel have found this to be the case for teaching associates with many of the modules, since there is a dearth of published material that deals directly with behavioral approaches to teaching severely and profoundly handicapped individuals. Therefore, the method being used is a combination of personalized, competency-based instruction and a traditional approach to college education. The courses consist of the self-contained modules with regularly scheduled seminars. The seminar sessions provide verbal feedback to the trainees, who are also given frequent written examinations.

The procedures for teaching the seminar sessions for each module are illustrated in a flowchart (Figure 1) and are outlined below.

1. Study all readings. Prior to directing the seminar sessions for a module, the primary and supplemental readings should be thoroughly read by the instructor. The supplemental readings contain more comprehensive information to add to the instructor's resources for group discussion and remedial sessions.

2. Assign teaching associate trainees (students) to the seminar class. It is suggested

TABLE 4

Teacher and Teaching Associate Informational Competencies: Module A—Right to Education

Informational Competencies (abbreviated)	Teachers	Teaching Associates
Prepare a written definition, description, statement of:		
1. Concept of "zero rejection"	X	X
2. Origins of "rights to treatment and education"	X	X
3. Constitutional provisions establishing "rights to treatment and education"	X	
4. Legal exclusion of handicapped from public education	X	
5. Difference between "class action" and "private action" suit	X	
6. Rationale for legal issue of equality of *access to* education	X	
7. Stages in Wyatt V. Stickney litigation	X	
8. The salient provisions of the Pennsylvania consent agreement	X	
9. Application of "least restrictive means" principle	X	X
10. "Cascade system" of educational placement	X	
11. Status of institutional residents in relation to "right to education"	X	X
12. Legally prescribed minimum standards for educational programs	X	
13. Economic aspects of court ordered minimum educational standards	X	
14. Court decision challenging use of testing instruments for special class placement	X	X
15. Negative aspects of purchasing special education services	X	
16. Concept of "institutional peonage"	X	X
17. Distinction between therapeutic and nontherapeutic work assignments	X	
18. Legal approaches to remediating "institutional peonage"	X	
19. Statutory definition of exceptional children	X	
20. Legal exceptions to providing special education services	X	

that no more than ten students be assigned to a class, in order to promote an informal environment and to facilitate discussions.

3. At the opening of the first class session, distribute the student manuals and explain the course procedures.

4. For the remainder of the first class session, explain the purpose of the pretest (to compare pre and post test differences for determining the effectiveness of training material). Then assign readings for the first unit (if there is more than one unit) and administer the pretest. (When a comprehensive pretest is developed and tested, the pretest will also give the student the opportunity to "test out" of the module.)

5. In the second class session, begin discussing the competencies in the first unit, using the test questions and answers as a discussion guide. This guide is recommended, since the test questions and answers may have more information and definitions than are included in the primary readings.

6. Once all of the competencies within the

TABLE 5

Teacher and Teaching Associate Performance Competencies: Module B—Introduction to Operant Behavior

Performance Competencies (abbreviated)	Teachers	Teaching Associates
Apply academic information by:		
1. Translating target behaviors from assessment scales into behavioral definitions	X	
2. Engaging in a procedure for identifying potential reinforcers	X	X
3. Using a measurement instrument to record performance of target behavior	X	X
4. Determining interobserver reliability of measurements	X	
5. Computing and plotting data points on a graph	X	X
6. Presenting programmed discriminative stimuli	X	X
7. Immediately presenting contingent reinforcers during training	X	X
8. Withholding the presentation of reinforcers during training contingent upon nontargeted responses	X	X
9. Interrupting responses which are incompatible with targeted responses	X	X
10. Following a specific programmed teaching sequence	X	X

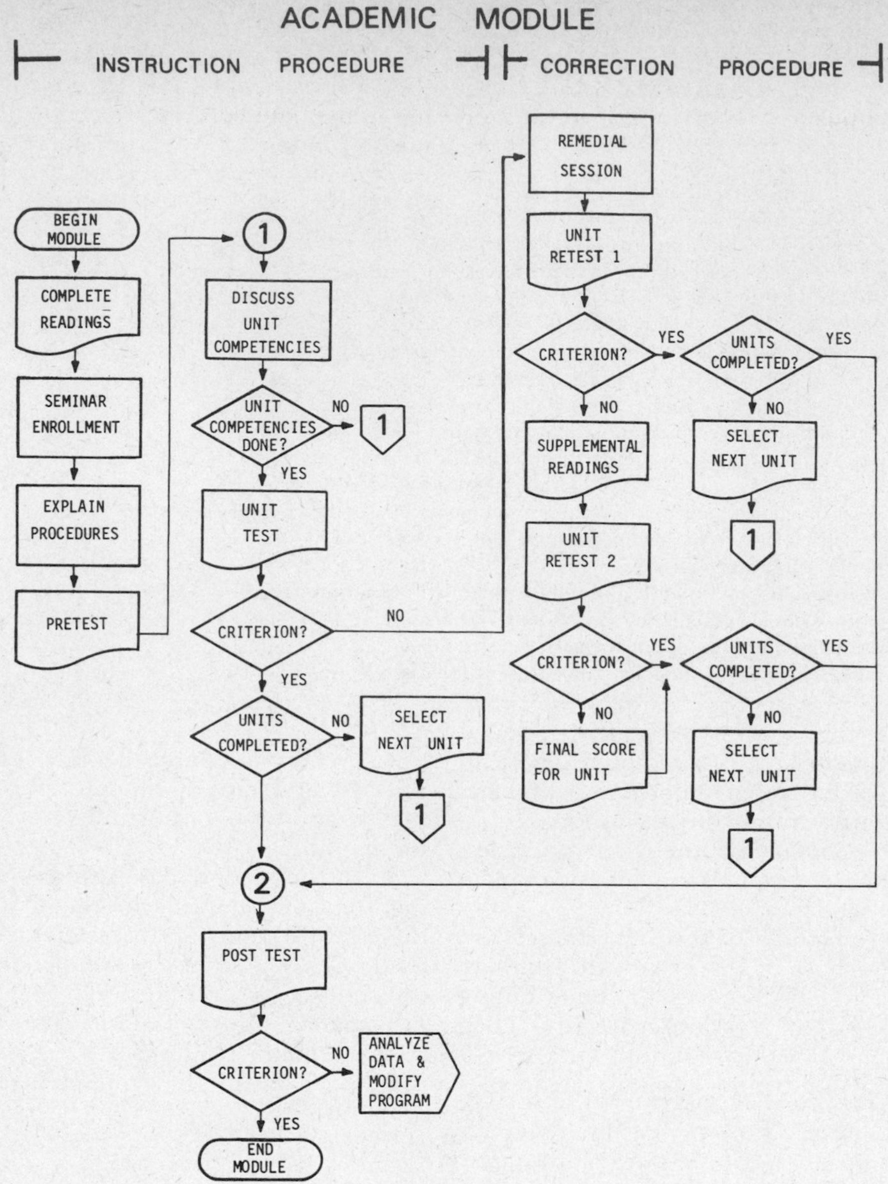

Figure 1. Instructor procedure flowchart: Academic module.

unit have been covered in the seminar, administer the unit test.

7. If a student reaches criterion on the unit test, cycle him back to the discussion of the next unit; when all the units have been covered, administer the post test.

8. If a student fails to reach criterion on the unit test, then cycle to the correction procedure, as follows:

a. Re-discuss those competencies for the questions the student answered incorrectly.

b. Administer the same unit test again (Retest 1).

c. If the student reaches criterion on the unit retest, cycle to the next units. When all the units have been covered, administer the post test.

d. If the student again fails to perform to criterion, assign the supplemental readings over the pertinent competencies and administer Retest 2 for that unit.

e. If the student reaches criterion on Retest

2, cycle to the next units. When all the units have been covered, administer the post test.

f. If the student again fails to perform to criterion, record the highest score for the unit and proceed to the next unit or post test.

9. Once all units have been tested, administer the post test to each student.

10. If criterion is reached on the post test, the student has successfully completed the module.

11. If criterion is not reached on the post test, analyze the data and modify the program so as to meet the needs of the training environment and the individual students.

In addition to discussion, the instructor can utilize various audio-visual aids as well as behavior rehearsal. Fawcett, Mathews, Fletcher, Morrow, and Stokes (1975), in their work with low-income paraprofessionals, have demonstrated the effectiveness of behavior rehearsal (consisting of an opportunity to practice, followed by feedback on practice performance) as an important link between information acquisition and performance acquisition of specific competencies. In the present primitive state of instructional technology for training paraprofessionals, the skill and resourcefulness of the instructor will play an important supplemental role to published instructional material for trainers of the severely and profoundly handicapped.

Evaluation of Informational Competencies. Written tests, including objective questions, as well as questions requiring written statements, have been developed for each training module within specified courses. A proficiency criterion, such as 90% correct responses for test completion, is necessary to demonstrate the informational competencies of each module. The difference in proficiency criteria between teachers and teaching associates is a quantitative difference, as opposed to a qualitative one. For example, in a given competency area, such as "Right to Education," a teacher is required to obtain 20 informational competencies, whereas the teaching associate is required to obtain only 6 of those 20 competencies. Nevertheless, 90% correct performance is required of both teachers and teaching associates.

Practicum Course Procedures. The training methods for practicum skills are being adapted from procedures developed by Carpenter (1976) which are similar to those suggested by O'Brien and Azrin (1972) and Horner and Keilitz (1975) for training handicapped persons. The procedure consists of five basic components: providing explicit instructions to the trainee; offering the opportunity to perform correctly with no assistance from the instructor; providing immediate corrective oral feedback; modeling or demonstrating the skill to be learned; and giving verbal guidance to the trainee in successive approximations to criterion performance. Specific procedures are as follows.

1. *Instructions*: At the beginning of a skill task, the practicum instructor provides explicit instructions on the procedures and components of the task, or instructional program, for the child. For example, if the skill task consists of an imitation program (Striefel, 1974), the instructor gives a copy of the program to the trainee for study and systematically goes through the program, step by step, until the trainee is familiar with what cues to give, what responses to expect from the child, how to reinforce correct responses, correction procedures for incorrect responses, criteria for correct responses, data collection procedures, and so on.

2. *No assistance*: The instructor then offers the trainee the opportunity to conduct the task correctly without assistance. If the trainee does perform correctly, the instructor gives positive feedback for correct responses. If the trainee makes an error, the instructor proceeds to the next component of the training procedure, immediate corrective verbal feedback.

3. *Immediate corrective feedback*: Immediately following an error by the trainee, the instructor gives corrective feedback. Carpenter (1976) defines corrective feedback as: "Stating the trainee's error in response to the child behavior, and/or giving corrective feedback why the child response required a certain response from the trainee" (p. 23). Analyzing the trainee's errors includes listing, describing, or providing additional information about what trainee behaviors are needed for a correct response. This statement is always put in positive form, and instead of pointing out what the trainee did incorrectly, the instructor explains the child's error, and what the correct trainee response should be. The trainee is then given the opportunity to correct his error by practicing the appropriate response.

4. *Model*: Typically, immediate corrective feedback with positive practice and praise is sufficient to obtain and maintain desirable performance by the trainee. However, if the trainee continues to make errors, the instructor models or demonstrates the appropriate response.

After the demonstration, the trainee is once again allowed to practice the task correctly.

5. *Verbal guidance*: If the trainee responds incorrectly, the instructor task-analyzes the skill and verbally guides the trainee through successive approximations of the task until criterion performance is achieved. It should be emphasized that the verbal guidance method is an alternate procedure that is rarely, if ever, needed to elicit correct performance by teaching associate trainees. Should this procedure be needed frequently, the skill task should be broken down into component parts as a means of simplifying the required activity.

In addition to this systematic training procedure, the trainees are exposed to other appropriate models in the classrooms throughout practicum training. It is assumed that these models also have an important effect on the teaching behavior of the trainees.

Evaluation of Performance Competencies. In determining skill proficiency, the difference in criteria for teachers and teaching associate trainees for demonstration of performance competencies remains the same, i.e., quantitative rather than qualitative. Skill proficiency is evaluated with the same tool for all teaching personnel. This project uses the Trainer Proficiency Checklists developed for evaluation of practicum performance by R. Don Horner, Department of Special Education, University of Kansas, and the Personnel Training Program, Kansas Neurological Institute. The checklists provide an objective evaluation of the trainer's ability to: establish the child's baseline performance; engage in appropriate teaching procedures for acquisition of a new behavior by the child; and engage in appropriate procedures for maintaining learned behavior by the child. Reliability for skill proficiency is established in two ways: by independent evaluations of separate instructors for the same competency, using the checklists; and by evaluation of the trainer's performance on teaching a second new behavior to the child. (Evaluation procedures are not shown here, but are included in this volume in "A Competency-Based Approach to Preparing Teachers of the Severely and Profoundly Handicapped," by R. Don Horner.)

The ultimate goal of the trainer of the severely handicapped is, of course, to increase the number of functional skills acquired by the child being trained. A teacher or teaching associate can perform perfectly according to academically structured objectives, but, if the child fails to learn, any number of programmatic variables may be responsible. Nevertheless, it is not sufficient simply to evaluate competencies during and at the completion of training; it is also necessary to establish their validity at the job placement site. This can be accomplished by monitoring on-the-job performance by site visits following placement.

Inservice Training Model

The teaching associate training program may be implemented as an inservice training program at the local educational agency (LEA). The primary terminal objectives for the trainees in the program are the attainment of: the specified applied skills for educating handicapped children by demonstration of criterion performance on practicum training; and the informational competencies to criterion on academic training.

The specified prerequisite for entry into the training program is a high school diploma or its equivalent. If an individual can demonstrate the required competencies without the formal prerequisites, a high school diploma is irrelevant. Nevertheless, most school districts have established a high school diploma as a minimum qualification for employment.

The LEA may need to provide staff inservice training in one of three basic categories: specialized training; generic, or generalized, training; or combined specialized and generic training.

Specialized Training

The purpose of specialized training is to instill specific competencies for a specific task. The main advantages of specialized training lie in the expedience and economy of training for a specific set of competencies in a specific environment, as compared with training for general competencies. The response cost involved in training a teaching associate in, for example, the procedures of a specific language training program with a given group of children, is considerably lower than the cost of training that same teaching associate in the basic components and concepts in all language training. The time spent in training, the financial cost of implementation, and the time lag between training and proficient performance of the trainee are all factors which favor specialized training.

However, there are major disadvantages in specialized training. From the standpoint of preservice instruction, specialized training is relatively impractical to implement. It is nearly impossible to know exactly what type of job placement each individual trainee will have. Will he be teaching language development, motor development, or other skills? Will he be working in a classroom for severely handicapped, moderately handicapped, learning disabled, deaf and blind, or all combinations of handicaps? Training each individual in the specialized skills for each position is obviously impractical and economically unfeasible. In addition, obtaining only specialized skills limits opportunities for employment.

Generic Training

The 23 modules of this training program are designed to provide general competencies for teaching associates. Although the program is geared to educating the severely handicapped, it provides generic competencies for teaching individuals with any or all handicaps.

The advantages to training in generic competencies are apparent. It is feasible to implement with the same information and skills. Academic instruction can be offered on a group basis or through self-paced instruction. Performance competencies can be provided through practicum exercises at individual practicum sites, which not only train students in specific competencies, but also expose them to specialized environments. It is assumed that, with specific competencies in the basic learning principles and teaching procedures, a teaching associate should have a better prospect for employment than an individual with a specialized skill. Another working hypothesis is that an individual with generic training should be able to generalize his knowledge to new and novel teaching environments more effectively than an individual with specialized training.

For these reasons, this project recognizes the importance and advantages of specialized training, but does not promote the development of a systematic program of specialized training for national dissemination. Nevertheless, specialized training is an important component and should ideally be provided through inservice programs at the local level for specific educational environmental needs. Perhaps the most obvious solution to using either specialized training for specific local environments or generic training for general competencies in a local environment would be a combination of both. The disadvantages of either model are irrelevant if generic and specialized training are combined into an inservice training program.

An Inservice Format

A staff inservice training program which offers both specialized and general competencies could be implemented by use of the program presented in this article. Depending on whether or not the local agency has a staff member to provide inservice training, two possible formats are available.

Staff Trainer. If the local agency employs an individual specifically for inservice training, the program could be used as outlined in this article. A seminar class meeting before or after school hours could be held on a regular basis for a group of staff trainees. The seminar would provide training in the informational competencies. The performance competencies could be taught in the staff member's assigned classroom, with the classroom teacher serving as the practicum supervisor, or trainer. This format for practicum training would be especially feasible if the classroom were arranged in the same manner as the model developed by Fredericks, et al. (1975), using the teacher as a classroom manager.

The content of the curriculum could easily consist of the modules developed by this project. If the trainee were assigned to a specialized subject, such as language training, the area supervisor, teacher, or consultant could provide the practicum training. This arrangement would provide a trainee with both generic training (seminar) and a specialized skill (practicum).

Classroom Teacher. An alternate format could utilize the classroom teacher to whom the trainee is assigned for providing training in both informational and performance competencies. With this format, the teacher could serve as coordinator of the training material for informational competencies on an individual, self-paced basis. The training in performance competencies could be handled in the manner previously stated. The competencies, materials, procedures, and evaluation tools could be those presented previously and could be used within either inservice format.

Career Advancement

The total program presented here provides comprehensive, performance-based training across a common set of competencies for both teachers and teaching associates, and an educational career ladder on which teaching associates may advance across ranks to become teachers. However, a program designed to train teaching associates for the severely handicapped will probably fail to attract many applicants unless it includes some visible and objective method for advancement. Current salaries for teaching associates are inadequate in relation to the educational opportunities open to those who have completed a functional performance-based training program. Thus, potential career advancement is currently the only real source of motivation for acquiring the competencies taught in a rigorous training program.

Although there may be multiple solutions to the question of advancement, we will consider only two at this point: advancement within the teaching associate ranks and advancement to the teaching ranks. Briefly, advancement within ranks could be based on experience (years on the job and number of children's behaviors changed), completion of this training program, and additional training (workshops and advanced courses with objective testing at critical points). Such continuation of training could lead to an associate degree (community junior college). This would be a natural step out of the realm of teaching associate to that of teacher through attendance at a four-year college for completion of a degree and certification as a special education teacher. It should be noted that most programs for certified special education teachers are at the graduate level because, in most cases, certification and experience in primary or elementary education are prerequisites. The authors believe this to be more myth than necessity.

Conclusion

The training of teaching associates and other paraprofessionals must be specific and precise if the goal of such training is to reduce the level of disability of the developmentally handicapped. The role a teaching associate should play in the classroom has been the subject of considerable debate. There are many who believe that teaching should be the sole responsibility of the professional teacher. The absolute necessity of individualized instruction for the more severely developmentally disabled renders this belief impractical; the success of well-trained teaching associates in teaching the severely handicapped shows that such beliefs are unfounded.

References

Blessing, K. R. Use of teacher aides in special education: A review and possible implications. *Exceptional Children,* 1967, *34,* 107–113.

Carpenter, C. J. *An experimental analysis of descriptive feedback and corrective practice as a paraprofessional training technique.* Unpublished doctoral dissertation, University of Kansas, 1976.

Clark, H. B., & Macrae, J. W. The use of imposed and self-selected training packages to establish classroom teaching skills. *Journal of Applied Behavior Analysis,* 1976, *9,* 105.

Cruickshank, W. M., & Haring, N. C. *A demonstration: Assistants for teachers of exceptional children.* Syracuse, New York: Syracuse University Press, 1957.

Esbensen, T. Should teacher aides be more than clerks? *Phi Delta Kappan,* 1966, *47,* 237.

Fawcett, S. B., Mathews, R. M., Fletcher, R. K., Morrow, R., & Stokes, T. F. *A community-based personalized instructional system: Teaching helping skills to low-income paraprofessionals.* Unpublished manuscript, University of Kansas, 1975.

Fredericks, H. D., Baldwin, V. L., Grove, D. N., Riggs, C., Furey, V., Moore, W., Jordan, E., Gage, M., Levak, L., Alrik, G., & Wadlow, M. *A data based classroom for the moderately and severely handicapped.* Monmouth, Oregon: Instructional Development Corporation, 1975.

Gardner, J. M. Teaching behavior modification to nonprofessionals. *Journal of Applied Behavior Analysis,* 1972, *5,* 517–521.

Gilhool, T. K. Education: An inalienable right. *Exceptional Children,* 1973, *39,* 597–609.

Horner, R. D. Teacher proficiency checklist. Personnel Preparation Program. Department of Special Education, University of Kansas (unpublished), 1975.

Horner, R. D., Holvoet, J., & Rinne, T. *Competency specifications for teachers of the severely and profoundly handicapped.* Unpublished manuscript, Personnel Preparation Program, Department of Special Education, University of Kansas, 1976.

Horner, R. D., & Keilitz, I. Training mentally retarded adolescents to brush their teeth. *Journal of Applied Behavior Analysis,* 1975, *8,* 301–109.

Hursh, D. E., Schumaker, J. B., Fawcett, S. B., & Sherman, J. A. *Training behavior modifiers: A comparison of written and direct instructional methods.* Unpublished manuscript, Department of Human Development, University of Kansas, 1973.

O'Brien, F., & Azrin, N. H. Developing proper mealtime behaviors of the institutionalized retarded. *Journal of Applied Behavior Analysis,* 1972, *5,* 389–399.

Panyan, M., Boozer, H., & Morris, N. Feedback of attendants as a reinforcer for applying operant techniques. *Journal of Applied Behavior Analysis,* 1970, *3,* 1–4.

Panyan, M., & Patterson, E. F. Teaching attendants the applied aspects of behavior modification. *Mental Retardation,* 1974, *12,* 30–32.

Reid, B. A., & Reid, W. R. Role expectations of paraprofessional staff in special education. *Focus on Exceptional Children,* 1974, *6,* 1–14.

Sailor, W., Guess, D., & Lavis, L. W. Preparing teachers for education of the severely handicapped. *Education and Training of the Mentally Retarded,* 1975, *10,* 201–203.

Sontag, E., Burke, P., & York, R. Considerations for serving the severely handicapped in the public schools. *Education and Training of the Mentally Retarded,* 1973, *8,* 20–26.

Striefel, S. *Managing behavior—7: Teaching a child to imitate.* Lawrence, Kansas: H & H Enterprises, Inc., 1974.

Tucker, D., Horner, R. D., & Hollis, J. H. Introduction to operant behavior module: Teaching associate training component. Unpublished manuscript, Personnel Training Program. Topeka: Kansas Neurological Institute, 1975.

DENNIS J. TUCKER is the co-Coordinator of the Teaching Associate Training Component of the Personnel Preparation Program for Education of the Severely Handicapped at Kansas Neurological Institute in Topeka, Kansas.

R. DON HORNER is Research Associate, Department of Special Education, University of Kansas, and Project Coordinator, Personnel Training Program for the Severely Handicapped.

A Competency-Based Approach to Preparing Teachers of the Severely and Profoundly Handicapped: Perspective I

BARBARA WILCOX

University of Illinois at Urbana-Champaign

Various factors are currently operating in special education to effect changes in service delivery. Landmark litigation, such as the PARC and Mills cases, has produced radical changes in the field, especially in the provision of services to severely handicapped citizens. As states continue to mandate services for the severely handicapped, the demand for teachers will be substantial, especially if states adopt a teacher/student ratio of no more than one to five (Stainbach, Stainbach, & Maurer, 1976). Because the pressure to implement programs is so intense and the shortage of trained personnel so acute, conditions now exist which may actually undermine the gains that the severely handicapped have made through court rulings.

The first problem is that school districts may be forced to respond to pressure by hiring and staffing classrooms with personnel who are *willing*, rather than *trained* or *qualified*, to work with the severely handicapped. The outcome of such a practice would be failure on a massive scale, since the role of the teacher of severely handicapped students is exceedingly complex and extends far beyond the traditional teaching role. There is a direct relationship between the level of a student's disability and the level of instructional competence required of the teacher: the more pronounced the disability, the greater and more precise the skills required of the teacher (Sontag, Burke, & York, 1973). Most graduates of those programs which prepare teachers of the mildly handicapped are simply not going to have the skills to toilet-train, to eliminate self-destructive and self-stimulatory behavior, to train eye contact and imitative responding, to systematically teach community survival skills, and so on. To hire teachers who lack these requisite competencies is to guarantee that schools will produce few significant changes in the lifestyle of the severely handicapped. However, if this is the only way that classes can be started, then there is an urgent need for comprehensive in-service training to develop competencies.

A second danger arising from current pressures to serve the severely and profoundly impaired is that history may repeat itself. We may find that teachers' colleges respond to training needs in the field in terms of quantity, rather than quality. Both Tawney (Note 1) and Meyen (Note 2) warn against a philosophy which encourages "every teachers' college in the country to train special class teachers" (in this case, teachers for the severely handicapped). The needs of handicapped students will not be served by poorly staffed and poorly conceived programs which turn out teachers with few technical skills, limited expectations for, and limited exposure to the severely impaired. Training programs should not serve teachers who enter the field simply because there are job opportunities and support for training.

If the increases in services for the severely and profoundly handicapped that have been achieved through legislation and parent advocacy are to be expanded or, indeed, maintained, it is clear that university training programs must play an important role. Not only must they prepare high-calibre personnel who can generate comprehensive educational services for the severely handicapped, but they must do so at both pre-service and in-service levels. Unfortunately, probably more has been

---

"Competency-based training" or "competency-based teacher education" has been defined and implemented in a variety of ways. In this paper, competency-based training refers to any training program which is defined by statements of trainee performance. The author discusses competencies or performances that she judges to be appropriate to training programs preparing personnel to work with the severely handicapped, but makes no assumptions about the system by which competent performance is to be achieved (e.g., there is no judgment that competency-based training is best handled in a modular format).

The author thanks Joseph R. Jenkins for his thoughtful comments on the manuscript and Nick Certo and Fred Orelove for their editorial assistance.

done to date to provide severely handicapped students with appropriate educational programs than has been done to ensure appropriate educational programs for their teachers!

This paper addresses itself to the task of specifying those competencies required for teachers of the severely handicapped. The intent is to present strategies for identifying, stating, and evaluating competencies to be developed in training programs; to provide a partial delineation of areas in which the teacher should demonstrate competence; to discuss the implications of the competency-based approach to training teachers of the severely handicapped; and to identify some general concerns in this area.

Identification of Competencies for Teachers of the Severely/Profoundly Handicapped

In a competency-based approach to teacher education, several strategies are typically employed to generate competency statements. Some trainers have simply translated existing program coursework into sets of competencies. The result, quite naturally, is that traditional training is offered in a traditional way with a change only in labels (Lilly, 1976). Fortunately, this option is not usually available to those concerned with training teachers of the severely handicapped, since few programs currently exist that could be so "translated." Training programs for teachers of the severely handicapped have both the luxury and the responsibility of building from the ground up.

Another common technique for identifying program competencies is to have professionals (teachers or teacher trainers) generate or respond to lists of behaviors presumed to be needed by teachers of a particular student population. Skill statements which result from professional consensus then serve as the backbone of a training sequence. Less frequently, employers or supervisors of teachers are asked to generate or respond to lists of skills hypothesized to be needed for successful teacher performance. The validity of competency statements totally based on professional judgment is naturally limited by the experience of those professionals with the student population in question. Administrators or supervisors who have had little direct contact with severely handicapped children may not be in a position to make enlightened recommendations about the content and focus of university training programs. On the other hand, to ask university faculty to specify the required skills is to fail to recognize the general naiveté with respect to this group of children and adults. Indeed, Meyen (Note 2) comments that, at best, most university departments react to the needs of the severely and profoundly handicapped "only academically." Nonetheless, one would probably want to empower university staffs to make their best guess about essential teacher competencies, and to modify that list according to their graduates' success in teaching the severely handicapped.

A more direct approach to the problem would be to observe "good" teachers as they work with their students, and to identify as necessary teacher competencies those skills required to meet role demands. The value of training statements or program competencies generated by such direct observation may be limited by several factors. First, there may be few "good teachers" of the severely handicapped for program developers to observe. Second, those competent teachers who do exist may not be operating in normal environments. That is, they may be teaching in institutional or private school settings, rather than within the public school system. As a result, anyone describing their performance would be bound to include some behaviors not expected of public school staff, and would similarly omit others that are central to public school functioning.

While none of these procedures for generating performance statements can stand alone, each of them may be used in combination to begin to delineate competencies for model personnel preparation for teachers of the severely handicapped. The initial information pool is small, but the training needs are too great to advocate that development be delayed until any single approach has undergone extensive replication and validation.

Even more than competency-based teacher education in other areas of disability, competency-based programs for teachers of the severely handicapped rely heavily on input from the severely handicapped students themselves. When one observes a teacher and describes his role-related behaviors, one naturally identifies competencies defined by student needs. With the severely impaired, however, this focus may be exaggerated: the behavior deficits and developmental needs of the pupils, rather than theories of retardation, define skills requirements for teachers. To hold that teacher competencies should be generated on the basis of pupil needs creates a somewhat paradoxical situation: when problems displayed by the severely handicapped define teacher competencies which, in turn, became the goals of university training programs, then the handicapped are, in fact, helping to educate the special educators.

An approach that evaluates competence in terms of the ultimate criterion of child behavior change is consonant with a position which focuses upon student behavior to generate competencies for the teacher trainee. While such a strategy for evaluating teachers is at odds with traditional trainee evaluation procedures (which may focus on attendance, appearance, compliance, progress through college course work, etc.) and even with certain competency-based approaches (those which focus on the acquisition of "knowledge" competencies), it is hardly a novel proposition:

> . . . potential teachers must be able to demonstrate that they can change public school students' behavior in prescribed ways *before* they receive a license to teach. (Brown & York, 1974, p. 7)

> Any "certification" program [should] require that the teaching credential be based on documentation of teacher change in child performance over time and on increasingly more complex tasks. . . Teachers should be expected to document that they have changed child behavior, and should be liable if they cannot. (Tawney, Note 1, p. 93)

> The ultimate test of the validity of a training program becomes the degree to which program objectives, when attained by student teachers, produce significant pupil gains in the classroom . . . [an] evaluation of the effects of program graduates on children's behavior is needed. (Stamm, 1975, p. 200)

An emphasis on documenting child behavior change, in fact, seems to be closely tied to the entire movement to secure services for severely handicapped citizens. Early advocates argued from a position that all children could benefit from appropriate educational programs, and presented behavior change data to support their case. Given the present state of the economy and the intense competition for federal training dollars, Tawney (Note 1) warns that programs for the severely handicapped must justify their existence by documenting their effectiveness in producing personal, social, and academic gains in their students.

It is clear that to hold child behavior change as the sole measure of teacher proficiency is an extreme and untenable position. Few programs would fail a teacher trainee for not producing satisfactory change in a severely handicapped student, if during the practicum, the trainee had been consistent in program implementation, had responded to his failure by systematic manipulations of program variables, and had incorporated supervisor suggestions regarding instructional delivery and development. Similarly, few would certify a trainee who did literally nothing, yet whose students were more skillful at the end of the semester. The focus on pupil change, however, does direct attention to the real function of teacher education programs.

In a framework which emphasizes child behavior change as a measure of teacher competence, all statements nominated for inclusion as training program competencies should be evaluated on the basis of whether they contribute to a teacher's success in changing children's behavior in desired directions. Much of the "knowledge" that programs find so easy to impart may lose importance when translated into program implications for children.

Statement of Teacher Competencies

Once teacher competencies have been identified—by examining the needs of severely and profoundly handicapped students and the teacher performances necessary to bring about behavioral changes in those students—then they must be formalized for consumer groups. Both potential students in the training program, and potential employers of program graduates, must be clear about what graduates should be able to do at the completion of training.

Partly because of the relative ease and familiarity of such an approach, many training programs have emphasized the development and verification of knowledge or informational competencies, at the expense of performance competencies related to effective interaction with pupils. A sampling of such informational competency statements might include:

> Discusses the history of service delivery to the severely and profoundly impaired.

> Writes a description of the "cascade system" for placement of handicapped individuals in educational programs.

> Discusses the relationship between frequency of a behavior and the length of an observational interval.

> Produces a written description of the purpose of conducting a task analysis of a concept.

> Is familiar with local and national agencies concerned primarily with the severely and profoundly impaired.

> Defines and identifies instances of the following: positive reinforcement; negative reinforce-

ment; primary, secondary, and generalized reinforcement; Premack principle.

The assumption behind such competency statements is, of course, that knowledge precedes application: information must be acquired before a teacher can be successful in delivering services to severely handicapped individuals, or be proficient in performances which incorporate positive or negative reinforcement, task analysis, and so on. Early program development efforts, it is argued, should focus on the identification of all those things a teacher of the severely handicapped should *know about* before he actually begins teaching a child. When one examines such competencies as "Lists common etiologies for severe and profound retardation," or "Prepares written discussion of the multiple baseline design," against such a criterion as, "Does this skill influence the teacher's ability to change children's behavior or to deliver quality services to severely handicapped pupils?," the argument that the former should serve as training program goals is not persuasive. Most informational competencies do not have much validity when one considers criterion performance for which teachers are trained. Seldom, if ever, are teachers called upon to "discuss developmental theory as it relates to assessing cognitive ability," or to "prepare a review of six studies using operant procedures with the severely handicapped." Meyen (Note 2) calls for institutions training personnel for work with the severely handicapped to resist the pattern of structuring competency-based programs which are "heavy on information."

In addition to the questionable validity of many knowledge competencies, their emphasis on information may undermine the power of competency-based programs in two important ways. First, when competencies are conceptualized as demonstrations of the mastery of discrete facts, then the number of individual competencies in any training program reaches a number great enough to defy any type of systematic implementation. Analysis of a training program into hundreds of competencies is elaborate and impressive, but hardly functional. Such a listing could represent an initial step in organizing a competency-based approach but, in this author's judgment, would require some consolidation and combination of entries before qualifying as a manageable training system.

A related problem is that, in such a system, the energy and attention of faculty trainers is consumed in monitoring student progress through the list of competencies. (Is the definition of akinetic seizures complete? Has he presented a coherent written description of how to remove and clean a child's braces?) Thus, the trainer's perspective is distorted, and the view of child behavior change as the goal of training is lost in the shadows of an elaborate checkoff system.

An alternative to requiring numerous informational competencies as prerequisites to application and performance would be a program whose competencies describe the roles and functions actually involved in a teacher's job (Lilly, 1976). Such statements would necessarily define fairly large units of behavior and involve several specific skills. Consider, for example, the following performance criteria:

1. Given at least two students, each exhibiting behavioral excesses that interfere with the delivery of instruction (e.g., self-injurious or stereotypical behavior), the trainee will design, write, and carry out an instructional program to eliminate or decrease the frequency of the target response.

   The completed instructional plan will include the following components:
   a. Behavioral statement of problem.
   b. Specification of program objective(s).
   c. Measurement procedures.
   d. Baseline performance data.
   e. Description of the intervention.
   f. Charted pupil performance data and evidence of formative evaluation.
   g. Procedures designed to enhance the generalization and maintenance of behavior change.

   Products must document behavior change or show systematic program revision on the basis of performance data and be acceptable to the supervisor/instructor.
2. In consultation with the classroom or agency teacher and university instructor, the trainee will identify one noncertified staff member or volunteer and train that individual:
   a. To state problems behaviorally.
   b. To collect and chart program data utilizing procedures and definitions already in effect.
   c. To implement an ongoing instructional program in an academic or pre-academic area.
   d. To implement an ongoing management program for a socially excessive behavior.
   e. To employ basic management techniques to accelerate desirable and decelerate undesirable behaviors throughout the day.

   The training program must include:
   a. Statement of specific training objectives and performance criteria.

b. Description of techniques to be used to modify staff and volunteer behavior.

c. A method to evaluate the effectiveness of training.

d. Summary of evaluation and suggestions for future training.

Both planning and outcomes must be judged acceptable by the instructor and the target audience.

Consider the first performance criterion above. In addition to some obvious requirements (e.g., to operationally define behaviors of concern, to collect and chart data), the trainee has to be able to list and define the basic procedures to weaken behaviors, to consider the factors influencing the effectiveness of the various alternatives, to rationalize his selection of a procedure, and so on. Each performance criterion requires a rather sophisticated process of integrating knowledge and performance into a whole which approximates the actual demands of the job. Trainee competence is assessed on this type of problem-solving, rather than on a series of splinter skills taken out of their natural context. To state training competencies as large performance units with a number of component skills is both efficient and criterion-valid.

Although mastery of information is inferred from successful application and generally is not evaluated independently, there are instances where informational competencies are appropriate. The roles for which personnel were being trained may require informational competencies in addition to, or in lieu of, performance criteria. For example, since a teacher might reasonably be expected to define verbally "least restrictive alternative" during an interdisciplinary staffing on a child, then mastery of that information is an appropriate competency statement. In situations where lack of information might result in physical harm to a student (e.g., moving or positioning a child with cerebral palsy, handling a seizure), then knowledge competencies are important prerequisites to performance. However, if the task is to train numeral discrimination, then prior independent assessment of the trainee's understanding of the discrimination training literature (e.g., the research on intra/extradimensional shifts, errorless learning, match-to-sample, etc.) is simply not justified. Rather, such areas should be evaluated as they are incorporated into the actual instructional task.

Competency statements represent terminal behaviors of the training program and, as such, bear a great resemblance to instructional objectives. Like their counterparts, all competency statements should identify a trainee behavior, the conditions under which that behavior is to be demonstrated, and the criterion for successful performance. So far it has been suggested: (a) that the trainee behavior be related to child behavior change rather than to paper-and-pencil performance; (b), that the conditions (location, complexity) of performance approximate those the teacher is likely to encounter on the job; and (c), that the criterion of training competency, in most cases, be documented pupil change.

Competency Specification

An inclusive list of the competencies required of an effective teacher of the severely and profoundly handicapped has yet to be drawn up. Traditionally a teacher's role (and its attendant competencies) has been limited to giving direct instruction in basic academic areas. Responsibilities for community involvement, parent liaison, training of paraprofessionals, and curriculum development activities have been minimal. However, given the lack of appropriately trained educational support personnel, the extreme characteristics of severely handicapped students, and the evolving pattern of providing services to them, the list of requisite teacher skills is growing at an alarming rate. Since it is likely that teachers entering the market during the next five to ten years will have major responsibilities for quality control and program development in the systems that employ them (Meyen, Note 2), it is imperative that their training do more than develop competence in direct instruction.

While there is probably no single set of competency statements that is "correct" for the role of teacher of the severely handicapped (because, for example, teachers in sparsely populated areas may need more or different skills than their counterparts in urban or suburban systems), many suggestions have been offered for grouping competency statements into clusters (e.g., Certo & York, Note 3; Horner, Holvoet, & Rinnie, Note 4; Stainbach et al., 1976). Focusing on child behavior change as the core of professional competence, one might try to organize competencies as they relate to the actual instruction of severely handicapped students. In Table 1, the author has tried to identify areas in which those working with the severely and profoundly handicapped need to be competent:

1. Management of the environment (political, social, and physical) to support the delivery

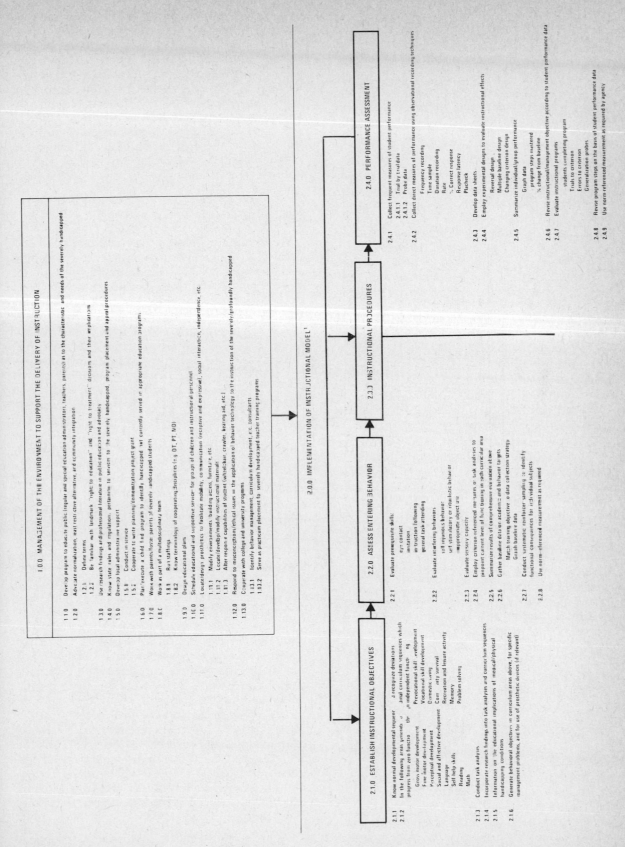

1.0.0 MANAGEMENT OF THE ENVIRONMENT TO SUPPORT THE DELIVERY OF INSTRUCTION

- 1.1.0 Develop program to educate public (regular and special education administrators, teachers, parents) as to the characteristic and needs of the severely handicapped
- 1.2.0 Advocate normalization, least restrictive alternative, and community integration
  - 1.2.1 Define terms
  - 1.2.2 Be familiar with landmark "right to education" and "right to treatment" decisions and their implications
- 1.3.0 Use research findings and professional literature in public education and advocacy
- 1.4.0 Know state rules and regulations pertaining to services to the severely handicapped, program placement and appeal procedures
- 1.5.0 Develop local administrative support
  - 1.5.1 Conduct in service
  - 1.5.2 Cooperate to write planning/demonstration project grant
- 1.6.0 Plan/execute a child find program to identify handicapped not currently served in appropriate education programs
- 1.7.0 Work with parents/foster parents of severely handicapped students
- 1.8.0 Work as part of a multidisciplinary team
  - 1.8.1 Run staffings
  - 1.8.2 Know terminology of cooperating disciplines (e.g. OT, PT, MD)
- 1.9.0 Design educational plans
- 1.10.0 Schedule educational and supportive service for groups of children and instructional personnel
- 1.11.0 Locate/design prosthetics to facilitate mobility, communication (receptive and expressive), social interaction, independence, etc.
  - 1.11.1 Modify environments (building access, furniture, etc.
  - 1.11.2 Locate/develop/modify instructional materials
  - 1.11.3 Alter response capabilities of student (wheelchair, crawler, hearing aid, etc.)
- 1.12.0 Respond to misconceptions/ethical issues in the application of behavior technology to the instruction of the severely/profoundly handicapped
- 1.13.0 Cooperate with college and university programs
  - 1.13.1 Identify behavior management, curriculum development, etc. consultants
  - 1.13.2 Serve as practicum placement for severely handicapped teacher training programs

2.0.0 IMPLEMENTATION OF INSTRUCTIONAL MODEL[1]

2.1.0 ESTABLISH INSTRUCTIONAL OBJECTIVES

- 2.1.1 Know normal developmental sequence and recognize deviations
- 2.1.2 In the following areas generate longitudinal curriculum sequences which progress from zero functioning through independent functioning
  - Gross motor development
  - Fine motor development
  - Perceptual development
  - Social and affective development
  - Language
  - Self help skills
  - Reading
  - Math
  - Prevocational skill development
  - Vocational skill development
  - Domestic living
  - Community survival
  - Recreation and leisure activity
  - Memory
  - Problem solving
- 2.1.3 Conduct task analyses
- 2.1.4 Incorporate research findings into task analyses and curriculum sequences
- 2.1.5 Information on the educational implications of medical/physical handicapping conditions
- 2.1.6 Generate behavioral objectives in curriculum areas above, for specific management problems, and for use of prosthetic devices (if relevant)

2.2.0 ASSESS ENTERING BEHAVIOR

- 2.2.1 Evaluate prerequisite skills:
  - eye contact
  - imitation
  - instruction following
  - general task attending
- 2.2.2 Evaluate interfering behaviors
  - self injurious behavior
  - self stimulatory or ritualistic behavior
  - inappropriate object use
- 2.2.3 Evaluate sensory capacity
- 2.2.4 Employ criterion-referenced measures or task analyses to pinpoint current level of functioning in each curricular area
- 2.2.5 Summarize results of comprehensive evaluation above
- 2.2.6 Gather baseline data on academic and behavior targets
  - Match training objective to data collection strategy
  - Graph baseline data
- 2.2.7 Conduct systematic reinforcer sampling to identify functional consequences for individual subjects
- 2.2.8 Use norm-referenced measurement as required

2.3.0 INSTRUCTIONAL PROCEDURES

2.4.0 PERFORMANCE ASSESSMENT

- 2.4.1 Collect frequent measures of student performance
  - 2.4.1.1 Trial by trial data
  - 2.4.1.2 Probe data
- 2.4.2 Collect direct measures of performance using observational recording techniques
  - Frequency recording
  - Time sample
  - Duration recording
  - Rate
  - % Correct response
  - Response latency
  - Placheck
- 2.4.3 Develop data sheets
- 2.4.4 Employ experimental designs to evaluate instructional effects
  - Reversal design
  - Multiple baseline design
  - Changing criterion design
- 2.4.5 Summarize individual/group performance
  - Graph data
  - program steps mastered
  - % change from baseline
- 2.4.6 Revise instructional/management objective according to student performance data
- 2.4.7 Evaluate instructional programs
  - students completing program
  - Trials to criterion
  - Errors to criterion
  - Generalization probes
- 2.4.8 Revise program steps on the basis of student performance data
- 2.4.9 Use norm-referenced measurement as required by agency

Table 1 (*Continued*)

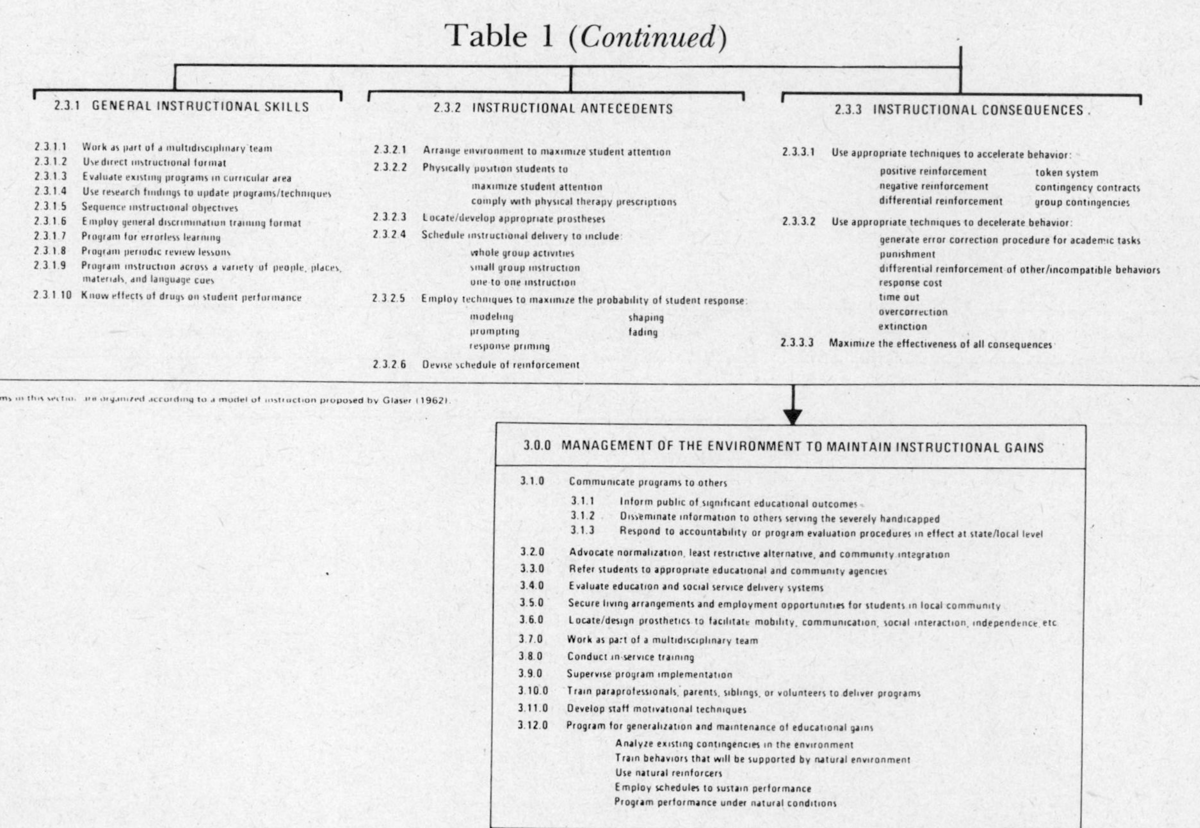

2.3.1 GENERAL INSTRUCTIONAL SKILLS

2.3.1.1 Work as part of a multidisciplinary team
2.3.1.2 Use direct instructional format
2.3.1.3 Evaluate existing programs in curricular area
2.3.1.4 Use research findings to update programs/techniques
2.3.1.5 Sequence instructional objectives
2.3.1.6 Employ general discrimination training format
2.3.1.7 Program for errorless learning
2.3.1.8 Program periodic review lessons
2.3.1.9 Program instruction across a variety of people, places, materials, and language cues
2.3.1.10 Know effects of drugs on student performance

2.3.2 INSTRUCTIONAL ANTECEDENTS

2.3.2.1 Arrange environment to maximize student attention
2.3.2.2 Physically position students to
- maximize student attention
- comply with physical therapy prescriptions

2.3.2.3 Locate/develop appropriate prostheses
2.3.2.4 Schedule instructional delivery to include:
- whole group activities
- small group instruction
- one to one instruction

2.3.2.5 Employ techniques to maximize the probability of student response:
- modeling
- prompting
- response priming
- shaping
- fading

2.3.2.6 Devise schedule of reinforcement

2.3.3 INSTRUCTIONAL CONSEQUENCES

2.3.3.1 Use appropriate techniques to accelerate behavior:
- positive reinforcement
- negative reinforcement
- differential reinforcement
- token system
- contingency contracts
- group contingencies

2.3.3.2 Use appropriate techniques to decelerate behavior:
- generate error correction procedure for academic tasks
- punishment
- differential reinforcement of other/incompatible behaviors
- response cost
- time out
- overcorrection
- extinction

2.3.3.3 Maximize the effectiveness of all consequences

[1]Items in this section are organized according to a model of instruction proposed by Glaser (1962).

3.0.0 MANAGEMENT OF THE ENVIRONMENT TO MAINTAIN INSTRUCTIONAL GAINS

3.1.0 Communicate programs to others
- 3.1.1 Inform public of significant educational outcomes
- 3.1.2 Disseminate information to others serving the severely handicapped
- 3.1.3 Respond to accountability or program evaluation procedures in effect at state/local level

3.2.0 Advocate normalization, least restrictive alternative, and community integration
3.3.0 Refer students to appropriate educational and community agencies
3.4.0 Evaluate education and social service delivery systems
3.5.0 Secure living arrangements and employment opportunities for students in local community
3.6.0 Locate/design prosthetics to facilitate mobility, communication, social interaction, independence, etc.
3.7.0 Work as part of a multidisciplinary team
3.8.0 Conduct in-service training
3.9.0 Supervise program implementation
3.10.0 Train paraprofessionals, parents, siblings, or volunteers to deliver programs
3.11.0 Develop staff motivational techniques
3.12.0 Program for generalization and maintenance of educational gains
- Analyze existing contingencies in the environment
- Train behaviors that will be supported by natural environment
- Use natural reinforcers
- Employ schedules to sustain performance
- Program performance under natural conditions

of instruction to the severely/profoundly handicapped.
2. Implementation of instruction.
3. Management of the environment (political, social, and physical) to maintain instructional gains.

The skills listed under each heading differ in the extent to which their presence or absence might have direct implications for the instructions pupils receive. Performance areas identified under "Implementation of the Instructional Model" are probably the most directly related to changing child behavior, while those related to support for instructional delivery and to programming for maintenance of instructional gains are somewhat indirect in their immediate educational impact.

The format of Table 1 violates earlier guidelines for how competencies should be stated: there are no conditions, behaviors, or criteria, nor are statements combined to describe a performance comparable to what a teacher would face on the job. Instead, in order to convey the tremendous range of necessary competencies, the outline superficially identifies relatively isolated skill areas. The listing is admittedly arbitrary at points (concern was more for identifying skill areas than for their placement under the only/suitable heading) and, in all probability, incomplete. In spite of the fact that table entries would have to be expanded and elaborated before they could be used in a training program, the presentation may, nonetheless, have the following advantages:

1. It provides a framework for identifying competencies that may have been overlooked.
2. It provides a model for differentiating the focus of competencies required of personnel at various levels of training or responsibility.

While there is clearly some sequence in which criterion performances are achieved on the job (producing change must precede any efforts to maintain that change), skills areas should not necessarily be developed in the order outlined here.

Impact of Teacher Competencies on Training Programs

Some have suggested that a necessary prerequisite for the development of programs for teachers of the severely handicapped is that the behavior of teacher trainers at colleges and universities be modified (Bijou & Wilcox, Note 5). Regardless of whether the metamorphosis in higher education comes before or after the conceptualization of a training program in the area of severely handicapped, there is no doubt that the changes will be wide-ranging. The expansion of teacher education to include the preparation of teachers of the severely and profoundly impaired will require significant change from the patterns of teacher training to date.

Teacher Trainers Must Significantly Expand their Concepts of Curriculum

It is no longer sufficient to prepare teachers with methods to teach reading, writing, and arithmetic. University trainers must concentrate on equipping their graduates with the skills to teach severely handicapped students to survive in the world from the moment they wake up in the morning until they go to bed at night. To undertake a program to train teachers of the severely handicapped is to assume responsibility for dealing with behaviors that have rarely been the concern of the public schools or the university trainer.

Teacher Trainers Must Be Increasingly Experimental in Outlook

It is imperative that university programs recognize that the skills of their graduates are limited by the information in the grasp of the program faculty. Given the relative naiveté of the field, it is unlikely that any one person or program has very many answers to the problems posed by the severely handicapped. To generate the necessary information, teacher trainers must form a partnership with researchers to develop and refine techniques that are responsive to and effective with the myriad problems presented by the severely and profoundly impaired. The long-standing dichotomy between teacher training and research cannot be allowed to stand if the student group is to be served.

Programs Must Draw upon Resources Outside of Special Education

New and functional alliances must be formed between teacher trainers and those in other disciplines who may have skills or information relevant to the severely handicapped. Those responsible for training teachers must be able to draw upon resources in physical and occupational therapy, therapeutic recreation, nursing, vocational and technical education, speech and language therapy, psychology, law, and social service delivery if they are to provide trainees with the necessary range of competence. A commitment to train teachers of the severely handicapped must include a genuine willingness to break down barriers between the university and the community, as well as the traditional departmental barriers within the university itself. Needs of the severely handicapped are not met by maintenance of territoriality and the professional status quo.

Training Programs Must Become Truly Field-Based

Practicum experiences and university course requirements must be integrated (not just correlated), and the latter must be continually reshaped by input from the field. Both the performance of teacher trainees and the particular needs of the severely handicapped students being served must be functional in modifying course content and sequence.

University Faculty Must Move into the Field

There are several factors that exert pressure on faculty to move out of their offices and into the schools. First, they ought not to be content with mere academic knowledge of the population for which they are training teachers. The demands of severely handicapped children and adults are significantly more dramatic than those of the mildly handicapped. In order for the training program to reflect this reality, the trainer would do well to expose himself to it. Besides providing an important form of faculty in-service, a move into the field would help meet another major need in severely handicapped personnel preparation: trainee supervision. Rarely do the teachers of the severely handicapped found in the public school system exhibit skills similar to those being developed in any given training program. Consequently, they cannot serve as appropriate models and supervisors for teacher trainees. Faced with a dearth of models in the environment and the responsibility to train students and document their competence, the university faculty member has few places to turn, other than to himself. The heavy responsibility of program supervision cannot be ignored. However, when competent program graduates are hired locally (which is, in part, the goal of any training program), then some responsibility for trainee supervision may be transferred to them.

Programs Must Be Capable of Delivering In-Service Instruction of High Quality

If the pressure for the delivery of educational services to severely handicapped students was, of necessity, relieved by the hiring of untrained personnel, then university trainers should devise a means of providing these teachers in-service instruction, supervision, and competency development comparable to that delivered to full-time students. In instances where the severely and profoundly handicapped are being taught by uncertified teachers, an in-service program would serve to integrate these experienced personnel into the educational mainstream. In-service training cannot be regarded as secondary; it is a major means of improving the services available to the severely handicapped.

Great Care Must Be Taken to Recruit and Select Students for Training Programs

Because the severely handicapped are a greater challenge than other special populations, and as a result programs training teachers of the severely and profoundly impaired are likely to be demanding and inclusive, it is important that students in those programs be both talented and committed. Brown and York (1974) have identified some of the difficulties in recruiting teacher trainees for the severely handicapped: (a) few students have had exposure to severely handicapped children or adults prior to college and, as a result, few start out intending to become teachers of the severely handicapped; (b) students see other disability areas in special education as more glamorous and interesting; (c) some university students may develop initial interest on grounds that may fail to sustain them throughout a rigorous teacher preparation program. If excellence in the training of teachers of the severely handicapped is to be achieved, these obstacles must be overcome. Program coordinators must develop systems for actively recruiting students and for developing in them over the course of training, not only skills but a commitment to serving the severely handicapped.

The recruitment of prospective teachers of the severely and profoundly handicapped should probably draw on disciplines outside of education and special education. The competencies required of those who will be responsible for the education of the severely handicapped are such that individuals whose preparation has been in psychology, speech and language therapy, and occupational or physical therapy have very appropriate backgrounds.

Training Programs Must Assume Some Responsibility for Student Motivation

Because the children and adults with whom the teacher trainee will work are by definition different, difficult, and on a low level of functioning, it is likely that the usual rewards available to teachers will be somewhat attenuated. In order to maintain student participation with high levels of effort and enthusiasm, programs must prepare teachers who are reinforced by child behavior change, and should consciously schedule academic and peer group events to maintain trainee morale. No one is the better if programs turn out graduates who are competent but "burned out."

Problems Facing Competency-Based Education for Teachers of the Severely Handicapped

In addition to the rather substantial tasks of identifying and generating appropriate competency statements and modifying program content in response to input from the field, several other dilemmas confront programs that train teachers of the severely handicapped. Perhaps the most significant of these is the availability (rather than non-availability) of appropriate (i.e., normal and least restrictive) practicum placements. The mere availability of severely handicapped students does not ensure a viable training situation. In states where education for the severely and profoundly impaired is not mandated or really implemented, teacher trainers are faced with the question of how to prepare public school teachers when no public school training sites are available, and of how to train students to evaluate the *educational relevance* of physical/medical conditions in facilities where only physical/medical *maintenance* is provided. While there is surely no single solution to this version of the chicken-or-the-egg dilemma (which comes first: the practicum sites or the teachers?), the problem of appropriate practicum placements is one which must be directly confronted by those who have committed themselves to the competency-based approach. Field sites are crucial, since students need an environment in which to develop and demonstrate those skills learned in the university training program.

In response to the problems of locating sites which are compatible with the goals of the training program, some (e.g., Meyen, Note 2) have suggested a return to the laboratory school concept and have argued in favor of university-operated direct service programs as vehicles for training. Such a pattern would be convenient for both the trainer and teacher trainee. However, since a lab school on a university campus is probably as non-normal as a private or institutional program (from both the pupils' and trainees' points of view), it would seem more appropriate in the long run for universities to continue their involvement in current practicum sites (whatever they may be), while at the same time investing their energy in working with public school systems to develop the local support and resources needed to serve the severely and profoundly handicapped in the public school domain.

The question of role differentiation is another problem facing those committed to competency-based training for teachers of the severely handicapped. Given current patterns of staffing, it is likely that personnel at a number of levels (paraprofessional, bachelor teacher, master teacher, administrator, and supervisor) will be involved in providing educational programs for severely handicapped children and adults. If universities offer training in a number of degree programs, then surely the competencies defining the various levels should delineate substantially different performance domains. But how *does* one differentiate the competencies required at various levels in the educational or administrative hierarchies? Just how should the repertoire of a master's degree student differ from that of a bachelor teacher (in sheer number of competencies, frequency of application, theoretical sophistication, magnitude of pupil change expected, etc.)? Precisely which competencies are required of which roles will depend in part on the educational service delivery model in the particular state. However, a possible solution to the dilemma would be to select appropriate competencies, using the scheme presented in Table 1. Paraprofessional training programs would be required to demonstrate student competency in the management of antecedents and consequences during instructional delivery (2.3.2 and 2.3.3). Training programs at the bachelor's level would be responsible for developing and verifying skills related to program development, pupil monitoring, and program revision (2.1.0, 2.2.0, 2.3.0, and 2.4.0). Thus their skills would extend far beyond those of the paraprofessional but would still be limited to the implementation of the instructional model. In addition to skillful performance of all competencies in the instructional model segment (2.0.0), programs training teachers at the master's level might be required to develop in their trainees selected indirect skills (such as working with parents and devising educational prosthetics) related to facilitating the delivery of instruction (1.0.0) and programming for generalization and maintenance (3.0.0). Programs training administrators should emphasize some selected skills in the performance assessment area (2.4.0), in addition to competencies in managing the environment to support delivery instruction and to maintain educational gains.

A final, and certainly futuristic, problem for competency-based programs training teachers for the severely handicapped arises from the expectation that such training programs can be effective. Teacher trainees, in the course of their education, will demonstrate that they can toilet train, eliminate self-injurious behavior, develop generalized imitation, and program for the acquisition of basic academic and self-care skills. The problem is what subsequent generations of trainees will do to demonstrate competence once a large percentage of the practicum population has been toilet trained, is no longer self-destructive, can imitate, and so on. At such a point, trainers could either fall back upon knowledge competencies (e.g., outline a program to toilet train) or simulation (e.g., "teach" a fellow trainee to imitate) in order to make judgments of trainee skill level. If either alternative is adopted, then the statement of training competencies must be modified to reflect such changes in trainee skills and experience.

Conclusion

Since the role of the teacher of the severely handicapped is immensely complex, and, as a result, the job of the teacher trainer equally so, it would be wise for those seriously involved in such efforts to share competency statements among themselves. In that way, programs could learn from one another and could spend their program development time more productively than by duplicating efforts. Along these lines, an effort is currently being made by a task force of the American Association for the Education of the Severely/Profoundly Handicapped to draft a set of minimal competencies which could be used as guidelines to develop or evaluate training programs preparing personnel to work with severely and profoundly impaired students (Certo, Bricker, Horner, Wilcox, & York, Note 6).

Given the current state of the art (or the technology, if you prefer), it is crucial to maintain open and constructive communication between disciplines and programs serving the severely handicapped. At the same time, however, it may be appropriate to limit the number of programs preparing teachers for this population to those locations which meet two criteria: some degree of faculty expertise and commitment to the severely handicapped and a sufficient number of severely handicapped students to support a training program. In that way, the probability of superior teacher training and services for the severely handicapped are increased without an accompanying proliferation of instant experts and instant programs, whose appearance can only serve to undermine public confidence and professional credibility.

Reference Notes

1. Tawney, J. W. *Prerequisite conditions for the establishment of educational programs for the severely retarded.* Paper presented at the National Association for Retarded Citizens conference on education of severely and profoundly retarded students, New Orleans, March, 1975.
2. Meyen, E. L. *Preparing educational personnel for the severely and profoundly mentally retarded.* Paper presented at the National Association for Retarded Citizens conference on education of severely and profoundly retarded students, New Orleans, March, 1975.
3. Certo, N., & York, R. Minimal competencies for teachers of severely and profoundly handicapped students. Madison, Wisconsin: Department of Studies in Behavioral Disabilities, University of Wisconsin, 1976.
4. Horner, R. D., Holvoet, J., & Rinne, T. *Competency specifications for teachers of the severely and profoundly handicapped.* Lawrence, Kansas: Department of Special Education, University of Kansas, 1976.
5. Bijou, S. W., & Wilcox, B. *The feasibility of providing effective educational programs for the severely and profoundly retarded.* Paper presented at the National Association for Retarded Citizens conference on education of severely and profoundly retarded students, New Orleans, March, 1975.
6. Certo, N., Bricker, D. D., Horner, R. D., Wilcox, B., & York, R. Teacher Competencies Task Force. (Working draft.) The American Association for the Education of the Severely/Profoundly Handicapped.

References

Brown, L., & York, R. Developing programs for severely handicapped students: Teacher training and classroom instruction. *Focus on Exceptional Children,* 1974, *6,* 1–11.

Glaser, R. Psychology and instructional technology. In R. Glaser (Ed.). *Training research and education.* Pittsburgh: University of Pittsburgh Press, 1962, pp. 1–30.

Lilly, M. S. Competency based teacher education: A personal perspective. *Behavior Disorders,* 1976, *1,* 105–111.

Sontag, E., Burke, P. J., & York, R. Considerations for serving the severely handicapped in the public schools. *Education and Training of the Mentally Retarded,* 1973, *8,* 20–26.

Stainbach, S., Stainbach, W., & Maurer, S. Training teachers for the severely and profoundly handicapped: A new frontier. *Exceptional Children,* 1976, *42,* 203–210.

Stamm, J. M. A general model for the design of a competency-based special education professional preparation program. *Education and Training of the Mentally Retarded,* 1975, *10,* 196–200.

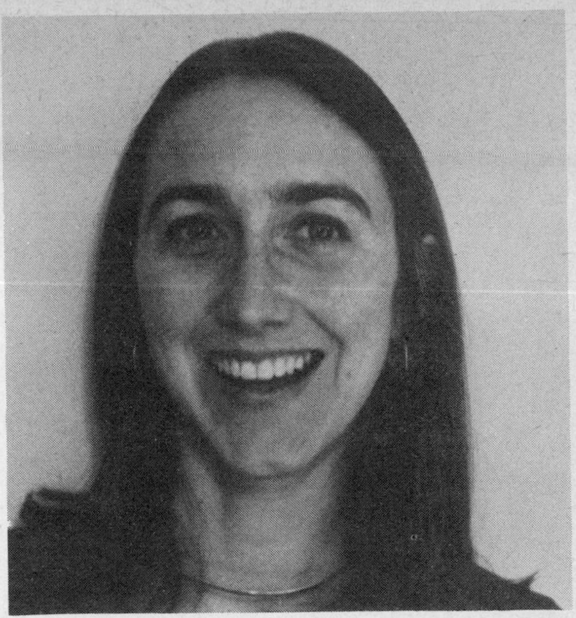

BARBARA WILCOX serves as Coordinator of the Severe Behavior Handicaps program at the University of Illinois in Urbana-Champaign. She previously taught at Temple University, Philadelphia, and also served as Education Coordinator at Woodhaven Center, a Philadelphia institution for the severely and profoundly retarded.

A Competency-Based Approach to Preparing Teachers of the Severely and Profoundly Handicapped: Perspective II

R. DON HORNER

University of Kansas

There are at least three major groups of students who might seek preparation as teachers of the severely and profoundly handicapped: high school graduates who have decided to embark upon a career in teaching; recent college graduates who have completed a program in regular education, psychology, human development, behavioral disabilities, occupational or physical therapy, or vocational rehabilitation, and regular and special education teachers in the field who have elected or have been assigned a class for the severely and profoundly handicapped.

Sontag, Burke, and York (1973) have pointed out that many of the new classes for the severely and profoundly handicapped are likely to be staffed by teachers with little or no preparation in this area. This is especially likely if pre-service preparation programs at the college and university level lag behind the implementation of legislative and judicial mandates requiring provision of educational opportunities for all school-aged children. Staffing a classroom for the severely and profoundly handicapped with a teacher who has no preparation in this area is somewhat akin to staffing a surgical unit of a hospital with an intern. This should not be done, but it may be the only way such classes can be started. If it *is* done, these teachers will have to be given in-service training. In this event, the only educational and professional prerequisites that can be required are those the teachers bring with them into the program. Sontag (1975) has called for institutions of higher education to put equal emphasis on pre-service and in-service training. In-service training programs as currently constituted are often expensive and inefficient, especially in predominately rural states. If an in-service preparation program is demanded by the needs of teachers in the field, it should be provided but viewed as a temporary program, rather than as a viable alternative to the pre-service approach.

A pre-service approach offers more options for the educational and professional prerequisites. If none are required, an individual could enter the preparation program directly from high school. However, Brown and York (1974) have pointed out that: (a) few college students have had exposure to severely handicapped children before entering college; (b) few start college intending to become teachers of severely handicapped students; (c) other disability areas attract more interest than do the severely handicapped; and (d) some may develop an initial interest on grounds that fail to sustain them through a rigorous teacher preparation program. At this time, it seems unlikely that an individual entering college could have either the information or experience necessary to select a career in teaching the severely and profoundly handicapped. Also, in those states where the completion of a teacher preparation program leading to certification in regular education is a prerequisite to preparing for certification in special education, it is often impossible or very difficult to enter a program in special education as a college freshman. The prerequisites for entering a preparation program in the area of the severely and profoundly handicapped would appear to be, at least, status as a member of the junior class and, at most, an undergraduate degree and certification in regular education. Thus, a program preparing teachers of the severely and profoundly

The preparation of this article was supported by grant OEG-0-74-2766 from the Bureau of Education for the Handicapped. However, the opinions expressed herein do not necessarily reflect the position or policy of the U.S. Office of Education and no official endorsement by the U.S. Office of Education should be inferred. The author wishes to acknowledge the contributions of Gary Campbell, Doug Guess, Leonard Lavis, Edward Meyen, Trudy Rinne, Wayne Sailor, Charles Spellman, Larry Thompson, and Dennis Tucker in developing the program and to offer a special acknowledgement to Debby Maxon, Jennifer Holvoet, and Bonnie Utley whose effectiveness as practicum site supervisors has been largely responsible for the success of the project.

handicapped should probably be developed so that a student could enter at either the senior year, as a final year of undergraduate specialized training, or as a first-year graduate student who has either just completed an undergraduate program or has elected to return from the field to pursue an advanced degree.

The provision for completing specialized training at the undergraduate level is compatible with the career ladder proposed for the teaching associate training program designed to provide additional personnel in classes for the severely and profoundly handicapped (Tucker, et al., in press). It is also compatible with public school system budgets that must continually absorb new programs despite a restricted tax base. School systems can employ individuals with undergraduate degrees at a substantial savings. This solution is not altogether compatible with effective training, if that training has to be compressed to fit within existing undergraduate degree requirements; nor is it compatible with the recruitment of individuals for preparation as teachers of the severely and profoundly handicapped who are pursuing undergraduate degrees in disciplines outside of education. The competencies required for teachers of the severely and profoundly handicapped are also a relevant part of the training of individuals whose undergraduate preparation has been in psychology, speech pathology, occupational or physical therapy, and the like.

Competency Specifications

Sontag, Burke and York (1973) pointed out the relationship between the level of the students' disability and the competence required of teachers. As they put it, "The more pronounced the level of disability, the more specific and precise are the competencies required of the teachers" (p. 23).

The basic teaching and training format used in competency-based programs for teachers of the severely and profoundly handicapped should be the same one advocated by Bijou and Wilcox-Cole (1975) for the education of those children served by such teachers. This format includes: "(a) setting goals in behavioral terms; (b) assessing current functioning with respect to these goals; (c) applying learning and motivational principles; (d) monitoring the effectiveness of teaching; and (e) arranging conditions to maintain and generalize the gains achieved" (pp. 13–14).

The objective of a curriculum to prepare teachers of the severely and profoundly handicapped should be to establish three broad blocks of competencies in the repertoire of each student teacher, as follows:

1. Competencies that are *directly* related to changing student behavior. This is in line with Brown and York (1974), who state that one view of an instructional competency is "a set of behaviors a teacher engages in that result in empirically verifiable changes in the behavioral repertoires of the students in his or her charge" (p. 5.). Such specific competencies as contingent use of attention, timing of prompts, and ignoring irrelevant behavior are included in this block. This block of competencies should be the primary focus of the teacher training program and must go well beyond the traditional "methods" courses of the past.

2. Competencies that are *indirectly* related to changing student behavior, including such specific competencies as determining potential reinforcers, performing a task analysis, and scheduling classroom activities.

3. Competencies that currently have an *unknown* relationship to student behavior but appear to be important to professional performance in the field. Such specific competencies as knowing the legal rights of the handicapped, the medical complications accompanying certain syndromes, and the principle of normalization fall into this block.

Within each block there should be both informational and performance competencies. Informational competencies are those that specify the information that must be acquired by a teacher trainee in order to achieve a performance competency. Often, several informational competencies are prerequisite to acquisition of a performance competency. For example, before a teacher trainee can acquire the performance competency requiring contingent use of a reinforcer, that trainee must have learned exactly what constitutes a reinforcer and a contingency.

A definitive listing of all the informational and performance competencies required to become an effective teacher of the severely and profoundly handicapped has not yet been drafted. Such a list would have hundreds of entries and is beyond the scope of this article. One attempt at such a list, with heavy emphasis on a behavioral approach, has been completed by Horner, Holvoet, and Rinne (1976). The list probably has omitted many required competencies and may include many that are not required. The total training program at the University of Kansas currently has 322 informational competencies and 128 performance competencies, compiled through an analysis of the literature, expert opinion, direct observation of teacher behavior, and lists prepared by teachers in the field and students in the program (*cf*. Rynders, Bruininks, & Gordon, 1974).

Once the competencies have been specified, they should be organized into clusters which form the basis for a training model. Certo and York (1976) have organized competencies into six broad clusters, as follows: general, miscellaneous, and indirectly related service delivery; curriculum; teaching techniques; assessment; measurement and evaluation; and behavior management. Stainback et al. (1976) have classified the training needs of prospective teachers of the severely and profoundly handicapped as: diagnostic evaluation, curriculum, methodology, inter-disciplinary teamwork, extensive field experience, parent training, and use of prosthetic aids.

Horner, et al. (1976) have organized the informational and performance competencies into 25 training modules, as follows:

1. *Right to Education*. Delineation of the history of the right-to-education and right-to-treatment concepts through relevant legislative and judicial actions, and the implications of these actions for the education of severely and profoundly handicapped individuals (*q.v*. Lippman & Goldberg, 1973; Mental Health Law Project, 1973; Sheldon & Sherman, 1974).

2. *Introduction to Operant Behavior*. Basic procedures and techniques that enable a teacher to establish functional relationships between teaching and the behavior of severely and profoundly handicapped individuals (*q.v*. Becker, Engelmann, & Thomas, 1971; Birnbrauer, Burchard, & Burchard, 1970; Gardner, 1971; Kazdin, 1975; Miller 1975; Neisworth & Smith, 1973; Thompson & Grabowski, 1972).

3. *A Behavioral Approach to Special Education*. An introduction to the application of operant procedures in a "classroom" context, specifically those procedures most relevant to the education of severely and profoundly handicapped individuals (*q.v*. Brown, 1973; Brown & York, 1974; Haring & Lovitt, 1967; Hollis & Gorton, 1967; Lake, 1974; Luckey & Addison, 1974; Shearer & Shearer, 1972; Sontag, Burke, & York, 1973; Williams, Brown, & Certo, 1975).

4. *Basic Classroom Participation*. A series of exercises leading to the acquisition of specific performance competencies while the student teacher assists the classroom teacher in educational programming.

5. *Measuring Operant Behavior*. Learning the measures used to convert behavior into a numerical form (*q.v*. Bijou, Peterson, & Ault, 1968; Browning & Stover, 1973; Cooper, 1974; Hall, 1971; Hursh, Wildgen, Minkin, Sherman, & Wolf, 1972; Kozloff, 1971).

6. *Evaluation of Operant Procedures*. The arrangement of baseline and training conditions in reversal and multiple baseline designs, probe procedures, and traditional pretest-posttest type evaluation.

7. *Strengthening Operant Behavior*. Procedures for developing and increasing operant behavior through such techniques as successive approximation, chaining, differential reinforcement, modeling, prompting, use of the Premack principle, etc. (*q.v*. Bandura, 1969; Whaley & Malott, 1971).

8. *Weakening Operant Behavior*. Procedures for decreasing operant behavior, such as extinction, time-out from positive reinforcement, contingent application of an aversive stimulus, overcorrection, differential reinforcement of other behavior, etc. (*q.v*. Forehand and Baumeister, 1976; Gardner, 1969).

9. *Schedules of Reinforcement*. The procedures for reinforcement control of operant behavior through such schedules as continuous, fixed-ratio, fixed-interval, variable ratio, variable interval, and differential reinforcement of high and low rates. (*q.v*. Spradlin, Girardeau, & Corte, 1965).

10. *Generalization and Discrimination of Operant Behavior*. The procedures for establishing, broadening, transferring, or reducing the capacity of stimuli to set the occasion for operant behavior (*q.v*. Gold & Scott, 1971; Terrace, 1963a; 1963b; Touchette, 1968, 1971).

11. *Programming for Normalization*. Understanding of the normalization principle and programs which effectively reduce dehumanizing practices and have as their goal progress toward and integration of an individual into the next highest level of a continuum of less restrictive environments (*q.v*. Wolfensberger, Nirge, Olshansky, Perske, & Roos, 1972).

12. *Programming Prosthetic Environments*. Procedures whereby prosthetic devices and procedures are used to build or set the occasion for behaviors currently absent or too weak to permit the individual to accrue naturally occurring reinforcers afforded by the environment (*q.v*. Bare, Boettke & Waggoner, 1962; Bergstrom & Coles, 1971; Finnie, 1970; Hoffman, 1970; Macey, Stancliffe, Beumer, & Roper, 1974; Robinault, 1973; Rosenberg, 1968).

13. *Programming Engaging Environments*. Procedures whereby reinforcers afforded by the environment are provided or strengthened, and procedures for the scheduling and zoning of activities (*q.v*. Bricker & Bricker, 1971, 1972, 1973; Connor, Batarseh, Massey,

& Cicenia, 1972; Doke & Risley, 1972; Hewett, Taylor, & Artuso, 1970; Jacobson, Bushell, & Risley, 1969; LeLaurin & Risley, 1972; Quilitch & Risley, 1973; Rodriquez & Sproles, 1967; Stabler, Gibson, Cutting, & Lawrence, 1974).

14. *Training Teacher Associates and Parents*. Methods that have effectively established extension of the application of operant procedures in the classroom, through teacher aides (*q.v.* Gardner, 1972; Panyan, Boozer, & Morris, 1970; Panyan & Patterson, 1974; Reid & Reid, 1974), and in the home and community, through parents (*q.v.* Fredericks, Baldwin, McDonnell, Hoffmann, & Harter, 1971; Galloway & Galloway, 1971; Salzinger, Feldman, & Portnoy, 1970; Schell & Adams, 1968; Seitz & Hoekenga, 1974; Terdal & Buell, 1969; Watson & Bassinger, 1974).

15. *Intermediate Classroom Participation*. A series of exercises designed to instruct the student teacher in bringing about a change in a single behavior in a single student.

16. *Assessment Scales*. Information on the administration, scoring, and use of such scales, instruments, and checklists as the Pennsylvania Training Model, the Balthazar Scales of Adaptive Behavior, the Camelot Behavioral Checklist, the Portage Project Checklist, the TARC Assessment System, etc. (*q.v.* Balthazar, 1971, 1973; Cain, Levine, & Elzey, 1963; Doll, 1947; Foster, 1974; Nihira, Foster, Shellhaas, & Leland, 1974; Sailor & Mix, 1975; Somerton & Turner, 1975; Shearer, Billingsley, Frohman, Hilliard, Johnson, & Shearer, 1970).

17. *Writing Instructional Objectives*. The process of determining and writing broad educational goals, general educational objectives, and specific instructional objectives (*q.v.* Mager, 1962; Wheeler & Fox, 1972).

18. *Curriculum Development*. The curriculum guides for educational programming for the severely and profoundly handicapped (*q.v.* Adams, 1975; Anderson, Hodson & Jones, 1975; Brody & Smilovitz, 1974; Brown, Williams, & Crowner, 1974; Gross & Cohen, 1975; Fredericks, Riggs, Furey, Grove, Moore, McDonnell, Jordan, Hanson, Baldwin, & Wadlow, 1976; Myers, Sinco, & Stalma, 1973; Tucker, 1974), and the procedures for identifying, defining, and sequencing behaviors in a teaching program for each individual in the classroom (*q.v.* Haring and Cohen, 1975; Merrill, 1971).

19. *Task Analysis and Instructional Programming*. Specific procedures for reducing a complex behavior to a number of single behaviors, reducing single behaviors into component parts, selecting and integrating a teaching strategy with the task analysis, and sequencing the components and single behaviors into a program (*q.v.* Davies, 1973; Freda & Loolioan, 1975; Gagne, 1971; Seigel, 1972).

20. *Motor Programs* (*q.v.* Chandler & Adams, 1972; Ethun & D'Angelo, 1963; Horner, 1971; Loynd & Barclay, 1970; McAulay & McMillan, 1965; O'Brien, Azrin, & Bugle; 1972; Striefel, 1974).

21. *Self-Help Programs* (*q.v.* Azrin & Armstrong, 1973; Ball, Seric, & Payne, 1971; Baumeister & Klosowski, 1965; Brett, 1960; Foxx & Azrin, 1973; Mahoney, Van Wagenen, & Meyerson, 1971; Martin, Kehoe, Bird, Jensen, & Darbyshire, 1971; O'Brien & Azrin, 1972; O'Brien, Bugle, & Azrin, 1972; Panyan, 1973; Song & Gandhi, 1974; Treffry, Martin, Samels, & Watson, 1970; Watson, 1972).

22. *Language Programs* (*q.v.* Bricker & Bricker, 1970; Carrier & Peak, 1975; Garcia & DeHaven, 1974; Kent, 1974; Miller & Yoder, 1972; Sailor, Guess, & Baer, 1973; Spradlin, 1966; Stremel, 1972; Stremel & Waryas, 1974).

23. *Socialization Programs* (*q.v.* Bradtke, 1972; Keeran, Grove, & Zachofsky, 1969; Whitman, Mercurio, & Caponigri, 1970; Twardosz & Baer, 1973).

24. *Pre-Academic Programs* (*q.v.* Brown, Scheuerman, Cartwright, & York, 1973; Brown & Sontag, 1972; Brown, Williams, & Crowner, 1974; Craig & Holland, 1970; Martin & Powers, 1967; Scheuerman, Cartwright, York, Lowry, & Brown, 1974; Sidman & Cresson, 1973; Sidman & Stoddard, 1966; Striefel & Wetherby, 1973; Twardosz, & Sajwaj, 1972; Whitman, Zakaras, & Chardos, 1971).

25. *Advanced Classroom Participation*. A series of exercises designed to enable the student teacher to progress from teaching one program to one individual or small group for a short period, under close supervision, to teaching several individuals or small groups throughout the school day, using a number of programs, with a minimum of supervision.

These 25 modules have been subsumed under courses leading to 18 credit hours toward a Master of Science degree through the Department of Special Education at the University of Kansas. These modular courses, plus general courses required of all students (six hours), two courses taken outside of special education (six hours), and thesis (four hours) constitute the entire teacher training program (*c.f.* Ulrich & Kent, 1966).

Development of Competency Training Modules

The process of module development has been broken down into a 20-step procedure.

1. A review of the literature about the education of the severely and profoundly handicapped and the assignment of each journal article, book chapter, program, or other published and unpublished manuscripts or parts thereof to one or more modules.
2. The tentative selection of the readings to be included in the modules and their assignment to the primary, supplemental, or optional reading list.
3. The formulation of the educational goal for each module.
4. The formulation and sequencing of the informational and performance competencies for each module, and specification of the instructional system and module format.
5. The final selection of those readings that are directly related to each informational and performance competency.
6. The development of test questions for each informational competency and practicum exercises for each performance competency.
7. The development of criterion answers for each test question, and criterion performance for each practicum exercise.
8. The organization of educational goals; informational and performance competencies; primary, supplementary, and optional readings; and practicum exercises into prototype student teacher manuals.
9. The addition of the test questions, criterion answers, and performance criteria to number 8 above for the prototype practicum site supervisor manuals.
10. The testing of the student teacher and practicum site supervisor manuals in the practicum sites with the student teachers and the supervisors.
11. The analysis of the data on the informational and performance competencies of the student teachers.
12. The revision of the informational and performance competencies, readings, and/or the test questions, practicum exercises, criterion answers, and performance criteria of the modules, based on data and feedback from the student teachers and the practicum site supervisors.
13. The planning of any audio-visual media production required to support the modules.
14. The organization of the readings of the modules into new written material to serve as a text.
15. The production of any prototype audio-visual support required for the modules.
16. The testing of the new written material and the audio-visual support of the modules in the practicum sites with the students and the practicum site supervisors.
17. The analysis of the data on the informational and performance competencies of the student teachers.
18. The revision of the new written material of the modules, based on the data and feedback from the students and the practicum site supervisors.
19. The revision of any audio-visual support required for the modules, based on the data and feedback from the students and the practicum site supervisors.
20. The arrangement of the publication of the written text and any audio-visual support for the modules.

Competency Training Sequence

Once the competencies have been identified, specified, and organized into clusters to form the basis for a training module, the next steps require the sequencing of the training of the competencies within a cluster, and the sequencing of the clusters within the teacher preparation program. A cursory review of the competencies within a cluster often results in the impression that they are so interrelated that they should all be trained simultaneously. While there are no hard and fast rules for sequencing the training of competencies, the following general rules may be useful:

1. Determine whether any of the competencies are prerequisite to other competencies. For example, learning the procedures for revising an instructional program should be preceded by learning the components that should be included in an instructional program.
2. Determine whether any of the competencies are typically used in a particular sequence. For example, the procedures involved in administering an assessment scale precede scoring an assessment scale.
3. Determine those competencies, grouped according to 1 and 2 above, that appear to be complex and those that appear to be simple, and organize the groups from simple to complex. The same general rules can also be applied to the sequencing of clusters.

Sometimes groups of competencies within a cluster or a number of clusters are so interrelated that training must proceed concurrently, rather than serially. In this event, it is helpful to develop a flow chart to show the interrelationships and to facilitate a student's progress through the competency sequence. This chart, in addition to presenting the required sequence, should also have time lines to suggest a pace for acquiring the competencies. One of the guiding principles of competency-based instruction is that individuals acquire the competencies at their own pace. Unfortunately, this is also one of the limitations of competency-based instruction. Many student teachers set a pace below that necessary for them to actually acquire the competencies and, too often, that pace is incompatible with the academic tradition of semesters, credit hours, and the assignment of grades (Johnson and Sulzer-Azaroff, 1975). A suggested pace that allows ample time for acquiring each competency can be developed over time, will help the student teachers progress through the competency sequence, will reduce the number of incomplete grades, and will diminish the probability of the student teachers' falling so far behind that they abandon their efforts.

The training program at the University of Kansas is centered around the basic (summer session), intermediate (fall semester), and advanced (spring semester) classroom participation modules, with the remaining modules providing information relevant to performance in the practicum site. A schedule showing the integration of information and practicum exercises for the summer session is presented in Figure 1.

The letters A through D represent modules; the numbers represent the informational competencies for Modules A through C and the practicum exercises (leading to acquisition of the performance competencies) for Module D (Basic Classroom Participation). Module A (Right to Education) is not directly related to the practicum exercises, so the suggested pacing displayed in Figure 1 spaces the completion of the informational competencies across the entire summer session. Module B (Introduction to Operant Behavior) is directly related to the practicum exercises of Module D. The first eight informational competencies of Module B are scheduled for completion before a student is prepared to start Exercise 1 of Module D. All of the informational competencies in Module B prepare the student teacher for readings related to the application of the principles of operant behavior in the area of special education. Thus, all of the informational competencies of Module B are scheduled for completion before a student teacher is prepared to start Module C (A Behavioral Approach to Special Education). Since Module C is indirectly related to completing the practicum exercises, the instructional objectives of Module C are spaced

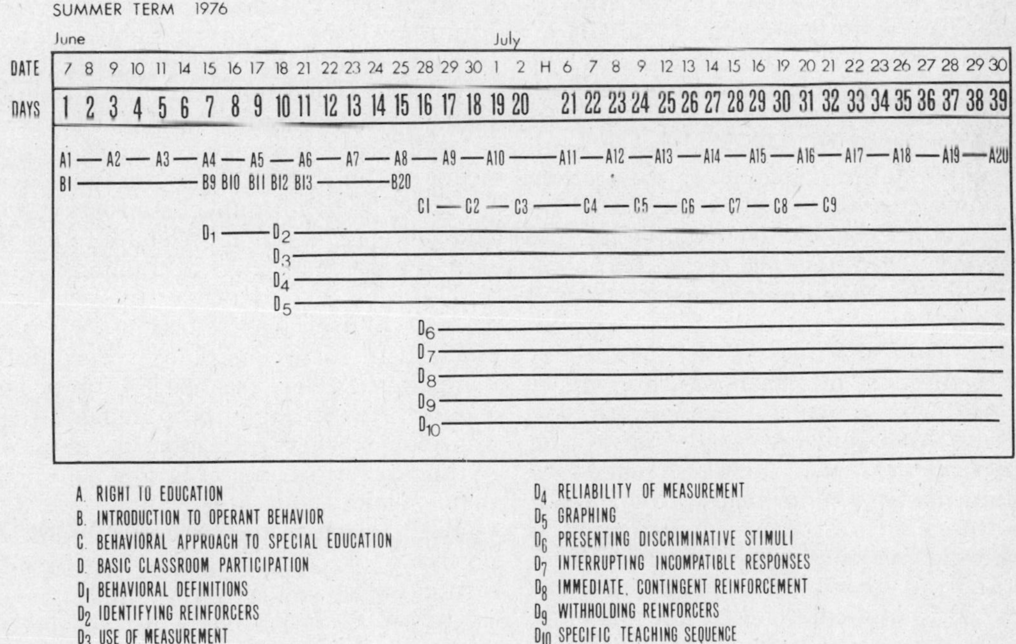

Figure 1. Suggested pace and required sequence for completing the informational competencies of training modules A, B, and C and the performance competencies of module D during the summer session.

for completion across the remainder of the summer session. A suggested pace and required sequence schedule, integrating the information and practicum exercises, has also been developed for the fall and spring semesters. Student teachers who begin the program sometime other than the summer session have a guide for estimating how far they will be able to progress during the semester, and can enroll accordingly. Student teachers who do not complete a sequence for which they have enrolled are given a grade of Incomplete which must be removed by completing the sequence during the next enrollment period.

Student teachers who enroll in a given sequence (summer, fall, or spring) must have completed all modules in the curriculum up to those subsumed under the courses for which they are enrolling. Once enrolled, the student teacher is given the opportunity to take a pretest on the first module(s) in the sequence. The pretests are designed to be administered on a group basis through overhead projection (Stalling, 1972). If the student teacher takes the pretest(s) and scores 90% or above on the written questions (as independently scored by two practicum supervisors), the student teacher may proceed to the next module in the sequence. If the pretest is not attempted, or the pretest score is below 90%, the student teacher must read the primary readings and relate these to the informational competencies. The informational competencies essentially serve as study questions (Semb, Hopkins, & Hursh, 1973). After completing the readings for each informational competency, the student teacher may elect to take the posttest or to go to the supplementary readings for additional information. If the student teacher completes the posttest on an informational competency without completing the supplementary readings, and the answer conforms to or exceeds the criterion stated in the instructor's manual (as independently scored by two practicum supervisors), the student may proceed to the next informational competency or proceed to a practicum exercise (Keller, 1968). Any disagreements about the scoring of written answers, on questions related to specific informational competencies, are resolved by the author, and this information is used to strengthen the scoring procedure. If student teachers fail to reach criterion on a practicum exercise, remedial instruction through modeling (Gardner, 1972; Panyan & Patterson, 1974) is given on those deficiencies that resulted in the failure. If student teachers fail to reach criterion on a written instructional objective, they are first directed to review the primary readings related to that informational competency, given reading assignments from supplementary readings, and required to rewrite their answers (Bostow & O'Connor, 1973). If any student should fail a second time, he would be given tutorial assistance in an interview format (Sheppard & McDermot, 1970).

Performance on practicum exercises is also assessed independently by two practicum supervisors through direct observation of the behaviors required by each of the practicum exercises. If performance conforms to or exceeds the performance criterion of the exercise, the student teacher proceeds to the next informational competencies of those modules in the sequence designed to prepare him for the next practicum exercise.

The nearly unrestricted access to the practicum site supervisors who serve as proctors (Farmer, Lachter, Blaustein, & Cole, 1972) leads to efficient scheduling, monitoring, and individualized instruction, and is an indispensible part of the training program.

Practicum Specifications

The informational competencies required of teachers of the severely and profoundly handicapped can be acquired and measured in a number of ways. The best format appears to be one that presents the material in a self-paced programmed instruction format, accompanied by audio-visual support and objective measures of acquisition (Lloyd & Knutzen, 1969; Myers, 1970). The acquisition of the performance competencies, however, depends upon the availability of well organized, tightly programmed practicum placements in classrooms for severely and profoundly handicapped students. As Brown and York (1974) put it, "We have found it necessary to provide teachers in training with intense and durable experiences with severely handicapped children" (p. 3). It is important that the teachers in such classrooms are skillful in the competencies that the teacher trainees are to acquire. It is strongly recommended that these classroom teachers be responsible to the director of the teacher training program. This may mean that colleges and universities will have to establish classes, and either support teacher positions or affiliate with the local school district for such support.

The professional training program for teachers of the severely and profoundly handicapped within the Department of Special Education at the University of Kansas and the Kansas Neurological Institute has led to the establishment of practicum sites at the Kansas Neurological Institute, the Topeka Public Schools, the Children's Rehabilitation Unit of the University of Kansas Medical Center, the Lawrence Public Schools, and the University Affiliated Facility of the Parsons State Hospital and Training Center. The goal of a practicum placement is not only to provide a setting in which competencies can be acquired, but also to duplicate as closely as possible the situation the teacher trainee will enter after graduation.

Evaluation of Teaching

Tawney (1975) suggests that "any 'certification' program requires that the teacher credential be based on documentation of positive change in child performance over time and on increasingly more complex tasks" (p. 93). Brown and York (1974) state "potential teachers must be able to demonstrate that they can change public school students in prescribed ways *before* they receive a license to teach" (p. 5). The measurement of teacher performance is a very difficult endeavor. One system for measuring the systematic application of operant techniques by student teachers is currently under development (Horner, 1975). The system uses three Teacher Proficiency Checklists to measure teacher performance during baseline, acquisition, and maintenance of specific behaviors taught by student teachers. The checklists are designed to be used with very specific skill-building programs (*q.v.* Horner, Billions, & Lent, 1974), but can also be used to evaluate a student teacher's performance in managing specific classroom behaviors.

During the Advanced Classroom Participation sequence, each student teacher must demonstrate criterion performance on teaching a student a motor, self-help, language, socialization, and pre-academic skill (provided there are handicapped students for whom assessment scales have indicated such programs are relevant targets). Criterion performance includes establishing the baseline performance of the skill, teaching the acquisition of the skill, and programming maintenance of the skill, once acquired. The acquisition checklist is presented in Figure 2.

The first seven items are information items. They are completed as follows:

1. The name of the student teacher conducting the acquisition session is entered in the space after "Teacher."

2. The name of the practicum site supervisor is entered after "Observer." If a second observer is also present for reliability checks, one observer

TEACHER PROFICIENCY CHECKLIST — ACQUISITION

1. Teacher ____________ 2. Observer ____________

3. Date ________ 4. Student ____________

5. Program ____________ 6. Session No. ________

7. Reinforcer(s) ____________

PRIOR TO THE ACQUISITION SESSION THE TEACHER:

8. has list of program steps YES NO 9. has prepared training area YES NO

10. has reinforcers YES NO

DURING THE ACQUISITION SESSION THE TEACHER:

11. records time session is started YES NO

12. begins session as specified in program YES NO

		1	2	3	4	5	6	7	8	9	10	11	12	13	14	15
13. presents programmed discriminative stimulus for each response as specified in program	YES NO															
14. presents reinforcer for each response that conforms to behavioral definition	YES NO															
15. withholds presentation of reinforcer for each response not conforming to behavioral definition	YES NO															
16. interrupts each response incompatible with conformance to behavioral definition	YES NO															
17. records results of each trial	YES NO															
18. proceeds to next step as specified in program	YES NO															

AFTER EACH ACQUISITION SESSION THE TEACHER:

19. records time session is ended YES NO

20. computes data point YES NO

21. plots data point on chart YES NO

Total YES ____ / Total YES & NO ____ = ____ %

90 - 100% EXCELLENT
80 - 89% GOOD
70 - 79% FAIR
60 - 69% POOR
59 and below UNACCEPTABLE

Figure 2. The acquisition Teacher Proficiency Checklist used to measure the systematic application of operant techniques by student teachers during the acquisition of specific behaviors by severely handicapped students.

writes "primary" after his name. The observations made by the primary observer are used for determining the teacher proficiency score.

3. The month, day, and year are entered after "Date."

4. The name of the handicapped student receiving acquisition training is entered after "Student."

5. The name of the program being used for acquisition training (e.g., use of spoon, self-dressing, grasping, etc.) is entered after "Program."

6. The number of the acquisition session is entered after "Session No." For example, a student who has had nine prior acquisition sessions (exclusive of baseline sessions) would be on session 10. If the student teacher has no record of prior acquisition sessions, a question mark is placed in the space (unless it is the first acquisition session). The student teacher is asked for the training record to determine the session number. The student teacher is not asked the session number, as this might encourage a false report to cover the absence of a training record.

7. If the observer witnessed the procedure (conducted prior to the first acquisition session) to identify reinforcers for the student to be trained, the reinforcer determined to be most effective is entered after "Reinforcer(s)." If the observer did not witness the procedure or none was conducted, a question mark is placed in the space.

The next three items are behaviors which are to be performed by the student teacher prior to conducting the acquisition session. They are scored as follows:

8. If the student teacher *has* the program or program steps in the immediate training area prior to starting the acquisition session, the observer circles "yes" after "has list of program steps." If the student teacher does not have the program or program steps in the immediate training area, the observer circles "no," and instructs the student teacher to obtain the program or program steps. If none exists nor is available, the observation is terminated and the session is scored "unacceptable."

9. If the student teacher *has* the required materials (e.g., data sheet, counters, etc.) and equipment (e.g., toothbrush, spoon, etc.) prior to starting the acquisition session, the observer circles "yes" after "Has prepared training area." If the student teacher does not have the required materials and equipment, the observer circles "no" and instructs the student teacher to obtain the required materials and equipment. If they are not available, the observation is terminated and the session is scored "unacceptable."

10. If the student teacher *has* "tangible" reinforcers (e.g., candy, cookies, juice, etc.) available in the immediate training area, the observer circles "yes" after "has reinforcers." If the student teacher does *not* have any tangible reinforcers available in the immediate training area, the observer asks, "What reinforcers do you plan to use?". If the answer is "a tangible reinforcer," the observer circles "no" and instructs the student teacher to obtain the tangible reinforcers. If none is available, the observation is terminated and the session is scored "unacceptable." If the answer is "an intangible reinforcer" (e.g., hugs, praise, etc.), the observer circles "yes" and instructs the student teacher to proceed with the session.

The next eight items are measures of behaviors which are to be performed by the student teacher during the acquisition session. They are scored as follows:

11. The acquisition session is officially started when the student teacher enters the time of day on the data sheet. If the student teacher enters the time before beginning the acquisition session, as specified in the program, the observer circles "yes" after "records time session is started." If the student teacher starts the acquisition session without entering the time on the data sheet, the observer circles "no." If the student teacher has no data sheet, the observer circles "no"' and instructs the student teacher to obtain the data sheet. If no data sheet exists, or is not available, the observation is terminated and the session is scored "unacceptable."

12. The observer must determine from the acquisition record the point in the program at which the student teacher should start the acquisition session (e.g., beginning, step 1, step 2, etc.). If the student teacher starts at the correct point, the observer circles "yes" after "begins session as specified in program." If the student teacher starts at a different point, the observer circles "no." The observer must carefully note the criterion for moving the student ahead in the program. An example of a criterion is three sessions with 90% correct responses or better on a specific program step; if this has been met on the acquisition record, the correct beginning step for the session would be the next step in the program.

13. The programmed discriminative stimuli are the instructions (as specified in the program) presented by the student teacher to set the occasion for a response by the student. This could be a verbal discriminative stimulus (e.g., "John, say 'cup' "); a visual discriminative stimulus, such as the student teacher's pointing to an object; a tactile discriminative stimulus, such as guiding a student's hand; or any combination or variation of instructional stimuli. Prior to the use of the checklists, the observer must determine the instructional discriminative stimuli to be presented by the student teacher during acquisition for each step in the program. The first 15 minutes of instruction are divided into one-minute intervals. The observer places a tally mark after "yes" in the appropriate interval (e.g., interval 5 during the fifth minute of instruction) each time the discriminative stimulus *is* presented by the student teacher exactly as specified in the program. The observer places a tally mark after "no" in the appropriate interval each time the discriminative stimulus is *not* presented by the student teacher exactly as specified in the program.

14. The reinforcer(s) as determined and entered in item 7, and/or determined to be present through item 10, must be given by the student teacher within three seconds of the termination of a response by the handicapped student which conforms to the behavioral definition of the response specified in the

program. The observer must have determined the behavioral definitions specified for each step in the program prior to the use of the checklists. The observer places a tally mark after "yes" in the appropriate interval each time a response conforming to the behavioral definition occurs and *is* followed within three seconds by the predetermined reinforcer. The observer places a tally mark after "no" each time such a response occurs and is *not* followed within three seconds by the predetermined reinforcer.

15. If the observer determines that a response by the handicapped student does not conform to the behavioral definition, item 15 is scored instead of item 14. The observer places a tally mark after "yes" in the appropriate interval if the response does not conform to the behavioral definition and the student teacher withholds the reinforcer, or a tally mark after "no" if the student teacher presents the reinforcer.

16. If the observer determines that a response by the handicapped student not only fails to conform to the behavioral definition but is incompatible with the response required by the behavioral definition, then item 16 is also scored. The observer places a tally mark after "yes" in the appropriate interval each time a response is performed by the student which is incompatible with the response required by the behavioral definition and *is* interrupted or stopped by the student teacher before it can be completed. The observer places a tally mark after "no" in the appropriate interval if such a response occurs and *is not* interrupted by the student teacher before it can be completed. Examples of incompatible responses might be attempts to leave the training area, throwing equipment or materials, crawling under a table, resisting physical assistance, etc.

17. Prior to the use of the checklist, the observer must determine from the program what constitutes a trial (e.g., each presentation of a discriminative stimulus; or each time a response occurs; or each time an opportunity is presented by events occurring in the individual's environment; or each time a specified time interval expires). The observer places a tally mark after "yes" in the appropriate interval each time the trial occurs, and the student teacher marks the results of that trial on the data sheet. The observer places a tally mark after "no" each time a trial occurs, and the student teacher does *not* mark the results of that trial on the data sheet.

18. The observer must determine which steps are in the program, prior to the use of the checklists. The steps might be each behavior in a sequence of behaviors to be completed by the handicapped student. If the program specifies that the student is to be trained on all the steps in the program at each acquisition session, the observer places a tally mark after "yes" in the appropriate interval each time the student teacher advances the handicapped student to the next step in the program sequence. The observer places a tally mark after "no" in the appropriate interval each time the student teacher advances the student to a step which is *not* the next step in the program sequence. If the program specifies the handicapped student is to be trained on one step at a time, this item would be scored only if the student reached criterion on a step during the observed session and should, therefore, be advanced to the next step. The observer places a tally mark after "yes" in the appropriate interval if the handicapped student reaches criterion on a step within the observed session and *is* advanced to the next step by the student teacher. The observer places a tally mark after "no" in the appropriate interval if the handicapped student reaches criterion on a step within the observed session and is *not* advanced to the next step in the program by the student teacher. When only one step is taught at a time, the decision to move to the next step in most programs is based on criterion performance over one or more entire sessions. In this event, the decision to move to a new step would occur only prior to the start of a session and would be scored in item 12 ("begins session as specified in program").

The last three items are behaviors which are to be performed by the student teacher to end the acquisition session. They are scored as follows:

19. Training during each acquisition session is officially ended when the student teacher enters on the data sheet the time of day the training ends. If the student teacher enters the time on the data sheet, the observer circles "yes" after "records time session is ended." If the student teacher does not enter the time on the data sheet, the observer circles "no."

20. The student teacher should summarize the data into either total frequency, average frequency, rate, total duration, average duration, percent correct, percent of total possible, or other score(s) for the session as specified in the program. If the student teacher computes the data point(s), the observer circles "yes" after "computes data point." If the student teacher does not compute the data point(s), the observer circles "no."

21. The student teacher should plot the summary score(s) on the chart at the point where a vertical line from the number of the session just conducted intersects with a horizontal line across from the number(s) which represents the

score(s) for the session. If the student teacher plots the data point(s), the observer circles "yes" after "plots data point on chart." If the student teacher does not plot the data point(s), the observer circles "no."

In scoring, one point for each "yes" circled and one point for each mark tallied after a "yes" is totaled and entered as total A. One point for each "no" circled and one point for each mark tallied after a "no" are added and entered as total B. The total of A and B are added and entered as total C. The total of A is divided by the total of C to obtain the percentage of "yes" scores. The category (Excellent, Good, etc.) which contains the percentage of "yes" scores obtained by the student teacher is circled by the observer. Ideally, total C should be around 100 (Guilford, 1965), in order for the computation of percentage of "yes" tallies to be a sensitive measure of student teacher performance. A percentage should not be computed if the divisor (total C) is less than 20. In this event, the data from such a session should be combined with the data from subsequent sessions until total C is greater than 20.

The reliability of the observers should be determined by dividing the sum of the number of times both observers circled "yes" or both observers circled "no," and the number of times both observers entered the same number of "yes" or "no" tallies in an interval by the number of agreements, plus the sum of the number of times one observer circled a "yes" and the other circled a "no," and the number of intervals in which one observer entered a different number of "yes" or "no" than the other observer (disagreements), and multiplying by 100. Any interval in which neither observer enters a "yes" or "no" tally should not be counted as either an agreement or disagreement, in order to avoid inflating the reliability quotient (Kazdin, 1975).

The reliability of the three checklists for evaluating teacher proficiency in the use of specific programs in both individual and small group sessions, as well as increases in proficiency in the use of programs by teacher trainees as a result of instructional feedback, is currently being studied.

Plans are also underway to expand the evaluation system into a classroom evaluation system. This system would be more global than the Teacher Proficiency Checklists and will be used to evaluate the total classroom, including the architectural and physical properties, the use of adaptive devices, general staff-student interactions, student-environment interactions, curriculum selection, curriculum utilization, the use of measurement systems, interaction with ancillary personnel, the use of teaching associates, and the involvement of parents. The system will be one of program evaluation, in the manner of PASS (Program Analysis of Service Systems; Wolfensberger and Glenn, 1975) and ALERT (Analyzing and Measuring Deinstitutionalization across Residential Environments with Alternative Living Environments Rating and Tracking System; Budde, 1976).

This system will provide a means to conduct follow-up evaluations on the extent to which the informational and performance competencies are implemented by teachers once they enter the field. It could also be used to determine the in-service training needs of teachers already in the field, and to provide a criterion by which State Departments of Education personnel could determine eligibility for renewal of certification for teachers of the severely and profoundly handicapped.

Conclusion

There are many different approaches that can be taken to prepare teachers of the severely and profoundly handicapped, but there seems to be a consensus of agreement in several areas. First of all, any teacher training institution considering establishing such a program should do so only if it is willing to make the necessary commitments in terms of staff, expenses, and time required for an effective program. Second, the program should provide for extensive interaction between student teachers and a variety of students with severe and profound handicaps in a number of practicum settings. Third, the program should stress performance by student teachers which results in specific changes in the behavior of handicapped students, with all other aspects of training designed to complement this goal. Finally, the program should be systematically evaluated to determine the extent to which its goals are being met and to provide a basis for remediation of any deficiencies.

The most serious need at the present time is the design, development, and dissemination of additional educational programs which have been empirically determined to produce positive change in the behavior of severely and profoundly handicapped students. The most pressing needs are in the motor development and pre-academic areas for younger students, and in the socialization and vocational areas for older students. Until the development of such programs receives high priority, and the programs are available for integration into teacher training programs, the cart will still be before the horse and the potential for backlash (Brown and York,

1974) is great. As Meyen (1975) put it, "Unless an investment is made in creating resources commensurate with the demand for personnel, we may find the 24-hour retarded child being taught by teachers who run out of skills after an hour and a half" (p. 144).

References

Adams, J. L. *An education curriculum for the moderately, severely, and profoundly mentally handicapped pupil.* Springfield, Ill.: Charles C Thomas, 1975.

Anderson, D. R., Hodson, G. D., & Jones, W. G. *Instructional programming for the handicapped student.* Springfield, Ill.: Charles C Thomas, 1975.

Azrin, N. H., & Armstrong, P. M. The "mini-meal"—A method for teaching eating skills to the profoundly retarded. *Mental Retardation*, 1973, *11* (1), 9–13.

Ball, T. S., Seric, K., & Payne, L. E. Long-term retention of self-help skill training in the profoundly retarded. *American Journal of Mental Deficiency*, 1971, *76* (3), 378–382.

Balthazar, E. E. *Balthazar scales of adaptive behavior, Part three: The scales of functional independence.* Palo Alto, Cal.: Consulting Psychologists Press, 1971.

Balthazar, E. E. *Balthazar scales of adaptive behavior II. Scales of social adaptation*. Palo Alto, Cal.: Consulting Psychologists Press, 1973.

Bandura, A. *Principles of behavior modification.* Chicago: Holt, Rinehart, & Winston, 1969.

Bare, C., Boettke, E., & Waggoner, N. *Self-help clothing for handicapped children.* Chicago: National Association for Crippled Children and Adults, 1962.

Baumeister, A. A., & Klosowski, R. An attempt to group toilet train severely retarded patients. *Mental Retardation*, 1965, *3* (6) 24–26.

Becker, W. C., Engelmann, S., & Thomas, D. R. *Teaching: A course in applied psychology.* Chicago: Science Research Associates, 1971.

Bergstrom, D., & Coles, C. H. *Basic positioning procedures.* Minneapolis: A-V Publications Office, Sister Kenny Institute, 1971.

Bijou, S. W., Peterson, R. F., & Ault, M. D. A method to integrate descriptive and experimental field studies at the level of data and empirical concepts. *Journal of Applied Behavior Analysis*, 1968, *1*, 175–191.

Bijou, S. W., & Wilcox-Cole, B. The feasibility of providing effective educational programs for the severely and profoundly retarded. In *Educating the 24-hour retarded child.* Arlington, Texas: National Association for Retarded Citizens, 1975, 9–25.

Birnbrauer, J. S., Burchard, J. D., & Burchard, S. N. Wanted: Behavior analysts. In R. H. Bradfield (Ed.) *Behavior modification—The human effort*. Sioux Falls, S. D.: Dimensions Publishing Co., 1970, 19–76.

Bostow, D. E., & O'Connor, R. J. A comparison of two college classroom testing procedures: Required remediation versus no remediation. *Journal of Applied Behavior Analysis*, 1973, *6*, 599–607.

Bradtke, L. M. Intensive play: A technique for building affective behaviors in profoundly mentally retarded young children. *Education and Training of the Mentally Retarded*, 1972, *7* (1), 8–13.

Brett, G. Dressing techniques for the severely involved hemiplegic. *American Journal of Occupational Therapy*, 1960, *14*, 262–264.

Bricker, W. A., & Bricker, D. A program of language training for the severely language handicapped child. *Exceptional Children*, 1970, *37* (2), 101–113.

Bricker, D., & Bricker W. *Toddler research and intervention project report—Year I.* Nashville, Tenn.: Institute on Mental Retardation and Intellectual Development, George Peabody College for Teachers, 1971.

Bricker, D., & Bricker W. *Toddler research and intervention project report—Year II.* Nashville, Tenn.: Institute on Mental and Intellectual Development, George Peabody College for Teachers, 1972.

Bricker, D., & Bricker, W. *Infant, toddler, and preschool research and intervention project report—Year III*. Nashville, Tenn: Institute on Mental Retardation and Intellectual Development, George Peabody College for Teachers, 1973.

Brody, J. F., & Smilovitz, R. *APT: A training program for citizens with severely or profoundly retarded behavior.* Spring City, Penn: Pennhurst State School, 1974.

Brown, L. Instructional programs for trainable level retarded students. In L. Mann & D. A. Sabatino (Eds.), *The first review of special education (Vol. 2)*. Philadelphia: Journal of Special Education Press, 1973.

Brown, L., Scheuerman, N., Cartwright, S., & York, R. *The design and implementation of an empirically based instructional program for young severely handicapped students: Toward the rejection of the exclusion principle. Part III*. Madison, Wis: Special Education Services, Madison Public Schools, 1973.

Brown, L., & Sontag, E. (Eds.) *Toward the development and implementation of an empirically based public school program for trainable mentally retarded and severely emotionally disturbed students. Part II*. Madison, Wis: Special Education Services, Madison Public Schools, 1972.

Brown, L., Williams, W., & Crowner, T. *A collection of papers and programs related to public school services for severely handicapped students*. Madison, Wis: Madison Public Schools Specialized Education Services, 1974.

Brown, L., & York, R. Developing programs for severely handicapped students: teacher training and classroom instruction. *Focus on Exceptional Children*, 1974, *6*, 1–11.

Browning, R. M., & Stover, D. O. *Behavior modification in child treatment.* Chicago: Aldine Publishing Co., 1973.

Budde, J. F. *Analyzing and measuring deinstitutionalization across residential environments with alternative living environments rating and tracking system (ALERT)*. Lawrence, Kansas: University of Kansas, 1976.

Cain, L. F., Levine, S., & Elzey, F. F. *Manual for the Cain-Levine social maturity scale*. Palo Alto, Cal: Consulting Psychologists Press, 1963.

Carrier, J. K., & Peak, T. *Non-speech language initiation program (Non-SLIP)*. Lawrence, Kansas: H & H Enterprises, 1975.

Certo, N., & York, R. *Minimal competencies for teachers of severely and profoundly handicapped students*. Madison, Wis: Department of Studies in Behavioral Disabilities, University of Wisconsin, 1976.

Chandler, S. S., & Adams, M. A. Multiply handicapped children motivated for ambulation through behavior modification. *Physical Therapy*, 1972, *52* (3), 399–401.

Connor, G. N., Batarseh, G., Massey, P. S., & Cicenia, E. F. Intensive programming for the severely/profoundly retarded using prerecorded audio tapes. *Mental Retardation*, 1972, *10*, 40–42.

Cooper, J. O. *Measurement and analysis of behavioral techniques.* Columbus, Ohio: Charles E. Merrill, 1974.

Craig, H. B., & Holland, A. L. Reinforcement of visual attending in classrooms for deaf children. *Journal of Applied Behavior Analysis*, 1970, *3* (2), 97–109.

Davies, I. K. Task analysis: Some process and content concerns. *AV Communication Review*, 1973, *21* (1), 73–86.

Doke, L. A., & Risley, T. R. The organization of day-care environments: Required versus optional activities. *Journal of Applied Behavior Analysis*, 1972, *5*, 405–420.

Doll, E. A. *Vineland social maturity scale—Manual of directions.* Minneapolis, Minn: American Guidance Service, 1947.

Ethun, C. A., & D'Angelo, R. J. Gait training for the severely mentally retarded. *Journal of the American Physical Therapy Association*, 1963, *43*, 179–180.

Farmer, J., Lachter, G. D., Blaustein, J. J., & Cole, B. K. The role of proctoring in personalized instruction. *Journal of Applied Behavior Analysis*, 1972, *5*, 401–404.

Finnie, N. R. *Handling the young cerebral palsied child at home.* New York: E. P. Dutton, 1970.

Forehand, R., & Baumeister, A. A. Deceleration of aberrant behavior among retarded individuals. In M. Hersen, R. M. Eisler, & P. M. Miller (Eds.). *Progress in Behavior Modification.* New York: Academic Press, 1976.

Foster, R. W. *Camelot behavioral checklist manual.* Lawrence, Kansas: Camelot Behavioral Systems, 1974.

Foxx, R. M., & Azrin, N. H. *Toilet training the retarded—A rapid program for day and nighttime independent toileting.* Champaign, Ill.: Research Press, 1973.

Freda, L. J., & Loolioan, J. K. Task analysis as the training determinator: One organization's approach. *Educational Technology*, 1975, *15* (9), 22–26.

Fredericks, H. D. B., Riggs, C., Furey, T., Grove, D., Moore, W., McDonnell, J., Jordan, E., Hanson, W., Baldwin, V., & Wadlow, M. *The teaching research curriculum for moderately and severely handicapped.* Springfield, Ill. Charles C Thomas, 1976.

Fredericks, H. D. B., Baldwin, V. L., McDonnell, J. J., Hofmann, R., & Harter, J. Parents educate their trainable children. *Mental Retardation*, 1971, *9* (3), 24–26.

Gagne, R. M. Learning hierarchies. In M. D. Merrill (Ed.). *Instructional design: Readings.* Englewood Cliffs, N. J.: Prentice-Hall, 1971, 118–133.

Galloway, C., & Galloway, K. C. Parent classes in precise behavior management. *Teaching Exceptional Children*, 1971, *3*, 120–128.

Garcia, E. E., & DeHaven, E. D. Use of operant techniques in the establishment and generalization of language: A review and analysis. *American Journal of Mental Deficiency*, 1974, *79* (2), 169–178.

Gardner, J. M. Teaching behavior modification to non-professionals. *Journal of Applied Behavior Analysis*, 1972, *5* (4), 517–521.

Gardner, W. I. Use of punishment procedures with the severely retarded: A review. *American Journal of Mental Deficiency*, 1969, *74*, 86–103.

Gardner, W. I. *Behavior modification in mental retardation.* Chicago: Aldine Publishing Co., 1971.

Gold, M. W., & Scott, K. G. Discrimination learning. In W. B. Stephens (Ed.). *Training the developmentally young.* New York: John Day, 1971, 420–444.

Gross, P., & Cohen, M. *Developmental pinpoints.* Seattle: Experimental Education Unit, Child Development and Mental Retardation Center, University of Washington, 1975.

Guilford, J. P. *Fundamental statistics in psychology and education.* New York: McGraw-Hill, 1965.

Hall, R. V. *Managing Behavior 1—Behavior modification: The measurement of behavior.* Lawrence, Kansas: H & H Enterprises, Inc, 1971.

Haring, N. G. & Cohen, M. Using the developmental approach as a basis for planning and sequencing different kinds of curricula for severely/profoundly handicapped persons. In *Educating the 24-hour retarded child.* Arlington, Texas: National Association for Retarded Citizens, 1975, 43–70.

Haring, N. G., & Lovitt, T. C. Operant methodology and educational technology in special education. In N. G. Haring & R. L. Schiefelbusch (Eds.). *Methods in special education.* New York: McGraw-Hill, 1967, 12–48.

Hewett, F. M., Taylor, F. D., & Artuso, A. A. The engineered classroom: An innovative approach to the education of children with learning problems. In R. H. Bradfield (Ed.), *Behavior modification—The human effort.* Sioux Falls, S. D.: Dimensions Publishing Co., 1970, 77–122.

Hoffman, R. B. *How to build special furniture and equipment for handicapped children.* Springfield, Ill.: Charles C Thomas, 1970.

Hollis, J. H., & Gorton, C. E. Training severely and profoundly developmentally retarded children. *Mental Retardation*, 1967, *5*. 20–24.

Horner, R. D. Establishing use of crutches by a mental retarded *spina bifida* child. *Journal of Applied Behavior Analysis*, 1971, *4* (3), 183–189.

Horner, R. D. *Teacher Proficiency Checklist.* Lawrence, Kansas: Department of Special Education, University of Kansas, 1975.

Horner, R. D., Billions, C., & Lent, J. R. *The toothbrushing program.* Seattle: Edmark Publishing Co., 1974.

Horner, R. D., Holvoet, J., & Rinne, T. *Competency Specifications for Teachers of the Severely and Profoundly Handicapped.* Lawrence, Kansas: Department of Special Education, University of Kansas, 1976.

Hursh, D., Wildgen, J., Minkin, B., Sherman, J. A., & Wolf, M. M. *The principles and procedures of behavior modification.* Lawrence, Kansas: Department of Human Development, University of Kansas, 1972, 10–25.

Jacobson, J. M., Bushell, D., & Risley, T. Switching requirements in a Head Start classroom. *Journal of Applied Behavior Analysis*, 1969, *2*, 43–47.

Johnson, K. R., & Sulzer-Azaroff, B. PSI for first-time users: pleasures and pitfalls. *Educational Technology*, 1975, *15*, 9–17.

Kazdin, A. E. *Behavior modification in applied settings.* Homewood, Ill.: The Dorsey Press, 1975.

Keeran, C. V., Grove, F. A., & Zachofsky, T. Assessing the playground skills of the profoundly retarded. *Mental Retardation*, 1969, 7 (3), 29–32.

Keller, F. S. "Good-bye teacher." *Journal of Applied Behavior Analysis*, 1968, 1, 79–89.

Kent, L. R. *Language acquisition program for the severely retarded.* Champaign, Ill.: Research Press, 1974.

Kozloff, M. A. *Measuring behavior: Procedures for recording and evaluating behavioral data.* St. Ann, Missouri: CEMREL, Inc., 1971, 1–63.

Lake, T. P. (Ed.). Programs providing alternatives: Educating the severely and multiply handicapped. *Education and Training of the Mentally Retarded*, 1974, *9*, 29–47.

LeLaurin, K., & Risley, T. R. The organization of day-care environments: "Zone" *versus* "man to man" staff assignments. *Journal of Applied Behavior Analysis*, 1972, *5*, 225–232.

Lippman, L., & Goldberg, I. I. *Right to education: Anatomy of the Pennsylvania case and its implications for exceptional children.* New York: Teachers College Press, 1973.

Lloyd, K. E., & Knutzen, N. J. A self-paced programmed undergraduate course in the experimental analysis of behavior. *Journal of Applied Behavior Analysis*, 1969, *2*, 125–133.

Loynd, J., & Barclay, A. A case study in developing ambulation in a profoundly retarded child. *Behavior Research and Therapy*, 1970, *8* (2), 207.

Luckey, R. E., & Addison, M. R. The profoundly retarded: A new challenge for public education. *Education and Training of the Mentally Retarded*, 1974, *9*, 123–130.

Macey, P. G., Stancliffe, J., Beumer, B., & Roper, W. *Mobilizing multiply handicapped children—A manual for the design and construction of modified wheelchairs.* Lawrence, Kansas: Division of Continuing Education, University of Kansas, 1974.

Mager, R. F. *Preparing instructional objectives.* Palo Alto, Cal: Fearon Publishers, 1962.

Mahoney, K., Van Wagenen, R. K., & Meyerson, L. Toilet training of normal and retarded children. *Journal of Applied Behavior Analysis*, 1971, *4* (3), 173–181.

Martin, G. L., Kehoe, B., Bird, E., Jensen, V., & Darbyshire, M. Operant conditioning in dressing behavior of severely retarded girls. *Mental Retardation*, 1971, *9*, 27–30.

Martin, G. L., & Powers, R. B. Attention span: An operant conditioning analysis. *Exceptional Children*, 1967, *33*, 565–570.

McAulay, M. E., & McMillan, M. Teaching severely retarded children to walk. *Developmental Medicine and Child Neurology*, 1965, 7 549–566.

Mental Health Law Project. *Basic rights of the mentally handicapped*. Washington, D.C: Mental Health Law Project, 1973.

Merrill, M. D. (Ed.) *Instructional design: Readings*. Englewood Cliffs, N.J: Prentice-Hall, 1971.

Meyen, E. L. Preparing educational personnel for the severely and profoundly mentally retarded. In *Educating the 24-hour retarded child*. Arlington, Texas: National Association for Retarded Citizens, 1975, 132–144.

Miller, J. F., & Yoder, D. On developing the content for a language teaching program. *Mental Retardation*, 1972, *10* (2), 9–11.

Miller, L. K. *Principles of everyday behavior analysis*. Monterey, Cal. Brooks/Cole Publishing Co., 1975.

Myers, D. G., Sinco, M. E., & Stalma, E. S. *The right to education child. A curriculum for the severely and profoundly mentally retarded*. Springfield, Ill: Charles C Thomas, 1973.

Myers, W. A. Operant learning principles applied to teaching introductory statistics. *Journal of Applied Behavior Analysis*, 1970, *3*, 213–220.

Neisworth, J. R., & Smith, R. M. *Modifying retarded behavior*. Atlanta: Houghton-Mifflin Co., 1973.

Nihira, K., Foster, R., Shellhaas, M., & Leland, H. *AAMD adaptive behavior scale manual*. Washington, D.C: American Association on Mental Deficiency, 1974.

O'Brien, F., & Azrin, N. H. Developing proper mealtime behaviors of the institutionalized retarded. *Journal of Applied Behavior Analysis*, 1972, *5* (4), 389–399.

O'Brien, F., Azrin, N. H., & Bugle, C. Training profoundly retarded children to stop crawling. *Journal of Applied Behavior Analysis*, 1972, *5* (2), 131–137.

O'Brien, F., Bugle, C., & Azrin, N. H. Training and maintaining a retarded child's proper eating. *Journal of Applied Behavior Analysis*, 1972, *5* (1), 67–72.

Panyan, M. *Managing behavior 4—Behavior modification: New ways to teach new skills*. Lawrence, Kansas: H & H Enterprises, 1973.

Panyan, M., Boozer, H., & Morris, N. Feedback to attendants as a reinforcer for applying operant techniques. *Journal of Applied Behavior Analysis*, 1970, *3* (1), 1–4.

Panyan, M., & Patterson, E. F. Teaching attendants the applied aspects of behavior modification. *Mental Retardation*, 1974, *12* (5), 30–32.

Quilitch, H. R., & Risley, T. R. The effects of play materials on social play. *Journal of Applied Behavior Analysis*, 1973, *6*. 573–578.

Reid, B. A., & Reid, W. R. Role expectations of paraprofessional staff in special education. *Focus on Exceptional Children*, 1974, *6* (7), 1–14.

Robinault, I. P. *Functional aids for the multiply handicapped*. Hagerstown, Md: Harper & Row, 1973.

Rodriquez, E. M., & Sproles, P. C. The use of a listening center with severely retarded children. *Education and Training of the Mentally Retarded*, 1967, *2*, 140–141.

Rosenberg, C. *Assistive devices for the handicapped*. Minneapolis: A-V Publications Office, Sister Kenny Institute, 1968.

Rynders, J. E., Bruininks, R. H., & Gordon, D. *Needs assessment: A vital step in designing an objectives-based training program for teachers of moderately and severely retarded pupils*. Paper presented at the 52nd Annual International Convention of the Council for Exceptional Children, New York, April, 1974.

Sailor, W., Guess, D., & Baer, D. M. Functional language for verbally deficient children: An experimental program. *Mental Retardation*, 1973, *11* (3), 27–35.

Sailor, W., Guess, D., & Lavis, L. Training teachers for education of the severely handicapped. *Education and Training of the Mentally Retarded*, 1975, *10* (3), 201–203.

Sailor, W., & Mix, B. J. *The TARC assessment scale*. Lawrence, Kansas: H & H Enterprises, 1975.

Salzinger, K., Feldman, R. S., & Portnoy, S. Training parents of brain-injured children in the use of the operant conditioning procedures. *Behavior Therapy*, 1970, *1*, 4–33.

Schell, R. E., & Adams, W. P. Training parents of a young child with profound behavior deficits to be teacher-therapists. *Journal of Special Education*, 1968, *2*, 439–454.

Scheuerman, N., Cartwright, S., York, R., Lowry, P., & Brown, L. Teaching young severely handicapped students to follow verbal directions. *Journal of Special Education*, 1974, *8* (3), 223–236.

Seigel, E. Task analysis and effective teaching. *Journal of Learning Disabilities*, 1972, *5* (10), 519–531.

Seitz, S., & Hoekenga, R. Modeling as a training tool for retarded children and their parents. *Mental Retardation*, 1974, *12* (2), 28–30.

Semb, G., Hopkins, B. L., & Hursh, D. E. The effects of study questions and grades on student test performance in a college course. *Journal of Applied Behavior Analysis*, 1973, *6*, 631–642.

Shearer, D., Billingsley, J., Frohman, A., Hilliard, J., Johnson, F., & Shearer, M. *The Portage guide to early education: Instructions and checklist (Experimental edition)*. Portage, Wis: Cooperative Educational Service Agency No. 12, 1970.

Shearer, M. S., & Shearer, D. E. The portage project: A model for early childhood education. *Exceptional Children*, 1972, *39*, 210–217.

Sheldon, J., & Sherman, J. A. The right to education for the retarded. *Journal of Education*, 1974, *156*, 25–48.

Sheppard, W. C., & McDermot, H. G. Design and evaluation of a programmed course in introductory psychology. *Journal of Applied Behavior Analysis*, 1970, *3*, 5–11.

Sidman, M., & Cresson, O. Reading and crossmodal transfer of stimulus equivalences in severe retardation. *American Journal of Mental Deficiency*, 1973, 77 (5), 515–523.

Sidman, M., & Stoddard, L. T. Programming perception and learning for retarded children. In N. Ellis (Ed.). *International review of research in mental retardation* (Vol. II). New York: Academic Press, 1966, 151–208.

Somerton, E. & Turner, K. *Pennsylvania training model: Individual assessment guide*. King of Prussia: Regional Resources Center of Eastern Pennsylvania for Special Education, 1974.

Song, A. Y., & Gandhi, R. An analysis of behavior during the acquisition and maintenance phases of self-spoon feeding skills of profound retardates. *Mental Retardation*, 1974, *12* (1), 25–28.

Sontag, E. The severely handicapped child in the public school—what we have to do. In *Educating the 24-hour retarded child*. Arlington, Texas: National Association for Retarded Citizens, 1975, 35–41.

Sontag, E., Burke, P. J., & York, R. Considerations for serving the severely handicapped in the public schools. *Education and Training of the Mentally Retarded*, 1973, *8*, 20–26.

Spradlin, J. E. Environmental factors and the language development of retarded children. In S. Rosenberg (Ed.). *Developments in applied psycholinguistics research*. Riverside, N.J: Macmillan, 1966.

Spradlin, J. E., Girardeau, F. L., & Corte, E. Fixed ratio and fixed interval behavior of severely and profoundly retarded subjects. *Journal of Experimental Child Psychology*, 1965, *2*, 340–353.

Stabler, B., Gibson, E. W., Cutting, D. S., & Lawrence, P. S. Zone planning for accelerating adaptive behavior in the retarded. *Exceptional Children*, 1974, *40*, 252–257.

Stainback, S., Stainback, W., & Maurer, S. Training teachers for the severely and profoundly handicapped: A new frontier. *Exceptional Children*, 1976, *42* (4), 203–210.

Stalling, R. B. Administering quiz and instructional material by overhead projection. *Journal of Applied Behavior Analysis*, 1972, *5*, 31–32.

Stamm, J. M. A general model for the design of a competency-based special education professional preparation program. *Education and Training of the Mentally Retarded*, 1975, *10* (3), 196–200.

Stremel, K. Language training: A program for retarded children. *Mental Retardation*, 1972, *10* (2), 47–49.

Stremel, K., & Waryas, C. A behavioral-psycholinguistic approach to language training. *American Speech and Hearing Association Monographs*, 1974, *18*, 96–124.

Striefel, S. *Managing behavior 7—Behavior modification: Teaching a child to imitate*. Lawrence, Kansas: H & H Enterprises, 1974.

Striefel, S., & Wetherby, B. Instruction following behavior of a retarded child and its controlling stimuli. *Journal of Applied Behavior Analysis*, 1973, *6* (4), 663–670.

Tawney, J. W. Prerequisite conditions for the establishment of educational programs for the severely retarded. In *Educating the 24-hour retarded child.* Arlington, Texas: National Association for Retarded Citizens, 1975, 90–98.

Terdal, L., & Buell, J. Parent education in managing retarded children with behavior deficits and inappropriate behaviors. *Mental Retardation*, 1969, *7* (3), 10–13.

Terrace, H. S. Discrimination learning with and without errors. *Journal of the Experimental Analysis of Behavior*, 1963a, *6*, 1–27.

Terrace, H. S. Errorless transfer of a discrimination across two continua. *Journal of the Experimental Analysis of Behavior*, 1963b, *6*, 223–232.

Thompson, R., & Grabowski, J. (Eds.) *Behavior modification of the mentally retarded.* New York: Oxford University Press, 1972.

Touchette, P. E. The effects of graduated stimulus change on the acquisition of a simple discrimination in severely retarded boys. *Journal of the Experimental Analysis of Behavior*, 1968, *11*, 39–48.

Touchette, P. E. Transfer of stimulus control: Measuring the moment of transfer. *Journal of the Experimental Analysis of Behavior*, 1971, *15*, 347–354.

Treffry, D., Martin, G., Samels, J., & Watson, C. Operant conditioning of grooming behavior of severely retarded girls. *Mental Retardation*, 1970, *8*, 29–33.

Tucker, D. J. *Skill acquisition program bibliography*. Lawrence, Kansas: Camelot Behavioral Systems, 1974.

Tucker, D., Hollis, J., Sailor, W., Horner, D., Kelly, P., & Guess, D. Preparing "paraprofessional" personnel for education of the severely handicapped: the teaching associate. *Education and Training of the Mentally Retarded*, in press.

Twardosz, S., & Baer, D. M. Training two severely retarded adolscents to ask questions. *Journal of Applied Behavior Analysis*, 1973, *6* (4), 655–661.

Twardosz, S., & Sajwaj, T. Multiple effects of a procedure to increase sitting in a hyperactive retarded boy. *Journal of Applied Behavior Analysis*, 1972, *5* (1), 73–78.

Ulrich, R., & Kent, N. D. New tactics for the education of psychologists. *American Psychologist*, 1966, *21*, 655.

Watson, L. S. *How to use behavior modification with mentally retarded and autistic children: Programs for administrators, teachers, parents and nurses*. Libertyville, Ill.: Behavior Modification Technology, 1972.

Watson, L. S., & Bassinger, J. F. Parent training technology: A potential service delivery system. *Mental Retardation*, 1974, *12* (5), 3–10.

Whaley, D. L., & Malott, R. W. *Elementary principles of behavior.* New York: Appleton-Century-Crofts, 1971.

Wheeler, A. H., & Fox, W. L. *Behavior modification: A teacher's guide to writing instructional objectives.* Lawrence, Kansas: H & H Enterprises, 1972.

Whitman, T. L., Mercurio, J. R., & Caponigri, V. Development of social responses in two severely retarded children. *Journal of Applied Behavior Analysis*, 1970, *3*, 133–138.

Whitman, T. L., Zakaras, M., & Chardos, S. Effects of reinforcement and guidance procedures on instruction following behavior of severely retarded children. *Journal of Applied Behavior Analysis*, 1971, *4*, 283–291.

Williams, W., Brown, L., & Certo, N. Components of instructional programs for severely handicapped students. *Theory into Practice*, 1975, *14*.

Wolfensberger, W., Nirge, B., Olshansky, D., Perske, R., & Roos, P. *The principal of normalization in human services.* Toronto: National Institute on Mental Retardation, 1972.

Wolfensberger, W., & Glenn, L. *Program Analysis of Service Systems III.* Toronto: National Institute on Mental Retardation, 1975.

R. DON HORNER is the Coordinator of the Teacher Training Component of the Personnel Preparation Program for Education of the Severely Handicapped, on subcontract to the Department of Special Education at the University of Kansas in Lawrence.

The Quest for Competence in Serving the Severely/Profoundly Handicapped: A Critical Analysis of Personnel Preparation Programs

PHILIP J. BURKE

Bureau of Education for the Handicapped

MARILYN COHEN

University of Washington

The purpose of this article seemed simple enough at the outset. With the growing emphasis on competency-based instruction and the attention now being focused on personnel preparation in the area of severely/profoundly handicapped (SPH) children, the authors felt it was extremely important to provide an overview of competency-based instruction as it is evolving in this new area. In order to provide this overview, the authors decided to examine twelve projects from across the nation, each designed to prepare personnel to work with the SPH. The written project descriptions would be examined and the competencies offered across projects would be carefully extracted, then sorted and classified. The results of this survey would be summarized in such a way as to allow one to compare and contrast projects, to consider the comprehensiveness of their approaches to their training problems, and to consider the applicability of the competencies identified to SPH training programs in general.

After a good deal of review, however, this task became considerably more complex. At this stage in the development of competency-based teacher education, little is certain and most issues are open for debate. Some would argue that the entire effort is a waste of time, that it is impossible to plan for and to train teachers to meet every problem that will confront them in educational settings. In this view, a better strategy would be to concentrate on a few basic skills that would serve teachers well in any setting. The trainer would program teachers to react to situations that might arise, using a well understood set of problem-solving techniques, so the argument goes.

If, on the other hand, one accepts the alternate approach of attempting to formulate and train in accordance with a prescribed set of competencies, another set of problems arises. Although there are literally thousands of competencies generated and depicted in the literature, most of them have not been validated (Shores, Cegalka, & Nelson, 1973). The usual procedure in generating competencies is to do a survey of field practitioners, followed by a literature search. The final set of competencies is usually selected by a panel of judges, but frequently the trainer makes the final implementation decision, matching the competencies with program resources such as practicum, personnel, children, and trainee capabilities—in other words, a compromise.

In the entire area of competency generation, the least effort appears to be spent on the actual validation process. A full consideration of this issue is probably the most important item in the competency-based training movement, most particularly in preparing personnel for the severely and profoundly handicapped.

Procedures

Given that the issue of competency-based teacher education is rife with discord, the authors developed a modest goal. They selected for review only Special Projects funded by the Division of Personnel Preparation, Bureau of Education for the Handicapped, and committed to the concept of stating competencies for the preparation of personnel for the education of the SPH. (The Special Projects Program funds model projects of national significance in high-priority areas of personnel preparation for the handicapped; for further information, see Burke, 1973).

There are, of course, excellent training programs not funded as Special Projects. However,

TABLE 1

*SPH Operational Special Projects**

Grant No. G007501220 University of Miami, Florida Dr. Diane D. Bricker, Project Director Training Personnel to Provide Educational Programs for the Profoundly Handicapped	Grant Nos. OEG-0-73-6137 (Completed) and G007501004 University of Wisconsin–Madison Dr. Lou Brown, Project Director A Graduate Level Training and Information Development Program for Professionals Working with Severely Handicapped Students
Grant No. G007402791 University of Northern Iowa Dr. Richard C. Brady, Project Director Development of Educational Personnel for Work with the Severely, Profoundly and Multiply Handicapped	Grant No. G007602994 University of New Mexico Dr. Gary Adamson, Project Director A Program for Training Teachers of Severely Handicapped
Grant No. G007402766 Kansas Department of Social and Rehabilitation Services Dr. Douglas Guess, Project Director Personnel Training Program for the Severely Handicapped	Grant No. G007602505 University of Vermont Drs. Hugh S. McKenzie and Robert T. York, Project Co-Directors Development of Graduate Training Programs which Facilitate Community Based Special Education for the Severely Handicapped in a Rural State
Grant No. G007402772 Maryland State Department of Education Dr. Camille Peck, Project Director Training Teachers for Severely and Profoundly Handicapped Children	Grant No. OEG-0-71-1673 University of Kentucky Dr. James Tawney, Project Director Practice What You Preach
Grant No. G007402775 Oregon State System of Higher Education, Teaching Research Division Dr. H. D. "Bud" Fredericks, Project Director Competency Training for Teachers	Grant No. OEG-0-73-6004 and G007501961 Pennsylvania State Department of Education Ms. Ellen Somerton, Project Director Pennsylvania Training Model for Preparation of Teachers of the Severely and Profoundly Mentally Retarded and Multihandicapped
Grant No. G007402771 University of Washington Dr. Norris G. Haring, Project Director Preparation of Personnel in the Education of the Severely Handicapped	

* Does not include the BEH/DPP SPH projects for the blind, deaf, deaf/blind, or seriously emotionally disturbed.

one might assume that those currently funded and functioning would be in a position to contribute to the literature, and information concerning them was readily available. One of the projects was not really designed to train teachers and was at such a preliminary state of development that it was not included in the analysis. Thus, all data is reported on the basis of eleven projects, shown on Table 1. (No attempt has been made to ascribe an order or ranking, and the data in later tables is reported randomly, with projects identified by the letters A through K.)

Table 1 shows that the projects and their training efforts focus on SPH children and adolescents, a population which is typically multi-handicapped but whose primary handicap is not sensory or emotional in nature. A number of Special Projects focus on the blind, deaf, deaf-blind, and seriously emotionally disturbed, but these are not included in the analysis.

The authors appreciate greatly the cooperation they received from each project in conducting this analysis. Being selected for such an honor can result in dubious rewards and the authors were reminded of the words of Scott in his *Legend of Montrose*: "I'll make thee famous by my pen, And glorious by my sword." Alas, the projects are listed in Table 1.

Outline

It was necessary to devise an outline of the areas of general competence that should be addressed in a comprehensive program. Unfortunately, in the opinion of the authors, none of the projects examined was fully comprehensive. Also, the authors were not familiar with any research or journal articles that had reported a comprehensive, validated outline that could be used to perform the desired analysis.

To conduct a comprehensive analysis of each project, it was first necessary to establish guidelines for the analysis, and to develop an outline to describe general areas of competency that one should expect to find in a well rounded training program. The formulation of this outline involved extensive review of the literature, surveys of current training programs (excluding the eleven under consideration), discussion with colleagues, and numerous analyses of curriculum materials available for both SPH youngsters and their teachers. The resulting outline describes the various components of a comprehensive training program as these components could be identified by the authors at this time. Some of the items are not totally independent of one another, but have been listed separately in order to indicate discrete bodies of information that should be considered.

It is assumed that applied behavioral analysis is an acceptable and desirable technology to use in training personnel to educate the SPH. However, upon full examination of the outline, one can see that affective and cognitive development and other major areas are clearly addressed. At best, the model suggested is eclectic and perhaps too detailed and cumbersome for actual implementation. It is assumed that some streamlining and consolidation would occur if the reader wished to implement such a program. In order to obtain a general overview of SPH training which might have applicability for all programs, it was necessary to ignore individual program characteristics and examine, instead, training components in terms of a comprehensive training rationale.

Having designed the master outline to describe a comprehensive training program, the authors then used this outline to provide an organizational plan for categorizing the wide variety of expected trainee behaviors they found across the eleven projects they surveyed. Each behavior listed was considered as a discrete entity as this major organizational effort was initiated. As the authors attempted to relate *each* behavior offered by each of the projects to their master outline, however, they found that some minor modifications of the outline were necessary. With these modifications, it became possible to include every behavior identified by the projects, thus providing an inclusive overview of present efforts toward defining competency-based teacher training programs. (See Table 2.)

Analysis

There is no agreement in the literature as to what constitutes a "competency." Some programs emphasize cognitive learning behaviors. Others speak of behavioral objectives, instructional objectives, competency components, competency clusters, competency specifications, and competency modules, almost as if the terms were interchangeable. Some projects grouped competencies as behavioral and informational. Others simply detailed the substantive items they wished the trainee to master in the program.

In the current analysis, statements relating to competency areas and/or statements actually specifying expected trainee behavior were carefully extracted from each of the eleven projects. The intent of the authors was not to judge the form of the competencies addressed but, rather, their content and substance. Thus, a simple but widely inclusive understanding of "competencies" has been used.

In all cases, the authors used the precise wording offered by the authors of these projects, as indicated in the 1975 project descriptions and in additional information received from the projects as of June 1976. In addition, whenever a project description indicated that further competency listings had been developed, the authors contacted project staff and obtained these listings. Once again, this material was cited without modification as it was offered by project staff.

There are significant differences among the programs in many major areas which might affect competency expectations. Among these are:

1. Whether the intent is preservice university training or inservice training offered by a university or state department of education.
2. Whether the trainees enrolled are undergraduates, master's or doctoral level people, or public school personnel selected to work with the SPH.
3. Whether the major emphasis is training individuals to function as classroom teachers, rural classroom teachers involved in a satellite system, consulting teachers, teacher trainers, administrators of pro-

TABLE 2

SPH Competency Outline

1. History
2. Right to Education
3. Interdisciplinary Communication
4. Parent Unit
5. Utilization of Local, State, and National Resources
6. Development of Community-Based Services
7. Administrative Skills
8. Classroom Organization
9. Public Speaking and Writing
10. Training Unit
11. Normal Child Development
12. Exceptional Child Development
13. Medical Basics Unit
14. Handling Health Problems
15. Prosthetic Strategies
16. Assessment
17. Applied Behavioral Analysis
    a. Rationale and Definitions
    b. Research Overview
        (1) General Research Emphasis
        (2) Behavioral Research Emphasis
    c. Instructional Procedures
        (1) Arranging Antecedent Events
        (2) Behavioral Slicing Procedures
        (3) Arranging Consequent Events
    d. Functional Analysis
        (1) Pinpointing Behaviors
        (2) Selecting Appropriate Measurement Systems
        (3) Reliability and Validity Issues
        (4) Selecting Devices to Collect Data
        (5) Selecting Appropriate Data Displays
        (6) Isolating Critical Variables
        (7) Data Collecting and Charting
        (8) Data Decisions
        (9) Applied Behavioral Analysis
18. Considerations for Curriculum Development
    a. Instructional Objectives
    b. Curricular Constructs
    c. Task Analysis
    d. General Sequencing Concerns
    e. Commercial Materials
    f. General Issues in Curriculum Development
19. Curriculum Units
    a. Motor Unit
    b. Sensory or Perceptual Development Unit
    c. Communication Unit
    d. Socialization Unit
    e. Recreation and Leisure Time
    f. Preacademic and Academic Skills Unit
    g. Vocational Education Unit
    h. Cognitive Unit
    i. Affective Unit
    j. Independent Living Skills
        (1) Self-Help
        (2) Domestic Maintenance
        (3) Community Living Skills
        (4) Sex Education

grams, and/or members of interdisciplinary teams.

Given this diversity in the programs, the analysis concentrated on the issue of total preparation to educate the children, as well as service in the role of advocate in the school and community for SPH children. If the bottom line tends to indicate that the field needs a "super teacher" to educate and represent these children properly, then so be it. No attempt has been made in this analysis to conclude that the preparation can be completed at a bachelor's, master's, or post-master's level. That is an issue to be decided by the trainer in future applications of the skills and expectations outlined here. Also, no effort is made to analyze how long it would take to complete such a comprehensive program. However, it would be safe to assume it would not be possible for a dedicated, bright, articulate potential teacher of the SPH to thoroughly master such a program in less than eighteen months of intensive training.

Table 3 shows that each project was fully analyzed in accordance with the outline developed by the authors. A monograph to be prepared at a later date will contain a sample of the actual competencies offered. In Table 3, the projects are represented as columns A through K, in random order, and shown as they relate to the competency outline shown in Table 2.

Classification of Table 3 was determined as follows:

1. The "d" means that a project simply indicated that a competency area was addressed in the training program, but that no competencies were contained in the written description of the project, nor submitted after a follow-up telephone request. Thus, "d" indicates some development, but without a statement of competence.

2. The "D" means that the comprehensive development of competencies was clearly evident in the project description. The form of the competency presentation was not of great concern. For example, in some projects, the competencies are stated as behavioral objectives and expected trainee behaviors are clearly indicated; in others, the need for the trainee to obtain a cognitive understanding of specified areas is indicated. The authors sought an indication of a detailed specification of learning needs for the trainee, not simply a general content outline. The "D" was assigned only when it was evident that an effort was made to define the competency area in a compre-

TABLE 3

An Analysis of Competency Areas by Project

Competency areas		Eleven projects											Totals		
		A	B	C	D	E	F	G	H	I	J	K	d	D	d + D
1. History							d			D		d	2	1	3
2. Right to Education				D		d			d		d	d	4	1	5
3. Interdisciplinary Communication		d	D			d				d	D	d	4	2	6
4. Parent Unit		D	D	d	D	d	d		D		D	d	4	5	9
5. Utilization of Local, State, and National Resources					d	d			d		D	d	4	1	5
6. Development of Community-Based Services				D		d	d			D	d	d	4	2	6
7. Administrative Skills				d						d			2	0	2
8. Classroom Organization			d	D	D					d	D	d	3	3	6
9. Public Speaking and Writing					D	d	d				d	d	4	1	5
10. Training Unit				D		d	D			D	D	D	1	5	6
11. Normal Child Development									D	d	d	d	3	1	4
12. Exceptional Child Development				d		d			d	D	d	d	5	1	6
13. Medical Basics Unit													0	0	0
14. Handling Health Problems							d		d		D	d	3	1	4
15. Prosthetic Strategies				D		d			D	D	d		2	3	5
16. Assessment		d		D	D	D	d		D	D	D	d	3	6	9
17. Applied Behavioral Analysis	a. Rationale and Definition			D		d				d	d	D	3	2	5
b. Research Overview	(1) General Research Emphasis						d			d		d	3	0	3
	(2) Behavioral Research Emphasis			D			d			d		d	3	1	4
c. Instructional Procedures	(1) Arranging Antecedent Events			D		d				d	d	D	3	2	5
	(2) Behavior Slicing Procedures			D								d	1	1	2
	(3) Arranging Consequent Events		D	D		d		d		d	D	D	3	4	7
d. Functional Analysis	(1) Pinpointing Behavior		D	d	d							D	2	2	4
	(2) Selecting Appropriate Measuring System	d	d	D						d	d	d	5	1	6
	(3) Reliability & Validity Issues			D							d		1	1	2

TABLE 3 (*Continued*)

Competency areas		Eleven projects											Totals		
		A	B	C	D	E	F	G	H	I	J	K	d	D	d + D
	(4) Selecting Devices to Collect Data			d	d	d					d		4	0	4
	(5) Selecting Appropriate Data Displays			d	d								2	0	2
	(6) Isolating Critical Variables		D	d	D	D	d		d		D	D	3	5	8
	(7) Data Collection and Charting		d	d	D	d					d		4	1	5
	(8) Data Decisions		D	D	D	d			d		d	d	4	3	7
	(9) Applied Behavioral Analysis			d		d			d		d		4	0	4
18. Considerations for Curriculum Development	a. Instructional Objectives		D	D	D	d			d	d	D	d	4	4	8
	b. Curriculum Constructs			D						d	D	D	1	3	4
	c. Task Analysis			D			d	d		d	D	D	3	3	6
	d. General Sequencing Concerns	D	D	D		d					d	d	3	3	6
	e. Commercial Materials			d	d						D	d	3	1	4
	f. General Issues in Curriculum Development		D								d	D	1	2	3
19. Curriculum Units	a. Motor Unit	d		D		D			D	d	D	d	3	4	7
	b. Sensory or Perception Development Unit									d		D	1	1	2
	c. Communication Unit	d		D					D	d	D	D	2	4	6
	d. Socialization Unit			D								d	1	1	2
	e. Recreation & Leisure Time			d								d	2	0	2
	f. Preacademic & Academic Skill			D						d		D	1	2	3
	g. Vocational Education Unit									d	d	d	3	0	3
	h. Cognitive Unit									d		D	1	1	2
	i. Affective Unit											d	1	0	1
	j. Independent Living Skills Unit (1) Self-Help			D					D	d	d	d	3	2	5
	(2) Domestic Maintenance											d	1	0	1
	(3) Community Living Skills									d		d	2	0	2
	(4) Sex Education										d	d	2	0	2

hensive manner. In several cases, projects addressed elements of a competency area but did not cover the entire area. For instance, several projects defined five or more competencies and expected trainee behaviors under "exceptional child development," but the competencies dealt primarily with cerebral palsy and not with the broad issue of exceptionality. In such cases, the "d" designation was assigned. (In general, the "D" designation was assigned conservatively.)

3. A blank represents no competency development whatsoever.

Competency Areas

This section presents the elements of each training unit, indicating the authors' expectations as to what should be covered in each area. This presentation, along with Table 3, shows that some of the areas are addressed by a large proportion of the eleven projects, while other areas are addressed only cursorily or not at all. The broad issues and implications concerning training are discussed in a later section of this paper.

1. History

The trainer may consider it important for students to place their programs of study in historical perspective, if for no other reason than the axiomatic belief that those who are uninformed of their past are destined to repeat its errors, a particularly undesirable thought when one considers the history of treatment for the SPH. Content for an historical unit might include tracing such issues as: diagnosis and definition of the severely handicapped; societal attitudes; instructional expansion; institutional care; workers who have contributed to this area of special education; organizational involvement, both government and private.

History was not of great interest to all programs in this study. One project had actually developed competencies in this area. Two indicated that history was covered in the project but had not developed competencies.

2. Right to Education

This training unit concerns the history of litigation affecting the severely handicapped, with particular emphasis on litigation in a particular program's state, as well as the current involvement of the federal government. Items covered should include: due process; right-to-education litigation and equal protection under law; severely handicapped children and the law; legal and legislative considerations.

Five projects made some provision for examination of legal and legislative considerations, but only one project had developed competencies.

3. Interdisciplinary Communication

Educators working with SPH individuals will be required to utilize the resources of professionals from many other disciplines, including physical and occupational therapy, nursing, communication disorders, medicine, social work, and engineering. Any comprehensive training program should train students in utilizing resource people, in functioning as members of interdisciplinary teams, and in synthesizing the suggestions of the various disciplines into a plan of action for the classroom. Because interdisciplinary effort may become a plan for action only through the determined efforts of all individuals involved, it is critical that the trainee begin to examine and practice some of the skills necessary to facilitate communication.

Six projects addressed this issue. Two of these presented detailed competencies.

4. Parent Unit

Continuing problems with transfer and generalization of skills taught in the school setting necessitate active involvement by all persons in the SPH child's environment. Some of the areas that must be included by a training unit are: learning to communicate with parents in an effort to determine priority areas for intervention; helping to establish home programs; utilizing parent information in school programs; encouraging and working with parents to help the child generalize his skills beyond the school setting. The acquisition of these skills requires that the trainee become familiar with parent training strategies, learn to utilize the parent as a resource person, and learn to discriminate essential information which may be incorporated into plans for total child management. The overall importance of this unit cannot be over-emphasized. Preliminary findings of the Oregon Project (Grant No. G007402775) indicate that an hour of teacher/child instruction, coupled with an hour of parent/child reinforcement of that instruction is more effective and efficient by a two-fold measure than is a straight two hours of teacher/child instruction with no parent reinforcement.

Nine of the projects surveyed delineated a variety of behaviors which trainees would be expected to perform. Of these nine, five included detailed competencies.

5. Utilization of Local, State, and National Resources

In preparing for the role of SPH educator, it will in many cases be imperative that the trainee understand established institutions in his community, studying organizational structures and procedures for dealing with the bureaucracy in attempts to meet SPH program needs. The trainee must also learn procedures for determining those resources which are already available in the community and in other communities, as well as national resources, including the Council for Exceptional Children and the American Association for the Education of the Severely/Profoundly Handicapped.

A critical competency area is that of understanding the State Department's commitment to SPH children. A review of litigation may be necessary, in that the trainee may need to relate legal rights to actual practice in the community. Further, the trainee should be introduced to some of the procedures considered valuable when attempting to ensure that these newly found rights will not be violated. The passage of Public Law 94-142 and the development of the individual education plan (IEP) for each child is critical to the protection of the child's and parent's rights. In terms of Public Law 94-142, it appears that "appropriate" education will be defined in relation to whether a specific area of education or therapy is included in the IEP. If it is included, then the child is entitled to it. In essence, the protection of the child's civil rights in an educational sense will be geared to the design of the IEP. Training programs should also have a special interest in examining available facilities for the older SPH individual, facilities which would be involved when individuals are no longer eligible for school programs. The commitment of the educator to studying longitudinal issues affecting the SPH individual clearly needs to be reflected in the training program.

Five projects addressed this issue. Only one presented detailed competencies.

6. Development of Community-Based Services

When attempting to utilize available community resources, some trainees may come to the realization that many of the services their pupils require are not available. Should the trainee ever hope to see these services develop, it will be necessary that he assume a more active role in his community. A review of litigation affecting the rights of the handicapped in the community would be an essential component of this unit, as well as exploration of the role a special educator should play in the process of developing services. The unit should also cover channels to pursue, procedures to follow in forming citizen advisory and/or advocacy groups, resource people to contact, possible obstacles to overcome, service delivery models to study, background information to obtain concerning establishing and maintaining community-based services, and integration of the handicapped into the mainstream. The trainee's role in recruiting other outstanding individuals into the field might also be explored.

Two projects had outlined extensive competencies in this area. Four others indicated that this area was covered in their training sequences, but did not give details as to competencies.

7. Administrative Skills

The teacher in a classroom for the severely handicapped will be placed in the position of directing teams of paraprofessionals, volunteers, and parents. Such positions will also necessitate some organizational management skills to ensure a program which is both efficiently and effectively handled. As the teacher moves into positions involving more than one classroom, these skills become even more critical. Moreover, as the teacher begins to design programs which require monetary considerations (many programs and materials for the SPH are quite costly), it will be essential to understand the ways in which monies are obtained and distributed.

In addition, the demonstration of pupil progress is an important component of SPH programs, used to justify and continue present levels of funding. Thus, the trainee must become skilled in summarizing pupil progress information across classrooms. Such summaries must address administrative concerns and express pupil gains clearly and concisely. If trainees are unable to summarize the large amount of information they have collected, they will continually require the services of others to help them in this task. Yet they may find themselves in situations where they are expected to have these skills; in fact, these skills may be important to their survival.

Unfortunately, the authors found no developed competencies in this area, and only two projects included such units in their training sequences.

8. CLASSROOM ORGANIZATION

A major finding of the Oregon study (Grant No. G007602994), designed to identify those competencies essential for successful teachers of the severely handicapped (those teachers whose pupils are making large gains), is that the length of the instructional day is a critical variable.

> The teacher and the aide must provide instruction for the child for as many minutes as possible during the day and thus must utilize a system of volunteers, scheduling, and materials arrangement so as to maximize instructional time. Little attention has been paid to this variable in the average teacher training institution. Moreover, little research is available regarding this subject. (Grant No. G007602994, Appendix, p. 11)

Because the broad variable that has been isolated here suggests many more questions than it answers regarding implications for training, we may only conclude that a unit concerning classroom organization bears careful consideration. Three projects appeared to concur with this opinion in offering detailed descriptions of student behavior and competencies in this area. Three other projects indicated that the area was covered in their training sequences, without the development of precise competencies.

9. PUBLIC SPEAKING AND WRITING

The people graduating from our training programs need not only to be skilled in their work with SPH individuals, but may also have to serve as advocates for the severely handicapped within their schools, communities, states, and possibly the nation. These professionals may be called upon to publicize their efforts, writing for various local and national publications, and speaking before local and national groups. Such skills are necessary, in our opinion, to fulfill the role of advocate.

The authors found one project with competencies in the area of writing, but not speaking. Four additional projects indicated this as an area generally covered in their training, but none of these had developed competencies.

10. TRAINING UNIT

Graduates from our training programs will, in all probability, be called upon to train others, including fellow professionals who, although they have not received any previous training specific to the task, have been asked to work with the severely handicapped and with parents and paraprofessionals. It is equally likely that many graduates will be given positions in which inservice and/or preservice training is a major part of their responsibility. If students have not received background in the preparation, design, and presentation of training modules, workshop activities, and lectures, and have been given no opportunity to supervise other trainees in practicum situations, they will have had little chance to develop some of the necessary skills which their new positions may require. When considering the gravity of these training responsibilities, we must examine our programs carefully to determine whether we are providing well designed sequences which will ensure carefully supervised experiences and opportunities for feedback as students begin to function in training roles.

Five projects have specified extensive listings of trainee behavior in this area, determined by the nature of the program (whether trainees are in preservice programs at undergraduate, master's, or doctoral levels, or are part of an inservice training effort for teachers and/or other interdisciplinary team members). One additional program indicates training in this area without specified competencies.

11. NORMAL CHILD DEVELOPMENT

With a firm foundation in normal development, the student may have some guidelines against which to compare the exceptional developmental patterns which he will confront in the classroom. This unit should, thus, include a study of the normal developmental sequence across each of the major developmental areas.

Although such a unit covers a very large area and would seem crucial in developing programs for severely handicapped individuals, most of the programs do not appear to have considered this topic in any great depth. Four training projects stressed the need to incorporate material about normal child development into the training sequence for a student in severely handicapped. Only one of the projects had actually developed competencies.

12. EXCEPTIONAL CHILD DEVELOPMENT

The authors discovered a number of attempts to present information about some of the more common problems with which the trainee will be expected to deal. In some cases, these efforts appear fairly fragmented; in others, greater effort has been devoted to delineating the crucial understandings in this area and to describing competencies that should be incorporated into training programs.

One project delineated in great detail the information that would be covered but has not, as yet, fully defined the competencies teachers would be required to demonstrate in this area. Five other projects listed no competencies, but addressed the area as important, indicating that it would be covered in some way in the project.

13. Medical Basics Unit

Special educators have generally avoided many of the medically related courses during their training for advanced degrees, although the SPH present numerous medically related problems and frequently have fragile medical existences. While the authors are not suggesting that trainees complete several years of medical school, they do feel that certain *basic* knowledge may be critical for a more thorough understanding of the child's presenting problem. A Medical Basics Unit could cover extremely basic introductory material in such areas as anatomy, physiology, and neurology. Help from professionals in such areas as neurology, pediatrics, nursing, and occupational and physical therapy will also be necessary if we are to begin to identify critical basic information in these areas.

These needs were underscored by the recent recommendations of the Maryland SPH Advisory Committee, which includes statewide representation from professional and parental groups concerned with SPH youngsters. This Committee identified neurodevelopment, neuroanatomy, and neurophysiology among areas necessary to SPH teacher preparation programs (Maryland Project, Grant No. G007402772, Appendix, p. 21). To date, however, examination of the eleven projects reveals little or no activity regarding development of competencies in this important area.

14. Handling Health Problems

Some SPH trainees express concern about being in a classroom situation where a health problem may occur that they will not be able to handle, but which will require immediate knowledge of correct procedures. A Health Problems Unit could provide the trainee with basic information regarding first-aid procedures for the most common types of emergencies, as well as information regarding convulsive disorders, which appear to be of continual concern to the entering trainee. A program on safety would also be helpful, as some trainees do not always make critical discriminations regarding classroom management and could benefit from guidelines, such as what to check before leaving a youngster alone in one part of the classroom. Still another consideration is nutrition, in that the SPH youngster may present many nutritional problems which relate to his total functioning. Teachers of the SPH will have great involvement with the child's nutritional status and, without basic information, may contribute to already present deficiencies. Thus, it is critical that trainees receive basic information to use in planning feeding programs, as well as for making selections regarding food reinforcers.

Only one project has developed competencies here. Three others offer a few ideas in this area, but have not developed competencies.

15. Prosthetic Strategies

Lindsley (1964) stated that three basic strategies have been successfully used in prosthetizing and rehabilitating the behaviorally handicapped: (a) construction of prosthetic devices, (b) prosthetic training, and (c) construction of prosthetic environments. Briefly, prosthetic devices are worn or carried about permitting the handicapped person to behave normally in an average environment. Some of the more common devices are eyeglasses, hearing aids, braces, dentures, and artificial limbs. Prosthetic training given to people with certain handicaps can permit them to behave efficiently in average environments. Among the common examples are training in receptor substitution through such techniques as lipreading or cane-tapping. Occupational and physical therapists may train individuals to use nondebilitated muscles to perform tasks which were previously dependent on injured or destroyed muscles. Training in the use of mnemonic devices for people with poor memories is still another example of a prosthetic training strategy. In the case of the prosthetic environment, the deficient behavior is not needed; rather, the environment is altered in such a way as to allow the individual to function effectively. Common examples are Braille books and magazines; ramps, elevators, and handrails; and specially designed homes and automobiles.

The trainee should receive information about available strategies, as well as the resources which may be used in obtaining necessary devices and/or further information about a given strategy. Although, as training progresses, it will be necessary to consider each of the available strategies in much more detail as they relate to particular units of curriculum (e.g., gross or fine motor functioning), it is also essential that the trainee be directed to consider some of the broader issues pertaining to this entire unit. Given the limited budgets of many SPH programs, these teachers may also have a tremendous need to learn to create new and inexpensive devices, as well as components for prosthetic environments. Locating and effectively communicating classroom needs to resource people (including parents, engineers, and local people with handyman skills) will also be an important endeavor for trainees.

In the past five years, the completely experimental area of prosthetic devices has seen developments that have been nothing short of spectacular, including the Opticon and the Kurzweil Reading Machine. The authors believe that trainers should collaborate with the best engineering minds on campus and in the field to construct means for surmounting additional handicaps through the use of technology. With computer chips and mini-circuitry, along with other developments, the possibilities appear almost boundless. The field has been dealing with a group of youngsters who were written off by educators long ago; why not also challenge the barriers in this area?

This survey indicates that three projects have particular concern with this area and have developed detailed competencies. Two additional projects listed this as an area of training but did not present competencies.

16. Assessment

Assessment units provide an introduction to those formal instruments and a few informal scales and tools currently available which the various programs have determined are applicable to the SPH. This appears to be an area of intensive development.

Nine projects addressed this area. Of these, six had defined competencies.

17. Applied Behavior Analysis

Because all programs surveyed use applied behavior analysis as their basis, they all placed major emphasis on competencies in this area. The following are those competency areas which seem to form the foundation upon which the trainee will be expected to build throughout his program.

a. Rationale and Definitions. This section introduces the trainee to the area by contrasting it with other approaches and by providing examples of current application. Five projects offered descriptions of the information they would include here, but only two had developed competencies.

b. Research Overview. This unit deals with research methodology and its general and specific application to the problem of educating SPH children, as follows.

(1) General Research Emphasis. The expectation is that the trainee would demonstrate knowledge of common research methodologies, especially as they have been applied to the study of problems in mental retardation and special education. There is also the expectation that the trainee would understand the difference between causal and correlational relationships and could isolate and define dependent and independent variables in the teaching situation. Only three projects addressed this area of training, and no project had actually defined detailed competencies.

(2) Behavioral Research Emphasis. While the previous unit would address general research concerns and cover large N research, here the emphasis would be small N. An introduction and overview of the research methodology, as well as the rationale for its selection in the study of specific problems would be presented. Also included would be an introduction to basic terminology (e.g., baseline, treatment). Surprisingly, only four projects addressed this area; of these, only one had what could be considered well developed competencies.

c. Instructional Procedures. As a result of extensive behavioral research, many instructional procedures have been described, and their effects on behavior have been documented. These procedures are defined functionally (e.g., a reinforcer may only be defined as such if it brings about an increase in behavior). Thus, the trainee will find basic information here necessary to later classroom functioning. Procedures are presented in three categories: those for arranging antecedent events (occurring before the child engages in the crucial behavior); those useful for behavior slicing (procedures for dealing with carefully isolated segments or aspects of behavior); those for arranging consequent events (occurring after the child has engaged in the crucial behavior). While the first two categories would be considered of major interest in this survey, the third has been demonstrated to be a particularly valid element for inclusion within a training program, according to the Oregon study (Grant No. G007402775).

(1) Arranging Antecedent Events. This includes skills in the ability to define and utilize instructional procedures that behavioral research has identified (e.g., prompting, fading, color cueing, exaggerated cue differences, modeling). Out of five projects with development in this area, two actually had extensively developed competencies.

(2) Behavioral Slicing Procedures. Those working with SPH youngsters will have need to teach many new behaviors; these behaviors may often only be developed slowly by first breaking the behavior into smaller component parts which may be more easily managed for teaching purposes. A thorough knowledge of procedures provided by behavioral research (e.g., shaping, chaining) will therefore be extremely valuable to the trainee. Two projects exhibited development in this area, but only one had specified competencies.

(3) Arranging Consequent Events. Included in this area, of course, would be topics such as reinforcer selection and scheduling of reinforcement. When considering this particular area, however, the finding of the Oregon Project (Grant No. GOO7402775) is especially interesting. This project has worked toward identifying competencies for teachers of SPH youngsters by comparing a group of teachers whose students made the greatest gains over an academic year with a group which did not demonstrate similar gains. Results indicated that one major area of teacher training that should be emphasized is delivery of appropriate consequences to the child being taught. This is hardly a startling finding; behaviorists have long emphasized the necessity for appropriate feedback. Yet, of the projects reviewed, only four showed detailed competencies, while seven indicated development in this area.

d. Functional Analysis. The application of skills in applied behavior analysis to solving daily classroom dilemmas may be termed "functional analysis." For the purposes of this paper, functional analysis is considered to have nine essential elements.

(1) Pinpointing Behaviors. The trainee must learn to offer precise behavioral descriptions of problems. In part, this would include translating potential target behaviors from assessment scales into precise behavioral definitions with written statements of the components of precise behaviors. Four projects included development in this area, and two had detailed competencies.

(2) Selecting Appropriate Measurement Systems. Another crucial component of functional analysis is selection of the appropriate measurement system to sensitively describe the behavior that has been pinpointed. The student should be familiar with basic measurement issues (e.g., will he choose to collect duration, percent, trials to criterion, or rate data, given a particular behavior?), and be able to present advantages and disadvantages of each measure. Six projects provided expected trainee behaviors here, but only one listed competencies.

(3) Reliability and Validity Issues. While reliability and validity are major issues whenever measurement is considered, one might be surprised to learn that only one project actually stressed providing extensive background information in this area and had developed competencies for it.

(4) Selecting Devices to Collect Data. After selecting the measure to collect data on the target behavior, the trainee should be able to select or design the appropriate devices for use in collecting data. It is important for the trainee to understand that data will not be collected under laboratory conditions where complex devices may be perfectly appropriate for data collection. The project with the greatest emphasis in this area highlighted the need for the teacher to use devices that are practical to classroom use. However, none of the four projects addressing this unit included detailed competencies.

(5) Selecting Appropriate Data Displays. Before the trainee begins to chart data, he must select an appropriate chart (bar graph display, arithmetic or semilogarithmic or logarithmic chart, etc.). He must also have basic information about graphs in general (drawing and interpreting various scales, the relationship between the ordinate and abscissa, etc.). Although all projects surveyed appeared to emphasize charting data, only two delineated trainee behaviors regarding basic knowledge of charts.

(6) Isolating Critical Variables Affecting the Pinpointed Behavior. Another skill vital to functional analysis is that of isolating critical variables which are affecting the child's performance. Various procedures can be used to accomplish this. Systematic observations involving observation tools designed to help the teacher analyze the environment may include having the trainee learn to use plan sheets

requiring the specification of potentially relevant variables that affect child performance. As he becomes proficient in this procedure, the trainee acquires a powerful tool which may be utilized in isolating classroom variables and systematically examining them. Five projects specified tools the trainee would be expected to use when conducting this analysis. Eight of the eleven projects stressed that skill in analyzing critical variables is an essential component of the applied behavior analysis unit of the training program.

(7) Data Collection and Charting. In the integration of all skills vital to functional analysis, one would assume that data collection and charting would be important areas. However, only one project set some minimum requirements here (the trainee was required to record for a certain period of time and with a certain criterion for reliability). Four others define a criterion for accuracy but have not detailed competencies.

(8) Data Decisions. To perform functional analysis successfully, the trainee must become skillful in using the data he has collected. The main thrust in this area would involve determining from baseline data when to implement the treatment procedure, and determining the effectiveness of treatment procedures by comparing data in the treatment conditions to data in the baseline conditions. Seven projects specified behaviors in this area. Of these, three had detailed competencies.

(9) Applied Behavior Analysis: General Considerations for Education. Here the attempt is to encourage the trainee to synthesize information about functional analysis into some general models for classroom functioning. Discussions of the systematic instructional model in the SPH classroom would, for example, be appropriate. Also, examination of existing programs as they have employed functional analysis in their development of instructional plans for SPH may be included. Four projects indicated work in this area, without the development of detailed competencies.

18. Considerations for Curriculum Development

Topics of particular relevance to curriculum development are: establishing instructional objectives, delineating curricular constructs, performing task analysis, general sequencing skills, using commercial materials, and general issues in curriculum development. Because there are so few totally applicable materials for an SPH classroom, the trainee will find curriculum development to be a major issue. Also, because each of these topics could appear repeatedly as the trainee considers separate curriculum units, the authors decided that a systematic introduction to general information pertinent to each topic would be an essential component in comprehensive training programs.

a. Instructional Objectives. Although the specification of instructional objectives concerned all projects surveyed, there are extreme differences in requirements and emphases. Eight projects included training units in this area; of these, four had developed competencies.

b. Curricular Constructs. A construct, by its very nature, is extremely broad, allowing room for the consideration of many and varied issues. Among the constructs emerging in this survey are: (a) the notion of stages in learning, defined as acquisition, proficiency, maintenance, generalization, and adaptation; (b) issues of pupil discrimination and generalization. Training the SPH in discrimination and generalization represents a major area of concern. What is important to consider is that applied behavior analysis offers important *procedures* useful in teaching these two *processes*, but the problems presented by each of these two processes merit special consideration.

Three projects outlined competencies in this area. One additional project emphasized development but had not defined competencies.

c. Task Analysis. Task analysis involves the analysis of a task, skill, or general competency area and provides a behavioral break-out of the essential component parts in a way which may be used for instructional purposes. Considering the dearth of appropriate curricular materials, teachers must be able to adapt and modify available materials and create many new materials to meet individual pupil needs. For this reason, task analysis is an area of major importance. Research of the Oregon Project (Grant No. G007402775) indicates that utilization of a task analyzed curriculum is an important variable in gains made by SPH youngsters. Indeed, results indicate that the type of material made no essential difference; what made the difference was task analysis of the material.

Six projects outlined development of training in task analysis. Of these, three had detailed competencies.

d. General Sequencing Concerns. In dealing with the broad sequencing problems presented in a curriculum unit, the trainee may begin to concern himself with grouping a number of task analyses he has conducted, then studying their relationship to each other as he considers larger instructional components. He might also consider the ways in which he would sequence various objectives when examining the child's entire curriculum as presented over several years. Six projects addressed this issue, and three of these presented competencies.

e. Commercial Materials. Although few materials are currently available for the SPH classroom without considerable adaptation, it is vital that the trainee become familiar with those materials which have the greatest potential, and to learn how to adapt them for individual use. Only four projects addressed this issue; of these, only one could be considered to have developed competencies.

f. General Issues in Curriculum Development. The authors believe that one major issue that should not be overlooked is that, while the student probably should have a firm foundation in applied behavior analysis, it is extremely important that he be made aware of the contributions of other workers and other orientations. Unfortunately, few projects offer trainee behaviors relating to this issue or make any effort to diversify in the area of teaching technology.

Comprehensive projects which involve empirical evaluation require integration of all the earlier issues covered in this unit. Indeed, when addressing curriculum development, many projects stressed to the trainee the importance of examining pupil performance. This need for continual examination of pupil data in relation to objectives is emphasized by several projects.

Finally, a few projects highlight the need to examine particular types of programs, such as an infant program, when curriculum issues are considered. Apparently, there is a need to examine the ways by which some of the issues presented would be applied to different age groups. As longitudinal training programs focusing on SPH are developed, there will be many questions involving the pupil's present and future life space that the trainee will want to examine in developing curricula. Issues of functionality, for example, may become of major concern and would surely seem worthy of careful consideration as one approaches an overview of educational programming.

Only three projects addressed this issue. Of these, two had detailed competencies and an orientation sensitive to the issues.

19. Curriculum Units

There are a variety of opinions regarding core curriculum units. As an example, the University of Washington project (Grant No. G007402771) offered the following curriculum units, specifying that trainees have competencies in the areas of: (a) language development, (b) fine and gross motor skills, (c) prevocational and vocational skills, (d) "life" skills such as personal hygiene, time-telling, change-making, (e) appropriate social behavior patterns, (f) and academic programming according to the levels of the children.

As another example, the University of Miami project (Grant No. G007501220) indicated that a comprehensive program should contain the following major curriculum areas: (a) language, (b) cognitive, (c) self-help, and (d) motor. Further, the University of Vermont (Grant No. G007602505) includes: (a) motor, (b) perceptual development, (c) social studies, (d) communication, (e) social functioning, (f) cognitive development, (g) self-care, (h) academic skills, and (i) occupational/vocational/practical skills.

Through studying numerous possibilities suggested by available curriculum materials, literature reviews, surveys of colleagues outside the projects under study and the projects themselves, the authors decided upon the following major units for their analysis: motor, sensory or perceptual development, communication, socialization, recreation and leisure time, preacademic and academic, vocational education, cognitive, affective, and independent living skills.

a. Motor Unit. To implement instruction within a unit covering both gross and fine motor programs, the authors feel that information pertaining specifically to medical aspects should be thoroughly reviewed, along with normal and exceptional development affecting motor skills. This unit might also consider prosthetic strategies pertaining to motor problems and relating to specific handicapping conditions. The major emphasis, however, would be to introduce specific programming strategies relative to motor programs, and an introduction to such basic information as lifting and positioning physically handicapped youngsters. The trainee should also develop an understanding of the roles of the physical and occupational therapist in the classroom and the ways therapists may participate as valuable resource persons.

As each of the core units is presented it should become apparent to the reader that information covered in other areas of the training program may provide an especially important foundation when the trainee considers the programming strategies relevant to any particular area. Here, the general information provided in the Medical Basics Unit, as well as the units concerning normal and exceptional development can now be developed and refined in such a way as to highlight, review, and expand upon topics of specific concern when examining motor skills.

Seven programs have begun to define the content for this motor unit. Of these, four could be considered to offer listings of expected trainee behaviors or competencies.

b. Sensory or Perceptual Development Unit. In this unit, specific effort should be devoted to examining and applying relevant programming strategies for dealing with sensory and perceptual disorders. Programming for sensory disorders as they may be associated with mental retardation (such as visual disorders or hearing disorders of varying degrees of involvement, as well as combinations of the above) may be extremely important. Perceptual disorders as they relate to auditory, visual, and tactile stimuli should also be included. Further, the often discussed topic of sensory stimulation for the SPH youngster could receive attention in this unit.

The authors found this area grossly underdeveloped in the projects reviewed. Only two projects addressed the unit, and only one of these had developed competencies.

c. Communication Unit. This component includes a review of normal receptive and expressive language development. Other modes of nonverbal communication, such as gestures, would also be introduced, and special emphasis should be given to certain crucial behaviors, such as establishing eye contact (an entering behavior in many programs, and a crucial early communication behavior). As is intended in the previous units, the trainee would be given background on only critical information, but would be provided with a variety of programming strategies to practice, including prosthetic techniques (e.g., manual communication, language boards, the Bliss symbol system).

Our survey indicated that six projects have begun to define the content for this unit by specifying required trainee behaviors. Of these, four could be considered to have detailed competencies.

d. Socialization Unit. Two subtopics merit consideration in this area: self-stimulatory behavior and social interaction.

(1) Primary among those behaviors that interfere with socialization programs are self-stimulatory behaviors. For this reason, programming strategies should become topics for intensive study. None of the programs surveyed, however, seemed to share our belief in providing a special emphasis here, as no competencies within this area could be found.

(2) Social interaction often presents major problems for the SPH, and this subject appeared to be of concern in some projects. The teacher trainers considering this issue are attempting to define behaviors related to socialization (smiling, cooperative play, verbalizations about particular things such as current events). Nonetheless, only one project addressed this area in a comprehensive manner.

e. Recreation and Leisure Time. The present and future life spaces for many of the SPH suggest that these individuals will have a good deal of "leisure time." It will therefore be necessary for trainees in this field to begin examining more systematically the ways in which individuals may spend this time. Training should concentrate on activities in which social interaction is essential, and on activities that can be done without the participation of others. Programming strategies for music, arts and crafts would be extremely appropriate here. Procedures to identify and utilize presently reinforcing activities, while simultaneously building new reinforcing activities to occupy free time, require much further exploration. There is little development in this area. Only two projects addressed the issue, and no competencies were developed.

f. Preacademic and Academic Skills Unit. Functional academic skills are essential to the SPH, in order that they may learn such basic behaviors as using the telephone, making change, writing one's name, reading basic survival words. As intensive, long-term programs are developed for SPH youngsters, teachers will need more intensive preparation in imparting preacademic and academic skills to those individuals who become ready to enter such programs. There is also the major issue of defining readiness. Trainees will have to be familiar with entering behaviors required by various reading and math sequences. They should also understand the various strategies for teaching reading and math skills to this population, and information on skill sequences in each of these subject areas should be presented to provide basic guidelines.

Unfortunately, only three projects addressed this area in their training, although two of these have developed an excellent set of competencies.

g. Vocational Education Unit. Vocational education relates directly to the SPH individual's functioning in the community. Certain SPH trainees will concentrate in this area of preparation, but we feel that all trainees should have basic information on vocational education if they are to understand issues affecting longitudinal functioning of the individuals with whom they are working. Those advocating the integration of the SPH into the community cannot afford complacency in regard to the actual situations they will face in the future. The pinpointing of prevocational skills is a continuing need, as is effort to identify and create job placements which may endure in a continually changing technological society.

A vocational education unit should concentrate on the examination of programming strategies that have been successful in ongoing vocational programs. Another critical issue is the consideration of life skills that are important in maintaining a job once placement has occurred.

Few projects surveyed have outlined trainee requirements in this area. In fact, only three have addressed the issue, and none of these has developed competencies.

h. Cognitive Unit. Although all units in a training program would certainly have a cognitive base, our rationale in providing a separate unit here is that the other units concern themselves largely with observable child behavior. A cognitive unit, on the other hand, would involve constructs, theories, and approaches that deal with cognitive processes. Topics would include problem-solving, concept building, visual and auditory memory, short and long term memory. In addition, Piagetian constructs should be examined thoroughly, particularly as they may relate to the functioning of the SPH. Years of study and research lie ahead in this area, but it is important that we begin.

The authors found only two projects with units on cognition. Of these, one had developed competencies for trainees.

i. Affective Unit. The affective domain presents interesting problems in that it is a domain which cannot be ignored as we consider our own daily lives, yet we continue to struggle with the definitional problems which it presents. This area may assume new importance as we consider a population which might have great difficulty utilizing some of our conventional means to provide feedback concerning the effect our efforts are having on their lives.

Inasmuch as the affective domain presents definitional problems, trainees should be offered the challenge to explore this area and define behaviors which might be used to develop program sequences. The importance of development in this area is not only that our affective behaviors relate our "humanness" to others, but also that success on the job and with co-workers is often dependent on the SPH adolescent's ability to relate appropriately to others. The lack of attention to affective behavior is underscored by the fact that only one project dealt with the issue at all, and no project had developed any competencies in relation to it.

j. Independent Living Skills. Regardless of his relative success in the vocational area, the child needs certain skills to help ensure his independence. The degree of independence he ultimately achieves in his future life space, whether a sheltered, partially independent, or totally independent environment, will depend upon his mastery of basic independent living skills. This unit is composed of self-help skills, domestic maintenance, community living skills, and sex education.

(1) The most basic self-help skills concern personal body maintenance, including programming and prosthetic strategies for handling, feeding, toileting, dressing, and grooming. These procedures receive major emphasis in most SPH programs, so it might be expected that all programs would require several trainee competencies here. Yet only five projects appear to have devoted major effort to this area and, of these, detailed competencies were presented in only two.

(2) Domestic maintenance skills involve doing laundry, cleaning house, planning and preparing meals, and the like. The authors were surprised to find an almost complete lack of attention to training needs in this area. Only one project indicated this as a need, and it did not include detailed competencies.

(3) The broad area of community living skills involves problems relating to the successful integration of the SPH individual into the

community. The trainee may be asked, for example, to consider and delineate minimal skill levels necessary for the individual to use stores, services, and transportation facilities. In examining those few contributions offered by the projects, it appears that trainee behavior is presently confined to discussion of relevant issues. Only two projects addressed community living skills, and no detailed competencies have been developed.

(4) One of the projects offered a set of topics on sex education which we feel that other projects should cover: moral, philosophical, and legal issues involving sex and the severely handicapped; the role of parents and schools in sex education; body functioning; birth control; masturbation; sexual intercourse; and menstrual hygiene. These issues should be appropriately addressed to the proper age and setting, and geared to whether the adolescent were living at home or in a residential setting. With the adolescent living at home, sex education should be coordinated with the parents or surrogates.

Although many of us agree that educators must not overlook the important issue of sex education, only two projects had outlined training in this area, and no competencies had been developed.

Discussion of Findings

When the initial analysis outlined in Table 3 was completed, the incidence of development for each competency was evaluated (Table 4). If a competency area was adequately developed in at least four projects (i.e., with defined competencies) and was addressed in at least six projects, it could be considered to have been moderately developed. On the other hand, if no more than one project had addressed a competency area fully, and if two or fewer projects were involved in the development of a competency, then the area was considered to be seriously under-developed.

Table 4 is an overall project-by-project comparison. Of the total of 50 areas of potential competency development suggested by the authors, full competencies have been developed in only 23 areas by the project ranking highest in competency development (Table 4, row 3, project C). Thus, any analysis would have to conclude that much work remains ahead in the whole area of competency development if we are to be successful in our quest for competence in serving the SPH. On the other hand, it is encouraging that four projects (C, I, J, and K) are well on the way to addressing the 50 areas of development, and one project (K) has developmental work underway in 42 of the 50 areas outlined by the authors.

Row 7 of Table 4 shows some idiosyncracies of projects (and probably of their directors). Some tend to indicate coverage of a broad

TABLE 4

Analysis of Project Competencies—Total Development

	Developmental Elements	Projects										
		A	B	C	D	E	F	G	H	I	J	K
1	d	5	3	11	5	18	10	2	8	21	19	29
2	Rank	8/9	10	5	8/9	4	6	11	7	2	3	1
3	D	2	9	23	8	3	1	0	7	6	15	13
4	Rank	9	4	1	5	8	10	11	6	7	2	3
5	d & D	7	12	34	13	21	11	2	15	27	34	42
6	Rank	10	8	2/3	7	5	9	11	6	4	2/3	1
7	% D	29%	75%	68%	62%	14%	9%	0%	47%	22%	44%	31%

1 Row indicates the number of competencies for which the project rated "d" (i.e., some development without full competency development).
2 The rank of the project on the variable "d."
3 Row indicates the number of fully developed competencies per project.
4 The rank of the project on the variable "D."
5 Row reflects the total competency development and comprehensiveness of each project.
6 The rank of the project on the combined variables "d" & "D."
7 Row reflects the % of the development in a project that has resulted in full competency development. Thus, project C has a combined d + D of 34, 68% of which represent competency development.

area of competency development but have actually developed few areas in relation to the total coverage projected (Projects E and F). Conversely, some projects develop competencies for a high percentage of the areas projected for coverage (Projects B and C, with 75% and 68%, respectively). One might infer, as an example, that Project B simply does not list competency areas as part of the training coverage until a full set of competencies have been developed. On the other hand, Project K indicates a broad package of training (42 of 50 areas covered) but a relatively low ratio of coverage to full competency development (13 areas of full development out of 42 areas covered, for a total of 31%).

Table 4 also reveals that a few projects have not devoted a great deal of effort to competency development in any of the identified areas. For example, Project G projects only two areas for coverage, both undeveloped.

Moderately Developed Competency Areas

Table 5 indicates that the greatest development of actual competencies has taken place in assessment. Six of the eleven projects had developed competencies for assessment, while three more of the eleven may be considered to have begun developmental efforts in this area. Apparently, there is some consensus regarding the importance of knowledge concerning assessment tools available, procedures for correctly administering these tools, and for interpreting results obtained.

TABLE 5

Competency Areas[1] Moderately Developed

Competency	D[2]	d + D[3]
IV. Parent Unit	5	9
X. Training Unit	5	6
XV. Assessment	6	9
XVI. Applied Behavioral Analysis		
C. Instructional Procedures		
3. Arranging Consequent Events	4	7
XVIII. Considerations for Curriculum Development		
A. Instructional Objectives	4	8
XIX. Curriculum Units		
A. Motor Unit	4	7
C. Communications Unit	4	6

1. An area that had a minimum D = 4 and d + D = 6 was considered significant. The numbers in the two columns indicate numbers of projects in each category.
2. Letter "D" indicates the development of competencies.
3. Letter "d" indicates some development without competences defined (d + D = total development effort).

Areas which also received project attention were the Parent and Training Units. Nine projects had begun developmental work on the Parent Unit, with five of the nine offering competencies in this area. Six projects show work on the Training Unit, and five of these have developed competencies.

Because all of the projects have placed emphasis upon the importance of using applied behavior analysis as a basis, it is especially interesting to note the areas within the Applied Behavior Analysis Unit which have thus far received most attention. Arranging consequent events appears to be the instructional procedure given most consideration. While some outside the area of applied behavior analysis have at times equated the area with a body of knowledge about consequent events, it is unfortunate that those within the area have not thus far devoted more effort to developing competencies related to the other important procedures, such as arranging antecedent events. Moreover, the authors' outline regarding the applied behavior analysis unit showed that functional analysis involves a number of component skills. Although it would appear that several projects have attended to those components involving a synthesis of skills, few have actually devoted much specific attention to earlier components which may be necessary to ensure success in these attempts at synthesis. For example, while several projects were interested in having their trainees utilize data for instructional decision-making, little effort was devoted in many of these projects to ensuring that the trainee actually had such critical skills as accurately pinpointing the behavior of concern, selecting an appropriate measurement system to monitor that behavior, selecting appropriate devices to reliably collect the data in a classroom situation, and actually demonstrating reliable data collection under carefully specified conditions. Without these necessary skills, the trainee may, in fact, accumulate unreliable and invalid data upon which he attempts to base his instructional decisions.

With the continued current emphasis on specification of instructional objectives, it is not surprising that our analysis should reveal instructional objectives as an area of moderate development, with eight of the eleven projects indicating developmental work. The reader may, nevertheless, find it somewhat unexpected that only four of the eleven projects have actually detailed competencies in this area.

When examining core curriculum areas, the reader will make a most interesting discovery.

TABLE 6

Seriously Underdeveloped Competency Areas[1]

Competency	D[2]	d + D[3]
VII. Administrative Skills	0	2
XIII. Medical Basics Unit	0	0
XVII. Applied Behavioral Analysis		
C. Instructional Procedures		
2. Behavioral Slicing Procedures	1	2
D. Functional Analysis		
3. Reliability and Validity Issues	1	2
5. Selecting Appropriate Data Displays	0	2
XIX. Curriculum Units		
B. Sensory or Perceptual Development Unit	1	2
D. Socialization Unit	1	2
E. Recreation and Leisure Time	0	2
H. Cognitive Unit	1	2
I. Affective Unit	0	1
J. Independent Living Skills		
2. Domestic Maintenance	0	1
3. Community Living Skills	0	2
4. Sex Education	0	2

1. Competency areas were considered to be seriously underdeveloped if D = 1 or 0 and if d + D indicated that no more than two projects had addressed the competency area. Numbers indicate number of projects in each category.
2. Letter "D" indicates the development of competencies.
3. Letter "d" indicates some development without competencies defined (d + D = total development effort).

Only two units, Motor and Communication, may be considered even moderately developed, according to the authors' guidelines. This finding may lead to some speculation as to why these two areas, over all others identified, have received the most attention. Certainly both are of major importance when the SPH population is considered. For both areas, there would appear to be a discrete body of knowledge vital to a trainee in SPH, a body of knowledge meriting special consideration. Apparently, this information cannot be covered in a cursory manner or integrated totally within other training units if valid educational programming is later to occur.

Seriously Underdeveloped Competency Areas

In examining Table 6 and those competency areas that were judged to be seriously underdeveloped, one finds that several of the curriculum units identified by the authors were not addressed by the projects.

Selecting Appropriate Data Displays. With reference to Table 6, this competency is not well developed. Since all eleven of the projects are committed to applied behavior analysis as a technology, the omission of this skill from all but two of the projects may be the result of refusal to state the obvious. Still, the omission of such a crucial proficiency should not occur in a detailed project description oriented to a competency-based training approach.

Administrative Skills. The inadequate development of competencies in administration is a serious concern. The authors feel strongly that the entire area of administrative skills (including management, supervision, helping relationships with other teachers, and community interaction) must be thoroughly spelled out in training programs. Otherwise, teachers of the SPH will not be able to fill their roles as advocates, resource persons, and community representatives for the SPH. If they cannot fulfill these responsibilities, then the problems of community reintegration will remain with us and become more complicated, and the reasons for educating the SPH will become blurred.

Medical Basics Unit. The need for solid understanding in this area has been presented earlier. What is suggested goes far beyond textbook presentations on the subject and should include the pros and cons of the various medical treatments designed to ameliorate or modify handicapping conditions through drugs and surgery. The authors believe that the teacher of the SPH must know the terminology, the frequently prescribed drugs and their side effects, and the risks involved in various corrective surgical procedures. Most important, the teacher must have a clear understanding of the relatively fragile medical existence of SPH children. Failure to know the limits that can be demanded of a child in his educational program will not only bring about the failure of the program, but could endanger the health, even the life, of the child.

Curriculum Units. The lack of development in administrative skills and medical basics, though of great concern, was not surprising to the authors. We were, however, disappointed by the failure of the projects as a group to address so many important curriculum areas.

As far back as Itard, professionals who work with the SPH have been discouraged by the difficulty of teaching them to generalize, to understand concepts. As Itard was frustrated when he could not successfully teach the concept of sharpness, though he could quite easily make his "wild boy" see that knives

A, B, and C were indeed sharp, we too have consummate difficulty in the area of generalization. Our graduates must have a good foundation in cognitive development if we are to look to them to devise the methods and procedures for resolving the difficult problems we have traditionally faced in this area.

The fact that affective development of the SPH is essentially unaddressed in personnel preparation programs leaves us in a particularly difficult position. Behavioral technology emphasizes skills, rather than affects. But if anything has remained consistent in the few pieces of data we possess, it is that we are dealing with a population of children who, left to their own devices, will most certainly become social isolates. Moreover, reports over the past thirty years show that the less severely handicapped face the same destiny. Failure to consider the affective area will not only promote serious areas of regression in SPH individuals, but will also have a profound influence on their employability. The lack of work in the Socialization Unit is directly related to these problems, and the combined under-development of these two areas is particularly distressing.

The need for full competencies in the Sensory or Perceptual Development Unit cannot be as strongly established as the need for other types of competencies because of the confusion on how deficiencies in these areas relate to actual behavioral outcomes. However, as progress is made in the field, particularly with the moderately handicapped, SPH graduates should be able to comprehend and stay abreast of developments. In addition, several trainers have reported that their SPH graduates have been hired to teach children with specific learning disabilities and, in this event, the argument for inclusion of this area has even greater merit.

Given the problems of idleness experienced with the SPH, especially in residential settings, the authors were surprised to see such a low level of emphasis on this area in the projects. It is quite important that future teachers of the SPH comprehend the importance of free time with these children, and fully understand how they can help plan the use of this time to complement the physical and mental well being of the children in their charge. This is also a greatly needed skill in working with parents on home management.

Finally, the greatest disappointment for the authors was the extremely low level of development in these projects in key areas of domestic maintenance, community living skills, and sex education. These three units should be absolutely fundamental to a good, comprehensive SPH training program. In fact, we feel that these are three of the most vital skills needed by teachers of the SPH if the entire deinstitutionalization movement is to succeed. Proper development in this area can do much to prevent the institutionalization of the older adolescent.

Conclusion

The authors have presented objective data and subjective opinions on the basis of eleven case studies. The reader must decide the relative usefulness of the findings, the appropriateness of the authors' judgments, and the applicability of both to the general problem of preparing personnel to educate the SPH.

The quality of what has been developed in terms of teacher competencies appears to be generally excellent. If the eleven projects studied here are any indication of the direction in which the field is proceeding, then, in the main, we are taking the proper direction, and the developmental work that remains to be done is within our collective grasp. The field of personnel preparation in the area of SPH has moved far and fast in the past five years, and we are quietly optimistic about the outcome of this quest for competence in serving the severely and profoundly handicapped.

References

Burke, P. J. The role of special projects in the preparation of personnel for educating handicapped children. *Education and Training of the Mentally Retarded*, February, 1973, *8*(1), 62–64.

Lindsley, O. R. Direct measurement and prosthesis of retarded behavior. *Journal of Education*, 1964, *147*, 62–81.

Shores, R. E., Cegelka, P. T., & Nelson, C. M. Competency based special education teacher training. *Exceptional Children*, 1973, *40*(3), 192–197.

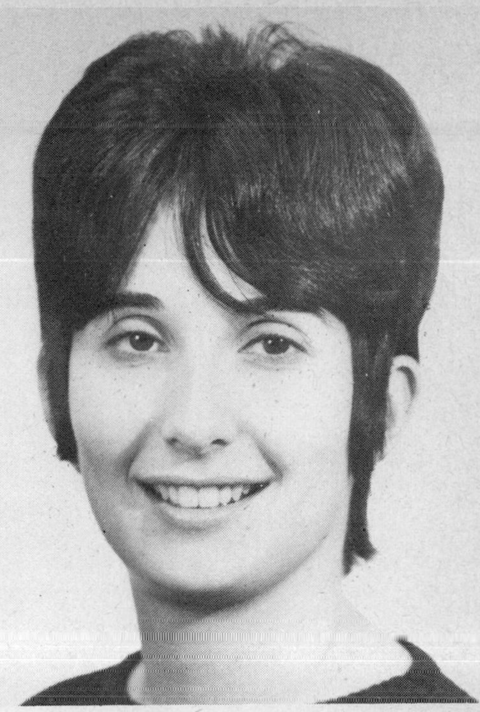

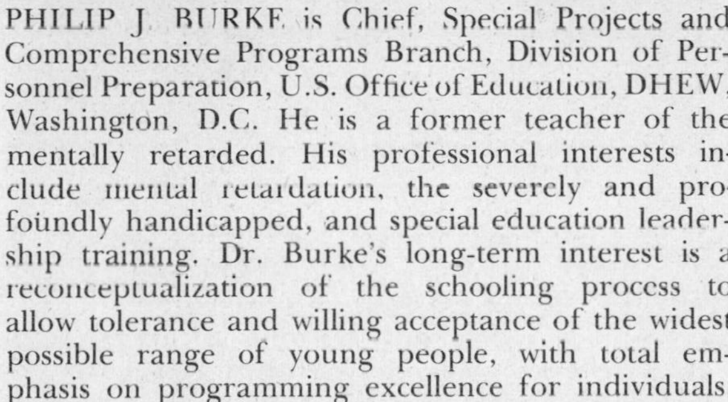

PHILIP J. BURKE is Chief, Special Projects and Comprehensive Programs Branch, Division of Personnel Preparation, U.S. Office of Education, DHEW, Washington, D.C. He is a former teacher of the mentally retarded. His professional interests include mental retardation, the severely and profoundly handicapped, and special education leadership training. Dr. Burke's long-term interest is a reconceptualization of the schooling process to allow tolerance and willing acceptance of the widest possible range of young people, with total emphasis on programming excellence for individuals.

MARILYN COHEN is Program Coordinator, Elementary and Secondary Training, Experimental Education Unit, for the College of Education and the Child Development and Mental Retardation Center, of the University of Washington. Dr. Cohen has served frequently as a consultant for teacher training programs and has conducted inservice teacher training workshops in Washington, South Dakota, Wisconsin, and Maryland.

XII Concluding Statement

Many parents, professionals, citizens, and children have participated in the recognized progress made in providing educational programs for the severely handicapped. Many more will join the cause because of their empathy, compassion, and willingness to assume responsibility for self and others. The late Dr. William Menninger, one of the founders of the famed Menninger Foundation, often said while advocating better services that there must be "brains before bricks." Menninger was speaking to the issue of humanistic individual and group commitment, plus concerted efforts, in behalf of the handicapped. This nation has the brains, in the collective wisdom of all citizens, and now must use them to build program bricks to the extent that those who have been unserved or ill-served may have the opportunity to contribute to the society of which they are a part.

Richard J. Whelan

We've Only Just Begun

RICHARD J. WHELAN

The University of Kansas and University of Kansas Medical Center

This brief chapter in what is a unique publication, and surely a milestone, conveys one person's impressions and perceptions of the forces which have influenced and will influence the actions that this nation's citizens, individually and collectively, will undertake in behalf of their severely handicapped brothers and sisters. Reflections and impressions are no more than one's subjective and objective mixing of events as they are, or at least as they are thought to be. Others may view the same events and form different impressions, or point to different and perhaps more important events related to the quest for humanistic services for the severely handicapped. Thus, the content which follows is neither comprehensive nor complete; it cannot be, because the realistic and desirable ends for which many people strive have not been reached.

Public awareness of the needs associated with severely handicapped children has grown in recent years. It will behoove advocates for this group of long neglected children to check awareness with activity. The two do not always coincide. Acquiring awareness is easy; acting on it and maintaining needed actions is something else again. Action is much more difficult, even though the satisfaction from achieving progress is great.

Some brief history, a definition of the population to be served, and advocacy positions are described in this chapter. The story of the severely handicapped needs telling. Perhaps this book will be a positive indication of things to come. That is to be hoped for and, when it happens, the work of many who contributed to this edition will be recognized and applauded for many years of a brighter future for all handicapped children.

A Little History

Almost twenty years ago a very famous and now historical interchange occurred between two prominent educators of the handicapped (Goldberg & Cruickshank, 1958). Many educators believed that the primary focus of the dialogue was whether the public schools should assume the responsibility of providing programs for trainable and severely handicapped children. Professor Goldberg argued in the affirmative, while Professor Cruickshank wrote in support of the opposite position. It was obvious that both were advocates for appropriate and quality-based instructional programs. The apparent disagreement was centered upon which agency should be assigned responsibility for provision of services. But, was agency location the real issue? No! A careful reading of the two positions reveals that the fundamental issue involved a difference in what constituted education, and what constituted training, e.g., should the public schools provide education or training, or should they do both? Cruickshank believed that the public schools should educate, e.g., help students to develop reasoning, to analyze, to critically evaluate, to abstract, to generalize. In contrast, Goldberg believed that public school resources could be used to promote behavior changes within large ability ranges or variances between the low and high starting points for program implementation. In essence then, the difference in the two positions was one of role function, and not whether public schools could or could not assume the responsibility.

Even at the time of the interchange, the issue was moot. Public schools were providing programs for the severely handicapped, although not nearly to the extent as they do at the present time. While educators may still debate the differences between the definitions of education and training, it is probably an academic exercise, a waste of scarce time and energy. A line could be drawn on a hierarchy of capabilities, and capabilities below the line could be called training, while those above could be labeled as education. Who would draw the line? Could consensus be reached? One can envision many years of debate on the issue, and it would detract from the primary task of implementing needed programs in national, state, and local jurisdictions. A glance into any standard dictionary obviates the compulsion to devote energy to differences in labels. For example, education is defined as development through instruction; training is defined as undergoing instruction to reach a level of proficiency or capability. Both definitions include the goal of change, to be different as a result of interacting in a planned environment. The public schools are capable, given adequate human and fiscal resources, of providing programs for severely handicapped children in proximity to and with children who are not handicapped.

On Definitions

The topic of the Cruickshank and Goldberg dialogue of eighteen years ago was trainable retarded children, even though the label "severely handicapped" was used, too. Now, the national dialogue has shifted to children with obvious multiple and global anomalies of the type that present an awesome challenge to educators who purport that they can make a difference in the functioning level of these children. Who are these relatively newly recognized children for whom public schools and educators must now provide programs? Descriptions of these children would probably vary with the numbers of professionals asked to describe them. However, a definition has been formulated as a part of federal policy. The Bureau of Education for the Handicapped, the agency responsible for the federal role in providing educational services for the severely handicapped, has published the following description:

> Severely handicapped children are those who because of the intensity of their physical, mental, or emotional problems, or a combination of such problems, need educational, social, psychological, and medical services beyond those which are traditionally offered by regular and special educational programs, in order to maximize their full potential for useful and meaningful participation in society and for self-fulfillment. (*Federal Register*, 1975, p. 7412)

The definition includes children with diagnostic labels of autistic, schizophrenic, cerebral palsied, deaf, etc. It also describes observable behaviors such as self-mutilation, self-stimulation, fragile physical condition, severe language deficits, chronic destructive behavior patterns, and lack of responsiveness to stimuli.

A definition does not add a great deal to knowledge, and it does not solve problems. Yet, it is a necessary step to circumscribing a problem, and the federal position has done just that. Improvements in the definition could be made, but for now it is both realistic and desirable. It provides flexibility for program development, implementation, and evaluation within a comprehensive and visable boundary of needed activities. The definition is further unique in that it departs from a listing of labels to include functional behavior descriptions, and a general design of services required to provide programs for the severely handicapped. If educators will use the definition for descriptive purposes, and not fall into the ubiquitious reification trap of using it to explain failure to bring about change in children and agencies, this nation will witness a true revolution in the growth of humanistic programs for that part of our population which has been out of sight, out of mind, and woefully neglected.

Reflections on Advocacy

It would be an easy task to chronicle and emphasize the advances we have made in programs for the handicapped. In the presence of such advances, why the title of this brief chapter? Indeed, there is a new era dawning in the education of handicapped children. This new era finds its roots in the progress made over a period of many years. Most active special educators can well remember times when society, friends, and neighbors had little awareness of the problems which handicapped children had to endure. They knew of children who were kept at home by loving but frustrated parents because the agencies created to serve people neither recognized nor accepted responsibility for giving services. They have seen children separated from parents and placed in institutions which, at best, could offer only custodial care because funds were insufficient to provide needed programs. Under these conditions, even the most dedicated staff members become disillusioned and stopped striving.

This new era of awakening and revolution is due to three concurrent events. These events can be traced to the recent struggle of minority groups for their civil rights as guaranteed under the Constitution. This is unfortunate in that awareness and responsiveness to the needs of the handicapped did not bloom earlier; it is fortunate that it did finally occur because of the active leadership of civil rights advocates. There is both blame for lateness, and credit for initiation of action to share among all, but the important aspect is that movement has been generated. These concurrent events may be referred to as the three L's, leverage, litigation, and legislation (Whelan & Sontag, 1974).

In a participatory democracy, it is not surprising that these important events occurred. Parents of the handicapped, with and without the help of professionals, organized to tell their story to representatives of various agencies, state legislatures, and the Congress. The parents and others used *leverage*. In actual fact, the parents were training and educating lay and professional people alike to the realities and conditions under which over ten percent of our population must function.

When various governmental units were not responsive in matching their "say" with "do" behaviors, parent groups turned to the courts, the second L, *litigation*, for an affirmation of fundamental rights. They had their day, as recorded in the various court decisions and decrees. Implementing educational services is a function of the states, not the federal government, as provided for in Article X (tenth amendment) of the Constitution. Article X stipulates that "the powers not delegated to the United States by the Constitution, nor prohibited by it to the States, are reserved to the States respectively, or to the people." Therefore, there is no constitutional right to an education, *but* if education is provided by public money, there must be equal access and equal opportunity to participate in it. Further, handicapped children must have access to the resources needed to develop and maintain adequate programs even if this means disproportionate distribution of personnel and funds when compared to those available for the nonhandicapped.

The Congress, with the enactment of Public Law 94-142, *The Education of All Handicapped Children Act of 1975*, recognized that if handicapped children are to have needed programs, there must be a federal, state, and local sharing of responsibility and resources. Thus, the third L, *legislation*, came to pass. State and federal representative bodies passed laws which mandated quantitative and qualitative educational programs for the handicapped, and are now in the process of backing these up with fiscal appropriations.

The Beginning

And yet, in recognization of the advancements brought about by the three L's, we've only just begun. There are more bright lights now, but they are few when contrasted with the remaining sea of darkness. Many people, some departed, some active, and some to come in the future, have labored and will continue to labor long and hard to develop quality programs for the severely handicapped. Some states are serving far fewer children than the sixty percent estimated on a national measure. In addition, even though quantitative improvement has occurred, there is still much to be done to enhance the quality of services. Many thousands of well prepared special educators are needed, and the two million general educators must be assisted in acquiring the knowledge, understanding, and skill needed to be both advocates and teachers of the handicapped. The many millions of non-handicapped children must be enabled to learn that their handicapped peers are children who happen to have handicaps but who have the same needs, faults, and strengths as all children.

Indeed, we've only just begun. This is the beginning of the beginning. In reflecting upon our past, the growing awakening of our present, and the hopes for the future, it is important to recall a statement which Andrew Carnegie made to an employee who reported "all records broken yesterday." Carnegie quickly asked, "But what have you done today?". Advocacy for the rights of severely handicapped children is a continous process. To plead and defend a cause is the easy part; to maintain the cause is the true test of advocacy and commitment. Maintenance requires constant vigilance, self criticism, self evaluation, and self improvement, a redoubling of effort without losing sight of the aim. Success is not measured by what has been accomplished. Rather, it is measured by what should have been accomplished in relation to abilities. Dr. Edwin W. Martin, Deputy Commissioner of Education, Bureau of Education for the Handicapped, described the issue well: "With the newly recognized rights of handicapped children to the education we offer, there must be an equal responsibility to see that those rights are truly filled" (Martin, 1974, p. 153).

Many parents, professionals, citizens, and children have participated in the recognized progress made in providing educational programs for the severely handicapped. Many more will join the cause because of their empathy, compassion, and willingness to assume responsibility for self and others. The late Dr. William Menninger, one of the founders of the famed Menninger Foundation, often said while advocating better services that there must be "brains before bricks." Menninger was speaking to the issue of humanistic individual and group commitment, plus concerted efforts, in behalf of the handicapped. This nation has the brains, in the collective wisdom of all citizens, and now must use them to build program bricks to the extent that those who have been unserved or ill-served may have the opportunity to contribute to the society of which they are a part. The ends are in view; now the means to reach them must be arranged. It will require (a) courage, taking responsibility, (b) strength, taking consequences for action, (c) fairness, ensuring that what is needed is provided, and (d) reason, managing both ends and means efficiently and effectively. All of these are within the nation's capabilities, and need only be used to accomplish the end of providing educational services for the severely handicapped.

Perhaps all of the history, descriptions, and advocacy positions are best summed up by the words of one who was disabled. Many Americans remember Glenn Cunningham as a famous miler, but few know that as a child he overcame a serious physical disability. He tells it like this:

> My legs are the weakest part of me. I run more from the hips up than the hips down. This is how it has to be with everybody—you go where your heart takes you.

The collective hearts of many have taken us in the right direction. They will continue to do so. The severely handicapped will be given the opportunity to participate as equals, not inferiors, with their fellow human beings. The handicapped will do their share, and the nonhandicapped must match their effort if the goal—the improvement of conditions for humans—is to be achieved. One cannot ask for more.

RICHARD J. WHELAN is Professor of Education and Pediatrics, the Ralph L. Smith Professor of Child Development, and the Director of Education, CRU/UAF, University of Kansas Medical Center, College of Health Sciences and Hospital. He was formerly Chairman of the Department of Special Education, University of Kansas and U.K. Medical Center. He was also Director of the Division of Personnel Preparation, Bureau of Education for the Handicapped, U.S. Office of Education, Washington, D.C.

References

Federal Register, 1975, *40*, 7412.

Goldberg, I. I., & Cruickshank, W. M. The trainable but non-educable: Whose responsibility? *National Educational Association Journal*, 1958, *47*, 622–623.

Martin, E. W. Some thoughts on mainstreaming. *Exceptional Children*, 1974, *41*, 150–153.

Whelan, R. J., & Sontag, E. Prologue: Special education and the cities. In P. H. Mann (Ed.). *Mainstream special education*. Reston Virginia: The Council for Exceptional Children, 1974.